ENCYCLOPEDIA OF ANTISLAVERY AND ABOLITION

Greenwood Milestones in African American History

Encyclopedia of the Great Black Migration
Edited by Steven A. Reich

Encyclopedia of Slave Resistance and Rebellion
Edited by Junius P. Rodriguez

Encyclopedia of American Race Riots
Edited by Walter Rucker and James Nathaniel Upton

Encyclopedia of the Reconstruction Era
Edited by Richard Zuczek

ENCYCLOPEDIA OF ANTISLAVERY AND ABOLITION

Volume 2, J–Z

Edited by
Peter Hinks and
John McKivigan

Assistant Editor
R. Owen Williams

Greenwood Milestones in African American History

GREENWOOD PRESS
Westport, Connecticut • London

Library of Congress Cataloging-in-Publication Data

Encyclopedia of antislavery and abolition : Greenwood milestones in African American history / edited by Peter Hinks and John McKivigan ; R. Owen Williams, assistant editor.

   p. cm.

   Includes bibliographical references and index.

   ISBN 0–313–33142–1 (set : alk. paper) — ISBN 0–313–33143–X (v. 1 : alk. paper) — ISBN 0–313–33144–8 (v. 2 : alk. paper) 1. Antislavery movements—Encyclopedias. 2. Slaves—Emancipation—Encyclopedias. 3. Slavery—Encyclopedias. I. Hinks, Peter P. II. McKivigan, John R., 1949– III. Williams, R. Owen.

   HT1031.E53 2007

   326′.803—dc22   2006026185

British Library Cataloguing in Publication Data is available.

This book is included in the African American Experience database from Greenwood Electronic Media. For more information, visit www.africanamericanexperience.com.

Library of Congress Catalog Card Number: 2006026185
ISBN-10: 0–313–33142–1 (set)   ISBN-13: 978–0–313–33142–8 (set)
     0–313–33143–X (vol. 1)   978–0–313–33143–5 (vol. 1)
     0–313–33144–8 (vol. 2)   978–0–313–33144–2 (vol. 2)

First published in 2007

Greenwood Press, 88 Post Road West, Westport, CT 06881
An imprint of Greenwood Publishing Group, Inc.
www.greenwood.com

Printed in the United States of America

The paper used in this book complies with the Permanent Paper Standard issued by the National Information Standards Organization (Z39.48–1984).

10 9 8 7 6 5 4 3 2 1

To the memory of our friend and teacher,
John W. Blassingame

CONTENTS

J

James, C.L.R. (1901–1989)

Cyril Lionel Robert James, commonly known as C.L.R. James or Nello, was a writer, political theorist and activist, journalist, and avid cricket spectator. James is best known for his book, *The Black Jacobins* (1938). In this book, James wrote a comprehensive historical account of the Saint Domingue Revolt, the most successful black revolt in the era of the transatlantic slave trade that liberated enslaved Africans and simultaneously gave birth to the first modern black nation in the Americas, Haiti. James was enthralled with world revolutions and sought to understand why the masses revolted against a political system. Although the book was written early in his career, he had already made contact with a number of Russian revolutionaries and various communist and socialist parties and organizations in England. These people and groups more than likely influenced his writings on the **Haitian Revolution**.

The Black Jacobins was a symbolic title, because James believed that the Jacobins of the French Revolution and the Black Jacobins of the Haitian Revolution shared universal political goals. Moreover, James was visionary for his comparative approach of the Haitian and French revolutions and his somewhat Atlantic approach in writing history. Like James's Russian colleagues, as well as the peasants of the French Revolution, James showed that the enslaved Africans, free blacks, and mulattos living in Saint Domingue suffered social injustices under the penal slave system. Furthermore, in this book, James illustrated the complex nature of the three-tier color stratification system found in Saint Domingue and prevalent in slave societies in the Caribbean. James revealed the disgruntled attitudes of mulatto men who formed temporary and, in some cases, permanent alliances with the former enslaved and free blacks, bringing down the French planter and ruling class in Saint Domingue. **Toussaint L'Ouverture**, a former enslaved African, was the hero and the protagonist of the book. James believed that he was largely responsible for the success of the revolution and achieving Haiti's sovereignty.

James was born on January 4, 1901 in Port of Spain, Trinidad. James's mother shaped his early education and his passion to write by introducing him to various English novels and literary works. His father was a schoolmaster. In 1910, James received a scholarship to attend the prestigious Queen's Royal College in Trinidad. He graduated in 1918 and was hired by the College as a teacher. During his years of service, he met and taught the young **Eric Williams**. James saw himself as a professional writer, and in 1932, he immigrated to England to pursue his career.

In England, James joined several Marxist organizations and took a special interest in world revolutions. In 1933, he traveled to France to carry out research on the Haitian and French revolutions. When he returned to England, James wrote the play *Toussaint L'Ouverture*, performed for London audiences in 1936. The play starred Paul Robeson, a prominent black actor and political activist. In 1938 James left England for the United States, where he familiarized himself with Marxist circles and writers. He continued to publish and collaborated with Leon Trotsky and Raya Dunayevskaya on various Marxist and socialist projects. He was deported from the United States in 1953, but was later granted entry status in 1968. James lectured at several universities and maintained employment as a faculty member in at Federal City College in Washington, D.C. and its successor, University of the District of Columbia, from 1968 through 1981.

James was admired by his students, readers, and colleagues and tends to be remembered more for his lifetime fight against colonialism, capitalism, and racism. However, James made an early and significant contribution to the historiography of antislavery, abolition, and emancipation in his works, *The Black Jacobins* and *A History of Negro Revolt* (1938). In 1987, James was awarded Trinidad and Tobago's highest honor, the Trinity Cross. James died in his Brixton apartment on May 31, 1989 and was buried in his native country of Trinidad. *See also* Saint Domingue, French Defeat in.

Further Readings: Buhle, Paul. *C.L.R. James: The Artist as Revolutionary.* London: Verso, 1988; Cudjoe, Selwyn R., and William E. Cain, eds. *C.L.R. James: His Intellectual Legacies.* Amherst: University of Massachusetts, 1995; Henry, Paget, and Paul Buhle, eds. *C.L.R. James's Caribbean.* Durham: Duke University Press, 1992.

Jennifer J. Pierce

Jay, John (1745–1829)

Jay served as a delegate to the New York constitutional convention in 1777. He planned on introducing an amendment calling for the gradual emancipation of slavery, but was called away before he could do so by the death of his mother. Jay's ally, Governor Morris introduced a similar amendment, which failed. Even when in Europe as minister to Spain, he kept up an interest in the issue. In 1780, he recommended to

John Jay. Courtesy of the Library of Congress.

longtime friend and New York legislator Egbert Benson that he propose an emancipation bill. On February 10, 1785, Jay and some friends founded the New York Society for Promoting the Manumission of Slaves. Jay served as the first president and remained a member until his appointment as chief justice of the Supreme Court in 1789. In 1795, Jay became governor of New York. He planned to propose emancipation in his first message, but decided instead to work behind the scenes to introduce it to the legislature. The bill failed the first time, but was reintroduced each session until its ultimate passage in 1799. The bill passed in April 1799 stated that all children born of slave parents after July 4, 1799 would be free. The bill also prohibited the export of slaves. *See also* Jay, William.

Further Readings: Alexander, DeAlva Stanwood. *A Political History of the State of New York.* vol. 1. New York: Henry Holt, 1906; Monaghan, Frank. *John Jay: Defender of Liberty.* Indianapolis: The Bobbs-Merrill Company, 1953.

Robert W. Smith

Jay, William (1789–1858)

William Jay, a prominent abolitionist, was born June 16, 1789, in New York City, the second son of **John Jay** and Sarah Van Brugh Livingston Jay. As a young man he studied with the Reverend Thomas Ellison, and later attended Yale where he graduated in 1808. Jay studied law with John B. Henry of Albany, but could not continue practicing law because of difficulty with his eyesight. He retired to his father's home in Bedford, New York to recuperate, and married Augusta McVicker in 1812. In 1818, Jay was appointed an associate justice to the Westchester County bench by Governor Daniel Tompkins. He remained on the bench until he was replaced in 1843 at the urging of proslavery Democrats.

While living at his father's home, Jay became increasingly involved in local reform movements. He was instrumental in the formation of the American Bible Society. He provided founder Elias Boudinot with the draft of a constitution that helped structure the society, which was formed in 1816. Jay continued to support that organization, even against criticism by many high officials in the Episcopal Church. Of particular significance was his ongoing debate with Bishop John Henry Hobart, who was critical of the society's interdenominational activities. Jay's reformist writings at this time were primarily concerned with temperance and respecting the Sabbath. But he also wrote *Essay on Duelling* (1830), decrying the practice as barbaric. The essay was awarded a medal by the Anti-Dueling Society of Savannah.

During this period, 1815–1835, Jay also began to display the deep concerns over slavery that would ultimately draw him into the abolitionist circle. In his private correspondence he was harshly critical of the **Missouri Compromise** of 1820, and expressed his wish that politicians behave morally to stop the westward expansion of slavery. In 1826, Jay was informed that a Westchester County free man, Gilbert Horton, had been arrested in Washington, D.C., and was being held as a runaway slave. Jay called a town meeting and requested the intervention of Governor DeWitt Clinton. It was largely through Jay's efforts that Horton was released. But the meeting also generated a petition calling for the abolition of slavery in the nation's capital. With the death of John Jay in 1829, William spent the next four years organizing his father's writings and letters into his book *The Life of John Jay* (1833). That same year the New York chapter of the **American Anti-Slavery Society** was formed. Jay was an early contributor to the society's antislavery newspaper, the *Emancipator*, and he offered legal advice to the fledgling organization, but he did not yet become actively involved in the society itself.

The years 1834–1835 witnessed increasing violence and criticism directed against abolitionists, and Jay was drawn more fully into the cause in response. In 1835, he answered criticism of the American Anti-Slavery Society by comparing its goals to those of the **American Colonization Society**. The work, *Inquiry into the Character and Tendency of the American Colonization and American Anti-Slavery Societies*, sold well and was reprinted in London. His next work, *A View of the Action of the Federal Government in Behalf of Slavery* (1839), was carefully documented and revealed abolitionist fears that the federal government was actively promoting slavery and its expansion. This work was also well received and debated, and saw many reprints. As a jurist, Jay also reviewed Daniel Webster's invocation of comity in the ***Creole Affair***, and published a work critical of Webster in *The Creole Case and Mr. Webster's Despatch* (1842).

A committed pacifist, Jay promoted the cause of world peace and served as president of the American Peace Society from 1848–1858. He saw a distinct linkage between slavery and war, and worked assiduously to eliminate both. In 1842, he published *War and Peace*, promoting the idea of stipulated arbitration as a method for peacefully resolving differences between nations. The work was well hailed by peace advocates, and in England Jay's plan was promoted on the floor of Parliament by Richard Cobden. Jay continued to promote peace when he published *Causes and Consequences of the Mexican War* (1849). This work was harshly critical of the United States government, and reveals none of the buoyant optimism of *War and Peace*.

In his later years, Jay continued the battle against slavery and his letters on such issues as **Henry Clay**'s **Compromise of 1850** provide valuable insight into abolitionist thinking. He also became increasingly critical of the Episcopal Church for its failure to properly address the issue of slavery as a sin. In 1853, a compilation of Jay's antislavery works, *Miscellaneous Writings on Slavery*, was published. That same year he addressed the American Peace Society and praised Richard Cobden for his promotion of world peace, while never mentioning his own contribution. Although in failing health, Jay did travel to England in 1856. He died in October 1858 at seventy years old. In eulogizing Jay, **Frederick Douglass** proclaimed Jay the father of immediatism, and a man who had helped create the foundation of the modern abolitionist movement.

Owing to health concerns, Jay was not one of the more visible abolitionist figures. He often remained at the Jay family home in Bedford, and contributed to the cause through his writings. Like many other members of the New York abolitionist circle, Jay was conservative and convinced that social problems were best remedied by recourse to the American institutions of law, politics, and the church. He never would have removed himself from participation in these institutions as many other members of the antislavery movement did. If these institutions were corrupt, as many asserted, then they needed to be changed, and the only way to change them was through active engagement. Because of these beliefs, Jay frequently clashed with other, more radical elements of the abolitionist movement. However, there were limits to Jay's engagement. In 1842, Jay was approached to replace **James Birney** as the presidential candidate for the **Liberty Party**, an offer Jay ultimately declined. *See also* Democratic Party and Antislavery; Immediate Emancipation; Whig Party and Antislavery.

Further Readings: Budney, Stephen P. *William Jay, Abolitionist and Anticolonialist.* Westport, CT: Praeger, 2005; Jay, Willam. *Miscellaneous Writings on Slavery.* Freeport, NY: Books for Libraries Press, 1970.

Stephen P. Budney

Jefferson, Thomas and Antislavery

Thomas Jefferson (1743–1826) is at the center of the most insurmountable paradox in American history. Prior to serving as the nation's first secretary of state, second vice president, and third president, Jefferson was the primary author of the **Declaration of Independence**, in which he insisted, "All men are created equal." Nevertheless, before he died on July 4, 1826, Jefferson owned hundreds of slaves, many of whom were sold to settle his notoriously unruly debts, but only eight of them (all members of the Hemings family) were ever freed (three during his lifetime and five at his death). Sally Hemings was Jefferson's slave, as well as half sister-in-law and, as a 1998 DNA analysis proved, mother to at least one of his children.

Born the son of a rich Virginia planter and educated with many of the nation's future leaders at William and Mary College, Jefferson inherited several hundred acres and a keen understanding of the value of slaves. He acquired even more land, the now famous Monticello, through marriage to Martha Wayles Skelton, who died in 1782 shortly before turning thirty-four. Martha Jefferson gave birth to six children, only two of whom reached adulthood. Jefferson never knew life without slaves.

Yet Jefferson's view of slavery has long been contested. In the infamous *Dred Scott v. Sandford* majority opinion of 1857, Supreme Court Chief Justice Roger Taney confidently observed: "[The Declaration] would seem to embrace the whole human family.... But ... the enslaved African race were not intended to be included ... the conduct of the distinguished men who framed the Declaration of Independence would have been utterly and flagrantly inconsistent with the principles they asserted .... They perfectly understood the meaning of the language they used and how it would be understood by others; and they knew that it would not in any part of the civilized world be supposed to embrace the negro race" (60 U.S. 393 [1856]). Before becoming president, **Abraham Lincoln**, in his 1858 U.S. Senate campaign debate with Stephen Douglas, responded to Taney and the *Dred Scott* decision: "While Mr. Jefferson was the owner of slaves, as undoubtedly he was, in speaking upon this very subject, he used the strong language that 'he trembled for his country when he remembered that God was just'" (Fifth Debate, October 7, 1858). Did Jefferson never intend that "all men" included blacks, as Taney suggested, or was he a reluctant and remorseful slaveowner, as Lincoln suggested?

Among historians, Jefferson's supporters insist that he often wrote or spoke against slavery and even tried, in Congress in 1784, to eliminate the slave trade. Jefferson detractors claim that his antislavery assertions were pitifully few and only appeared in private letters. While some biographers portray Jefferson as a frustrated but tireless proto-abolitionist, still others proclaim he did almost nothing to end slavery. As it turns out, determining Jefferson's stance on slavery is anything but simple.

Jefferson recognized the detestable character of slavery, and he seems to have been at least theoretically bothered by it. His most significant repudiation of the institution can be found in *Notes on the State of Virginia*, written and rewritten by Jefferson in the 1780s. In Query XVIII of that collection, Jefferson observed, "There must doubtless be an unhappy influence on the manners of our people produced by the existence of slavery among us." Of Jefferson's concerns regarding slavery, none are more quoted than this line from an1820 letter to a friend: "We have the wolf by the ear, and we can neither hold him, nor safely let him go. Justice is on one scale, and self-preservation is on the other."

Although Jefferson often advocated freedom for slaves, there is little indication he made much effort toward emancipation. Furthermore, any effort he did make was predicated upon the complete removal of freedmen from the United States. More remarkable than anything he wrote in *Notes on the State of Virginia* rejecting slavery are his reflections relating to the inferiority of blacks. The pages of *Notes* are filled with pseudo-scientific descriptions and observations of blacks like the following:

- "the preference of the Oranootan for the black women over those of his own specie;"
- "they secrete less by the kidnies ... which gives them a very strong and disagreeable odour"
- "seem to require less sleep [and] ... will be induced by the slightest amusements"
- "brave, and more adventuresome. But ... from a want of forethought"
- "they are more ardent after their female"
- "their griefs are transient"
- "An animal whose body is at rest, and who does not reflect, must be disposed to sleep ... in memory they are equal to the whites; in reason much inferior."

Some historians insist that Jefferson was a product of his age; his racism, like his spelling, was indicative of the times. Opposition to slavery, they say, was socially and legally impossible for a wealthy Virginian. Still other historians disagree, insisting that some among Jefferson's contemporaries did far more to contain or even end slavery.

In 1782, the Virginia legislature passed a law allowing manumitted slaves to remain in the state. That law stood for twenty-three years, during which time George Washington freed all his slaves in his will. Unlike Jefferson, Washington also refused to break up slave families through sale, "as you would do cattle at a market." Another fellow Virginian and member of the state council, Robert Carter III, not only freed over 500 slaves, he also provided them with land to farm. Edward Coles, a neighbor of Jefferson, wrote the ex-president in 1814, seeking endorsement for a plan he had to free all his slaves. Jefferson dissuaded Coles, contending slaves were "incapable as children of taking care of themselves" and that emancipated slaves were "pests in society by their idleness." Ignoring Jefferson's advice, Coles moved to Illinois where he became the state's second governor and the man most responsible for keeping Illinois a free state prior to the Civil War. As for Jefferson, he remained a slaveholder all his life, and his antislavery seems to have been little more than rhetoric.

Further Readings: Ellis, Joseph J. *American Sphinx*. New York: Vintage, 1996; Finkelman, Paul, *Slavery and the Founders*. Armonk, NY: M.E. Sharpe, Inc., 2001; Miller, John Chester. *Wolf by the Ears*. Charlottesville: University of Virginia Press, 1991; Peterson, Merrill, ed. *Thomas Jefferson: Writings*. New York: The Library of America, 1984. See especially, *Notes on Virginia, Queries XIV, XVIII*.

R. Owen Williams

Jerry Rescue (1851)

One of the most important episodes in the history of antebellum antislavery, the Jerry Rescue involved the forcible rescue by Northern abolitionists of a captured fugitive who was being returned to slavery in the South. The incident occurred on October 1, 1851, in Syracuse, New York, which had become by that time a hotbed of abolitionism and reform activity. The rescue constituted deliberate and open defiance of the **Fugitive Slave Law** that had been passed by the U.S. Congress as part of the **Compromise of 1850**. Signaling an increasing radicalism and aggressiveness in the abolitionist movement, the Jerry Rescue marked the beginning of a shift away from the moral persuasion and legal reform tactics of the 1840s, advocated most notably by the **Garrisonians**, towards more open acts of resistance and civil disobedience that would characterize abolitionist agitation in the years leading up to the Civil War.

William Henry, known as "Jerry," was an escaped slave from Missouri who had lived in Syracuse for about two years, working in a carpentry studio as a cooper. On October 1, federal marshal Henry Allen and his deputies arrested Jerry under the false charge of petty theft. Jerry offered no resistance while the deputies handcuffed him and transported him to the office of U.S. Commissioner Joseph L. Sabine. Only at the Commissioner's office was Jerry informed that he had been arrested under the authority of the Fugitive Slave Law. His arrest marked the first time a fugitive slave had been captured in Syracuse under that law and accordingly drew much immediate attention.

At the time, many visitors were in Syracuse attending both a county agricultural fair and a local convention of the **Liberty Party**, the political arm of the abolitionist movement. When news of Jerry's arrest reached that convention, the abolitionists were outraged and the meeting was immediately adjourned. Its delegates included prominent philanthropist and abolitionist **Gerrit Smith**, Unitarian minister Samuel J. May, and Reverend Jermain W. Loguen, a fugitive slave and leader of the **Underground Railroad** network. Church bells were tolled to alert the members of the local Vigilance Committee to the arrest of a fugitive slave. A crowd of abolitionists, residents, and curious spectators flocked to the Commissioner's office.

Jerry's hearing was delayed while court officials attempted to find a large room to accommodate all the people who had crowded into the office. Not allowed to testify on his own behalf and fearing a guilty verdict, Jerry attempted to escape with the help of some sympathetic members of the crowd. Recaptured by police officers and volunteer agents, he was taken to the police office and placed in a back room under heavy guard with his legs shackled. As the crowd grew to what historians have estimated to be nearly 2,000 people, the local authorities began to fear a riot. Marshal Allen wanted to call out the militia to prevent disorder, but it never arrived.

Early that evening, the local Vigilance Committee met secretly to plan the rescue. By 8:30 p.m., a group of approximately fifty-two abolitionists marched down the street toward the police office carrying a long wooden beam that they then used as a battering ram to destroy the windows and doors of the office. As the abolitionists forced their way into the building, Marshal Allen and the other authorities fled. The crowd carried Jerry into the street, transporting him to a horse and buggy that had been waiting for him. Jerry was taken to a safe house in the city where he waited for four days before he left for Oswego, New York, on the shores of Lake Ontario. He then sailed for Kingston, Canada West (Ontario), where he died of tuberculosis in 1853.

Although abolitionists regarded the rescue of Jerry as the action of virtuous citizens defying an unjust law, most Northerners who desired reconciliation and compromise with the South held the opposite opinion. Indeed, newspapers outside of central New York frequently denounced the rescue as mob rule. Fearing prosecution, many participants in the rescue, including Loguen, fled to Canada West. Thirteen men were eventually arrested. After a number of postponements, the trials of the rescuers began in January 1853. However, only one person, Enoch Reed, was found guilty. He appealed, but died before the appeal was heard. Another rescuer was acquitted, and the remaining cases were postponed, adjourned, and then the charges were dropped against all the other rescuers. In a bold counter move, the abolitionists charged Marshal Allen with kidnapping a citizen of Syracuse. Although a grand jury indicted and tried him in June 1852, Allen was acquitted of the kidnapping charges because the court determined that he was merely enforcing federal law.

In Syracuse, abolitionists held public commemorations of the Jerry rescue every October 1 until the Civil War. They hoped to promote the same spirit of resistance to slavery and the legal system that supported it as the rescuers demonstrated in 1851. The Jerry rescue came to be so celebrated because successful rescues of fugitive slaves were rare in the 1850s; the vast majority of slaves who were captured by federal agents were returned into slavery. *See also* Canada, Antislavery in.

Further Readings: Roach, Monique Patenaude. "The Rescue of William "Jerry" Henry: Antislavery and Racism in the Burned-Over District." *New York History* 82, 2 (Spring, 2001): 135–154; Sokolow, Jayme A. "The Jerry McHenry Rescue and the Growth of Northern Antislavery Sentiment during the 1850s." *Journal of American Studies* 16, 3 (December, 1982): 427–445.

Michelle Orihel

Jews. *See* American Jews and Antislavery

Jim Crow. *See* Segregation and Disenfranchisement in the American South

Journalism. *See* Antislavery Journalism in the United States and Great Britain

Jubilee

Jubilee is mandated by the Sabbath laws given to **Moses** on Mount Sinai, as found in Leviticus 25. Expanding from the weekly Sabbath of creation or biblical day of rest in Genesis, a Sabbath of every seventh year is commanded, when the land is to lay fallow. After a "week" of Sabbath years (seven times seven years), a year of Jubilee or Sabbath of Sabbath years was to be observed. Beginning with the sounding of a ram's horn on the Day of Atonement in the fiftieth year, the entire society was to change, both in jubilee or sacred festival celebration and in liberation or release.

Along with giving the land a year of rest from being worked, the Jubilee year was to substantially equalize the Israelites' socio-economic world. This utopian recreation of society, where both excessive wealth and poverty were eliminated, was intended to maintain a more egalitarian society of families, clans, and tribes. Ancestral lands that had changed ownership were to be returned to their original occupants. Debts were to be forgiven (this is sometimes compared to the remission of debts that came with the accession of a new king in Mesopotamia).

The text of Leviticus makes several references to slavery. The laws state that Israelites, during the Sabbath year of the land, must feed their slaves equally to themselves. People of Israelite birth, whom God had permanently freed from slavery in Egypt to become His servants, could not be permanently enslaved. Persons who had been forced by economic reverses, unpaid debts, or bankruptcy to pawn or indenture themselves into servitude or slavery were to be freed in the Jubilee and allowed to regain their lands and homes.

The imagery of the Jubilee is echoed in messianic biblical texts and continues into the present day.

> The Lord hath anointed me to preach good tidings unto the meek; he hath sent me to bind up the brokenhearted, to proclaim liberty to the captives, and the opening of the prison to them that are bound;
> To proclaim the acceptable year of the Lord, and the day of vengeance of our God; to comfort all that mourn;
> To appoint unto them that mourn in Zion, to give unto them beauty for ashes, the oil of joy for mourning, the garment of praise for the spirit of

heaviness; that they might be called trees of righteousness, the planting of the Lord, that he might be glorified. (Isaiah 61:1–3, compare Luke 4:18–19)

In the modern world, the remarkable efforts of proponents—such as Bono of the band U2—of Jubilee 2000, a campaign to cancel the debts of Third World nations, have resulted in the cancellation of some debts owed by African countries to Western nations and banks. The campaign argues that this Jubilee-liberation of African peoples is especially appropriate, since the debts for which they are held responsible were incurred by dictatorships characterized by the very sort of inequality Jubilee is meant to address.

Further Readings: Jubilee 2000 Web site: www.jublilee2000uk.org.

Gordon C. Thomasson

Just War Theory as Justification for Slavery

Just war theory was used to justify slavery in several ways. Just war theory remains one of the more complex justifications for slavery because its original purpose was to prevent war or justify going to war based on a nation's right to self-defense. Only later was it used to justify slavery. When a nation's need for slave labor increased, the likelihood of wars of conquest justified through just war theory increased. Typically, opposing nations each used just war arguments to defend its decision to engage in war. The victor's just war arguments were then used to justify enslaving the opposing side. When slavery and war were linked in this way, the moral implications of slavery were rarely considered because the society had established the morality of the war through just war theory. Just war is then believed to produce just slavery because the slave is seen to have forfeited a right to freedom by engaging in an unjust war.

Just war theory assumed that peace was the natural state of neighboring nations. For each war the theory assumed the existence of an aggressor nation and a nation that was the victim of aggression. By implication one nation was just and the other unjust. However, many scholars point out that while a nation's reasons for going to war are often complex, nations tend to engage in wars that are in their economic interest. They also note that self-defense can be broadly categorized. For instance, wars fought on religious grounds are often a product of the belief that the opposing religion is immoral and therefore a threat to the nation's existence. From this point of view, a war fought on religious grounds is then characterized as a war of self-defense because the existence of the other religion is seen as a threat. While many religions included provisions for slaves who were willing to convert, nations often failed to adhere to these provisions. Judaism, for instance, held provisions that allowed converts who also married into the religion to be freed and absorbed into the society. When just war arguments were used to justify slavery, the institution of slavery was seen as a permanent extension of the state of war.

Just war theory as a justification for slavery increased with the expansion of agricultural societies that required a large supply of cheap labor. Through the use of slave labor, these societies sustained a surplus of food that allowed them to keep slaves with minimal expense to the slaveholder. Through the use of slave labor, Rome, for instance, was able to transform itself from a subsistence economy with very little surplus to a market economy capable of producing and consuming a large surplus by increasing agricultural productivity on large farms. As Rome's productivity increased, so too did the need for slave labor. While the primary purpose of just war theory was to prevent war, when the theory was used in connection with slavery it increased the profitability of war and, in turn, increased the likelihood of war. When the just war theory was used as a justification for slavery, it allowed the society to remove the social obstacles that might have prevented individuals from justifying slavery because it made slavery part of the war sanctioned by social institutions. *See also* American Jews and Antislavery.

Further Readings: Finley, M.I. *Ancient Slavery and Modern Ideology.* New York: Viking Press, 1980; Meltzer, Milton. *Slavery: A World History.* New York: Decappo, 1993.

Shelinda Pattison

K

Keith, George (1638–1716)

George Keith was a Scottish theologian who settled in Pennsylvania in 1689 and wrote the first published tract objecting to slavery in colonial America. Having been born into a Presbyterian family, and studied at Aberdeen University, Keith converted to the Society of Friends (**Quakers**) in the 1660s, and ended his life as an Anglican rector in the south of England. His changes of denominational allegiance evinced Keith's restless quest for self-improvement and his disputative temperament. His longstanding association with prominent Quakers such as William Penn and Robert Barclay first attracted him to America in the 1680s, where he rapidly became controversial because he insisted that the Philadelphia Society of Friends adhere more rigorously to original Christian teachings. Keith's preaching urged American Quakers to accept a degree of scriptural authority and orthodoxy, although many rejected such ideas as antithetical to their core beliefs in revelation and the Inner Light.

Keith's ideas sharply divided the Quakers of Pennsylvania. The Quaker slaveholding and merchant elite were challenged by the suggestion that their customary authority in Meeting Houses over doctrine and procedure had no root in scripture. Conversely, poorer and marginal Quakers found Keith's ideas to be empowering, and in 1692, labeling themselves "Christian Quakers," his supporters seceded to form new Meetings. Prosecuted for slander and prohibited from preaching by the colonial elite, Keith returned to Britain in late 1693 only to find London Quakers similarly censuring his views.

One of George Keith's last acts as a Quaker in America was to issue an "Exhortation and Caution to Friends Concerning Buying or Keeping of Negroes," on August 13, 1693. This short message echoed concerns first raised by a group of Mennonite Quakers in Germantown who circulated a petition in 1688 protesting the unchristian nature of slavery and its incompatibility with the mission of the Society of Friends. Keith's "Exhortation" argues that not just whites, but "Negroes, Blacks, and Taunies are a real part of Mankind," and that true believers should look beyond their own souls to "liberty both inward and outward." The tract condemns the evils of slavery and the slave trade, and urges each Quaker to do what he or she can to limit its spread. While it did not advocate full abolition, it did suggest a series of smaller measures, including urging readers to purchase slaves only with the intent to buy their freedom, to undertake to free bondspeople they already owned, and to pledge to educate black children.

Keith based his opposition to slavery on five premises, all grounded in Scripture. First, he noted that to engage in the slave trade was to deal in stolen goods, and all Quakers were pledged to avoid such un-scriptural conduct. Second, he observed that since no person would want to be reduced to chattel property, slavery thus contravened the Christian directive, "to do unto others as you would have them do unto you." Keith identified a third reason in a biblical passage that insisted that runaway servants were not to be returned to their masters, but were to be harbored and to have the Gospel extended "to them as well as others." Keith's fourth argument cautioned that the involvement of Quakers with the horrors of slavery demeaned Christianity and undermined its global mission. Any cruel slaveholders will face repercussions for their behavior at the hands of the Almighty. Finally, Keith observed that any earthly riches gained through the exploitation of others are corrupted and to be abhorred.

George Keith's antislavery tract, like many other challenges to the institution during the later colonial era, relied heavily upon the Quaker faith and its egalitarian and non-violent principles. Yet Quakers were the largest slaveholders in the Middle Atlantic colonies and played a prominent role in the international slave trade by the end of the seventeenth century. Thus, while the "Exhortation" helped launch antislavery protests, it must also be understood in the context of its own time and place: Keith sought through the manifesto to rally his separatist supporters against the wealthier, more commercially oriented Quaker elite in Philadelphia and to reform Quaker worship and administration. However, the arguments Keith articulated would be central to the Quaker antislavery philosophy which would emerge over the eighteenth century.

Keith returned to America briefly as an Anglican missionary between 1702 and 1704, and successfully converted hundreds of disillusioned Quakers in the Jerseys to Anglicanism, but never returned to the issue of slavery again in published form.

Further Readings: Keith, George. "An Exhortation & Caution to Friends Concerning Buying or Keeping of Negroes." Printed by William Bradford, New York, 1693. [Online, July 2004]. Quaker Writings Home Page, www.qhpress.org/quakerpages/qwhp/gk-as1693.htm; Kirby, Ethyn Williams. *George Keith (1638–1716)*. New York: Appleton-Century Company, 1942; Soderlund, Jean R. *Quakers & Slavery: A Divided Spirit*. Princeton, NJ: Princeton University Press, 1985.

Ben Marsh

Kelley, Abby. *See* Foster, Abby Kelley

Kemble, Fanny (1809–1893)

Frances Ann Kemble was born November 27, 1809 into one of the most famous theater families in England. Her father, Charles Kemble, had joined the company of his brother, John Phillip, at Covent Garden, and her mother, Maria Theresa, was a famous actress in her own right. Fanny was born in the midst of the "Old Prices Riots," during which mobs protested nightly against the inflated ticket prices of her uncle's recently rebuilt Covent Garden Theatre. As a child, Fanny was rebellious and precocious, and her parents tried to tame her by sending her to boarding schools abroad. Fanny's teachers recognized her intelligence and literary talent, and during her school days she developed a love of theology that influenced her later in life.

When Fanny was sixteen years old, her mother allowed her to be exposed to smallpox, hoping that a mild case would immunize the girl, but Fanny's case was serious and scarred her for life. The family's trials continued when, in 1829, Covent Garden was repossessed, and Charles faced a lawsuit for one-sixth of the debt. Maria Theresa began training Fanny in Shakespeare in the hope that the young woman would save the family from ruin.

On October 5, 1829, Fanny debuted in *Romeo and Juliet* to critical and popular acclaim. She quickly became the most beloved actress in England, and her fame and newfound fortune averted her family's financial disaster. In 1832, against her wishes her father arranged a two-year tour of the United States. She and Charles arrived in New York on September 4. The American critics praised her, but she hated the nation, citing the rudeness of its citizens. As she continued her tour through Philadelphia, Baltimore, Washington, D.C., and Boston, she gradually warmed to Americans. Fanny eventually decided to marry Pierce Butler, heir to a plantation near Savannah, Georgia.

The couple wed at Christ Church in Philadelphia on June 7, 1834 and moved to a house near the city. Fanny bore daughter Sarah on May 28, 1835. That year she read William Ellery Channing's abolition tract "Slavery" and decided to write one too. Fanny had been against slavery since her youth and quickly befriended Philadelphia's famous abolition family, the Sedgewicks. Being married to a man who was set to become the second-largest slaveholder in Georgia strengthened her convictions against the institution. Fanny tried to append an antislavery essay to her book, *Journal of America*, but her publishers refused, and in 1835, they published the book without the essay.

In 1836, Butler inherited his family's Georgia Sea Island plantation. He grew increasingly difficult and Fanny decided to leave him and flee to England that year. Butler traveled to England to retrieve her and they moved back to Philadelphia, where their daughter Frances was born in 1838. Maria Theresa died that year, and Fanny was devastated. Butler decided to take her to his plantation to alleviate her grief.

The family arrived on the Butler plantation on December 20, 1838. Fanny arrived believing that her husband's slaves were well-treated and happy, but the reality of life on the plantation quickly changed her mind. She witnessed horrors wrought against the slaves and decided to take action. Fanny opened a hospital for her husband's slaves, as well as a nursery. She taught the children hygiene, and gave wages to her personal servants. When she taught a young slave named Aleck the alphabet, she broke the law.

In her journal, she gathered stories of atrocities committed against female slaves at the hands of white men. She was the first writer to condemn slavery as an institution of sexual exploitation, and much of her writings focused on the degradation of both female slaves and white women living on plantations. Upon their return to Philadelphia in the spring of 1839, Fanny threatened to leave Butler unless he manumitted his slaves. Pierce refused and the two became estranged. Editor **Lydia Maria Child** wanted to serialize Fanny's Georgia journal and publish her correspondence with Elizabeth Sedgwick, but Pierce would not allow it. Meanwhile, Fanny became aware of her husband's infidelities after he dueled with the husband of one of his lovers. She left Butler in 1845, taking her daughters back to England.

She returned to the stage to support her children and eventually organized a successful Shakespearean repertory company. In 1849, Butler formally divorced her on grounds of desertion, and daughters Sarah and Fan moved back to America to live with him. Fanny returned in 1856. Sarah eventually married into a Northern family and continued to agitate against slavery. Daughter Fan, however, remained loyal to the South and to her father, who was arrested in 1861 for disloyalty to the Union.

Fanny published her *Journal of a Residence on a Georgian Plantation* in 1863 to persuade the English to stop supporting the South. The book received good reviews in England. British readers had not read anything like it—a book on the horrors of slavery seen through the eyes of a civilized Englishwoman. The Ladies Emancipation Society of London reprinted several lithographs from the book and distributed them in pamphlets. The American edition was published that same year, and Frederick Law Olmstead, author of his own encounters with late antebellum slavery, endorsed the book.

Later in life, Fanny published *Records of a Girlhood, Records of a Later Life,* and *Further Records.* Daughter Fan tried to block the publication of her mother's memoirs in an unsuccessful effort to discredit her. In her later years Fanny met Henry James and remained friends with him until her death on January 15, 1893. *See also* Literature and Abolition.

Further Readings: Clinton, Catherine. *Fanny Kemble's Civil Wars.* New York: Simon and Schuster, 2000; Kemble, Fanny. *Fanny Kemble's Journals.* Cambridge, MA: Harvard University Press, 1990; Kemble, Fanny. *Journal of a Young Actress.* New York: Columbia University Press, 1990; Kemble, Fanny. *Journal of a Residence on a Georgian Plantation in 1838–1839.* London: Longman, Green, Longman, Robert and Green, 1863.

Susan Fletcher

King, Boston (1760–1802)

Boston King freed himself twice, became a leader of a black Loyalist community of freed slaves in America and then in Africa, and wrote and had published one of the most revealing and poignant memoirs of an individual's struggles in slavery and in freedom. Over the course of his eventful life, King was born into slavery in South Carolina, escaped to British lines during the American Revolution, was evacuated from New York to **Nova Scotia** in 1783, joined the migration from Nova Scotia to **Sierra Leone** in 1792, and spent two years in England training to be a Methodist missionary before returning to Sierra Leone.

As with so many slaves who freed themselves, in King's first 25 years, he combined luck, ingenuity, and persistence to escape slavery and to stay free. King was born on the South Carolina plantation of the Waring family; his father was a Christian, a native African, and a leader of the local black community, and his mother was most likely born in America and may have been at least partly American Indian. A favorite of his horse-racing owner, King traveled extensively in the colonies as a stable attendant before being apprenticed to a Charles Town (now Charleston) carpenter. The American Revolution offered the young, resourceful man a chance to escape the abusive carpenter; in 1780, King fled and joined the British army in Charles Town. After a series of adventures, including being accidentally left behind by his regiment, being recaptured and reenslaved by American forces, and a daring nighttime escape during low tide from New Jersey to Staten Island, King was in British-occupied New York City when peace was declared in 1783. He joined the 2,700 others listed in the Book of Negroes whom the British, at their own expense, evacuated to Nova Scotia and promised land and supplies for farming. Like many of the free blacks in Nova Scotia who suffered poverty and hardship, King struggled to make ends meet, though eventually was able to parlay his carpentry skills into a modest living.

But it was King's inspiration by **Methodism** that led to his remarkable Atlantic-World career. King's most memorable childhood experience involved a religious revelation during a dream, and he continued to study the Bible as best he could during the American Revolution. However, he did not consider himself fully converted to Christianity until his first few years in Nova Scotia. After that, he began preaching and managed to gain a pulpit. When John Clarkson came to Nova Scotia in 1792 to recruit settlers for the new British-sponsored colony in West Africa, Sierra Leone, King convinced Clarkson to include him as a missionary despite the fact that King's modest living excluded him from the Sierra Leone Company's requirements that only very poor people be taken. Though his wife became sick on the journey to Africa and died soon after their arrival, King survived and began his work as a teacher and missionary, with limited success. In 1794, he accepted an invitation to go to England at the Sierra Leone Company's expense to study; he spent the next two years at a Methodist school in Bristol, during which time he wrote his memoirs, published serially in the *Methodist Magazine*. King then returned to missionary work in Nova Scotia, where he died in 1802.

Along with his amazing success at establishing himself as an educated free man and community leader, King's main legacy lay in his autobiography. King's 9,000-word account in some ways typified the abolitionist-sponsored, conversion narratives of former slaves; his description of his slavery and freedom is paralleled by the story of his call to Methodism and his growing sense of brotherhood with white Methodists. While compared to the writing in his own letters, the narrative's language clearly bears the mark of an editorial hand; yet it conveyed his distinctive sense both of religious inspiration and of passion for freedom which was never surpassed by any other slave narrative. Although not as widely acknowledged at the time of its publication as was that of **Olaudah Equiano**'s, the memoir offers an eloquent account of one man's spiritual journey and efforts to gain and keep freedom through the turmoil of the American Revolution, the black Loyalist colony in Nova Scotia, and the free black colony in Sierra Leone.

Further Readings: King, Boston. "Memoirs of the Life of Boston King, a Black Preacher. Written by Himself, during his Residence at Kingswood School." In Vincent Carretta, ed. *Unchained Voices: An Anthology of Black Authors in the English-Speaking World of the Eighteenth Century.* Lexington: University of Kentucky Press, 1996, pp. 351–368; Walker, James W. St. G. *The Black Loyalists: The Search for a Promised Land in Nova Scotia and Sierra Leone, 1783–1870.* Reprint. Toronto: University of Toronto Press, 1993; Black Loyalists: Our History, Our People [Online, June 2005]. Canada's Digital Collections, http://collections. ic.gc.ca/black-loyalists/index.htm.

Andrew M. Schocket

Koran. *See Qur'an* and Antislavery

Kossuth, Louis (1802–1894)

Louis Kossuth led Hungary's failed revolution for independence from Austria in 1848 and 1849. In December 1851, seeking aid for his cause, he began an almost eight-month tour of the United States. But his efforts to obtain military and financial aid for Hungary's defense failed, in part because Kossuth became entangled in debates about slavery that were engrossing American political culture at the time. When Kossuth refused to stand publicly for or against slavery, both abolitionists and proslavery Southerners accused him of running to the other side, and in July 1852, Kossuth returned to Europe without substantial support.

Kossuth was escorted to America from exile in Turkey aboard a naval steamer, and at first, many observers, including a young **Abraham Lincoln** in Illinois, cheered this gesture as a fitting show of national support for the revolutions of 1848. Many viewed those struggles as successors to America's own revolution; Kossuth, who was greeted in many places by parades and throngs of people, was often compared to George Washington. In many cities, he made a triumphal entry, complete with well-attended parades and honorary banquets. Some Americans, particularly hawkish politicians who were part of the nationalistic "Young America" movement, supported Kossuth's designs because of a desire to expand the global influence of the United States. But although Kossuth was feted repeatedly, he raised few funds. He made even fewer converts to his paradoxical doctrine of "intervention for non-intervention," by which he hoped the United States would interfere militarily to stop the interference of Austria in Hungarian affairs.

Among the reasons for Kossuth's lack of success was his uncertain posture toward slavery. Initially, abolitionists hoped, and Southerners suspected, that Kossuth would identify with Northern antislavery forces coalescing around the Free Soil Party and resistance to the Compromise of 1850. His image as a romantic liberal shaped this presumption, as did his policies as provisional governor of Hungary, which had included the emancipation of serfs. Kossuth was introduced to abolitionists in England while en route to the United States, and antislavery tracts, including **Theodore Dwight Weld**'s *American Slavery as It Is*, were reportedly placed in his hands.

But speculations about Kossuth's allegiances were usually premised on the belief that he intended to stay in the United States, and Kossuth made it clear that he came for assistance, not asylum. He avoided divisive issues. Kossuth declared within a week of arriving that he would not meddle with "domestic" concerns, a euphemism that all understood to mean slavery. This professed neutrality, while failing to convince Southerners that Kossuth was not antislavery, enraged Northern abolitionists. His severest critics were the followers of **William Lloyd Garrison,** who published a lengthy open letter denouncing Kossuth.

In various ways, all participants in the national debate over slavery tried to turn the notoriety of Kossuth to their advantage. Free Soil politicians in Congress tried to link Kossuth's liberal principles with theirs and thus capitalize on his popularity in the elections of 1852. **Harriet Beecher Stowe** alluded to him and recent European revolutions in *Uncle Tom's Cabin,* which was completing its serial publication while Kossuth toured the country. Despite Kossuth's reticence, Stowe, like other moderate antislavery figures, was optimistic that Hungary's freedom would augur well for abolitionism. Free African Americans in the North tended to be encouraged by Kossuth's popularity. Some argued that if his revolution was justified, so were slave insurrections; others used Kossuth's arguments for national self-determination in their rhetorical attacks on colonization. Although abolitionists never united behind Kossuth, the antislavery connotations they attached to his name impeded his campaign in the South. Near the end of his tour, a frustrated Kossuth thus complained of being placed between the upper and lower millstones of Northern abolitionism and Southern proslavery.

Further Readings: Morrison, Michael A. "American Reaction to European Revolutions, 1848–1852: Sectionalism, Memory, and the Revolutionary Heritage." *Civil War History* 49 (2003): 111–132; Reynolds, Larry J. *European Revolutions and the American Literary Renaissance.* New Haven, CT: Yale University Press, 1988; Spencer, Donald S. *Louis Kossuth and Young America: A Study of Sectionalism and Foreign Policy, 1848–1852.* Columbia: University of Missouri, 1977.

W. Caleb McDaniel

L

Labor Movements and Antislavery

In both Britain and the United States, the attitude of labor reformers toward the abolition of slavery represented a missed opportunity. It might have seemed natural for those seeking to elevate the condition of white working people to focus on alleviating the degradation of enslaved Africans in both the United States and the Caribbean, on the grounds that eliminating slavery would help to decrease some of the stigma associated with manual labor. In fact, many abolitionists explicitly made this connection, arguing that slaveholders were in league with Northern factory owners to promote the chattelization of white workers. In actuality, because the vast majority of abolitionists had a different interpretation than labor reformers about the value of competition in the labor market, they found themselves on opposite sides of this issue, with labor reformers calling their own condition "white slavery" or "wage slavery" and calling for it, rather than chattel slavery, to be the main focus of reformist attentions.

With some notable exceptions, British and American abolitionist leaders were largely drawn from the middle rather than the working classes, and tended to share certain views. Most abolitionists agreed that the meaning of freedom was "self-ownership," rather than a level economic playing field. They accepted labor-market competition and claimed that poverty spurred workers on to virtues like sobriety and thrift. Moreover, poverty seemed to them an intractable problem that admitted no easy solution, while slavery was clearly a man-made and more easily abolished institution, and thus should have priority. While some abolitionists, impelled by Christian humanitarianism, may have felt that Northern employers should pay a reasonable level of wages, their commitment to freedom of contract led them to oppose labor's central vehicle for achieving higher wages—labor unions. Abolitionist political economy was notoriously underdeveloped.

In response, labor reformers on both sides of the Atlantic played the race card in the nineteenth century by creating an imagined community of whiteness. This imagined community of whiteness was strengthened in the United States by the affiliation of labor reformers with the antebellum

Democratic Party, which was proslavery and very comfortable with racial inequality. Labor songs and poetry pointed out the hypocrisy of emancipationists, who focused their largesse on black people while white factory children starved and worked themselves to death. This argument was aided by the coincidence in the early 1830s of the English campaign to extirpate slavery in its West Indian colonies with labor reformers' battle for a ten-hour day for children working in factories.

Thus, in Britain, Tory radical Richard Oastler railed against factory masters who reserved their only compassion for black workers whom they had never seen. Referring to work in factories as "wage slavery" emphasized the additional injustice implicated in ignoring workers in the abolitionists' own racial community. Later, Chartists broke up abolitionist meetings in an attempt to reinforce their belief that real slavery was the exclusion of white working men from the suffrage. In America, New England journeyman and labor leader Seth Luther, and New York labor legislator Mike Walsh, compared the plight of the Northern workingmen unfavorably to that of the slaves; Walsh's newspaper, *The Subterranean*, was filled with racial slurs. Catholic writer Orestes Brownson used the analogy between factory work and slavery to damn the entire wage labor system. Some artisans did sign antislavery petitions, but their decision to do so was not supported by the discourse of labor reform.

One of the only labor movements in which any credence was given to abolitionism was the land reform movement. **Gerrit Smith,** a well-known abolitionist, not only supported the movement to gain homesteads for white workers, but also supplied a number of black workers with free homesteads on his own land in upstate New York. George Henry Evans, the leader of the National Reform Association and the editor of the longest-running antebellum labor newspaper, the *Working Man's Advocate,* had long been an opponent of slavery, going so far as to support the **Haitian Revolution** and **Nat Turner**'s Rebellion. Others in the land reform movement, including antirent leader Thomas Devyr, and labor unionist John Commerford, were more strident Democrats, but Evans's role as the editor of the main land-reforming newspaper meant that movement was able to offer some support for an end to slavery.

The ideological basis of land reform also caused it to harmonize with antislavery. Land reformers promised to alleviate the overcrowding in the labor market. Readily available and affordable land would be a safety valve, alleviating the fear that if the labor market were swamped with freed blacks, the price of labor would plummet. Despite this potential underlying sympathy between abolition and land reform, abolitionists sparred with Evans in their newspapers throughout the late 1840s. Each side tried to convince the other to make its cause a greater priority.

The land reform movement was not the only point of contact between the antislavery movement and labor reform. White working men seeking sympathy for their position could also look to abolitionists like John Collins, who combined abolitionism with communitarianism; Nathaniel P. Rogers, editor of the *Herald of Freedom*, who called for a rethinking of all coercive labor systems; and William Goodell, another antimaterialist abolitionist. By the 1850s and 1860s, even abolitionists like **Harriet Beecher Stowe** were using the labor movement's own racial beliefs and arguments to try to engage Northern working men, by pointing out the light skin color of many enslaved blacks, the result of many generations of amalgamation with slaveholders. If wage slavery was wrong because it fell upon white men, then surely chattel slavery was wrong when it fell upon people who were nearly white. Despite these overtures, and the fact that abolitionists and labor reformers were both seeking to secure for the laborer the value of his labor, abolitionists and labor reformers remained mostly estranged from each other throughout the antebellum period. *See also* Democratic Party and Abolition.

Further Readings: Bolt, Christine, and Seymour Drescher, eds. *Anti-Slavery, Religion, and Reform: Essays in Memory of Roger Anstey.* Hamden, CT: Archon Press, 1980; Bronstein, Jamie L. *Land Reform and Working-Class Experience in Britain and the United States, 1800–1862.* Stanford: Stanford University Press, 1999; Glickstein, Jonathan. "The Chattelization of Northern Whites: An Evolving Abolitionist Warning," *American Nineteenth-Century History* 4 (2003): 25–58; Huston, James L. "Abolitionists, Political Economists, and Capitalism," *Journal of the Early Republic* 20 (2000): 488–521; Perry, Lewis, and Michael Fellman, eds. *Antislavery Reconsidered.* Baton Rouge: Louisiana University Press, 1979; Roediger, David. *The Wages of Whiteness: Race and the Making of the American Working Class.* New York: Verso, 1999.

Jamie Bronstein

Lane Seminary Debates (1834)

Theodore Weld, a student at Lane Seminary, Cincinnati, organized a series of debates regarding slavery in February 1834. Son of a Presbyterian minister, Weld and twenty-four other students had recently transferred to the new school from Oneida Institute, New York. Most of these students were men of some accomplishment and maturity. The debates addressed two main questions: first, whether or not slavery should be immediately abolished; and second, whether Christians should support colonization of American blacks in Africa.

For the times, these were two highly controversial issues. Even those who held antislavery views did not agree upon methods with which to end slavery. The debates, held over two weeks, were moving and far-reaching. They systematically challenged the audience, mostly other students, to thoughtfully examine these issues. The nation tuned-in to the debates through antislavery newspapers. In their remarks, Weld and the former Oneida students revealed the strong influence of revivalist **Charles G. Finney** and his ideas of moral **perfectionism**.

Finney had taught students how to generate a conversion experience or change in beliefs. The first step was sharing solid facts that appealed to reason. The second was creating an emotional connection. In these debates, that connection was building empathy for enslaved persons. Student speakers related first-hand experiences observing injustices endured by slaves. Henry Thompson of Kentucky, Andrew Benton of Missouri, and Colemen

Hodges of Virginia spoke of cruelty to slaves that each had witnessed, including separation of families, torture, and murder. Finney had taught that once reason and emotional connection were brought to bear, time and individual reflection could create a sincere change in a person's beliefs.

The issue of colonization, or the plan to deport free blacks to Africa, was also debated. At this time many believed whites and blacks could not live together peacefully in freedom. Some feared numerous free blacks would deprive white Americans of what was often seen as limited resources including jobs, food, and land. In addition, a widely held view of racial inferiority led many people to believe free blacks would remain dependent upon whites. This supposed inferiority was long used to justify racial, hereditary slavery. This pervasive false belief caused racial prejudice in the 1830s and continued to do so for more than a century to come.

Examples of racial equality were often used by antislavery debaters to help dispel this myth. James Bradley, a former slave, spoke of being taken by force from Africa. Yet he rose to manage his master's Kentucky plantation, while saving to purchase his freedom. He was an articulate and forceful example of how a black person, despite adversity, was more than equal to persons of other races.

The debates succeeded in converting nearly all Lane students to support both immediate emancipation and oppose colonization. Following the debates, Lane students formed an antislavery society. They also raised money to support a library and aid Cincinnati blacks. Students also conducted night school and Sunday school for free blacks living in Cincinnati. Some Lane students even resided in free black homes.

The debates, as well as the mission work among black residents, angered authorities at Lane Seminary. The next fall trustees took disciplinary action against the students who organized the debates and then performed mission work among free blacks. As a result, Theodore Weld and William T. Allan and a group of at least seventy-three other Lane students withdrew from the school in the fall of 1834. They became known as the Lane Rebels. Soon the student group issued their own account of events at Lane and "The Statement of Reasons" for withdrawal. It was signed by fifty-one students.

Some Lane Rebels continued to study in nearby Cumminsville and work with Cincinnati's black community. In the fall of 1835, part of the group removed to Oberlin College in northern Ohio. That new school had agreed to accept black students, thanks to pressure from this group. But most significantly, a number of Lane Rebels, including Weld and Allan, went on to devote themselves to the antislavery cause. Lane Rebels eventually fanned out across the North as ministers, speakers, and reformers. Many years of their hard work helped bring about a change in how the public viewed slavery and African Americans. *See also* American Colonization Society.

Further Readings: Hagedorn, Ann. *Beyond the River: The Untold Story of the Heroes of the Underground Railroad*. New York: Simon & Schuster, 2002; Horton, James Oliver, and Lois E. Horton. *In Hope of Liberty: Culture, Community, and Protest among Northern Free Blacks, 1700–1860*. New York: Oxford University Press, 1997; Lesick, Lawrence Thomas. *The Lane Rebels: Evangelicalism and Antislavery* *in Antebellum America.* Studies in Evangelicalism, No. 2. Metuchen, NJ: Scarecrow Press, 1980.

Jennifer Harrison

Las Casas, Bartolomé de (c. 1474–1566)

Born into a merchant class household in Seville, Spain, in about 1474, Bartolomé de Las Casas achieved international recognition as a Roman Catholic (Dominican) priest, diplomat, historian, spiritual writer, traveler, and advocate for the indigenous peoples in the Spanish colonies of South and Central America. In the face of much opposition, Las Casas, known as the "Protector of the Indians," worked diligently to change European policies about colonization of the New World and to improve the treatment of its native population.

Bartolomé's father accompanied Christopher Columbus on his second voyage to the Caribbean, and the younger Las Casas edited Columbus's travel journals. Prior to his first voyage across the Atlantic Ocean in 1502, Las Casas studied law at the University of Salamanca; this background served him well in his fifty-year struggle for Indian rights. Because of family and personal connections, he received an *encomienda* (a royal land grant) on Hispaniola (modern Haiti and the Dominican Republic) in 1502. While Spain's colonial policy did not condone the enslavement of the Indians, the colonists' demand for tribute from the indigenous people turned into a form of forced labor (***repartimiento***). The Crown viewed the New World's conquered peoples as Spanish subjects and generally sought to protect and "Christianize" them. In reality, however, Madrid had little control over what colonial landowners did to the native peoples on their own *encomiendas*. This abusive situation, combined with the spread of new diseases, caused many deaths among the indigenous tribes of Hispaniola and in much of Latin America.

Around 1507, Las Casas began training as a Roman Catholic priest, since he wanted to participate in the conversion of the indigenous tribes to Christianity. After admission into holy orders in 1510, Bartolomé still retained his *encomienda*, but the teaching of the Dominicans had a profound influence on him. As a landholder himself, he observed the exploitation of the Indians firsthand and eventually relinquished his claim to land and rejected a social and economic system that was cruel and inhumane.

Two specific events occurred early in Las Casas's priesthood that changed his views concerning Spanish colonial policy in America. The first event occurred in 1511, on Hispaniola, when Fray Bartolomé heard the Dominican friar, Antonio de Montesinos, deliver a sermon condemning the *encomienderos* and their exploitation of the native people. Montesinos said "'I am the voice of one crying in the wilderness.' You are in mortal sin ... for the cruelty and tyranny you use in dealing with these innocent people.... Tell me, by what right or justice do you keep these Indians in such cruel and horrible servitude? ... Are these not men? ... Have they not rational souls, are you not bound to love them as you love yourselves?" These words from Montesinos, along with the teaching of other Dominicans (e.g., Vasco de Quiroga, Bernardino de Minaya), eventually led Las Casas to object to the harsh system by which Spanish landowners exploited the Indians.

The second event occurred during the Spanish conquest of **Cuba** in 1513, when Bartolomé accompanied the Spanish soldiers as a chaplain. During this invasion, he witnessed the brutality of the *conquistadors* toward the Indians; he felt that all of the colonists needed to share the crisis of conscience he had experienced. He freed the native workers living on his *encomienda* and sailed back to Spain in 1515, hoping to convince the Spanish government to do away with the *encomienda* system and improve the conditions of the Indians. This was the first of many diplomatic trips Las Casas made between Spain and the colonies until his final voyage back to Spain in 1547; this journey marks the beginning of his active role in the abolitionist cause.

Las Casas did not object to the colonization of the New World per se, but he tirelessly attempted to persuade the Spanish to work with Indians in humanitarian and peaceful ways. On many of his trips to Spain, Las Casas went before King Charles V of Spain (grandson of Ferdinand and Isabella), other Spanish officials, or representatives of the Roman Catholic hierarchy. On his first trip back to Spain, Las Casas called for an end to the *encomiendas* and the system of forced labor that existed in Spain's colonies. Bartolomé enlisted the support of Cardinal Francisco Jiménez de Cisneros, who appointed him as "priest-procurator" of the Indies.

Bartolomé de Las Casas pled his cause in Spain through persuasive speech and writing, but he also returned to the New World and sought to bring about reforms in the colonies. In 1520, Las Casas, with the help of Charles V, founded the first of several free Indian villages in Venezuela as a place where the native population and Spaniards could farm together in peace. This experiment, along with similar ventures in other territories, failed for lack of support from the colonial landowners and uprisings from the Indians. Although he was discouraged when these utopian communities failed, Las Casas did not admit defeat. He did, however, withdraw from his active work, and, in 1523, joined the Dominican order in Santo Domingo, Hispaniola. A ten-year retreat from public activity allowed Bartolomé to reflect on the situation and prepare for three more decades of work as writer, debater, and advocate for fair treatment of the Indians.

Two European decrees advanced Las Casas's abolitionist efforts. The first came in 1537, when Pope Paul III issued a papal bull (*Sublimis Deus*), stating that all Indians were rational human beings, capable of receiving the Gospel. The second came in 1542, when King Charles V signed the New Laws (*Leyes Nuevas*), which were designed to eliminate the *encomiendas* by limiting them to one generation. Although these new laws exemplified the changing attitude of Europeans toward the Native Americans, the colonists rejected them in practice. Indeed, even as Bishop of Chiapas, Fray Bartolomé was unable to enforce the New Laws in his own diocese.

Through his polemical writing and debates, Las Casas advanced the cause of freedom for the Indians. Bartolomé produced four works that focused on the relationship between the colonists and the natives, criticizing what had happened in the past and suggesting ways to make a better future. He wrote his first work in 1537: *Del único modo de atraer a todos los pueblos a la verdadera religión* (*Concerning the Only Way of Drawing All Peoples to the True Religion*). This book contains Las Casas's ideals on the proper way of converting the Indians through patient persuasion and affection.

The second work, entitled *Brevísima relación de la destrucción de las Indias* (*A Brief Report on the Destruction of the Indians*), published in 1542, documented the Spanish violence against conquered peoples. In this work, Las Casas estimated the number of indigenous peoples killed during the Spanish conquest of the New World and named the different methods of torture and execution used to control the Indians. He offered this evaluation of the Spaniards:

> Yet into this sheepfold, into this land of meek outcasts there came some Spaniards who immediately behaved like ravening wild beasts, wolves, tigers, or lions that had been starved for many days.... Their reason for killing and destroying such an infinite number of souls is that the Christians have an ultimate aim, which is to acquire gold, and to swell themselves with riches in a very brief time and thus rise to a high estate disproportionate to their merits.

Some historians question the reliability of this polemical work, claiming that Las Casas exaggerated the numbers and cruelties or misrepresented the meek nature of the New World's indigenous peoples—who reacted in a variety of ways to the conquistadors.

The third book, *Apologética historia,* a defense of his historical interpretation of the Indians, served as the introduction to a fourth, and major, work: *Historia de las Indias* (*The History of the Indies*). Las Casas completed these studies in 1562, but requested that they be published posthumously. His *Historia* recorded events of the Spanish conquest and passed judgment upon the Spaniards for their cruelty. In these books, Fray Bartolomé apologized for a suggestion that he made earlier in his public career—viz., that the colonists should use more Africans in their labor force to protect the Indian population from total annihilation. As he retracted his earlier statement, Bartolomé de Las Casas insisted that Africans deserved the same right of self-determination that he sought for the Indians. Indeed, in his *History of the Indies*, Fray Bartolomé argued for the essential unity of all humankind.

Las Casas also participated in a major debate, a *junta* called by Charles V, to consider philosophical, theological, and legal questions about Spain's conquest and control of the New World colonies. In this debate, which took place in Valladolid, Spain, in 1550–1551, Las Casas faced a worthy opponent, the Spanish philosopher Juan Ginés de Sepúlveda. The debate asked whether the Indians were fully human and whether Spain had the legal or moral right to conquer the Indians before they received Christian instruction; both speakers built their arguments with citations from the Bible, early church fathers, and medieval and Renaissance thinkers. Sepúlveda defended the Spanish conquest of the New World as a just war and justified the harsh treatment of the Indians on the basis of Aristotelian theory, arguing that the Indians were violent and inferior and were, by nature, slaves. Bartolomé claimed that the Indians acted violently in response to mistreatment by the Spaniards. On the basis of medieval legal precedent, Las Casas argued that Spain could not claim authority over the indigenous peoples until they peacefully converted to Christianity. Neither side of the debate claimed a decisive victory, but the Valladolid controversy provided Bartolomé with yet another means of placing human rights before the public eye.

Bartolomé de Las Casas died in 1566, while working in a monastery in Madrid. Throughout his long, controversial career, Las Casas advocated philosophical, theological, and legal concepts that challenged Spain's policies related to the conquest, settlement, and evangelization of the New World. Some liberation theologians have claimed him as a pioneering thinker and activist, while critics have suggested that Las Casas did more harm than good by inciting a determined opposition. Without a doubt, his tireless efforts as writer, diplomat, and missionary advanced the cause of abolition in Latin America and contributed to the modern ideals of human dignity and freedom. *See also* Just War Theory as Justification for Slavery; Roman Catholic Church and Antislavery and Abolitionism; Spanish Empire, Antislavery and Abolition in.

Further Readings: Friede, Juan, and Benjamin Keen, eds. *Bartolomé de las Casas in History: Toward an Understanding of the Man and His Work.* DeKalb: Northern Illinois University Press, 1971; Hanke, Lewis. *All Mankind Is One: A Study of the Disputation between Bartolomé de Las Casas and Juan Ginés De Sepúlveda in 1550 on the Intellectual and Religious Capacity of the American Indian.* DeKalb: Northern Illinois University Press, 1974; Magnaghi, Russell M. *Indian Slavery, Labor, Evangelization, and Captivity in the Americas.* Lanham, MD: Scarecrow Press, 1998; Sevilla-Casas, Elias, ed. *Western Expansion and Indigenous Peoples: The Heritage of Las Casas.* The Hague: Mouton, 1977; Traboulay, David M. *Columbus and Las Casas: The Conquest and Christianization of America, 1492–1566.* Lanham, MD: University Press of America, 1994.

Gerald L. Mattingly and Leslie A. Mattingly

Latin America, Antislavery and Abolition in

The long military struggle for Latin American political independence from Spain, beginning in 1808 and ending with the withdrawal of the Spanish armies from mainland Latin America in 1824, culminated in the creation of the new republics of Latin America. The civil wars across Latin America also fatally weakened the colonial institution of slavery, which had helped to prop up Spanish colonialism. It took some time for all the independent republics to abolish slavery with formal legislative acts, but the death knell had been sounded well before the institution actually disappeared. The wars of national independence fought across Latin America were not in themselves wars of abolition, but these wars began a process that led to the abolition of slavery within the independent countries of Latin America.

The Latin American wars of independence had part of their origin in the age of revolution that preceded them. The American Revolution had provided a powerful example of how to throw off European colonialism, and the French Revolution had spread the ideas of the Enlightenment throughout Europe and beyond. French revolutionary ideas had helped to precipitate the overthrow of slavery in the French colony of Saint Domingue, and this, in turn, led to the independent black republic of Haiti, an evocative symbol of revolutionary change for the Americas. The idea of liberty now was no longer an abstract intellectual term; for the slaves of the Americas, rumors of the **Haitian Revolution** meant freedom from the hated institution which imprisoned them. For their masters, however, it inspired the fear of slave rebellion and the loss of their slave property.

The leaders of the Latin American independence movements embraced the rhetoric of the Enlightenment to promote their cause. They accused Spain of enslaving the peoples of Latin America and called for freedom from this Spanish colonial servitude. The language of political freedom which gained ground as the civil wars slowly led to the collapse of Spanish colonialism was directed at Spain, but collective and individual freedoms were inextricably connected. Slaves who were persuaded to fight for the freedom of a country in return for personal freedom made the connection very quickly. However much slave owners who had lived off slave labor wanted to retain the institution, in the minds of slaves the catchword of liberty meant individual freedom just as much as it meant collective freedom. Even slaves who were illiterate, and most were, were attuned to the words and rhetoric of the civil wars in which they played such an important part.

Historians do not agree on how many slaves there were in Latin America on the eve of independence, but they agree that outside Brazil and Cuba slave labor was dominant only in selected areas of Latin America. The largest slave numbers were to be found in Brazil, but in the remainder of mainland Latin America, slaves did not exceed 10 percent of the population. Slave populations were concentrated in the cacao and sugar plantations of Venezuela, the coastal regions of Peru and Ecuador, the mining communities and the port towns of what would become Colombia, and the area around Buenos Aires in the Rio de la Plata. They were to be found wherever their labor was deemed essential. In urban areas they dominated as domestic servants and worked at a variety of artisan positions. One recent estimate found approximately 30,000 in the Rio de la Plata, 78,000 in New Granada (Colombia), nearly 65,000 in Venezuela, and less than 90,000 in the Viceroyalty of Peru, of whom up to 6,000 were located in Chile.

Abolition of the Slave Trade in Latin America

As soon as Britain abolished the African slave trade within her own colonial empire in 1807, British politicians and diplomats embarked upon a campaign to persuade other countries to follow Britain's example so that slave traders could not use flags of these countries to carry on the slave trade. When the Latin American independence movements began, their leaders were anxious to secure British support, and one way was to embrace the new liberalism of equality by proscribing the Atlantic slave trade. The British government would not accept declarations alone or even legislation. It insisted on including articles banning the slave trade in all treaties it signed with the newly independent countries of Latin America recognizing their independence, seeking to bind these new nations together in a campaign to enforce the abolition of the slave trade. By 1826, Britain had succeeded in signing treaties with Mexico, Colombia, and Buenos Aires, and in each, a standard clause prohibiting the slave trade was included.

Apart from Brazil and Cuba where an illegal slave trade flourished into the second half of the nineteenth century, the most difficult area confronting British diplomacy was Uruguay and the surrounding La Plata region. The British feared a renewal of the slave trade as a means of supplying more slaves to the flourishing plantation areas of southern Brazil. Here it took until 1842 before a treaty including a binding antislave-trade provision was ratified. By checking the possible renewal of the slave trade through the La Plata region, the British government was striking a blow at the continuing slave trade to Brazil. Slaves were also being brought from Uruguay to Buenos Aires from the latter 1820s. Governor Juan Manuel de Rosas reopened the slave trade into Buenos Aires from 1831 to 1833. British pressure again forced a halt, and a new Anglo-Argentine antislave-trade treaty of 1840 effectively suppressed it.

British support for the antislave-trade campaign was occasionally misinterpreted. When a British army invaded and occupied Buenos Aires in 1806, the African slaves in the city apparently believed that their emancipation was at hand. The British general obliged the creole elite in Buenos Aires by issuing a decree saying that he had no intention of abolishing slavery. When, in turn, the inhabitants of Buenos Aires expelled the British, they were assisted by slaves fighting with arms issued by the town council. Slavery would continue in Buenos Aires and Argentina until much later.

Venezuela was the first independence movement to ban the slave trade in a decree issued by the Supreme Junta of Caracas in 1810. The banning of "the vile traffic in slaves" was then included in the first Venezuelan constitution promulgated in 1811. The independence movement in Chile banned the slave trade in the same year and also provided that children of slaves would subsequently be born free, thus beginning a free womb process that would be followed eventually by most of the newly independent Latin American countries. In Chile, this step prompted some slave owners to free their slaves. Some 300 slaves then marched to the government in Santiago, armed with knives, asking the new government for their freedom and offering to defend the new republic. The republican government of Buenos Aires issued an executive decree in 1812, prohibiting the slave trade, and confirmed it in legislation the following year. The constitution of the new state of Cartagena in 1812 included a clause banning the slave trade, although the civil war conditions made enforcement of this provision highly doubtful. Not all of these early antislave-trade declarations remained in force, but the overall effect was to seal the fate of the African slave trade to mainland Latin America and to weaken Latin American slavery.

Just as **Simón Bolívar** would try to set an example for abolitionists in northern South America, the liberator José de San Martín did the same in the former Viceroyalty of Peru, issuing a decree in Lima in 1821, banning the slave trade and initiating the free womb concept throughout the new republic of Peru. In Mexico the earliest revolutionary leaders went even further, as Miguel Hidalgo proclaimed the abolition of slavery in 1810, which his successor José Maria Morelos confirmed. The ultimate failure of their social revolution postponed the abolition of slavery in Mexico until after formal independence had been achieved. The cumulative effect of these decrees and early legislative acts was to signal that the demise of slavery throughout Latin America was inevitable, even though it would take much longer to eliminate it completely. Of the mainland Latin American republics, only Chile and Central America abolished slavery immediately following independence. Chile abolished slavery in 1823, the first mainland Latin American republic to do so, and once the Central American Federation had broken away from Mexico and declared its own independence it, too, abolished slavery in 1824. When the Central American Federation dissolved in 1839, none of the Central American successor states reverted to legal systems of slavery. In Santo Domingo, now the Dominican Republic, Haitian occupation forces abolished slavery in 1822.

By 1851, Britain had succeeded in signing antislave-trade treaties with nearly all the newly independent states of Latin America, ensuring that the flags of these nations would not be used in the African slave trade. Latin American willingness to assist Britain in suppressing the slave trade helped to ensure that it would not spread and also cut off the external supply of slaves that the institution had depended upon. Without that supply, slavery could not last long in any of the new nations. That it survived as long as it did is testimony to the lack of any strong antislavery commitment among the ruling classes of the new republics.

Slave Emancipation in Venezuela and Colombia

Following the decree ending the slave trade to the region, the Venezuelan patriot, Francisco Miranda, proclaimed a slave enlistment decree in 1812, seeking to lure slaves to enlist in the republican army by promising them eventual freedom after fighting (and surviving) for four years. Slave owners who feared that the experience of Haiti would be repeated in Venezuela forced Miranda to limit the number of slaves included, but the precedent of recruiting slaves to fight in the civil wars had been set. Both sides, the royalists and the republicans, would use this device and slaves, themselves, would join the armies in an effort to obtain their freedom, just as some would later desert if they saw an opportunity to throw off the legal shackles of slavery. Thousands of slaves utilized the continuing civil wars in northern South America, as they did in other areas of South America, to flee their masters. An estimated 5,000 joined Bolívar's army in Colombia between 1819 and 1821, and up to a third of recruits in Ecuador were slaves hoping to gain freedom. The civil wars provided the opportunity, but it was the slaves themselves who seized the chance of fighting with all its attendant risks to escape their past servitude. Many became casualties of the wars, either killed or suffering wounds which would leave them incapacitated in years to come. Slaves and former slaves did much of the fighting throughout Latin America, and their contribution to the independence movements has often been overlooked.

In 1816, Simón Bolívar promised President Pétion of Haiti that in return for the president's political and financial support in the struggle against Spanish colonialism, he would issue a proclamation declaring freedom for all slaves. In this and subsequent pronouncements, Bolívar repeated his commitment to the abolition of slavery, but he was never able to persuade his countrymen to live up to the promise he had made. He did, however, free his own remaining slaves in 1820 as an example to others. Later, in October 1821, he passed a law freeing the slaves of Spaniards who chose to leave Gran Colombia rather than live in the newly independent republic.

In 1820, Bolívar wrote that "it seems to me madness that a revolution for freedom expects to maintain slavery." He was unable to resolve the central contradiction of his statement. As the leader of the independence forces in northern South America, Bolívar was trying first of all to seduce slaves to fight for the republican side with offers of freedom following the wars. His real message was that slaves who wanted their freedom would have to fight as republicans to gain it, but time would prove that the eradication of the institution needed even more than the sacrifices of individual slaves. It required clear legislative action. In spite of the ringing declarations of freedom from Bolívar, and the important contribution of slaves and ex-slaves to the republican victory, the institution of slavery survived into the independence period in northern South America.

Bolívar summoned legislators to a Congress at Angostura in 1819 to create a constitution for the newly independent nation of Gran Colombia, encompassing present-day Venezuela, Colombia, and Ecuador. The legislators, many of whom were creole planters and slave owners, refused to ratify Bolívar's abolition policy. Instead they postponed effective and complete abolition through a series of rhetorical statements affirming eventual slave emancipation. Two years later, in 1821, legislators passed the Cúcuta Slave Law, decreeing the free birth of all children born to slave mothers. This set in motion a process of gradual emancipation with conditions. To ensure compensation to slave owners, the child had to serve the mother's master for eighteen years. Even then, full legal freedom would only occur if a local board of manumission approved.

Bolívar continued to issue decrees against slavery in the new republic of Gran Colombia, at least four more, in 1822, 1823, 1827, and 1828, but none succeeded in bringing complete emancipation. The slave owners used every method available to them in opposing emancipation and in preserving what was left of an institution they relied upon for labor and wealth. Slave labor, although in slow and steady decline, remained deeply entrenched in the economic and cultural fabric of the society, and those possessing slaves fought the idea of emancipation as long as possible. Although the number of slaves in Caribbean New Granada (Colombia) fell to less than 7,000 by

1835, urban elites still relied upon female slaves for their domestic labor, and the census figures did not include the labor of the children who had ostensibly been freed by the free womb legislation but still were performing servile labor for the slave masters. It remained true throughout the region that the majority of slave women were to be found as domestic laborers in the cities and the majority of slave men worked in rural areas. The failure to achieve genuine emancipation in Gran Colombia meant that with the breakup of the state in 1830 and the emergence of Venezuela, Colombia, and Ecuador, the end of the institution was left to the new states to resolve.

Slavery in the new state of Gran Colombia, and after 1830 in the successor states of Venezuela, Colombia, and Ecuador, was by then an institution affecting only a small minority of the population. Two of these states, Venezuela and Colombia, along with Peru, however, had possessed the largest slave populations in Spanish South America at the beginning of the independence period. Slave populations had steadily declined due to the end of the African slave trade, the severe disruptions of the civil wars over many years, natural death and the impact of the free womb law of 1821, along with growing opportunities readily seized by slaves to obtain their own freedom. Slavery remained concentrated in the plantation areas of Venezuela and the port towns of the future Colombia. By 1844, less than 2 percent of Venezuela's population still remained slaves. These slaves, however, carried on working as servile laborers and also functioned as sources of financial credit for their often financially over-stretched owners. But in the years following independence, fewer slaves were willing to put up with slavery. They became more aggressive in seeking freedom through flight, abandoning plantations to join bands of guerrillas and finding other ways to escape from servitude. Yet, even when slavery as an institution was clearly in its last stages with the number of slaves steadily diminishing, Venezuelan slave owners were unwilling to abolish slavery without adequate compensation. Their demand for compensation held up final abolition in 1854 when the bill was being debated. The formal abolition of slavery in Venezuela occurred on March 24, 1854. Emancipation in New Granada, or Colombia as it became in 1856, had occurred two years earlier at the beginning of 1852.

Slave Emancipation in Peru

Complete emancipation of slavery throughout Peru seemed to be just a matter of time in 1821, following San Martín's declaration that the country itself was free from Spanish colonialism. That declaration proved premature as was the hope for immediate emancipation. Not until 1824 and the final defeat of Spanish forces at the battle of Ayacucho was a republican victory secured. In Peru and in the neighboring Latin American states, complete emancipation of slavery had to wait for another thirty years. No antislavery movement powerful enough to overcome the vested interests of the conservative property-owning elite existed. Peru's slave population at independence amounted to some 50,000 individuals, which was less than 4 percent of the total population of 1,325,000. Slave labor, therefore, did not play a vital role in the economy as a whole, but it did play a role where the slave population was concentrated: in the plantations of the Peruvian coastal river valleys and around Lima itself. Here, the importance of slaves, as sources of wealth and as symbols of social status, was much greater. Peruvian slave owners succeeded in postponing effective emancipation as long as possible. Peru's experience mirrored that of the neighboring states; emancipation was characterized by gradualism and the preservation of the social structure underpinning slavery even as the institution itself slowly withered away.

Emancipation finally occurred in Peru in 1855, at approximately the same time period as it happened in Venezuela, Bolivia, Colombia, Ecuador, and the Argentine Confederation. All these countries were no doubt influenced by the liberal ideas of the 1848 revolutions in Europe, but in each country there were unique circumstances dictating the timing of emancipation. When it came, slave emancipation in Peru, as in other Latin American countries, was a product of a steadily disintegrating slave structure and the unremitting efforts of the slaves themselves to use every means possible to obtain their own freedom. Flight, legal suits brought before the courts, self-purchase and a variety of challenges to slave owners, both active and passive, slowly undermined what remained of a once dominant colonial institution.

Following his successful invasion of Peru, San Martín proclaimed the law of free womb on August 12, 1821, and later that same year he issued a decree on November 20, prohibiting the slave trade. Further decrees strengthened the trend toward emancipation in Peru, including proclamations of freedom for slaves who joined the patriot army. The arrival in Peru of Bolívar in 1823 to consolidate the independence that San Martín had won reinforced the hopes of the antislavery elements in the country. These were soon disappointed by the absence of any substantive measures to implement the complete abolition of slavery. Neither San Martín nor Bolívar was prepared to risk an open confrontation over abolition with the creole elites who were now in power. The two liberators set in motion policies of gradual emancipation, but that is as far as they would go. Neither contemplated the emancipation of slaves without compensation for the slave owners whose loyalty was essential if republicanism was to succeed. Abolishing slavery without compensation might have quickly converted the creole slave owners back to royalists. The desperate financial state of the new republics precluded the use of scarce funds for solely humanitarian purposes.

After Peru's independence from Spain, writers, politicians, and landowners alike attributed the decay of Peru's agriculture, especially the decline of the coastal plantations, to the lack of slaves. Labor shortages were viewed as the major problem, and rural labor was still equated with slave labor. The country's governing elites continued to make a strong mental connection between agricultural prosperity and the continuation of slave labor. Even as slave numbers declined, the remaining slaves continued to be seen as indispensable in a variety of occupations, both rural and urban. For slave owners, slaves also proved to be a significant financial investment, and they could bring a high rate of return. On rural estates the total value of the slaves often reached a substantial portion of the overall value of the estate. Slaves could serve as collateral for loans and mortgages and they could earn money for their master by being hired out. Because slavery was such a profitable enterprise in many varied ways, in the midst of the political and financial chaos that characterized Peru's existence in the post independence period, slave owners and the governing elites firmly opposed immediate abolition. Instead, the Peruvian slave owners focused their energies on trying to re-establish the remnants of Peruvian slavery upon a stronger foundation. Peru's landowning elites proved strong enough to persuade the government to re-open the slave trade beginning in 1846, permitting the importation of slaves from neighboring American republics for a trial period of six years.

The Peruvian government in 1839, acting in response to pressure from the landowners, modified the free womb provision to ensure that former slaves would not be freed until they reached the age of fifty. Previously, between 1837 and 1842, as the children of the free womb laws reached their age of freedom, Colombia, Uruguay, and Venezuela had raised the age of these "libertos," as they were termed, to twenty-five, to retain their labor. In each of these cases, the policy of gradual emancipation embodied in the free womb laws was being twisted into a last ditch defense of slavery by the creole slave owners of the new republican states.

No strong abolitionist movement appeared in Peru during the first half of the nineteenth century, but by the middle of the century there were signs of growing repugnance towards the continued existence of slavery, evident in newspaper columns and letters to the editor from individuals. As Peru's neighboring countries moved towards emancipation in the early 1850s, more Peruvians began to believe they should follow this wider Latin American example not to be seen as uncivilized. The Peruvian government, however, remained obdurate in its defense of slavery, as first Bolivia abolished it in 1851, then Colombia and Ecuador in 1852, the Argentine Confederation in 1853, and finally Venezuela in 1854.

The eruption of a civil war in Peru in 1854 created the context in which Peruvian emancipation took place. President José Echenique, seeking to continue in power, issued a decree on November 18, 1854, encouraging slaves to enlist in his army in what has been described as a "self-serving, opportunistic gesture." Any slave enlisting and serving for two years would be freed, as would his legitimate wife. The president's rival, a man named Ramón Castilla, responded in early December with a decree, extending freedom to all slaves. His decree, too, was also self serving and opportunistic, but both decrees followed a well-established tradition going back to the liberators, Bolívar and San Martín, who had lured slaves to fight with promises of freedom. When Castilla became president of Peru in 1855, he found that he had to ratify his promise of emancipation. In order to retain the support of slave owners, he also had to pay compensation. Eventually, over 25,000 remaining slaves were freed with compensation exceeding seven million pesos. The emancipation of Peru's slaves did not lead to a social revolution in the country, nor did it mean any significant improvement in their economic or social status. It did fulfill the long delayed promise of liberation given by both San Martín and Bolívar that Peru's landowning elite had fought so hard and so long to thwart.

Slave Emancipation: Buenos Aires, Argentina, and the La Plata Region

The declaration of independence in Buenos Aires in 1810 coincided with expressions of racial equality, but even in 1810 the Buenos Aires City Council was not willing to contemplate the abolition of slavery. Property rights were viewed by these Buenos Aires creoles as sacrosanct, and slaves were still seen as property. Here, as in northern South America, the outbreak of civil wars that would endure for years created a demand for soldiers that caused the military leaders to look to slaves to fulfill. Beginning in 1813, slave owners were required to sell some of their slaves to the state. The slaves were enlisted in army units and promised their freedom after the fighting had ended. Many died during the fighting, others returned with wounds of varying severity, and still others seized any opportunity they were given to desert and find freedom. The 1813 impressments of slaves into the republican army followed a free womb decree passed by the republican Constituent Assembly of Buenos Aires and opened the door for future forced slave enlistments.

Half of San Martín's army of liberation, which crossed the Andes in 1816 to free Chile from Spanish rule, consisted of slaves conscripted into military service from Buenos Aires and its surrounding territory, and promised their freedom after the fighting was over. The former slaves who fought in San Martín's army participated in a remarkable military campaign in which they fought battles in Chile, Peru, and Ecuador, but less than 150 of the original 2,000 or so former slaves actually returned to Argentina following the end of the wars. Desertion, death, and wounds or disease determined the fate of the others.

San Martín was certainly not the only military leader in the southern cone of South America to use slaves in his army. Historians estimate that from 4,000 to 5,000 slaves served with the republican forces in the Río de la Plata region between the years 1813–1818. José Artigas, the caudillo leader in the Banda Oriental (the future Uruguay), encouraged slaves to fight with him, although in reality most were probably fighting for themselves. He was eventually defeated by a Portuguese army that came from Brazil supported by the landowners of the region. With slavery restored in the future territory of Uruguay and the Portuguese triumphant, Artigas fled to Paraguay in 1820. The former slaves who were the core of his army accompanied him to Paraguay and settled in communities there.

Under the dictatorship of Francia, slavery in Paraguay flourished until Francia's death in 1840 when his own slaves were freed, steps were taken to stop the slave trade, and a free womb law was adopted, guaranteeing the gradual emancipation of the slaves in Paraguay. It took until 1869, however, before Paraguay accepted the abolition of slavery.

In Argentina, the Constitution of the Argentine Confederation of 1853 contained a clause abolishing slavery, but the province of Buenos Aires delayed ratifying the constitution and joining the state until 1861, thereby preserving slavery a little longer. By 1861, however, slavery in all areas of Argentina had effectively ended.

Abolition of Slavery in Mexico

The Hidalgo revolt witnessed the beginnings of the independence movement in Mexico. Following the outbreak of revolution in 1810, Hidalgo broadened the appeal of his revolutionary movement by issuing an emancipation proclamation that caused many more slaves to enlist in Hidalgo's revolutionary army. Mexico possessed very few slaves on the eve of the Latin American independence movements, perhaps some 6,000 out of a total estimated population of six million. The slaves were concentrated in the port regions of Veracruz and Acapulco and their hinterlands.

The eventual defeat of Hidalgo and his successor, Morelos, did not end the Mexican slaves' own efforts to procure their freedom. Mexico's independence from Spain came in 1821, and the Mexican leader of independence, Iturbide, issued a proclamation freeing slaves who had fought on the republican side, one indication that slaves had continued to fight for their freedom throughout the civil wars preceding independence. Although several Mexican states abolished slavery in the mid 1820s, the final Mexican legislation emancipating all slaves in the country came in October 1829, during the brief presidency of Vicente Guerrero, a Mexican of mixed-race background and a veteran of Mexico's pre-independence civil wars.

This emancipation measure was clearly directed at stopping the immigration of slave owners from the United States into Texas along with their slaves, a migration that would turn Texas into a slave plantation state. The emancipation decree was not enforced immediately, but outside of Texas, it was accepted throughout Mexico. Once Texas seceded from Mexico in 1836 and became the Republic of Texas, slavery was legalized once more and the United States' annexation of Texas in 1845 recognized Texas as a slave state. Within Mexico, the Constitution of 1857 included an article again abolishing slavery.

Conclusion

With the outbreak of the independence struggle in Latin America, the rhetoric of the Enlightenment embraced by the republican leaders signaled that freedom would come not only collectively for the colonies of Spain, but individually for slaves as well. The rhetoric obscured the reality of a Latin American society where property rights took precedence over slaves' rights to individual freedom. The creoles who found themselves in power after the elimination of Spain from mainland Latin America put their own self interest ahead of the concept of freedom where slaves were concerned.

Slavery was fatally weakened by the long and damaging civil wars, which characterized the independence period both in the northern and southern parts of South America, as well as in Mexico. Nevertheless, the institution of slavery took a long time to die. The final emancipation of slavery in many Latin American countries did not occur until the 1850s, and even then the social and economic reality for the former slaves was not significantly altered.

The wars of independence did open new opportunities for the slaves to grasp their own freedom by fighting for one side or the other, and, following independence, gradual emancipation was solidified through free womb laws and the abolition of the slave trade. Yet the story of slave emancipation in Latin America is one of a protracted struggle in which the slave owners fought every step of the way to protect their slave property even as slave numbers declined continuously and the institution of slavery slowly, but steadily, disappeared. *See also* Cuba, Emancipation in; Spanish Empire, Antislavery and Abolition in; Texas, Annexation of.

Further Readings: Blackburn, Robin. *The Overthrow of Colonial Slavery, 1776–1848.* London: Verso, 1988; Blanchard, Peter. "The Language of Liberation: Slave Voices in the Wars of Independence." *Hispanic American Historical Review* 82, 3 (2002): 499–523; Blanchard, Peter. *Slavery and Abolition in Early Republican Peru.* Lanham, MD: SR Books, 1992; Klein, Herbert S. *African Slavery in Latin America and the Caribbean.* Oxford: Oxford University Press, 1986; Lombardi, John V. *The Decline and Abolition of Negro Slavery in Venezuela.* Westport, CT: Greenwood, 1971; Lynch. John. *The Spanish American Revolutions.* 2nd ed. New York: W.W. Norton and Company, 1986.

David Murray

Lavigerie, Charles (1825–1892)

As an archbishop and then a cardinal of the Catholic Church, Charles Lavigerie was the founder of the modern Catholic antislavery movement. Born in southwestern France, Lavigerie became a priest in 1849. The Catholic Church had since the French Revolution been hostile to progressive movements which it associated with anticlericalism and the effort during the revolution to create a state-controlled church. In 1863, Lavigerie was appointed Bishop of Nancy. As bishop, Lavigerie struggled to disengage the church from reactionary forces in Nancy. In 1867, he was appointed Archbishop of Algiers. In 1868, he founded the Society of Missionaries to Africa, better known from the color of their robes as the White Fathers. Their mission was first defined as carrying the Christian message to Muslim peoples. The white robes were chosen because they resembled Arab robes. They had little success in North Africa, and thus, from 1878, they focused on sub-Saharan Africa, though they maintained an interest in Islam. They quickly became one of the more important Catholic mission orders.

In 1884, Lavigerie became a cardinal. By this time, Lavigerie's missionaries were confronting the ravages of the slave trade. Many missions in the interlacustrine area and the eastern Congo became armed camps trying to protect those fleeing the violence. Convinced that slaving was an obstacle to mission work, he devoted his considerable oratorical and organizational talents to creating an antislavery movement in a religious community that had hitherto not been involved. He sought states that could protect the victims, briefly tried to organize a movement of armed volunteers, and pleaded with the Pope to lead an antislavery crusade. Finally, in 1888, the reforming Pope, Leo XIII, gave his approval. That year, Lavigerie made a tour of Europe, starting with an emotional sermon in Paris lashing out at the cruelties of the slave trade and the suffering it caused. Before the year was out, antislavery committees had been formed in every Catholic country he visited. Parish priests all over Europe carried his message to Catholic communities. In Belgium, he met with King Leopold, who was looking for an ideological cover for his effort to colonize the Congo basin. He also forged links with the British abolitionists, but not with the existing French abolition movement. **Victor Schoelcher** and most early French antislavery people were anticlerical. Lavigerie was too committed to the Catholic Church to be able to work with them. The stimulus Lavigerie gave to the antislavery movement led to the **Brussels Conference** of 1889–90, which committed European powers to the suppression of the slave trade, though it provided few hard measures to guarantee this. The revitalization of antislavery also created a pressure on colonial regimes to take actions against slavery once they had established control of the areas they had staked out for themselves. Lavigerie died in 1892, but the Société Antiesclavagiste de France (Antislavery Society of France) remained an important force in French colonial politics, and the White Fathers continued to play a role in the mission field. *See also* Roman Catholic Church and Antislavery and Abolitionism.

Further Reading: Renault, François. *Lavigerie, L'Esclavage Africain et L'Europe.* Paris: E. De Broccard, 1971.

Martin A. Klein

League of Nations and Antislavery and Abolition

The League of Nations, established in 1919, played an important role in the campaign to abolish slavery. Article 23 of the League Covenant bound its members to "ensure fair and humane conditions of labor" for men, women, and children, not only in their own countries but also in all countries with which they had commercial and industrial relations, and to secure the "just treatment" of the natives under their rule. The League established the League Permanent Mandates Commission to ensure that the powers, which acquired former enemy territories as the result of the First World War, administered them in the interests of their inhabitants. Among other things, they were to suppress the slave trade and to end slavery as soon as "social conditions" allowed it.

However, the League itself, apart from the Mandates Commission, might never have been drawn into the general campaign for the abolition of slavery had not the Secretary of the British Anti-Slavery and Aborigines Protection Society, John (later Sir John) Harris, lobbied members of the League after he had heard that slave raiding and trading were rife in southwestern

Ethiopia. Finding that for political reasons the British government did not intend to take any action, Harris persuaded the delegate for New Zealand, Sir Arthur Steel-Maitland, to propose in September 1922 that the Council of the League launch an inquiry into slavery. The League then solicited member governments and asked for information on slavery. When this failed to produce much information, it established the Temporary Slavery Commission to inquire into slavery worldwide. Unable to prevent this, the European colonial powers limited the commission's evidence to published works and information supplied by governments, or government approved non-governmental organizations (NGOs).

The commission consisted of former colonial governors or officials, who had experienced slavery first hand, as well as a member of the International Labor Organization (ILO). A Haitian was included as window dressing. These were "independent experts." Hitherto, slavery to most Westerners meant only chattel slavery. Chattel slaves were property. They could be bought, sold, and inherited. Their servitude was lifelong and hereditary. Some were state owned, but most were private property and only their owners, or a court, could free them. They were captured, inherited, bought, paid as tribute or given away. Some sold themselves or their children in times of famine. The leading members of the commission knew that the main problem for colonial peoples was not the chattel slavery still legally practiced in parts of Africa and Arabia, but the labor demands of the colonial powers themselves. Against the wishes of the colonial governments, the Temporary Slavery Commission extended the definition of slavery to include debt-bondage, peonage, serfdom, forced marriage, the adoption of children to exploit them, and the forced labor imposed by governments.

As the result of pressure from this commission, and the drawing up of a draft treaty by its British member, Sir Frederick (later Lord) Lugard, the League negotiated the **Slavery Convention of 1926.** This was followed in 1930 by the negotiation of the Forced Labor Convention by the International Labor Organization (ILO). Its aim was to protect colonial peoples from the various forms of forced labor demanded by their colonial rulers.

The League appointed two more slavery committees, backed by Britain, anxious to display its antislavery zeal. The first, the Committee of Experts on Slavery, met in 1932. This time only the European colonial powers were represented. Its evidence was even more restricted than that of its predecessor, and it was marked by friction particularly between its English and French members. It complained that, owing to the rules of procedure, it did not have enough information, and recommended the appointment of a permanent League Slavery Committee.

The result was the appointment by the League of the Advisory Committee of Experts on Slavery, which met from 1934 to 1938. It consisted of delegates of the colonial powers, and, as before, its sources were strictly limited to protect the colonial governments. After a halting start, this committee was soon dominated by its British member, Sir George Maxwell. His plan was to collect as much information as possible to concentrate on freeing the remaining chattel slaves, mainly in Ethiopia and parts of Arabia where slavery was still legal. He wanted to pass such matters as the exploitation of adopted children, which theoretically ended when the child grew up, and debt bondage, which ended when the debt was paid, to the ILO and more influential League bodies, such as the Social Questions Committee and the Child Protection Committee. When this was achieved, he believed that the committee could be disbanded—its work successfully accomplished. Meanwhile, he insisted on honest reports from the British government and bombarded his colleagues with reports on all aspects of slavery. To the dismay of the Colonial Office, the result was that as Maxwell produced most of the committee's reports, it seemed that slavery existed mainly in the British Empire. Maxwell had not succeeded in his aims when, to his great disappointment, the outbreak of the Second World War ended all hope of further meetings.

However, the League committees had some impact. The first treaty against slavery in all its forms had been negotiated and ratified by a number of powers. A great deal of information had been collected on the practices that the Temporary Slavery Commission had designated as slavery. Both the French and the British reviewed their antislavery laws. On the downside, Italy used the suppression of slavery to justify its conquest of Ethiopia in 1935.

Slavery was now well and truly in the public arena, and after the war it was taken up by the United Nations, which succeeded the League of Nations.

It should be noted that these committees did not discuss the new forms of slavery and forced labor that were taking shape in the form of gulags in the Soviet Union from the 1920s, or the concentration camps of Nazi Germany. Meanwhile, other League bodies dealt with such questions as forced prostitution (sometimes called the White slave trade), and forced recruitment for contract labor from Liberia to the Spanish island of Fernando Po.

Further Readings: Miers, Suzanne. *Slavery in the Twentieth Century: The Evolution of a Global Problem.* Walnut Creek, CA: Altamira Press, 2003; Reports of the Temporary Slavery Commission, 1924–25, League of Nations Archives, Geneva (also available in the British Library); Reports of the Committee of Experts on Slavery, 1932, League of Nations Archives, Geneva, (also available in the British Library); Reports of the Advisory Committee of Experts on Slavery 1934–38, League of Nations Archives, Geneva (also available in the British Library).

Suzanne Miers

League of Nations Covenant, Articles 22 and 23

The Covenant, or Charter, of the **League of Nations** embodied the paternalistic colonial worldview of the victorious powers in World War I. Colonized peoples deemed too uncivilized to govern themselves were placed under a League of Nations mandate, to be administered by a League member. Parts of Articles 22 and 23 of the Covenant bear on slavery and the slave trade, and nominal mandate responsibilities for these areas, as well as in colonies.

The League Covenant was hardly ambiguous, and included, in Article 22, a "prohibition of abuses such as the slave trade," and in Article 23, the following clauses regarding labor:

(a) [colonial and mandate powers] will endeavor to secure and maintain fair and humane conditions of labor for men, women, and children, both in their own countries and in all countries to which their commercial and industrial relations extend, and for that purpose will establish and maintain the necessary international organizations; (b) undertake to secure just treatment of the native inhabitants of territories under their control; (c) will entrust the League with the general supervision over the execution of agreements with regard to the traffic in women and children.

The League's enforcement actions in many of these areas were almost non-existent, as the interests of its members who were colonial powers in commerce, tax revenues, and political stability outweighed almost all other considerations. Great Britain, for example, did not act to end slavery in the interior of Sierra Leone until 1928. The colonial head, hut, and other taxes which natives usually had to pay in the coin of the realm forced colonized peoples to work for European enterprises—the only source of such legal tender—in *de facto* slavery for less than subsistence wages in order to avoid jail. None of the European colonial powers did much more than pay lip service to their covenant obligations in their own colonies or mandates.

Only one League member, **Liberia,** came under systematic investigation and censure for its failure to uphold the covenant. Local and national elites in Liberia had, if anything, expanded labor abuses through exploiting the traditional pawning or indenture system while eroding the protections of traditional practices. Tribal and village labor quotas resulted in widespread *corvee* labor and individual forced recruitment for tasks such as porterage which included carrying outsiders through the interior in hammocks, and road-building. Forced labor was also required for development of farms and plantations for district commissioners and other members of the Americo-Liberian elite, often during the crucial peak labor demand of the village farming season, so that starvation often followed such coerced labor. Overseers of such labor, having quotas to meet, were essentially unsupervised; consequently, violence and many other abuses commonly occurred. With the United States-promoted 1926 contract between the Monrovia government and the American Firestone Rubber Company, demand for forced labor outside the local economy increased dramatically. Chiefs coerced the powerless, rivals, alcoholics, and others perceived as troublemakers to work at Firestone, the labor force of which expanded to over 10,000. The final outrage, however, came when troops under the orders of members of the Americo-Liberian elite, themselves former slaves who had settled in Liberia with the motto "The Love of Liberty Brought Us Here," engaged in systematic night-raiding, kidnapping, and shipping of villagers to Spanish plantations on the island of Fernando Po. Even the then Liberian Vice President Allen Yancy was accomplice to a trade that brought as much as $45.00 a head for each of 3,000 men exported. This brought down the government (1920–1930) of then President C.D.B. King and led to some reform and a decline in international opprobrium. Short-term coerced labor on private and on nominally government projects continued in the hinterlands, however, at least into the 1980s.

While criticisms of Liberia were justified, both Britain and France had held designs on Liberian territories and sovereignty. The publicity they gave to Liberia's violations was clearly self-serving. Only objections from the United States, which had its own neo-colonial agenda in Liberia, had repeatedly prevented the African republic's dismantling by neighboring colonial powers whose treatment of their own subjects, excepting the literal export of slaves to other countries, was little if any better, and certainly no more in conformity with the League's ideals. *See also* United Nations and Antislavery.

Further Readings: Liebenow, J. Gus. *Liberia: The Quest for Democracy.* Bloomington and Indianapolis: Indiana University Press, 1987; Sawyer, Amos. *The Emergence of Autocracy in Liberia: Tragedy and Challenge.* San Francisco: Institute for Contemporary Studies, 1992.

Gordon C. Thomasson

Les Amis des Noirs

From its first recorded meeting in February 1788, the first French antislavery society, the *Société des Amis des Noirs*, had very few friends but, indeed, many enemies. Its archenemies were, quite naturally, the planter interest. During the revolutionary period in 1789 and after, colonial planters and merchants, represented in the *Comité national* or at the *Club de l'hôtel Massiac*, expressed pointed hatred toward the *Société des Amis des Noirs*. They blamed it for much of the turbulence that had rocked their plantations and businesses to the ground, and accused it of scheming the ruin of the colonial interest as a whole. In a letter dated September 8, 1791, the Marquis de Rouvray, a planter in Saint Domingue, wrote to his daughter, "No doubt the Friends of the Negroes have been the first cause of our woes," as a mass slave insurrection broke out in this most lucrative of French colonial possessions. This was typical of the arguments aimed at the *Société* by its enemies.

Cautious not to be drawn into such controversial debates, the antislavery societies that came into existence in the first half of the nineteenth century, such as the *Comité pour l'abolition de la traite* and the *Société française pour l'abolition de l'esclavage*, never fully acknowledged their vital relationship to the first antislavery society. Participating in the same obfuscation, historians have until very recently ignored the existence of the second *Société*, the Friends of the Negroes and of the Colonies, that was active under the Directory (1795–99) and which became even more internationalist than the first one. The first problem with the *Société des Amis des Noirs* was thus to disentangle its actual activities from previous misrepresentations. For reasons of space, this article focuses only on the first société.

The *Société des Amis des Noirs* had a three-fold paternity. On the one hand, it was the natural heir of the Enlightenment in which writers like **Montesquieu,** the Abbé Prévost, or Bernardin de Saint-Pierre denounced slavery as immoral. From the 1770s onward, the moral condemnation of slavery gave way to a much more radical antislavery which celebrated the institution's violent destruction. Two famous examples are the *Histoire philosophique et politique du commerce et des établissements des Européens dans les deux Indes* by the **Abbé Raynal** and *L'An 2440* by Louis Sébastien Mercier. Mercier and Raynal constructed the literary figure of the black, indomitable rebel, while predicting the general insurrection of all slaves and the eventual demise of plantation societies in general. While such writers were not true abolitionists seeking an immediate end to slavery, they used radical rhetoric to ameliorate plantation regimens. The members of the *Société des Amis des Noirs* used a quite different, and far less radical, strategy of promotion, but it is difficult to separate its creation from the earlier work of Raynal and Mercier.

The *Société des Amis des Noirs* may have been the first antislavery society in France; it was not, as we know, the first antislavery society in the Atlantic World. It was modeled after the English *Society for Effecting the Abolition of the Slave Trade*, which was founded in London in 1787 by Granville Sharp, **Thomas Clarkson, William Wilberforce,** James Ramsay, and James Philips. As Brissot and Clavière, the two original founders of the French *société*, explained in their correspondence, the *Société des Amis des Noirs* was an offshoot of the English Society. From the very start, the *Société* existed as part of a complex Atlantic web of antislavery societies—including the **Pennsylvania Abolition Society**—that shared data and methods.

The members of the *Société des Amis des Noirs* were roughly of three kinds: liberal-minded aristocrats animated by the ideas of the Enlightenment, such as the Marquis de la Fayette, Condorcet, the Lameth brothers, François-Xavier Lanthenas, the Comte de Mirabeau, and the Abbé Grégoire; *gens de lettres* and jurists such as Jérome Pétion, Brissot, and Mercier; and representatives of the business interest such as Clavière or Mollien.

The *Société des Amis des Noirs* cannot truly be described as an abolitionist society. Much like its English counterpart, the *Société*'s prime objective was not the immediate abolition of slavery in the French colonies. Its members clearly did not intend to make slaves the agents of their own liberation, as they became in French Saint Domingue. If the *Société* did petition to grant equal rights to free blacks in Saint Domingue, it did so, in part, to keep the rebellious slaves of the colony under control. The *Amis des Noirs* was not a philanthropic association either, but a new kind of political society in which a new form of political association was attempted. It was open to men and women alike and to Frenchmen and foreigners. Chapter 3 of its *Statutes* made the *Société* explicitly internationalist: "The members of the London and American associations, which share the objective of the *Société des Amis des Noirs*, will of right be accepted in the general assemblies." Its aim was to exert pressure on public authorities at the same time it endeavored to instruct the public on the history of slavery and slave labor and on the possible ways of reforming the French colonies.

The first objective of the *Société des Amis des Noirs* was to abolish the Atlantic slave trade. Its second objective was to bring about a gradual abolition of slavery as a form of labor. Its third objective was to reform the system of French colonization by rationalizing and modernizing the plantation labor system and by creating new colonies in Africa. The use of black labor was still desired, but it could be achieved without the costly transportation of slaves across the Atlantic.

The *Société des Amis des Noirs* used newspapers, journals, pamphlets, and books to constantly disseminate information about its cause. As true heirs of the Enlightenment, the founding members of the *Société* believed that the question and character of slavery had to be illuminated fully for the public. The minutes of the first meeting illustrate this strategy. The *Société* had just received books on slavery from London. The *Amis des Noirs* firmly believed that "The translation and publication of those works must be one of the first objects of consideration of the committee." The committee stressed the importance of republishing all out-of-print French books that sponsored the abolition of the slave trade. The members of the *Société* were also asked to be familiar with the books and pamphlets written by the planter interest so as to better counter their arguments. The *Société* was, finally, to encourage research on slavery in the colonies and was to publish, on a regular basis, the accounts of its activities. It did so in such newspapers as the *Patriote Français*, *L'analyse des papiers anglais* and *Le Cercle Social*.

The *Société des Amis des Noirs* was active until the fall of 1791 when it began to become indistinguishable from the activities of such members of the emerging Girondins group as Brissot and Grégoire. Its main success was the granting of equal rights to free people of color in Saint Domingue and other French colonies in March 1792. The *Société* reemerged for a short period of sixteen months between the end of 1797 and the early months of 1799. Its demise was followed a few years later by its worst defeat: the reestablishment of slavery in the French colonies under the Consulate. *See also* Brissot de Warville, Jacques-Pierre; French Colonies, Emancipation of; Saint Domingue, French Defeat in.

Further Readings: Dorigny, Marcel and Bernard Gainot, eds. *La Société des Amis des Noirs*. Paris: Unesco, 1998; Soboul, Albert, ed. *Dictionnaire historique de la révolution française*. Paris: Presses Universitaires de France, 1989; Thésée, Francoise. *Autour de la Société des Amis des Noirs: Clarkson, Mirabeau et l'abolition de la traite, août 1789–mars 1790*. Paris: Présence africaine, 1983.

Jean-Pierre Le Glaunec

Levy, Moses Elias (1782–1854)

Moses E. Levy was a Jewish-American abolitionist and reformer who achieved celebrity in London during the height of the British antislavery crusade. Both as a Jew and as a U.S. citizen, Levy's position within the evangelical-led abolitionist movement was unprecedented. His anonymous *Plan for the Abolition of Slavery* (London, 1828) garnered favorable notice and resulted in the formation of a new antislavery organization that promoted

Levy's unique approach to gradual emancipation. During a time when conversionist activity was rife among the evangelical leadership—earning the enmity of even secular Jews—and when public activism of any sort was avoided in the Anglo-Jewish community, Levy's mere presence during this crucial period made his achievements even more noteworthy.

The son of a merchant and courtier to the sultan of Morocco, Levy fled as a youngster with his family to British Gibraltar after anti-Semitic violence engulfed the entire Moroccan Jewish community. In 1800, Levy left for St. Thomas, Virgin Islands where he established himself as a merchant/shipper. After a successful career in the West Indies, Levy underwent a spiritual epiphany and abandoned his lucrative trade in favor of a life centered on social, educational, and religious reform. He arrived in the wilds of east Florida in 1821 and founded Pilgrimage Plantation, the first Jewish communal/farming settlement in the United States. A few years later, after suffering a series of setbacks, he departed for England where he hoped to elicit support for his fledgling colony. In London, Levy took on the role of social activist during 1827–1828, and his writing and oratory became well known in the metropolis.

Many of Levy's ideas evolved from his practical experience as a planter in Cuba, Puerto Rico, and Florida—a background that few British abolitionists could claim. From his perspective, immediate emancipation would be catastrophic since blacks were not only psychologically debilitated by slavery, but were hindered by illiteracy as well. As a solution, Levy advocated universal education for slave children, a humane system that would stress reading, writing, and the fundamentals of science, as well as practical training in agriculture. All students—both male and female—would also be instructed in the Bible and raised as Christians; freedom would be awarded at the age of twenty-one, and each male would be given land for farming. Influenced by the utopian philosophy of Robert Owen and the innovations of Swiss educator Johann Heinrich Pestalozzi, Levy envisioned an organized group of philanthropic businesses that would enact his tenets. In theory, these companies would own slaves until the time when their newly trained, free-labor force would supplant slavery in the plantation economy.

Levy's *Plan* was praised for addressing pragmatic issues that other abolitionists avoided. Despite the publication's anonymity, Levy's authorship was well-known in reform circles, and his activities were followed closely by the London press. Some evangelicals compared his benevolent character to the renowned **William Wilberforce.** Levy returned to the United States shortly thereafter. *See also* American Jews and Antislavery.

Further Readings: Levy, Moses E. *A Plan for the Abolition of Slavery,* 1828. Chris Monaco, ed., Reprint. Micanopy, FL: Wacahoota Press, 1999; Monaco, C.S. *Moses Levy of Florida: Jewish Utopian and Antebellum Reformer.* Baton Rouge: Louisiana State University Press, 2005.

C.S. Monaco

Liberated Africans at the Cape of Good Hope

Those captured as slaves, but released at the Cape of Good Hope, were known as "Prize Slaves" or "Prize Negroes" at the time, because they were seized by the British navy as "prizes"; today they are more commonly known as "Liberated Africans," the term frequently used for such people in West Africa. Over 4,000 en route to the Americas were landed at the Cape, at the southern tip of the African continent, between the end of the British slave trade in 1808 and the mid 1840s. Though formally liberated from slavery, they were freed into what was virtual slavery, for the fourteen-year apprenticeship system they all had to undergo amounted to a new form of slavery. For some, conditions were harsher than for the slaves. Whereas many of the Sierra Leonean "Liberated Africans" returned to what is now Nigeria and other places of origin when they could, those who were released at the Cape remained in what is now South Africa, the great majority becoming part of those who would be given, and accept, the name "Coloureds."

Liberated Africans arrived at the Cape in two main waves. Once the British ended their own participation in the Atlantic slave trade in 1808, they were anxious, for both economic and humanitarian reasons, to persuade others to follow suit and cease trading in slaves. A British naval squadron, based in Simon's Town on the Cape Peninsula, south of Cape Town, sought to prevent slave ships traversing the waters of the southern Indian Ocean from reaching the Americas. Numerous slave ships that had set out from ports up the East African coast were seized, along with their human cargoes, and declared "prizes" by the Vice-Admiralty Court that sat in Cape Town. Between 1808 and 1825, approximately 1,500 "Prize Slaves" were taken into service at the Cape. Most arrived before 1815, for in the aftermath of the Napoleonic wars, the British were not successful in persuading the Portuguese government to sign an antislave-trade treaty that would allow British ships to intercept, search, and seize ships flying the Portuguese flag. It was Portuguese nationals who were most heavily involved in slaving in southern waters in this period. A treaty that was signed in 1817 applied only north of the equator, and British naval officials had no powers to search Portuguese ships south of that. In the two decades after the end of the Napoleonic wars, therefore, there was only one major addition of Liberated Africans to the Cape population: in 1818 a Portuguese ship was wrecked in Table Bay and its large cargo of slaves abandoned.

After the British Parliament passed legislation empowering British naval officers to search any ships flying the Portuguese flag, and capture them if they were carrying slaves or were fitted out as slave ships, the Portuguese agreed to sign the kind of treaty the British had long sought from them. The 1842 Anglo-Portuguese treaty gave Britain the right to search Portuguese ships anywhere. If such ships were found to be engaged in slaving, they were to be brought before a court of mixed (British and Portuguese) commission, one of which had been established in Cape Town in 1843. This second wave brought an even larger number of liberated Africans to the Cape in the early 1840s than had the first. When the governor of the island of St. Helena visited Cape Town in December 1841, he reported that there were 1,700 liberated Africans there, captured at sea by the West African squadron. Cape Town businessmen at once offered money to meet the expense of bringing them to the Cape, and some 1,360 liberated Africans, most of them children, arrived at the Cape from St. Helena between March and June 1842. As British naval vessels patrolled further up the East African cost, it became impractical for them to return to release the captured slaves at the Cape. Of the 444 slaves on one slave ship captured off Madagascar, over half died before it reached the Cape fifty days later. After Natal became the second British colony in South Africa 1843, some were released there, and others in the Seychelles. The last liberated Africans to be freed at the Cape landed in 1864, but in fact very few were landed after 1846.

This new influx of liberated Africans was very convenient for the property-owning colonists, for it eased the transition to the post slave-trade era and provided a new supply of "apprentices" after the four-year period of apprenticeship for ex-slaves came to an end in 1838. The liberated Africans were much in demand as a labor force that cost nothing and was controlled with relative ease, for there was no possibility of them returning to their places of origin. The majority was placed on farms, but others worked in Cape Town itself, where some were able to acquire education and were assimilated to Cape society. Some followed the example of many of the ex-slaves and adopted the Muslim religion. In Sierra Leone, the liberated Africans came to dominate the pre-existing population, and, to a quite remarkable extent, were able to fashion their own destiny. At the Cape, by contrast, the end of slavery left intact the basic class division of the society, and the liberated Africans, after release, automatically entered the dominated classes in the settler-ruled society. *See also* Cape of Good Hope, Antislavery and Emancipation at.

Further Readings: Mason, John. *Social Death and Resurrection: Slavery and Emancipation in South Africa.* Charlottesville: University of Virginia Press, 2003; Reidy, Michael. "The Admission of Slaves and 'Prize Slaves' into the Cape Colony, 1787–1818." Unpublished Master's thesis, University of Cape Town, 1997; Saunders, Christopher. "Liberated Africans in the Cape Colony in the First Half of the Nineteenth Century." *International Journal of African Historical Studies* 18, 2 (1985): 223–239.

Christopher Saunders

Liberia

Liberia was founded in 1822 along the West African coast by the **American Colonization Society** (ACS) as a site to settle emancipated slaves from the United States, making it the first American colony. It became an independent country in 1847. Between its founding and the outbreak of the United States Civil War, approximately 12,000 Americans migrated to **Liberia.**

The idea of colonizing freed blacks in Africa was not new when the ACS was organized in December 1816. The concept was discussed by Americans dating back before 1800, and the British founded what would become **Sierra Leone** for that purpose in 1787. The ACS was supported by many prominent white Americans, such as Henry Clay and Bushrod Washington, and in 1819 Congress allocated $100,000 for the encouragement of

A Vey town (i.e. Vai) near Monrovia. Courtesy of the Library of Congress.

relocating former slaves. The capital city, Monrovia, would even be named for President James Monroe. Chapters of the ACS would open in several states in addition to the creation of other independent state and city colonization societies.

An abortive effort was made to found the colony in 1820. In 1821, with the assistance of a U.S. Navy vessel, land was purchased from the West African natives. Another effort to establish a colony was made in 1822, and this time succeeded in laying the foundation for Liberia. Other state colonization societies such as in Maryland also founded colonies in the same regions and would eventually be incorporated into a larger Liberia.

Liberia was a colony from 1822 to 1847. Among those who resided in the colony were freed slaves from the United States who gained their freedom on condition of leaving, and free blacks who were looking for a better life away from the openly racist white America. The former slaves from the United States would become Americo-Liberians. Former slaves from the Caribbean would become the Congo People. Both Americos and Congo peoples would eventually become separate ethnic groups in modern Liberia. The population was augmented by recaptureds, blacks liberated from illegal slave ships working along the West African coast, as a well as a large indigenous population. With attitudes somewhat similar to whites who migrated to the United States, many of the new settlers saw themselves as coming to civilize the native population. The new society they created was based on the American culture, including the Southern plantation culture they knew in the United States. The expense of maintaining Liberia for the ACS was great, and there were potential threats from colonial powers. In 1846, the colony voted to become an independent state and a year later it did so. Joseph Jenkins Roberts was elected its first president. While an American creation, independent Liberia was not recognized by the United States until after the start of the Civil War because of persistent Southern opposition.

The supporters of Liberia had varied reasons for endorsing it. For those who did not believe freed slaves could be integrated into American society, it was a way to rid the nation of their presence and to return blacks to their supposedly "natural" home in Africa. Some whites even believed the presence of Liberia would hasten the end of slavery by affording a site where hesitant slaveholders might require their slaves to go as a condition of manumission. Slave owners would also benefit by getting rid of those free blacks whose presence "corrupted" slaves and who might even encourage the murder of slave masters or whites in general.

The society's efforts were opposed vigorously in the 1820s by black anti-colonizationists, and they gained some significant white support in the early 1830s as they won more whites over to oppose the ACS, Liberia, and slavery. Abolitionists, white and black, understood the colony as an effort to strengthen slavery by eliminating the free black presence. Blacks themselves were not enthusiastic about abandoning their native land for an Africa that was no more their homeland than it was that of white Americans.

The country of Liberia was ruled by "Americo-Liberians" from 1847 to 1979. The role of indigenous tribes in the rule of Liberia was sharply curtailed throughout much of the nation's history. In 1862, they were declared subjects with limited political rights, but there was only a very gradual acceptance of their role in society. In a 1979 coup the rule of Americo-Liberians was ended and replaced by a period of turmoil lasting over two decades. In modern Liberia, Americo-Liberians have become just one of many ethnic groups in the country, constituting approximately 2.5 percent of the population, with Congo people comprising another 2.5 percent. *See also* Africa, Antislavery in; Africa, Emancipation in.

Further Readings: Burin, Eric. *Slavery and the Peculiar Solution: A History of the American Colonization Society.* Gainesville: University Press of Florida, 2005; Beyan, Amos Jones. *African American Settlements in West Africa: John Brown Russwurm and the American Civilizing Efforts.* New York: Palgrave, 2005; Clegg, Claude Andrew. *The Price of Liberty: African Americans and the Making of Liberia.* Chapel Hill: University of North Carolina Press, 2004; Reef, Catherine. *This Our Dark Country: The American Settlers of Liberia.* New York: Clarion Books, 2002.

Donald E. Heidenreich, Jr.

Liberty Party

The Liberty Party developed from a split in the antislavery movement over the question of participation in the political process and acceptance of the Constitution as a valid form of government for the United States. Supporters of political involvement wanted a new, third party committed to the elimination of slavery. Those who favored forming such a third party included **Gerrit Smith** and Myron Holley of New York, Edwin Stanton of Ohio, and Joshua Leavitt of Massachusetts, editor of the *Emancipator*.

In 1839, a series of meetings beginning at the national convention of the **American Antislavery Society,** led to the formation of the Liberty Party and its nomination of **James G. Birney** of Michigan for president and Thomas Earle of Ohio as his running mate. The Liberty Party's effort in the 1840 election was minimal, and the party received little more than 7,000 votes nationally.

The Liberty Party platform in 1840 focused on a single issue, slavery, and took no position on other important issues of the day such as the tariff and internal improvements. The party enjoyed some success at the state and local levels during the early 1840s in the Northern states, drawing support largely from members of the **Whig Party.** In 1844, Birney was again nominated for president and was seen as enough of a threat to be attacked by the Whig Party press with a forged letter calling into question his opposition to slavery. The Liberty Party attracted some 62,300 votes in the election, which was very close between the two main party candidates, James K. Polk and **Henry Clay.** In New York State, Birney's vote exceeded the margin between Polk and Clay; carrying New York would have made Clay president. The Liberty Party was strengthened by these results and saw itself as now holding the balance between the two principal parties.

This success and political issues of the post-election period, especially the Mexican War, led many in the party to seek alliances with other reform groups and reform or antislavery members of the Whig and Democratic parties. This "broad platform" approach had been discussed prior to 1844, but gained strength afterwards and had prevailed by the 1848 election. Coalitions between the Liberty Party and other reform groups, or antislavery elements of other parties, led to a number of electoral successes for Liberty Party members in a number of Northern states.

In 1848, the Liberty Party nominated **John P. Hale** of New Hampshire for president. When Martin Van Buren bolted from the Democratic Party over the issue of slavery, Hale and his running mate, Leicester King, withdrew in favor of the new Free Soil Party candidate. Van Buren, however, was not acceptable to the entire "broad platform" faction because of his record on other reform issues and his earlier, much softer, stand on slavery. A rump convention formed the National Liberty Party and nominated Gerrit Smith for president. A coalition of several reform groups also nominated Smith, but with a different running mate.

The Liberty Party did not survive this division. Some of its more politically successful and ambitious members returned to the Democratic or Whig parties. Those with stronger antislavery views joined the Free Soil Party. The Liberty Party was replaced by the Free Soil Party, if anything a more committed antislavery party, but with a much broader base. Both the Liberty Party and the Free Soil Party made little, if any, effort to attract Southern voters for support, as did the later Republican Party. The Liberty Party had succeeded in its principal goal—bringing the debate over slavery into electoral politics. *See also* Democratic Party and Antislavery.

Further Readings: Holt, Michael F. *The Rise and Fall of the Whig Party.* New York: Oxford University Press, 1999; Sewell, Richard H. *Ballots for Freedom: Antislavery Politics in the United States, 1837–1860.* New York: Oxford University Press, 1976; Volpe, Vernon L. *Forlorn Hope of Freedom: The Liberty Party in the Old Northwest, 1838–1848.* Kent, Ohio: Kent State University Press, 1990.

William H. Mulligan, Jr.

Libreville

Libreville, today the capital of Gabon, began as a coastal settlement on the Gabon Estuary occupied by Mpongwe clans since at least the sixteenth century. Mpongwe men struggled in the early nineteenth century with one another to act as middlemen between European and South American—mainly Portuguese, Spanish, and Brazilian—slave traders and interior networks bringing captives down to the coast. Ironically, the collection of villages that relied on slave exporting became home to a brief and poorly organized establishment to house slaves captured by the French navy. Under pressure from England, the French navy by the 1840s began to patrol the South Atlantic African coast for vessels carrying slaves. Admiral Bouet-Willaumez forced several Mpongwe clan chiefs to accept French rule between 1839 and 1845 and built a small fort on the present site of Libreville to shelter repatriated Africans.

After several attempts to find adequate labor for the fledging fort failed, in part due to the fact free Mpongwe people could earn more money trading slaves and natural resources than doing menial labor, French officers considered using liberated captives as a source of workers. In 1846, the French warship *Australie* nabbed the slaver *Elizia* off the coast of Cabinda where the Congo River meets the sea (now part of Angola). Most of the slaver's unfortunate passengers were members of Vili clans from present-day Congo-Brazzaville. Though many of the crew and some slaves fled from the boat, the roughly 270 slaves remaining were shipped to the Senegalese port of Gorée. In the following year, French officers decided to send the former slaves to the French fort on the Gabon Estuary. One of the main reasons for this plan was the dearth of manpower in the region, which especially vexed the French navy because the settlement was the headquarters of slave patrols in the area. This move also annoyed some of the former slaves, a number of whom resisted the relocation, although they faced imprisonment for doing so. About fifty or so of the ex-slaves were finally transported to Libreville by 1849.

Officials and Roman Catholic missionaries designed a model township that assumed former slaves would be docile and loyal workers would accept Christianity. The plans unraveled soon after the first group of former slaves arrived. The 1848 Revolution in France disrupted supplies and funding to the fort and its new village of Libreville. Some former slaves ran off, established their own village several kilometers away, and began to raid Libreville for women to take as wives in 1849. Though a small amount of state aid in rations and tools helped the remaining ex-slaves, most residents of Libreville began to join the larger Mpongwe town society rather than follow the dictates of French commandants. They also shed their former slave status as soon as possible. Free Mpongwe were outnumbered by slaves from other parts of Gabon, and considered bondsmen and women to be fit only for menial labor and farming. Thus, the "Librevillois" had little incentive to remain in the state-run village. By the late 1850s, the French administration stopped assistance to the settlement and did not bring in any other rescued slaves. Only the name of Libreville left any reminder of the plan to resettle former slaves.

Another irony about Libreville is that domestic slavery continued to exist in the town for many years. The French never made any formal attempt to emancipate slaves owned by Mpongwe masters. Some wily Mpongwe continued to sell slaves to Brazilian and Spanish buyers into the 1850s. At the end of the same decade, the French government initiated an "emigration" program to send slaves to their Caribbean colonies, but halted the program after protests from American missionaries and others. Open execution of slaves by African masters for those accused of using supernatural forces to harm free people continued through the 1870s. When French commandants took a harsher line towards slave executions, a bloodbath began as slaves were killed by mysterious men dressed as leopards between 1877 and 1879. Though the exact causes and directors of these murders never came to light, circumstances suggest masters who wished to keep control over their slaves lay behind the brutal assaults. As late as 1927, some missionaries noted that a dwindling number of old slaves remained in bondage to free Mpongwe families. The end of open slave sales in the late-nineteenth century ensured the slow end of bondage in Libreville. People of slave descent gradually became seen as members of free Mpongwe families.

Far from being the French equivalent of Freetown, Libreville only briefly became a place where former slaves found a new home. French concerns about workers, rather than antislavery rhetoric of liberation, brought bondsmen to the port. Such ambivalence about the colony and the treatment of slaves would make itself felt throughout much of African territories controlled by France. In Gabon as in much of French West Africa, administrators had mixed feelings about banning slavery outright. Libreville failed as a home for ex-slaves, but did eventually succeed in becoming a foothold that later generations of French would exploit to conquer all of Gabon.

What makes Libreville's name even more incongruous today is that slaves still can be found in the city. West Africans, especially from Benin and Togo, have brought children to work as maids and as vendors selling food and knickknacks on Libreville's streets. Many of these children are not paid and are not allowed to go to school or return home. Child trafficking is a serious problem in the city. One can only hope the Gabonese government will one day be more successful in stamping out these practices than the French were over a century ago.

Further Readings: Bucher, Henry. "Liberty and Labor: The Origins of Libreville Reconsidered," *Bulletin de l'IFAN* 41, 2nd series (1979): 477–495; Lasserre, Guy. *Libreville: La ville et sa région.* Paris: Armand Colin, 1958; Patterson, K. David. *The Northern Gabon Coast to 1875.* Oxford: Clarendon Press, 1975; Rich, Jeremy.

"Eating Disorders: A Social History of Food Consumption and Food Supply in Colonial Libreville, ca. 1840–1960." PhD thesis, Indiana University, 2002; Schnapper, Bernard. *La Politique et le commerce français dans le golfe du Guinée, 1838–1871.* Paris: Mouton, 1961.

Jeremy Rich

Lincoln, Abraham (1809–1865)

On February 12, 1809, Abraham Lincoln was born in Kentucky to Thomas and Nancy Lincoln. In 1816, the family moved to Indiana, "partly on account of slavery; but chiefly on account of the difficulty in land titles in Ky," according to Lincoln. Lincoln's year of formal schooling was in Indiana, but most of his time was spent working on the farm or as a hired hand. In 1830, the Lincoln family moved to Illinois, and shortly thereafter Lincoln struck out on his own. When the Black Hawk War broke out in 1832, Lincoln joined a volunteer company and was elected captain, gaining his first experience as an elected leader.

After the war, Lincoln ran unsuccessfully for the state legislature. He ran again in 1834 and won. While in the legislature, Lincoln began studying law and had gained his license by 1836. Lincoln was reelected three times, and was soon the leader of the Illinois Whigs. In 1837, reacting to the murder of abolitionist **Elijah Lovejoy,** the legislature passed a resolution condemning abolitionist societies, declaring the right of property in slaves to be sacred, and asserting that the federal government could not abolish slavery in the capital. Lincoln was one of six legislators who voted against the resolution, and in March he helped to write a protest declaring, "The institution of slavery is founded on both injustice and bad policy." However, Lincoln also asserted, "The Congress of the United States has no power, under the constitution, to interfere with the institution of slavery in the different States."

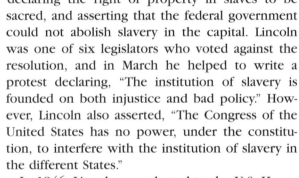

In 1846, Lincoln was elected to the U.S. House of Representatives. During a break in the session in 1847, Lincoln represented a slaveholder in a lawsuit, arguing that the man should not be deprived of his slaves. In 1849, Lincoln authored a referendum calling for the gradual, compensated abolition of slavery in the District of Columbia, but could not get support for the measure. Lincoln did not run for reelection, and for the next ten years practiced law.

Abraham Lincoln. Courtesy of the Library of Congress.

As slavery became an increasingly important issue, the new antislavery Republican Party began to siphon members, including Lincoln, away from the Whigs. In 1858, Lincoln campaigned against Stephen Douglas for a senatorial appointment. In a series of debates, Douglas, who favored not interfering with slavery where it already existed and allowing popular sovereignty to decide on it in the territories, argued that Lincoln sought equality between the races. Lincoln stated his preference that no new slave states be admitted to the Union, and that slavery be abolished in the District of Columbia, but also asserted, "I am not, nor ever have been in favor of bringing about in any way the social and political equality of the white and black races ... I am not nor ever have been in favor of making voters or jurors of negroes, nor of qualifying them to hold office, nor to intermarry with white people." Lincoln did not receive the appointment, but the debates brought him national attention.

In February 1860, Lincoln spoke at the Cooper Institute in New York, arguing that slavery should not be allowed to spread to new areas, but neither should it be abolished where it already existed. While the position was unacceptable to extremists on both sides, the majority of Northerners agreed with Lincoln's moderate stance, earning him even more national prominence. Lincoln was not the favorite to receive the Republican nomination in 1860, but he was acceptable to most factions of the party, and when the frontrunners ran into opposition, it was Lincoln who was nominated. In November, Lincoln was elected to the presidency even though he received less than half the popular vote and did not appear on the ballot in most Southern states.

By the time Lincoln assumed the presidency, seven states had already left the Union, and soon afterward four more followed them. Lincoln knew he had to keep the border-states—Delaware, Maryland, Kentucky, and Missouri—in the Union, something he could not do if he moved against slavery, so he held off, even rescinding early freedom proclamations issued for runaways by military commanders John Frémont and David Hunter. However, by July 1862 and after the successful implementation of the First and Second Confiscation Acts, Lincoln saw that he could move against slavery as a military measure, thereby forestalling much criticism, and drafted an Emancipation Proclamation freeing the slaves in areas that were in rebellion. After showing the draft to his cabinet, they encouraged him to keep the document secret until the Union forces had won a major battlefield victory so as to avoid appearing desperate. Lincoln took their advice, kept the proclamation to himself, and waited for a victory. On August 14, 1862, Lincoln met with a group of African Americans and advocated colonization, the voluntary deportation of former slaves, saying that the racism and distrust on both sides would never allow the races to live together. In the months prior to this meeting, Lincoln had actually appointed some individuals to inquire into the possibility of creating a site for African American colonization in the black republic of Haiti. Nowhere, however, in the draft of the Emancipation Proclamation did he mention colonization.

Eight days later, Lincoln wrote, "My paramount object in this struggle *is* to save the Union, and is *not* either to save or to destroy slavery. If I could save the Union without freeing *any* slave I would do it, and if I could save it by freeing *all* the slaves I would do it; and if I could do it by freeing some and leaving others alone I would also do that." In September, after the Union victory at Antietam, Lincoln announced the preliminary

Emancipation Proclamation. Foreign intervention, which had recently seemed a possibility, became a dead letter because no nation wanted to be seen as interfering in a war for freedom. While Lincoln may have wavered on slavery before signing the Emancipation Proclamation, afterward there was no doubting how he felt. In 1864, Lincoln wrote, "I am naturally anti-slavery. If slavery is not wrong, nothing is wrong. I can not remember when I did not so think and feel."

In 1864, Lincoln worked hard for his reelection and a constitutional amendment abolishing slavery. In November, Lincoln was reelected easily and in January the **Thirteenth Amendment** was passed. Lincoln's second inaugural address, delivered just over a month before he was assassinated by Southern sympathizer John Wilkes Booth, showed just how far he had come: "Fondly do we hope, fervently do we pray, that this mighty scourge of war shall soon pass away, yet if God wills it continue till all the wealth piled by two hundred years of bondage shall have been wasted, and each drop of blood drawn by the lash shall have been paid for by one drawn by the sword, the judgments of the Lord are true and righteous altogether." In his 1876 "Oration in Memory of Abraham Lincoln," **Frederick Douglass** proclaimed "in his heart of hearts he loathed and hated slavery." *See also* Democratic Party and Antislavery; Radical Republicans; Whig Party and Antislavery.

Further Readings: Basler, Roy P., ed., and Marion Dolores Pratt and Lloyd A. Dunlap, asst. eds. *The Collected Works of Abraham Lincoln*, 9 vols. New Brunswick, NJ: Rutgers University Press, 1952–1955; Oates, Stephen B. *With Malice Toward None: The Life of Abraham Lincoln*. New York: Harper and Row, 1977.

Jared Peatman

Literature and Abolition

The institution of slavery in the United States galvanized the literary community as writers sought to present the cruelties meted out against human beings to preserve a social system that defied the founding principles of the revolution and the basic tenets of Christian beliefs. From the introduction of the slave trade at the Jamestown colony in 1619 to the Emancipation Proclamation of 1863, freed and enslaved African American and white writers, many of whom were active in religious organizations, revolutionary movements, and women's rights groups, along with individuals compelled by indignation against social injustice, sought to press upon the emerging nation's conscience the inherent wrong of forcing men, women, and children into bondage and maintaining a caste system that terrorized the powerless to enrich the privileged white landowners, particularly of the Southern states.

The term "abolition" in this context refers to the abolishing of slavery throughout the United States, especially as it concerned the trafficking of Africans from their native lands to be sold as property, the oppression of those descendents of enslaved Africans within a primarily agrarian system of labor, and the denial of these people from achieving self-determination through laws and prohibitions, both by individual states and the federal government. The survey of literature concerned with abolition includes sermons, speeches, political tracts and essays, autobiographical narratives, poetry, and fiction.

In the seventeenth century, although few voices spoke out against "the peculiar institution," one remarkable group, the **Quaker** community, began to organize on behalf of freedom of worship for black slaves. In their yearly meetings from the 1680s on, the Quakers called for the abolition of slavery, which they referred to as the "traffick in menbody." They pointed out that such a practice undermined the "democratic egalitarianism" of Christianity. The early eighteenth century witnessed an awakening of the American conscience against slavery with Puritan Samuel Sewell's antislavery pamphlet "**The Selling of Joseph,** A Memorial" (1700). The pamphlet was published during the heated controversy about the holding of slaves, which the Puritan-enacted *Body of Liberties* had established in New England in 1641. By 1700, the slave trade was an institution. A burgeoning population of slaves brought the need for a reconsideration of such a practice as it contradicted egalitarian Christian beliefs that all people were children of God and therefore heirs to God's kingdom, principles that the Quakers had voiced earlier. Puritan leader of the Massachusetts Bay Colony, Cotton Mather lamented the practice of slavery in 1702 in his famous work *Magnalia Christi Americana*. In 1706, he published an *antislavery* sermon, "The Negro Christianized," which spoke of the need to view African Americans as part of the body of Christ, to treat them as brothers and sisters in the faith, and to encourage literacy to make the Bible available to them.

In the period from the mid-eighteenth century to the beginning of the nineteenth, voices spoke out against slavery and urged abolition. John Woolman of Massachusetts (1720–1782) published an essay dealing with the issue in "Some Considerations on the Keeping of Negroes" (1754). Meanwhile, African writers very early on recounted their experiences with slavery from first-hand experience. Among those slaves was Lucy Terry (born in West Africa in 1730), considered the first African American writer, whose poetry was passed down in the oral tradition. Only one of her poems, "Bars Fight," has survived, published in 1855, over thirty years after her death. Although the poem itself does not deal with abolition, Terry is acknowledged to be one of the first women to fight for equality, unsuccessfully arguing the case for the admittance of one of her sons to Williams College.

In New England, African American men of the cloth represented another voice for equality and abolition. John Marrant, a black preacher, led a congregation of black loyalists in Nova Scotia, impressing on his brethren the idea of a Zion, a promised land, which, according to his view, would be the return of blacks to Africa and the establishment of an all-black community in **Sierra Leone.** He died before realizing his vision, but paved the way for others, such as David George, who saw the resettlement of African American slaves as a solution to the problem of slavery. Marrant's autobiography of his life as a preacher, published in 1790, was one of the first to reach a wider audience. In Boston, two other notable black writers, Prince Hall and **Boston King,** spoke out against slavery in the years leading up to the Revolutionary War. Hall's petition to abolish slavery in Massachusetts in 1777 affected the eventual end to slavery in the Commonwealth in 1783. Connecticut's **Lemuel Haynes,** writer and preacher of the New Light Ministry, contributed to abolition in his essay "Liberty Further Extended: Or Free Thoughts on the Illegality of Slave-Keeping," which was first published in 1783 in the *William and Mary Quarterly*. Although these black Atlantic writers called for abolition, Prince Hall and Boston King considered a return to Africa a more viable way to release their brothers and sisters from bondage and fulfill their dream of a new Zion. Later, whites would take up the idea of colonization, returning blacks to Africa, as an alternative to abolition, most notably Thomas Jefferson himself.

The Founding Fathers addressed the issue in the late-eighteenth century as they grappled with the inherent contradiction of slavery within a new democracy. **Benjamin Franklin** published an editorial, "On the Slave Trade" (1790), where he urged readers to abolish the institution. Thomas Jefferson, in his *Notes on the State of Virginia*, "Queries XIV and XVII" (1785), strongly condemned the institution of slavery, but argued that emancipation should be accompanied by the removal of blacks to a separate colony, where they could be "free and independent people." As leaders of the new republic searched for a compromise, slave narratives began to circulate, bringing the conditions by which people were stolen from their homes, forced to endure the Middle Passage to the United States, humiliated through the slave trade, and denied the most basic of human rights as outlined in the **Declaration of Independence. Olaudah Equiano,** kidnapped from what is now Nigeria, published *The Interesting Narrative* in 1789, an autobiography of his life as a slave and later a freeman. Ignatius Sancho was the author of a publication, *Letters of the Late Ignatius Sancho, an African* (1782), which included correspondences with British writer Laurence Sterne. Sancho's letters described the inhumane conditions of blacks forced into slavery and helped raise awareness of their plight.

In the early nineteenth century, three developments gave momentum to both sides of abolition: the Fugitive Slave Act of 1793, which handed slave owners legal recourse to reclaim runaway slaves captured in the North; the **Missouri Compromise** of 1820−21, allowing Missouri to enter the Union as a slave state; and **Nat Turner**'s Rebellion in 1831. Turner, a black preacher in Virginia, exhorted his parishioners to rise up against their white oppressors. Their fury led to a massacre of both adults and children before the rebellion was forcibly put down. Turner, arrested, tried, and convicted, was sentenced to death, but before his execution in 1831, his confession was recorded by Thomas R. Gray, whose publication of these last words, *The Confessions of Nat Turner, the Leader of the Late Insurrection in South Hampton, Va.,* was circulated to a reading public curious about the man and the events. The description of his life and times created an uneasy stir among both Northerners and Southerners. In fact, shortly after these events, several states passed laws forbidding slaves to learn to read, citing the fact that Turner had been able to read to study the Bible and preach in the black churches. Additionally, it became increasingly difficult for black preachers to operate freely in the South. In short, the Nat Turner Rebellion created a generalized suspicion and hostility toward blacks. The Missouri

Compromise demonstrated that legislators were unwilling to champion the cause of abolition. The Fugitive Slave Act of 1793 was superseded by the **Fugitive Slave Law** of 1850, which was more injurious to blacks. This legislation stripped runaway slaves of any legal guarantees that their liberty would be protected in the North. By mid-century, the promise of emancipation had become remote.

Given the political climate of these decades, abolitionists began to speak out forcefully, only to be met with scorn and violence. Many of these social reformers, ministers themselves, wrote essays and political tracts condemning the situation in the South. Meanwhile, the slave narrative gained a wider readership. **Frederick Douglass,** a runaway slave, orator, and leader of the growing antislavery movement in the Boston area, published his *Narrative of the Life of Frederick Douglass, an American Slave* in 1845. The author of the preface was the famous abolitionist **William Lloyd Garrison.** In this account of the cruelties he endured, Douglass brought the conditions of this institution to the conscience of the white readership of the North. Later, he published the essay, "What to the Slave Is the Fourth of July?" returning to the inherent contradiction of a nation built on democratic principles and denying at the same time, liberty to millions of black Americans. **Henry Highland Garnet,** another black writer of the mid-nineteenth century, addressed the gradual incorporation of African Americans in the society. He gave a speech, later published as *An Address to the Slaves of the United States of America, Buffalo, N.Y., 1843*, at a Negro National Convention. Another slave narrative, but unique in that it spoke for the black woman, was published in 1861. Although it was several years later than Douglass, Harriet Jacobs' account of being a slave and a woman impressed upon the nation's conscience that the issue of disenfranchisement was twofold. In *Incidents in the Life of a Slave Girl*, Jacobs assumes a fictional protagonist to deal not only with the conditions of the blacks, but specifically of black women: sexual harassment, concubinage, and the selling of children. Her narrator pleads, "Pity me and pardon me, O virtuous reader. You never knew what it is to be a slave; to be entirely unprotected by law or custom; to have the laws reduce you to the conditions of chattel, entirely subject to the will of another." The confluence of these two movements was to give voice to **Sojourner Truth,** the sisters **Angelina** and Sarah **Grimké,** and **Harriet Beecher Stowe** at mid-century.

Radical abolitionists brought the controversy to the public forum. Most notable was William Lloyd Garrison, whose antislavery tracts raged against the idea of "gradual abolition," and called for a militant "immediate" abolition of slavery. The abolitionist movement found a charismatic leader in Garrison, whose weekly newspaper, *The Liberator* (1831–1865), gave voice to many categories of social reformers in the North. Among those who worked with Garrison was John Greenleaf Whittier, whose *Justice and Expediency* was an antislavery tract. In the 1830s and 1840s, abolitionists were often met with mob violence. However, such writers as Garrison, Whittier, and Frederick Douglass persevered, passionately arguing the rightness of their cause. Whittier's poem "Massachusetts to Virginia," is based on an account of fugitive slave George Lattimer, who pleaded for his freedom in Boston against the attempt of his former owner to return him to the South. Eventually, Lattimer was given his free papers. The poem illustrates the hypocrisy of the Fugitive Slave laws.

William Garrison was unswerving in his crusade against slavery. Inspired by another editor, **Benjamin Lundy,** whose newspaper *The Genius of Universal Emancipation* (1828) was the only publication exclusively devoted to the cause, Garrison, however, disagreed with Lundy's position of gradual, not immediate, emancipation and colonization in Africa. In 1831, he and Isaac Knapp began publishing issues of *The Liberator,* pressing upon Americans the crime perpetrated on millions of black Americans. Garrison maintained that only immediate emancipation would redeem the nation. Included in his vision of universal emancipation were women. Among the early abolitionists, Garrison was preeminent, tirelessly promoting other writers, such as Frederick Douglass, whose narrative saw print through Garrison's efforts.

Garrison's influence on women writers was profound. **Lydia Maria Child,** a young, white novelist of the genteel tradition, turned her efforts toward abolition after meeting with Garrison. Her first abolitionist pamphlet, *An Appeal in Favor of That Class of Americans Called Africans* (1831) was directed to middle-class women. The Grimké Sisters, Angelina and Sarah, were also profoundly moved by Garrison and joined the abolitionist movement in the 1830s. Alarmed by the angry mobs in Boston who attacked women abolitionists, both sisters began lecturing throughout New England. Sarah Grimké, in her *Appeal to the Christian Women of the South* (1836), argues the urgency of the cause by appealing to their Christian principles. The abolition movement clearly found allies in the women's movement.

One woman instrumental in turning the tide of public opinion in favor of abolition was Harrier Beecher Stowe, daughter of an illustrious churchman, Lyman Beecher, and wife of a learned theologian. A New Englander, she became aware of the **Underground Railroad** while living in Cincinnati, Ohio, and felt compelled to address the cause and wrote the novel that dramatized the cruelties of slavery. *Uncle Tom's Cabin,* published serially and then as a volume in 1852, captured the hearts and minds of readers across the nation and became perhaps the nation's first bestseller, selling 300,000 copies in the first year. Although from our contemporary perspective her characters seem stereotyped, the story led readers of her day to understand how the system of slavery tore at the fabric of the family. Even the term "Uncle Tom" later became a label for those African Americans who accommodated themselves to the white racist system, rather than rebel against it. By the end of the decade, the divisions deepened to the point that any compromise to Southern slavery had become remote. Stowe wrote other sketches, stories, and essays, one concerning Sojourner Truth (1797–1883), a black evangelist, abolitionist, and women's rights activist. Her piece, "Sojourner Truth, the Libyan Sibyl" (1863) is a lively exchange, an authentic record of the colloquial speech of her time. Although others recorded her speeches, Olive Gilbert transcribed Sojourner Truth's powerful *Narrative* (1850), one of several slave narratives that fueled the abolitionist movement.

Other black women emerged to speak out against such injustices. Frances Ellen Watkins Harper, writing at mid-century, is regarded as the first black woman to publish a short story in the United States, "The Two Offers," which describes the problems created within the black family—drunkenness and child abuse—resulting from the slave system. Her poetry directly concentrates on the issues of slavery and the need for moral reform. "The Slave Mother" dramatizes the mother's anguish when she is forced to give up her child. Her speeches, published in 1857, urge an end to slavery and the equal treatment of women.

One important literary figure, William Wells Brown, an escaped slave from Kentucky, became active in the antislavery movement and spoke as a delegate to the National Negro Convention, held in Buffalo in 1843. He published his own slave narrative in 1847. Brown's novel, *Clotel*, published in London in 1853, later in New York in 1861, is considered one of the earliest fictional renderings of life from a black antislavery perspective. As the novel crossed the Atlantic, it was heavily revised, published in installments in the *Weekly Anglo-African* and finally brought out in 1867 as the novel *Clotelle: or The Colored Heroine*. Other novels by black men of the late-antebellum period included Frank Webb's *The Garies and Their Friends* and **Martin Delany**'s *Blake*.

As President **Abraham Lincoln** took office in 1861, the nation was so deeply divided on the issue of slavery that any compromise or accommodation had become untenable. The secession of South Carolina and the firing on Union troops at Fort Sumter in April of that year plunged the nation into a civil war that was to last for four wrenching years, during which time Lincoln's Emancipation Proclamation, delivered in 1863, formally ended slavery in the United States. The Proclamation demanded a release of all persons from bondage. As the war continued for one more year, the slaveholding states eventually surrendered their arms, their lands, and their way of life to the more powerful, rapidly industrializing North. In the years to come, African Americans would continue to struggle for equal rights and equal protection under the law, but the abolition of slavery, in principle, had been achieved. Writers, both black and white, had borne witness to the "peculiar institution" that deprived human beings of life and liberty; they had, by speaking out, contributed to the demise of an unjust system that undermined the democratic ideals upon which the nation has been founded. *See also* Garrisonians.

Further Readings: Brooks, Joanna, and John Saillant, eds. *Face Zion Forward: First Writers of the Black Atlantic, 1785–1798*. Boston: Northeastern University Press, 2002; Gates, Henry Louis, ed. *The Slave Narratives*. New York: Signet, 1987; Gates, Henry Louis, and Nelly Y. McKay, eds. *The Norton Anthology of African American Literature*. New York: Norton, 1996; Gould, Phillip. *Barbaric Traffic: Commerce and Antislavery in the Eighteenth-Century Atlantic World*. Cambridge, MA: Harvard University Press, 2003; Lauter, Paul, and Richard Yarborough, eds. *The Heath Anthology of American Literature*. vol. 1. 4th ed. New York: Houghton-Mifflin, 2001; Merish, Lori. *Sentimentalism Materialism: Gender, Commodity Culture, and Nineteenth-Century American Literature*. Durham, NC: Duke University Press, 2000.

Sonja Lovelace

Livingstone, David (1813–1873)

Born into a poor Blantyre, Scotland, household in 1813, David Livingstone achieved fame as a Christian missionary, energetic explorer, and formidable opponent of the slave trade. Livingstone spent over half of his life in Central and Southern Africa, from his arrival in 1841 until his death in 1873. Through his speaking tours and popular books, he raised the awareness and increased knowledge of Westerners about Africa and its problems.

From age 10 through 21, the young Livingstone worked full days in cotton mills, while receiving his education through night school and self-discipline. As a young adult, he chose to follow his father in the practices and piety of the Independent Congregational Church. Livingstone felt the call to the mission field in 1834, after hearing about the need for medical missionaries in China. He began his medical and theological training at the University of Glasgow, and became a member of the London Missionary Society (LMS) in 1838. In 1840, the LMS ordained Livingstone, and he passed the exam to qualify as a doctor. He learned that the Opium War (1839–1842) prevented missionary work in China at that time. Therefore, after hearing a speech by Robert Moffat, his future father-in-law, about evangelistic endeavors in southern Africa, Livingstone changed his life's course by sailing to Cape Town in 1841.

David Livingstone initially joined Moffat at the LMS mission station at Kuruman, where the new missionary met Mary Moffat, whom he married in 1845. In the hopes of finding new converts to Christianity, David and his family pushed farther north into Mabotsa and Kolobeng, toward the Kalahari Desert. Living and working in one place for a long time, however, proved unsatisfactory for Livingstone. He hoped to discover new ways of converting and evangelizing the Africans. During these early years in Africa, Livingstone acquired skills in speaking the local languages, finding his way through the African terrain, and surviving in places far removed from other Europeans. Between 1849 and 1851, he achieved some measure of fame by traveling to Lake Ngami and exploring the Zambezi River. After living in south Africa for a decade, Livingstone decided to send his wife and children back to Britain in 1852, as he prepared for the first of three extended periods of exploration into the heart of central Africa.

During his thirty-two years in Africa, Livingstone led three major expeditions. First, in 1853–1856, he crossed the southern part of the continent from Luanda to Kilimane, from the coast of Angola to the coast of Mozambique. Second, in 1858–1864, Livingstone

David Livingstone. Courtesy of the Library of Congress.

explored the Zambezi River and the surrounding area; Mary accompanied David on this trip but died in 1862. Third, in 1866–1873, he searched for the source of the Nile River and continued his exploration of the Zambezi. The Royal Geographical Society provided enthusiastic support—and gave special recognition—to Livingstone during his second and third journeys.

In between these three major excursions into Central Africa, Livingstone returned to Britain on two occasions, once in 1856–1857, and again in 1864–1866. During these furloughs, Livingstone published his two famous books: *Missionary Travels and Researches in South Africa* (1857) and *Narrative of an Expedition to the Zambezi and Its Tributaries* (1865). These books instantly captured a wide reading audience, and they also played a crucial role in informing the West about the African slave trade. At the same time, Livingstone's work put pressure on Portugal and other European nations that had not aggressively opposed the slave trade.

It is clear that Portuguese explorers had already traveled some of the same routes Livingstone had traversed, but he mapped these trails and recorded information about the flora, fauna, tribes, and landscape as had no other explorer before him. In addition to these geographical discoveries, these expeditions also allowed Livingstone to document the escalation of the African slave trade and the atrocities that accompanied it. His British background and Christian vocation made him keenly aware of the evil of slavery. Because of the reform work of Sir **William Wilberforce** and Sir **Thomas Fowell Buxton,** among others, the British government outlawed the ownership of slaves in 1807 and, in 1833, had abolished the slave trade throughout the Empire.

Livingstone and his travel companions saw the devastation and destruction of the slave trade—in burned villages, ruined crops, rotting corpses, skeletons along the trails, and orphaned and dying children. Sometimes his party saw the villages on fire and even encountered the Arab, Swahili, or Portuguese slavers leading captured Africans yoked or chained together. In some instances, Livingstone and his colleagues exchanged fire with the slavers to free the enslaved men, women, and children. Hoping to show the rest of the Western world the enormous loss of life due to the increased activities of the traders, Livingstone recorded these atrocities in his books and letters.

Livingstone fought the slave trade aggressively, especially as it increased because of new markets in the Indian Ocean. Through the influence of abolitionists like Buxton, Livingstone sought to establish commerce and Christianity—and to "civilize" Africa. He wanted Africans to exchange local goods (e.g., ivory) for Western products (e.g., cloth), but this ideal depended on the goodwill of the tribal leaders and foreign investment. Livingstone's explorations opened up new territory for missionary activities, but he also hoped that his travels would pave the way for legitimate commerce and eliminate the African role in slave trade. Unfortunately, his famous expeditions also provided new trails for the movement of slavers, a paradox that frustrated Livingstone immensely.

After his famous encounter with Henry M. Stanley in 1871, Livingstone died on his last expedition at Chitambo, in modern Zambia, in 1873. David

Livingstone's African colleagues mummified his body and transported it to the coast; the British people received his body with great reverence and honored him with burial in Westminster Abbey. To be sure, Livingstone left a mixed legacy. Many historians suggest that he failed as a missionary and opened the continent for further colonization. Other critics suggest that he had low regard for the African peoples. In any case, Livingstone made significant contributions to science, and his tireless opposition to slavery also contributed to its ultimate demise.

Further Readings: Jeal, Tim. *Livingstone*. New Haven, CT: Yale University Press, 2001; Liebowitz, Daniel. *The Physician and the Slave Trade: John Kirk, the Livingstone Expeditions, and the Crusade Against Slavery in East Africa*. New York: W. H. Freeman & Company, 1998; Lloyd, Brendan W. *A Bibliography of Published Works by and about David Livingstone, 1843–1975*. Cape Town: University of Cape Town Libraries, 1978; "The Paradox of David Livingstone," seven articles on Livingstone's life and work in *Christian History*, 16, 4 (Fall 1997); Ross, Andrew C. *David Livingstone: Mission and Empire*. New York: Hambledon & London, 2002.

Gerald L. Mattingly and Leslie A. Mattingly

Locke, John (1632–1704)

John Locke was an Oxford-educated English physician and philosopher whose work addressed broad issues of government, politics, religion, and economy. His book on epistemology, *An Essay Concerning Human Understanding* (1690), brought Locke wide renown. To this day, however, he is best known for his works in political philosophy, of which his *Second Treatise of Government* (1689) is the most notable. In large part, it is in this work that Locke lays out his opposition to slavery.

Labor, according to Locke, was a fundamental component not just of the economy, but also of society in general for it produced rights as well as things. Slavery attributed only very limited rights, if any, to the enslaved, while defying those basic rights to which all humans were entitled through their labor. Thus slavery was an unjust institution because the society sanctioning it refused to recognize evident human rights and to safeguard the freedom they accorded. Locke's contention that an individual's labor entitled the individual to certain rights influenced antislavery thought in fundamental ways.

Locke opposed slavery both on philosophical and political grounds. He did not devote significant space to the matter in general, although he did devote a chapter to the topic in his *Second Treatise of Government* where he wrote: "The natural liberty of man is to be free from any superior power on earth, and not to be under the will or legislative authority of man but to have only the law of nature for his rule." The law of nature was "a state of perfect freedom" and a "state also of equality, wherein all the power and jurisdiction is reciprocal, no one having more power than another."

Politically, Locke opposed slavery for two key reasons. First, he argued that slavery was a violation of liberty because it was not established by the common consent—that is, slaves, although they were under the legislative power of the State, were nevertheless denied a role in determining their own rights and laws. Second, he maintained that slavery was fundamentally opposed to freedom in that "a standing rule to live by, common to every one of that society" was absent from political life.

Locke's political opposition to slavery was informed by what he considered the authoritarianism of the Stuart dynasty in England. He perceived the Stuart rule of his time as tyrannical in general, and its policies, in particular, as intent upon enslaving the English. Thus, the genesis of Locke's opposition to slavery had little to do with any antipathy to the African slave trade. Indeed, Locke was a shareholder in the Royal Africa Company—the sole British company in the latter decades of the seventeenth century chartered to participate in the African slave trade—and had commercial interests in the slave-based colony of South Carolina.

In practice, Locke was far from an abolitionist. He was the author in 1669 of *The Fundamental Constitutions of Carolina*, although it

John Locke. Courtesy of the Library of Congress.

was drafted in conjunction with others and ultimately never ratified. Here, he laid out designs of an intentionally organized feudal society, mirroring in some senses the hierarchical political organization of British society at the time. In this context, and despite his philosophical views that slavery infringed upon individual liberty and personal freedom, Locke supported the establishment of slavery in the colony of the Carolinas, arguing that it would increase production and, therefore, the commercial success of the colony. *See also* Atlantic Slave Trade and British Abolition.

Further Readings: Locke, John. *Second Treatise of Government*. C.B. Macpherson, ed. Indianapolis: Hackett, 1980; Locke, John. *An Essay Concerning Human Understanding*. Kenneth P. Winkler, ed. Indianapolis: Hackett, 1996.

Noah Butler

Long, Edward (1734–1813)

Edward Long was born in England, the fourth son of Samuel Long who owned properties in Longville, Jamaica, in Tredudwell, Cornwall, and in London. He was educated in England, and only when his father died in 1757 did he travel to Jamaica, an important British sugar colony. He became a private secretary to the lieutenant governor of the colony and, thereafter, was appointed a judge of the Vice-Admiralty Court in Jamaica. Shortly after his arrival, he married a Jamaican heiress, Mary Ballard, by whom he had six children. However, he spent only twelve years in Jamaica, returning to England on account of ill health in 1769.

His great-grandfather, Samuel Long, had been involved in the English capture of Jamaica from Spain in 1655 and was rewarded with a large land grant at Longville. Edward was inspired by his great-grandfather, who was active in Jamaican politics, and by **John Locke**'s argument in his *Two Treatises of Government* (1690) that sovereign power derived from the will of a nation's subjects. Drawing on them, he argued in his major work, *The History of Jamaica* (1774), that the elected Assembly should be the foremost political power in the colony. His history was widely read in his own time and remains important today on three counts. First, he described the topography and history of the island, and proposed that Jamaica should emulate the commercial economy of Britain to improve trade, accessibility to consumer goods, and the intellectual and moral fiber of the local population, including whites as well as slaves. Second, he indicted the white inhabitants of Jamaica for their moral and intellectual laxity. And third, he advanced a view of African slaves, slavery, and interracial sexuality that has made Edward Long the byname of English racism.

His purpose in writing the book was to draw Britain's attention to the value of its colonies, which he considered neglected, and to identify the means by which the colony could both be protected from the incursions of maroons and made lucrative for Jamaica and Britain. Motivated in part by the notion that trade and consumer desire could positively influence the social evolution of Jamaica's slave population, he wrote several pamphlets and letters that explained his perspective on trade and slavery: "Candid Reflections upon the judgments of the Court of King's Bench on what is commonly called the Negroe-Cause, by a Planter" (1772); "Letters on the Colonies" (1775); and "A Pamphlet on the Sugar Trade" (1782).

Although Long believed that slavery was divinely ordained in that God had appointed some people in all societies to labor, his familiarity with Jamaican society inclined him to believe that planter and white families were degenerating in both their sexual morality and linguistic facility through domestic contact with African slaves. His solution was to uplift the intellectual capacity and moral probity of slaves. He proposed to accomplish this end by providing education, encouraging conversion to Christianity, instilling European habits of consumerism, and assigning special privileges to certain groups in the hope of reducing the gulf between Africans and Europeans and, thus, of fostering a more stable, safe, and prosperous community for all. His criticism of the white class in Jamaica was, indeed, seized upon by abolitionist readers as an indictment of an institution that corrupted both owners and slaves.

Long's views on race are, however, the keystone of his modern reputation. When he wrote his *History,* his racialist and a historical view of Africans was not then widespread, although elements were adopted by influential figures such as **Thomas Jefferson**. His negative characterizations of black Africans, to name but a few, included the likelihood that they constituted a separate species from Europeans; that they possessed a distinctive, distasteful odor; that they were naturally slothful and gluttonous; that they indulged in sexual intercourse with apes; and that they had never developed arts and letters. His view represented the beginning of a negative sense of color consciousness that became entrenched in British discourse and gave new impetus to American racism. Long considered Africans inferior to Europeans physically, intellectually, and morally, and he theorized that the disparities between Africans and Europeans had arisen primarily from the stagnation of African culture, its defiance of progress. However, he believed that Africans could be improved overall by social, sexual, and economic contact with the English. And, while he disapproved of interracial sexuality, he considered the mulatto (a cross between a Negro and a European) an important participant in his new social order. In particular, he believed that the improved physical stature of mulattos would prove a benefit to the military defense of the colony. He justified the institution of plantation slavery by claiming that Britain had introduced Africans to civil society and saved them from slaughter at home while purging Africa of its criminal elements. Long's editing of Robert Norris's *Memoirs of the Reign of Bossa Ahadee, King of Dahomey* (1789), which was published with a tract entitled "The African Slave Trade," was a supplementary effort to substantiate his proslavery point of view. Bossa Ahadee (who ruled from 1732 to 1774) appears as a cruel tyrant responsible for diminishing the Whydah slave trade and depopulating Africa, while "The African Slave Trade" closely follows Long's *History* in arguing the beneficial effects of slavery on Africans and Britons.

Further Readings: *The Dictionary of National Biography.* Leslie Stephen and Sidney Lee, eds. Vol. 12. London: Oxford University Press, 1917; Long, Edward. *The History of Jamaica, or General Survey of the Ancient and Modern State of that Island: With Reflections on its Situations, Settlements, Inhabitants, Climate, Products, Commerce, Laws and Government.* 3 vols. George Metcalf, ed. London: Frank Cass & Co. Ltd., 1970; Norris, Robert. *Memoirs of the Reign of Bossa Ahádee, King of Dahomey, an Inland Country of Guiney. To Which Are Added, the Author's Journey to Abomey, the Capital; and A Short Account of the African Slave Trade.* London: W. Lowndes, 1789; Wheeler, Roxann. *The Complexion of Race: Categories of Difference in Eighteenth-Century British Culture.* Philadelphia: University of Pennsylvania Press, 2000.

Susan B. Iwanisziw

Lord Dunmore's Proclamation

On November 7, 1775, the Earl of Dunmore, the last royal governor of Virginia, issued a proclamation imposing a state of martial law on the rebellious colony that he had governed since 1771. In an unusual, indeed unprecedented, step he declared free those slaves "appertaining [belonging as a possession or right] to Rebels" who would abscond and fight for the king. It was a daring act by a desperate man, short on troops and trying unsuccessfully to govern the colony from on board a warship. Despite not being a professional soldier, Dunmore was looking to raise an army not only of slaves but also of Indians with which to quell the rebellion. Most Virginians, Tory and Patriot alike, were slaveholders, as was Dunmore himself. Many thought that suborning slaves to desert en masse was opening Pandora's Box. It might lead to a slave revolt—a prospect too dreadful to contemplate. Such an uprising would be difficult to contain; it would inevitably spread from the slaves of rebels to the slaves of Tories; together they would make common cause against the common oppressor, slaveholders. Normally, martial law would place slaves—all slaves—under greater restrictions; no slave would ever be declared free in return for military service.

Slaves were not loyal or disloyal subjects; they were not subjects at all. They owed allegiance only to their master, not to the king. The rationale of Lord Dunmore's proclamation was that the treason of the rebels had discharged their slaves from allegiance. Invoking martial law gave the governor the right to invade and expropriate private property, which the slaves were. He was not freeing slaves so much as confiscating them. Fugitive slaves (the property of rebels) thus became wards of the crown, and, at the pleasure of the crown, could "earn" their liberty by taking up arms in its defense. In the manner of convicts released into military service, the slaves were to be mercenaries paid in the coin of their own freedom. Though royal authority was scarcely enforceable anywhere in Virginia, many slaves, thinking compulsory military service not too high a price to pay for liberty, responded to Lord Dunmore's proclamation and rushed to the governor's assistance. Many were slaughtered at the battle of Great Bridge in December 1775; the survivors spent the next few months cruising off the coast of Virginia with the governor and his little fleet. Most died from disease.

The proclamation served little purpose other than to inflame further popular feeling against Lord Dunmore. The patriot convention responded by issuing an edict to the effect that fugitive slaves taken in arms would be summarily executed. An unintended result was that slaves loyal to their patriot owners were armed by them and fought against the British, as was their duty. Subsequent proclamations by British army commanders liberated slaves who fled rebel masters, but they were never allowed to fight. A punitive war measure rather than an antislavery measure, Lord Dunmore's proclamation was an experiment in brinkmanship too risky to repeat. Declaring slaves of rebels free so that they could help put down a rebellion by their masters was thought to be impolitic, a menace to the very fabric of the socio-legal order to which both parties to the conflict wholeheartedly subscribed. Some eighty-seven years later, during a much greater rebellion and civil war in which slavery was the central issue, Lord Dunmore's proclamation would find its echo in President Lincoln's Emancipation Proclamation.

Further Readings: Berkeley, Francis L. *Dunmore's Proclamation of Emancipation . . . .* Charlottesville, VA: The Tracy W. McGregor Library, University of Virginia, 1941; Caley, Percy B. "Dunmore, Colonial Governor of New York and Virginia, 1770–1782." Ph.D. dissertation, University of Pittsburgh, 1939; Quarles, Benjamin. "Lord Dunmore as Liberator." *William & Mary Quarterly* 3rd ser. 15 (1958): 494–507.

Barry Cahill

L'Ouverture, Toussaint (1743–1803)

Born into slavery in 1743, Toussaint grew up on Bréda Plantation, near Le Cap in the north of Saint Domingue. Though slim and short in stature,

Toussaint was energetic and acquired an extensive knowledge of animals, especially horses, and developed a keen knowledge of horticulture, plants, and roots. Portraits of him are contradictory, but he was not handsome, although he exhibited the charisma of a natural leader.

Little is known about Toussaint's parents. Legend has it that his father was named Gaou-Ginou and was an African chieftain of the Arada tribe from Dahomey, also known as Bénin. Toussaint had some mastery of the Arada language, but he also received some education on Bréda Plantation. He cultivated an air of mystery about his past and heritage, but had been protected from the harsh conditions of slavery in Saint Domingue.

Even before the **Haitian Revolution** of 1791, Toussaint achieved the status of a free person. By the age of thirty-three, he had married Suzanne Simone Baptiste and had two children by her. He also rented a plot of land and employed thirteen slaves. By 1791, Toussaint owned at least one slave himself, but he awarded his slave freedom following the initial insurrection.

Following the outbreak of the black revolution of 1791, Toussaint joined the rebel insurgents. Even though the Spaniards of Santo Domingo (Dominican Republic) were allied with the French, the Spaniards hated the French Revolution of 1789 and decided to encourage the rebel insurgents as a means of fomenting trouble for France in the Caribbean. Toussaint and his allied insurgents received arms and ammunition from the Spaniards, but Toussaint joined the French forces when the French abolished slavery in the island in 1793. As an insurgent, he first worked as a doctor, but achieved leadership as a military commander. His skill in battle was legendary, and he was both feared and respected by allies and enemies alike.

Toussaint was not immune to expediency, but he did more than most leaders to promote the ideals of the French Revolution—liberty, equality, and fraternity, as expressed in the Declaration of the Rights of Man and Citizen. Indeed, he took extraordinary measures throughout his military and political life to treat all groups equally and with fairness. The trust he engendered helped him solidify his control of the colony. However, when a regiment of mulattos defected to the enemy, causing him to lose a battle against the British at St. Marc, he vowed never to trust the free colored completely again.

In August 1793, Toussaint took the name L'Ouverture in an official document for the first time. The origins of the name are unclear, but one explanation is that he took the name because of his uncanny ability to find and exploit openings on the battlefield. As skilled as he was on the battlefield, Toussaint was also skilled at politics and diplomacy. By exhibiting tireless dedication to the freedom of his people, "Papa Toussaint," as he came to be called, was seen as their protector from enslavement by the European colonial powers.

By 1799, Toussaint had consolidated his control of the colony and set about securing its independence. He achieved the trust of many former planters, whom he invited back to the island; he realized that he needed their knowledge and skills to make the island prosperous again, and many thousands responded to Toussaint's proclamation of peace and safe passage. He also proposed a constitution that ensured equal treatment for all groups and made himself governor general for life. He negotiated informal trade agreements with Britain and the United States, and he instituted labor policies intended to expand the colony's production of key tropical staples—sugar, coffee, cotton, and cocoa.

Between 1797 and 1802, Toussaint's power reached its zenith. He was the quasi-independent ruler of the quasi-independent government of Saint Domingue, and he negotiated with the great powers as if he were the sovereign equal of Great Britain, the United States, and France. But the freedom and independence of Saint Domingue were threatened by events in France. By 1802, the French Revolution had passed thru its radical phase of liberty and equality and had now become much more preoccupied with the restoration of order and business. Toussaint pleaded with the new ruler of France, **Napoleon Bonaparte,** to recognize him as ruler and to respect the freedom of the black cultivators recently escaped from bondage. He assured Napoleon and the French that he only wanted to achieve commonwealth status within the French empire. But the former planters of Saint Domingue resident in Paris insisted that the productivity of the plantations would only be completely restored if slavery and the old regime were restored. Their opinions deeply influenced Napoleon's plans for the island.

In 1802, Napoleon sent General Victor Leclerc and 20,000 soldiers against Toussaint and the freed slaves of Saint Domingue. The Leclerc expedition was charged with the mission of retaking the island and reestablishing bondage. Toussaint's rebel forces fiercely resisted and caused Napoleon to commit 40,000 additional troops. Under the leadership of the former slave **Jean-Jacques Dessalines,** the black revolution defeated and expelled the white Frenchmen from Saint Domingue, as it had defeated and expelled the Spaniards and English earlier in the 1790s. As for Toussaint, he was seized duplicitously by the French during peace negotiations held under a flag of truce and transported to a prison in the French Alps. He died at Fort de Joux on April 7, 1803, unaware that his army had rallied behind the leadership of Dessalines, to win the colony's independence and proclaim the new Republic of Haiti on January 1, 1804.

Despite his untimely death, Toussaint L'Ouverture was one of the leading freedom fighters of the modern world. Even though his origins were wretched, he was a brilliant general and wise administrator who expelled the British, Spanish, and French forces sent against him, emancipated the slaves of Saint Domingue and Santo Domingo, and strived to reform Haiti's politics and society. His extraordinary efforts at reaching across lines of race and class set him apart from contemporaries, and his vision of an independent country of equals was finally ahead of his time. *See also* French Colonies, Emancipation of; Saint Domingue, French Defeat in.

Further Readings: Geggus, David. *Slavery, War, and Revolution: The British Occupation of Saint Domingue, 1793–98.* Oxford: Oxford University Press, 1982; James, C.L.R. *The Black Jacobins: Toussaint L'Ouverture and the San Domingo Revolution.* 2nd ed. London: Vintage, 1989.

Tim Matthewson

Lovejoy, Elijah (1802–1837)

Elijah Parish Lovejoy was an educator, newspaper publisher and editor, religious leader, abolitionist, and political activist. Lovejoy was murdered by an angry mob of men on November 7, 1837 in Alton, Illinois. Many of the local residents opposed his antislavery beliefs printed in the local newspaper, the *Alton Observer*. After the shocking incident, the **American Anti-Slavery Society,** American abolitionists, free blacks, and enslaved Africans commemorated Lovejoy as a hero and martyr of the U.S. antislavery movement.

Lovejoy was born near Albion, Maine to the Reverend Daniel and Elizabeth (Moody) Lovejoy on November 9, 1802. Lovejoy boasted Puritan roots and was raised in an evangelical household. The young Lovejoy first studied at home and later attended local academies in Monmouth and China, Maine. He graduated from the Baptist-supported Waterville College, now Colby College, in September 1826. Upon his graduation, Lovejoy became a schoolmaster at China Academy.

In 1827, Lovejoy moved to St. Louis, Missouri, where he established a private high school, the curriculum for which was grounded in classical education. Three years later, he entered a partnership with T.J. Miller and became the editor of the *St. Louis Times*. In 1833, he graduated from Princeton Theological Seminary, and was later licensed as a preacher. He returned to St. Louis to edit the *St. Louis Observer*, which espoused politics informed by Christianity and antislavery. In 1835, he married Celia Ann French.

Abolitionist Elijah P. Lovejoy denouncing slave-owners before the U.S. Congress, 1830s. Courtesy of the North Wind Picture Archives.

The *Observer*, however, came to disturb local residents, primarily because of Lovejoy's abolitionism. In 1835, Lovejoy was denounced by residents for shipping the *Emancipator*, a New York newspaper published by the American Anti-Slavery Society, with a box of Bibles to a Jefferson City branch of the American Bible Society for St. Louis. In 1835, a mob destroyed his press and he witnessed the lynching of a man named Francis J. McIntosh. Lovejoy then decided to move to Alton, Illinois with his wife, Celia, and their son, Edward Payson. In 1836, Lovejoy established the *Alton Observer* and resumed his antislavery publishing. Angry residents in Alton twice destroyed Lovejoy's press and during the latter attack, he was murdered when he sought to defend his office. *See also* Bible and Slavery.

Further Readings: Curtis, Michael Kent. "The 1837 Killing of Elijah Lovejoy by an Anti-Abolition Mob: Free Speech, Mobs, Republican Government, and the Privileges of American Citizens." *UCLA Law Review* 44 (1997): 1109–1184; Dillon, Merton L. *Elijah P. Lovejoy: Abolitionist Editor*. Urbana: University of Illinois Press, 1961; Simon, Paul. *Freedom's Champion: Elijah Lovejoy*. Carbondale: Southern Illinois University Press, 1994; Educational Resources: Elijah Lovejoy [Online, August 2005] Center for State Policy and Leadership, http://pphsp.uis.edu/elijah_parish_lovejoy.htm.

Nadine Hunt

Lundy, Benjamin (1789–1839)

Benjamin Lundy, the most significant American antislavery advocate of the 1820s, edited *The Genius of Universal Emancipation*. Born to Joseph and Elizabeth Shotwell Lundy on January 4, 1789, in Sussex County, New Jersey, Lundy was a birthright **Quaker.** He witnessed the dehumanizing effects of slavery firsthand while learning the trade of saddlery in Wheeling, Virginia. He relocated to Ohio, where he married Esther Lewis and established his own shop in 1815. He soon began his activist career, helping to cofound the Union Humane Society in 1816 in Mount Pleasant, Ohio. Short-lived though this group proved, its tenets would remain consistent across Lundy's career: opposition to slavery through both moral and political means, use of all legal means to free slaves, and assisting free blacks.

After a frustrating sojourn in Missouri during the tumultuous statehood debates of 1819–1820, Lundy recognized the importance of an antislavery press. With the 1820 death of Elihu Embree, the Tennessee editor of the *Emancipator*, Lundy picked up his mantle with *The Genius of Universal Emancipation* in June 1821. The next year he moved his family and his paper from Ohio to Greeneville in eastern Tennessee, to foster antislavery sentiments in the South.

From the beginning, Lundy based his abolitionist analysis on the ideals of the **Declaration of Independence,** decrying the blatant hypocrisy that slavery entailed politically, ethically, religiously, and economically. Though he embraced the Quaker heritage of John Woolman and **Anthony Benezet** and counted on Friends' support, his paper was never partisan, maintaining an ecumenical, even eclectic tone. He supported efforts to prove that free labor was more profitable than slavery. Lundy was ambivalent toward colonization; he saw through its underlying racism, and ridiculed the impossibility of relocating all American blacks to Africa, but he also appreciated any movement that freed slaves and provoked reflection on the benefits of manumission. One result of this was a trip to Haiti in 1826 to investigate possibilities for American blacks resettling there. Not only was the trip a failure, but also Lundy's wife died while he was away; relatives raised their five children.

Based in Baltimore since 1824, *The Genius of Universal Emancipation (GUE)* became the national voice of antislavery. Through Lundy's paper, forces that shaped abolition and related movements first came to prominence. Lundy cautiously supported Frances Wright's Nashoba project, and more enthusiastically published **Elizabeth Heyrick**'s bold *Immediate, not Gradual Abolition*. His serious treatment of women as coworkers and intellectuals continued with his mentoring of the Quaker poet Elizabeth Margaret Chandler, who would become editor of the women's page of *GUE* in 1829. Lundy also befriended free blacks in Baltimore, including William Watkins, and published their writings occasionally.

In 1828, Lundy traveled north to raise funds, meeting with many Northern philanthropists, such as William Goodell and George Benson. But the most important meeting was with **William Lloyd Garrison.** Inspired by Lundy, and choosing to focus his energies on antislavery, the young Garrison became an associate editor of *The Genius* in 1829. His more strident tone resulted in legal problems for himself and the paper. Once Garrison was out of prison, he and Lundy amicably ended their business relationship, leaving Garrison free to launch *The Liberator* in 1831. Despite ideological differences and public quarrels over the next decade, the importance of Lundy's influence in converting Garrison to antislavery and encouraging his editorial skills cannot be underestimated: it cements Lundy's role in bridging earlier antislavery movements to later abolitionists.

In the spring of 1832, Lundy traveled to Texas, investigating conditions in this part of Mexico for black American settlement. While negotiations with the Mexican government ultimately evaporated, he gained intimate knowledge of Southern white American plans to usurp this land and, he feared, turn it into several new slave-holding states. He wrote two widely circulated pamphlets in 1836, *The War in Texas* and *The Origin and True Causes of the Texas Revolution*. **John Quincy Adams** used Lundy's writings and testimonies to delay the annexation of Texas to the United States.

Texas propelled Lundy from a nearly forgotten relic to a central player in the growing antislavery movement of the late 1830s. However, he was suffering ill health and losing his hearing. While preparing for his move to Illinois to live with his children, Lundy's papers were destroyed in the mob arson of Pennsylvania Hall in 1837. Arriving in Illinois the next year, antislavery forces there saw Lundy and *The Genius* filling the gap left by **Elijah Lovejoy**'s martyrdom, and so the paper resumed for twelve issues. Lundy died August 22, 1839, in Lowell, Illinois, from fever brought on by overwork on his farm. Lundy was widely eulogized, but his contributions have still been underestimated, now and then. His newspaper fanned a flame of abolition that was nearly extinguished, and brought its fire to a new generation. His ecumenical approach was not only religious, but sectional, too. He consistently tried to reach the conscience of white Southerners, and to place slavery in international perspective. He was tireless (to his own detriment), almost always impoverished, open-minded to new ideas, and consistent in his principles. Relatively free of class snobbery, he evaluated ideas on their merits rather than on the respectability of their authors. He intuitively grasped the difficulties involved in ending slavery, and thus encouraged a pluralism of ideas to further that goal.

Further Readings: Armstrong, William C. *The Lundy Family and Their Descendents.* Belleville, Ontario, Canada: Mika Publishing Company, 1987; Dillon, Merton L. *Benjamin Lundy and the Struggle for Negro Freedom.* Urbana: University of Illinois Press, 1966; Earle, Thomas. *The Life, Travels and Opinions of Benjamin Lundy.* New York: Arno Press, 1969 [originally published 1847]; Landon, Fred. "Benjamin Lundy in Illinois." *Journal of the Illinois State Historical Society* 33 (March 1940): 53–67; Lundy, Benjamin. *The War in Texas.* Upper Saddle River, NJ: Literature House, 1970 [reprint of 1836 edition]; Lundy, Benjamin. *The Origin and True Causes of the Texas Revolution Commenced in the Year 1835.* Philadelphia, 1836; Lundy, Benjamin. *The Poetical Works of Elizabeth Margaret Chandler, With a Memoir of her Life and Character.* Mnemosyne Press, 1969; Miller, Randall M. "The Union Humane Society." *Quaker History* 61, 2 (1972): 91–106; Sandlund, Vivien. "'A Devilish and Unnatural Usurpation': Baptist Evangelical Ministers and Antislavery in the Early Nineteenth Century: A Study of the Ideas and Activism of David Barrow." *American Baptist Quarterly* 13, 3 (1994): 262–277.

Jennifer Rycenga

M

Macaulay, Zachary (1768–1838)

Zachary Macaulay was born on May 2, 1768 in the Scottish town of Inverary, one of the twelve children of Reverend John Macaulay and Margaret Campbell. As a child, Zachary's formal schooling was limited, but his father instilled in him a love of reading and tutored him in art, literature, and a number of foreign languages. Despite his love of learning, his father preferred he pursue a career in business, apprenticing fourteen-year-old Zachary to a Glasgow merchant.

After three years, Macaulay left to seek employment in Jamaica, but arrived with few prospects and no money. Using a friend's connections, he was hired as a bookkeeper on a sugar plantation, an experience he found laborious but eye-opening. Working on a sugar plantation, Macaulay saw firsthand the experiences of slaves and their mistreatment at the hands of masters and overseers. At age twenty-one, he returned to England.

Following a brief period of inactivity, Macaulay was introduced to members of the Clapham Sect by his brother-in-law, Thomas Babington, who was a considerable influence on the young man. The Clapham Sect of reformers included evangelicals such as **William Wilberforce**, Henry Thornton, **Thomas Clarkson** and others. Macaulay's exposure to the supposed evils of slavery made him a natural fit in this group, which was becoming increasingly involved in antislavery reform. He was virtually unique among the Clapham reformers as one of few with any firsthand exposure to the institution of slavery.

Shortly thereafter, Zachary Macaulay joined the London Abolition Committee and was appointed secretary of the Sierra Leone Company, whose charge it was to develop the new colony of **Sierra Leone**. In 1794, the company appointed Macaulay as governor of the struggling possession, and except for a brief vacation, Macaulay served in that capacity until 1799. Although overall he was a tireless and successful administrator, Macaulay was faced with unrest on the part of black Nova Scotian settlers, land allocation problems, and attacks from French naval squadrons involved in the Napoleonic Wars. Macaulay's tenure as governor saw a sizable expansion of the capital, Freetown, before his permanent return to Britain in mid-1799.

In that same year, Macaulay married Selina Mills, and the couple ultimately had nine children. One child was the politician and commentator Thomas Babington Macaulay, while another, Hannah, was the mother to politician and historian Sir George Otto Trevelyan.

After his marriage, Macaulay immersed himself even further in antislavery reform efforts. As the British slave trade was ending, in April 1807 he was instrumental in the founding of the African Institution, the premiere antislavery group in Britain until the 1820s. Macaulay served as the group's first secretary, was given a special award for service to the group in 1813, and in 1814 was chosen to represent the abolitionists at the Congress of Vienna. In 1823, he helped form the **Anti-Slavery Society** and edited its newspaper, *The Antislavery Reporter.* Macaulay's efforts towards antislavery reform were crucial to the movement, as by the early 1820s many other leaders (such as Wilberforce) were suffering from declining health or old age.

Macaulay's life in this period was not easy, however. Business problems and lack of attention to financial matters caused considerable hardship, remedied only after several years of intervention by one of his sons. Nonetheless, partly due to Macaulay's diligence, Britain passed an Emancipation Act in August 1833, which went into effect on August 1, 1834, ending the institution of slavery in the British colonies. In bad health and with lingering financial problems, Zachary Macaulay passed away in 1838. *See also* Atlantic Slave Trade and British Abolition; British Slavery, Abolition of.

Further Reading: Booth, Charles. *Zachary Macaulay.* London, 1938.

Wayne Ackerson

Manumission

Manumission involves the liberation of individual bondpersons in a society that continues to maintain slavery. It is distinct from emancipation, which connotes the freeing of all slaves within a society. Wherever slavery existed, manumission occurred. Manumission rates varied across time and space, a heterogeneity borne of disparate demographic, economic, geopolitical, and social conditions. Dissimilar manumission rates in the Americas produced free black and "free colored" populations that differed in size, composition, and outlook. Even so, the actual process of manumission was remarkably uniform. Everywhere, manumission was a protracted enterprise involving multiple parties. Critical negotiations between slaveholders, bondpersons, and others came before and after the bestowal of freedom. In short, manumission was a ubiquitous and complex practice, one whose frequency, character, and consequences changed as historical circumstances changed.

Manumission rates varied among societies. Slave liberations occurred more frequently in Brazil than in the United States, to give an oft-cited example. Yet even in the most manumission-adverse societies, some slaveholders emancipated bondpersons.

Manumission rates also varied within societies. Brazil provides an illustrative example. The differences could be regional: in the early nineteenth century, manumission rates were higher in Minas Gerais than in Sao Paulo. The distinctions could be temporal: in the sugar-producing regions of northeast Brazil, slave liberations were relatively uncommon in the dynamic mid-seventeenth century, but they increased thereafter as the economy sputtered. The dissimilitude could be demographic: in Brazil (as elsewhere), some slaveholders and bondpersons were more likely to engage in manumission than others.

Intersocietal and intrasocietal differences in manumission rates influenced the size of free black and free colored populations. In Spain's mainland colonies, free people of color outnumbered slaves by the early nineteenth century. In Brazil, the freedperson population approximated the slave population by the early 1800s and surpassed it by mid-century. In most areas colonized by northern Europeans, the free colored population was smaller than the white population and usually dwarfed by the slave population. All totaled, by 1800, there were close to two million free persons of color in the Americas, compared with approximately three million slaves.

Governmental authorities outlined the means by which slaveholders could legally free bondpersons. The most common methods of manumission were gratis, conditional, delayed, self-purchase, postmortem, and state-sponsored. When slaveholders emancipated bondpersons gratis, they did not explicitly demand compensation. In conditional manumissions, slaves obtained liberty, but additional requirements were made of them, such as attending to their ex-owner until his or her death. Delayed manumissions were instances wherein slaveholders withheld immediate liberty, but promised to grant freedom at a future date. In self-purchase arrangements, bondpersons bought their liberty, the price for which could be above, below, or at the market price for slaves. In postmortem manumissions, slaveholders liberated bondpersons upon their demise, usually with a testamentary decree. State-sponsored manumissions took many forms, including bestowing liberty to slaves who revealed insurrection plots and to those who served in the military, with the latter policy sometimes resulting in mass liberations. Although these modes of manumission differed in many respects, they shared at least one characteristic: normally, they granted freedom to select slaves only—large-scale, state-sponsored manumissions notwithstanding. Put another way, slaveholders rarely emancipated bondpersons en masse.

Manumission was not just a legal act. It was also a social process, often a lengthy one, in which important events preceded and followed the official confirmation of liberty. At each stage of the process, bondpersons, slaveholders, and other parties sought to advance their own interests.

For slaves, the trek to freedom was often difficult. Not surprisingly, some bondpersons were better situated to make the journey than others. The law inhibited a number. Restrictions on emancipating superannuated slaves were common, for instance. Even more important were the economic, demographic, and social forces that molded manumission patterns. The result was a distinctive population of freedpersons: females, mixed-race persons, skilled workers, urbanites, and creoles were overrepresented among the manumittees' ranks, largely because their sex, color, occupation, residence, and level of acculturation gave them greater access to the avenues of freedom. While no single characteristic predetermined whether a slave would achieve liberty, bondpersons with the aforementioned traits generally had the most opportunities for freedom.

Female slaves were more likely to secure liberty than male slaves. Despite the fact that bondmen usually outnumbered bondwomen on slaving vessels and large plantations, sixty to sixty-five percent of manumittees in the Americas were females. This overrepresentation occurred for a number of reasons. In some cases, male slaveholders liberated their bonded sexual partners. In others, slaveholders emancipated bondwomen because they assumed the latter would be dependent on them, and therefore would remain an accessible, exploitable labor force. A gendered division of labor also contributed to the preponderance of freedwomen. Traditionally "female" occupations such as housekeeper, cook, nurse, laundress, and vendor allowed some bondwomen to make money and meet sympathizers, and thereby increased their opportunities to obtain freedom. Sex-specific customs could have the same effect, as was the case in eighteenth-century Surinam, where some planters transferred pregnant slaves to urban Paramaribo in order to better monitor their health, a procedure that introduced such women to persons and practices that bolstered their chances for freedom. Like slavery itself, manumission was a gendered experience.

It was also a familial endeavor. Freedom was usually not given gratis, so slaves who wanted to liberate themselves and their kin had to pool their resources and gradually buy their way out of bondage. The objective was to have one family member buy his or her freedom, and then that manumittee would accumulate funds and purchase other kin. Strategy was essential, and gender and sex influenced bondpersons' deliberations. Often the choice was between liberating a male, whose comparatively high wages could underwrite additional manumissions, or freeing a female, whose children after emancipation would be born free. To complicate matters, different slaveholders often owned different members of a slave family. In these situations, familial reconstitution necessitated enlarging the strategy for manumission. Expansive undertakings of this sort sometimes irked neighboring slaveholders. Protests were most common in places where manumissions occurred infrequently, such as the nineteenth-century U.S. South. Slaves' familial bonds thus rendered manumissions intricate affairs, ventures that required determination, sagacity, and deftness on the slaves' part.

Counterpoised against the slaves' objectives were their owners' ambitions. Individuals freed bondpersons for any number of reasons. Some manumitted their bonded concubines. Other emancipators, especially free black ones, liberated their own kin. Still others were moved by humanitarian, religious, or philosophical considerations. To dismiss manumitters' professions concerning morality, gratitude, and affection as mere rationalizations for pecuniary objectives is to overlook how non-economic forces influenced manumission practices and to ignore slaves' own efforts to attract the positive attention of their owners, and thereby increase their odds for liberation. Nevertheless, it is clear that many slaveholders initiated manumissions for financial reasons.

Slaveholders freed bondpersons during good times and bad. Manumission rates usually increased when the economy declined. Rising manumission rates in Pernambuco, Brazil during the late-seventeenth century and in the Chesapeake region during the late-eighteenth century, for example, coincided with downturns in sugar and tobacco production, respectively. On occasion, food shortages prompted slaveholders to liberate bondpersons. This was the case in eighteenth-century Curacao, where spikes in manumission rates corresponded with periodic famines. In some instances, however, manumission rates rose during eras of economic growth. In early nineteenth-century Baltimore, manumission abetted commercial and industrial expansion. A similar story unfolded during the early to mid-1700s in the gold-mining region of Sabara, Minas Gerais, Brazil. Viable during both booms and busts, manumission was a protean practice.

From the slaveholders' perspective, manumission promised an exceptionally productive and flexible labor force. This was especially true in regard to self-purchase arrangements. Slaveholders assumed that bondpersons who were trying to buy their freedom would work harder and be less apt to run away. They also figured that self-purchase agreements would allow them to slowly liberate their older, less profitable slaves and use the manumittees' ransom money to purchase additional bondpersons. And all the while, slaveholders retained the legal rights to would-be manumittees' children. In some instances, children born to self-purchasing women were deemed slaves for life; in others, the offspring were entitled to freedom at a later date—when they reached adulthood, for example. Either way, slaveholders could take possession of the youngsters or leave them with their parents, depending upon the costs of child upkeep and their need for child labor. For many slaveholders, manumission meant profit maximization.

Some slaveholders were more likely to embrace manumission than others. Proportionally speaking, small, urban, and free black slaveholders liberated bondpersons more frequently than their large, rural, and white counterparts. In a like manner, females were overrepresented among the manumitters' ranks. Such women were not exhibiting antislavery sympathies. If anything, slaveholding women, having fewer vocational options and less material wealth than most slaveholding men, were particularly dependent on slave-generated revenue, and they wanted their bondpersons to labor diligently and faithfully. Thus, the profusion of female manumitters was attributable to legal strictures, gender conventions, familial concerns, and slave acumen, not tenderheartedness. Throughout the Americas, lawmakers impaired females' property rights. Generally speaking, only unmarried and widowed women exercised full control over their property. As a result, female slaveholders' options regarding slave management were comparatively circumscribed, and this may have made them more reliant on manumission than men. Similarly, gender norms, while varying from society to society, restricted female slaveholders' management choices, especially in regard to personally inflicting corporal punishment, and manumission may have emerged as a favored method of motivating bondpersons. Familial concerns may have also contributed to the overrepresentation of females among manumitters. Whereas male slaveholders might expect bondpersons to serve their widows and children, widows may have had more discretion in disposing of their property, a flexibility that could bode well for favored slaves. Finally, bondpersons understood female slaveholders' legal, social, and familial situation, and manipulated it to their advantage. In short, slave-owning women were as invested in bondage as their male counterparts, but differing circumstances led many to utilize manumission as a way to protect their profits.

Slaves and slaveholders were not the only ones involved in the domain of manumission. Other parties made their presence felt, including lawmakers. The legislators' influence fluctuated over time. Until the mid-1700s, manumission statutes tended to be unobtrusive. Thereafter, government officials made manumission a more cumbersome process, although Brazil was somewhat of an exception to this trend. In Martinique, Barbados, and Jamaica, the crackdown reflected growing white fears about free black economic competition and servile revolt. The same anxieties were evident in the nineteenth century in the United States and Cuba where the profitability of the cotton and sugar revolutions fuelled slaveholders' concerns that the supply of bondpersons would diminish due to restrictions on the Atlantic slave trade. By the early nineteenth century, legislators not only required emancipators to post bonds to insure that manumittees would not become public charges, they also prohibited various methods of liberation such as testamentary emancipations and banned the freeing of certain bondpersons, especially the elderly.

Public opinion also affected manumission patterns. When local attitudes countenanced slave flight, bondpersons had greater leverage in negotiating for manumission. In the post-Revolutionary Northern United States, for example, slavery collapsed more quickly than lawmakers had intended, partially because slaves used the burgeoning antislavery sentiment to exact promises of expeditious freedom from their owners. Comparable events transpired in northeastern Brazil 100 years later, when private manumissions outpaced the statutory timetable for gradual abolition. Conversely, when public opinion was not in the slaves' favor, bondpersons had more difficulty securing freedom. Simply put, outside parties always affected emancipatory ventures.

The ventures did not end once slaves obtained liberty. There was also the question of the freedpersons' place in the social order. Two important factors in determining manumittees' status was their relationship with their former owner and the character of the larger society. Some ex-slaves fared better than others, but none enjoyed socioeconomic and political equality.

Manumission conferred freedom, not independence. Many emancipators expected subordination and fealty from their former slaves. Consequently, freedpersons struggled to escape their ex-owners' control. For some, the terms of manumission obliged them to additional labor. For others, the law demanded that they show deference to their former owners and serve them dutifully. For still others, affective bonds with enslaved kin kept them within their ex-owner's sphere of power. Destitution likewise impaired manumittees' quest for autonomy. Self-purchase agreements could leave freedpersons penniless and past their most economically productive years, with the result being that they remained dependent on their old owners. Even individuals with valuable occupational skills found that white antipathy might stall their drive for independence. Similarly, rural manumittees who could not acquire land were frequently at their ex-owners' mercy. In sum, the mode of manumission, legal regulations, familial considerations, and economic matters affected freedpersons' chances for self-determination.

A multiplicity of variables also influenced freedpersons' status in the larger society. Racial attitudes, demographic trends, economic conditions, and legal codes were among the most important. This tumult of forces never produced a racially egalitarian culture in the Americas, but by the early nineteenth century three distinctive societal patterns had emerged. First, in most of the Spanish- and Portuguese-speaking areas, freedpersons' numerical strength (25 to 50 percent of the population) and economic power (especially in urban locales) provided opportunities for upward mobility, but white racism and civil disabilities limited their prospects, rendering free people of color a large and diverse caste unto themselves. Second, in many parts of the British and French Caribbean, as well as in Dutch Surinam, "free coloreds" served as a racial buffer between an overwhelming slave majority and a white minority that feared servile insurrections. The free people of color exploited their advantage, sometimes becoming large slaveholders and even citizens, yet they still labored under the stigma of their mixed-racial ancestry and former servile status. Last, in the antebellum United States, free blacks constituted only 6 to 8 percent of the Southern population, but they faced a level of enmity that was perhaps unparalleled in the history of slavery, a hostility that inspired laws that required the departure of new manumittees and a colonization movement that championed the removal of African Americans beyond the country's borders. Thus Southern free blacks probably understood better than anyone that manumission was a protracted, multiparty undertaking that resulted in liberty, not equality.

Further Readings: Brana-Shute, Rosemary, and Randy Sparks, eds. *From Slavery to Freedom: Manumission in the Atlantic World.* Columbia: University of South Carolina Press, forthcoming; Burin, Eric. *Slavery and the Peculiar Solution: A History of the American Colonization Society.* Gainesville, Fl.: University Press of Florida, 2005; McGlynn, Frank, ed. *Perspectives on Manumission,* special issue of *Slavery and Abolition* (Dec. 1989); Nash, Gary B., and Jean R. Soderlund. *Freedom by Degrees: Emancipation in Pennsylvania and its Aftermath.* New York: Oxford University Press, 1991; Patterson, Orlando. *Slavery and Social Death: A Comparative Study.* Cambridge, MA: Harvard University Press, 1982; Tannenbaum, Frank. *Slave and Citizen.* New York: Alfred A. Knopf, Inc., 1946; Whitman, T. Stephen. *The Price of Freedom: Slavery and Manumission in Baltimore in Early National Maryland.* Lexington: The University Press of Kentucky, 1997.

Eric Burin

Maroons of Jamaica/Tacky Rebellion

The Maroons are fundamental to the history of resistance in the Caribbean, and next to the Guianas, Jamaica had the largest Maroon community in the British-colonized Caribbean, with Portland, St. Thomas-in-the-East, St. Mary, Trelawny, and St. Elizabeth having been the parishes with the largest centers of Maroon settlement. The meaning of the word *Maroon* has been subject to debate. Some writers insist that it derives from the Spanish word *cimmaron*, meaning cattle that had escaped to the wilds, and later applied to Tainos and Kalinagos and later Africans, who escaped European colonization across the Americas (including Brazil where *quilombos* emerged) and established free communities in the forests and mountains. The earliest Maroons in Jamaica were the Tainos who escaped Spanish exploitation. They were joined later by runaway Africans. *Marronage*, derived from *Maroons*, signifies flight to the forest or mountains (or by sea to other territories) and the formation of Maroon communities. The height of marronage was after the British capture of Jamaica from the Spanish in 1655. Between 1655 and 1739 [when the first Maroon war ended], Maroon Towns had been established firmly at Accompong (St. Elizabeth), Trelawny Town (the Leeward Maroons in the Cockpit country), Scott's Hall (St. Mary), and at Crawford Town, Nanny Town and Moore Town in the Blue Mountain range of eastern Jamaica (the Windward Maroons).

The Maroons secured their freedom through treaties in 1739 and 1795, respectively, after the first and second Anglo-Maroon wars. Several individual Maroon leaders have come to light, including Cudjoe and Nanny (the most famous), who fought for freedom for the Windward (Blue Mountain area) Maroons. The post-treaty history of the Maroons has been contentious. Their treaty obligations required them to assist the British in suppressing revolts and returning runaways (although many Maroons did not collaborate with the treaty agreement) in exchange for land for their villages and their own freedom. This collaborative role that many played has been resented by many Caribbean people.

One example of this collaborative role was during the suppression of the Tacky Rebellion. Tacky, said to have been from the Coromanti ethnic group in Guinea, West Africa, is said to have been the leader of the 1760 slave revolt in Jamaica's northern parish of St. Mary. At the time, he was headman on Frontier sugar plantation, meaning that he was among the supervisory group. This revolt broke out on Easter Sunday, April 8, 1760, and it involved arson, the killing of about sixteen whites, and the destruction of several sugar estates. Weapons were obtained from Fort Haldane in Port Maria, the capital city of St. Mary, to which Tacky led a small band of other enslaved peoples to capture the weapon-stocked fort. After killing the storekeeper, Tacky and his men took four barrels of gunpowder and forty firearms. The band of rebels went on to set fire to the sugar works at Heywood Plantation. They took over Frontier and Trinity plantations, destroyed Esher Estate and Ballards Valley Estate and engaged the British troops at Bagnolds, drawing the troops into an ambush. Martial law was imposed by the governor of Jamaica who also enlisted the aid of the Windward Maroons [from Crawford Town, Nanny Town], as well as from Scotts Hall, in an effort to quell the rebellion. Oral history indicates that not all of the Maroons fought against Tacky.

By June 1760, the rebellion had been crushed. Tacky himself is said to have been killed by a Maroon, Davy; and many of his followers were said to have committed suicide in a cave near what is now Tacky's Falls. Oral tradition indicates that Tacky escaped. As in other rebellions, those freedom fighters captured were brutally punished either by being burnt alive, whipped, imprisoned, executed, or deported. Tacky's revolt inspired over 1,000 enslaved people in Westmoreland, Hanover, and St. Thomas-in-the-east to revolt. By the end of 1760, over 60 whites and 300 enslaved had been killed as a result of wars of rebellion. *See also* Palenques (Colombia).

Further Readings: Carey, Beverly. *Maroon Story*. Kingston: Agouti Pub., 1993; Craton, Michael, *Testing the Chains*. Ithaca: Cornell University Press, 1982; Sherlock, Philip and Hazel Bennett. *The Story of the Jamaican People*. Kingston: Ian Randle Pub., 1998; Beckles, Hilary and Verene Shepherd. *Liberties Lost: The Indigenous Caribbean and Slave Systems*. Capetown: Cambridge University Press, 2004.

Verene Shepherd

Martineau, Harriet (1802–1875)

Harriet Martineau was an English reformer who opposed slavery in books and speeches as well as in her travels to the United States. She was born in Norwich to a merchant family of Huguenot descent. Her parents encouraged intellectual growth for both male and female children, though the destiny of their daughters remained in their eyes bound to the household.

Harriet proved to be a precocious child. She translated Tacitus and read Thomas Malthus's work on population at the age of fifteen. Within a short time she embraced the political economy of Adam Smith and David Ricardo. Under their influence she became a reformer on a number of issues, including her opposition to slavery.

In the early 1830s, Martineau published "Demerara," a short story condemning slavery, as well as two antislavery articles. At first she stressed that slavery was bad economics and business, but more substantially she argued that it was an unspeakable wrong committed against the blacks. For a while Martineau supported the plan for emigration of slaves back to Africa, but she came to feel that the numbers of those who had chosen this path were so small it was a failure, and also a moral failure because she abhorred the notion that blacks and whites could not live together in the same society.

In 1834, Martineau embarked on a trip to the United States; she was already identified as an abolitionist. When she arrived in New York, the captain hesitated to let her off the ship because of the recent race riots in that city. He was convinced to do so only when her traveling companion assured him that although Martineau was an abolitionist, she was not an activist.

In her later book about this trip, Martineau describes one particular incident in 1835 in Boston that seemed especially important. There she attended a meeting of the ladies auxiliary of the antislavery society, and during its course was asked to comment on the question of abolition. Martineau hesitated at first because, although she had voiced her opinion in England, this would be her first public statement in America. Finally, she did make a public statement in favor of abolition and for that Martineau received death threats and threats that she would be tarred and feathered.

Another consequence of Martineau's trip was that she came in contact with **William Lloyd Garrison**, and through his influence she strengthened her position against the evil of slavery. Martineau saw for herself what conditions were really like and, like Garrison, came to see that there was no possible justification for it. Conditions could be improved and the black made equal through education.

During her travels in the United States, Martineau also became more aware of another reforming issue, the subjugation of women. She saw this vividly portrayed in the South, but it also was a notable factor in the North. In 1837, for example, the clergy of Massachusetts issued a pastoral letter criticizing the unfeminine activities of women in the antislavery movement. One thing that became clear to her was the close kinship between the liberation of women and the liberation of slavery. One gets another perspective on this close connection from her later book about the Middle East, where she strongly condemned the way in which the Turkish Sultan held his harem in virtual slavery.

Another revealing aspect of Martineau's American trip came when she decided to adopt a slave girl who, it seemed, could no longer be maintained by her owner. Martineau planned for her education either as a domestic servant or worker. The child never came to live with her, but some scholars have found it patronizing that she did not set higher goals for the girl, while others have looked at it in the context of the time.

On her return to England, she continued to support the antislavery movement through such means as raising money and welcomed the United States Civil War as the way to achieve abolition. It is thought that Martineau may have influenced English public opinion in favor of the Union. An ardent reformer who campaigned for the rights of blacks, women, and the underprivileged, she died in 1875. *See also* American Colonization Society; Gender and Slave Emancipation; Gender Relations within Abolitionism.

Further Readings: Hoecker-Drysdale, Susan. *Harriet Martineau, First Woman Sociologist.* New York: Berg, 1992; Pichanick, Valerie K. *Harriet Martineau, The Woman and Her Work, 1802–76.* Ann Arbor: University of Michigan Press, 1980.

Marc L. Schwarz

Memorialization of Antislavery and Abolition

Throughout the history of slavery, there have been individuals of various races and from various countries who have fought for its abolition. Several of these abolitionists have been honored with memorials, including statues and plaques, conventions, celebrations, and the naming of various buildings and public spaces.

One of the most famous American abolitionists was **Sojourner Truth**. Born Isabella Van Wagenen in New York in 1797, Truth was sold many times as a slave. Although she escaped from slavery and helped others to do the same, her freedom was not fully secured until after abolition in New York, in 1827. Truth eventually made Battle Creek, Michigan, her home for more than twenty years, and that city has erected a Monument Park in which Truth has a memorial dedicated to her fight for women's rights and to her efforts to guide escaped slaves through the **Underground Railroad**. There have also been numerous other monuments built in her honor. A portion of highway I-194 and M-66 in Michigan has been designated the Sojourner Truth Memorial Highway. Other noteworthy commemorations of Truth include her induction into the Michigan Women's Hall of Fame in Lansing in 1983 and, in 1986, a postage stamp issued by the United States government. In 2002, the bronze Sojourner Truth Memorial Statue was erected in Florence, Massachusetts; it stands atop an eight-foot pedestal surrounded by gardens and flowers.

The renowned abolitionist, **William Lloyd Garrison**, has also been memorialized, although not as extensively as Truth. In Boston, a statue of William Lloyd Garrison is prominently situated in the Commonwealth Mall with the inscription "My countrymen are all mankind." The statue sits in the middle of one of the busiest streets in Boston.

Harriet Elizabeth Beecher Stowe knew Garrison well. Stowe was born in Litchfield, Connecticut and is best remembered for her book *Uncle Tom's Cabin* and other literary efforts attacking slavery. She also assisted fugitive slaves on the Underground Railroad. Today Stowe has a library and museum named after her in Hartford, Connecticut, where her papers and memorabilia are housed along with many unique works and correspondence of other noteworthy abolitionists.

A memorial was erected in honor of the highly regarded orator and abolitionist **Frederick Douglass** in New Bedford, Massachusetts, where he lived in the late 1830s. The statue sits outside of the New Bedford City Hall and mentions that Douglass changed his name from Frederick Baily to Frederick Douglass to make it more difficult for Southern slave catchers to find him. Douglass and his dedication to freedom are memorialized in innumerable sites in the United States and beyond.

As antislavery and abolition did not only take place in the United States, the United States is not the only place where one finds them memorialized. The centennial of the abolition of slavery in Cuba was celebrated with the holding of several conferences in 1986. Also, in 1988, conferences were held to commemorate the abolition of slavery in Brazil, an event that involved numerous historical congresses and other ceremonies. The editor of the journal *American Historical Review* decided to dedicate the entire August 1988 issue to mark the anniversary. Also, a statue of **Abraham Lincoln** freeing the slaves stands nearby London's famed Westminster Abbey.

A memorial to the slaves at Mount Vernon, the former home of President George Washington, was dedicated on September 21, 1983. The memorial sits on the slaves' burial site, where it is believed over 300 enslaved people were interred. In 2001, in Lawnside, New Jersey, the Peter Mott House officially opened to the public. The house is a memorial for those who ran the Underground Railroad. The house stands as a museum to those who helped the slaves find their way to freedom. The house, constructed over 160 years ago, was inhabited by black businessmen and farmers whom helped escaped slaves to freedom.

On January 1, 1883, in Washington, D.C., a large and important celebration took place. It was the twentieth anniversary of the signing of the

Emancipation Proclamation and a celebration of black abolitionist men. This was the first time an assemblage of influential African American leaders had gathered together. It was at this dinner and all across the country that African Americans first began to commemorate their struggles for freedom. January 1 became Emancipation Day and was celebrated within the African American communities in the North and South. This celebration and commemoration was the first of many in 1883, most of which memorialized black and white abolitionists and their fight for freedom and equality.

The Robert Gould Shaw Memorial to the Massachusetts Fifty-Fourth and Fifty-Fifth Colored Regiments is one of the most eminent commemorations of African Americans' struggle against slavery. It was dedicated in the Boston Common in May 1897 with a large, solemn parade that included veterans from the two regiments and over 3,500 cadets, seamen, militia, and mounted police. It remains the single most important memorial to the over 180,000 black men who fought against Southern slavery from January 1863 to the Civil War's end. Many of the Fifty-Fourth's men died at the Battle of Fort Wagner in Charleston Harbor in July 1863, a battle that the *New York Tribune* proclaimed, "made Fort Wagner such a name to the colored race as Bunker Hill had been for ninety years to the white Yankees." This memorial was of enormous significance for it served to remind an American public of a fact that most had forgotten by the century's end—that the bloody and ultimate Union victory in April 1865 had been very dependent upon the tens of thousands of courageous black troops from the North and South who enthusiastically volunteered to smash the institution which had beleaguered them for so long.

The timing for the Shaw installation was propitious for the nation as a whole, as the South, in particular, was actually then engaged in a very contrary memorialization. Throughout the South, Confederate soldiers were being commemorated with statues and large monuments for their brave defense of their states and the Confederacy. As laws disenfranchising and segregating blacks were being passed throughout the South at century's end, and Northerners were encouraged to leave the white South alone to resolve its race "problem," a new and amicable reunion between the white North and South was promoted. Newly erected memorials both North and South celebrated only white veterans and their heroism, and all but denied the vast involvement of African Americans in the great struggle. The acme of this process of forgetting was the great encampment of white veterans in Gettysburg, Pennsylvania, in July 1913 to celebrate the fiftieth anniversary of the terrible battle. No black veterans were invited to this event, which highlighted the renewed bond of national fellowship between Southern and Northern white men.

In the early decades of the twentieth century, many historians who wrote about the Civil War and the crisis preceding it in the 1850s blamed the abolitionists and irresponsible antislavery forces in the North for causing the war. Through their ceaseless and distorted propaganda against slavery and supposed support for John Brown's raid on Harpers Ferry in 1859, they had needlessly inflamed an anxious South about the security of their control over their legal property—the slaves—and led them to choose secession as their only feasible recourse. By the mid-twentieth century, however, a vast revision of the history of slavery, antislavery, and the causes of the Civil War were undertaken, which highlighted the causative significance of Southern intransigence in the 1850s and the bold courage rather than corrupt fanaticism of the abolitionists. The bravery and dedication of Civil Rights workers in the South in the 1950s and 1960s helped stimulate a rethinking of the role and importance of the abolitionists in antebellum America. The civil rights movement and the reevaluation of the role of antislavery in antebellum America contributed to a new endeavor to commemorate the struggles of those who had fought against slavery before and during the Civil War. Along with a host of Web sites affording a positive history of abolitionism, the most prominent example of this drive to memorialize antislavery is the recent completion in Cincinnati of the National Underground Railroad Freedom Center.

Further Readings: Blight, David W. *Race and Reunion: The Civil War in American Memory.* Cambridge, MA: Belknap Press. 2001; Drescher, Seymour. *The Abolition of Slavery and the Aftermath of Emancipation.* Durham, NC: Duke University Press, 1988; Foster, Gaines M. *Ghosts of the Confederacy: Defeat, the Lost Cause, and the Emergence of the New South.* New York: Oxford University Press, 1987; Hedrick, Joan D. *Harriet Beecher Stowe: A Life.* New York: Oxford University Press, 1994.

Johnathan L. Carter

Mennonites

American Mennonites had a consistent record of opposition to slavery, principally by not permitting any church member to own a slave, but they did not generally take part in public campaigns for abolition. As early as 1663, Dutch Mennonites in Pieter Plockhoy's short-lived colony in Delaware banned slavery and slave traders from their settlement. The 1688 Germantown protest against slavery emerged from a group of **Quakers** of Mennonite origin, some of whom organized the first Mennonite congregation in America a decade later.

In the eighteenth century, Mennonites settled in southeastern Pennsylvania and western Virginia, where slave-owning was more a status symbol than an economic necessity. As with their Quaker neighbors, simple living was one source of Mennonite antislavery testimony. John Hunt, a contemporary New Jersey Quaker, pointed to the practice of Lancaster County, Pennsylvania, Mennonites in rejecting "superfluities" like owning slaves. John Woolman cited the example of a York County, Pennsylvania, Mennonite who chose to sleep in a field rather than be waited on by his friend's slaves. Unlike Quakers, some of whom owned slaves and had to be convinced to give them up, the Mennonite ban on slave owning was complete; Pennsylvania tax records reveal no slave owners among Mennonites or the related Dunkers (Church of the Brethren). As early as 1761, Dunker Elder Christopher Sauer wrote against the slave trade as "an evil and a sin."

The prohibition against church members owning slaves was universal in the nineteenth century too. A Mennonite catechism published by Peter

Burkholder at Winchester, Virginia, in 1837 repeated the admonition against slavery and the slave trade because "all are free in Christ." In one of the earliest extant records of the Virginia Conference, it was "Decided that inasmuch as it is against our creed and discipline to own or traffic in slaves; so it is also forbidden for a brother to hire a slave unless such slave be entitled to receive the pay for such labor by the consent of his owner."

The Dunkers reiterated their ban on members owning slaves at their annual meeting in 1782, but, in 1787, permitted candidates for baptism who already held slaves to keep them long enough to recover the purchase price before freeing them. They went on record in 1812 that both slavery and the slave trade "should be abolished as soon as possible."

Although generally wary of political activity, Mennonites in eastern Pennsylvania signed petitions to Congress in the 1830s for the abolition of slavery. They also opposed the **Fugitive Slave Law** of 1850. The **Underground Railroad** appealed to Mennonite sensibilities, giving aid to strangers in need. Pennsylvania Mennonites Daniel Kauffman, Deacon Samuel Kendig, Christian Frantz, and Augustus W. Cain were arrested for smuggling slaves to freedom. Lancaster County Mennonites were accused of voting for abolitionists, although this assertion cannot be documented. Areas with a substantial Mennonite vote certainly returned antislavery candidates, such as Thaddeus Stevens. *See also* Germantown Antislavery Petition.

Further Readings: Longenecker, Stephen L. *Piety and Tolerance: Pennsylvania German Religion, 1700–1850*. Metuchen, NJ: Scarecrow Press, 1994; MacMaster, Richard K. *Land, Piety, Peoplehood: The Establishment of Mennonite Communities in America 1683–1790*. Scottdale, PA: Herald Press, 1985; Schlabach, Theron F. *Peace, Faith, Nation: Mennonites and Amish in Nineteenth-Century America*. Scottdale, PA: Herald Press, 1988.

Richard MacMaster

Methodists and Antislavery

Founded in England in the eighteenth century by John Wesley, the Methodist Episcopal Church grew rapidly and, by the eve of the Civil War, was one of the largest denominations in the United States. Like other Christian churches, the Methodists divided in the wake of increased agitation against the institution of slavery. Although some Methodists joined the abolitionist movement in its earliest days and the Wesleyan embrace of the doctrine of holiness lent itself to a theological opposition to slavery, the church was unable to maintain unity in the face of such a divisive issue.

Created by the revivals led by John Wesley in England, Methodism came to the United States in the era of the Revolutionary War, a period during which antislavery sentiment swept the nation. Accordingly, the first Methodist discipline in America was decidedly antislavery, condemning both slave ownership and the slave trade as sinful. This was in keeping with John Wesley's own antislavery stance in England, but the American church soon broke with that tradition. As the church grew during the Second Great Awakening, church discipline was one of its defining characteristics. Its top-down church government emphasized a strict discipline that was inflexible.

In the North, especially in New England, ministers and superintendents had no problem with enforcing the regulations against slavery as their congregations grew in the wake of revivalism. Indeed, revivalism fed into social reform, and Northern Methodists were actively involved in antislavery as well as other benevolent activities. In the South, however, revivalism coincided with a social conservatism that restricted the scope of social reform, and rapid membership growth brought the question of slavery to the fore. To maintain unity and encourage church expansion, the Methodist Church began to accommodate slave ownership by not enforcing the rules against it. Sectional unity was maintained by official silence on the issue.

When the abolitionist movement came to prominence in the 1830s, such official silence was no longer possible. New England Methodists readily joined abolitionist organizations and began pushing for enforcement of the discipline on the issue. They did not believe they could have Christian fellowship with the owners of slaves. In the mid-Atlantic and mid-West, some Methodists joined the abolitionist movement, but most kept the silence needed for unity. In 1836, the increasing power of abolitionism required official action. This led to the Methodist General Conference condemning the evils of slavery, but the leaders of the church tried to keep unity by also denouncing the methods of abolitionism. Although this mixed message managed to sustain church unity, it only served to increase the dissatisfaction of Methodist abolitionists. As the years went by, more and more antislavery Methodists began to realize that their church would not take action against the peculiar institution. Increasingly, the only alternative for them seemed to be to join **come-outer** churches that would split from the main denomination and form smaller organizations dedicated to purity in both theology and politics. In 1841, this led to the creation of the Wesleyan Methodist Connection, which opposed slavery and emphasized the holiness doctrine of entire sanctification. This doctrine, taught by Wesley, held that Christian perfection (holiness) was achievable in the face of a corrupt and sinful world. Northern Methodists and other proponents of sanctification believed that individuals could live without sin through the grace of God and the power of the Holy Spirit. This led them to denounce the sin of slave owning along with such other practices as the use of tobacco and alcohol. If Christian perfection could be lived in the real world, then it was not necessary to compromise on issues of discipline.

Meanwhile, opponents of slavery who remained members of the Methodist Episcopal Church continued trying to overturn the policy of silence. They cried out against the slaveholding of Bishop James O. Andrew of Georgia and called for church action to remove him from the episcopate. This set the stage for the General Conference of 1844 in New York City, where everyone realized the issue would be debated. In a dramatic meeting, the conference delegates struggled with the issue of slavery for two long weeks. The question of slavery raised the question of discipline, which in turn raised the question of church government. Many Methodists flattered themselves by arguing that their church was uniquely American in that it was democratic and individualistic. But the official church government was autocratic and provided for a strong episcopacy. Should the church be centralized or decentralized?

Should slave-owning be considered a sin or not? Could a compromise be reached? After a vigorous debate, the delegates voted and decided, by a vote of 111 to 69, that Bishop Andrew should step down from his position as long as he owned slaves. Outraged Southerners began planning to break with the church, while Northerners insisted that, if the church did not discipline the bishop, they would secede from the ecclesiastical union.

In response, moderate Southern delegates tried to forge a compromise, presenting a plan that called for the creation of two general conferences instead of one. While some Northerners resisted the plan, others supported it in hopes of achieving an amicable resolution to the problem. When the vote was taken, the plan was rejected. Amid calls for a friendly separation, the conference ended. Almost immediately, the Southerners called for a conference of Southern churches and they convened in Louisville, Kentucky, in May 1845, where they created the Methodist Episcopal Church, South. Northerners were unable to achieve the conciliatory break that some had hoped for. Despite the fact that the Southern church sent a delegate to the Northern conference in hopes of cooperating where possible, the Northern churches further divided on the issue. Abolitionists and other Northern Methodists cried out against Southern secession, arguing that the move was unconstitutional. One major point of contention was the matter of the Methodist publication empire, which both sections had long shared. In 1848, the Northern church refused to accept the Southern delegate and voted to reject any plan for peaceful separation. Tensions mounted as some Northern conferences extended into slave states, and there were arguments over where the boundary between the sectional churches should be drawn. When the division of the publication arm of the church could not be resolved, the Southern church took the matter to court and was awarded a pro rata division in the 1850s.

Thus, the antislavery movement and the question of whether or not slave-owning was a sin divided the Methodist Episcopal Church. Although the division slowed the come-outer movement, the Northern church was not able to recover the lost members who had joined smaller groups like the Wesleyans. The piety of the holiness movement called for stricter discipline and a devotion to entire sanctification that the larger church simply could not provide. A similar split among the Baptists soon followed the division of the Methodists. These religious secession movements foreshadowed political division and remained long after the Civil War. The Methodist Episcopal Church did not reunite until 1939, although dissenting Southern churches again seceded the following year. *See also* First Great Awakening and Antislavery.

Further Readings: Bucke, Emory S., ed. *The History of American Methodism.* 3 vols. New York: Abingdon Press, 1964; Goen, C.C. *Broken Churches, Broken Nation: Denominational Schisms and the Coming of the Civil War.* Macon, Ga.: Mercer University Press, 1985; McKivigan, John R. *The War against Proslavery Religion: Abolitionism and the Northern Churches, 1830–1865.* Ithaca: Cornell University Press, 1984.

A. James Fuller

Mexican War and Antislavery

The Mexican War (1846–1848), prosecuted by the Democratic administration of James K. Polk, inspired the emergence of a broad-based, politicized antislavery movement that eclipsed the abolitionism of the 1830s and intensified the bitter debate over whether to prohibit or recognize slavery in the federal territories.

Antislavery Northerners complained that the Mexican War was an unprovoked act of aggression whose territorial accessions would mainly benefit Southern (slaveholding) migrants. South Carolina Senator John C. Calhoun had boldly asserted the annexation of Texas (the primary cause of war with Mexico) was necessary to provide slavery a western outlet for expansion. This alarmed many Northern free-white-labor advocates who hoped to see slavery restricted to the existing Southern states. The seemingly proslavery nature of the war inspired Henry David Thoreau to write his essay *Civil Disobedience*. Nevertheless, most Northerners of both parties accepted the war.

Still, many people tried to prevent slavery's expansion into territories gained in the war, though not all for the same reason. On August 8, 1846, David Wilmot, an obscure Democratic representative from Pennsylvania, authored an amendment to a war-time appropriations bill that stipulated "as an express and fundamental condition of the acquisition of any territory from the Republic of Mexico ... neither slavery nor involuntary servitude shall ever exist in any part of said territory." Though Congress failed to adopt it, the Wilmot Proviso's principle of congressional prohibition of slavery's expansion would serve as the ideological foundation of the new antislavery Free Soil Party in 1848.

The proviso was not an abolitionist document. It made a broader appeal to Northerners' self-interest in defending freedom, especially free labor, rather than to their moral objections to slavery. Wilmot authored his proviso in part out of contempt for black labor and a desire to keep it out of the West. Notwithstanding such instances of racism, many antislavery proponents were quite progressive at the time. Although some Free Soilers, such as **Salmon P. Chase**, Charles Sumner, and Joshua Giddings, consistently promoted citizenship and voting rights for free black men, they were a distinct minority. Most antislavery supporters had never espoused immediate abolitionism, believing instead that to restrict the expansion of slavery was to set it on the path to peaceful extinction.

In the **Compromise of 1850**, the antislavery movement met with partial success in prohibiting slavery from the territories gained in the Mexican War. That compromise, an omnibus bill consisting of several elements, admitted California as a free state. Importantly, it also allowed for popular sovereignty—a doctrine by which territorial settlers would determine, among other matters, whether or not to recognize slavery—to govern the New Mexico Territory. Inspired directly by the conflicts over the Mexican War, popular sovereignty achieved only limited acceptance among the antislavery movement. When it was incorporated into the 1854 bill to organize the Kansas and Nebraska territories, antislavery leaders bitterly resisted since those territories had previously been pledged to freedom by the provisions of the **Missouri Compromise.** Yet, by 1856, popular sovereignty in Kansas meant internecine warfare between antislavery and proslavery settlers. The Mexican War further inflamed the dispute over slavery and the territories. Antislavery and proslavery forces would clash over "ownership" of the territories with increasing frequency throughout the 1850s, indeed, until secession and the United States Civil War itself. *See also* Immediate Emancipation; Texas, Annexation of.

Further Readings: Hietala, Thomas. *Manifest Design: Anxious Aggrandizement in Late Jacksonian America.* Ithaca, NY: Cornell University Press, 1985; McPherson, James M. *Battle Cry of Freedom: The Civil War Era.* New York: Oxford University Press, 1988; Potter, David. *The Impending Crisis, 1848–1861.* Completed and edited by Don E. Fehrenbacher. New York: Harper Torchbooks, 1976; Sewell, Richard. "Slavery, Race and the Free Soil Party, 1848–1854." In Alan M. Kraut, ed. *Crusaders and Compromisers: Essays on the Relationship of the Antislavery Struggle to the Antebellum Party System.* Westport, CT: Greenwood Press, 1983, pp. 101–124.

Matthew Isham

Mill, John Stuart (1806–1873)

John Stuart Mill is perhaps best known for his formulation of "Utilitarianism," a moral philosophy predicated on an individual's right to seek happiness. Mill's later political philosophical writings on liberty, political economy, and individuality are equally noteworthy. Indeed, toward the end of his life, Mill became increasingly active in political affairs and devoted to causes of social justice.

While slavery and its abolition were not primary concerns of Mill, a majority of his writings dealt with contemporary social and political issues; slavery thus became a recurrent theme. In general, Mill was against slavery yet he never systematically delineated that opposition in any one work. Rather, his arguments against slavery were peppered throughout his writings.

For Mill, slavery was both a political and a philosophical problem. Politically, Mill argued that it was the duty of more powerful nations to entreat other and less powerful nations to enhance liberty. A fundamental way to expand and improve liberty was to abolish slavery. Thus Mill favored a British international policy that would not support slavery in America or elsewhere. Philosophically, Mill opposed slavery because it impeded individuals' realization of liberty and happiness.

He developed this understanding more fully in one of his most famous works, *On Individuality*, in which he argued that slavery was an

John Stuart Mill. Courtesy of the Library of Congress.

institution predicated on harm and as such constituted a clear social problem: "Acts, of whatever kind, which, without justifiable cause, do harm to others, may be, and in the more important cases absolutely require to be, controlled by the unfavorable sentiments, and, when needful, by the active interference of mankind. The liberty of the individual must be thus far limited; he must not make himself a nuisance to other people."

Mill found slavery problematic for two reasons. First, it did not allow enslaved individuals to attain and develop his or her full individuality. Second, it allowed some individuals—the slave owners—to harm other individuals, physically and psychologically. The unequal distribution of power enabled the abuse of one class of individuals by another. Slavery epitomized such a misappropriation of power: "[T]he only purpose for which power can be rightfully exercised over any member of a civilized community, against his will, is to prevent harm to others."

For Mill, slavery represented a hindrance to the development of a just society: Its abolition would necessarily be a contribution to "human advancement."

Further Readings: Alexander, Edward, ed. *The Subjugation of Women*. New Brunswick, NJ: Transaction Publishers, 2001 [1869]; Bromowich, David. "A Note on the Life and Thought of John Stuart Mill." In David Bromowich and George Kateb, eds. *On Liberty*. New Haven, CT: Yale University Press, 2003, pp. 1–27; Mill, John Stuart. In David Bromowich and George Kateb, eds. *On Liberty*. New Haven, CT: Yale University Press, 2003 [1859]; "One Simple Principle." In Michael Rosen and Jonathan Wolff, eds. *Political Thought*. Oxford: Oxford University Press, 1999.

Noah Butler

Millennialism and Abolitionism

The Book of Revelation, the last book of the **Bible**, prophesies a 1000-year period of peace to be enjoyed by the faithful. Another name for the Book of Revelation is the Apocalypse, and the millennium has often been termed the New Jerusalem. Questions about the millennium began preoccupying European and American Protestants in the seventeenth century. When would the millennium occur, or had it already begun? Was its beginning sudden or gradual, violent or pacific? Who would enjoy it, and how could the faithful prepare for it? Was it a state in the world or in the hearts of believers? Would it be accompanied by the corporeal resurrection of the faithful deceased as well as by the reappearance of Christ in history, either before (premillennialism) or after (postmillennialism) the golden age? Were there signs of the dawning of the millennium, such as the commonly accepted one of the return of Jews to the Holy Lands? Answers to some of these questions became intertwined with protests against the slave trade and New World slavery.

One influential millennialist was **Jonathan Edwards**, the eighteenth-century Calvinist American theologian, whose prophetic description of the irenic thousand years included black and Indian divines. Edwards believed that the forces of evil—those followers of Antichrist—had been losing battles to the forces of good since the beginning of the Protestant Reformation, but that Antichrist was still waging war against God. Edwards's literary executor and theological heir, **Samuel Hopkins**, infused his mentor's ideas with abolitionism by arguing in his *Treatise on the Millennium* (1793) that the slave trade and slavery were among the worst sins committed by Antichrist's followers and were part of the final battle between the forces of good and those of evil. Believers should root out slavery, not only because it was sinful but also because in doing so they were participating in the advent of the millennium. Edwards's grandson, Timothy Dwight, a leading theologian and president of Yale College, enhanced the connection between the millennium and abolitionism in two *Discourses* (1812). Dwight elevated the end of the British and the American trade in slaves (1807 and 1808) to the level of major steps in God's plan to bring forward the millennium. In his book-length poem *Greenfield Hill* (1794), Dwight envisioned, in a postmillennial mood, the human ideal of a harmonious society created at last in America. Harmony among all races was a crucial part of Dwight's vision: "All mingling, as the rainbow's beauty blends/Unknown where every hue begins or ends."

In the early nineteenth century, postmillenialism became the American Protestant consensus. Progress in America—religious, political, economic, material—was to open the gates of the golden age, after which Christ would reappear in triumph. Yet this progress might well be accompanied by great conflict with further chapters in the ongoing struggle between good and evil. For both many Northerners and many Southerners, the battle over slavery was one such chapter. Throughout the several decades before the Civil War, some Americans voiced premonitions of hostility and destruction. A trial by fire or a baptism by blood was, in the abolitionist view, to purge the nation of the sin of slaveholding or, in the proslavery mind, remove the influence of the corrupt North from the plantation South. Apocalyptic notions and images were found widely in American arts, religion, and politics. Indeed, in the most famous antislavery novel, **Harriet Beecher Stowe**'s ***Uncle Tom's Cabin*** (1852), when the black protagonist is sold away from his family and, ultimately to his death, his master intones, "'It's done!'. . . ; and, fetching a long breath, he repeated, "'It's done!'" Stowe was alluding to one of the key passages from the Book of Revelation describing the violent judgment of God:

> And the seventh angel poured out his vial into the air; and there came a great voice out of the temple of heaven, from the throne, saying, It is done. And there were voices, and thunders, and lightnings; and there was a great earthquake, such as was not since men were upon the earth, so mighty an earthquake, so great. And the great city was divided into three parts, and the cities of the nations fell: and great Babylon came in remembrance before God, to give unto her the cup of the wine of the fierceness of his wrath. (Revelation 16:17–19)

The slavetraders and slaveholders were, of course, in Stowe's mind, inviting such divine judgment upon the nation as well as upon themselves.

Scholars of the twentieth and twenty-first centuries have sometimes been critical of millennialist abolitionism, which seems not to have concerned itself with black freedom except insofar as it was part of a vast divine design. Black men and black women seem to have been merely figures in the progress of the millennium, not individuals deserving civic freedom in their own right. Uncle Tom himself, for instance, is an ideal type with the qualities of a saint, not a flesh-and-blood man. An answer to this criticism is that millennialists tended to understand all things and events as part of the divine design, so they were scarcely capable of comprehending civic freedom, whether of black or white, as a good in and of itself. Moreover, their absorption of the battle against slavery into the progress toward the millennium did make abolitionism a matter of the utmost moral urgency. A millennialist element was a crucial part of the nineteenth-century crusade that helped end North American slavery. *See also* Antislavery Evangelical Protestantism.

Further Readings: Aamodt, Terrie Dopp. *Righteous Armies, Holy Cause: Apocalyptic Imagery and the Civil War*. Macon, GA: Mercer University Press, 2002; Moorhead, James H. "Apocalypticism in Mainstream Protestantism, 1800 to the Present." In Bernard J. McGinn, John J. Collins, and Stephen J. Stein, eds., *The Continuum History of Apocalypticism*. New York: Continuum International Publishing, 2003, pp. 467–492.

John Saillant

Missouri Compromise (1820)

In 1803, when President Thomas Jefferson authorized American negotiators to purchase Louisiana from Emperor **Napoleon Bonaparte** of France for $15 million, Jefferson believed that he had secured the independence of the yeoman farmer for centuries. Jefferson, however, lived to see his purchase become a fierce battleground between North and South over the issue of slavery. As Americans moved westward, so too did slavery. Matters came to a head in 1819, when Missouri Territory applied for statehood. Missouri had the requisite number of inhabitants to apply for statehood, but it also had roughly 3,000 slaves. Missouri thus threatened to become the first slaveholding state that lay completely west of the Mississippi River.

On February 13, 1819, Representative James Tallmadge, a Jeffersonian Republican from New York, offered an amendment to the Missouri statehood bill. This amendment contained two parts. The first part called for a ban on further importations of slaves into Missouri. The second part outlined a gradual emancipation plan similar to that of New York's, in which the children of adult slaves would receive their freedom at the age of twenty-five. Adult slaves would remain in bondage. Tallmadge's amendment created a political firestorm that lasted for two days in the House of Representatives, and two years in the nation.

The House of Representatives, in which the North enjoyed a numerical majority, voted to support the Tallmadge Amendment, but the Senate, which was evenly divided between free and slave states, rejected it. This voting alignment repeated itself throughout most of the Missouri Crisis of 1819–1821. Supporters of slavery in the Senate not only enjoyed the balance of free and slave states, but also the support of senators from states such as Illinois and Indiana, technically free states, but ones with a pronounced Southern influence.

As the House and Senate failed to agree, the bill could not proceed and had to wait until the next session of Congress before any action could occur. While Congress was between sessions, the Missouri issue caught fire in the Northern states. Large assemblies of citizens around the North met and wrote petitions that they sent to their members of Congress, asking them to support Missouri statehood without slavery. Residents of Missouri, likewise, held meetings to protest the actions of the House of Representatives. These meetings also produced petitions, urging Congress to grant Missouri statehood without restriction as to slavery.

The Sixteenth Congress began its first session in this highly charged atmosphere in November 1819. Missouri took up much of the agenda from November until early March 1820. Speeches poured forth from representatives and senators, as did essays in newspapers. Men argued about the place of slavery in the American republic, the effect of slavery on national character, the degrading influence of slavery on free labor, the three-fifths clause and its impact on national politics, whether Congress had the power to restrict slavery in a territory and a state, and whether Congress had the power to regulate the movement of slaves across state lines. Antislavery Northerners, such as Representatives Timothy Fuller of Massachusetts and Arthur Livermore of New Hampshire, had railed against slavery as an institution in the previous session, going so far as to call it a sin. Some Southerners, such as Senator William Smith of South Carolina, openly defended slavery in the session in late 1819 and launched a new intellectual trend in the South. Representative William Plumer, Jr., of New Hampshire, reported that talk of secession regularly dropped from the lips of Southern members of Congress, should Missouri enter the Union without slavery.

A compromise was already in the works, designed to prevent the possibility of secession. Speaker of the House **Henry Clay** of Kentucky and Senator James Barbour of Virginia were in close contact with President James Monroe. Monroe favored Missouri becoming a slave state, but he also supported the idea of a compromise. Maine had been a province of Massachusetts for several decades, but its residents had grown both in numbers and desire for independence. The Massachusetts legislature granted them the opportunity to apply for statehood in 1819. The Senate linked the statehood bills of Maine and Missouri. If Missouri failed to enter the Union, Maine would suffer the same fate. Despite howls of protest from antislavery Northerners, the Senate approved the bills for Maine without slavery and Missouri without restriction as to slavery. After much debate, the solidarity of the Northerners in the House of Representatives broke, and by a vote of 90 to 87, the House approved the bill for Missouri to form a state government without restriction as to slavery. As part of this package, the House and Senate approved legislation that created a geographic line at 36° 30', the southern boundary of Missouri. There was to be no slavery north of this line, with Missouri being the only exception to this rule.

The compromise was unpopular in much of the North, as well as in Virginia. Antislavery Northerners believed that this failed effort to halt the westward spread of slavery represented a capitulation to the South, a conclusion buttressed by Representative John Randolph of Virginia, who sneered that the men who voted with the South were doughfaces. Many Virginians felt much the same as many antislavery Northerners. These

Virginians believed that the slaveholding South had given up too much territory in this compromise.

The compromise reached earlier in 1820 almost came undone that summer when the Missouri legislature wrote a state constitution that called for a ban on free black and mulatto immigration into the new state. This proposed clause angered many Northerners, as well as some Southerners. The clause raised the issue of black citizenship and whether the proposed ban violated the privileges and immunity clause of the United States Constitution. Under the terms of this clause, all citizens share federal rights in all of the states in the Union. There was much debate over the place of African Americans in the republic, but no consensus. Congress finally agreed to require Missouri's legislature never to pass any law that might infringe on the privilege and immunities of an American citizen. The Missouri legislature agreed, and Missouri entered the Union in August 1821. With this second compromise the American republic had navigated its way through the most threatening political crisis that had yet gripped the nation. The compromise would last until the Kansas-Nebraska Act of 1854 repealed it. *See also* Compromise of 1850; Mexican War and Antislavery.

Further Readings: Foley, James C. "'Make the iron enter into their souls': Slavery and Race in the Missouri Crisis, 1819–1821." Ph.D. Dissertation, University of Mississippi, 2005; Forbes, Robert Pierce. "Slavery and the Meaning of America, 1819–1837." Ph.D. Dissertation, Yale University, 1994; Moore, Glover. *The Missouri Controversy, 1819–1821.* Lexington: University of Kentucky Press, 1953.

James C. Foley

Montesquieu, Charles de Secondat, Baron de (1689–1755)

Charles de Secondat, Baron de Montesquieu, was a French intellectual whose writings were influential not only in Enlightenment Europe but in North America as well. Montesquieu is best known for his lengthy book *The Spirit of Laws*, published in 1748. In this famous work, Montesquieu examined the evolution of law by comparing a wide variety of political, social, and historical contexts from throughout the world.

Montesquieu articulated his views on slavery in Part 3 of *The Spirit of Laws*. First, he offered a definition: "Slavery in its proper sense is the establishment of a right which makes one man so much the owner of another man that he is the absolute master of his life and his goods." His opinion of slavery was frank: "it is not good by its nature."

For Montesquieu, slavery was problematic for two reasons. First, it limited the choices a slave had. In so doing, it prevented a slave from fully developing a sense of "virtue" and acting from it because slaves were forced instead to act in accordance with their masters' wishes. Second, the masters contracted "all sorts of bad habits from their slaves."

While he acknowledged the economic and social complexity of slavery, Montesquieu concluded that slavery was essentially a form of despotism and thus primarily a political issue. While considering the origins of slavery, Montesquieu compared the Roman enslavement of other Romans, the Spanish enslavement of Native Americans in the New World, and the French

Charles de Secondat, Baron de Montesquieu. Courtesy of the Library of Congress.

enslavement of blacks in the French Colonies (e.g., the West Indies). He ultimately determined that slavery was rooted more in political organization ("civil slavery") than in nature ("natural slavery"), and looking for its origin was a complicated, if not fruitless, endeavor.

Categorizing slavery by the type of labor performed and the space in which it was performed, he distinguished two forms of it: "real" slavery and "personal" slavery. Real slavery was tied to land and was predominantly agricultural; personal slavery was characterized by domestic service. The two were not mutually exclusive and, according to Montesquieu, the worst form of slavery was when real and personal slavery were superimposed.

While he lauded the fact that slavery was illegal in most of eighteenth-century Europe, because Montesquieu noted the complexities surrounding the institution of slavery, he failed to call for a total global abolition of the practice. Instead, he stressed the importance of law: "But whatever the nature of slavery, civil laws must seek to remove, on the one hand, its abuses, and on the other, its dangers." *See also* Rousseau, Jean-Jacques.

Further Reading: Montesquieu, Charles Secondat Baron de. *The Spirit of Laws.* Cambridge: Cambridge University Press, 1989 [1748].

Noah Butler

Moravians

The Moravian Church was a Protestant religious denomination whose members settled in both Pennsylvania and North Carolina prior to the American Revolution. The Moravians were originally the Unitas Fratum (Unity of the Brethren), a group of German Protestants descended from followers of John Hus in Eastern Europe. The sect first immigrated to the American colonies in 1735, where they settled in Georgia. Their pacifist views and the high death rate due to the Georgian climate forced the denomination to move northward to Bethlehem, Pennsylvania, in 1741. In 1749, the British Parliament declared the sect an organized church in the colonies. The legislation recognized the sect as the "Ancient Protestant Episcopal Church," and referred to the members of the church as "Moravians." In 1752, Lord Granville agreed to sell to the Moravians roughly 100,000 acres in the piedmont region of North Carolina. A year later, settlers from Pennsylvania migrated to an area later named "Wachovia," which is located in modern-day Forsyth County, North Carolina.

While building their communities in the Carolina Piedmont, the Moravians came into contact with the institution of slavery. Their Board of Supervisors (Aufseher Collegium) was officially opposed to slavery, since it conflicted with their religious concepts of free labor and community ownership of property. In addition, members of the church saw African Americans as a potential missionary opportunity. In 1785, a member of the sect went against official church policy and purchased a slave. Other members of the denomination soon began to purchase slaves to assist in tasks that most of the membership deemed unworthy. In addition, the closed religious community began to attract neighbors who were not Moravians, and used slaves for labor and capitol. These individuals founded the community of Winston, which was located next to the Moravian community of Salem. The influx of industry into both Winston and Salem increased the need for labor. By 1847, the Board of Supervisors removed all restrictions against church members purchasing, hiring, or selling slaves. During the American Civil War, a number of Moravians volunteered to serve in the Confederate Army.

In regards to the institution of slavery and African Americans, the Moravians were decidedly different than most of their white Carolina neighbors. The denomination struggled with the notion of slavery, but embraced the notion that slaves were individuals and were capable of worship and belief in a higher deity. This notion of individual worth governed that relationship built around the slaves and their masters. African Americans were allowed to worship with the brethren in their churches. In the 1820s, the church acted upon a desire of a number of African American church members to form their own congregation within the confines of Salem itself. A log church was constructed in 1823. This black congregation was not allowed to meet at times when the local white population was concerned about the possibility of a slave revolt. In 1861, the log structure was replaced by a brick building named St. Philips Moravian Church.

Further Readings: Africa, Philip. "Slaveholding in the Salem Community, 1771–1851." *North Carolina Historical Review* 54 (1977): 271–307; Hamilton, J. Taylor. *History of the Moravian Church; the Renewed Unitas Fratrum, 1722–1957*. Bethlehem, PA: Interprovincial Board of Christian Education, Moravian Church in America, 1967.

William H. Brown

More, Hannah (1745–1833)

Hannah More was born on February 2, 1745. In her formative years, More was educated by her schoolmaster father, Jacob More, and attended a boarding school in Bristol, England—a leading port in Britain's Atlantic slave trade. She became an educator, playwright, essayist, and English poet. As an activist and author, More advocated for female education and improving the moral values of lower-class Britons. She also vigorously supported the abolition of the slave trade and slavery.

John Newton and **William Wilberforce** nurtured More's abolitionism. Newton, captain of a slave-trading vessel who turned against the traffic and became an outspoken clergyman and author of *Thoughts upon the African*

Hannah More. Courtesy of the Library of Congress.

Slave Trade (1788), provided her with knowledge about the slave trade. Upon meeting William Wilberforce in the summer of 1787, More became an active supporter of abolition and soon began composing antislavery poetry. In 1788, she published her first work, "Slavery: A Poem" which was republished in 1816 as "The Black Slave Trade." This was followed by other popular poems, including "The Sorrows of Yamba; or, The Negro Woman's Lamentation" (1795) and "The Feast of Freedom; or The Abolition of Domestic Slavery in Ceylon" (1816).

These poems sought to influence pending antislavery legislation before Parliament. At the request of Wilberforce, More began composing "Slavery: A Poem" in late December 1787 to coincide with parliamentary debates over Sir William Dolben's Slave Limitation (or Middle Passage) Bill. The poem made vivid the realities of the Middle Passage where Africans were crammed into ship holds and chained closely to each other. These intolerable conditions produced contagious and fatal diseases and required disposal of corpses on almost a daily basis. The Middle Passage Bill proposed to reduce the number of slaves on British slave ships. This legislation had the potential to save the lives of Africans and British seamen.

In "Slavery: A Poem," More methodically illustrated the spiritual, psychological, and economic cost of Britain's continuing involvement with the slave trade. Using sentimentality and literary allusions, she imagined the feelings of enslaved Africans and implored Britain to abolish the traffic. In "Slavery: A Poem" and her other antislavery poetry, More spoke ardently on behalf of enslaved populations and laid the foundation for generations of British women to voice their objections to the slave trade and slavery.

Further Readings: Demers, Patricia. *The World of Hannah More*. Lexington: The University Press of Kentucky, 1996; Ford, Charles Howard. *Hannah More: A Critical Biography*. New York: Peter Lang Publishing, Inc., 1996; Stott, Anne. *Hannah More: The First Victorian*. New York: Oxford University Press, 2003; Wood, Marcus. "Hannah More." In Marcus Wood, ed., *The Poetry of Slavery, An Anglo-American Anthology 1764–1865*. New York: Oxford University Press, 2003, pp. 99–119.

Marilyn Walker

Moreau de Saint-Méry, Médéric-Louis Elie (1750–1819)

Moreau de Saint-Méry was born in Martinique and trained as a lawyer in Paris before establishing a practice in Saint Domingue in 1774. When the French Revolution began in 1789, he represented Martinique in the

National Assembly and was chosen as president of the electors of Paris. He engaged actively in legislative debates about colonial policy and was a key member of the *Club Massiac*, a procolonial lobbying group. His tenure as a Revolutionary statesman was cut short by the Terror, however. Faced with an arrest warrant issued by the Jacobin government in Paris, Moreau de Saint-Méry fled to the United States. From October 1794 until August 1798, he lived in Philadelphia, where he opened a bookstore and a printing press.

Before the Revolution, Moreau de Saint-Méry had written a multi-volume work on colonial legislation in the French Caribbean. In exile, he resumed his research and writing about the colonies. He is perhaps best known for creating a system of racial taxonomy. Using "fully white" and "fully black" as the poles of a racial hierarchy, Moreau de Saint-Méry created designations for 110 different combinations of the two races. Suggesting that race was an indelible marker carried in the blood, Moreau de Saint-Méry insisted that African traits would endure in mixed-race children, no matter their education, upbringing, or proportion of European ancestry.

Moreau de Saint-Méry's "scientific" belief in the permanence of racial marking and his political convictions about colonial autonomy informed his strident opposition to any metropolitan interference in the political status of *gens de couleur*. He imagined that such interference undermined the whites' positions as masters, as slaves might then imagine there was a greater power to which they could petition for redress. Moreau de Saint-Méry argued that colonial legislative autonomy was the only way to protect the white population and guarantee the economic benefits of colonial production. Throughout the 1790s, Moreau de Saint-Méry insisted that the colonies should have their own special laws, instead of being subjected to the French constitution. This position would give plantation owners unfettered control over their slaves and prevent the *gens de couleur* from obtaining full political rights.

Moreau de Saint-Méry returned to France during the Consulate. He became an advisor to **Napoleon Bonaparte**, taking a position in the Colonial Ministry, where he worked alongside others who had defended colonial autonomy and slavery. Bonaparte's own proslavery, procolonial views were reflected back to him by men like Moreau de Saint-Méry. Having this nucleus of support cleared the way for Bonaparte to send the Leclerc expedition to Saint Domingue in 1802 and to reimpose slavery in the French colonies in 1804. Moreau de Saint-Méry thus stands as an exemplar of French thought about slavery and race at the beginning of the nineteenth century. While supporting the amelioration of slave conditions, his convictions about the benefits of colonial production made Moreau de Saint-Méry a champion of plantation slavery. His attitudes about race, which resonated with the growing trend toward scientific racism, justified this view. *See also* French Colonies, Emancipation of; Haitian Revolution; St. Domingue, French Defeat in.

Further Readings: Dayan, Joan. *Haiti, History and the Gods*. Berkeley: University of California Press, 1995; Dubois, Laurent. *Avengers of the New World: The Story of the Haitian Revolution*. Boston: Harvard University Press, 2004.

Jennifer J. Pierce

Mormons. *See* Church of Jesus Christ of Latter-Day Saints and Antislavery

Moses

Moses, the biblical figure bearing a rather common Egyptian name, flourished sometime between the sixteenth and thirteenth centuries B.C.E. Perhaps due to national embarrassment, he is unmentioned in contemporary ancient Egyptian records, although Canaanite slaves are known to have been held in Egypt at that time (following the defeat of the final Hyksos Dynasty and the great exodus of most Canaanites from Egypt ca. 1540 B.C.E.). Nevertheless, biblical texts give significant details about Moses in terms of slavery, and he becomes a symbol of freedom and abolition for the ages.

The story of Moses logically begins with Joseph who had been sold into slavery in Egypt, rose to a position of great political power and trust under the then pharaoh (probably a Hyksos pharaoh), and saved Egypt as well as his birth family from a great famine (Genesis 37–50). The Israelite population later grew and apparently was seen as a threat to Egypt. To control them they had been enslaved by a later pharaoh, "which knew not Joseph." Later, to further prevent the Israelites' population growth, a genocidal program of killing sons born to the Israelites was instituted. Moses is depicted as a unique survivor of this genocide, whom an Egyptian princess was tricked into raising (Exodus 1–2). As an adult, Moses killed an Egyptian who was smiting one of the Hebrew slaves. He then fled to the land of Midian, settled, and married. God later revealed himself to Moses and called him to return to Egypt and free his people from slavery in accord with the Lord's covenants with the patriarchs Abraham, Isaac, and Jacob/Israel.

Egypt refused to free the Israelites, but a series of miracles culminating in the death of the firstborn Egyptian males helped Moses lead the Israelites to freedom. He subsequently delivered God's laws to Israel, beginning with commanding observance of the Passover Seder, often known as the "Festival of Freedom," which celebrates their being freed from slavery. Later he gave Israel the Ten Commandments and other laws, including a command to observe the **Jubilee** year in which people whose impoverished circumstances had forced them to indenture or pawn themselves into slavery for a fixed period of time were to be set free. The image of freedom from slavery becomes, through Jubilee symbolism, part of the biblical image of messianic redemption—such as the formal year of release declared by Jesus in a Nazareth synagogue (Luke 4:18–19, compare Isaiah 61:1–3).

Moses remains, from antiquity to the present, a symbol or archetype of the liberator from slavery and champion of freedom. In his lifetime, George Washington was often associated with Moses, leading his people to freedom, as was **Abraham Lincoln**. With more justification, **Harriet Tubman** was frequently referred to as the Moses of her people. The figure of Moses is found in the struggle against slavery and oppression to the present day, from Negro spirituals such as *Go Down Moses*: "Go down Moses/Way down in Egypt Land/Tell ole Pharaoh/To let my people go," to the freedom songs of Bob Marley such as *Exodus*: "Send us another Brother Moses gonna cross the Red Sea." Finally, Martin Luther King, Jr.'s 1964 Nobel Peace laureate speech perfectly reflects the image of Moses as it has continued in history: "Oppressed people cannot remain oppressed forever .... The **Bible** tells the thrilling story of how Moses stood in Pharaoh's court centuries ago and cried, 'Let my people go,'" just as his prophetic April 3, 1968 speech in Memphis just before his assassination painfully echoes Moses's death: "I just want to do God's will. And He's allowed me to go up to the mountain. And I've looked over. And I've seen the promised land. I may not get there with you. But I want you to know tonight, that we, as a people, will get to the promised land" (compare Deuteronomy 34:1–5). *See also* Book of Exodus, Story of Joseph.

Gordon C. Thomasson

Mott, Lucretia Coffin (1793–1880)

Lucretia Coffin Mott was a Quaker minister and advocate of abolition, women's rights, and peace. She was born on January 3, 1793, on the island of Nantucket, Massachusetts, the daughter of Thomas and Anna Folger Coffin. Like many on Nantucket, her father engaged in the East India trade; Mott later attributed the independence of Nantucket women to the frequent absence of men from the island. At home, school, and in meeting, Mott absorbed **Quaker** theology and antislavery sentiment. In 1804, her family moved to Boston and Mott soon left to attend Nine Partners, a Quaker Boarding School in Dutchess County, New York. She chafed against the authority of her instructors, but eventually became a teacher at the school and learned first-hand of sexual discrimination through her unequal salary. She also met fellow teacher James Mott, a Quaker from Westchester County, New York, whom she married in 1811.

After their marriage, the couple moved to Philadelphia, where Mott soon discovered her skill as a public speaker. James embarked on several unsuccessful careers before finally settling on a cotton commission business in 1822. Mott gave birth to the first of her six children in 1812, and her youngest daughter was born in 1828. She also taught in a Quaker school in 1817. But her son Thomas died in 1817, plunging Mott into a spiritual crisis from which she emerged renewed as a minister and follower of Elias Hicks, the radical Quaker preacher from Long Island, who railed against the Philadelphia Elders and their complicity with slavery. In 1827, the Motts and other Hicksites left the Philadelphia Yearly Meeting of Friends to form a parallel organization more sympathetic to Hicks's teachings. Lucretia Mott became one of the most famous and controversial Hicksite preachers, as she found the new denomination disappointingly conservative. In her sermons, she castigated the Society of Friends for not taking a strong enough stand against slavery, and for allowing superficial indications of spirituality to outweigh the individual's inner experience of God's teachings. She adopted as her motto "truth for authority, not authority for truth."

In the 1820s, the Motts first began to advocate the use of free produce, or goods made without slave labor, and James gave up his cotton commission

Lucretia Coffin Mott. Courtesy of the Library of Congress.

business for wool in 1830. Both James and Lucretia Mott attended the founding meeting of the **American Anti-Slavery Society** in Philadelphia in 1833. James signed the Society's declaration, but Mott, as a woman, did not, although she was the only woman to speak at the meeting. Shortly thereafter, Mott and other white and black women formed the Philadelphia Female Anti-Slavery Society, which thrived for the next thirty-six years with Mott as its frequent president. She participated in the Anti-Slavery Convention of American Women, speaking at its first meeting in New York in 1837. When the Convention met in Philadelphia the following year, an angry antiabolition mob burned Pennsylvania Hall, the meeting site, to the ground, and then headed for the Motts' house before being diverted at the last moment by an abolitionist ally.

In 1840, Mott was one of several female American delegates to the **World Anti-Slavery Convention** in London, who were refused seats by British abolitionists upon their arrival. This rebuff, following so soon after the American Anti-Slavery Society split over the proper role of women in the movement, galvanized Mott and another American woman, **Elizabeth Cady Stanton**. Mott began speaking more frequently on women's rights, motivated also by further factionalism in the Society of Friends over slavery and women's authority. Mott's visit to her sister, Martha Coffin Wright, in Auburn, New York, prompted the organization of the first women's rights convention at nearby Seneca Falls in 1848.

Mott spent the next three decades traveling the country, attending meetings on a variety of reforms. Mott viewed the antislavery, women's rights, temperance, and peace movements as contributing to the spread of true democracy and Christianity. She spoke against the false authority men derived from organized religion, tradition, politics, and law, urging people to follow their personal understanding of God's will, not society's prescriptions. In 1853, Mott gave an antislavery speech in Maysville, Kentucky. While local slaveholders feared she would incite rebellion, her lecture was so well-received that the audience demanded she speak again on women's rights. Mott tolerated no compromises with slavery, but she did seize every opportunity to talk individually with slaveholders. But when the Civil War loomed, Mott would have preferred that President Lincoln allow the South to leave the Union.

Committed to the peaceful and non-violent doctrine of non-resistance, Mott deplored the Civil War, but she celebrated emancipation with other abolitionists. She never attributed this success to the military, however, but to the moral warfare waged by **William Lloyd Garrison** and other abolitionists. Like many abolitionists, Mott turned her attention to aiding former slaves, joining the Friends Association for the Aid and Elevation of the Freedmen. After the war, Mott devoted herself to women's rights, peace, and free religion, an antisectarian movement committed to a liberal understanding of Scripture. Her beloved husband James died in 1868, but Mott continued her struggle for human progress, attending an anniversary meeting of the Seneca Falls Convention in 1878. However, her increasingly failing health limited her ability to attend reform meetings, and she died at home on November 11, 1880. *See also* Gender and Slave Emancipation; Gender Relations within Abolitionism; Seneca Falls Convention; Women's Antislavery Societies.

Further Readings: Bacon, Margaret Hope, *Valiant Friend: The Life of Lucretia Mott*. New York: Walker and Company, 1980; Palmer, Beverly Wilson, Holly Byers Ochoa, and Carol Faulkner, eds. *The Selected Letters of Lucretia Coffin Mott*. Urbana: University of Illinois Press, 2002.

Carol Faulkner

Muscat and Oman, Abolition of Slavery in

Slavery was widely practiced in Muscat and Oman where slaves were used as domestics, laborers in the date plantations, and pearl divers along the coast of Oman. Slaves continued to arrive in Oman in the late 1940s from the Makran coast and from Baluchistan in Pakistan, despite the fact that the institution had been abolished in neighboring Bahrein in 1937. For Oman it was clear that abolition had to be accomplished from within, otherwise any attempts to do so from without would have met with problems of compliance. Accordingly, Britain, the dominant power in the region, used its influence to persuade the states in the region to end domestic slavery. This in itself, however, was not a sufficient deterrent; the demand for slave labor, for instance, on date plantations in Oman in the mid-twentieth century was quite crucial in affecting the prevalence of the institution. At least two more decades would pass before slavery was finally abolished there after a palace coup deposed Sultan Said Ibn Taimur, an owner of hundreds of slaves.

As with some of the other states in the region, the British did not directly pressure the ruler of Oman to suppress slavery. They argued that they could not force him to end an institution that was recognized by Muslim law. Moreover, they believed he opposed abolition because he was unwilling to pay compensation to former owners. In the 1950s, the British manumitted slaves—excluding those in the Sultan's possession—at the rate of about eighteen a year on the grounds of ill-treatment, and understood the Sultan's tolerance of these actions as evidence of his good faith.

There were, of course, inconsistencies in the British position here as elsewhere. Their claims that manumitted slaves still in the service of their former masters were free to leave were proven to be untrue when they learned that domestic slaves in Batinah were, in fact, prevented by force from seeking full freedom. Furthermore, while the rulers of the northern six states (which included Dubai) and later Abu Dhabi agreed to sign a treaty in May 1963 declaring that slavery, like the slave trade, had long been banned in their territories, no such pressure was brought to bear on Oman to do the same, despite the fact that conservative Saudi Arabia had just abolished slavery. It was thus no surprise that Britain faced continuous attacks at the United Nations over the next several years for being a supporter of the autocratic Sultan. The British position was dictated by their economic, political, and strategic interests to maintain the flow of oil from the region and to retain their air base in Masirah. They continued supporting the despotic Sultan whose son, Qabus, was still too young to replace him.

Both domestic and foreign opposition to the Sultan grew more vociferous by the mid-1960s, especially once oil was discovered. At the same time, Britain came increasingly under attack from the leading Arab states for its involvement in Oman. The anticolonial atmosphere both at home and in the Arab world forced the Labor government to announce its intention to leave the Gulf and Oman by 1971. Before this could happen, however, a palace coup took place in July 1970 in which Qabus, with the British endorsement, deposed his father and assumed the crown for himself. One of the first reforms of his new administration was to outlaw legal slavery in that year. Oman now ceased to be the only country in the region in which slavery was legal. *See also* Arabia and Nineteenth- and Twentieth-Century Slavery; Islam and Antislavery; *Qur'an* and Antislavery.

Further Readings: Earth, Frederick. *Sohar: Culture and Society in an Omani Town*. Baltimore: John Hopkins University Press, 1983; Gordon, Murray. *Slavery in the Arab World*. New York: New Amsterdam, 1989; Hutson, Alaine. "Enslavement and Manumission of Africans and Yemenis in Saudi Arabia, 1926–1938." *Critique* 11, 1 (2002): 49–70; Miers, Suzanne. *Slavery in the Twentieth Century*. Walnut Creek, CA: Altamira Press, 2003.

Abdin Chande

Myers, Stephen (1800–1870) and Myers, Harriet (1807–1865)

Stephen Myers came to be the most important leader of the **Underground Railroad** movement in Albany, New York, in the 1830s, 1840s, and 1850s. Together with his wife, Harriet, they were the focal point of assistance in helping freedom seekers, or fugitives from slavery, who had arrived in Albany on their way to **Canada** or settling in New York State. While there had been other significant figures of the Underground Railroad in Albany, they met untimely fates, or moved to other theaters of action. It is well documented that Stephen and Harriet Myers assisted thousands of individuals to settle in or move through Albany to points west, north, and east on the Underground Railroad. Initially, in the 1830s, Myers used his own resources. By the 1840s, Myers organized *The Northern Star Association*, utilizing its resources in support of freedom seekers and in support of the publication of The Northern Star and Freeman's Advocate newspaper. By the 1850s, Myers was the principal agent of the Underground Railroad in Albany, and was receiving financial assistance from a broad range of backers. Under his leadership the Albany branch of the Underground Railroad was regarded by some as the best-run part of the Underground Railroad in New York State.

Stephen was born a slave in 1800 in Rensselaer County in Hoosick Four Corners. While not much is known of his early years, it is known that at the age of twelve he was in the service of Albany's General Warren of Revolutionary War connections, and was freed at the age of eighteen. Over the next decade and a half he worked as a grocer and steamboat steward, starting his journalistic enterprises in the late 1830s and early 1840s. His first newspaper venture was short lived. It was called *The Elevator*. It concentrated on news and information targeting the free African people in Albany. Stephen and Harriet were married in 1827. Harriet worked with him on his newspaper ventures. He was a leading spokesperson for antislavery and the rights of free blacks in Albany in the late 1840s and 1850s. His newspaper, *The Northern Star and Freeman's Advocate*, was a vehicle for reform around education, temperance, black rights, and the need to abolish slavery. Toward the end of the 1840s, the newspaper may have taken on the name *Northern Star and Colored Farmer* when Myers was involved in organizing an economic project call the Florence Farming and Lumber Association. Later in his life he had other publishing ventures including the *Pioneer*, and *Telegraph and Temperance Journal*. Stephen Myers was an active speaker and shared the podium with other black orators of his day, such as **Frederick Douglass** and William H. Johnson. He spoke in Albany and Troy, as well as in Massachusetts and the New York City area.

Myers was not only involved in abolitionist activity, but he showed leadership in addressing a wide range of civil rights issues. Through his newspapers he was deeply involved in education and advocacy. He also provided leadership as the superintendent of one of the area's first schools for black children, The Free Colored School in Albany based at Israel African Methodist Church in 1843. He was active in organizing Suffrage Clubs to encourage Black voting rights, petitioning the state legislature for reforms, and the early organization of free black labor. He was also involved in economic development through the Florence Farming and Lumber Association where he worked with philanthropist **Gerrit Smith** to provide farms and farming skills to black farmers.

Harriet Myers was born in 1807 as Harriet Johnson. While the source of her education is not known, she collaborated with her husband in the production of the various newspaper projects and was known for providing a "skilled" editorial hand in proofreading. She was also involved in various women's organizations popular among black women that raised funds through bazaars and sewing circles to support the work of the Underground Railroad.

Harriet Myers died in August 16, 1865. In the obituary, which appeared in the Philadelphia *Christian Recorder* of September 2, 1865, she was described as one of "nobleness" of heart, "unselfish hospitality," and "Her house was ever a refuge for the oppressed and friendless." Stephen Myers was buried February 16, 1870, but no record has been thus far found identifying the specific date of his death.

Paul Stewart

N

Nabuco, Joaquim (1849–1910) and Abolition in Brazil

Brazil's gradual process of abolition during the nineteenth century gave rise to the development of competing ideologies of labor and citizenship among elites troubled by the transition from slavery to free labor. Great Britain's abolitionist agenda and trade interests in Brazil resulted in a series of treaties between the two nations during the first half of the century, culminating in the end of Brazil's involvement with the transatlantic slave trade in 1851. The subsequent decline in the availability of slave labor in the Brazilian Empire and the escalating presence of antislavery sentiment in international politics pushed both elite abolitionists and non-abolitionists to consider what was to be made of "free" labor in a slave society. In contrast to the popular abolitionism that flourished in the United States, abolition remained an issue of debate among Brazilian political elites only for most of the nineteenth century. The political career of Joaquim Nabuco (1849–1910) traces the shifting political climate surrounding abolitionism in Brazil and the more popular overtones it acquired by the 1880s. Nabuco's abolitionism was primarily expressed in fiery parliamentary speeches, in several written works, and in popular campaigns, which eventually emerged in the streets. He remains Brazil's most renowned abolitionist leader.

In 1870, while still a law student in São Paulo, Nabuco wrote his first abolitionist essay, *A Escravidão*, which was only posthumously published. In this work, he described slavery as legal, yet unjust and degrading to Brazilian society because it furthered the feudal-agrarian structure, it gave unlimited power to landowners and slaveholders, and it stripped man—including Africans—of his "natural" rights. Nabuco located the essential immorality of slavery in its denial of the natural right of man to property in himself and to free labor. This viewpoint led him to support agrarian reform, which would give poor workers and ex-slaves access to land and production. He discussed a transition from slavery to freedom that would integrate the national worker, which included African-born and Brazilian-born ex-slaves, into a peasantry based on small landholdings. Although

Nabuco later favored European immigration as a means of securing the development of the free-labor economy in Brazil, he initially believed that the ex-slave population would supply adequate labor, and the experience of working within a free labor system would gradually "season" and educate ex-slaves, traumatized by the experience of slavery, into responsible and productive workers. Nabuco viewed the right to property not only as an inalienable right, but also as a "rational" destiny fulfilled by the transformative power of free labor. With the passage of the Free Womb Law in 1871 which freed children born to slave mothers, Nabuco became more committed to the abolitionist cause, as ending slavery in Brazil seemed more possible.

After law school, Nabuco spent almost a year in New York (1876–1877), coinciding with the election that resulted in the Compromise of 1877 and the election of Rutherford B. Hayes as president. Scholar Carlos Daghlian has argued that Nabuco learned much about public speaking from observing the debating and oratory of the presidential candidates. After this experience, he went back to Brazil and was elected deputy from the province of Pernambuco. The speeches he gave while serving in the Chamber of Deputies between 1879 and 1880 earned him a reputation as a great orator and leader of the abolitionist cause. Numerous politicians recalled the power of Nabuco's early parliamentary speeches and how his talent for improvisation, his magnetic, clear voice, and his physical attractiveness conquered crowds, all of which would strengthen his popular abolitionist campaigning in the 1880s.

The years 1879 and 1880 proved crucial for the abolitionist movement in Brazil. Having failed at the first attempt to legalize immediate emancipation through parliamentary action, abolitionists turned to other means of building support. They published newspapers, such as *A Gazeta da Tarde* and *O Abolicionista*, and formed such abolitionist societies as the *Sociedade Brasileira Contra a Escravidão* and the *Associação Central Emancipadora*. These abolitionists, mainly based in Rio de Janeiro, formulated ideas about economic development and the restructuring of free labor modeled after the postemancipation labor policies of the United States. Abolitionist pamphlets appealed to literate and educated urban dwellers likely to identify with the antioligarchic language adopted by the movement after 1880. *O Abolicionista* indicted slavery as the cause of Brazil's industrial and urban underdevelopment. Abolitionists credited the success of the United States South's reconstruction to the industrialization of the cotton industry, which had shifted toward the development of local textile industries and away from the export economy.

The concern with the legacy of slavery and its impact on people of African descent was a widely discussed topic throughout the nineteenth century. Anxious about rehabilitating Brazil's economy and liberating it from the legacy of slavery, abolitionists emphasized the benefits liberal capitalism would have upon free labor and the modernizing of agriculture. The French Revolution, they argued, had eradicated feudalism by not only democratizing the countryside through wage labor, but by industrializing its cities and giving workers a greater choice of occupations. France was a model for urban abolitionists aspiring to weaken the proslavery rural oligarchy and give leverage to a small urban bourgeoisie inclined toward industrial development.

Abolitionists also argued that abolition was essential for the advance of universal citizenship. Throughout the nineteenth century, political elites debated the voting rights of free blacks and freedpersons, granting *libertos* (free/freed blacks) the right to vote if they possessed a certain minimum income or property. Those in Parliament who argued for limiting *libertos'* right to vote contended that the experience of slavery had forever incapacitated people of African descent from exercising their natural rights responsibly. Moreover, they believed the realities of race further crippled the African slaves. Being black was in and of itself a badge of degradation and precluded their citizenship. Yet Nabuco and other abolitionists responded that, while slavery had in some way damaged *libertos*, education would rehabilitate the ex-slave population and render them a responsible citizenry capable of fully exercising their natural rights.

Nabuco addressed these problems of citizenship in Parliament in 1879–1880, problems further complicated by an influx of Chinese immigrant labor into Brazil to overcome what planters asserted was a shortage of labor. Nabuco argued that a shortage of labor was not Brazil's problem, and instead advocated agrarian reform and the education of ex-slaves. Nabuco stated that Chinese labor would only sustain slavery by promoting poor labor and removing the need to free and elevate the enslaved. Resorting to his own racial preconceptions, Nabuco claimed the Chinese would degrade, rather than strengthen, Brazil and its people. Rather, he supported the importation of European migrant workers to "revitalize" the Brazilian race and help the ex-slaves overcome their "African" past by a process of "whitening" through intermarriage.

Despite heated debates in 1879–1880, the oligarchy in Parliament continued to favor slavery, as well as relationships of dependency between ex-slaves and ex-masters, as a means of protecting planter interests. Nabuco was defeated as a candidate for Parliament in 1881. Nabuco then retreated to London where he established contact with the **Anti-Slavery Society** in efforts to revitalize the abolition movement in Brazil. There he wrote *O Abolicionismo* in 1883, the single most important printed work of the abolitionist movement in Brazil. In this work, Nabuco examined the history of Brazil's antislavery struggle throughout the nineteenth century. Nabuco defined abolitionism as a social and political reform movement that went beyond the issue of abolition by acknowledging slave emancipation alone would not solve Brazil's problems. Nabuco identified slavery as the real ruler of Brazil: "the master over all available capital . . . it has the commerce of the city at its mercy, all the property of the country behind it, and, finally, a formidable clientele in every profession: lawyers, doctors, engineers, priests, teachers, and public employees." Thus, Nabuco's abolitionism was a struggle to increase access to and diversify capital, a movement to initiate land reform and to open Brazil for bourgeois development and federalism. The latter objective was the particular focus of Nabuco's 1884 election campaign in Recife, during which he defined the abolitionist cause as a movement of social, economic, and political reform that went beyond slave emancipation. His campaign's renewed abolitionist agenda returned him to the seat in the Chamber of Deputies he had lost in 1881, when the popular appeal of the abolitionist struggle seemed to fade.

During this election, abolitionism shifted from a topic of parliamentary debate to one engaging both popular abolitionists and urban working classes. This shift was in large part due to the electoral reform of 1881, which enfranchised a portion of the urban working class who were sympathetic to abolition. During the 1884 Recife election campaign, Nabuco appealed to these new voters in a populist manner and posited abolition as crucial to the development of urban labor and industry. His speeches concentrated on the "emancipation" of free urban workers rather than on the emancipation of slaves. Although Nabuco's advocacy of immigrant European labor seemed contrary to this optimistic belief in the national urban working class, it nonetheless illustrated the influence of the new urban electorate on abolitionist political campaigning. Nabuco and other abolitionists recognized the great significance the emerging urban-industrial economy would play in the new, post-emancipation Brazil.

Although the Golden Law of 1888 abolished slavery in one act, its isolated singularity does not justly illustrate the shifting moral attitudes toward slavery that developed throughout the nineteenth century—not only among abolitionists, but also among planters who interpreted slavery as a "necessary evil" for Brazil's economic progress. After abolition, Nabuco continued to be active in politics and defended the Brazilian monarchy, which was toppled in 1889 by a coup d'état that established Brazil's first republican regime. By the early 1900s, Nabuco had embraced republicanism and worked for the Brazilian embassy in London. In 1905, Nabuco became the ambassador for Brazil in Washington D.C., where he defended a pan-American approach to international politics, influenced by the Monroe doctrine, and where he lived out the last years of his life. *See also* Atlantic Slave Trade and British Abolition; Latin America, Antislavery and Abolition in.

Further Readings: Conrad, Robert. *The Destruction of Brazilian Slavery, 1850–1888.* Berkeley: University of California Press, 1972; Correia de Andrade, Manuel, ed. *Joaquim Nabuco: O Parlamentar, O Escritor, e O Diplomata.* Recife: Fundação Joaquim Nabuco, Editora Massangana, 2001; Daghlian, Carlos. *Os Discursos Americanos de Joaquim Nabuco.* Translated by João Carlos Gonçalves, Recife: Fundação Joaquim Nabuco, Editora Massangana, 1988; Graham, Richard, ed. *The Idea of Race in Latin America, 1870–1940.* Austin: University of Texas Press, 1990; Nabuco, Carolina. *The Life of Joaquim Nabuco.* Translated by Ronald Hilton. Stanford, CA: Stanford University Press, 1950; Nabuco, Joaquim. *Minha Formação.* Rio de Janeiro: Livraria José Olimpio Editora, 1957.

Patricia Acerbi

Napoleon. *See* Bonaparte, Napoleon

"Negro Exodus" (1879–1881)

The "Negro Exodus," first black migration after slavery in the United States, was a three-year period in which as many as 40,000 African Americans migrated to Kansas from the Mississippi Valley (Louisiana, Mississippi, Tennessee, and Northern Texas). The Exodus was motivated by failing legislation designed to increase blacks' socio-economic opportunities. The African Americans who participated in the Exodus took an important step toward Black Reconstruction and civil rights for blacks all over the United States.

Black migration had been considered a remedy to racial conflict and slavery since before the United States Civil War. During slavery, **Abraham Lincoln** advocated, and the **American Colonization Society** (ACS) funded, the emigration of blacks from America to Liberia in West Africa. Despite the 11,000 blacks transported, many were hesitant to relocate to foreign lands. At the close of the Reconstruction Era, Henry Adams and Benjamin "Pap" Singleton began to entreat blacks to leave the South for Kansas, which proved a more palatable suggestion. Jim Crow practices impeded legal remedies for racism, and over time, racial violence and voter intimidation in the South became intolerable for many African Americans. In response, Adams and Singleton began planning the Exodus in their respective home states, Louisiana and Texas.

In 1877, Singleton, an escaped slave and often referred to as the "Father of the Exodus," began organizing his migration efforts in Texas, while Adams, who bought himself out of slavery, began speaking publicly about black subjugation and voting restrictions in Louisiana. Although he initially attempted to use the services of the ACS, Adams came to recognize the unwillingness of many blacks to remove to Africa. He also noticed the success of Singleton's Kansas migration, and in 1879, Adams changed his strategy and began leading his followers to Kansas as well. Although Singleton and Adams never met, they were the key coordinators of the Negro Exodus. They organized thousands of African Americans to abandon the South and relocate to Kansas between 1879 and 1881.

The Exodus's success drew attention from Congress. Early in 1880, Adams and Singleton were subpoenaed to testify separately about the motivations for the phenomenon before the Unites States Senate Committee in Washington, D.C. The mass migration of the "Exodusters," as the migrants are often referred, was initially successful. Many of the migrants became landowners and entrepreneurs. Initially, black men were able to exercise their voting rights and several were elected to public offices. Additionally, African Americans remaining in the Mississippi Valley capitalized on the migration, which made jobs more readily available and the negotiation of improved tenant farming contracts easier.

The impoverished condition of these migrants eventually forced them into wage labor and domestic jobs, however, while others remained unemployed or homeless. By 1884, some of the migrants returned to their home states. Others who remained in Kansas became destitute. Shortly after the conclusion of the Exodus concern arose among poor whites about the influx of African Americans into Kansas. As a result, the socio-economic circumstances experienced by African Americans in the Mississippi Valley became recognizable in Kansas.

Further Readings: Athearn, Robert G. *In Search of Canaan: Black Migration to Kansas, 1879–80*. Lawrence: University of Kansas Press, 1978; Painter, Nell Irvin. *Exodusters: Black Migration to Kansas after Reconstruction*. New York: W.W. Norton & Co., 1992.

Ellesia A. Blaque

New Divinity

The New Divinity was a movement extending the Calvinist theology of **Jonathan Edwards** after the great divine's sudden death in 1758. Its leaders were Joseph Bellamy and **Samuel Hopkins**, both associates of Edwards, and its influence was great, particularly in New England. It was a controversial movement, articulating strong views of predestination and divine providence, as well as a demanding standard of personal ethics contained in its doctrine of disinterested benevolence. It was also an evangelical movement, leading some New Divinity men, along with lay people, to preach to African Americans. Christian ideals of missions to Africans and the Christianization of the continent were bolstered by the New Divinity.

A number of men and women in the New Divinity camp became active in both abolitionism and charitable efforts to improve the lives of African Americans. The ethical standard of benevolence seemed to mandate an immediate end to the slave trade and slavery, the cruelties and viciousness of which seemed self-evident. Whether or not disinterested benevolence should unite blacks and whites affectionately and equally in a free society was less obvious. Some adherents of the New Divinity endorsed an interracial society, while others favored the expatriation of free blacks, also known as colonization. Indeed, some individuals wavered between these two approaches to a postslavery America.

Because of their ardent patriotism in the War of Independence, the New Divinity men have sometimes been understood as jingoes who retreated from abolitionism as the new nation accepted slavery in the South and the slave trade for two decades after the ratification of the U.S. Constitution. This understanding is inaccurate. The New Divinity remained committed to divine standards of ethical behavior and civic freedom, and they never accepted a slaveholders' status quo in America. If the New Divinity approach to race seems flawed from a twenty-first-century viewpoint, it is because some of them were pessimistic about the prospects of an interracial society and thus favored colonization.

Further Readings: Brooks, Joanna. *American Lazarus: Religion and the Rise of African-American and Native American Literatures.* New York: Oxford University Press, 2003; Conforti, Joseph A. *Samuel Hopkins and the New Divinity Movement: Calvinism, the Congregational Ministry, and Reform in New England between the Great Awakenings.* Grand Rapids, MI: Wm. B. Eerdmans Publishing Company, 1981; Saillant, John. "Slavery and Divine Providence in New England Calvinism: The New Divinity and a Black Protest, 1775–1805," *New England Quarterly* 68, 4 (December, 1995): 584–608.

John Saillant

New England Antislavery Society (NEASS)

Founded in 1832 in Boston, the New England Antislavery Society (NEASS) was the first American abolitionist organization to embrace the doctrine of immediatism. The NEASS thereafter became the model for all "second wave" abolitionist organizations, including the **American Anti-Slavery Society**, founded in Philadelphia in 1833. The NEASS also proved innovative by hiring traveling agents and publishing a short-lived organizational maga-zine, *The Abolitionist*. The group also offered a public platform to some of the most important antislavery activists of the nineteenth century, including **Frederick Douglass**. The NEASS was perhaps best identified with its founding figure, **William Lloyd Garrison**, publisher of the radical aboli-tionist newspaper, *The Liberator*. But the group also drew inspiration and support from Boston's black community, which offered intellectual and monetary capital to the burgeoning immediate abolition movement, both in New England and nationally. Garrison himself was influenced by black Bos-tonian David Walker who authored *An Appeal to the Colored Citizens of the World* (1829), a rousing rejection of prevailing abolitionist tactics of gradualism and colonization. In addition, African Americans provided nearly a quarter of the seventy-two signatures to the group's constitution at the first annual meeting of the NEASS. In this sense, the NEASS was the first biracial reform organization in America—a significant achievement when considered against the history of segregation in early abolitionist societies such as the **Pennsylvania Abolition Society**.

The NEASS's activism rested on attacking Southern slavery and routing racial prejudice in Northern states. Just as the group hoped to convince and coerce Southern masters to liberate enslaved people, so too did it aim to challenge racial injustice above the Mason-Dixon Line. As the group's consti-tution boldly put it, "the objects of the society shall be to endeavor, by all means sanctioned by law, humanity and religion, to effect the abolition of slavery, to improve the character and condition of the free people of col-or... and obtain for them equal civil and political rights and privileges with the whites." Group activists challenged Massachusetts's laws prohibiting racial intermarriage and aided in early school desegregation lawsuits. They also signed petitions against both slavery and the slave trade in the District of Columbia. Despite espousing ideals of racial equality, white activists within the NEASS could also practice a form of "romantic racialism," which depicted African Americans—both free and enslaved—as desperately in need of white leadership.

Outside of attacking Southern slaveholders (and antiabolitionist Northern-ers), the NEASS struggled against members of the **American Colonization Society**, who argued that abolitionism was folly and removal by transporta-tion of freed blacks was the only safe solution to America's racial ills. NEASS members constantly debated the efficacy of colonizationist policies in town meetings throughout New England, and waged a similar war against coloni-zationist thinking in printed publications.

In February 1835, the NEASS was officially renamed the Massachusetts Anti-Slavery Society (MASS), and it functioned for several years as an auxiliary to the American Anti-Slavery Society. Although female activists in New England created a bevy of their own abolitionist organizations, the MASS supported women's activism, admitting female reformers and hiring female agents. While schisms within the broader antislavery movement—particularly over women's roles and political abolitionism—certainly impacted the MASS, the group functioned through the Civil War, holding a memorable thirtieth anni-versary meeting in 1862. *See also* Garrisonians; Immediate Emancipation.

Further Readings: Mayer, Henry. *All on Fire: William Lloyd Garrison and the Abolition of Slavery.* New York: St. Martin's Griffin, 2000; Newman, Richard. *The Transformation of American Abolitionism: Fighting Slavery in the Early Republic.* Chapel Hill: University of North Carolina Press, 2002.

Richard Newman

New Mexico Slave Trade. *See* Indian-Mestizo Captives, Liberation of

New York Committee of Vigilance

One of the most radical African American abolitionist societies of the 1830s, the New York Committee of Vigilance was organized on November 21, 1836, although its activities began informally the year before. The New York Committee of Vigilance especially sought to halt the practice of kidnapping of self-emancipated slaves and free blacks from the streets of the city. Slave catchers, using the 1793 Fugitive Slave Act as a pretense, would bring their captives before a city magistrate, who would then rule the person a fugitive slave. Quickly, the black person would be taken in chains to a waiting ship and spirited off to slavery in the Southern states. The **New York Manumission Society**'s radical wing had contested such practices since the 1790s and local blacks had commonly demonstrated and even rioted against slave catchers, calling them man stealers.

Organizing the Committee was an important step in uniting middle class blacks, sympathetic whites, and the black working class against kidnapping. At the organizing meeting, **David Ruggles** was appointed secretary. A radical abolitionist, Ruggles already had experience accosting slave catchers and indicting sea captains taking part in the illegal slave trade. Other significant members included Thomas Van Rensellaer, a former slave and now a prominent black restaurateur and community leader, William Johnston, an English-born abolitionist, George R. Barkers, a New York City broker, and James W. Higgins, a local grocer. Ruggles found a number of enslaved people held illegally by their masters who were often on Northern tours. This integrated group, led by Ruggles, embarked on a number of sensational slave rescue cases, using a legal device known as a *writ de homine replegiando* that freed individuals imprisoned or held by a private party by giving security that the accused would appear in court. It is now replaced in American law by the writ of *habeas corpus*; Ruggles and the committee cooperated with the New York Manumission Society in the Dixon Case, which forced the judiciary to grant jury trials to fugitives. In 1838, Ruggles created the nation's first black magazine, the *Mirror of Liberty*, to chronicle the hundreds of instances in which the committee helped fugitive slaves. Ruggles's zeal eventually caused trouble when he printed a letter in the *Colored American* accusing a local black boardinghouse keeper of hiding fugitives for slave catchers. The boardinghouse keeper successfully sued Ruggles, the newspaper, and the committee for libel. An ensuing investigation uncovered financial irregularities and Ruggles was forced to resign his post. In 1840, lobbied by the manumission society, the New York State Legislature passed a bill requiring jury trials for blacks, although it was weakened several years later in the *Prigg v. Pennsylvania* case. The Committee continued on into the 1840s but on a lower profile. It inspired the New York State Committee, innumerable local organizations, and was a key, early safe harbor on the **Underground Railroad**.

Further Reading: Ripley, Peter C., et al. *The Black Abolitionist Papers.* Chapel Hill: University of North Carolina Press, 1991, Vol. 3, pp. 168–180.

Graham Russell Gao Hodges

New York Manumission Society (NYMS)

Founded in 1785 in New York City, the New York Manumission Society (NYMS) was one of the most important abolitionist groups of the early national period. Counting elite statesman such as **John Jay** and Alexander Hamilton as members, the group helped shepherd the gradual emancipation act through the state legislature in 1799. Less well-known group members—particularly adherents of the Religious Society of Friends, also known as **Quakers**—pestered ship captains engaged in the international slave trade through the port of New York, aided free black kidnapping victims, and even helped fugitive slaves. Together with the **Pennsylvania Abolition Society** and the **American Convention of Abolition Societies**, the NYMS put a tactical face on the early antislavery movement.

Originally called the New York Society for Promoting the Manumission of Slaves and Protecting Such of Them as Have Been or May be Liberated, the NYMS was formed during the country's first broad public debate over slavery's status in post-Revolutionary culture. Beginning with Pennsylvania in 1780, every Northern state passed a gradual abolition law during the next twenty-five years. Although New York's law, which took effect July 4, 1799, was the second to last Northern abolition act (New Jersey's statute passed in 1804), debate over abolitionism in the state dated back to 1777. The New York Manumission Society took shape in January 1785 to bolster the passage of such a law. Although the group attracted support from some celebrated New York politicians and merchants, Quakers and Anglicans dominated its day-to-day membership. The Society's constitution declared that slavery violated the religious and political underpinnings of American culture—equality and justice for all. By the time NYMS members helped push through the abolition act in 1799, New York contained roughly 21,000 enslaved people. The law stipulated that all slaves born after passage of the act would be freed gradually, women at twenty-five and men at twenty-eight. The law was revised in 1817 so that all slaves would be liberated on July 4, 1827.

As Patrick Rael has written, the New York Manumission Society also "worked to tighten loopholes in other state laws: it sought to strengthen prohibitions on the import and export of slaves to the state, to prevent inhuman treatment of slaves, and to remove provisions of the slave code permitting courts to deport slaves deemed guilty of crimes." Perhaps the Society's most unheralded act was the creation of an African Free School in November 1787. By the 1820s, abolitionists watched over roughly 800 students in seven different schools. Eventually, protest in the first half of the 1830s by the black community compelled abolitionists to turn over running the schools to African American leaders. The city of New York incorporated the two principal African Free Schools into the public school system in 1834.

Like other gradual abolitionist groups of the early national era, the New York Manumission Society did not admit black members—it was a segregated group. Moreover, its members were accused of treating New York City's free black community paternalistically and even as inferiors. By the 1830s, when second wave abolitionists appeared nationally declaring black activists "coadjutors" of a new movement to destroy slavery immediately, the New York Manumission Society was in decline. The group officially folded in 1849. Yet its several decades of abolitionist activism formed an integral part of the early antislavery movement, particularly the sectional erosion of slavery in Northern states via gradual abolition laws. *See also* New York Committee of Vigilance.

Further Readings: Davis, David Brion. *The Problem of Slavery in the Age of Revolution.* Ithaca, NY: Cornell University Press, 1976; Rael, Patrick. "The Long Death of Slavery." In Ira Berlin and Leslie Harris, eds. *Slavery in New York.* New York: New Press, 2005.

Richard Newman

Newton, John (1725–1807)

John Newton, the author of *Amazing Grace*, worked as a slave trader, an ironic twist of history that has given rise to a mythology about the writing of one of Christianity's greatest hymns. Stories about John Newton and his hymn abound, filled with tales of him penning the words on the night of his conversion or asserting that he immediately gave up his work as a slave trader because of the freedom his own salvation had given him, and he wanted to grant that same release to others. While the myths are mostly inaccurate, the historical account of John Newton's life might be even more dramatic than those stories.

Born in London, England, in 1725, he was the son of a merchant sea captain. Newton's mother, a pious woman, raised her son in the faith, exerting considerable influence over the boy while her husband plied his trade at sea. She dedicated her son to the ministry and taught him to read by the age of three. Her plan for his education was largely biblical, with much time dedicated to the scriptures and catechism. When his mother died when John was seven years old, his father enrolled him at a boarding school in Essex. There, he continued his education by learning Latin, but his father took him from the school to go to sea on his eleventh birthday.

Over the next seven years, Newton sailed with his father and learned to be a sailor. His father encouraged John to live morally, but did not push him toward spiritual things. Throughout his teenage years, he occasionally read Christian books and studied the **Bible**, but also lived the life of a sailor, which he later termed "profane" and "sinful." Yet, his early education led him to further spiritual interest and he often attempted to reform his behavior. This was especially true during times of crisis. But his reformation was mostly superficial. His habit of living a good life on the surface while also indulging in pleasure and sin continued into adulthood.

At sixteen, he went to Kent to conduct some business for his father and met Mary Catlett, the daughter of a friend of his mother's. He quickly fell in love with the fourteen-year-old girl and extended his visit despite his father's instructions. About a year later, Newton was impressed into service on board an English man-of-war. His father was unable to secure his freedom and he was forced to serve in the navy. He threw off his faith and became openly hostile, even attempting to desert, which resulted in a brutal whipping and his demotion. Finally, his unruliness prompted his being traded to a passing merchant ship. Not long after that, he found himself bound to service as the servant of a slave trader.

For the next year or so, Newton worked on an island plantation on the coast of Africa. His slavetrader master was married to an African woman who disliked the young man because her husband treated him like a son. She mistreated him in every way she could, especially when her husband was away on business. He found himself in bondage, picking limes, and suffering under humiliating conditions. He was nearly a slave. Traded to another master who treated him better, Newton learned much about the slave trade and saw its profitability, and his skills led to his promotion to manager of his master's factories. Rescued in 1747, he returned to the sea.

During a voyage, he read *The Imitation of Christ* by Thomas à Kempis, which renewed his interest in spiritual things. Over the next few years, he experienced a gradual spiritual growth that led to his conversion. Newton finally married Mary Catlett in 1750 and soon became the captain of his own ship. He had worked in the slave trade for a number of years before his conversion, and he continued to do so after. He could not ignore the horrors of the Middle Passage, and he deplored the conditions under which the slaves were transported across the Atlantic. He felt that it was his Christian duty to improve those conditions, but he did not yet believe that slavery itself was a sin. This was indicative of his strict Calvinist theology, which emphasized man's fallen nature and doing one's duty in whatever context God placed the individual. In his autobiography, Newton wrote that, as a slave trader, "I never had the least scruple to its lawfulness. I was upon the whole satisfied with it as the appointment providence had marked out for me." However, he was "sometimes shocked with an employment that was perpetually connected with chains, bolts, and shackles. In this view I had often prayed that the Lord, in His own time would place me in a more humane calling."

When he was about to embark on yet another voyage in 1754, Newton suffered a seizure that left him temporarily paralyzed. His doctor refused to allow him to sail again and he resigned his position. At about the same time, his wife also became seriously ill and her health steadily declined thereafter. John now focused on nursing his wife and studying for the ministry. In 1764, he was appointed to the curacy at Olney, where he became close friends with William Cowper. Together, they wrote hundreds of hymns and published "The Olney Hymns," a collection that became standard for decades. There in Olney, he wrote *Amazing Grace* and put it to a tune that may have originated with slaves. In 1779, he moved to London as pastor of St. Mary Woolnoth Church, where he continued his ministry until his death in 1807.

Later in life, Newton began to oppose slavery. When Parliament debated the slave trade, Newton testified about the atrocities of it and publicly supported the legislation that abolished the slave trade throughout the British Empire in 1808. The former slave trader lent his name to the antislavery cause and became widely known for his ardent opposition to the institution. *See also* Atlantic Slave Trade and British Abolition.

Further Readings: Newton, Rev. John, et al. *The Life and Spirituality of John Newton: An Authentic Narrative.* Reprint of 1764 ed. London: Regent College Publishing, 1998; Phipps, William E. *Amazing Grace in John Newton: Slave Ship Captain, Hymn Writer, and Abolitionist.* Macon, GA: Mercer University Press, 2001; Pollock, John. *Newton the Liberator.* London: Hodder and Stoughton, 1981.

A. James Fuller

Nonviolence. *See* Violence and Nonviolence in American Abolitionism

North Africa and Abolition

Abolition of the slave trade in North Africa occurred piecemeal, elements of the slave trade effectively suppressed as early as 1816 and some continuing well into the twentieth century. While export slavery diminished considerably under pressure from European and Ottoman powers, domestic slavery, which could be conducted privately, persisted throughout North Africa. The slave populations involved were diverse; historically, North Africa was the center of the oriental trade in slaves. Slaves trafficked through North Africa were "white" Christian Europeans from the Mediterranean region and "black" pagan Africans, but only very rarely "white" Circassians and Georgians, who generally traveled the Black Sea route. Located from west to east on the southern Mediterranean coast, the countries we now know as Morocco, Algeria, Tunisia, Libya, and Egypt were motivated in banning the slave trade or in forestalling abolition by various cultural and economic considerations. Among the motivations for action or inaction were threats of foreign or imperial intervention, diplomatic and trade advantages, local and religious custom, the importance of slaves as domestic and agricultural workers, and the revenue generated from slave-trading markets and ports.

Historically, Europeans from the Mediterranean region and Africans from the Gold Coast, the Sahara, and the Sudan comprised the major human commodities for North-African Muslim slave traders. International trade for European countries depended on access to the Mediterranean Sea, and, centuries before fifteenth-century Europeans initiated the Atlantic slave trade in Africans, the Muslim states of Morocco, Algiers, Tunis, and Tripoli trafficked in European, as well as African slaves, both for domestic use and for sale in the east. According to Muslim law, or *Shari'a*, which sanctioned servitude, those who did not conform to Islam, those without peace treaties, and those forcibly defeated in accordance with the rules of *jihad* (or holy war) were all subject to enslavement.

Mediterranean Christian Slavery and Abolition

Mediterranean slaves came from nearly every part of Europe, acquired as prisoners in open warfare, by corsair (pirate) raiding in coastal regions, on merchant shipping, and by shipwreck. From the Middle Ages, both France and Spain had encouraged friars of their Trinitarian and Mercedarian Orders, respectively, to negotiate the ransom or redemption of Christian Europeans. Some historians claim that as many as a million Europeans were subjected to North African or Turkish slavery, but the numbers have always been far lower than those for the oriental traffic in black Africans. With the expansion of international trade in the sixteenth century, most European countries involved in Mediterranean trade and, later, the United States of America, endeavored to limit the enslavement of seafaring nationals in North Africa by means of treaties with the individual states or with the Ottoman Empire, which, for many years, exerted direct or nominal control over Algiers, Tunis, Tripoli, and Egypt. Not all treaties specifically denied North African states the right to enslave Europeans, but even when they did, European and American nationals were sometimes captured and sold. Narratives about European servitude became popular among the reading public; some publications describing Englishmen in North African bondage include *A True Description and Breefe Discourse, of a Most Lamentable Voiage, Made Latelie to Tripolie in Barbarie ... Set Foorth by Thomas Saunders* (1587), Francis Knight's *A Relation of Seaven Yeares Slaverie under the Turkes of Argeire ...* (1640), Simon Ockley's edition of *An Account of South-West Barbary Containing What Is Most Remarkable in the Territories of the King of Fez and Morocco. Written by a Person Who had been a Slave* (1713). Famous captives include the Spanish author Miguel de Cervantes (1547–1616) and the French priest and reformer Vincent de Paul (1581?–1660), who was later sanctified, as well innumerable naval and military officers. Except for women inducted into seraglios (harems) or sailors and artisans detained for their valuable technical skills, the period of bondage was often brief—an average of about five years. Although many perished in North African galleys and public works projects, some slaves were ransomed, redeemed, or exchanged for Muslim prisoners; some escaped, making their own way home; and some converted to Islam, thus securing their own freedom. From 1580 to 1680, the total number of Europeans held captive at any one time in North Africa probably amounted to about 35,000, with the numbers declining thereafter.

After the abolition of the Atlantic slave trade by several European nations and the United States of America, Britain, in particular, turned its attention to the abolition of the Mediterranean-Christian slave trade. In 1814, British Admiral William Sidney Smith stepped up to champion the end of Christian slavery by demanding military action against the corsair states of North Africa. Smith founded an international charity to finance the effort, naming it the Society of Knights Liberators of the White Slaves in Africa. His mission was forestalled, however, by the pivotal bombardment of Algiers by Britain's Lord Exmouth in 1816, which freed the remaining 3,000 or so Christians held in Algiers and across North Africa. After Exmouth's military intervention, the North African states generally capitulated to their European and American trading partners by signing treaties that included non-enslavement clauses. Moreover, the British and American navies spearheaded military efforts to enforce compliance. The northern Circassian trade to eastern markets continued unabated, with a large influx of agricultural slaves in the 1860s. The Ottoman Porte was reluctant to interfere, but by the 1890s only a few women of slave-status were acquired for harem service, and the institution of Circassian slavery in Islamic culture gradually died out.

Abolition of the African Trade

The abolition of the African slave trade in North Africa was more difficult to accomplish than the abolition of the white slave trade. From the mid-seventeenth to the mid-eighteenth century, some 10,000 Africans were sold into enslavement annually, destined for labor in various parts of North Africa, the Ottoman Empire, and Arabia. Attempts to end this commerce came from Europe and from the Ottoman Porte, but most official declarations to end the slave trade or slavery itself had no provisions for enforcement. Humanitarian efforts, whether prompted by antislavery zeal or diplomatic and trade considerations, came from the east and west. Efforts from the east included several nineteenth-century Ottoman edicts; the most important of these are the Ferman of 1847, which attempted to prohibit the African export trade to Asia and censured the involvement of government officials, and the Ferman of 1857, which gave legal and moral authority to the Ottoman abolition of the trade. Despite its domestic adherence to antislavery, the Turkish government was able to exert very little pressure to ensure that its satellites conformed. However, the 1880 Convention for the Suppression of the Slave Trade between Britain and Egypt gave Britain the right to search Ottoman ships and to seize contraband slaves, a power that allowed Britain to act as the international enforcer throughout the Mediterranean region. In the west, Britain persuaded the United States and all the major European maritime powers, except France, to sign treaties outlawing the slave trade, and it promoted the right of each state to search the others' shipping. However, even when backed up by naval power, such treaties often proved a hindrance to slave traffickers rather than a true impediment.

Humanitarian concern for slaves continued to have an effect in official circles, but once North Africa was partitioned by the colonial powers, reform was frequently nominal rather than actual. Between 1890 and 1919, the European powers established several agencies to oversee the end of slavery. The Brussels Conference of 1889 declared slavery criminal. The resulting **Brussels Act** of 1890 reaffirmed that the welfare of Africans susceptible to enslavement was an international responsibility and required the signatories to prevent slave raiding and trafficking, to repatriate or resettle freed or escaped slaves, and to curtail arms dealing in slaving areas. While this Act actually facilitated colonialism and the further exploitation of Africa under the guise of antislavery legislation, it also created two international bureaus—one in Zanzibar and the other in Brussels—to maintain records of slave trafficking and antislavery legislation by the signatories. These offices, however, had no provisions for enforcing antislavery policies except by resort to public opinion.

Between 1892 and 1914, all the colonial powers attempted to reduce large scale slave raiding and trading, including the export of slaves from Africa, but none was successful in imposing an immediate end to the institution of slavery. By 1919, the **League of Nations** agreed to suppress slavery in all its forms, but little was accomplished until the British Anti-Slavery and Aborigines Protection Society, piloted by John Harris (1874-1940), lobbied the League to promote effective antislavery measures. Even Britain, which complacently regarded itself as the world's emancipator, ducked the issue of slavery in its own colonies. Spurred by Harris's agitation, the League appointed the Temporary Slavery Commission of 1925–1925 to inquire into slavery worldwide, and the **Slavery Convention of 1926** became the first international body with a specific mandate to end slavery. This treaty remains in force today. Other committees were convened and discussion about slavery and other forms of forced labor continued, but chattel slavery was legally abolished only on a country-by-country basis, the last capitulation coming in 1970—although slavery is not, even now, completely eradicated. Anti-Slavery International, a contemporary agency dedicated to eradicating slavery, monitors continuing incidents, including small-scale European domestic, agricultural, and sex slavery; Asian child and sex slavery; and Sudanese slavery, which recently erupted as a result of military conflicts and famine. Perhaps tens of thousands of Sudanese children and adults have been snatched as war booty from their homes in the south and transported north, to work for Islamic owners.

Many international policies have lacked effective enforcement procedures, relying on the integrity of the signatories, who, often enough, had other interests to pursue. In the nineteenth and twentieth centuries, most of North Africa came directly into French control during this period of legislation about and oversight of slavery, and French colonials were more interested in preserving local rights and peaceful coexistence than in pursuing the humanitarian agenda of abolition.

Abolition of the African Trade in Algeria, Tunisia, and Morocco

France acquired these territories in the nineteenth and early twentieth centuries, although, for hundreds of years previously, Portugal and Spain had controlled vital ports and maintained a military presence across North Africa.

Algeria (the nation that emerged from the city-state of Algiers) fell to French control in 1830. The actual number of African slaves in nineteenth-century Algeria is not known, but they were a significant factor in the economy. In the lands along the Mediterranean coast, slaves were mainly employed in agriculture, and in the Sahara region to the south, slaves worked in date production, the construction and maintenance of irrigation systems, and herding. From 1844, the local French bureaucracies—*les Bureaux arabes*—were set up to administer local populations, and these authorities became responsible for implementing emancipation when the 1848 French imperial law that abolished slavery took effect. French administrators in Algeria viewed the prospective emancipation of slaves with skepticism, for abolition would not only affect the revenues arising from the trans-Saharan caravans (which were subsidized by slave trading) but also the support of the Arabs who would resent the loss of personal wealth tied up in slaves. In 1857, 1858, and 1887, governmental circulars insisted—without result—on the implementation of abolition, even though, in 1880, France decreed that the relationship between a slave and his owner would no longer be recognized by law. Algerian, Moroccan, and Tunisian slaves learned to flee from their owners to regions controlled by the French authority in Algeria in search of emancipation, but only in 1906 did the president of the French Republic issue a decree on the illegal character of the slave trade in Algeria. As a consequence, slavery declined but did not cease altogether.

Like Algeria, Tunisia (the nation emerging from the city-state of Tunis) had also been a satellite of the Ottoman Empire since the end of the sixteenth century. However, the Husseinic dynasty founded in 1705 was able to assert a good deal of autonomy for more than 100 years. Sandwiched between Algeria, which fell to France in 1830, and Tripolitania (now Libya), which was reclaimed by the Ottomans in 1836, the Tunisian ruler, Ahmad Bey (1837–1855), favored European protection over Ottoman submersion, and he initiated a number of reforms to modernize Tunisia. Tunisia was not a major slave trading country, and, persuaded by Britain and protected by its naval force, the Bey abolished slavery in Tunisia in 1846. However, his successor, Muhammad Bey (1855–1859) reversed the law, claiming that slavery was an integral part of Muslim tradition. Crisis during the reign of Muhammad al-Sadiq (1859–1882), who carried on the process of modernization, drew Tunisia into a series of economic and social reversals, which led to Tunisia's realliance with the Ottomans in 1871. The Bey soon severed this tie, but, several years later, Britain traded its de facto protection of a highly vulnerable but independent Tunisia for French acquiescence in the British administration of Cyprus. Tunisia was reduced to a French protectorate in 1883. As such, it was subject to French imperial law, with its lax enforcement policies regarding abolition.

An empire in its own right from the time of Ahmad al-Mansour (d. 1603), Morocco was a Muslim state accustomed to slaving revenues from both the "white" and "black" trades. From al-Mansour's time, the empire included the Songhay (a once powerful empire in the Sahel region immediately south of Morocco), which provided a rich source of both gold and slaves who were routinely trafficked through Morocco and across North Africa to the east. Moroccans also used slaves domestically in households, in agriculture, in the military, and in public works. The Ottoman edicts had no effect in Morocco, and the slave trade, traditionally conducted either privately or in open markets in most of the major cities, was not abolished until the end of the nineteenth century when the sultan succumbed to European pressures. However, the Moroccan historian Ahmad al-Nāsirī assisted in creating abolitionist sentiment by a strong indictment of slavery in his *History of the*

Maghrib (1881), in which he argued that Islamic law was broken by the enslavement of Africans who were, for the most part, already Muslim.

Britain protected Morocco from European colonization by supporting its nineteenth-century sultans, some of whom attempted to impose reform along modern European lines, but Britain finally ceded Morocco to the French in 1912 in return for a free hand in Egypt. In the French Protectorate of Morocco, the series of laws for the abolition of slavery enacted by the French government had little effect until 1925, when a law was passed that explicitly prohibited slavery. Even then, there was no sudden end to slavery, and freed slaves and their former masters continued to relate to each other in substantially the same manner.

Abolition of the African Trade in Libya

Libya, previously known as Tripolitania, developed in the region of the port of Tripoli, and spread as far as the western border of Egypt. It was under Ottoman domination from 1551 until 1722. With sparse agricultural development and a comparatively low population, Tripolitania had little domestic demand for slaves. Thus, most of the Africans transported along the northern route from the Sudan and Morocco or along the trans-Saharan slave routes were exported to the east; indeed Tripoli was a major slave outlet from the late-sixteenth century onward. After 1722, the country was ruled by a hereditary sultanate, which continued to facilitate the slave trade until 1835, when the Ottomans invaded and resumed control. Current estimates place the total traffic at about 784,000 African slaves between the years 1550 to 1857, when the Ottomans abolished the slave trade. Ottoman prohibition in Tripolitania proved itself somewhat effective; a major influence on abolition was the dreadful deaths in 1849 of 1,600 slaves and the slave merchants who accompanied them when they crossed the desert from Bornu to Fezzan, an event that spurred the British government to urge the Ottoman Porte to take steps to prevent the recurrence of such suffering. As a result, the Porte required the Governor of Tripoli to monitor slave trading more carefully, although he was not commissioned to prohibit slave imports altogether. Yet, after the 1857 edict, Tripolitanian governors did attempt to end raids and to repatriate enslaved Africans. Until that point, perhaps two thirds of the caravan trade across the Sahara involved slaves. Owing to Ottoman abolitionist measures, British pressure, and the spread of French imperial power in Africa, which removed important slave catchment areas from predation, by 1869 the numbers of slaves in transit had dropped substantially. This suppression of trafficking along the traditional Tripoli route led, however, to increased traffic along the more arduous Algerian and Egyptian routes. Slaves were sold for domestic use in twentieth-century Libya, even after the Italians expelled the Ottomans in 1911.

Abolition of the African Trade in Egypt

Egypt was sequentially subject to foreign powers with different slave policies. Mamluk Egypt fell to Ottoman domination in 1517, although the

Mamluk Sultanate managed to regain control by the late-eighteenth century. Curiously, throughout this period the Ottomans strove to restrict the transportation of slaves for sale in Egypt. This restriction was not premised upon humanitarian principle but upon military pragmatism, a ploy to debilitate the Mamluks who relied on male slaves for their army. When the Ottomans restored direct rule in Egypt in 1786, they simultaneously prohibited any slave imports into Egypt, a prohibition that lasted through the French occupation (1789–1801) and into the Anglo-Ottoman reoccupation that followed, and indeed, until the 1850s, when the Ottoman Empire abolished slavery. Of course, slaves were imported despite the ban, some entering Egypt overland when the Tripoli route was jeopardized by active policing of the slave trade, and some entering from the Sudan, especially after the Egyptian occupation in 1820. Slave-trading that originated in the Sudan was difficult to suppress, but the slave markets in Khartoum were closed by 1864, and a river police patrol was established to track down traders' boats and seize their slave cargoes. Meanwhile, Britain strove to abolish slavery within Egypt, but met with sustained religious resistance. Following the Convention for the Suppression of the Slave Trade between Britain and Egypt in 1877, abolition remained elusive. When Sir Evelyn Baring was appointed Agent and Consul General in Egypt in 1883, he did nothing to promote the cause of abolition, having concluded that slavery in Egypt did not exist by any act of the government but rather as a Muslim religious law, and, hence, could not be abrogated by legislative action. However, the British established Manumission Bureaus in Egypt, which emancipated any slave who applied, and by 1907, the institution was largely eradicated. Nevertheless, in 1907, Egypt established a Slavery Repression Department to ensure oversight of continuing slave trafficking in the north. *See also* Africa, Antislavery in; Africa, Emancipation in, Africa Squadron; Arabia and Nineteenth- and Twentieth-Century Slavery; Atlantic Slave Trade and British Abolition; Barbary Wars and White American Enslavement in North Africa; British Slavery, Abolition of; East African Slave Trade; Islam and Antislavery; Livingstone, David; Muscat and Oman, Abolition of Slavery in; Ottoman Empire; Decline of Slavery in; Slave Narratives.

Further Readings: Anti-Slavery Reporter. Anti-Slavery International, July 2004; Barbour, Nevill. "Northwest Africa from the 15th to 19th Centuries." In *The Last Great Muslim Empires.* Hans J. Kisling et al., eds. Princeton: Markus Weiner Publishers, 1969, pp. 97–147; Bennett, Norman. "Christian and Negro Slavery." *Journal of African History* 1, 1 (1960): 65–82; *Children in Sudan: Slaves, Street Children and Child Soldiers.* Human Rights Watch, September 1995. http://www.hrw.org. reports/1995/Sudan.htm, September 16, 2004; Clissold, Stephen. *Barbary Slaves.* London: P. Elek, 1977; Colley, Linda. *Captives.* New York: Pantheon Books, 2002; Erden, Y. Hakan. *Slavery and the Ottoman Empire and Its Demise, 1800–1909.* Basingstoke: Macmillan Press, Ltd., 1996; Julien, Charles-Andre. *History of North Africa.* John Petrie., trans. and ed. C.C. Stewart, ed. Routledge & Kegan Paul, 1970; Harris, Joseph E. *The African Presence in Asia: Consequences of the East African Slave Trade.* Evanston, IL: Northwestern University Press, 1971; Miers, Suzanne and Martin Klein, eds. *Slavery and Colonial Rule in Africa.* London: Frank Cass, 1999; Segal, Ronald. *Islam's Black Slaves: The Other Black Diaspora.* New York: Farrar, Straus and Giroux, 2001; Snader, Joe. *Caught Between Worlds: British Captivity*

Narratives in Fact and Fiction. Lexington: University Press of Kentucky, 2000; Toledano, Ehud R. *The Ottoman Slave Trade and Its Suppression, 1840–1890.* Princeton: Princeton University Press, 1982.

Susan B. Iwanisziw

Northwest Ordinance (1787)

The Northwest Ordinance is perhaps the most significant piece of national legislation passed by the U.S. Congress during the period when the Articles of Confederation formed the basis for national government. Enacted on July 13, 1787, it was among the last measures passed by the Confederation Congress.

Designed to facilitate the orderly settlement of the territory west of the Appalachian Mountains and north of the Ohio River, the Ordinance had several elements. Most generally, it established the principle that new territories, when sufficiently settled, would become states, fully equal to the original thirteen, and not remain permanently or even for very long in a subordinate position. Land in the territories would be sold directly to occupiers in small parcels, not in large parcels to speculators and others with political connections. Federal land would be surveyed prior to sale using a grid system and specific lots were set aside to support public education. These principles continued to govern the territorial expansion of the United States for the next century as the nation reached its current borders. Finally, slavery was prohibited from the entire territory, although provision was made for the return of fugitive slaves from the territory when claimed by their owners or their owners' agents. The exclusion of slavery from the territory was not controversial at the time, unlike later efforts to legislate on the status of slavery in the territories, and reflects both the spirit of equality that emerged from the Revolution and the general sense in the 1780s that slavery was an economically marginal institution and would soon disappear.

While the ordinance appeared to free those slaves already in the territory, territorial governor Arthur St. Clair did not move to free slaves already in the territory and acted to prevent slaves being freed by court order, ruling that pre-1787 slaves must remain in bondage.

When Indiana was established as a separate territory, it permitted the importation of African Americans as indentured servants who were bought and sold openly. When Illinois became a separate territory, it adopted the same practice. There were 746 indentured blacks in Illinois as late as 1830. Both territories continued this practice, as well as lax enforcement of anti-slavery provisions in their constitutions, after attaining statehood. Both indenture and slavery in the Northwest Territory and the states formed from it were largely limited to areas near the Ohio River.

Further Readings: Hyman, Harold M. *American Singularity.* Athens: University of Georgia Press, 1986; Onuf, Peter S. *Statehood and Union: A History of the Northwest Ordinance.* Bloomington: Indiana University Press, 1987; Taylor, Robert M. *The Northwest Ordinance of 1787: A Bicentennial Handbook.* Indianapolis: Indiana Historical Society, 1987; Williams, Frederick D. *The Northwest Ordinance: Essays* *on its Formulation, Provisions, and Legacy.* East Lansing: Michigan State University Press, 1989.

William H. Mulligan, Jr.

Nova Scotia

Nova Scotia became home to **Canada**'s first significant community of freed blacks in the aftermath of the American War of Independence. These communities were settled by refugee slaves who had fled behind British lines in response to proclamations freeing the slaves of rebels. Article VII of the Treaty of Paris ending the war provided that American slave-property not be sequestrated, or separated from other property returned to the victorious Patriots. Sir Guy Carleton, British commander-in-chief in America, refused to comply with this provision on the grounds that it constituted bad faith with his predecessors who had promised freedom to fleeing slaves under the terms of the Philipsburg (NY) Proclamation of June 30, 1779. Carleton thus assumed the logistical, if not the moral responsibility for evacuating the freed blacks, as well as Loyalists both white and black, from New York City. Between April and November 1783, some 3,000 freed blacks were transported to greater Nova Scotia (including today's New Brunswick), where they hoped to be treated as immigrant settlers on equal terms with other refugees. Systemic racism, however, prevented such a favorable reception.

A freed black was simply a fugitive slave in disguise, and not even blacks who had served with the army were privileged with equal rights. Culturally there was no difference between Nova Scotia and most of the Thirteen Colonies; fugitive slaves, war or no war, were not the same as legally manumitted slaves or freeborn blacks. Moreover, Nova Scotia was no better prepared for an influx of 3,000 irregular freedmen than it was for ten times that number of Loyalists. There were already hundreds of slaves in Atlantic Canada, and as many as 2,500 more were imported by the Loyalists. An unreconstructed slave society such as Nova Scotia was in 1783 readily determined that a freedman who was actually a refugee and fugitive from slavery in revolted neighboring colonies was inassimilable. The coming of the Loyalists and their slaves reinforced slavery, while the coming of the freed blacks, but recently slaves themselves, at once undermined and complicated it.

The ports of debarkation for the freed blacks were Saint John, Port Roseway, Halifax, Annapolis Royal, Fort Cumberland (Amherst), and Port Mouton. The largest group—some 1,500—went to Port Roseway, where, at the head of the northwest arm of Shelburne Harbour, they established Birchtown, at the time the largest freed black settlement in North America. In so doing, they immortalized the name of the one-time military commandant of New York City, Brigadier Samuel Birch, who had issued many of their safe-conducts which certified their freedom. The second largest group was set down with the Loyalists at the mouth of the Saint John River (City of Saint John), whence they proceeded northwards and settled on the Kingston Peninsula. In Halifax they established the historic black quarter in the north suburbs of the old town, which survives to this day. On the eastern side of

Halifax Harbour, beyond the village of Dartmouth, they took over the new Loyalist township of Preston, which has forever since been identified with them, and where a subsequent wave of black refugee immigrants was settled after the War of 1812. On the fringe of the Loyalist settlement of Digby, on the western shore of the Annapolis Basin, they established Brindley Town. Among other communities they founded were Birchtown, "Niggertown Hill" [Sunnyville] and Tracadie Road in Guysborough County, and Birchtown in Annapolis County.

The freed blacks were treated little better than the slaves that they had formerly been, and did not flourish despite their best efforts. Disqualified from fully exercising their property and civil rights in a society which viewed blacks as property almost by definition, many of the freed blacks were receptive in 1791 to a proposal from the Sierra Leone Company, a London-based antislavery philanthropy, to relocate to West Africa. Officialdom in Nova Scotia encouraged the venture because they were glad to see the freed blacks go; they feared that ex-slaves could not coexist with slaves without undermining the very institution of slavery. As a result, many of the freed black communities were depopulated and some disappeared altogether. Of all the settlements founded by the freed blacks, only Birchtown (Shelburne County), the largest of them, remains intact. Yet the majority of the freed blacks were not seduced by the blandishments of the Sierra Leone Company and decided to stay in Nova Scotia, where their descendants live to this day. They stoutly resisted efforts by Loyalists to reenslave them and many lived to witness the disappearance of slavery. At a time when most blacks were unfree, those freedmen who could not prove that they were not slaves were apt to be pressed into slavery by Loyalists who had lost slave property in America for which they could not obtain compensation. The presumption was in favor of the master, not the purported slave, and before the 1790s no court would uphold the constitutional liberty of freed blacks if it were challenged.

While it is by no means easy to distinguish descendants of the freed blacks from those of the slaves, who established their own communities after the end of slavery, it is clear that the children and grandchildren of the freed blacks were not entirely displaced by the post-War of 1812 "Black Refugee" immigrants. The very presence of the freed blacks encouraged the slaves, beside whom they lived and with whom they probably intermingled, to assert and test their right to freedom. If the slaves of rebels could be emancipated by royal fiat, why not also the slaves of Loyalists? Thanks to the initiative of the Black Loyalist Heritage Society, the freed black experience of 1783–1792 has become the prime focus of black historical interest in Nova Scotia. The tendency to assimilate the freed blacks to the Loyalists expresses retrospectively the hope of the freed blacks themselves—that, like the Loyalists, they would find in Nova Scotia a promised land where they would be free indeed, endued not only with the fundamental right of freedom but also with the legal rights deriving from it. Instead they found themselves half-free in a slave society overflowing with acquisitive slaveholders from the very colonies where they themselves had formerly been enslaved. The continual struggle to maintain their newfound, qualified liberty under the most difficult conditions imaginable bedeviled their efforts to form sustainable communities and build a free society in the midst of a slave one.

Further Readings: African Nova Scotians in the Age of Slavery and Abolition [Online, June 2004]. Nova Scotia Archives and Records Management Web site. http://www.gov.ns.ca/nsarm/virtual/africanns; Walker, James W. St. G. *The Black Loyalists: The Search for a Promised Land in Nova Scotia and Sierra Leone, 1783–1870* [1976]. 2nd ed. Toronto: University of Toronto Press, 1992; Wilson, Ellen Gibson. *The Loyal Blacks*. New York: Capricorn Books, 1976.

Barry Cahill

O

O'Connell, Daniel (1775–1847)

Daniel O'Connell was a Catholic landowner who became the preeminent Irish statesman of his time. His abolitionist activities came late in his life, after he had already established his reputation as a champion of Irish and Catholic rights, but O'Connell was staunchly opposed to both British and American slavery. Abolitionists on both sides of the ocean welcomed his support. Nonetheless, because O'Connell's political priority was always with Ireland, and because his career was in its twilight by the 1840s, he remained on the margins of organized abolitionism, never allowing himself to be identified fully with a particular group of antislavery reformers.

O'Connell rose to prominence in the 1810s and 1820s, when he helped mobilize an impressive popular movement in Ireland against the Protestant ascendancy in politics, which was only strengthened by the Union of 1800 formally joining Ireland to the United Kingdom. By denouncing the disenfranchisement and marginalization of Catholics, O'Connell became a hero among the populace. After mobilizing impressive displays of popular dissent, he was elected to the House of Commons in 1828, despite the prohibition of Catholics from seats in Parliament. O'Connell's defiant election pressured the British government to grant Catholics legislative representation in 1829, and to allow O'Connell—nicknamed the "Liberator"—to take his seat. This was his most important political achievement, the act that became known as Catholic emancipation.

Once in Parliament, slave emancipation also occupied O'Connell's attention. In the parliamentary debates that produced the Emancipation Bill of 1833, he sided with abolitionists against the West Indian lobby. After 1834, he criticized **apprenticeship** and supported its overthrow in 1838. Yet O'Connell's antislavery sentiments did not subside after emancipation. He encouraged British abolitionists as they turned their attention to universal emancipation, and particularly to the United States.

O'Connell's renown as an antislavery spokesman and his philippics on American hypocrisy impressed abolitionists, especially **William Lloyd Garrison,** who met him while visiting England in 1833. O'Connell supported

Daniel O'Connell. Courtesy of the Library of Congress.

Garrison's efforts to expose the shortcomings of the **American Colonization Society** before British abolitionists. **Garrisonians** were also impressed in 1840 when O'Connell criticized the exclusion of women from the **World's Anti-Slavery Convention.** After the Convention, O'Connell added his name, along with that of the popular temperance reformer Father Theobald Mathew, to the so-called "Irish Address." In the Address, which carried an additional 60,000 Irish signatures, O'Connell urged Irish-Americans to side with the abolitionists and spurn prejudice against African Americans. It was brought to the United States at the end of 1841 by black abolitionist Charles L. Remond.

In January 1842, Garrisonians triumphantly produced the Irish Address at a public meeting in Boston, hoping that O'Connell's influence would win over Irish immigrants to the antislavery cause. But for a variety of reasons, including the racism of many Irish Americans and their own struggle against nativism, Irish immigrants did not respond to the Address enthusiastically. Many persisted in their antiabolitionism despite their respect for O'Connell. The Address thus crystallized what would be a recurring problem for the Irish "Liberator." On the one hand, he wanted to garner Irish-American support for political reforms at home, but on the other hand, he refused to recant his opposition to American slavery.

This dilemma surfaced again in 1843, when O'Connell spearheaded a yearlong campaign for the repeal of the Union of 1800. O'Connell had long favored a distinct Irish Parliament and a form of home rule; he saw his nationalism as continuous with his fight for religious toleration and the political equality of Catholics. Thus, in 1843, with his political alliances in Parliament eroding, O'Connell renewed his calls for Repeal. Repeal associations sprung up among Irish Americans, who sent financial aid across the Atlantic. O'Connell welcomed the money despite the often virulent antiabolitionism of the senders. Garrisonians criticized what they saw as O'Connell's equivocation, just as they would later criticize the Free Church of Scotland for accepting contributions from the South. But O'Connell did not withdraw his condemnation of slavery. In a long 1843 letter rebuking the Cincinnati Repeal association, which had defended American slavery, he made clear that his commitment to Repeal did not lessen his commitment to abolition. At any rate, O'Connell was arrested by the British government at the end of 1843 for his Repeal activities, and his influence among Irish radicals declined thereafter, though his popularity remained considerable.

Despite his antislavery commitments, O'Connell was politically wary of being associated with the Garrisonians. In 1843, he publicly criticized what he saw as Garrison's infidel religious beliefs, which he said were opposed to Catholic faith. An infuriated Garrison felt betrayed by these remarks, but he was similarly wary of O'Connell. Since radical abolitionists often denounced both politicians and Catholicism, O'Connell's status as a Catholic politician was problematic. Even so, Garrisonians gladly praised his strictures on slavery, frequently publishing his speeches. They also applauded his opposition to the use of violence for political ends, even for Ireland's independence. When Hungarian revolutionary **Louis Kossuth** later vacillated on slavery, Garrisonians chided him by pointing to the constancy of O'Connell, whom many of them eulogized in 1875 on the centennial of his birth. Despite his death in 1847, O'Connell's memory thus lived on among antebellum American abolitionists. *See also* Hibernian (Irish) Anti-Slavery Society; Roman Catholic Church and Antislavery and Abolitionism.

Further Readings: Ignatiev, Noel. *How the Irish Became White.* New York and London: Routledge, 1995, pp. 6–31; Osofsky, Gilbert. "Abolitionists, Irish Immigrants, and the Dilemmas of Romantic Nationalism." *American Historical Review* 80 (1975): 889–912; Riach, Douglas C. "Daniel O'Connell and American Anti-Slavery." *Irish Historical Studies* 20, 77 (1976): 3–25.

W. Caleb McDaniel

Oman. *See* Muscat and Oman, Abolition of Slavery in

Oroonoko and Early Antislavery Literary Works

Authors who expressed a profound sensitivity to the histories of individual slaves or disgust for slave abuse were often motivated by simple compassion, rather than by antislavery sentiment. Sympathetic fictional treatments, biographies, plays, and poems, whose numbers grew incrementally throughout the long eighteenth century (1660–1832), nevertheless helped build the ideological foundation from which abolitionist writers were able to create a public antislavery constituency. Writers from Britain, North America, the Caribbean region, and Europe all contributed to the development of this constituency, which, ultimately, influenced antislavery legislation in Great Britain, the United States, South America, and elsewhere.

Oroonoko, or the Royal Slave (1688), a novella by **Aphra Behn,** has been promoted by several twentieth-century scholars as an early antislavery text. The nameless narrator purports to have lived in Surinam and befriended the Coramantien Prince, Oroonoko, who led a failed slave rebellion during the English colonial administration (1649–1667). To punish his revolt, the deputy governor of the colony has the prince cruelly whipped, but, once restored to health, Oroonoko kills his wife, Imoinda, to preserve her and their unborn child from the indignities of slavery. While the narrator is absent, the colonists brutally execute the prince by dismemberment and burning. The depiction of Oroonoko's noble character and tragic history is highly flattering, but the narrator's romanticization of his life is accompanied by a rather matter-of-fact acceptance of the harsh conditions suffered by the ordinary slaves. Indeed, Oroonoko is clearly identified as a trader in African slaves in his own country, his capture the trick of an English sea captain to whom he had previously sold prisoners of war. In light of Behn's royalist convictions and the fact that the transatlantic slave trade was sanctioned by Charles II who issued African trade monopolies to the Company of Royal Adventurers (1663) and to the Royal African Company (1672), her attitude toward slavery is unlikely to be wholly disapproving. However, the dramatic adaptation of the colonial part of the story, first by Thomas Southerne in 1695 and then by a series of eighteenth-century adapters, drew Behn's sympathetic account of the royal slave inexorably into the province of the abolitionists.

Southerne's play held the stage for over 100 years, one of the mainstays of British theater. If Behn's text must remain an ambiguous record of her attitude toward slavery, Southerne's play cannot, with any justice, be similarly categorized. In debating a slave's right to rebel, Southerne's Oroonoko argues that he is a legitimate purchase with no cause to defraud his owner. Displeased with the dramatic Oroonoko's character, mid-eighteenth-century adapters transformed the play in order to emphasize the horrors of slave life and to press readers and playgoers into recognizing the cruelties of the institution. Only in John Ferriar's *Prince of Angola* (1788), an adaptation sponsored by the Manchester Society for Abolition, did the play become unambiguously abolitionist. The antislavery agenda is made explicit in Ferriar's preface, but it surfaces implicitly in his redrawing of Oroonoko as an eighteenth-century man of sentiment and, especially, in his excision of Oroonoko's involvement with slave-trading activity.

Plays were not a major vehicle for arousing antislavery advocacy, but several dramas depicted sympathetic slaves in French, English and North American theaters. These included Pierre Antoine de La Place's French translation of *Oroonoko* (1742); Isaac Bickerstaff's *Padlock* (1768), featuring the slave Mungo, which was performed in England and in various North American locations as early as 1771; and Olympe de Gouges's *Zamore et Mirza* (transformed into *L'Esclavage des Nègres* or *Negro Slavery*) published in France in 1788. Most important in terms of the antislavery cause is George Colman the Younger's **Inkle and Yarico** (1787). In this extremely popular comic opera, Colman transformed the well-known Caribbean story about a pregnant Indian woman named Yarico, who was sold into slavery by her callous English lover, into a celebration of two interracial marriages.

Behn's novella, that sparked much of this dramatic reflection on slaves and slavery, did not, overall, have much impact on fiction writing. Indeed, her *Oroonoko* was marketed as a "true history" rather than a fiction. Early novels certainly mentioned slaves and freed slaves; for example, Maria Edgeworth's *Belinda* (1801) includes a brief episode about the marriage of a capable Jamaican slave to a young Englishwoman. But **Harriet Beecher Stowe**'s ***Uncle Tom's Cabin*** (serialized in 1851–1852) provided the archetype for the antislavery novel. On the other hand, the personal histories of African slaves became popular reading. These include **Ottobah Cugoano**'s *Thoughts and Sentiments on the Evil and Wicked Traffic of the Slavery and Commerce of the Human Species* (1787); **Olaudah Equiano**'s *The Interesting Narrative of the Life of Olaudah Equiano* (1789), which was translated into Dutch, German, and Russian; and the anonymous American autobiographical poem, *The American in Algiers, or the Patriot of Seventy-Six in Captivity* (1797).

The greatest literary contribution to the antislavery movement arose in the form of poetry. Many verses expressing sympathy for African slaves were composed by writers who were not professionally dedicated to the poetic arts. Some appeared within antislavery treatises, such as Thomas Tyron's *Friendly Advice to the Gentleman-Planters of the East and West Indies* (1684). Daniel Defoe, better known for his novels and tracts, expresses his contempt for the exploitation of Africans and Native Americans in his poem *Reformation of Manners: A Satyr* (1702). Other critiques of contemporary slavery include Bernard Mandeville's *The Planter's Charity* (1704), several poems about Inkle and Yarico, and Richard Savage's *Of Public Spirit in Regard to Public Works* (1737).

When the abolitionist movement gathered momentum, many poems became vehicles for propaganda. Published in the hundreds during the last decades of the eighteenth century, poems were composed by men and women, both black and white, from various social classes and religious affiliations. *The Dying Negro, A Poem* (1775) by Thomas Day is prefaced by an anguished description of the slave trade, while the poem addresses the suicide of an escaped slave who is forced back into slavery on the eve of his marriage to an English woman. At **William Wilberforce**'s request, William Cowper wrote two moving poems concerning the slave trade: *The Negro's Complaint* (1778) and *Pity for Poor Africans* (1788). Also commissioned by the British Anti-Slavery Society in support of Wilberforce's bill, **Hannah More**'s *Slavery, A Poem* (1787) was widely distributed in Britain and in the United States. Ann Yearsley, or Lactilla, the "milkmaid poet," wrote *A Poem on the Inhumanity of the Slave Trade* (1788). For obvious reasons, African poets living in North America, such as Phillis Wheatley and Jupiter Hammon, were less forthright in condemning the slave trade. However, abolitionists used their poetic genius to challenge common white assumptions of African intellectual inferiority.

Romantic poets also contributed to the public cause with topical poems. William Blake wrote *The Little Black Boy* (1789); Robert Southey composed a sonnet sequence on the slave trade (1794); and Samuel Taylor Coleridge penned, in Greek, *The Wretched Lot of the Slaves in the Islands of West India*. William Wordsworth wrote a sonnet dedicated to the end of slavery, entitled *To* **Toussaint L'Ouverture** (1803).

As well as poets and writers, public activists of all stripes were inspired to commemorate in verse the triumphs and struggles of William Wilberforce's parliamentary campaign and the eventual abolition of the slave trade in Britain. Activists included Anna Letitia Barbauld, John Walsh, James Grahame, and Sir Thomas Edlyne Tomlins. Distanced by revolution and circumstance from British parliamentary activity, Americans countenanced their own abolition of the slave trade without the same outpouring of poetic propaganda. However, William C. Foster, a working man, called for an end to slavery worldwide in *An Address, Presented to the Readers of the* Waterford Gazette, *January 1, 1803. See also* Literature and Abolition.

Further Readings: "Abolition Literature." http://www.users.muohio.edu/mandellc/projects/aronowml/LitHome/htm; Basker, James G., ed. *Amazing Grace: An Anthology of Poems about Slavery, 1660–1810.* New Haven, CT: Yale University

Press, 2002; Brown, Gregory S. "Abolitionism and Self-Fashioning: Olympe de Gouges and her *Esclavage des Noirs,* 1783–1792." *Western Society for French History: Selected Papers of the 1999 Annual Meeting.* Barry Rothaus, ed. Vol. 27. Denver: University of Colorado Press, 2001, pp. 210–219; Iwanisziw, Susan B., ed. *Oroonoko: Adaptations and Offshoots.* Aldershot, Hants: Ashgate Publishing Ltd, forthcoming; Lipking, Joanna, ed. *Oroonoko: Aphra Behn.* New York: W.W. Norton & Co., 1997.

Susan B. Iwanisziw

Ottoman Empire, Decline of Slavery in

Approved by custom and sanctioned by law, slavery was an institution of vital importance in Ottoman society. Ottoman law regulated all aspects of the slaves' status. It laid down the obligations of masters and slaves, and determined the relationship between them. In theory, slaves could only be obtained from non-Muslim countries with which a state of war existed. Muslim prisoners of war or rebels could not be enslaved. Legally, slaves could not be used for "inappropriate" uses, for example as thieves, beggars, or prostitutes (although they could be for concubines). The law reflected ideals of a male-dominated society.

Culturally, slavery was an important channel for recruitment and socialization and a means of linking individuals into patronage networks. While the law did not make any distinction among types of slaves, in practice clear social stratification emerged. Part of the complexity of studying slavery in the Ottoman Empire arises from the continuum of degrees of slavery rather than a clear distinction between slave and free. At the top, we have the officeholders (e.g., Grand Vazirs), state functionaries and harem ladies of slave origin. Their decisions affected the lives of both slave and free, and in most cases had both slave and free reporting directly to them. There was little to distinguish these slaves from the free. At the other end of the spectrum we have the agricultural slaves, the most restricted of Ottoman slaves.

During the early period of the Ottoman Empire (c. 1446–1556), prisoners of war (especially children) were converted to **Islam** and taught how to practice their new faith. These *kul* slaves were also taught the Turkish language and customs. Depending on their abilities and aptitudes, they were trained for a career in government (religious, military, or administrative) with elite status. The women who came to the *harem* as slaves were taught and trained to be Ottoman ladies. Like the *kul* slaves, they went through rigorous training to learn all the domestic and social roles attached to their position. As they grew up, they were paired with *kul* slaves—an appropriate match for Ottoman society. With the stabilization of frontiers, *kul* slaves were recruited through *devshirme* (a child-levy imposed on the empire's non-Muslim subjects). During the seventeenth century, the child-levy was abandoned and a different strategy for recruitment and socialization emerged.

Wealthy families "adopted" children of slaves, educated them and endowed them for life. This custom of *besleme* was encouraged by Ottoman culture and served a dual purpose of freeing the slave and expanding the patronage network of the family. The complexities and richness of such situations often developed into lifetime relationships that entailed protection, patronage, loyalty, and mutual affection.

The *kul* and *harem* slavery survived until the demise of the empire in the second decade of the twentieth century. Emanating from the palace and permeating into the elite, only the abolition of the sultanate and the physical removal of the royal family from Turkey finally ended the practice.

Demand for skilled labor in Ottoman cities was partly met by industrial slaves. Slaves were immune from seasonal migration and were more productive than free labor, as they could buy their freedom by working for a specified number of years or by producing a specified quantity of goods.

Domestic slaves, because of where they served, were intimately connected with the decision makers of the family. Hence, they could negotiate their position and influence family decisions. A suckling relationship, for example, could evolve into a "mothering" relationship with freeborn children of the house. By extension, slave children would be considered "part of the family." Ottoman law had legal mechanisms to grant manumission. One was for the master to voluntarily grant freedom (encouraged by Ottoman ideals). Another was for the slave to buy his/her freedom (*mukatebe*). Offspring of free-slave unions were considered free, and the bonded mother was free upon the master's death. Once free, it was illegal to be enslaved again. If mistreated, slaves could and did, seek redress through the courts; however, in most cases, the courts abstained from regular interference in the treatment and punishment of slaves by owners.

Ottoman law forbade the enslavement of freeborn Muslims, and *Zimmis* (protected minorities). The absence of slave breeding practices and cultural attitudes resulted in a steady decline of the slave population. Ottoman slavery hence depended on a vast and complex slave-trading network that provided the lion's share of slaves. In the eighteenth century, an increasing number of the Ottoman elite were educated in European institutions and in such European values as equality, individual rights, and political freedom, which influenced Ottoman culture. The Ottomans adopted a negative stance towards slavery and gradually disengaged from it on moral grounds.

During the 1850s and 1860s, Circassian refugees from Caucasus entered the empire in large numbers. Although the Circassians were Muslims, their culture, including their treatment of slaves, was closer to that practiced in the Balkans. The Porte (Ottoman government) was reluctant to interfere with established custom, and sought to limit agricultural slavery through existing means. Laws prohibiting the sale of free individuals into slavery were strengthened and enforced. Slaves who wanted their freedom used the *mukatebe*—sometimes with assistance from the state treasury. Realizing that slaves typically could not afford the manumission fee, the government offered land as part or full compensation. Finally, laws mandating military service of refugees sped up manumission.

In the 1840s, the abolition movement in Britain started looking at slavery in the Ottoman Empire. The British abolitionists treated all types of bondage within the Ottoman Empire as one homogeneous entity. Hence, an agenda to emancipate only the most restrictive slaves was never considered. This lack of differentiation may have contributed to prolonging the most oppressive forms of slavery. The Ottomans viewed the attack on their slavery system as an affront to their sensibilities and culture. Hence, foreign efforts at abolishing slavery in the empire were met with considerable resistance; even though some of the high-ranking ministers were themselves "of slave origin," i.e., either slaves with elite status or offspring of slaves.

The British government then focused its efforts on curtailing the trafficking of slaves on humanitarian grounds. The goal was to get the Porte to issue edicts forbidding the trade in slaves. British diplomatic and commercial representatives monitored the implications of these edicts, and reported to London. Eventually, the Ottoman government participated in negotiations leading to the **Brussels Act** against slave trading in 1890.

The Ottomans felt morally and spiritually superior to the Europeans. This feeling coexisted with the recognition of their technological and economic inferiority, and bred resistance to yielding to British pressures. Thus, even when the Porte issued a number of edicts, their enforcement often lagged behind and required reiteration and reenactment. Ideologically, the statesmen responded defensively to British pressure for abolition. While they accepted the need to prevent human suffering, their laws restricted the slave-trade without addressing slavery itself. The reform-minded activists were too absorbed in their struggle for political rights and only marginally addressed slavery. During the 1870s, the playwrights, novelists and poets made the most impressive effort to grapple with the issue of slavery. All three groups seem to project the least restricted forms of slavery to Europe (i.e., the *kul* and *harem* slaves), where there is virtually no practical difference between slave and free. While at home, they addressed the most restrictive forms of bondage.

The Ottomans did not adopt a policy of abolishing slavery *per se*. Instead, they enacted laws that effectively choked off the slave trade, hindered the travel and transfer of slaves, and encouraged manumission, sometimes using the state treasury to compensate slaveowners. These measures severely curtailed slavery in the empire. This attitude was in keeping with the Ottoman political culture, which was patient, mindful of the long term, gradual, indirect, very pragmatic, and in most cases quite effective. *See also Qur'an* and Antislavery.

Further Readings: Ayalon, David. *Eunuchs, Caliphs and Sultans, a Study in Power Relationships.* Jerusalem: Magnes Press. 1999; Clarence-Smith, William, ed. *The Economics of the Indian Ocean Slave Trade in the Nineteenth Century.* London: Frank Cass Publishers. 1989; Crone, Patricia. *Slaves on Horses: The Evolution of the Islamic Polity.* Cambridge: Cambridge University Press. 1980; Erdem, Hakan. *Slavery in the Ottoman Empire and its Demise 1800–1909.* New York: Macmillan. 1996; Lewis, Bernard. *Race and Slavery in the Middle East: An Historical Enquiry.* Oxford: Oxford University Press. 1990; Miura, Toru, ed. *Slave Elites in the Middle East and Africa, a Comparative Study.* London: Kegan Paul International. 2000; Pipes, Daniel. *Slave Soldiers and Islam; the Genesis of a Military System.* New Haven, CT: Yale University Press. 1981; Savage, Elizabeth, ed. *The Human Commodity: Perspectives on the Trans-Saharan Slave Trade.* London: Frank Cass Publishers. 1992; Toledano, Ehud. *The Ottoman Slave Trade and its Suppression: 1840–1890.* Princeton, NJ: Princeton University Press. 1983; Toledano, Ehud. *Slavery and Abolition in the Ottoman Middle East.* Seattle: University of Washington Press. 1998.

Mohammed Hassanali

P

Paine, Thomas (1737–1809)

A printer, pamphleteer, author, and statesman, Thomas Paine is best known as the author of two critical Revolutionary-era treatises, "Common Sense" (1776) and "The Rights of Man" (1791–1792). Thomas Paine was also an important antislavery figure in the late-eighteenth century western world. In 1775, Paine published "African Slavery in America," a vigorous attack on both the slave trade and the institution of slavery itself. Referring to slaves as "an unnatural commodity" and the slave trade as "wicked," Paine chastised Anglo-Americans for sanctioning chattel bondage. Paine found religious justifications of slavery particularly troubling. Far from chattel possessions devoid of rights, enslaved people, Paine observed, had "a natural, perfect right" to freedom. The essay, published in *The Pennsylvania Journal and the Weekly Advertiser*, marked Paine as one of the rising antislavery voices of the 1770s, along with fellow Pennsylvanians **Benjamin Rush** and **Anthony Benezet**.

Paine solidified his antislavery credentials by joining the **Pennsylvania Abolition Society**, the first antislavery organization in the Western world. In 1780, Paine also helped draft Pennsylvania's gradual abolition law, which declared that all enslaved people born after that year would be liberated at the age of twenty-eight. As the first so-called "post-nati" abolition law passed in the United States—post-nati referring to the fact that the individual's liberation occurred at some established date after their birth—it became the basis for similar statutes in New York, New Jersey, Connecticut, and Rhode Island over the next twenty years. Paine's particular genius as an antislavery writer and statesman was to link antislavery principles to the democratic institutions of

Thomas Paine. Courtesy of the Library of Congress.

governance appearing in America. Abolition could not be achieved, Paine concluded, by relying on masters' private manumission of slaves; rather, emancipation must be compelled by positive government enactment. For Paine, abolition was nothing less than common sense.

Further Readings: Davis, David Brion. *The Problem of Slavery in the Age of Revolution.* Ithaca, NY: Cornell University Press, 1975; Nash, Gary, and Jean Soderlund. *Freedom by Degrees: Emancipation and Its Aftermath in Pennsylvania.* New York: Oxford University Press, 1991; Soderlund, Jean. *Quakers and Slavery: A Divided Spirit. New York.* Princeton, NJ: Princeton University Press, 1985.

Richard Newman

Palenques (Colombia)

Palenques were communities of runaway slaves formed since the late-sixteenth century all along Colombian territory. These became important centers for resistance to colonial slave society, especially in those areas surrounding key economic regions like Cartagena and Santa Marta on the Caribbean coast where domestic and agricultural slaves were widespread, and Cauca and Antioquia close to the Pacific coast where mining was more common. The most important *palenques* were San Basilio, west of the Magdalena River in the Caribbean, and El Castigo, close by the Patía River in the southern Andean province of Popayán. The symbolic power of *palenques* was recognized by the colonial state, which barred their formation and existence. Yet finding this an impossible goal, by the eighteenth century the state promoted arrangements with some *palenques* in order to achieve some control over them while granting them the right to be free communities.

Slave resistance in colonial Colombia took many forms. Legal strategies afforded one form whereby the enslaved appropriated Hispanic judicial spaces and language for the defense of their rights. These strategies had been customary since the seventeenth century and became more frequent in the eighteenth century when more tolerant Bourbon legislation created more judicial opportunities for the enslaved. Rebellion, on the other hand, was not always a safe path as colonial authorities and slave owners punished rebels severely with mutilation or death. A more feasible alternative for slaves was to run away and form free communities, or *palenques*, beyond the reach of the Spanish state or slave owners.

Flight represented an elemental form of resistance to slavery and led to the emergence of autonomous communities, which deeply threatened the institution of slavery. *Palenques* were transgressive because they symbolized the possibility to achieve freedom for enslaved populations. In their communities they generally created agricultural economies and sometimes organized themselves politically on the basis of African tribal structures. But the members of these communities also continuously attacked plantations to obtain goods and helped to destabilize colonial society.

The earliest fugitive communities formed in the late-sixteenth century around the city of Cartagena, the most important port of trade for African slaves on the Caribbean coast. After numerous Spanish expeditions attempted to overpower the runaways, their communities did not disappear.

The most important *palenque*, San Basilio, was formed by groups of Kongo, Angola, Arará, Mina, and Karabalí runaway slaves from *haciendas* around Cartagena, who successfully defended their freedom against these assaults.

In the seventeenth century, the colonial government abandoned the project to pacify the **maroons** and instead determined to recognize them as autonomous black communities. The name "community of San Basilio" was given to them by governor Juan de Torrezar Diaz y Pimienta in 1774 in recognition of their free status, granting them the right to have land, name a political leader, and exclude all white men, except the priest, from the town. These were among the first free towns in America. The crown's decision to legalize their existence, however, included the mandate that they henceforth observe Spanish law as well as prevent other runaways from joining their communities. These negotiations were the most notable to occur between the state and a maroon community in colonial Colombia.

The southwestern maroon community of "El Castigo" affords another important illustration of the relation between the state and a Colombian *palenque*. Located in the province of Popayán, in the Patía River Valley, it comprised two villages, each one with a church, and included runaway slaves from the *haciendas* near Popayán and Valle del Cauca, and from the mines in Barbacoas, Panamá, and Chocó. Initial negotiations with the state secured a priest to live among them, but without the community accepting any political compromise with the state or formal integration into colonial society. Such adamant conditions asserted by this *palenque* spurred rising tensions with the state, and Spanish authorities viewed these maroons as intractable throughout the eighteenth century. However, during the wars of independence in the early 1810s, the Patía maroons defended their own freedom by allying with the Spanish army against the revolutionaries. They became some of the war's most feared guerrillas, and their military organization safeguarded their territory and guaranteed their permanence as a free community. The *palenque* allied with the royalists because they were very suspicious of the patriots' position on race and their communities and they feared that independence might bring a revocation of their hard-won rights acquired during the colonial era.

Palenques resisted slavery and forged autonomous communities which built innovative political structures, merged their residents' African ancestral beliefs with those of Catholicism, and created an alternative economy which allowed them landed property and independent production and exchange. *Palenques* were the first examples of collective Afro-Colombian culture and were the predecessors of Colombia's contemporary black communities. *See also* African American Communities.

Further Readings: Escalante, Aquiles. "*Palenques* in Colombia." In Richard Price, ed., *Maroon Societies: Rebel Slave Communities in the Americas*. Baltimore and London: The Johns Hopkins University Press, 1979, pp. 74–81; McFarlane, Anthony. *Cimarrones and Palenques: Runaways and Resistance in Colonial Colombia*. In Gad Heuman, ed., *Out of the House of Bondage. Runaways, Resistance and Marronage in Africa and the New World*. New York: Frank Cass, 1986, pp. 131–151; Zuluaga, Francisco. *Guerrilla y sociedad en el Patía*. Cali, Colombia: Universidad del Valle, 1993.

Marcela Echeverri

Parker, John Percial (1827–1900)

A former slave from Virginia, John Percial Parker is believed to have aided 900 or more slaves during his fifteen-year career as an **Underground Railroad** conductor. At age eight, he was sold by his master, probably also his father. Purchased by a Mobile, Alabama, doctor, he drove the doctor to see his patients, and became friends with the doctor's two sons, who secretly taught him to read and write.

After being separated from his master's sons when they went north to complete their educations, Parker's master apprenticed him to a plasterer. An argument with his employer landed him in a slave hospital, from which he fled after a fight with the hospital's sadistic caretaker. He spent several months on the run, and was only accidentally reclaimed by his master.

Following this abortive escape, his master arranged employment for him in a foundry. Parker quickly became a skilled iron molder, but his tendency to quarrel with his employer and coworkers led to trouble. His master decided to sell him south as a field hand. Desperate to avoid this fate, Parker persuaded one of his master's patients to purchase him with the understanding that he would pay her back his purchase price plus interest, in exchange for his freedom.

By working hard, Parker was able to repay the widow in eighteen months. In 1845, he was given his freedom papers, traveled north to Cincinnati, and found employment as an iron molder. Though he states in his autobiography, *His Promised Land*, that his master never mistreated him, he nevertheless harbored a deep resentment for having been enslaved. Therefore, he was not averse to the idea of assisting in the escape of two Kentucky slave girls. This first experience of guiding fugitive slaves from Kentucky to the home of a Ripley, Ohio, abolitionist, was the start of his career as an Underground Railroad conductor.

Parker married in 1848, after which he moved from Cincinnati to Ripley, where he had already been working with the town's many abolitionists. For the next fifteen years, he was actively involved in conducting escaping slaves across the Ohio River. Among his many antislavery colleagues were Ripley Presbyterian minister John Rankin, as well as Levi Coffin. Although he had a $1,000 price on his head, he made almost-nightly trips into Kentucky to bring groups of fleeing slaves to Ripley. He recounted many of his harrowing (and sometimes amusing as well) adventures in *His Promised Land*.

Although the traditional lore of the Underground Railroad has painted a picture of a movement organized and headed by Caucasian abolitionists, without whom runaway slaves would never have been able to make their bids for freedom, the truth is quite different. They were much more apt to trust fellow African Americans over white men, and their first contact after they had entered a Northern state was most often with a free black like Parker. Many cities had sizeable free black communities; their residents frequently concealed runaways, forwarding them further north to both black and white abolitionists when it was safe to do so.

These Northern blacks, despite being free, did not find life easy. They encountered bitter prejudice from whites, which limited jobs they might hold and where they might live. The Ohio Black Laws, originally enacted in 1804, for example, required that all free blacks entering the state not only possess free papers, but also register themselves with the clerk of courts in the county they resided in. Later Black Law legislation required that free blacks coming into the state post a $500 bond to ensure that they would not become a public charge. Other Northern states enacted similar laws. In addition to such obstacles, they also ran the risk of being kidnapped and sold into slavery by white slave hunters.

John Parker was a respected member of the Ripley, Ohio, community. He established himself not only as a successful businessman, running his own foundry, but also as an inventor. One of the first African Americans to hold patents for his inventions, he manufactured and marketed his soil pulverizers and tobacco presses throughout the Midwestern United States.

Further Readings: Gara, Larry. *The Liberty Line: The Legend of the Underground Railroad.* Lexington: University Press of Kentucky, 1961; Griffler, Keith R. *Front Line of Freedom: African Americans and the Forging of the Underground Railroad in the Ohio Valley.* Lexington: University Press of Kentucky, 2004; Hagedorn, Ann. *Beyond the River.* New York: Simon & Schuster, 2002; Horton, James Oliver, and Lois E. Horton. *In Hope of Liberty.* New York: Oxford University Press, 1997; *Ripley, Ohio: Its History and Families.* Ripley, OH: Ripley Historical Committee, 1965; Sprague, Stuart Seely, ed. *His Promised Land: The Autobiography of John P. Parker, Former Slave and Conductor on the Underground Railroad.* New York: W.W. Norton & Company, 1996.

Susannah C. West

Paul, Nathaniel (1793–1839)

Born in Exeter, New Hampshire, Nathaniel Paul was an outspoken African American clergyman and abolitionist during the 1820s and 1830s. He founded the First African Baptist Church in Albany, New York, in 1820, where he served as pastor for ten years. The son of a veteran of the American Revolution, Paul adhered uncompromisingly to the republic's founding principles of liberty and equality for all. He was one of the earliest agitators for complete and **immediate emancipation**, staunchly opposing the **American Colonization Society**'s scheme for **gradual emancipation**. Throughout his career, he pursued various avenues to end slavery and racial discrimination.

Paul was instrumental in founding the nation's first African American newspaper. In 1827, spurred by racially disparaging comments from white journalists, Paul joined with other free black abolitionists including Presbyterian minister Samuel E. Cornish and Episcopal pastor Peter Williams, Jr., to establish *Freedom's Journal* (1827–1829), in New York City. As an authorized agent for the paper in Albany, New York, Paul promoted its efforts to present a black voice in the nation's debate over slavery.

Paul is probably best known for his address at Albany's First African Baptist Church on July 5, 1827, celebrating New York's official termination of slavery, which took effect on July 4, 1827. In lauding the New York legislation as a triumph "over tyranny and oppression," Paul employed religious, sometimes prophetic, language to denounce slavery as "contrary to the laws" of God. He declared that "not only throughout the United States of America, but throughout every part of the habitable world, where slavery exists, it will be abolished."

Despite his opposition to African colonization, Paul and his brother, Benjamin, moved in 1830 to Wilberforce Colony, Canada, a free black community led by former slave and Rochester businessman, Austin Steward. After a year of acting as the colony's agent and minister, Paul departed to travel throughout the British Isles, raising funds to establish a manual labor college at Wilberforce. Although his expenses exceeded the $8,000 he raised, his many lectures before thousands of people attracted attention and support from leading British and American abolitionists such as **George Thompson, Thomas Clarkson,** and **William Lloyd Garrison**. Upon his return to the United States in 1836, he continued his public antislavery work with the Albany Anti-Slavery Society and as a supporter of Cornish's new newspaper, *Colored American*.

A strong proponent of education, Paul believed that black religious, social, and moral improvement would advance the antislavery cause and weaken racial prejudice. Consequently, he devoted considerable attention to African American self-improvement efforts, becoming the first president of Albany's Union Society for the Improvement of the Colored People in Morals, Education and Mechanic Arts. In addition, Paul continued in the ministry, leading Albany's Union Street Baptist Church until his death.

Further Readings: Pease, William H. and Jane H. Pease. *Black Utopia: Negro Communal Experiments in America.* Madison: State Historical Society of Wisconsin, 1963; Quarles, Benjamin. *Black Abolitionists.* New York: Oxford University Press, 1969; Swift, David E. *Black Prophets of Justice: Activist Clergy before the Civil War.* Baton Rouge: Louisiana State University Press, 1989.

Dianne Wheaton Cappiello

Pennsylvania Abolition Society (PAS)

Founded in 1775, "The Pennsylvania Society for Promoting the Abolition of Slavery and for the Relief of Free Negroes Unlawfully Held in Bondage," also known as the Pennsylvania Abolition Society (PAS), was the world's leading antislavery organization during the early republic. Indeed, only the rise of Garrisonian reformers in the 1830s dethroned the PAS as the abolitionist vanguard in the United States. The Pennsylvania Abolition Society remains in existence today, supporting African American educational endeavors and the memory of the abolitionist struggle, among other things.

After its initial organization, the PAS lapsed during the Revolutionary War, but was revived in 1784. Reorganized in 1787, the PAS formed a constitution, created a committee system assigning specific abolitionist tasks to members (from educational activities in the free black community to raising funds among philanthropists), and organized a legal aid system for endangered blacks that became a model for other abolitionists. The group was officially incorporated by the state in 1789. According to its constitution, the PAS would "use such means as are in their power to extend the blessings of freedom to every part of the human race." The PAS's committee of correspondence communicated with abolitionists and reformers in England, France, the Caribbean, and almost every state in the American union. Indeed, under the PAS's leadership, Philadelphia became a worldwide capital of the first-wave abolitionism.

The PAS's first incarnation comprised a small group of men who wanted to expand **Quakers**' attacks on slavery. The Society of Religious Friends, commonly known as Quakers, had a long history of antislavery activism, particularly in Pennsylvania, where figures from Ralph Sandiford to **Anthony Benezet** had published consciousness-raising essays against bondage. The PAS grew from these roots, attracting support from other religious denominations as well as statesmen and governing elites. During the late-eighteenth and early-nineteenth centuries, nearly 2,000 members would officially join the PAS, and many more reformers would express sympathy with its motives. While men of standing joined the group—including America's leading statesman, **Benjamin Franklin,** who served as president of the group from 1787 to 1790; its leading doctor, **Benjamin Rush;** and its leading jurist, William Rawle—so too did tailors, middling merchants, and candle makers.

The PAS advocated gradual abolitionism, both in Pennsylvania and other states. PAS members, including **Thomas Paine,** helped pass the Quaker State's gradual abolition statute in March 1780. The first of its kind in the western world, the law outlined slavery's gradual demise in Pennsylvania: all slaves born after the law's passage would be free at twenty-eight. This statute, combined with PAS lawyers' advocacy of black rights in state and federal courts, compelled even fugitive slaves to run away to "free" Pennsylvania.

Tactically, the PAS favored action in legal and political venues rather than mass organizing of American citizens. The PAS was the first abolitionist group to issue antislavery petitions to federal institutions. In 1787, the group asked PAS member Benjamin Franklin to present an antislavery memorial to the Constitutional Convention then meeting in Philadelphia (Franklin pocketed the petition for fear of its divisive consequences). In February 1790, the PAS petitioned the first federal congress for an end to overseas slave trade and consideration of gradual abolitionism. "We have observed with great satisfaction," the petition told Congress, "that many important and salutary powers are vested in you for 'promoting the welfare' and 'securing the blessings of liberty' to the people of the United States." Such power should be aimed at slavery. The memorial infuriated Deep South slaveholders and was not acted upon by Congress. Subsequent PAS memorials were less radical in tone. Nevertheless, both on its own and as the leader of the **American Convention of Abolition Societies,** a biennial meeting of local and state abolitionist groups from 1794 to 1836, the PAS presented many other petitions to state and federal governments on subjects ranging from ending the domestic slave trade to abolishing slavery in the federally controlled District of Columbia.

The PAS had a complex relationship with Pennsylvania's free black community. On the one hand, the group rendered important aid to African Americans by finding apprenticeships for former slaves, opening schools for free blacks, and even offering business loans to black leaders such as **Richard Allen** and Absalom Jones. On the other hand, the PAS remained a segregated organization until the 1830s. The group would not ask black leaders to become fellow activists, as did **Garrisonians,** because they believed that abolitionism should be left to legal and political elites. African Americans could be helped by white abolitionists but they could not be considered coadjutors of the movement.

As slavery expanded both geographically and numerically during the nineteenth century, the PAS faced its toughest challenges. Indeed, slavery's growth in the South and Southwest offset the passage of gradual abolition laws in every Northern state. In addition, the creation and expansion of the **American Colonization Society** (or ACS, formed December 1816) allowed Northern and Southern citizens to unite behind a quasi-antislavery movement, one that pictured free blacks—and not bondage—as America's major problem. While the majority of blacks opposed the ACS, the PAS did not publicly rebuke colonizationism until the late 1820s. Although some PAS members believed that colonization would fail, others, such as well-known reformer Roberts Vaux, considered the ACS a worthy reform group.

By the 1820s and 1830s, as blacks in Philadelphia, New York, Boston, and other locales engaged in more radical forms of abolitionism (from mass pamphleteering to confrontational fugitive slave defenses), and a new generation of white reformers began embracing the doctrine of immediate abolitionism, the PAS was further marginalized. Labeled "modern" abolitionists, these new reformers included white evangelicals, black elites, and for the first time in mainstream antislavery organizations, women. Modern abolitionists formed the **American Anti-Slavery Society** (ironically in the PAS's home of Philadelphia), supported Garrison's *Liberator*, and spawned a whole new wave of local and state abolitionist societies. By the mid-1830s, the era of PAS dominance was over. "Has abolition gone defunct in Pennsylvania," some old-time activists wondered?

Still, the PAS remained active over the next several decades, with some members joining the modern abolitionist crusade (the first immediatist antislavery society appeared in Philadelphia in 1834, attracting some key PAS supporters). Other PAS members worked with fugitive slaves, became further involved in black education efforts and remained dedicated to a more moderate brand abolitionism. The group has never folded.

Though it receives little credit in contemporary histories of antislavery, the PAS was an important part of American abolitionism. During the post-Revolutionary era in particular, when many statesmen supported antislavery ideals but feared abolitionist action, the PAS attacked slavery in a highly efficient and formally organized manner. The group helped launch gradual abolitionism in Northern states and establish (with black runaways and kidnapping survivors) the concept of "free" Northern culture well before the Free Soil and Republican Parties would do so. And the group was among the first to put slavery on the federal radar via petitions against the overseas slave trade. Even Garrison would salute the PAS as among the most "thorough-going" antislavery reformers prior to the 1830s. In sum, the group formed a critical part of first-wave abolitionism. *See also* Democratic

Party and Antislavery; Gradual Emancipation; Immediate Emancipation; Radical Republicans; Whig Party and Antislavery.

Further Readings: Nash, Gary, and Jean Soderlund. *Freedom by Degrees: Emancipation and Its Aftermath in Pennsylvania.* New York: 1991; Newman, Richard S. *The Transformation of American Abolitionism: Fighting Slavery in the Early Republic.* Chapel Hill: University of North Carolina Press, 2002.

Richard Newman

Perfectionism

Perfectionism, also known as "Christian Perfection," was a religious doctrine developed in the United States in the 1830s and 1840s, which found expression in evangelical Protestant theology, social reform activism, and experimental utopian communities. Phoebe Worall Palmer, a Methodist lay preacher, proclaimed the possibility of perfect Christian love at a series of weekly, interdenominational prayer meetings in New York City in the late 1830s. Perfectionist doctrines were formulated systematically in the mid-1830s at Oberlin College by the Reverend **Charles Grandison Finney** and by Oberlin's first president, the Reverend Asa Mahan. As developed by Finney and Mahan, the doctrine of Christian perfection traced its theological origins back to the writings of John Welsey, the founder of Methodism, who first advanced the argument that devout Christians could experience a state of grace known as "perfection" or "holiness." Breaking with Martin Luther and John Calvin's views on human sinfulness, Wesley argued that God not only justified an individual by forgiving sin, but sanctified that individual, i.e., enabled that individual to be thereafter "perfectly holy," or free from sin. Drawing upon Wesley's writings, Finney laid out the basic tenets of Christian perfectionism in a series of lectures delivered in 1836 in New York City, later published as *Lectures to Professing Christians* (1837): the doctrines of "entire sanctification" and of "perfect holiness."

The scriptural foundation for the doctrine of perfection is the Gospel of Matthew 5:48, "Be ye therefore perfect, even as your Father which in heaven is perfect." For Finney, who throughout his career remained a Calvinist (meaning he remained committed to the theological doctrines associated with New England Puritanism), this scriptural passage supported a legalistic interpretation of perfection. "Sanctification is holiness," Finney lectured, "and holiness is nothing but obedience to the law." Christian perfection, accordingly, involved "perfect obedience to the law of God." The key innovation in Finney's perfectionist theology, which set him at odds with Old School Presbyterians and other ultra-orthodox Calvinists, was his assertion that through entire sanctification God provided the means by which devout Christians could meet this standard of perfect obedience.

The perfectionist doctrine that Christians could know and fully obey God's commandments led to a widespread belief that these commandments constituted a divine or transcendental **higher law** that Christians were duty-bound to obey even if it put them at odds with society's civil and criminal codes. Belief in the existence of a higher moral law led many perfectionists to participate in abolitionism and other nineteenth-century social reform movements. Taking the position that sin was entirely voluntary, many perfectionists believed both individuals and American society could be rid of all vice, corruption, and sinful behavior through moral suasion and concerted social activism. The first triumph of perfectionist social reform came with the Temperance Movement, a moral crusade against Americans' drinking habits that resulted in a dramatic decrease in the per capita consumption of alcohol. Perfectionists also identified prostitution, gambling, the penal system, and Sabbath-breaking as other pressing social problems urgently in need of reform.

Perfectionist social activism found its clearest expression in the rise in the 1830s of the abolitionist or radical antislavery movement, and in the abolitionist doctrine of "immediatism," which demanded the immediate, unconditional end of slavery. Drawing upon strands of perfectionist thought found in Quaker theology and in the peace or pacifist movement, **William Lloyd Garrison** and his abolitionist followers, known as **Garrisonians,** proclaimed slavery an absolute evil and a national sin, sought to persuade slaveholders of the irredeemable sinfulness of their actions, and condemned Northern politicians for their willingness to compromise on the issue of slavery and for supporting half-hearted antislavery reforms like **gradual emancipation** and the **American Colonization Society**. By the late 1830s, however, leading antislavery perfectionists like **Gerrit Smith** became frustrated with the Garrisonians' inability to effect decisive social change through moral suasion. Turning to politics, antislavery perfectionists founded the **Liberty Party** and nominated **James G. Birney** as the Party's presidential candidate in the elections of 1840 and 1844.

Other perfectionists, believing the social ills and moral corruption occasioned by the Market Revolution placed the nation beyond hope of reform, turned away from American society and founded experimental utopian communities. The best-known and longest-lived perfectionist commune, the Oneida Community, was established in 1847 by John Humphrey Noyes. Ordained a Congregationalist minister after attending Yale Divinity School, Noyes' license to preach was revoked in 1834 after he proclaimed that he had "received the holy spirit," and therefore was free from sin. Over the next decade Noyes refined his radical perfectionist vision in periodicals like the widely read *Perfectionist*, and in correspondence with other perfectionists like Charles Grandison Finney and Gerrit Smith. After receiving a large inheritance from his father, Noyes established a perfectionist community in 1843 in his hometown of Putney, New York. The Putney and Oneida communities are best known for Noyes's controversial doctrine of "complex marriage," which rejected the sanctity of monogamous marriage, and mandated sexual relations between adult male and female members of the community. Scandalous at the time, Noyes's unorthodox views on sexual relations were in fact consistent with his socialist interpretation of perfectionist doctrine, which he termed "biblical communism," and which critics descried as "Antinomian Perfectionism." Asserting a "higher law of perfection," Noyes declared that neither he nor other community members were bound by or obligated to respect society's civil codes or traditional Protestant interpretations of Scripture.

Noyes's relation to the abolitionist movement was complex and ambiguous. Evidence suggests that Noyes influenced Garrison's views on immediatism and non-resistance. Noyes also praised the formation of the Liberty Party, denounced Southern malfeasance during the Kansas-Nebraska Crisis and condemned the Supreme Court decision in the Dred Scott case. Yet Noyes later criticized Garrison and John Brown for inciting the reactionary violence that assailed the abolitionist movement. Like other perfectionists and utopian reformers influenced in whole or in part by the doctrine of **come-outerism,** Noyes's ultimate concern was the spiritual regeneration of the individual rather than the institutional reform of society. *See also* Antislavery Evangelical Protestantism; Bible and Slavery; Congregationalism and Antislavery; Immediate Emancipation; Methodists and Antislavery; Millennialism and Abolitionism.

Further Readings: Flew, R.N. *The Idea of Perfection in Christian Theology: A Historical Study of the Christian Ideal for the Present Life*. London: Oxford University Press, 1934; Jones, Charles Edwin. *Perfectionist Persuasion: The Holiness Movement and American Methodism, 1867–1936*. Metuchen, NJ: Scarecrow Press, 1974; Klaw, Spencer. *Without Sin: The Life and Death of the Oneida Community*. New York: Allen Lane, 1993; Passmore, John. *The Perfectibility of Man*. London: Duckworth, 1970; Thomas, Robert Davis. *The Man Who Would Be Perfect: John Humphrey Noyes and the Utopian Impulse*. Philadelphia: The University of Pennsylvania Press, 1977.

Neil Brody Miller

Phillips, Wendell (1811–1884)

One of the most effective and influential abolitionist orators of the nineteenth century, Wendell Phillips was born on November 9, 1811 as the eighth child of John Phillips, a wealthy lawyer, politician, and philanthropist, and Sarah Walley. His family occupied the highest caste in Boston, tracing their North American roots back to early seventeenth-century Salem, Massachusetts.

First educated at the Boston Latin School, Phillips later attended Harvard and graduated in 1831. Although he harbored an interest in studying history, he was recognized as a skilled debater and carried that talent with him to Harvard Law School. A Boston attorney and member of the Suffolk County bar, Phillips quickly grew bored with the legal profession.

In Ann Terry Greene, Phillips found both a wife and a vocation. Ann was the daughter and heir to one of Boston's wealthiest families, and a political radical. She was an avowed abolitionist, a supporter of antislavery newspaper editor **William Lloyd Garrison,** and a member of the Boston Female Anti-Slavery Society. Phillips followed her both down the aisle and into the ranks of Boston's abolitionists, dedicating himself to the cause at a March 1837 meeting of the Massachusetts Anti-Slavery Society. He was married on October 12, 1837, and only weeks later found the voice that would define his career.

Phillips' revealed his oratorical powers at a critical moment in the antislavery movement. In Alton, Illinois, on November 7, 1837, a proslavery mob murdered abolitionist newspaper editor **Elijah P. Lovejoy** and destroyed his printing press. Barricaded in the warehouse where he had hidden a new press—three others had been thrown into the nearby Mississippi River—Lovejoy was killed when he tried to prevent the mob from setting fire to the building. Word of the event electrified anti- and proslavery activists, and a month later, on December 7, Phillips attended a heated meeting at Faneuil Hall in Boston to discuss the case. What he heard enraged him. James T. Austin, the Massachusetts attorney general, denounced Lovejoy and compared the murderous mob to the Revolutionary War patriots who threw off British rule in 1776. For Phillips, this was too much; at the urging of friends, he rose with a spontaneous address celebrating Lovejoy's intrepid resistance. The gathered crowd was stunned by Phillips's clarity and eloquence, and thus, at the age of twenty-six, Phillips thrust himself to the forefront of the antislavery movement.

Following that debut, Phillips became a confidant of Garrison. The two saw abolitionism as a larger cause that embraced women's rights, rejected religious denominations, and was set apart from politics itself. Like Garrison, Phillips believed that the partisan electoral system was tainted by slavery; to be successful, abolitionism would have to be radical and revolutionary. He was even more hostile to proslavery forces than Garrison, dissenting from the latter's pacifism. For Phillips, a war against slavery would be a just war.

In 1840, Phillips and his wife were traveling in Europe where they attended the **World's Anti-Slavery Convention** in London as representatives of the **American Anti-Slavery Society**. Hoping to win support from British abolitionists for their movement, they were disappointed by their inability to convince the international gathering to allow women to vote at the event. The couple's failure in Britain demonstrated that a trans-Atlantic abolitionist movement would be less radical and more conventional than what Garrison and his cohort sought. Mainstream abolitionism continued to work through elections and politics to achieve its ends; Garrison, Phillips, and their associates continued to pursue a broader and more ideological reform agenda.

Throughout the 1840s and 1850s, Phillips continued to be at Garrison's side, professing before audiences the sentiments Garrison conveyed in print. Among his other writings, he penned two pamphlets on the defects of American politics: *The Constitution—A Proslavery Document* (1842), and *Can an Abolitionist Vote or Hold Office under the United States Constitution?* (1843). Both pamphlets laid out the Garrison-Phillips argument that abolitionists who continued to be involved in American politics were coconspirators in a corrupt system. The **United States Constitution,** as he saw it, was inherently proslavery.

Despite his power as a public speaker, Phillips also engaged in social reforms and civil disobedience in the cause of racial equality and abolition. He was a member of the executive committee of the American Anti-Slavery Society and the Boston Vigilance Committee; in the latter capacity, he helped protect fugitive slaves from capture in Boston after the passage of the 1850 **Fugitive Slave Law**. He also worked to overturn segregation in the city's public schools. Phillips wanted such activities to heighten, rather than assuage, the growing tensions between free and slave states. Agitation, he believed, could eventually split the Union; years before any slave states contemplated secession, Phillips advocated that Northern states peel away from the United States, leaving only the slaveholding states behind.

Phillips made this case throughout the 1850s, touring as a lecturer who delighted audiences with discourses on all kinds of topics, from natural science to the arts and architecture. But most came to hear him discuss slavery, blending his quick wit and accessible style with his uncompromising platform. He traveled throughout the northeastern and mid-western United States, never using a script, lending rhetorical support to the increasingly confrontational tactics of antislavery activists like the Free Soilers in Kansas, John Brown's followers at Harpers Ferry, and those who spirited away fugitives.

When war came, however, Phillips reversed his course. While supportive of the idea of Northern states seceding to escape slavery, he was now unwilling to permit Southern states to leave the Union to protect their peculiar institution. Demanding war and the return of the slave states, Phillips became one of the most radical of Republicans during the **Lincoln** Administration. He wanted the war to be about slavery, a radical revolutionary conflict that would result in emancipation and aggressive land redistribution in the South.

Parting ways with Garrison after the war, Phillips did not view emancipation as the endpoint of the abolitionist struggle. Reconstruction represented a new beginning, and in 1865 Phillips succeeded Garrison as president of the American Anti-Slavery Society. He served in that position until 1870, when the Fifteenth Amendment was passed.

In that year, Phillips ran for governor of Massachusetts as the candidate of both the Labor Reform and Prohibitionist Parties, garnering 20,000 votes. Phillips continued his activism on behalf of freed African Americans and began to speak out on issues of labor relations. In 1871, he supported former Civil War General Benjamin Butler's candidacy for governor of Massachusetts. In public, he called for eight-hour workdays and cooperative workplaces. Phillips made his last public speech on December 26, 1883 and died on February 2, 1884. *See also* Bleeding Kansas; Radical Republicans; Underground Railroad.

Further Readings: Bartlett, Irving. *Wendell Phillips: Brahmin Radical*. Westport, CT: Greenwood Press, 1973. Originally published in 1961; Stewart, James Brewer. *Wendell Phillips: Liberty's Hero*. Reprint ed. Baton Rouge: Louisiana State University Press, 1998.

Brian Murphy

Pitt, William, the Younger (1759–1806)

William Pitt was born in 1759, the second son of his famous father of the same name. The elder William Pitt was the legendary prime minister who, in the year of his son's birth, had secured victories for England in America, India, and the West Indies, thus creating a much enlarged British Empire and subduing its French rival. Known as the "Great Commoner," he tended to favor conciliation with the colonies, but failed to avert conflict with

America when he became prime minister again in 1766. Given the title Earl of Chatham, he suffered from mental instability, collapsed in the House of Lords in 1778, and died shortly thereafter. Neither the younger Pitt nor his contemporaries ever forgot the example of the elder Pitt. Educated at home, he went to Cambridge at the age of fourteen, and then attended law school at the Inns of Court in London.

Following his father's lead, Pitt entered Parliament and, in a stunning move, King George III appointed him prime minister at the age of twenty-four; he remained in this post, with one short intermission, until his death in 1806. He is frequently credited with having revived England after the debacle of the American Revolution and the bitter factional politics that followed it.

Pitt quickly gained esteem as an expert government manager and economist. At the same time he was also regarded as a reformer because of his stand on a number of issues. For example, he improved the operation of the East India Company, tried unsuccessfully to bring about reform of parliamentary constituencies, and failed in his attempt to establish Catholic Emancipation. Pitt's concern for reform was considerable; in particular, he was dedicated to ending the slave trade and abolishing slavery. In 1787, Pitt appointed his close friend, the prominent opponent of slavery, **William Wilberforce,** as head of the antislavery movement in Parliament.

Pitt also spoke openly in support of antislavery in the House of Commons. For instance, in 1788, Pitt presented a motion for an end to the slave trade. The motion was passed, but its opponents managed to place such obstacles in its path that it never took effect. Wilberforce proposed antislavery bills annually, and in 1792 Pitt gave a powerful speech on abolition. Many contemporaries (and later historians) considered this to have been among the greatest orations the prime minister ever gave. Pitt made it clear in his address that he would issue a sustained attack on slavery, arguing against the assumption that Africans were ill-suited to civilization and could not rise above the status of a slave, which, as he pointed out, was the same thing Romans had said about ancient Britons. Yet, just as the British had shown the capacity to move beyond their early culture, so the African slaves, given the right circumstances, could emerge into a similarly higher civilization.

Pitt continued to support antislavery measures until his death in 1806, a year before the abolition of the slave trade. Some abolitionists believed that he was only half-hearted in this support for their cause because he never made it a government bill. Yet his defenders argue that such a radical action could have caused the demise of his cabinet. It is clear, however, that his actions did much to keep the antislavery cause alive. *See also* Atlantic Slave Trade and British Abolition; British Slavery, Abolition of.

Further Readings: Derry, John W. *Politics in the Age of Fox, Pitt, and Liverpool.* New York: Palgrave, 2001; Duffy, Michael. *The Younger Pitt.* New York: Longman, 2000; Hague, William. *William Pitt the Younger.* London: HarperCollins, 2004; Oldfield, J.R. *Popular Politics and British Anti-Slavery: The Mobilisation of Public Opinion against the Slave Trade, 1787–1807.* New York: St. Martin's Press, 1995; Turner, Michael J. *Pitt the Younger.* London: Hambledon and London, 2003.

Marc L. Schwarz

Plato (c. 427–c. 347 B.C.E.)

Plato, the Athenian philosopher and founder of the school called the Academy, made a major contribution to Western thought. Although he never endorses the abolition of slavery, his philosophy is based to a considerable extent on the value of individual thought, upon the questioning of conventional assumptions, and upon the rejection of tyranny; thus his philosophy provides an ethical paradigm which by its very nature challenges the premises underlying the institution of slavery. Plato was the teacher of **Aristotle,** and the precise points of agreement and disagreement between the two philosophers have been argued about for over twenty-three centuries.

Plato was descended from the old aristocracy of his native city. He is reported to have been persuaded by Socrates to abandon the composition of dramatic poetry in favor of philosophy. After the execution of his beloved teacher Socrates in 399, Plato remained a student of philosophy, and his teaching is delineated, sometimes subtly, in the dialogues he wrote, many of them featuring Socrates as principal interlocutor, representing in more or less dramatic form the rhetorical and dialectical discussion of philosophical issues.

Though slavery was a normal part of life in classical Athens, where, as elsewhere in Greece, there prevailed a pragmatic acceptance of the rights conveyed by possession of superior power, Plato's dialogues are based upon a concept that undermined arbitrary authority. The remarkable power of Socratic argument is often found to be irresistible, and, though Socrates possessed neither wealth nor political power, he is conspicuously superior to many of those who confront him. Socrates' oft-repeated assertion that he merely sought the truth (as he demolished one conventional belief after another) posed a challenge to all arbitrary social conventions.

In the Platonic dialogue *Meno*, Socrates engages in a demonstration of a geometric proof simply by questioning a slave. He asks the right questions, and the slave provides the correct answers, and though Socrates goes on to argue from the slave's apt responses that knowledge must be a matter of recollection, clearly he has demonstrated as well that the potential of one human being is very much like that of another, a result which makes slavery one of the kinds of convention that Socrates' truth-seeking method tends to threaten. This disregard for convention infuriated many Athenians, particularly those who enjoyed a status enhanced by these socially and politically protected institutions, and eventually led to Socrates' indictment and execution.

Two other major Platonic dialogues also reckoned with slavery. The *Republic*, which described a conversation in which Socrates and two of Plato's brothers attempt to define justice by describing a hypothetical just city, seems to maintain that considerable restrictions of individual liberty—possibly intended to suggest those of Spartan life—are necessary for a city's survival. At the same time, however, the dialogue argues that the perfection of the city can only occur if philosophers are in charge, which suggests the political desirability of a wise harmony between *nomos* ("convention" or "law") and *physis* ("nature"). Within the just city proposed by Socrates and his friends, one law will forbid the enslavement of Greeks by other Greeks (Book V), and, though the immediate rationale for this prohibition is that the Greeks should remain united against the threat posed by the non-Greeks (*barbaroi*), the argument suggests that a critical examination of the convention of slavery is fitting and proper.

The *Laws*, written late in Plato's life, set forth another perhaps more practical model régime. As background for the construction of this model, the speaker, the Athenian, described Persia, the great military power that had forced the independent Greek city-states to band together to resist its military power, as a nation in which slavery had been taken to an extreme. Athens, according to the Athenian, had taken freedom to an equally undesirable extreme (Book III). Though this dialogue included some theoretical legislation which stipulated cruel penalties for disobedient slaves, it also suggested a certain underlying sophistication of terminology, for the Athenian nostalgically refers to the past as a better time when his fellow citizens were "willing slaves of the laws," a phrase which almost invites reconsideration of the concept of slavery, since "laws" (*nomoi*) are also conventions. But such subtlety, which characterized many points in Platonic discourse, remains matter for interpretation, and slavery in Plato never met a direct challenge.

Plato himself, according to one story, may have been enslaved for a while. He had gone to Syracuse to give political guidance to the tyrant Dionysius I. The tyrant, however, soon found Plato's independence of mind so objectionable that he arrested the philosopher and had him sold into slavery. Friends soon had him liberated.

The importance of Plato's thought on slavery is evident in the works of several great philosophers from antiquity. Socrates, much of whose influence in subsequent philosophy derives from Plato's account of him, was also a paradigm for such groups as the Cynics and the Stoics. Both of these groups valued personal freedom highly although measured it in somewhat different ways. The Stoic Epictetus, in the Roman era, was a freed slave who asserted that the freedom of his own intellect was within his own power. A key Stoic maxim which stated that the good are always free while the evil are always slaves demonstrated an important figurative development of the concepts of freedom and slavery. Plato also influenced Aristotle whose *Politics*, where he argued that some people are slaves by nature, discussed many issues raised in Platonic works. *See also* Classical Greek Antislavery.

Further Readings: Klein, Jacob. *A Commentary on Plato's Meno.* Chapel Hill: University of North Carolina Press, 1965; Plato. *Laws.* In Edith Hamilton and Huntington Cairns, eds., *The Collected Dialogues of Plato.* Bollingen Series 71. Princeton, NJ: Princeton University Press, 1961, pp. 1225–1513; Plato. *Republic.* In Edith Hamilton and Huntington Cairns, eds. *The Collected Dialogues of Plato.* Bollingen Series 71. Princeton, NJ: Princeton University Press, 1961, pp. 575–844.

Robert W. Haynes

Pointe Coupée Rebellion (1795)

The settlement of Pointe Coupée, located 150 miles north of New Orleans, was founded by French settlers in 1717. It remained a small, isolated frontier post for most of the French period. From the start, racial intermixture was prevalent in Pointe Coupée, and for a long time its slave population did not experience any marked developments. The slaves in Pointe Coupée numbered a mere 70 in 1731 and about 400 in the 1740s. In the Spanish period, however, its slave population increased, especially in the 1780s when the reexport trade in African slaves from Jamaica and Dominica reached its apogee. More than 4,000 slaves, many from the Bight of Biafra and most of them men, arrived in Louisiana from those two islands in the 1780s. The slave population reached the number of 1,500 in 1788 and about 1,600 in 1797. Both the 1788 and the 1797 censuses indicate a ratio of approximately one white settler for every three slaves. With an influx of Africans from both the Atlantic and Caribbean slave trades, the average number of slaves on plantations increased, which resulted in very imbalanced sex ratios, which in turn augmented the possibilities for resistance. The Pointe Coupée plantation was also unusually large for Louisiana.

While Pointe Coupée was not a slave society on the scale of Saint Domingue, many a planter there could only understand the attempted rebellion in 1795 in Pointe Coupée as the narrowly averted replica of the 1791 slave rebellion on the island. "If our information is correct, the Saint Domingue insurrection did not have a more violent beginning," argued one planter to the New Orleans Cabildo, the municipal body of representatives. If the secret dealings of the conspiracy had not been disclosed, it was believed that the rebel slaves would have reenacted the ceremony of the Bois Caïman, behind the plantation of Jacques Vignes at False River, and would have set fire to the Poydras Plantation, raided its ammunition store, killed all white men, unsupportive creoles and other slaves, before seizing the white women and fleeing. The planned rebellion of 1791 contrasted in scope and intensity with the slave plot that had been discovered at the Pointe Coupée. Slave involvement in the 1791 slave plot was much more limited and it also suffered from ethnic tensions between African and creole slaves. The plot leaders, among whom was Cesar, a Jamaican slave, were liberated a few years later, and the scale of the repression was very limited indeed.

On the contrary, the 1795 plot in Louisiana came to the attention of the Spanish authorities in the early days of April, after months of preparation that had taken slave leaders from one plantation to another trying to enlist fellow slaves and free people of color. Less than two months later, fifty-seven slaves were found guilty of having prepared a rebellion. Twenty-three were executed, their heads placed on pikes across Lower Louisiana to impress slaves into submission. Two free people of color were also convicted of involvement, as were three white men. Joseph Bouyavel, a Walloon teacher, was one of them. The fact that he had in his possession a copy of the *Declaration of the Rights of Man* was enough to raise the specter of Saint Domingue in most planters' eyes. Between the discovery of the plot and the execution of the convicted slaves, the planters' dread led them to exercise fierce and arbitrary power: slave patrols were sent to search for weapons in and around the plantations of Pointe Coupée and in other rural districts, and regular troops were called in for help, as hysteria spread across lower Louisiana.

The rebellion was centered on the heavily African plantation of Julien Poydras. Antoine Sarrasin, a mulatto driver, or *commandeur*, who belonged to the plantation, was one of the leaders of the conspiracy. The other leaders included Grand Joseph, Antoine, Philipe, and Baptiste who belonged to Colin Lacour and the widow Lacour. But the conspiracy spread to several other plantations and included slaves from different African ethnic groups as well as creole slaves, lower-class non-slaveholding whites, and free people of color. As Governor Carondelet remarked, "all appearances indicate that all the slaves from Pointe Coupée to the capital ... had knowledge of what was going on there." Like four years earlier, a Jamaican creole slave was among the leaders. Because of their noted history of resistance, Jamaican slaves were regarded by Louisiana planters as prone to rebellion, just as much as slaves from Le Cap in Saint Domingue.

In the past fifteen years, the many myths of Pointe Coupée that had deprived slaves of their agency in the conspiracy have been finally debunked. The Pointe Coupée slave rebellion is now broadly understood in two ways. It is, on the one hand, described as a multi-racial, cross-ethnic and universalist, abolitionist movement modeled after the Saint Domingue slave rebellion and directly inspired by the ideology of the rights of man. The conspiracy was discovered only four years after the outbreak of the Saint Domingue slave revolution, only three years after free people of color were given full civil and political rights in Saint Domingue, and just one year after slavery was abolished by the French Convention. Louisiana may have been a marginal colony within the Spanish Empire, but the winds of the revolutions blew in its direction and slaves heard and read about such upheavals. One of the rumors that motivated the conspirators was that slaveholders had concealed news of their freedom. According to this model of interpretation, the conspiracy, if it had gone through, would have rapidly spread from Pointe Coupée to Natchitoches, Opelousas, the German coast, and New Orleans, making it a cross-regional and not just a parochial affair. It is thought that slaves received the support of lower-class white Jacobins, many of them sailors and soldiers. Traditionally, the conspiracy has been interpreted as a simple story of brutal slave control leading to slave rebellion in which few slaves actually participated and the scope of which should not be exaggerated, certainly not to the point of understanding it as a widespread movement of abolition that crossed boundaries of race, class, and ethnicity. If one looks at the conspiracy from this angle, slave unrest was mostly centered on Pointe Coupée and hardly concerned the outlying areas. The plot is thus seen either through the lengthy and at times contradictory correspondence of the Spanish authorities and planters or through the eyes of the slaves they interrogated.

Some uncertainty still lingers as to what the plot really amounted to, but it was, in the end, a clear example of overt slave resistance and more importantly, a potent attempt to impose, by force, the abolition of slavery in a disproportionately slave-dominated, isolated frontier region of Spanish Louisiana. *See also* Saint Domingue, French Defeat in; German Coast (Louisiana) Insurrection of 1811.

Further Readings: Aptheker, Herbert. *American Negro Slave Revolts*, 5th ed., New York: Columbia University Press, 1987; Din, Gilbert C. *Spaniards, Planters and Slaves: The Spanish Regulation of Slavery in Louisiana, 1763–1803*, College Station: Texas A&M University Press, 1999; Hall, Gwendolyn Midlo. *Africans in Colonial Louisiana. The Development of Afro-Creole Culture in the 18th Century*, Baton Rouge: Louisiana State University Press, 1992; Holmes, Jack D. "The Abortive Slave Revolt at Pointe Coupée, Louisiana, 1795." *Louisiana History* 10 (Spring 1969): 97–124; Ingersoll, Thomas. *Mammon and Manon in Early New Orleans. The First Slave Society in the Deep South, 1718–1819*. Knoxville: University of Tennessee Press, 1999.

Jean-Pierre Le Glaunec

Port Royal (South Carolina)

One of the oldest place names on the eastern coast of North America, Port Royal is an important site in the history of New World slavery. In 1562, Jean Ribaut, while seeking a haven for French Huguenots in the New World, sailed into a broad harbor on the coast of South Carolina and named it Port Royal. Since then, the name has applied to the region, to the harbor, to an island, a river, and a town.

As a region, Port Royal includes the Sea Islands of South Carolina. The Sea Islands were one of the great incubators of the Gullah culture that combines elements of several African cultures with those of Europe. Thousands of African slaves from Senegambia, Angola, and other parts of Africa came to the Sea Islands to grow indigo, cultivate rice, and produce the famed Sea Island cotton. Living isolated lives away from commercial centers, the Sea Island slaves developed their own language, arts and culture.

The harbor and river of Port Royal were the training grounds for African American pilots and sailors. African Americans not only produced the staples that made white Beaufortonians rich, but they also took the crops to markets in Charleston and Savannah. In the first decades of European settlement in the region, these waterways were escape routes for hundreds of slaves who fled to St. Augustine. So many slaves fled South Carolina that the Spanish officials allowed them to settle and govern their own town—Garcia Real de Santa Teresa de Mosa north of St. Augustine. The settlement was the site of a major defeat for Carolina troops during General James Oglethorpe's siege of Saint Augustine in 1740.

The Sea Islands were also home to the "Port Royal Experiment"—an effort to transform the lives of the former slaves through education and religion. After the surrender of Forts Beauregard and Walker, federal troops occupied the Sea Islands in 1862. One of their immediate challenges was to care for the slaves who lived in the area, as well as the thousands of others who fled to the Union lines for freedom. A public-private response involved abolitionist teachers and preachers from Pennsylvania, Massachusetts, and other Northern states who came South and opened schools for the freedmen. Later, the **Freedmen's Bureau** provided housing and food, negotiated labor contracts, and tried to reconnect broken families. A few fortunate freedmen acquired land and many became successful farmers, craftsmen, and small businessmen.

One of the first schools founded during the Port Royal Experiment was the Penn School on St. Helena Island. This school trained and educated African Americans in the Port Royal area for decades. Today, it continues its mission as the Penn Community Center.

The Sea Islands, with their large African American majorities, were politically significant during Reconstruction. Robert Smalls of Beaufort served as a U.S. Congressman and was a member of both the South Carolina Constitutional Conventions of 1868 and 1895. He remained a political power in the region until his death. The Carolina low country was the last bastion of black power in the state.

The island of Port Royal was the site of Old Fort Plantation. From there on New Year's Day 1863, the Reverend William Brisbane read the Emancipation Proclamation to thousands of freedmen with great ceremony. Also, the Reverend Mansfield French presented regimental colors to the First Regiment of South Carolina Volunteers, a troop of freedmen who had enlisted in the Union army. The First Regiment of South Carolina Volunteers, later known as the 33rd U.S. Colored, was the first African American regiment commissioned during the Civil War. Federal forces raised both the First and Second South Carolina Regiments in the Port Royal area. Therefore, the Port Royal region and name have deep, multifaceted significance for the history of slavery and African Americans. *See also* African American Communities.

Further Readings: Helsley, Alexia Jones. *Beaufort, South Carolina: A History.* Charleston: The History Press, 2005; Rose, Willie Lee. *Rehearsal for Reconstruction: The Port Royal Experiment.* New York: Oxford University Press, 1964; Rowland, Lawrence S., et al. *History of Beaufort County, South Carolina.* Vol. 1, *1514–1861.* Columbia: University of South Carolina Press, 1996.

Alexia Helsley

Portuguese Colonies, Abolition in

Portugal had reached an abolition agreement with Britain as early as 1815, although that agreement allowed Portugal to continue its slave trade in the Southern Hemisphere. This began a tragic series of decrees that declared the abolition of slavery in Portuguese colonies, but never actually abolished the institution.

Due to its dependence on the Angolan slave trade, Portugal's decision to abolish the slave trade entirely came quite late, being delivered only in 1836. For several decades the prohibition went unenforced. Citing fears of political unrest and the lack of reliable access to inland areas, Portugal was particularly slow to support abolition even following a variety of official abolition decrees.

Initially the continuation of the slave trade in Portuguese colonies was tied to ongoing trade with Brazil, which was a Portuguese colony until 1822. In Brazil the demand for slaves remained high into the late-nineteenth century, and throughout that time Portugal relied on the economic network with Angola and Brazil. Although Brazil abolished the slave trade in 1850, slavery remained legal until the "Golden Law" of 1888 abolished slavery itself, making Brazil the last country in the Western Hemisphere to do so officially.

Slave market at Rio de Janeiro, Brazil. Courtesy of the Library of Congress.

Portuguese and Brazilian slave ships traveled unhindered from African coastal settlements until as late as 1845. Lacking local naval bases, as it had secured in West Africa, the Royal Navy was ineffective in searching ships traveling from Portuguese southern African ports until the late 1800s. Overall British naval efforts represented a stunning failure, as they managed to rescue only around 3,000 slaves per year. At the same time, an estimated two million slaves were transported from the western coasts of Africa in the decades just before and just after 1850.

Angola built its overseas commerce almost entirely on slave trading, and given Portugal's reliance on Angolan revenues, there was little movement from the colonial rulers to enforce abolition. Slave shipments from the ports of Luanda and Benguela on the Angolan coast continued until the late 1860s, with Portuguese, Brazilian, and Cuban slave traders replacing British and French merchants. Despite passage of an 1842 treaty with Britain that declared the trade to be piracy, the slave trade from Angola was continued with shipments going to Brazil until around 1853 and to Cuba into the 1860s. Exports only began to decline, not by any prohibition from Portugal, but with the closure of Brazilian slave markets. Even with this, however, the trade continued with slave shipments from Angola to the island colonies of Sao Tome and Principe. These shipments continued for decades, hiding behind the guise of "contract labor" to elude external pressure against the trade.

Other Portuguese colonies, however, did not experience the cessation of the external slave trade that occurred in Angola. The slave trade from

Mozambique, for example, while being reduced in numbers, continued as that colony's slave exports were simply redirected towards the networks of the Indian Ocean. Thus slaves from Mozambique were forced into the unacknowledged slavery of contract labor systems in French sugar planting colonies or the slave markets of eastern Africa. This shift in Mozambique's slave trade from an Atlantic to an eastern orientation would continue until the last decades of the 1800s. The use of slaves from Mozambique as contract labor on French plantations lasted until Napoleon III abolished the practice by a decree in 1864.

A Portuguese decree of 1869 and a later decree of 1875 sought the complete abolition of slavery, not simply the external trade. The problem of enforcement remained, however, and with the exception of decreased activities in some Angolan coastal towns, slave trade continued. Merchants and slave dealers who opposed the abolition of slavery as an institution actively resisted the decrees from Portugal and other supporters of the decision to end the external slave trade.

Even though slavery was finally abolished officially in 1878, many Africans continued to suffer as slaves under the ongoing programs of contract, and increasingly forced, labor. Many freed slaves had few options but to remain with their former owners under conditions that were largely unchanged. Others who attempted to maintain small farms were pushed into forced labor, especially through the use of taxes, in order to satisfy the demand for cheap labor. Many of the labor contractors or local authorities were former slave traders. The extensive use of vagrancy laws meant that any Africans not regularly employed could be drafted into contract labor or forced to work without remuneration. Under these programs unacknowledged slavery and the slave trade continued into the twentieth century. *See also* Africa, Antislavery in; Africa, Emancipation in; Atlantic Slave Trade and British Abolition; Nabuco, Joaquim and Abolition in Brazil.

Further Readings: Martin, Phyllis. *Historical Dictionary of Angola.* Metuchen, NJ: Scarecrow Press, 1980; Miers, Suzanne, and Richard Roberts, eds. *The End of Slavery in Africa.* Madison: University of Wisconsin Press, 1988; Miller, Joseph C. *Way of Death: Merchant Capitalism and the Angolan Slave Trade 1730–1830.* London: James Currey, 1988; Minter, William. *Portuguese Africa and the West.* Harmondsworth, England: Penguin Books, 1972.

Jeff Shantz

Postal Campaign (1835)

In May 1835, at the second annual meeting of the **American Anti-Slavery Society** (AASS), AASS Publications Committee Chair **Lewis Tappan** announced an aggressive campaign to deliver each week issues of the society's four publications to social and political leaders throughout the United States. Tappan called upon abolitionists throughout the country, including especially women and children, to donate generously toward the cost of publishing and mailing AASS materials through the federal mails to "*inquiring, candid, reading* men" who had not yet embraced the message of immediate emancipation. Although the Society targeted religious leaders, educators, businessmen, and politicians throughout the nation, the campaign was designed especially to reach leaders in the Southern states who might throw their influence behind abolition.

Tappan and editor Elizur Wright, Jr., who orchestrated much of the great postal campaign, counted upon a certain degree of violent opposition to help put their cause at the forefront of national attention. As Wright stated in the first issue of the serial *Human Rights*, published in July 1835, "If you wish to draw off the people from a mad or wicked custom ... you must make an excitement, do something that everybody will notice." During the following year, the AASS mailed more than one million pieces of antislavery literature to post offices throughout the nation, triggering a public outcry against abolitionism that far exceeded their expectations. The postal campaign was premised upon the mistaken assumption that antislavery sentiment ran wide and deep within the Christian public, including Southern churches, and that a determined appeal to Christian conscience would persuade many leaders to ally themselves with the cause of the slave. Instead AASS leaders found themselves vilified in both Northern and Southern states as advocates of disunion and racial war. Although free blacks were not on the AASS mailing list, it was widely rumored that they were the chief target of abolitionist organizing efforts, leading to a spate of new state laws to police free negroes and demands for more vigorous enforcement of existing race laws.

The postal campaign triggered a dramatic rise in antiabolitionist violence during the summer of 1835. Almost every major city in the nation saw antiabolitionist rallies and torchlight parades. News of mobs and antiabolitionist speeches filled the newspapers each day. In both North and South, pastors took to their pulpits to denounce abolitionists as irresponsible incendiaries who deserved to be censured by the public and prosecuted by the government for crimes against humanity. In many towns, committees formed to inspect the mails and destroy offensive abolitionist literature, an action that Postmaster General Amos Kendall virtually endorsed. On July 29, 1835, a mob broke into the Charleston, South Carolina, post office and carried off recently arrived mailbags filled with AASS literature. Identifying themselves with the patriots of the Boston Tea Party in 1773, the following night the thieves held a rally on the Charleston parade grounds attended by over 2,000 citizens, who watched approvingly as the abolitionist mail was burned beneath a large mock gallows where antislavery leaders hung in effigy. A grand jury in Virginia indicted and demanded the extradition of all officers of the AASS, while many Southern vigilance committees offered large bounties to anyone who would deliver prominent AASS officers to them dead or alive.

The postal campaign was a defining moment in the history of antislavery. The campaign helped to drive a wedge between more conservative churchmen and those who wished to see the evangelical churches align themselves with the cause of emancipation. The concerted opposition to the campaign across the nation and the virtually universal condemnation expressed by Southern citizens underscored the futility of antislavery tactics based upon moral suasion and helped to provide impetus to political approaches to the problem. Just as importantly, the violence sparked by the postal campaign succeeded in making the abolitionist cause a topic of daily conversation. According to Elizur Wright, Jr. the violence directed at the AASS did more to advance the cause of antislavery than the arguments of 1,000 agents could have accomplished. Between May 1835 and May 1836, more than 15,000 people subscribed to AASS publications and the number of AASS auxiliaries grew from 200 to 527 chapters. Abolitionism could never again be dismissed as a fringe movement.

Further Readings: Richards, Leonard D. *"Gentlemen of Property and Standing." Anti-Abolition Mobs in Jacksonian America.* New York: Oxford University Press, 1970; Snay, Mitchell. *Gospel of Disunion: Religion and Separatism in the Antebellum South.* New York: Cambridge University Press, 1993; Wyatt-Brown, Bertram. *Lewis Tappan and the Evangelical War Against Slavery.* New York: Atheneum, 1971; Wyly-Jones, Susan. "The 1835 Anti-Abolition Meetings in the South: A New Look at the Controversy Over the Abolition Postal Campaign." *Civil War History* 47 (2001): 289–309.

James R. Rohrer

Prince, Mary (c. 1788–c. 1833)

Mary Prince was a West Indian slave, born about 1788 in Bermuda, a British colony. Prince's mother was a household slave and her father was an enslaved workman. She had seven brothers and three sisters, who like herself, would all be sold into slavery. Her autobiography, *The History of Mary Prince, A West Indian Slave, Related by Herself*, was published in London and Edinburgh in 1831. *History* detailed the life of Prince under the consecutive ownership of Charles Myners, the Williams family, Captain I—, Mr. D—, and the Woodses. Legally considered property of these various slaveholders, Prince would experience physical and psychological abuse. Her narrative exposed the brutalities of colonial slavery and was critical in the struggle to rally the British populace for the abolition of slavery in the British colonies.

In 1826, Prince traveled with her last owners, the Woodses, from Antigua to England where they journeyed to retrieve their daughters from school and enroll their son in school. At her own request, Prince accompanied the Woodses on the trip. During the sea voyage, Prince had been unable to fulfill the demanding laundry duties Mrs. Woods assigned her. After continual mistreatment, abuse, and being threatened with expulsion from the Woods' home after they had reached England, she fled, realizing that, in England, her status as their slave had no validity. Aided by Mash (a shoe black), **Moravian** missionaries, and the **Anti-Slavery Society,** Prince found sporadic work and sought to attain her freedom in Antigua. In 1829, she was employed as a domestic servant by Thomas Pringle, the secretary of the Anti-Slavery Society. Under the employment of Pringle, Prince suggested that her history be recorded.

Prince, unable to read or write, required assistance to compose her autobiography. A guest in the Pringle home, Susanna Strickland, transcribed *History* truthfully and without embellishment. Pringle would edit *History*.

Invested in preserving the veracity of Prince's narrative, he wrote a "Preface" verifying Prince's pamphlet, provided supplementary documents recounting his first meeting with Prince, and provided a copy of a letter from Mrs. Pringle to the Birmingham Ladies Society for Relief of Negro Slaves about the inspection of Prince's body.

In *History*, Prince revealed the inhumane nature of slavery. She testified to the trauma of being separated from family, sold on the auction block, and abused violently by slave owners. For example, after Prince accidentally broke a jar, she was flogged with 100 lashes. She also described the daily regimen of life in West Indian bondage, especially for women. The enslaved nursed children, washed clothing, worked on farms, and extracted salt from mines and the numerous salt ponds of Turk Island. Prince's autobiography was very popular and influential; by the end of 1831, three editions of *History* had been published. Little is known of Mary Prince's life after 1832.

Further Readings: Bracks, Lean'tin L. *"The History of Mary Prince, A West Indian Slave, Related by Herself*: History, Ancestry, and Identity." *Writings on Black Women of the Diaspora, History, Language and Identity.* New York: Garland Publishing Inc., 1998, pp.29–54; Ferguson, Moira. "Introduction." *The History of Mary Prince, A West Indian Slave, Related by Herself.* Moira Ferguson, ed. Ann Arbor: The University of Michigan Press, 1993, pp. 1–26; Midgley, Claire. *Women Against Slavery: The British Campaigns, 1780–1870.* London: Routledge, 1992; Prince, Mary. *The History of Mary Prince, A West Indian Slave, Related by Herself.* London: F. Wesley and A. H. Davis, 1831.

Marilyn Walker

Prison Reform and Antislavery

Antebellum American advocates of **immediate emancipation**—the immediate, uncompensated emancipation of slaves without expatriation—were generally unconnected with contemporaneous institutional experiments in the incarceration and rehabilitation of criminals. Yet, their absence from the penitentiary movement did not mean that abolitionists were unconcerned with crime in society or with the treatment of society's law-breakers. On the contrary, as fortress-like prison structures began to garner support among reformers and state legislators in the 1820s and after, a vocal abolitionist minority unleashed a rhetorical assault against these prisons and the society that supported them.

No immediatist abolitionist mindful of the nation's criminal justice system surpassed the level of activism of the physician, educator, social reformer, and signer of the **Declaration of Independence, Benjamin Rush**. In 1787, Rush helped found the Philadelphia Society for Alleviating the Miseries of Public Prisons. In the decades following the American Revolution, he vigorously opposed—in lectures, pamphlets, petitions, and personal correspondence—punishments public and capital, and was among the earliest proponents of private confinement, religious instruction, and physical labor for prison inmates. Such positions placed Rush in the vanguard of penal reform. Indeed, his wide-ranging philanthropic pursuits included antislavery, Bible distribution, temperance, and humane treatment for the mentally ill, and anticipated the more focused efforts of evangelically inspired Protestant reformers of the 1820s and beyond. Rush judged the death penalty as a moral blight on society and utterly inconsistent with Christian precepts and with republicanism. "An execution in a republic," he asserted, "is like a human sacrifice in religion."

Yet little in Rush presaged the radical positions opponents of carceral and capital punishment would assume in the 1830s. When peace activists assembled in Boston on May 18, 1838, to establish an organization different from the more conservative American Peace Society, the participants understood capital punishment as only one malevolent symptom among many that plagued society and prevented humanity's progress. Their assembly launched the New England Non-Resistant Society, led by the fiery and controversial abolitionists **William Lloyd Garrison** and **Henry Clarke Wright**. They envisioned a world free of violence and of coercive institutions and relationships. To achieve the universal peace and human perfection that would usher in God's millennial Kingdom on earth, non-resistants sought the eradication of slavery, all warfare, military armaments, and imprisonment, and capital punishment. Regarding the latter, the society's *Declaration of Sentiments* announced to readers that Christ's compassionate teachings effectively abrogated the Old Testament's eye-for-an-eye injunction. "[F]orgiveness instead of punishment of enemies," it explained, "has been enjoined upon all his [Christ's] disciples, in all cases whatsoever. To extort money from enemies, or set them upon a pillory, or cast them into prison, or hang them upon a gallows, is obviously not to forgive, but to take retribution." In this way, non-resistants employed the same logic as Benjamin Rush. Whereas the latter invoked Jesus Christ to defend the rehabilitative potential of penitentiaries, the former did so to repudiate institutions in general. For non-resistants, the solution to social ills lay in nonsectarian faithfulness to Christ; thus, they declared their allegiance first of all to the government of God rather than any merely human institutions or denominations.

The Non-Resistant Society did not monopolize efforts to abolish the death penalty in antebellum America. Additional organizations such as the Massachusetts Society for the Abolition of Capital Punishment and a New York analogue were established in 1844 and were followed by a national society in 1845. The Harvard-educated lawyer and **Garrisonian** abolitionist **Wendell Phillips,** and the **Quaker** poet and non-Garrisonian immediatist John Greenleaf Whittier, were among the founders of the Massachusetts organization; the Unitarian minister, Garrison ally, and nonresistant Samuel Joseph May helped found the New York group. Other important abolitionists including Theodore Parker, Charles Burleigh, and **Lydia Maria Child** would also contribute to these movements. These societies, however, were not exclusively composed of antislavery agitators, but of humanitarians of several stripes—ministers, politicians, journalists, and physicians alike. Yet those abolitionists active in penal reform espoused the least popular and most radical aspects of that movement. Rather than embrace the expansion of penitentiaries and praise the reformation prison life supposedly afforded, these abolitionists protested against the execution of criminals. Still, so long as African Americans remained in bondage, opposition to the gallows was but a peripheral cause for immediatists.

It does not follow, however, that everyone involved in the antebellum antislavery campaign absolutely opposed criminal incarceration and the rehabilitation mission of penitentiaries. For example, although the Andover Theological Seminary graduate and Congregationalist minister, Louis Dwight, advocated the cause of the slave, improvement of prison conditions preoccupied his reformist activities. From 1825 until 1854, Dwight, as the founder and secretary of the Boston Prison Discipline Society, diligently spread the gospel of penal reform as he understood it: a system of solitary confinement and congregated productive labor for the incarcerated; Bible and common school provisioning for inmates; and the organization of prison populations according to age, mental health, and criminal record. Despite obvious divergences in objectives from nonresistance exponents, the proceedings and events of Dwight's Prison Discipline Society often appeared in Garrison's abolitionist weekly, *The Liberator*. The association also extended life memberships to the noted philanthropists and immediatists, **Arthur Tappan** and **Gerrit Smith**. And although the renowned educator of the handicapped, Samuel Gridley Howe—a future financial backer of John Brown's failed attempt to incite slave rebellions—disagreed with Dwight on certain penal fundamentals, as well as the latter's seeming dominance over organizational leadership, Howe nonetheless numbered himself among the society's affiliates. Yet, whoever aligned with the Boston Prison Discipline Society likely shared the regenerative philosophy of its leading member. For Dwight, "They [the convicted] are capable of love; but generally, when committed to Prison, they are filled with malice.... The very aggravation of their guilt is the loud call for your pity and prayers, and efforts. And their case is not hopeless." Upon such sentiments lay a strong impetus for the penitentiary movement, if not early nineteenth-century evangelical social reform more broadly. *See also* Antislavery Evangelical Protestantism; Bible and Slavery.

Further Readings: Davis, David Brion. "The Movement to Abolish Capital Punishment in America, 1787–1861," *The American Historical Review* 63, 1 (1957): 23–46; Lewis, W. David. *From Newgate to Dannemora: The Rise of the Penitentiary in New York, 1796–1848*. New York: Cornell University Press. 1965; Masur, Louis P. *Rites of Execution: Capital Punishment and the Transformation of American Culture, 1776–1865*. New York: Oxford University Press, 1989; Rothman, David J. *The Discovery of the Asylum: Social Order and Disorder in the New Republic*. Rev. ed. New York: Aldine de Gruyter, 1990.

Raymond James Krohn

Pugachev's Revolt

The largest peasant insurrection in Europe before the French Revolution took place in southeast Russia, and was led by Yemelian Pugachev, a Cossack born around 1742 in the village of Zimoveiskaia, also the birthplace of Stepan Razin, who led a similar revolt in the preceding century. Born in modest circumstances, Pugachev apparently did not attend school, and remained illiterate his whole life. After service in the army during the Seven Years War, Pugachev survived a bout of severe illness caused by a plague epidemic in 1770. Refused his request for military discharge, he then became a fugitive but was captured and placed in chains under guard. Establishing a pattern, he soon escaped, was recaptured and escaped again, four times within fifteen months. Finally he found refuge in the rural environs of Yaitsk, an outpost of Cossacks between the Ural Mountains and the Caspian Sea.

Here there had already been rebellions against Czarist authority, which had a double policy of attempting to secure Cossack loyalty by accommodations to traditional tribal forms of governance and cultural customs, and severe repression of dissidents. The entire region of southeast Russia was characterized on the one hand by the advance of the centralized Czarist government and indigenous resistance from peoples such as the Kalmyks. The Cossacks themselves took pride in their semi-barbarous skills as cavalrymen; when the Russians obtained their allegiance, it was never fully secured, as their independence remained a dominant factor. The centralized government favored the formation of a political elite among the Cossacks, giving rise to a division between "obedient" and "disobedient" factions. These tensions resulted in a short, but fierce, armed conflict in January, 1772, during which scores were killed and government records were destroyed.

Having found receptive listeners in the Yaitsk district, Pugachev conspired with a handful of others to suddenly announce to the world on September 1773 that he was actually Czar Peter III, and thus was seeking the restoration of the Fatherland under his name. Conditions of public information and knowledge were so primitive in rural Russia at that time that no one in the immediate region seemed to be able to discern the difference between Pugachev and the real Peter III, who had died in 1762. The manifesto then issued promised "land, grasses, money, lead, powder, and bread." The small band of rebels quickly grew when "Czar Peter" appeared at villages and towns, where he was greeted by the traditional bread and salt by peasants and even priests of the Orthodox Church. Typically, alcohol was then distributed freely. Soon whole units of Cossacks deserted to the rebellion; towns were besieged, burned and sacked, with army and government officials hanged or shot.

Local and regional government authorities were undermanned and often incompetent. While Pugachev promised much to those thronging to his side, he also threatened and delivered severe punishment to all who either opposed him or denied him necessities. With his military experience, Pugachev was able to make use of the assortment of artillery that he seized, for use in sieges. However, brutal though most of his sieges were, few were completely successful. The revolt took on the nature of a large, fluid band of marauders plundering the country, moving rapidly from place to place. This meant that the core of rebel leaders, which they labeled a "State War College," evaded capture, but also that the rebellion lacked stability. Insurgent forces could number in the thousands, suddenly mustering to the call of the rebels.

The prevailing status of the lower classes in Russia was some form of serf-dom, involving age-old traditional obligatory labor and service to feudal authority, either nobility or the church, and equally traditional ties to the land. When the rebels arrived in a new locale, they typically announced liberation from private serfdom, in favor of service to the government itself under "Peter III," the end of obligatory head-taxes, and cheap or even free salt (essential to the preservation of food). Peasants were also asked if local masters or stewards merited punishment, and if so, they were executed and hanged on the gates of wealthy estates.

In the Urals, forms of industrial serfdom prevailed, as the district was quickly being developed into a major metal-mining and refining zone. Sometimes hundreds of such "factory serfs" joined Pugachev's forces, while others would simply disappear into the mountains. Their expertise was often useful in producing weapons for the rebellion, including artillery, but these were improvised and not always safe to use (they often exploded when discharged).

After several months of confused fighting, the central government began to respond, with skilled commanders placed in charge, with sufficient forces to begin defeating the rebels. The siege of Orenburg, for instance, which had lasted six months, was lifted in March, 1774. Ever resourceful, Pugachev escaped encirclement, to seek refuge in the Ural Mountains, where again a series of small battles ensued. Finally, he broke out to the west and dramatically attacked the city of Kazan on July 12, 1774, burning it to the ground. However, he was quickly forced to turn south, toward Tsaritsyn, which was too powerful for him to attack. In a last phase, thousands of serfs along the Volga rose in revolt, but Pugachev continued to retreat toward the Caspian Sea.

Realizing that in spite of their intrepid struggle defeat was imminent, Pugachev's own men turned him over to the government in mid-September, and the revolt ended. At least 3,000 noblemen, clergymen, military officers, and officials were killed by the rebels, often by gruesome means, such as bludgeoning or torture. Destruction of records by rebels eliminated files that could confirm debts or property rights. During the repression that followed the defeat, thousands of serfs were executed in summary fashion. Pugachev and several of his associates were executed in Moscow on January 10, 1774.

In the short time of one year, the rebels had convulsed the entirety of southeast Russia, though they never had sufficient forces to threaten the central government itself. Pugachev's promise of "freedom" attracted the momentary allegiance of hundreds of thousands, and formed the basis of a great legend in Russian history. After his execution, Catherine the Great renamed the city of Yaitsk and the Yait River "Uralsk" and the "Ural River." Even public discussion of the rebellion was suppressed, though the memory of it resurfaced in the now classic account by Pushkin, published in 1833.

Further Readings: Alexander, John T. *Emperor of the Cossacks: Pugachev and the Frontier Jacquerie of 1773–1775.* Lawrence: Coronado, 1973; Pushkin, Alexander. *The History of Pugachev.* London: Phoenix, 2001.

Fred Whitehead

Q

Quakers and Antislavery

The Christian denomination of the Society of Friends, better known as the Quakers, has a long history of involvement with antislavery causes. While the Quakers have been hailed as leaders in the antislavery struggle, they sometimes suffered internal dissension over the issue. The Friends, started in England in the 1640s as a radically egalitarian reaction to the left of the Puritans, always maintained a strong tenet of human spiritual equality. As the denomination developed, Quakers possessed the intellectual and communal forms for critiquing slavery, as well as its attendant ills of racism, formalism, and inherited institutional power. This did not ensure, however, that Quaker antislavery testimony would be consistently applied, nor skillfully articulated at all points in their history. While the common impression that the Quakers were in the forefront of antislavery activism should be tempered, they were nevertheless in the antislavery vanguard among predominantly white groups.

As Quakers settled in the growing colonies of North America and the Caribbean, the founder of the Society, George Fox (1624–1691), began to express qualms about slavery. His concerns, though, were not directed against the institution of slavery, but focused on the proper obedience and religious instruction of slaves, and upon the conduct of masters. On a 1671 visit to Barbados, Fox took more care to dispel rumors that the Quakers were inciting slave revolts than he did to condemn the institution of slavery. Fox's travel companion, William Edmundson (1627–1712), however was shocked by the slavery he saw in North America in the 1670s. In his widely circulated journal, he speculated that Christianity and slavery were incompatible.

More forthright in their criticisms were a brave group of Dutch Quaker immigrants to Pennsylvania. In 1688, they addressed a strongly-worded denunciation of slavery to their monthly Meeting, pointing out the incompatibility of slave-holding with the Golden Rule: "There is a saying that we shall do to all men like as we will be done ourselves; making no difference of what generation, descent or colour they are .... Is there any that would be done or handled at this manner? viz. To be sold or made a slave for all the time of his life?" This remonstrance disappeared from history until republished by abolitionists in 1844. A similar denunciation of slavery from the schismatic followers of **George Keith** in 1693 was likewise fleeting in its impact.

Through the early eighteenth century, increasingly prosperous Quakers involved themselves in all aspects of slavery and the slave trade, economic success undercutting any strict application of their ideals of equality. These ideals did not, however, disappear. A few lone voices were raised against slavery in the 1720s and 1730s, most notably Ralph Sandiford (1693–1733) and Benjamin Lay (1682–1759), each of whom published antislavery arguments. However, the outstanding individual leaders of the movement to purge slave-holding from American Friends were **Anthony Benezet** (1713–1784) and John Woolman (1720–1772). Benezet's pamphlets on slavery had wide currency in both America and Europe, among Quakers and outside of the Society; his writings are credited with awakening the conscience of English abolitionist **Thomas Clarkson.** Furthermore, Benezet, who opened a school for free blacks in Philadelphia in the 1760s, became one of the first antislavery advocates to denounce as well the ideology of racial inferiority which undergirded slavery: "I have found amongst the negroes as great a variety of talents as amongst a like number of whites; and I am bold to assert, that the notion … that the blacks are inferior in their capacities, is a vulgar prejudice."

John Woolman's method included the written word, but succeeded more through a quiet but persistent personal witness. He would visit slave-holding Quakers, speaking against the practice, then insist on giving wages to slaves who had assisted him during his stay. He attended meetings in many districts, raising the inconsistencies of slavery and Christianity, without condemning slaveholders as individuals. By the late 1740s, slaveholding was decreasing among Quakers, and in 1754 the Philadelphia Quarterly Meeting declared slave-holding a sin, a resolution with which the Yearly Meeting concurred in 1758. Other Quaker meetings followed them; by 1780 slave-holding among Quakers was virtually unknown, as it had been determined an offense requiring disowning by other Friends. John Woolman's gentle, unrelenting style achieved ongoing resonance through his *Journal*, which became standard devotional reading for generations of Friends.

As Jean Soderlund demonstrates, Woolman's personal quest could not have succeeded without a change in the economic status of Quaker leadership. In the 1730s, many of those who deliberated and published the proceedings of Yearly Meetings were, themselves, slaveowners. By the late 1750s, leadership had passed to more reform-minded, middle-class Friends, who had no personal stake in upholding slavery.

Even as Quaker political power dissipated during the American Revolution, Friends seized on the congruency between republican language and antislavery. In April 1775, Anthony Benezet called the initial meeting of the Society for the Relief of Free Negroes Unlawfully held in Bondage. **Thomas Paine** was among the attendees of this first interreligious abolition group, but the majority were Quakers. Moses Brown (1738–1836), a wealthy merchant destined to play a key financial role in the industrialization of New England, manumitted his slaves and joined the Friends on the eve of the Revolution. Brown used his social prominence to fund numerous anti-slavery organizations over the next half-century. In the decades following the Revolution, a large-scale internal migration of Quakers occurred because of slavery; large numbers of Quakers in Southern states relocated to Ohio and Indiana, removing themselves from slave culture and governments that eyed their ideological differences with suspicion. Others moved to **Canada,** where they would later assist escaped blacks.

Arguably the most important international action of American Quakers during the Revolutionary era came when the Philadelphia Yearly Meeting urged their London counterparts to action. This resulted in English Friends submitting the first formal petition to Parliament opposing the slave trade in 1783, which would deeply influence the men who would become the leaders of the English movement to abolish the Atlantic slave trade including **William Wilberforce,** Thomas Clarkson, and **Thomas Buxton,** none of whom were Quakers. Quaker meetings would also form a crucial grass-roots backbone for the antislavery cause.

With the slave trade officially banned in 1808, white American and English antislavery entered a more quiescent, gradualist phase. The most notable Quakers in this period were the American editor **Benjamin Lundy** (1789–1839) and the English woman writer **Elizabeth Heyrick** (1769–1831). Lundy edited an antislavery newspaper, *The Genius of Universal Emancipation*, which kept the flame of abolition alive in the 1820s by entertaining all approaches to mitigating and ending slavery. One such approach came in the stirring tones of immediatism, first enunciated by Elizabeth Heyrick. Her call for an immediate end to the sin of slaveholding jarred her more conservative Quaker brethren in England when her pamphlet, *Immediate, not Gradual Abolition*, was published in 1824. However, her logic impressed women's antislavery groups in England, and, when republished in Lundy's paper in 1826, initiated a radicalization of white abolitionists in the United States.

Immediatism was the rampart of the English Quaker abolitionist **Joseph Sturge** (1793–1859), who led the struggle to end slavery in all English territory in 1835. Realizing that Parliament's recent passage of gradual, compensated emancipation in the British colonies could be compromised by racism, apprenticeship requirements, and the persistence of proslavery sentiments, Sturge undertook visits to the Caribbean and the United States to eradicate slavery in the British West Indies once and for all. He also helped organize the 1840 **World's Anti-Slavery Convention** in London which extended antislavery internationally.

With the advent of more radical abolitionist organizations in the United States after 1830, Quakers were divided amongst themselves on questions of tactics. There had been schismatic movements among the Friends in the early nineteenth century which resulted in an official distancing of those called Orthodox Quakers from abolitionist causes, despite a high level of individual Quaker participation in the movement. Quakers who played key roles in the abolitionist struggle included poets John Greenleaf Whittier

(1807–1892) and Elizabeth Margaret Chandler (1807–1836), and especially Philadelphians **Lucretia Coffin Mott** (1793–1880) and her spouse James Mott (1788–1868).

Lucretia Mott's antislavery activism highlights the contradictions present among Quakers. Because women had always participated equally in the Society, functioning as traveling ministers as well as speaking at meetings, Quaker women nurtured many organized women's antislavery groups. But as Quakers became more religiously conventional, they adopted some of the prejudices of their time, and objected to women's public political presence. Mott was also criticized for bringing black women to Quaker meetings; despite Benezet's early witness, Quakers had long discouraged African Americans from joining. Even though Mott was a member of the more socially radical Hicksite group, her actions left her threatened with disownment. The famous 1840 London conference refused to seat her as a full delegate; this led to her meeting **Elizabeth Cady Stanton** and planning what would eventually become the **Seneca Falls Convention.**

Many other abolitionists had been born Quakers, or sojourned with them, but had to leave the Society to continue their antislavery activism. Isaac Hopper (1771–1852), Arnold Buffum (1782–1859), **Angelina Grimké** (1805–1879), Sarah Grimké (1792–1873), **Abby Kelley Foster** (1811–1887), **Prudence Crandall** (1803–1890), Laura Haviland (1808–1898), Susan B. Anthony (1820–1906), and even Elias Hicks (1748–1830) himself, all found themselves at odds with Quaker meetings. Ironically, many of them are now claimed as Quaker heroes.

Similar tensions marked Quaker involvement in the **Underground Railroad.** Many Quakers assisted runaway slaves, but those who made it a priority were often chastised. Along the border states of Indiana and Ohio, heated disputes led to ruptures. Levi Coffin (1798–1877) and his wife Catherine White Coffin (d. 1909) were among those who were dismissed for meeting with non-Quaker abolitionists and for their willingness to break the law against harboring runaways. They and other radicals started the Indiana Yearly Meeting of Anti-Slavery Friends in 1843, which rejoined the main branch once most Quakers evolved to a similarly militant stance by 1857. Another noted Quaker "conductor" on the Underground Railroad was Lucretia Mott's associate, the Hicksite Thomas Garrett (1789–1871). Positioned strategically in Delaware, he assisted over 2,000 runaways, and provided financial and logistical support to **Harriet Tubman** (ca. 1820–1913).

The American Civil War posed the ultimate test for the pacifist Quakers, dramatically pitting their ideal of equality against their non-violence. Some, such as Garrett and Mott, had already reconciled themselves to the likely need for violence to overthrow the slave power. A few Iowa Quakers allied with John Brown (1800–1859) as he planned for his raid at the Harpers Ferry arsenal. Once the war began, Confederate states imprisoned Friends on suspicion of being against both slavery and the war. In the North, individual Quakers agonized over support for the war, and young men faced the even more grueling decision about whether to fight. Records show that as many as a quarter of eligible Quaker men did enlist; very few disownments were made despite this blatant disregard of a foundational tenet of the denomination.

Quakers remained active as missionaries during the late-nineteenth century expansion of British imperialism in Africa. In Zanzibar and Kenya, slaves were held under a variety of indigenous Muslim and Swahili social systems. Quakers vociferously maintained the need for immediate abolition. Henry S. Newman, the Honorary Secretary of the Friends Foreign Mission Association, established the "industrial mission" of Banani on the island of Pemba in 1897. Former slaves were welcomed, providing Newman with the means to agitate for abolition throughout the region. However, the Quakers of the time did not question the presumptions of imperialism, the paternalism of racism, or the exploitations of British capitalism; Friends had become part of the establishment, even if still occasionally a gadfly. While slavery was abolished in most colonial territory of East Africa by 1909, labor relations between the former slaves and the plantation owners was virtually unchanged. Quakers continued their antislavery agitation following World War I, joining in petitions to the **League of Nations** to monitor imperialist labor practices verging on slavery.

Contemporary Quakers are rightfully proud of their legacy of involvement in antislavery, but have not rested on their laurels. The American Friends Service Committee continues the struggle by working against debt-bondage, sexual slavery, and slavery in civil wars.

From the time they renounced slave-holding among themselves, Quakers became an integral part of antislavery struggles internationally. Because of their strong intra-group communication, they provided activists with organizational models and access to existing networks. The prominent public role of women in Quaker polity paved the way for the emergence of feminism from within the awakened political consciousness of female abolitionists. Yet Quakers have also suffered from their own internal problems including an incomplete dismantling of racial prejudice and debilitation from internal disputes, which have limited their cohesion at key moments in the struggle. *See also* Gender and Slave Emancipation; Gender Relations within Abolitionism; Germantown Antislavery Petition.

Further Readings: Anstey, Roger. *The Atlantic Slave Trade and British Abolition, 1760–1810.* London: Macmillan, 1975; Bacon, Margaret Hope. *Mothers of Feminism: The Story of Quaker Women in America.* San Francisco: Harper and Row, 1986; Coffin, Levi. *Reminiscences of Levi Coffin.* New York: Arno Press, 1968 (Reprint of 3rd edition, 1898); Cooper, Frederick. *From Slaves to Squatters: Plantation Labor and Agriculture in Zanzibar and Coastal Kenya, 1890–1925.* New Haven: Yale University Press, 1980; Davis, David Brion. *The Problem of Slavery in Western Culture.* Ithaca: Cornell University Press, 1966; Dorland, Arthur Garratt. *The Quakers in Canada, A History.* Toronto: Ryerson Press, 1968; Drake, Thomas E. *Quakers and Slavery in America.* New Haven: Yale University Press, 1950; Frost, J. William. *The Quaker Origins of Antislavery.* Norwood, PA: Norwood Editions, 1980; Hamm, Thomas D. "Indiana Quakers and Politics, 1810–1865." In *The Quaker Presence in America: "Let us then try what Love will do."* Barbara A. Heavilin and Charles W. Heavilin, eds. *Quaker Studies* Volume 5. Lewiston, NY: Edwin Mellen, 2003, pp. 219–242; Hamm, Thomas D. *The Quakers in America.* New York: Columbia University Press, 2003; Hewitt, Nancy A. "Feminist Friends: Agrarian Quakers and the Emergence of Woman's Rights in America." *Feminist Studies* 12, 1(Spring 1986): 27–49; Hornick, Nancy Slocum. "Anthony Benezet and the

Africans' School: Toward a Theory of Full Equality." *Pennsylvania Magazine of History and Biography* 99, 4 (1975): 399–421; Jennings, Judith Gaile. "The Campaign for the Abolition of the British Slave Trade: The Quaker Contribution, 1757–1807." Ph.D. dissertation, University of Kentucky, 1975; Nelson, Jacquelyn S. *Indiana Quakers Confront the Civil War.* Indianapolis: Indiana Historical Society, 1991; Newman, Henry S. *Banani: The Transition from Slavery to Freedom in Zanzibar and Pemba.* London: Headley Brothers, 1898 (Reprint edition. New York: Negro Universities Press, 1969); Nwulia, Moses D.E. *Britain and Slavery in East Africa.* Washington, D.C.: Three Continents Press, 1975; Soderlund, Jean. *Quakers and Slavery: A Divided Spirit.* Princeton: Princeton University Press, 1985; Walvin, James. *England, Slaves, and Freedom, 1776–1838.* Jackson, MS: University of Mississippi, 1986.

Jennifer Rycenga

Quok Walker Decision (1783)

In 1783, in *Commonwealth of Massachusetts v. Jennison*, the Supreme Court of Massachusetts under Chief Justice William Cushing pronounced Quok Walker—and all other slaves in Massachusetts—free. Through that single action, the court transformed Massachusetts from the first colony to legalize slavery into the first state to deny any of its citizens the right to hold human property.

This historic decision did not emerge, however, until Massachusetts courts oversaw two years of legal battles. In 1781, Quok Walker sued Nathaniel Jennison of Barre for assault and battery. While Quok considered himself a free man, Jennison thought Walker was his runaway slave. When Jennison found him working for John and Seth Caldwell, and Walker refused to accompany Jennison back to his home, Jennison and two other men beat him. After this brutal beating, Jennison imprisoned Walker in a barn.

Within a month, Quok Walker sued Jennison on a plea of trespass. The Worcester County Inferior Court of Common Pleas ordered Jennison to appear for the case *Walker v. Jennison* (1781). People illegally enslaved usually used a charge of trespass to sue for freedom. Trespass, the unlawful injury of another's person or property, determined status because a master could legally injure a slave, but not a free person. Therefore, if the jury found the defendant had injured the plaintiff, they had decided that he or she was free. From Jennison's perspective, injury was not possible, for he could not injure his own property. As his property, Jennison had a right to beat or restrain Walker as he willed. Walker and his lawyers responded that Walker was a free man and had therefore suffered injury. Before Jennison owned him, Walker had made an agreement with James Caldwell, Walker's original owner, to free him at the age of twenty-five. Jennison acquired Walker through marriage with one of Caldwell's daughters. After the daughter died and Walker came of age, Jennison refused to uphold Caldwell's agreement. The jury found Walker's argument most convincing and decided that Jennison had injured Walker, and, thus, Walker was free.

The initial case blossomed into three other cases between Walker, Jennison, and the Caldwell family. In each of these cases, the attorney, Levi

Lincoln, offered an impassioned plea for the abolition of slavery in Massachusetts; yet none of these cases declared anyone free, but Walker himself. The scope of the case would change, however, when the Commonwealth of Massachusetts arrested Jennsion for imprisoning and beating Walker in the final and most important case, *Commonwealth of Massachusetts v. Jennison* (1783).

The remarkable aspect of this case was Chief Justice Cushing's charge to the jury. Cushing pushed aside the traditional adherence to points of law and looked to the State Constitution of 1780 to instruct the jury. He thought that the concept of natural rights bound the framers to "declare *that all men are born free and equal"* and stated furthermore that *"every subject is entitled to liberty."* In his legal instruction he deemed slavery "as effectively abolished as it can be." He, therefore, ordered the jury not "to consider whether the promises of freedom to Quaco . . . amounted to manumission or not." After issuing his oral charge, Cushing wrote out his instructions in his legal notebook. Almost in amazement of what had happened, he ended the entry with a statement in his notebook that explained the significance clearly: "The preceding Case was the one in which by the foregoing Charge, Slavery in Massachusetts was forever abolished."

Despite this seemingly unequivocal assertion, slavery did not instantaneously end in Massachusetts. The immediate legacy of these cases was very murky. Most importantly, the abolition of slavery by judicial decree did not result in a mass emancipation but made it impossible for masters to maintain their ownership when brought to court. For this reason, some scholars have questioned whether the case indeed ended slavery. As legal scholar A. Leon Higginbotham expressed it, however, the court had indeed "signaled that it would no longer protect the legality of slavery." But the burden lay upon the enslaved men and women who had to assert their freedom to their master. The first substantial evidence that slaves actually became free was the 1790 Census when Massachusetts reported no enslaved inhabitants.

Further Readings: Blanck, Emily. "Seventeen Eighty-Three: The Turning Point in the Law of Slavery and Freedom in Massachusetts." *New England Quarterly* 75, 1 (2002): 24–51; Cushing, William. Massachusetts Historical Society, William Cushing Papers, Notes on Law Cases, 1783, 98; Higginbotham, A. Leon. *In the Matter of Color: Race and the American Legal Process, The Colonial Period* (1978); O'Brien, William. "Did the Jennison Case Outlaw Slavery in Massachusetts?" *William and Mary Quarterly* 17, 2 (1960): 219–241; Zilversmit, Arthur. "Quok Walker, Mumbet, and the Abolition of Slavery in Massachusetts." *William and Mary Quarterly* 25, 4 (1968): 614–624.

Emily V. Blanck

Qur'an and Antislavery

Like the revelations of the *Torah* and the *Gospel* before it, the revelation of the *Qur'an* was a profoundly transformative event in human history. Within 150 years of the death of the Prophet Muhammad, in 632 C.E., much of the inhabited world—stretching from Spain to India—had become

Muslim, responding to the vigorously asserted new faith and an entirely new legal system in ways that have had, and continue to have, a tremendous impact on world events. What impact did the revelation of the *Qur'an* have on the age-old institution of human slavery? A cursory review of the text and of the early Islamic history following its revelation might lead one to the conclusion that the *Qur'an*, much like the other Abrahamic scriptures that preceded it, left the institution of slavery just as it found it. Many scholars have contended that, while the Quranic text contains a number of ameliorative provisions lessening the harshness of the treatment of slaves and encouraging manumission, the Holy Book of the Muslims does not suggest abolition and it cannot be read as an antislavery document.

Closer analysis of the Quranic text and a critical approach to the history surrounding the revelation of the text shows that this conclusion is not completely accurate. It is important to note that the early revelations of the *Qur'an* exhorted the Prophet Muhammad and his small band of followers to embrace a dynamic new worldview. This worldview emphasized, in newly phrased and uncompromising terms, the oneness of God and the unity of the human race. It ardently rejected the domination of any group in human society by any other individuals or group of oppressors. The Quranic message, first revealed in an Arabian society riven by tribal rivalries, warfare, and socio-economic strife, was initially directed to members of the Prophet Muhammad's own tribe, the dominant and aristocratic Quraish of Mecca. Ultimately the message became a universal call, directing all human beings to seek justice and upright moral and ethical conduct in all their affairs. It demanded the abolition of worldly distinctions between human beings based on ethnicity, language, class, caste, wealth, lineage, or geographic origin.

The *Qur'an*'s egalitarian message is likely why slaves, the poor, and the disenfranchised in Mecca were among the first converts to the new religion. Slaves who converted to Islam endured particularly harsh retribution from their masters. For example, Muslim schoolchildren are familiar with the story of Bilal ibn Rabah, an Ethiopian slave who was tortured by his Meccan owner for days in the hot midday sun because he refused to renounce his conversion to the newfound faith. One of the Prophet's companions, Abu Bakr, a wealthy man and a new Muslim himself, interceded, purchasing Bilal and instantaneously freeing him. Bilal enthusiastically took up the cause of the new religion and ultimately originated the *adhan* ("the call to prayer"), first used by him at the Prophet's Mosque in Medina and now heard all over the world five times a day. Bilal thus was Islam's first *muaddhin* ("caller to prayer"). We owe our enjoyment of the melodious tones of the Muslim call to prayer to this emancipated slave, Bilal ibn Rabah.

In those early days of Islam, there were many more events like the instance of the emancipation of Bilal. Those events did not just concern slavery and persecution. They also involved other practices of the Meccan aristocracy that were viewed as corrupt, immoral, or oppressive. The texts of the early Meccan Quranic revelations, while powerfully condemnatory of Meccan immorality, tribalism, and polytheism, make only oblique references to the actual events that prompted the revelations. Instead, most accounts of the actual facts will be found in the historical literature and in the Traditions of the Prophet. A review of those facts leaves no doubt, however, that the early Muslim experience led to the liberation of many new Meccan Muslims from lives of slavery and degradation.

This reality is confirmed by the fact that all the important Quranic rules on slavery are emancipatory. There are no provisions in the *Qur'an* that actively promote or counsel the continuation of the institution of slavery. The message of the *Qur'an* rather exhorts mankind to work toward the achievement of a slavery-free society. This message was, unfortunately, deemphasized after the death of the Prophet Muhammad and ultimately lost in the rapid expansion of the Islamic Empire. Although the *Qur'an*'s assertions of absolute human equality, the inviolability of human dignity, and the importance of earthly justice were key rhetorical factors in fueling the rapid expansion of Islam, those messages did not result in any impulse or movement seeking the widespread abolition of the slave trade or of the system of chattel slavery. Yet, consistent with the core Quranic message, manumission of slaves in the Muslim world was a common and frequent occurrence. In some places, notably Egypt, former slaves rose to occupy the highest positions in political and religious hierarchies. Thus, in spite of the existence of a 1,300-year horrific and anti-Quranic history of plunder and trading in slaves, an examination of the *Qur'an*'s textual provisions on slavery and its more general discussions of the ideas of social justice and human equality shows the clear presence of a theological and jurisprudential basis for an antislavery position. As we have noted, not all of the Quranic usages are equally significant in determining the *Qur'an*'s attitude toward slavery, and in some cases they are ambiguous or neutral, displaying a matter-of-fact acceptance of the existence of chattel slavery in Arab society at the time of the revelation. Yet, in many other instances the antislavery message is unmistakable. The most effective way to analyze the Quranic treatment of the issue is to group its provisions on slavery by Arabic linguistic usage. Using a linguistic lens in our analysis helps separate the *Qur'an*'s neutral provisions from its antislavery provisions and will make the Holy Book's intendment clearer to the reader.

The *Qur'an* generally uses three linguistic forms in its references to slaves and slavery. The first linguistic form involves the use of the Arabic masculine noun *'abd*, which literally means "slave," but is also frequently used in the *Qur'an* to describe a servant or worshiper of God. Although the form is often used in a neutral way, a number of the usages of this form carry emancipatory messages. The second Quranic linguistic form describes chattel slaves with the use of the Arabic idiomatic expression, *ma malakat aymanukum* ("those whom your right hands possess"). This phrase describes war captives and others who may fall into a state of enslavement as a result of hostilities, negotiations between belligerents, or as tribute or war booty. The phrase, or some variant of it, is used thirteen times in the *Qur'an* (4:3, 4:24, 4:25, 4:36, 16:71, 23:6, 24:31, 24:58, 30:28, 33:50, 33:52, 33:55, 70:30). Although many of the verses using this phrase do nothing more than lay down rules of etiquette or decorum involving treatment of prisoners, a number of them also clearly contemplate a lightening of the burden of the captive or outright emancipation. The third linguistic form uses variants of the metaphorical expression *raqabah* ("the neck") to describe slaves, an obvious reference to the ancient practice of yoking captives by the neck. The Quranic usage of this form is much more graphic, and the verses employing this usage give us the most direct expression of the *Qur'an*'s overarching purposes in regard to slavery. In all of the verses using this form, God instructs the believers to free "the neck" or substantially lighten the burden placed upon it. Several of the instances of this usage are found in chapters and sections that convey a powerful message of equality and human freedom. The most important Quranic linguistic usages for descriptions of slavery are the first and the third forms, and we will discuss both usages here, focusing most of our attention on the metaphorical *raqaba* ("the neck") usage.

In a number of the instances in the *Qur'an* where *'abd* usage is employed, the *Qur'an* instituted an important change in how slaves were to be treated under the law. For example, verses 2:178 and 2:179 established the principle of equality in terms of punishment for homicide, abolishing distinctions based on social status or tribal affiliation. After the revelation of verses 2:178 and 179, slaves in Muslim society no longer feared being sacrificed as satisfaction to the victims of homicides committed by free persons, and, more importantly, they were protected by the law of homicide in the same way that free persons were protected. This was a revolutionary change in the Arab tribal customary law, and, as the criminal law often does, it sent a powerful rhetorical message of equality to all of the new Muslims. In the area of personal relations, the *Qur'an* also made profound changes in the law governing slaves. Prior to the emergence of Islam, slaves were often either not allowed to marry or they faced difficulties in establishing and maintaining marriage ties. Sometimes prisoners of war, captured and enslaved during hostilities, were allowed to bring a spouse with them into captivity, but this did not guarantee that the marriage tie would be respected. The *Qur'an*, to a large extent, changed these and other rules governing slave marriages. At verses 2:221 and 24:32, the *Qur'an* exhorts Muslims to permit their slaves to marry and, using the *'abd* linguistic form, extols a preference for marital partnerships between believing slaves and believing free persons over those between slaves and unbelievers, even though they might be free. While the social taboo associated with marriage to a slave may have persisted, the text clarifies that such relationships should no longer be legally taboo and that marriage among believing slaves and between believing slaves and believing free persons were henceforth to be viewed as acts of piety. It is important to remember that, while a slave's conversion to Islam did not automatically result in emancipation, a free person's marriage to his or her slave would result in the slave's emancipation, based on the jurists' Quranic interpretation that it was legally impossible to own one's spouse. Although these provisions might cause a male owner of a concubine to eschew marriage to her, preferring ownership and unrestrained access, the Caliph Ali, the fourth Caliph of Islam, acting within thirty years after the revelation, nullified the untoward results of this practice by ordering that a female slave mother of children by her free male owner (known as *umm walid* or "mother of the child" in Arabic) could not be sold and that she must, by operation of law, be emancipated upon the death of her owner. The Islamic law, drawn from interpretations of the *Qur'an* and Traditions of the Prophet, also stipulated that the children of such unions were free at birth. These rules encouraged meaningful and long-term humanitarian relationships between slaves and masters, ultimately ending in emancipation, and many prominent figures in Islamic history, including heads of state, military leaders, poets and scholars, were products of such unions.

Each Quranic use of the metaphorical Arabic word *raqaba* ("the neck") is also unmistakably emancipatory. Each time this word is used, the *Qur'an* orders or strongly urges that "the neck" be freed. Perhaps the most frequently referenced passage using the "neck" description of slaves is the verse that immediately precedes the verses announcing the ordinance that the law of equality must be applied in homicide, referred to above. The verse, 2:177, counsels the believers to eschew blind adherence to religious ritual, and, in imparting that counsel, it gives an express definition of righteous behavior. The verse requires that every righteous believer "spend of your substance . . . for the ransom of slaves."

The exhortation to righteous behavior is not the only way that the *Qur'an* encouraged the freeing of slaves. Again using the harsh linguistic phrase "the neck," the *Qur'an* announced that slaves were to be freed in partial expiation for the crime of unintentional homicide (4:92), for failure to comply with an oath or for taking false or futile oaths (5:89), and as penalty for inappropriate or unjust behavior by a husband toward his wife (58:3–6).

Two other instances of the use of the "neck" linguistic form in the *Qur'an* involve explicit pronouncements of legal injunctions and are of major importance for the Islamic law of slavery. A third instance, while only hortatory, is of nearly equal importance because of its delineation of the Islamic ethic in regard to slavery. Each will be considered in turn.

The first instance, at verse 9:60, is widely cited in legal treatises because it sets out the eight classes of persons in society who are entitled to receive public charity or *Zakat*, one of the five "pillars" of the Islamic faith. Those classes of persons are: (1) the poor; (2) the needy; (3) *Zakat* workers; (4) new Muslims; (5) slaves; (6) debtors; (7) those struggling "in the cause of God"; and (8) travelers. Although this verse does not expressly suggest that the heads of Islamic states should affirmatively work to eliminate or abolish slavery, it commands the authorities to consider the plight of slaves as one of their highest categories in the social welfare context.

The next instance of the *Qur'an*'s use of the "neck" metaphor is at verse 47:4, which sets out provisions for the treatment of prisoners of war. The verse provides that the Muslim military commander is permitted to capture and enslave non-believing enemy prisoners of war but, when hostilities are concluded, efforts must be made to free the prisoners or to ransom or repatriate them back to their communities. Despite a fair amount of scholarly opinion suggesting that the verse is only advisory, rather than mandatory, and the fact that, during the medieval era, heads of Islamic governments often ignored the verse's provision, the plain meaning and imperative tense of the Quranic language seem to mandate that heads of government must free captives at the cessation of hostilities.

The third and last instance of the use of the "neck" metaphor is perhaps the most compelling evidence of a Quranic philosophy in favor of individual freedom and an insistence on emancipation and abolition in the case of slaves. This philosophy, summed up in the wonderfully terse chapter entitled *al Balad* ("The City"), was revealed to the Prophet Muhammad early in his prophetic mission. The revelation, addressed to the Prophet, concerns his relationship with Mecca, the city of his birth, and the struggle he was about to undertake, which would eventually require him to flee the city in order to save his life and continue his mission. The chapter first points out that he, the Prophet, is a "freeman" or "dweller" of the city, but, like other men, he will face toil and struggle in life, of which many other men cannot fathom the meaning. The chapter then announces that there are two roads in life, one steep, and difficult, and the other flat, and easy. The steep road is the preferred road, but how is one to know the steep road? The *Qur'an* answers this question, stating that the steep road, among other things, involves freeing slaves, protecting orphans, and uplifting the indigent in society.

The *Qur'an*'s exhortation to the Prophet in *al Balad* describes the struggle required of the Prophet if he is to succeed in creating the virtuous society contemplated by the Holy Book. Every Muslim who emulates the Prophet in his or her individual effort to create this virtuous society must behave similarly. The good Muslim therefore frees slaves and works for abolition and the virtuous society contemplated by the *Qur'an* will ultimately be one that is free of slavery. *See also* Arabia and Nineteenth- and Twentieth-Century Slavery; Bible and Slavery; Islam and Antislavery.

Further Readings: Ali, A. Yusuf, trans. and comm. *The Holy Qur'an.* 9th ed. Maryland: Amana Publications, 1997; Ali, Syed Ameer. *The Spirit of Islam, a History of the Evolution and Ideals of Islam, with a Life of the Prophet.* London. Christophers. 1922; Arberry, A.J., trans. *The Koran Interpreted.* New York: Touchstone, 1996; Bell, Richard. *Introduction to the Qur'an.* Rev. William Montgomery Watt. Edinburgh: Edinburgh University Press, 1977; Esposito, John L. *Islam: The Straight Path.* 3rd ed. New York: Oxford University Press, 2004; Greenidge, C.W.W. *Slavery.* London: Allen and Unwin, 1958; Margoliouth, D.S., and H. Carless Davis, eds. *Mohammed and the Rise of Islam.* New York: Putnam, 1905; Pickthall, Marmaduke, trans. *The Glorious Koran.* Albany: State University of New York Press, 1976; Qutb, Sayyid. *In the Shade of the Qur'an. (Fi Zilal al-Qur'an)* Translated by M.Adil Salahi, Ashur A. Shamis. Vol. 30. New Delhi. Idara Ishaat E. Diniyat, n.d; Rodinson, Maxime. *Muhammad.* Translated by Anne Carter. New York: Pantheon Books, 1980; Watt, William Montgomery. *Muhammad at Mecca.* Oxford: Clarendon Press, 1953; Watt, William Montgomery. *Muhammad at Medina.* New ed. New York: Oxford University Press, 1981; Watt, William Montgomery. *Muhammad: Prophet and Statesman.* London: Oxford University Press, 1961.

Bernard K. Freamon

R

Radical Republicans

The Radical Republicans earned their label by advocating policies of radical social change during the Civil War era. Radicals interpreted the United States Constitution's guarantee of republican government in the several states as a mandate for vastly expanded national power during the Civil War and Reconstruction. Inspired by this view, Radical Republicans invoked federal power not only to destroy slavery, which they viewed as antithetical to republican freedoms, but also the political and economic systems that had supported it. Especially through Reconstruction, radicals envisioned remodeling the entire South into a region of small producers and free laborers, characterized by political equality for all men, regardless of race. Though not wholly successful in implementing their goals, they did inaugurate dramatic social and political change in the South, and throughout the United States.

Pointing to slavery as the fundamental cause of the Civil War, radicals prodded President **Abraham Lincoln** early in the conflict to wage war for emancipation. Lincoln's shrewd reluctance to propose emancipation prematurely—so as to preserve the loyalty of slaveholding Unionists in the border states—greatly frustrated radicals. For the most part though, they supported Lincoln's policies and greeted his preliminary Emancipation Proclamation in September 1862 with great enthusiasm. Through their leadership of the Joint Committee of the Conduct of the War, radicals also sought to aid the president in prosecuting the war, assistance that likely complicated his management of the war as much as it helped.

Radicals also differed with Lincoln on the subject of Reconstruction. The president sought the quick restoration to the Union of seceded states in which 10 percent of the adult, male population pledged their allegiance to the Constitution. Radicals, though, thought the destruction of the South's old political regimes was more important than hasty restoration to the Union. In July 1864, Senator Benjamin F. Wade of Ohio and Congressman Henry Winter Davis of Maryland sponsored a Reconstruction bill that required oaths of allegiance from over half of a state's adult males and disenfranchised Confederate leaders. Lincoln pocket-vetoed the bill, but radicals did not abandon demands for harsher Reconstruction measures.

Thaddeus Stevens of Pennsylvania, a leader in the House of Representatives, advocated redistributing plantation property to freedmen in small freeholds, and other radicals proposed legislation to guarantee black male suffrage. However, few Americans supported land redistribution, and several Southern states passed Black Codes in 1865 and 1866 that severely circumscribed black freedoms and voting rights. President Andrew Johnson (who succeeded to the presidency on Lincoln's assassination) vetoed the **Freedmen's Bureau** and Civil Rights bills in 1867, which had been designed to protect the freedoms and rights of freedmen. In response, Charles Sumner led other radicals in holding up congressional passage of the Fourteenth Amendment in 1867 until it incorporated protection of citizenship rights and suffrage regardless of color. Radicals also combined with moderates to assume control of Reconstruction in 1867 and orchestrate the impeachment of Johnson the following year.

Inspired in large part by George Julian, Stevens, and other radicals, Congress's **Reconstruction Acts** of 1867 divided the South into five military districts, directed the military to register voters for new state constitutional conventions, and enfranchised adult, black males to vote in those elections. These measures enfranchised over 700,000 African American voters, outnumbering the region's white voters, and led to the first biracial state governments in the nation's history. Those governments funded public education and other social programs designed to enhance economic and social opportunities for small producers, both white and black.

However, this radical change proved short-lived. Waning Northern support for the ongoing, costly Reconstruction process caused many moderates to abandon Radical Reconstruction by 1868. The combination of Southerners' dissatisfaction with new state taxes and a wave of racist violence aimed at Republican voters soon toppled Republican governments in the South. Democrats' return to power in most Southern states by 1872 effectively ended Radical Reconstruction. Though Radical Republicans' policies proved short-lived in the South, they had paved the way for greater political and social equality for Northern blacks and greatly expanded the powers of federal and state governments to effect social change. *See also* Democratic Party and Antislavery; Whig Party and Antislavery.

Further Readings: Foner, Eric. *Reconstruction: America's Unfinished Revolution, 1863–1877.* New York: Harper & Row, 1988; Hyman, Harold. *The Radical Republicans and Reconstruction, 1861–1870.* Indianapolis, Indiana: Bobbs-Merrill, 1967; Perman, Michael. *The Road to Redemption: Southern Politics, 1868–1879.* Chapel Hill: University of North Carolina Press, 1984; Trefousse, Hans. *The Radical Republicans: Lincoln's Vanguard for Racial Justice.* New York: Knopf, 1969.

Matthew Isham

Rama V, King of Siam. *See* Chulalongkorn, King of Siam

Rankin, John (1793–1886)

John Rankin was a Presbyterian minister and a prominent leader of the **Underground Railroad** in southern Ohio from the 1820s until the abolition of slavery in the United States. Along with a handful of others, he is considered to be one of the first antislavery activists to call for an immediate abolition of slavery. **William Lloyd Garrison** considered Rankin his antislavery mentor and cited Rankin's writings as inspiring him to enter the antislavery movement.

Of Scottish descent, Rankin was born near the village of Dandridge in Jefferson County, Tennessee, on February 4, 1793. Rankin attended Washington College in southeastern Tennessee where, in 1816, he married Jean Lowry, the granddaughter of Samuel Doak, the college's founder and president.

Rankin's antislavery activism began the year before, when he helped organize the Manumission Society of Tennessee in 1815. Soon after being licensed by the Abingdon Presbytery in 1817, Rankin began preaching against slavery. Opposition to his activism led Rankin to make plans for his family's removal to the town of Ripley in Brown County, Ohio. Their exodus in 1817 took the Rankin family through Kentucky, where their only horse died and their travel funds ran out, leading Rankin to accept a position as the minister of the Concord Presbyterian Church near the town of Carlisle in Nicholas County. In Kentucky, Rankin was active in the Kentucky Abolition Society until 1822, when he moved his family to Ripley, Ohio, their original destination.

In Ohio, Rankin joined the Chillicothe Presbytery, which installed him over the church at Ripley. In 1824, Rankin began publishing letters, addressed to his brother, a slaveholder in Virginia, which called for immediate abolition. Originally published in a serialized format in Ripley's local newspaper, the *Castigator*, Rankin's *Letters on Slavery* were republished in book form in 1826. By 1850, as many as twenty editions had been published, including one by the **American Anti-Slavery Society** in 1833.

At Ripley, Rankin emerged as a prominent leader of the Underground Railroad. His house on the bluff overlooking Ripley, with a lantern lighted every night, became a beacon guiding runaway slaves to freedom. Thousands of slaves made their way along the Ripley Line, frequently receiving help from Rankin and his family. Rankin's notoriety grew on the southern side of the Ohio River, where a $2,500 bounty was eventually placed on his head. In 1835, Rankin joined with **Theodore Weld, James G. Birney**, Horace Bushnell, and others to form the Ohio Anti-Slavery Society. The following year, Rankin traveled in Ohio as an organizing agent of the American Anti-Slavery Society.

After the national governing body of the New School Presbyterians refused to exclude slaveholders from membership, Rankin joined the **"come-outer"** movement. In 1847 he led the effort to form the Free Presbyterian Church, a new denomination that barred slaveholders or advocates of slavery from becoming members.

Rankin's contribution to the antislavery cause went beyond his organizing and publications. Rankin is the source of the real-life story that inspired **Harriet Beecher Stowe**'s fictional character, Eliza Harris, in *Uncle Tom's Cabin*. In 1838, Rankin and his family helped a runaway slave who crossed the partially frozen Ohio River, carrying her two-year-old baby in her arms. Rankin lived to see the abolition of slavery, dying in 1886, having personally helped hundreds of slaves escape their bondage and having helped shift popular sentiment in favor of immediate abolition. *See also* Immediate Emancipation.

Further Readings: Grim, Paul R. "The Rev. John Rankin, Early Abolitionist." *Ohio Archaeological and Historical Quarterly* 46 (1937): 215–256; Hagedorn, Ann. *Beyond the River: The Untold Story of the Heroes of the Underground Railroad*. New York: Simon & Schuster, 2002; McKivigan, John R. "The Antislavery 'Comeouter' Sects: A Neglected Dimension of the Abolitionist Movement." *Civil War History* 26 (1980): 142–160.

Andrew Lee Feight

Raynal, Abbé Guillaume-Thomas (1713–1796)

Abbé Guillaume-Thomas Raynal wrote *Philosophical and Political History of the European Settlements and Commerce in the Two Indies*. It was central to the eighteenth-century French debate about slavery and the slave trade. This collaborative project went through three editions (1770, 1774, 1781) and many printings, and while it bears Raynal's name and editorial influence, many of the arguments were supplied by philosophers such as Jean de Pechméja and Denis Diderot. Essentially a celebration of European expansion in Asia and the Americas, the *History* was similar to the more popular *Encyclopedia* in being a laboratory of ideas advanced during the Enlightenment. As a work of advocacy, it helped to frame the terms of the growing abolitionist movement in the second half of the eighteenth century.

Beginning with the satirical critique of slavery in **Montesquieu**'s *Spirit of the Laws* in 1748, an abolitionist movement emerged in France to denounce both slavery and the slave trade that made it possible. Despite the popularity of the Enlightenment's humanitarian and reformist ideals, France by the mid-eighteenth century still controlled more than half a million black slaves. The mercantilistic French economy profited from the sugar and other plantation staples produced in its West Indian colonies. From French port cities, over 4,000 slaving ships visited Africa between 1650 and 1850 to procure workers for the colonies of Saint Domingue, Guadeloupe, and Martinique. In the decades before the Revolution, there were some calls for gradual abolition of slavery, but they were never enacted. There were more substantial examples to follow, such as the fledgling English abolitionist movement begun by **William Wilberforce** and the antislavery initiatives of the Quakers in Pennsylvania. Moreover, the Physiocrats, a cluster of progressive French economic reformers, urged the advantages of free over slave labor and undercut primary arguments for colonial slavery. By the 1770s, slavery and the slave trade were being attacked on humanitarian and economic grounds for the first time.

After the *Spirit of the Laws*, Raynal's *History* was the most discussed critique of slavery and abolition. Raynal's *History* included an extensive description of the system of enslavement from Africa to the Antilles. Raynal attacked widely supported proslavery arguments. He asserted that religions had no right to support slavery for the purpose of conversion; people of African descent were not born slaves or for slavery; prisoners of war—supposedly enslaved legitimately—actually were created by European-sponsored conflicts to produce captives; the protests and the resistance of the enslaved made clear that they were not content to labor in the Americas. At its core, the system of Atlantic slavery was a vast violation of human freedom and Raynal called upon the world's monarchs to oppose slavery. But his was not an egalitarian perspective. Like most of his contemporaries, Raynal saw his project as part of a "civilizing mission" to regenerate an Africa which was yet in its historical infancy. This effort would parallel the reforms that he recommended in the American colonies. In the third edition of the *History*, he even recommended mixed marriages between French subjects and natives in other lands as a way of further civilizing the latter.

Raynal advanced one of the Atlantic World's first systematic plans for **gradual emancipation**. Raynal extolled the advantages of cultivation by Africans in Africa and the dissemination of European arts and industry to Africa; he did not favor the immediate liberation of present slaves but, oddly, he recommended the continued importation of those who were slaves in Africa so that they would become free in America. Female slaves could be emancipated once they bore enough children to augment the colonial population. Those blacks already enslaved in the colonies would not be emancipated, as they were unprepared for freedom. Younger slaves would have to work until the age of twenty, and then for five additional years with salary for the same master. Then they could become independent cultivators or agricultural laborers. Raynal (or Pechméja) warned that the alternative to refusing to end black slavery would be a slave uprising that would lead to reprisals and destruction. Raynal prophesized the appearance of a "Black Spartacus" who would restore human rights and perhaps, vengefully, replace the black code with a white code.

Yet Raynal's increasingly radical antislavery did not continue long past his third edition. By 1785, Victor-Pierre Malouet, an associate and colonial official, deeply influenced Raynal with his *Essay on the Administration of Saint-Domingue*. Raynal now revised his policies and argued that tropical agricultural products could be cultivated only by blacks. Until they could produce among themselves a Montesquieu, blacks were closer to humanity as New World slaves with their labor productively directed than as victims of their own barbaric and hostile societies in Africa.

As a collective enterprise that underwent three major editions, struggling through an era when humanitarian ideals were being balanced with economic realities, the *History* was frequently inconsistent. But even with its contradictions, Raynal's *History* was a seminal work in the emergence of a vigorous antislavery in the eighteenth century. To its contemporaries it was a synthesis of Enlightenment antislavery ideas with its dedication to strong and articulate advocacy. Abbé Raynal was an oracle to his peers in the march toward abolition. *See also* The Enlightenment and Antislavery; French Colonies, Emancipation of; Roman Catholic Church and Antislavery and Abolitionism.

Further Readings: Canizares-Esquerra, Jorge. *How to Write the History of the New World: Histories, Epistemologies, and Identities in the Eighteenth-Century Atlantic World.* Stanford: Stanford University Press, 2001; Duchet, Michele. *Anthropologie et Histoire au siècle des lumières.* Paris: François Maspéro, 1971; Pagden, Anthony. *Lords of All the World: Ideologies of Empire in Spain, Britain and France c.1500–c.1800.* New Haven, CT: Yale University Press, 1998; Seeber, Edward. *Anti-Slavery Opinion in France during the Second Half of the Eighteenth Century.* Baltimore: The Johns Hopkins Press, 1937; Wolpe, Hans. *Raynal and His War Machine.* Stanford, CA: Stanford University Press, 1957.

William H. Alexander

Reconstruction Acts in the United States (1867–1868)

Between March 1867 and March 1868, the U.S. Congress passed four Reconstruction Acts to facilitate the reentry of the former Confederate states into the Union. The First Reconstruction Act divided the South into five military districts under the command of army generals. The act also subjugated the citizens of those districts to the authority of military courts. The first district was comprised of Virginia, the second of the Carolinas, the third of Georgia, Alabama, and Florida, the fourth of Arkansas and Mississippi, and the fifth of Texas and Louisiana. Tennessee was not part of any district as it had already ratified the Fourteenth Amendment and was considered reconstructed. In addition to establishing military districts, the First Reconstruction Act barred former high-ranking Confederates from holding public office, demanded that states enact new constitutions guaranteeing universal male suffrage regardless of race, and required states to ratify the Fourteenth Amendment. President Andrew Johnson vetoed the bill, but was overridden by Congress. The presidential veto and ensuing congressional override was a pattern that would be upheld for all of the Reconstruction Acts. In response to the passage of the First Reconstruction Act, President Johnson removed Secretary of War Edwin Stanton from office in an attempt to curb the power of the **Radical Republicans**. However, Stanton was sustained in office by the Tenure of Office Act, and Johnson was impeached and nearly removed for his actions.

Faced with a choice of granting suffrage to former slaves or living under continued military occupation, many Southerners decided they would rather deal with the army than enfranchised African Americans. Recognizing this, Congress waited less than a month before passing the Second Reconstruction Act and giving the military district commanders directions on holding state constitutional conventions. The act proscribed the loyalty oath that was required of former Confederates, established the system for choosing delegates to write the new state constitutions, and laid out the methods and procedures for elections. The federal government was going to make sure the Southern states wrote new constitutions and ratified the

Fourteenth Amendment whether they wanted to or not. President Johnson, unhappy with compelling citizens to write a new constitution against their will, interpreted the bill as narrowly as possible.

In July 1867, Congress passed the Third Reconstruction Act, allowing district commanders to remove state officials from office. The act also declared that former U.S. government officials who then served in the Confederate government were not entitled to register to vote, and established who could serve on the voter registration boards and how they would work. In March 1868, the Fourth Reconstruction Act allowed the new state constitutions to be approved by a simple majority vote. By the summer of 1870, all of the former Confederate states had been readmitted to the Union, bringing an end to the necessity of the Reconstruction Acts. *See also* Lincoln, Abraham.

Further Reading: Foner, Eric. *Reconstruction: America's Unfinished Revolution, 1863–1877.* New York: Harper & Row, Publishers, 1988.

Jared Peatman

Redpath, James (1833–1891)

An immigrant to the United States from Scotland, James Redpath launched a career in journalism by working as a reporter for Horace Greeley's New York *Tribune*. He journeyed in the South in the mid-1850s, interviewing slaves clandestinely. After the third trip, Redpath published these interviews together with his impressions of the South in a book entitled *The Roving Editor: or, Talks with the Slaves*. In this book, Redpath allowed the slaves to express their discontent and willingness to revolt.

In 1855, Redpath moved to Kansas where he reported on the dispute over slavery in that territory. During these years, Redpath became a close associate of militant abolitionist John Brown. In 1858, Brown encouraged Redpath to move to Boston to help rally support for his plan for a Southern slave insurrection. After the failure of Brown's attack on Harpers Ferry, Virginia, in 1859, Redpath wrote a highly sympathetic biography of the executed abolitionist, *The Public Life of Capt. John Brown*.

In 1860, Redpath toured Haiti as a reporter and returned to the United States as the official Haitian lobbyist for diplomatic recognition, which he secured within two years. He simultaneously served as director of Haiti's campaign to attract free black emigrants from the United States and Canada. Redpath hoped that a selective immigration of skilled blacks to Haiti would elevate conditions on that island nation and thereby dispel racial prejudice in the United States. Redpath eventually also abandoned emigration, when he recognized that North American blacks preferred to remain at home once the Civil War seemed to promise a new day of freedom for their race. In 1863 and 1864, Redpath redirected his efforts to pioneering the publishing of cheap paperbound books principally intended for distribution to a reading audience of bored Union soldiers.

Later in the Civil War, Redpath served as a frontline war correspondent with the Union army in Georgia and South Carolina. In February 1865, federal military authorities appointed Redpath the first superintendent of public schools in the Charleston region. He soon had more than 100 instructors at work teaching 3,500 students of both races. In May 1865 in Charleston, Redpath organized the first-ever Memorial Day service to honor buried Union Army dead there. His reputation as a radical abolitionist and his tentative steps toward integrating South Carolina's schools caused worried military officials to replace Redpath and remove an irritation to Southern-born President Andrew Johnson.

In 1868, Redpath organized the first professional lecturing bureau in the United States and had as his clients, such notables as Charles Sumner, **Wendell Phillips**, Henry Ward Beecher, Susan B. Anthony, and **Frederick Douglass**. Redpath ended his professional career as the editor of the *North American Review* and ironically, given his abolitionist credentials, as the ghost writer for the former Confederate president Jefferson Davis. Despite suffering a stroke in 1887, Redpath continued to lead an active life until he was killed by a trolley car accident in New York City in 1891.

Further Reading: Horner, Charles F. *The Life of James Redpath and the Development of the Modern Lyceum.* New York: Barse and Hopkins, 1926.

John R. McKivigan

Re-emergence of Slavery During Era of World War II

While serfdom and chattel slavery were abolished in nations like Russia and the United States in the mid-nineteenth century, the nature of modern conflict eighty years later meant that for total war, total mobilization of the work force became necessary. Several nations engaged in practices of forced labor that were tantamount to slavery, whether permanent as in the case of Nazi treatment of Jews and Slavs, or temporary as in the relocation and internment of Japanese citizens of the United States and Canada.

Classic serfdom entailed a complex web of ties of families and even entire clans or tribes to feudal masters. Chattel slavery meant the actual ownership of persons by individuals, with property titles, deeds, and invoices. In the United States, the vast majority of slaves were Africans. The Nazi idea similarly involved racial themes, but with more concentration on "the Jewish question," as well as such other groups branded as inferior as Gypsies, Slavs, etc. There was some dispute whether such *untermenschen* should be killed outright, or dedicated to slave labor.

With the advent of the Nazis to power in 1933, concentration camps were quickly established throughout Germany. Almost all of these had ancillary labor camps, factories, and the like in the vicinity, where inmates worked without pay. There was no individual "title," but rather, entire races were simply the property of the German State, processed by the *Schutzstaffel* (commonly termed the S.S.), and rented out to factories, farmers, etc. There was some recognition that inmates such as engineers, technicians, and skilled workers should be particularly designated and deployed in industry and agriculture.

Once the war began, and especially once the Eastern Front was opened in June 1941, a policy of extermination of the Jews was set in motion. Whole communities were massacred. One's racial identity was sufficient to be a "crime" worthy of death. But there developed a split within the Nazi hierarchy, as one faction was set on extermination pure and simple, while another faction had a realization on some level that such a policy would set the subject populations against the Nazis based on the need to survive and also that this ran counter to the need for forced labor to keep German industry going. Throughout the war, this tension was never really resolved. Significantly, once the extermination camps got into full operation, the process of selecting was well developed. Upon arrival, those judged unable to work—the very young, the old, the sick—were sent at once to the gas chambers, while another cohort was destined for the nearby factories. There was a kind of industrial efficiency, wherein clothing, hair, gold from teeth, etc. was processed and recycled. Hence the people were not only slaves, but they became industrial products themselves. Similarly, prisoners were utilized as clinical material for medical research and cruel experiments on a wide scale.

Of the 35,000 slave laborers who worked in the I.G. Farben plants in the Auschwitz complex, 25,000 died there. The rations for workers in such factories were so small that malnutrition was epidemic. The life expectancy of the typical slave laborer was three-and-a-half months. In classic chattel slavery, the slave was valuable, but in the Nazi context, he or she was worthless, as population reduction was a main goal, and there were always more slaves to be had. In addition to Jews, vast numbers of prisoners and civilians from the East were brought into this system. Frequently these laborers were so weak from malnutrition and illness that they were useless for factory work.

From the Western Front, hundreds of thousands were transferred to Germany to work in factories; some 1.3 million from France alone. In some cases these were prisoners of war, while others were simply rounded up, and yet others "volunteered" because the alternative was starvation. By the end of 1944, one fifth of the work force in Germany was foreign, totaling 5 million.

Those who deny the Holocaust have argued that the crematoria in camps like Auschwitz were used merely to deal efficiently with the corpses of those who died of natural causes in nearby factories. This position tacitly acknowledges the existence of forced labor on a massive scale during the Nazi era.

Forced labor under the government of the Soviet Union took on a slightly different character. In 1931, Stalin stated that the Soviets were fifty to one hundred years behind the industrialized countries; they had ten years to make it up or they would be crushed. Hence, the Great Famine in the Ukraine was caused by a need to accumulate capital by selling grain on the world market, thus enabling the Soviets to purchase entire factories from Ford. In a similarly ruthless fashion, the Purge trials and Terror produced a compliant bureaucracy that would strive to meet production goals because failure to do so meant imprisonment or death. The "Gulag Archipelago" of labor camps stretching across Russia and far into Siberia was a vast system of industrial development on a "crash basis." Though there was usually a pretext of "crimes" having been committed by inmates—sabotage, conspiracy, and the like—the actual purpose of this system was industrial production at all costs. Whole social classes such as the wealthy peasant Kulaks were arrested, and either shot or transported to labor camps. The basis for the Soviet forced labor system was not race for the most part, but social class. "Class traitors" or other dissidents went to their deaths, or to the camps. A memorable literary portrait of this process is Yevgeny Yevtushenko's long poem *Bratsk Station*, in which dedicated Bolsheviks found themselves building electrical power plants in Siberia. As in Germany, the State was the "owner" of the person, rather than individuals. Even whole families could be deported, and thus the familial character of the old system of serfdom was replicated. The numbers involved in this system are disputed, but it was certainly in the tens of millions.

In the Far East, the Japanese Empire, allied with Nazi Germany, developed a vast system of slave labor to fuel factory and mine production in China (especially Manchuria), Korea, and in Japan itself. Hundreds of thousands of Chinese and Korean workers were brought into industry, with mortality rates as high as fifty percent in the mines. This system is powerfully depicted in the classic film trilogy "The Human Condition," directed by Masaki Kobayashi (1959–1960), where a young and somewhat liberal Japanese engineer is sent to a remote Manchurian factory where he is soon horrified by its brutal conditions. The sponsoring corporation is depicted as a cynical bureaucracy, indifferent to the suffering from which it profits so handsomely.

As in Germany, the Japanese engaged in medical experiments on prisoners of war, during which hundreds died in gruesome ways. These included experiments in germ warfare. Thus human beings were transformed into mere clinical material, in which they had no rights.

In addition to factory and mine labor, the Japanese developed a system of "comfort women," in which tens of thousands of women were forced into brothels for the Japanese military. In Korea alone, some 200,000 women were so conscripted; many did not survive the experience. Women of all races from the entire reach of the Japanese empire were included in this system.

Even in the western democracies, such as the United States and Canada, forced labor was also introduced, albeit with significant differences from the fascist model. In both countries, citizens of Japanese ancestry were quickly interned after Pearl Harbor was attacked. In the United States, they numbered 112,000, and in Canada, 21,000. They were transported to hastily constructed camps, often in remote desert regions. Some internees began work on nearby farms, producing food for themselves and in place of those who went off to join the war. As their "crime" consisted only of their racial origin, and there was no evidence of antigovernment sabotage or conspiracy, such internments bore a distinct resemblance to the camps in Germany. One difference was that it seemed to be more in the nature of a wartime emergency measure, rather than a result of a racial stigma that could never be overcome. Indeed, hundreds of Japanese-Americans interned in the camps actually served in the United States Army, though in Europe rather than in the Pacific. It is also significant that unlike in Germany there was nothing in place resembling extermination procedures, nor was there a high mortality rate for internees, compared to that for forced laborers under the Japanese. Still, the existence of internment and forced labor in the democracies suggests that the dynamic of such systems was not unique to the fascist powers.

While there had been isolated revolts by Jewish militants, both in the camps and in incidents like the Warsaw Rising of 1943, these had not been sufficient to shake the system, let alone destroy it. As with the end of chattel slavery in the United States at the end of the Civil War, the end of slave labor under the fascists was brought about only through the allied victory and the total defeat of the fascist armies.

After the war, a handful of military officers and corporate leaders in both Germany and Japan were tried for war crimes, including the use of forced labor. Some were convicted and sent to prison. However, the "comfort women" of Korea who survived sixty years after the end of the war, were still endeavoring to obtain reparations from the Japanese government.

Further Readings: Daniels, Roger. *Concentration Camps: North America Japanese in the United States during World War II.* Malabar, FL: Robert E. Krieger, 1981; Harris, Sheldon H. *Factories of Death: Japanese Biological Warfare, 1932–1945, and the American Cover-up.* New York: Routledge, 2002; Herbert, Ulrich. *Hitler's Foreign Workers: Enforced Foreign Labor in Germany under the Third Reich.* Cambridge: Cambridge University Press, 1997; Homze, Edward L. *Foreign Labor in Nazi Germany.* Princeton: Princeton University Press, 1967; Solzhenitsyn, Alexandr I. *The Gulag Archipelago.* New York: Harper, 1974; Suhl, Yuri, ed. *They Fought Back: The Story of Jewish Resistance in Nazi Europe.* New York: Crown, 1967.

Fred Whitehead

Repartimiento

In the Spanish New World Empire, *repartimiento* represented the allocation of Native Americans for compulsory labor, though it also could include goods and services. In Hispaniola, Christopher Columbus promised his men salaries, but he rarely paid them. Disgusted with meager earnings, settlers revolted against the Columbus family authority during the admiral's absence. Upon his third voyage in 1498, Columbus learned that colonists opposed his brother Barolomé's command in Hispaniola. To preserve stability, Columbus sanctioned the distribution of Indians that his adversaries disbursed to specific settlers. These allotments, termed *repartimientos*, designated a particular chieftain and his people to an *encomendero* to work in mines or agriculture. Early Spanish colonists coveted the *repartimiento* because it guaranteed labor supply and bestowed prestige to the *encomendero*.

In colonial Spanish America, the *repartimiento* evolved into the *encomienda* system. Repartimiento laborers were coerced into arduous work in agriculture, textile factories, and mining. Horrific working conditions and starvation under the *repartimiento*, coupled with contagious diseases, contributed to Caribbean native population decline. Edicts such as The Law of

Burgos (1512) failed to reverse this catastrophe. The Dominicans, under **Bartolomé Las Casas** (1474–1566), protested the mistreatment of Native Americans under the *repartimiento* system. Las Casas angrily denounced the Spanish abuse of Indians through his writings, which influenced the Spanish Crown to promulgate the New Laws of 1542. The New Laws banned Indian slavery and undermined the *encomienda* system. However, the *encomenderos* forcefully resisted implementation of these decrees. The Crown then allowed for an extension of the *encomienda* system, which thereafter gradually declined in central Mexico and Peru. However, the *encomienda* and *repartimiento* continued in Paraguay, the Yucatán, and Central America.

After the promulgation of the New Laws, Indian communities substituted cash tribute for previous non-monetary payments, though this transition remained inconsistent. For tributaries to meet annual payments they had to produce commercial goods and work for wages. By 1600, Native American communities were reorganized to fulfill their economic obligations to the colonial state and the **Roman Catholic Church**. However, financial requirements alone failed to compel enough Indians to abandon traditional production for *repartimiento* labor. To resolve this labor shortage, a system of rotational labor drafts, called the *repartimiento* in Mexico and the mita in Peru, was instituted.

Formal *repartimiento* and mita drafts were established in New Spain in the 1550s and in the central Andes in the 1570s. Under this system, the Indian communities supplied labor quotas for two to four months of the year. These minimal wages paid for tribute and other required payments. In New Spain the *repartimiento* dominated in agriculture and silver mining. In Peru, the mita furnished labor for silver mines, coastal plantations and road maintenance. In Quito, the *repartimiento* provided workers in the textile factories. In Peru, Ecuador, and Central America, the *repartimiento*/mita system mobilized Indian labor until the independence era.

Indigenous population decline and Spanish population growth rendered the *repartimiento* system inadequate for resolving labor scarcity. In central Mexico, large landowners and mine owners procured a stable workforce by contracting directly with Indians by offering wages slightly higher than those for *repartimiento* labor. Eventually wage labor replaced forced labor as Indians, being displaced due to land confiscation or sale, became wage earners. By 1630 wage labor replaced the *repartimiento* in New Spain, though Spanish and Creole landowners and mine owners deliberately kept salaries low.

Peruvian Indians fought against the *repartimiento* with uprisings from the 1740s through the 1770s. The most intense uprisings occurred under the leadership of José Gabriel Condorcanqui, also known as **Tupac Amaru II**. As a local chief from the Cuzco region, his insurgency wanted to abolish the mita, the *repartimiento* of goods, and the corregidores (provincial colonial administrators). In November 1780, the uprising grew as rebels executed a nefarious corregidor (magistrate). A colonial militia sent from Lima defeated the insurgency, and in May 1781, Tupac Amaru II was executed but the rebellions still continued. Before peace was restored in 1783,

10,000 people died during the insurrection that ultimately destroyed the *repartimiento* system. *See also* Latin America, Antislavery and Abolition in.

Further Readings: Bray, Warwick, ed. *The Meeting of Two Worlds: Europe and the Americas, 1492–1650*. New York: Oxford University Press, 1993; Thomson, Sinclair. *We Alone Will Rule: Native Andean Politics in the Age of Insurgency*. Madison: University of Wisconsin Press, 2002.

Kimberly Welch

Republicanism and Antislavery

In their struggle to convince Americans of the necessity of immediate, uncompensated emancipation of slaves without expatriation, and to persuade them of the sinfulness of human enslavement, antebellum abolitionists directly and indirectly invoked the legacy, language, and values of republicanism (as well as those of liberalism and evangelical Christianity). Indeed, to justify their cause, to embolden adherents and inspire converts, and to realize the nation's libertarian pretensions, immediatists often enlisted the past—particularly the memory of the American Revolution—to achieve a more perfect future (and union for that matter). The republican ideological heritage that partly informed abolitionist perceptions of slavery and helped shape abolitionist arguments against slaveholding was distinctive and sophisticated, extending across great amounts of space and time—from classical antiquity, Renaissance Italy, seventeenth- and eighteenth-century England, and Revolutionary America—and embracing such theorists and writers as Niccolo Machiavelli, James Harrington, Algernon Sidney, Thomas Gordon, John Trenchard, and **Thomas Jefferson**, to name only several.

Although abolitionists espoused that lineage, they never systematically adhered to a unitary framework of republican thought; nor, for the most part, did their intellectual ancestors. That is, American republicanism, hardly a static concept, has been shaped and reshaped, applied and reapplied, depending on the individual and the context. Indeed, the manner in which abolitionists utilized republican ideas often differed markedly from the usages of their contemporaries—Whig and Democratic politicians, urban laborers, slaveholders, and so on. Yet, despite republicanism's protean nature, certain central tenets nonetheless define that term and distinguish that worldview.

At the epicenter of republicanism was liberty, specifically how best to secure and preserve it. Liberty could mean different things to different people; for Americans, however, liberty referred to traditional rights, such as the ones guaranteed by the state and federal constitutions. To ensure liberty's enjoyment and existence, citizens must restrain their private desires and interests for the sake of the common good and be ever vigilant against plots that might endanger the body politic and jeopardize established freedoms. Should such conspiracies remain undetected, unchecked, or ultimately succeed, tyranny and oppression would assuredly follow (late-eighteenth-century colonial American rebels deployed similar rhetoric in defense of independence from England). Because of such ever-present threats, civic-minded republicans were the perpetual sentinels against arbitrary arrangements and encroachments of power. Such responsibilities, at least in the antebellum United States, ceased to be the exclusive domain of property holders—those individuals originally deemed appropriately independent, sufficiently capable of disinterested decision making, and necessarily invested in a republic's proper maintenance. Yet, the democratization of America in the early-nineteenth century, particularly the expansion of the suffrage to include all white adult males regardless of land ownership, incorporated greater numbers among the ranks of the productive, responsible, and virtuous citizenry. At about the same time, abolitionists completely undercut newly created racial and gender strictures for republican guardianship that matured during the Jacksonian era—for white male activists embraced not only black men as among those worthy of vigilant citizenship, but also black and white women as crucial participants. (It does not follow, however, that white-male antislavery agitators were without racial prejudices and gender biases.)

According to one historical argument that has asserted the strongest link between republicanism and abolitionism, immediatists believed that slavery "embodied the frightening force of arbitrary power [and] acted as an expansive and conspiratorial menace that smashed all barriers to authority, infected the moral character of a people, created widespread misery, and destroyed the fragile principles of human liberty" (McInerney, 8–9). To be sure, republican-sensitive abolitionists judged human enslavement utterly reprehensible, if only because masters were virtually all powerful and slaves nearly powerless. Such an extreme was a blatant contradiction of basic republican hallmarks, balance and order on the one hand, and self-control and self-determination on the other. And if power corrupted, republican-inspired abolitionists specifically feared the direful consequences that might arise from the absolute power that slave masters wielded.

Yet, when numerous antislavery delegates, primarily from across the North, gathered in Philadelphia in 1833 to establish what became the **American Anti-Slavery Society**, the national movement that they inaugurated did not originate in counter subversion. That is, at the outset of their campaign, antebellum abolitionists espied anything but a scheming planter oligarchy that, because of its determination to safeguard the "peculiar institution," threatened to subvert the liberty of everyone else. The suppression of traditional civil rights (the abolitionist postal and petition campaigns of the middle 1830s, for example), the decades-long debates over the status of slavery west of the Mississippi River, and the perceived attempt to seemingly nationalize the institution of slavery (the 1850 **Fugitive Slave Law** and the proslavery decision in the 1857 Supreme Court case, *Dred Scott v. Sanford*), all unequivocally stirred in abolitionists' republican misgivings. By the time the slave states of the Deep South greeted the election of Republican candidate **Abraham Lincoln** to the presidency in 1860 with secession from the Union, abolitionists had proven themselves the inveterate foes of what was called the Slave Power and the most outspoken agitators against the conspiracy thought to be waged by a cabal of aggressive and rapacious slaveholders to extend and protect slavery wherever slaveholders might travel or reside.

Indeed, soon after the founding of immediate abolitionism's national organization, antislavery activists confronted violence and endured hostility—in the press, in the streets, and in legislative halls, and against their property, against their persons, and against their basic rights—for nearly three decades before the eruption of sectional military conflagration. Because of the accumulated negative reactions that **immediate emancipation** intentionally and unintentionally provoked (largely stemming from abolitionist-instigated controversies surrounding the repeated incursions of the slavery issue into the national public and political discourse), abolitionists-cum-republicans were convinced that some malevolent, designing force impeded the emancipation of slaves, wrought havoc on the sanctity of liberty, and prevented the nation's return to founding principles as enshrined in the opening paragraph of the **Declaration of Independence**, thereby assisting in the republic's desolation and approaching demise. The Civil War, however, allowed for the potential of an appropriately restored republican course, one that extended personal freedoms to and protected the individual liberties of all the country's inhabitants. Such a hope enabled normally nonviolent and antiwar abolitionists to tentatively support the Union cause. Such a hope, moreover, ensured that abolitionists would remain ever vigilant on behalf of the enslaved, as they continually agitated for stronger antislavery measures from the Republican-controlled Congress and Executive. *See also* Democratic Party and Antislavery; Slave Power Argument; Whig Party and Antislavery.

Further Readings: McInerney, Daniel J. *The Fortunate Heirs of Freedom: Abolition and Republican Thought.* Lincoln: University of Nebraska Press, 1994; Rodgers, Daniel T. "Republicanism: the Career of a Concept." *The Journal of American History* 79, 1 (June 1992): 11–38.

Raymond James Krohn

Roma and Emancipation

The Emancipation of the Roma has specific features that result from the way in which the Roma have been perceived and disenfranchised since their arrival in Europe. The Roma arrived in Europe in several waves following the great Mongol invasion of 1241. They settled down gradually in Eastern Europe, Central Europe, and finally Western Europe. If at the beginning they were regarded with curiosity and fascination, gradually the traditional animosity between the sedentary and the nomads contributed to the construction of the Roma as the dangerous Other who would steal children, cast destructive charms, and try to subject the natives to unorthodox practices.

Such friction led to juridical decisions to expel the Roma beyond national borders. In 1530, King Henry VIII of England banned the Gypsies from his country. In 1524, King Gustav Vasa of Sweden ordered all Gypsies to leave the country, and in 1637 a new anti-Gypsy law was passed in Sweden. The great round up of all Gypsies in Spain in 1749 was probably the most aggressive anti-Gypsy legislation in Europe before the Holocaust (Porojmas, the destruction of the Roma).

The Western European feudal states with a powerful central authority succeeded in putting these aggressive policies into practice, banishing the Roma and inflicting very severe punishments on any one sheltering or helping them. The few Roma who continued to live in Western Europe never posed the same problems as in Eastern Europe. Firstly, their numbers were and are much smaller, with the exception of Spain, which has a larger number of Roma. Also, the much earlier modernity of Western Europe influenced the emancipation of the Roma. They were designated citizens of these modern states and were granted better economic opportunities in their developing industrialized economies. This did not prevent, however, the discrimination and the marginalization of the Roma, whose efforts to preserve their culture were often seen as standing against modernization and integration.

In Eastern Europe, which, during the Middle Ages, was under increasing Ottoman threat, the Roma were not banished, but many of them came to be enslaved. Probably they had been assimilated with the Tartars or the Turks, because they often came after the enemy troops and their racial visibility singled them out as aliens from the South. There were quite large numbers of Roma slaves on the territories of present-day Hungary, Romania, Serbia, and Russia. Roma women were often housemaids, whereas men worked on the fields. They were appreciated as musicians (lautari) and/or practitioners of such traditional crafts as blacksmiths or metal engravers. However, unlike the black slaves working on the plantations in the American South, the labor of the Roma slave was not the fundamental economic basis of all East European societies. These societies relied mostly on the exploited labor of the serfs and the peasantry, not on slave labor.

The emancipation of the Roma came slowly and mostly as a consequence of the influence of the Enlightenment ideology. In this respect, the Roma slaves and the American slaves were often regarded similarly. In Hungary and Transylvania, the Roma slaves were emancipated by Maria Theresa and Joseph II. The abolition of slavery was justified as the abolishment of an institution shameful for the age of **Enlightenment.** The manumission was accompanied by drastic measures against nomadic Roma. The idea was to turn the Roma into *New Hungarians*, citizens with stable whereabouts, that they be controlled and contained. The Roma had to become individuals who paid taxes to the state and had a clearly defined profession as their source of income. All these were considered to be valuable steps in diminishing the crime rate among the Roma. Roma children were obliged to attend schools where classes were in Hungarian and where musical education was offered as well.

Russians also had concerns about the nomadic Roma. In 1759, Czarina Elisabeth II passed a law forbidding the Roma to settle in St. Petersburg. This prohibition was repealed only in 1917. In 1783, the Roma were invited to "settle" and this obligation was reenacted in 1800, 1809, and 1839. The new authorities that came into power after the fall of the Czar in 1917 also encouraged the Roma to settle down and become farmers. In 1925, a Union of Gypsies was formed which developed many cultural programs promoting the foundation of Romany schools and encouraging Romany culture. In

1928, the Romany Theatre was founded. All this rich cultural activity came to an abrupt halt in 1938 when Stalin decided that the Roma were not a nation and an end was put to all the cultural activity in Romany. Only the Romany Theatre survived. It was only Mikhail Gorbachev's glasnost policy after 1985 that made Romany culture visible again and also allowed free manifestations of Romany organizations.

Macedonia, Bulgaria, and Serbia were parts of the **Ottoman Empire** for half a millennium. The Roma were levied higher than the Serbians, but otherwise they were treated like any other minority in the Empire. The Ottoman authorities also tried to discourage nomadism because it prevented the accurate taxation of the Roma. During this historical period, many Roma converted to **Islam**. The nineteenth century was the century of successful nationalisms in the Balkans. The emancipation of the Roma became part of the creation and consolidation of these new states. The new national authorities were also interested in forbidding nomadism and turning the Roma into settled citizens easier to contain, supervise, and tax. Many Roma became urban residents and were attracted by the urbanizing and industrialization policies developed mostly after World War II. The Holocaust seriously affected the Roma communities in these countries. Numerous Roma were placed in labor or extermination camps.

Cultural emancipation stagnated during this period, but, on the whole, in the twentieth century significant efforts were made to create a written Romany language and found Romany theatres. In the 1930s in Bulgaria, fragments from the Bible were published in Romany dialects, in Serbia Trifun Dimić published the New Testament in Romany, and in 1980, Shaip Jusuf published the first Romany grammar in the Romany language. The Pralipe Theatre was founded in Skopje (it operated until 1990s) and the Theatre Roma functioned in Sofia between 1947 and 1951. For a short period after World War II, Communist authorities allowed magazines and newspapers in Romany language, but it was only after 1990, in post-Communist societies, that the cultural emancipation of the Roma truly became visible. Journals and magazines, many of them funded internationally, were published, and television and radio programs were broadcast (at Tetovo and Skopje in Macedonia, in Cluj-Napoca and Bucharest in Romania). On the other hand, the post-Communist freedom of expression also gave vent to racist and xenophobic voices, which sometimes overwhelmed the voices of tolerance, ethnic cooperation, and mutual understanding.

In the Romanian Principalities (Wallachia and Moldavia), the Enlightenment influence continued all through the 1850s and coincided with the challenging influence of the American abolitionist discourse. For instance, only one year after its publication in the United States, *Uncle Tom's Cabin* was translated into Romanian. Mihail Kogalniceanu, an important Romanian writer and historian, and one of the champions of Roma emancipation, wrote the preface to this translation, which was supposed to influence the general public in favor of the emancipation of the Roma. Already in 1844, in an article published in the periodical *Propasirea*, Kogalniceanu talked about the necessity to emancipate the Roma. He made a comparison with the American colonies where the blacks were oppressed and the legislative bodies teemed with supporters of slavery. The situation was much better in the Romanian Principalities, in his opinion. The emancipation of the Roma became part of the nationalist discourse. The emancipation of the Romanian nation could not be complete and convincing while slavery, a barbaric and shameful custom, was still accepted. In 1855, on the eve of the emancipation of the Roma, Alecu Russo, a prominent writer and journalist, tackled the problem in an article published in the periodical *Steaua Dunarii*. In his opinion, slavery had to be abolished for humanitarian reasons, but also for economic reasons. It was not profitable. The appearance of the modern agricultural machines made the existence of so much labor force unnecessary. Turning the former Roma slaves into free workers who sold their labor force and bought wares for their necessities was much more profitable.

A much less remembered factor in the emancipation of the Roma in this part of Europe was the influence of the Freemasonry. The Freemasons considered that the human being can only be the slave of God; any other form of enslavement was to be rejected. Many of the personalities of the eighteenth and nineteenth centuries were Masons, including Joseph II and Mihail Kogalniceanu.

In the Romanian Principalities, the process of Roma emancipation began with Alexandru Mavrocordat's Act (1746 in Wallachia and 1749 in Moldavia). Alexandru Mavrocordat forbade the separation of spouses when Roma slaves were sold, and he also decreed that the offspring of a free individual and a slave was free. Before Mavrocordat's Act, matrimony to a slave meant slavery for both spouses. In Moldavia, particularly, there was fierce opposition to this law. In 1766, priests were forbidden to give their blessing to such unions. In 1785, there was a backlash and religious practice reverted to the previous "custom of the country." However, in 1780, in Wallachia the *Pravilniceasa Condica* (the *Law Record*) imposed the immediate separation of a Roma who married a free woman, but the offspring of such a union were free. The slaves owned by the state were manumitted in Wallachia in 1843 and in Moldavia in 1844. In the last year in Moldavia, the slaves owned by monasteries also became free. The same manumission process occurred in Wallachia in 1847. The manumission of the Roma slaves, who were the property of individuals, occurred in 1855 in Moldovia and in 1856 in Wallachia. Former owners were to receive compensation for their losses but most of them refused, so much had the idea of Roma manumission as a sign of modernity in the Romanian Principalities become influential. However, juridical emancipation did not solve the problem of the Roma. The social and economic needs of this new group of free individuals were not addressed at all. No programs of vocational training or social integration and education were conceived, and even less were implemented. Singular voices, such as that of Gheorghe Sion, would call for some form of vocational education for the manumitted Roma, but nothing practical would be done. As Romania was mostly an agricultural society, there was no significant industrial boom to absorb these newly free individuals. A solution would have been their transformation into farmers by allotting them land from the estates where they had previously been slaves. Nothing like that was even considered in the public discourse of the time. The Rural Act from 1864 did not refer to the former slaves who would be left out of the mainstream society.

The consequences of this situation can be seen even today. The Roma developed a marginal way of life somewhere in-between survival and crime, which increased the prejudice against them. Emancipation still has a long way to go. The situation is clearly grasped by the Roma themselves. The prevalent attitude was (and it is not yet extinct) that there was an intrinsic negative nature of the Roma that pushed him to crime and harmful idleness. Voices, which called for humaneness, tolerance, and an honest evaluation regarding the circumstances that pushed the Roma to marginalization, were neglected and even laughed at.

Significantly, it was the Roma themselves who tried most successfully, in the period between the two World Wars, to manage their own emancipation. Several political organizations of the Roma appeared. The most prominent leaders, such as G.A. Lazareanu-Lazurica or Calinic I. Popp-Serboianu, insisted on the necessity of assisting the Roma to find practical solutions to their social and economic needs.

A peculiar aspect of modern Roma emancipation was the reappearance of the so-called Roma kings, dukes, voivodes, etc. This new form of leadership resumed a medieval tradition when the Roma had their own leaders who represented the Roma in their relations with the mainstream authorities. At the end of World War II, the Kalderash from Poland, for instance, elected their own kings and formed the Kwiek dynasty (Michal II, Janusz Kwieck, and Rudolf Kwieck), which was recognized by the Polish authorities of the time.

These efforts to have a dialogue with mainstream society and develop typical Roma leadership were brutally interrupted by the dictatorships that ruled in Eastern European countries from the 1930s until 1990. During World War II, many Roma were deported to death camps in order to cleanse society of their reputed evil influence and actions. After World War II, Communist regimes did not recognize the Roma as a minority, with the significant exception of Yugoslavia. The situation of the Roma was analyzed several times by the Communist parties in plenaries dedicated to ethnic problems. For instance, in 1983 there was a report by the Propaganda Section of the Central Committee of the Romanian Communist Party about the Roma. The idea was that the Roma had to be bleached and assimilated to the majority. Compulsory secondary education and the obligation to be integrated into the labor force were the prevalent strategies.

After the fall of the Communist regime, the dismantling of the huge industrial complexes and of the collective farms affected the Roma more than other people. As they usually held the lowest positions in a factory, those that required fewer qualifications, they were the first to lose their jobs in the case of privatization or restructuring. The disappearance of the collective farms was another severe blow because land was given back to the former owners and usually the Roma did not own land. On the other hand, the free trade and free initiative opportunities were beneficial for other Roma who were able to integrate more quickly into the new economic structures of the East European countries.

But Roma emancipation is still an ongoing process because centuries of neglect and marginalization cannot be overcome by the success of few. Affirmative action policies in higher education, as well as increasing educational and social opportunities, publications in Roma language, and encouraging the appearance of a Roma elite are all aspects of the contemporary Roma emancipation process. *See also* Russian Serfs, Emancipation of.

Further Readings: Achim, Viorel. *The Roma in Romanian History.* Budapest: Central European University Press, 2004; Kenrick, Donald, and Clare Paul, research assistant. *The Romani World: A Historical Dictionary of the Gipsies.* Hatfield, UK: University of Hertfordshire Press, 2004; Mayall, David. *Gypsy-Travellers in Nineteenth Century Society.* Cambridge: Cambridge University Press, 1988; Copoiu, Petre. *Rromane paramica. Povesti tiganesti.* Bucuresti: Kriterion, 1996; Rossetti, Radu. *Scrieri.* Catalina Poleacov, ed. Mircea Anghelescu, preface and notes. Bucuresti: Minerva, 1980; Sion, Gheorghe. *Emanciparea tiganilor.* Bucuresti: Petru V. Hanes Publishing House, 1924.

Marcela Echeverri

Roman Catholic Church and Antislavery and Abolitionism

Slavery was a normal social institution, justified both scripturally and legally, in the world in which early Christianity spread. Mosaic law (Exodus 21; Deuteronomy 15) mandated moderate treatment of slaves, and Romans owned slaves and legislated regarding slavery. Jesus and the Apostles never sought to overturn the social institution of slavery, but they emphasized the equality before God of all believers, whether free or enslaved. On the one hand, this emphasis implied that slaves should work loyally and, if necessary, suffer patiently while keeping in mind the rewards of faith and the prospect of heaven. On the other hand, it implied that a social institution in which individuals were locked into inequality must be immoral. In most of Roman Catholic history, this tension has been resolved by the acceptance by canonists and theologians of the legitimacy of the institution of slavery along with a desire to ameliorate the condition of slaves themselves. An amelioration of slave life would, according to traditional Catholic thought, encourage dignity and faith.

Saint Paul exemplifies early Church teaching on slavery. Christian faith created one people, regardless of enslavement or of liberty, before God (Galatians 3: 27–28), yet slaves were still to obey their masters (Ephesians 6:9; Colossians 3: 22–24). In Philemon, Saint Paul urged a master to accept a runaway slave, Onesimus, returning as the courier of the letter itself, "not now as a servant, but above a servant, a brother beloved, ... both in the flesh, and in the Lord" (Philemon 16). The ambiguity of this letter allowed both proslavery and antislavery advocates to claim it as their own. Moreover, an idea found in the Gospels as well as in Saint Paul's letters that sin itself was a form of slavery would centuries later imply to believers that slavery was a kind of sin.

From the time of the early Church to the eighteenth century, Catholic teaching promoted amelioration while still tolerating slavery. While slavery disappeared in most parts of Europe and was replaced by serfdom, it continued to thrive in the Mediterranean and in some border regions. Some churchmen and monasteries held slaves, while others were instrumental in manumissions. Theologians like **Saint Augustine** and Saint Thomas Aquinas justified enslavement as part of the fallen world that had followed original sin. Natural law was, in Aquinas's views, silent on slavery itself, but not on the basic rights of slaves to sustenance, family life, worship, and the like, or on the masters' obligations of benevolence and guardianship to the enslaved. The exploration and settlement of the Atlantic World by Catholics beginning in the fifteenth century initiated a gradual decline of the ameliorationist-tolerationist stance. A 1435 papal bull commanded Catholics to free those of the native people of the Canary Islands, who had recently been enslaved by European settlers. A 1537 papal bull extended the command to Europeans in the West Indies, followed by mandates for the Philippines (1591), Brazil (1639), South America (1781), and all areas where native Americans or Africans were enslaved (1839). An influential figure in this process was **Bartolomé de las Casas** (1474–1566). Las Casas's father had accompanied Christopher Columbus on one of his expeditions to the New World, and Bartolomé moved to Hispañola in 1502. Soon ordained, las Casas, a slaveowner himself, came to object to the treatment of the indigenous people in the *encomienda* system, which allowed Spanish settlers to command the labor of local people. Widely used to exploit native peoples grossly, *encomienda* was replaced by an apparently less harsh system of draft labor, *repartimiento*, which ended the enslavement of natives while expanding that of Africans. Despite the efforts of Catholic missionaries to uphold the provisions of *repartimiento*, abuses by colonial officials continued. For example, following las Casas, a cohort of Jesuit missionaries sought both to convert the Guaranis of Paraguay and protect them from enslavement by Europeans. From 1609 to the 1750s, the Jesuits held other Europeans at bay, but finally the Paraguayan towns were attacked and the Jesuits expelled. Other Brazilian and Spanish clerics such as Tomas de Mercado, Bartolome de Albornoz, Alonso de Sandoval, and Pedro Claver were also among the first in the New World to speak against the Atlantic slave trade, doubting that such a cruel and murderous commerce could be sustained by Christian ethics. Yet they focused their ministrations on assisting and converting recently arrived Africans rather than on upending the commerce itself.

Las Casas reveals the mental and moral journey typically made by abolitionists in the era that more efficaciously opposed the slave trade and slavery (1775–1875). Thus, las Casas is important not only as a defender of the natives in the Spanish colonies and as a chronicler of early settlement, but also as an exemplary figure. The stages of this journey were an acceptance of slavery as a just social institution, skepticism about its justness and a personal crisis over its continuance, a provisional rejection of slavery, and, finally, a critique of the institution itself. Las Casas was a slaveowner. Experience in the Spanish colonies convinced him that the native peoples would inevitably be overworked, mistreated, and degraded by their Spanish masters. He passionately advocated Church protection of the natives, but he urged that their place as laborers be taken by sub-Saharan African slaves. He was not, however, the first to propose African slaves for labor in the Spanish colonies. His 1518 proposal came more than a decade after the first importation of African slaves. Las Casas has often been castigated as a proponent of the enslavement of Africans, but he did finally admit that it, too, was immoral. It is more accurate—both in the case of las Casas and of most abolitionists—to identify the process by which people came to understand that the slave trade and slavery were wrong than to expect a consistent opposition to slavery.

Las Casas was not alone. Many prelates and Church authorities supported his call for more humane treatment of the Indians. Yet the idea that the institution of slavery itself was immoral—an idea that negated centuries of Church teachings—was as slow dawning to Catholics as to Protestants. For both branches of the Christian faith, the decisive period for abolitionism ran from the end of the eighteenth century to the middle of the nineteenth century. European settlers in Catholic colonies almost always resisted the efforts of the Church to ameliorate slavery. Brazilian colonists, for instance, expelled the Jesuits and disobeyed royal orders when the use of Indian labor was threatened by ameliorationist or emancipationist policies. The 1685 *Code Noir*, effective in the French colonies, mandated religious privileges and days of rest for slaves, but the slaveholding planters refused to enact these protections. Such circumstances helped to convince Catholic intellectuals that ameliorationism would never work, that the only solution to the problems of the slave trade and slavery was their abolition. By the nineteenth century, leading Catholics like the Irish "Liberator" **Daniel O'Connell** (1775–1847) and the French educational reformer Comte de Montalembert (1810–1870) were arguing for the abolition of the slave trade and slavery. In 1888, the largest number of slaves freed by a national emancipation in a Catholic country occurred in Brazil, after several decades of internal abolitionist agitation, international pressure, and immigration of laborers whose wages were often lower than the upkeep required to maintain slaves. Yet even that liberation sparked widespread protest from slaveholders, most of whom were Catholic. Cardinal **Charles Lavigerie** (1825–1892), would spearhead the Catholic antislavery movement in sub-Saharan Africa in the late-eighteenth century as European colonialists divided the vast continent among themselves. Appalled not only by the indigenous slavery but also by the savage exploitation of the Africans by the colonizers, especially in the Belgian Congo, Lavigerie struggled with mixed results to secure a humane modification of these policies by Belgium's King Leopold.

Is there, finally, one Catholic teaching on slavery? For lay people, the slave trade and slavery probably seem right or wrong insofar as they cohere with society and culture at large. Thus, Catholics were once active in the slave trade and in enslaving Indians and Africans and papal bulls threatened excommunication. American Catholics of the Northern states fought in the U.S. Civil War, and today Catholics worldwide feel a visceral revulsion at the thought of slavery. For Catholic intellectuals and theologians, it seems certain that Church tradition is still influential. Slavery can be seen as in institution of the fallen world, not inherently evil but so prone to the abuse of slaves that it should be outlawed. To return to Aquinas, if natural law is silent on slavery, but if rights and duties that are required by natural law are incommensurable with the enslavement of some people, then the slave trade and slavery must be immoral. *See also* Antislavery Evangelical Protestantism; Bible and Slavery; Book of Exodus; Buddhism and Antislavery; Islam and Antislavery; Story of Joseph.

Further Readings: Davis, David Brion. *The Problem of Slavery in Western Culture.* New York: Oxford University Press, 1966; Noonan, John T., Jr. *The Church that Can and Cannot Change: The Development of Catholic Moral Teaching.* Notre Dame, IN: University of Notre Dame Press, 2005.

John Saillant

Rome and Antislavery. *See* Classical Rome and Antislavery

Rousseau, Jean-Jacques (1712–1778)

Jean-Jacques Rousseau was a leading intellectual of the French **Enlightenment.** He wrote on a variety of topics and in genres as diverse as opera and autobiography. Rousseau, however, is best known for his treatises on political philosophy, the two most famous of which are *The Social Contract* (1762) and *The Discourse on the Origin of the Foundation of Inequality among Men* (1775).

Rousseau, together with Thomas Hobbes, **John Locke,** and others, is recognized as a theorist of the social contract. For Rousseau, the "social contract" was a product of a fundamental change in social organization. Rousseau postulated that humans existed originally in a "state of nature"—a state, put as simply as possible, devoid of exploitation and political organization. The creation and nature of private property, according to Rousseau, indicated a fundamental departure from the reciprocity of the state of nature. In this context, the genesis of individual rights as the foundation of society stems from a tacit agreement (a "social contract") between the governed and their government.

Slavery according to Rousseau's system was an entirely social institution, based on private property and opposed to the social contract. There was no "natural" basis of slavery because, for Rousseau, there was no private property in nature. Rousseau, however, was far more concerned with the historical evolution of property than slavery. Nevertheless, he was influential in reshaping ideas about both individual and human rights, especially the doctrine that humans existing in the state of nature were fundamentally "good." The idea of a social contract presupposed a concern for the general good of the citizens to whom it attached. Slavery was contrary to this end and as such was an immoral institution. The problem of slavery, however, was not primary in Rousseau's philosophy; while he opposed slavery, its abolition was not one of his central preoccupations or a topic he visited frequently in his writings. *See also* Montesquieu, Charles de Secondat, Baron de.

Further Readings: Rousseau, Jean Jacques. The Discourses *and Other Early Political Writings.* Gourevitch, trans. and ed. Cambridge: Cambridge University Press,

1997; Rousseau, Jean Jacques. The Social Contract *and Other Later Political Writings* Gourevitch, trans. and ed. Cambridge: Cambridge University Press, 1997.

Noah Butler

Ruggles, David (1810–1849)

David Ruggles was a prominent African American abolitionist, publisher, and bookseller. He was born in Norwich, Connecticut, on March 15, 1810, the first of eight children of David and Nancy Ruggles, a free black couple. David Sr., was a blacksmith; his wife Nancy was a locally famous cook and caterer. Ruggles spent his early years in the family home in an old tenement located on a tiny triangular plot just off the main road in Bean Hill, a prosperous rural neighborhood of Norwich. Though his parents were members of the Methodist Church, David was educated at a charity school operated by the First Congregational Church. In his teens, he worked as a mariner on coastal vessels. At seventeen, he left home, moved to New York City and opened a grocery store on Courtland Street. Initially he sold alcohol, but soon announced his conversion to temperance in an advertisement in the *Freedom's Journal*, the newspaper of black New Yorkers.

Ruggles became active in the local antislavery and anticolonization movement. By the early 1830s, he employed self-emancipated slaves in his grocery. In 1833, he abandoned the store to concentrate on antislavery work as an agent for the *Emancipator*. He traveled around New England and the Mid-Atlantic states, making speeches, honing his ideas and making valuable contacts. He attended the National Conventions of Colored Peoples in Philadelphia and New York City and was a founding member of the Phoenix Society of New York, the Garrison Literary and Benevolent Association, and the New York Temperance Society, groups that combined reform, education, and antislavery. He opened the nation's first African American bookstore and lending library at his home at 67 Lispenard Street in New York City and operated it until a mob destroyed it in late 1835. In 1834, Ruggles published his first pamphlet, the anticolonization satire, *Extinguisher Extinguished . . . Or David M. Reese, M.D. Used Up*. In this pamphlet and an 1838 piece entitled *An Antidote for the Furious Combination*, he attacked Dr. David M. Reese, a prominent doctor and proponent of colonization policies. In 1835, Ruggles published the Abrogation of the Seventh Commandment, on his own press, another black first. This pamphlet appealed to the nascent feminist movement to shun Southern wives and daughters of slave masters. Ruggles began to write dozens of letters to the editors of abolitionist and other newspapers, extolling the value of education and antislavery journalism.

Ruggles began working with local abolitionists, Barney Corse and Isaac Hopper, to counteract the illicit slave trade, kidnappings of free blacks and capture of self-emancipated slaves in New York City. Working with them or by himself, Ruggles took part in highly publicized arrests of sea captains smuggling slaves in New Bedford, Massachusetts and New York City. He also routinely boarded vessels in New York harbor or entered private homes in search of blacks held unlawfully by masters and mistresses. In 1835,

Ruggles formalized such activities by organizing the **New York Vigilance Committee**. Over the next few years, the committee enabled hundreds of blacks including **Frederick Douglass** to avoid arrest and help them to freedom and work in New England or Canada.

Ruggles worked equally with whites and blacks. Between 1838 and 1841 he chronicled his activities in the *Mirror of Liberty*, the nation's first black magazine. He also published an annual report of the vigilance society. In 1839, his fervor proved his undoing. A successful suit for libel brought against Ruggles and Samuel Eli Cornish, the editor of the *Colored American* threatened to bankrupt the newspaper. Ruggles had made hasty claims that a local black boarding house keeper was hiding slaves. Ruggles and Cornish parted ways over the suit; accompanying audits of the vigilance society revealed unexplained deficits attributed to Ruggles's careless bookkeeping. Alienated, broken in health (he suffered from declining sight, stomach ailments, and other diseases), Ruggles fought his old colleague Cornish bitterly for two years before quitting New York.

After a fundraising tour of New England where many black organizations feted him for his courage, Ruggles showed his old grit in 1841 by refusing to move to the segregated cars on a railroad between New Bedford and Boston, Massachusetts. Tossed off the train, Ruggles suffered more injuries. This injustice sparked numerous protests, including attempts by **William Lloyd Garrison** and the newly famous Douglass to integrate the trains. Ruggles meanwhile had settled at the Northampton (Massachusetts) Association of Education and Industry, a communitarian society formed by abolitionists. There he mended his body, though he eventually lost his sight. He continued his work on the **Underground Railroad**. Ruggles studied hydrotherapy and opened first a clinic and later a hospital where he treated and cured patients ranging from **Sojourner Truth** to the wife of a Southern slaveholder. By the late 1840s, Ruggles was a respected practitioner and was on the cusp of expanding his business when he died on December 16, 1849, of a severe bowel inflammation. *See also* Methodists and Antislavery.

Further Reading: Hodges, Graham Russell Gao. "David Ruggles: The Hazards of Anti-Slavery Journalism." *Media Studies* (Summer 2000): 11–18.

Graham Russell Gao Hodges

Rush, Benjamin (1746–1813)

A famed physician, statesman, and reformer, Benjamin Rush was also one of the leading abolitionists of the early national period. A native of Pennsylvania, Rush was an active member of the Pennsylvania Society for Promoting the Abolition of Slavery (best known as the **Pennsylvania Abolition Society**), the world's leading abolitionist organization before the 1830s and based in Rush's longtime home of Philadelphia. Rush served as secretary of the group (1787–1789) and worked on various abolitionist committees during his life. He corresponded with leading abolitionists in America and England and served as a delegate to the **American Convention of Abolition Societies** several times during the 1790s. Like other members of the

Pennsylvania Abolition Society, Rush advocated **gradual emancipation** and supported Pennsylvania's 1780 law guaranteeing enslaved blacks born after that date freedom at the age of twenty-eight.

Years before this, Rush had authored one of the first broad attacks on slavery and the slave trade in the American colonies, a 1773 essay entitled "An Address to the Inhabitants of the British Settlements in America, Upon Slave-Keeping." Rush was also a patron of free blacks in post-revolutionary Philadelphia, helping to raise money for the first autonomous free black churches. Although some of his racial pronouncements sound odd to modern ears—Rush once argued that African Americans suffered from a form of leprosy, which accounted for their darker pigmentation—he was also part of an antislavery vanguard in late-eighteenth-century transatlantic culture which not only envisioned slavery as a moral wrong, but abolitionism as a practical good. Ironically, but not unlike some members of first-generation abolition societies in both New York and Virginia, Rush owned at least one enslaved person during his life.

Further Readings: Brodsky, Alfred. *Benjamin Rush: Patriot and Physician.* New York: Truman Talley Books, 2004; Nash, Gary B. *Race and Revolution.* Madison, WI: Madison House, 1990.

Richard Newman

Russian Serfs, Emancipation of (1861)

The statutes emancipating the serfs in the Russian Empire were signed into law by Tsar Alexander II on February 19, 1861. Twenty-two million serf men, women, and children—around 40 percent of the total peasant population of the empire—were freed from servile dependence on their noble landowners. The statutes also set in motion a land reform that, in time, would enable the freed serfs to buy land allotments from their former owners through the intermediary of the government. Similar reforms for the rest of the peasantry, those who lived on lands belonging to the state and imperial family, were also implemented. The intention of the bureaucrats who designed the reforms was to create, over a couple of generations, a landed as well as a free peasantry. It has become a clique in the historical literature to state that the alleged shortcomings of the reform were among the long-term causes of the Russian Revolution of 1917. Over half a century separated 1861 and 1917, however, during which a great deal happened that had more direct and immediate bearing on the collapse of the tsarist regime. Such a judgment disregards, moreover, the scale and ambition of the abolition of serfdom and related reforms that constitute among the largest pieces of social reform carried out by a government anywhere in the world prior to the twentieth century. The emancipation of the Russian serfs was a far more extensive measure than the near simultaneous emancipation of the slaves in the American South, where there was no land settlement. The Russian reform is more directly comparable in content to the gradual abolitions of serfdom that had been carried out elsewhere in central and eastern Europe, in particular the German states and Austrian Empire, over a few decades prior to 1848. In Europe, only Romania retained serfdom, for a few years, after Russia.

There were a number of motives for reform in Russia. There were long-standing economic, humanitarian, and political reasons to abolish serfdom that had been discussed both inside and outside the government for decades. The reasons for abolition and the immediate requirements of the state came together in the mid-1850s, when the defeat in the Crimean War highlighted the need for major reforms of the existing order. It seems that Alexander II accepted the argument for abolition that was put to him by reform-minded bureaucrats in 1856. It took a further five years, however, to plan the reform and overcome the opposition of conservatives in the government and nobility as a whole. The reform unfolded in a number of stages that did not reach their conclusion until 1907.

Tsar Alexander II (1855–1881) came to the throne in the middle of the Crimean War. He inherited a legacy of considerable discussion of reform of serfdom in secret in the inner circles of his father's government, but the only signifi-

Russian serfs greeting a noble, 1800s. Courtesy of the North Wind Picture Archives.

cant reforms that had been enacted concerned peasants who lived on state and imperial family lands and on noble land in the southwestern provinces, where the landowners were rebellious Poles. If he was going to go a stage further, Alexander faced the prospect of compelling the Russian nobility to give up their serfs. The general arguments for reform were well known in government circles and among the intelligentsia. The principles of free-market economics dictated that free labor was more productive than bonded labor, and that emancipation would create the conditions for economic development in a country that was increasingly lagging behind the industrializing states of northwestern Europe. The humanitarian arguments—that it was degrading for both serfs and serfowners to be part of a system where some human beings were owned by others—had roots in both Christianity and the secular ideas of the Enlightenment. Serfdom also posed a threat to internal security. The government was very well aware of, and concerned about, serfs' discontent with their status. While violent revolts were few and far between, the most recent was the **Pugachev's Revolt** of 1773–1774; the secret police reported what seemed to be a rising tide of small-scale protests, and advocated reform to diffuse a potentially explosive situation. The original reason for serfdom, moreover, had become an anachronism by the nineteenth century. The tsars had created serfdom by decrees issued between the late-sixteenth and mid-seventeenth centuries as a way of compensating nobles for compulsory service in the armed forces and administration. The tsars paid their servitors with landed estates and peasants bound to those estates rather than money. Compulsory state service for nobles had been abolished in 1762, however, and the government increasingly depended on professional military officers and bureaucrats, most of whom still came from the nobility, but who were paid with monetary salaries. There was, therefore, no reason to retain the system except inertia and a fear that emancipation could spark a revolt by either the nobles, who resented the loss of their serfs, or the serfs themselves, who might seek a more far-reaching reform than any tsar would concede.

All the motives for reform were familiar to Alexander II's predecessors from Catherine the Great (1762–1796). What seems to have spurred him to act was Russia's defeat by Turkey allied with Britain and France in the Crimean War of 1853–1856. The defeat on home territory indicated the need for major reform. A key point, however, was that serfdom was an impediment to reforming the system of military recruitment. Since the reign of Peter the Great (1682–1725), a small proportion of the male peasant population, usually under 1 percent, had been drafted into the army every year for long terms of service (two years in the first half of the nineteenth century). Recruits were freed from serfdom on joining the armed forces and very rarely returned home, even if they survived their service. Thus, in times of peace and war, the state maintained a vast and expensive army of former peasants. Other European states, however, were moving towards a system of drafting far larger numbers of men for much shorter terms of service, after which they were released into the reserves to be called up in times of war. This was a much cheaper option, and the money saved could be invested in reequipping and retraining Russia's outmoded and defeated army. Drafting large numbers of young men for a few years and then sending them home was incompatible with serfdom for two reasons. First, if draftees were still freed from serfdom, then the institution would be abolished by default over a number of years. Second, it would mean sending back men with military training to the villages. Given the government's concern for serf discontent, this was not a viable option. The argument for abolishing serfdom as a necessary precursor to military reform was put to Alexander II by deputy minister of war Dmitrii Miliutin in March 1856. Shortly afterward, Alexander impressed on the nobles of Moscow province the need for reform, and asked them to put forward proposals for how it might be carried out.

At the same, Alexander II entrusted planning the reform in secret to a trusted and conservative advisor, Yakov Rostovtsev. The government's initial plans were for a relatively modest measure that did not envisage a large-scale land reform. When the nobles, not altogether surprisingly, did not respond to the tsar's call for proposals, Alexander engineered a response from the Lithuanian provinces of the empire in November 1857. His reply was published and, thus, his decision to act was out in the open. Over the following couple of years, provincial nobles formed committees and drew up moderate proposals for reform, most of which left them in control of the land. Meanwhile, in St Petersburg, reform-minded bureaucrats, for example Dmitrii Miliutin's brother, Nicholas, were working with Rostovtsev to plan a more radical measure that would enable the freed serfs to acquire land. As a result of hard work on their part and friends in high place, in particular the tsar's brother Constantine and his aunt Elena, the reform-minded bureaucrats were able to triumph over more conservative elements in the government and the nobility.

It was their reform that was signed into law on February 19, 1861 and implemented. The serfs became personally free in 1861, but nothing else changed immediately. The first two years from 1861 to 1863 were a transitional period. In 1863, an indefinite period of "temporary obligation" began. The freed serfs continued to work for or pay dues to their landowners, but their obligations were strictly regulated by law. After 1863, on the initiative of their landowners, the freed serfs could enter the third stage—the redemption operation—during which they bought their land allotments by making payments to the government, which advanced compensation to the landowners. The terms of the redemption operation were deliberately favorable to the landowners to encourage them to initiate this final stage of the reform. Redemption became compulsory in 1881 for the minority of freed serfs who were still temporarily obligated to their landowners. Redemption took forty-nine years and was brought to a slightly premature conclusion with effect from January 1, 1907.

Most nobles resented the loss of their serfs, but gained financial compensation for the land they transferred to them. They were also compensated by the creation of provincial and district councils (*zemstva*) in 1864, in which they were disproportionately represented and thus gained renewed influence in rural areas. The nobles' days as the elite of the empire were numbered, however. Neither were the freed serfs particularly happy with the reform. There were widespread protests in the spring of 1861, when the measures were announced and, rather badly, explained to the rural population. Grudgingly, the freed serfs went along with the reform and sought to get the best deal they could. In time, their representatives learned to work with their former owners in the *zemstva*, and managed their own affairs at the village level in new institutions of local administration and justice set up after 1861. Russia's peasants, moreover, gradually adapted to and took part in the wider social and economic changes, such as the start of industrialization and urbanization and the expansion of schooling that unfolded in the late-nineteenth and early-twentieth centuries. In 1905–1907, however, Russian peasants took part in a massive rural revolution in which they seized land from non-peasants and tried to drive nobles from the countryside. In 1917–1918 they staged a successful repeat. The rural revolutions of 1905–1907 and 1917–1918 have often been seen as evidence for the failure of the reform. Recent research, however, has drawn into question the extent to which the freed serfs lost land they had worked for themselves prior to the reform and paid too much for it. The "land hunger" that spurred the peasant revolutions was to a large extent the result of massive population growth over the preceding decades—the population of the empire increased two-and-a-half fold between 1858 and 1917—rather than the land settlement enacted in 1861. The peasants clearly did resent the fact that they had not been given all the land free of charge in 1861, but this was not a realistic option politically for any tsarist government.

Further Readings: Emmons, Terence. *The Russian Landed Gentry and the Peasant Emancipation of 1861*. Cambridge: Cambridge University Press, 1968; Field, Daniel. *The End of Serfdom, Nobility and Bureaucracy in Russia, 1855–1861*. Cambridge, MA: Harvard University Press, 1976; Hoch, Steven L. "Did Russia's Emancipated Serfs Really Pay Too Much for Too Little Land? Statistical Anomalies and Long-Tailed Distributions." *Slavic Review* 63 (2004): 247–274; Moon, David. *The Abolition of Serfdom in Russia 1762–1907*. London: Longman, 2001; Moon, David. *The Russian Peasantry 1600–1930: The World the Peasants Made*. London: Addison Wesley Longman, 1999; Zaionchkovskii, Petr Andreevich. *The Abolition of Serfdom in Russia*. Edited and translated by Susan Wobst. Introduction by Terence Emmons. Gulf Breeze, FL: Academic International Press, 1978.

David Moon

S

Saint Augustine (354–430)

Augustine was one of the most influential Christian theologians of Late Antiquity. Born in 354 in North Africa, he taught rhetoric in Carthage, Rome (382), and Milan (385). Under Ambrose, bishop of Milan, he was converted in 385. In 388 he went back to Africa, and in 395 became bishop of Hippo Regius, where he remained until his death in 430. As in the case of other Church Fathers such as St. Ambrose (337–397 C.E.) and Isidore of Seville (602–636 C.E.), Augustine's ideas of slavery combined Greco-Roman and Christian views, a tradition that could be traced back to the New Testament, in whose texts the legitimacy of slavery was not questioned and the slave was depicted as someone whose body was liable to physical punishment and sexual abuse. The endorsement of slavery was deepened by the common characterization of the relationship between man and God as one between a master and slave. Slavery was thus understood as integral to the social and religious order.

The problem of slavery in Augustine's works is bound up with the issue of social order. The prime cause of slavery is sin. Before the Fall there was no slavery either to man or to sin. In the *City of God*, Augustine argued that it was "sin, so that man was put under man in a state of bondage; and this can be only a judgment of God, in whom there is no unrighteousness, and who knows how to assign divers punishments according to the deserts of the sinners." Slavery was thus penal, and a remedy for sin. Since Adam had misused the freedom he had been given by God in the natural state, all men became sinners, deserving punishment from God. Slavery was one of those punishments and therefore must be accepted. Moreover, Augustine stated that both masters and slaves were all slaves of sin and further blurred the boundary between free and slave: "And surely it is a happier lot to be slave to a man than to a lust; for the most cruel overlord that desolates men's hearts, to mention no other, is this very lust for overlordship." In the treatise *In Johannis Evangelium*, Augustine remarked: "O what a wretched thing is slavery! It is very common for men when suffering under bad masters to put themselves up for sale. Their aim is not to do without a master, but to change masters. But what is the slave of sin to do? To whom is he to turn? Whither is he to turn? Whither is he to seek to sell himself. ... A bad conscience cannot escape itself, there is nowhere for it to go." In this latter case, Augustine adopted the Stoic view of slavery. The Stoics, in spite of focusing on legal slavery, turned their attention to moral slavery, in accordance to the paradox that "every good man is free and every bad man a slave." The philosophers Seneca (4 B.C.E.–65 C.E.) and Epictetus (55–135 C.E.) argued that what really mattered was to avoid becoming a slave of passions and emotions. Being a slave was an accident due to Fate or Providence. True freedom was achieved only by living according to Nature and despising the lust for material things.

On the other hand, the Augustinian view that slavery was a punishment for sin resembles the Ciceronian justification for slavery, although Greco-Roman ideas of moral fault are not identical with Christian notions of sin. According to Cicero (106–43 B.C.E.)—an author well known to Augustine—slavery was a consequence of warfare. Rome had conquered the world waging just and defensive wars. The people conquered were thus guilty and deserved either death or slavery. If the life of the defeated enemy was preserved, he was made a slave of a Roman citizen. And if he redeemed himself, he could be manumitted and become a free man and a citizen. That Augustine had in mind the theory of just war when formulating his own conception of slavery is attested in a passage from his *City of God*:

> The origin of the Latin word for "slave" is believed to be derived from the fact that those who by the law of war might have been put to death, when preserved by their victors, became slaves, so named from their preservation. But even this could not have occurred were it not for the wages of sin; for even when a just war is waged, the enemy fights to defend his sin, and every victory, even when won by wicked men, humbles the vanquished through a divine judgement, correcting or punishing their sins.

For Augustine, redemption occurred not in the earthly city: freedom was achieved only eschatologically. No one in this life can be free.

Augustine was one of the Church Fathers who most emphasized the connection between slavery and sin, a connection that would become a key theme for the modern antislavery movement in the eighteenth century, as the **Quakers** in particular exemplified. However, in the age in which Augustine lived slavery never achieved the status of a problem, as it did in the modern world. In the fourth century C.E., slavery was still a pervasive institution in the urban and rural areas of the Roman Empire. And for Pagans and Christians alike it was inconceivable for a society to exist without slaves. *See also* Classical Rome and Antislavery.

Further Readings: Bradley, Keith R. "The Problem of Slavery in Classical Culture" (Review article). *Classical Philology*, 92 (1997): 273–282; Davis, David Brion. *The Problem of Slavery in Western Culture*. Ithaca, NY: Cornell University Press, 1975; Deane, Herbert A. *The Political and Social Ideas of St. Augustine*. New York: Columbia University Press, 1963; Dumont, Jean-Christian. *Servus: Rome et l'esclavage sous la République*. Rome: École Française de Rome, 1987; Garnsey,

Peter. *Ideas of Slavery from Aristotle to Augustine.* Cambridge: Cambridge University Press, 1996; Glancy, Jennifer. *Slavery in Early Christianity.* New York: Oxford University Press, 2002; Klein, Richard. *Die Sklaverei in der Sicht der Bischöfe Ambrosius und Augustinus.* Stuttgart: Franz Steiner Verlag, 1988; Rist, John M. *Augustine: Ancient Thought Baptized.* Cambridge: Cambridge University Press, 1997.

Fábio Duarte Joly

Saint Domingue, French Defeat in (1803)

In January 1802, the French Captain-General, Victor Charles Leclerc, arrived at Samaná Bay in the West Indian island of Hispaniola in the Greater Antilles. The following month the general occupied the charred city of Cap François, a provincial capital of the French colony of Saint Domingue, or present-day Haiti, which had been burned by its fleeing black inhabitants. France's First Consul, **Napoleon Bonaparte**, had decided to reduce the colony's black leader, **Toussaint L'Ouverture**, to reestablish the old regime, and to recover the rich colony inhabited by 500,000 blacks from their leaders, whom he derided as the "gilded Africans." Over the next twenty-one months, Bonaparte added more than 30,000 troops to Leclerc's army of 20,000 soldiers and sailors, but in November 1802 the survivors of the French expedition, 7,000 in number, were compelled to withdraw. Following the French withdrawal, the blacks declared themselves the independent Republic of Haiti on January 1, 1804, the first republic after the United States to win its independence.

Preparing for the Leclerc expedition, Napoleon Bonaparte had made peace with England on October 1, 1801. Bonaparte had received reports from several observers, including even **Léger F. Sonthonax**, claiming that Toussaint was the only obstacle to the restoration of French power in the Caribbean. The French expedition sailed from Brest on December 14, 1801 and was one of the largest ever sent out from France. But before Leclerc departed from France, Bonaparte secured the cooperation of the recently inaugurated President **Thomas Jefferson** in Washington, D.C., believing that the support of the American government and American merchants would be essential to the victory of the French over the blacks.

On July 11, 1801, Louis A. Pichon, French chargé to the Jefferson administration, met

Toussaint L'Ouverture. Courtesy of the Library of Congress.

with Secretary of State James Madison to inquire how the newly inaugurated Jefferson administration would respond to a French effort to recover its wayward colony of Saint Domingue. The regime of Toussaint had moved in the direction of independence and indeed was independent in all but name. Toussaint had proclaimed himself governor general for life and promulgated a constitution for Saint Domingue that put all power in his hands. He also conquered the Spanish part of the island Santo Domingo (which is now named the Dominican Republic) and asserted the indivisibility of the eastern and western portions under his control. Expanding the area of free soil in the Americas, Toussaint abolished slavery in Spanish Hispaniola. Pichon's interview with Secretary Madison did not yield a firm commitment to U.S. support for the Leclerc expedition, so Pichon secured an appointment with President Jefferson. On July 19, Jefferson proposed to Pichon a concert between England and France against Toussaint and his followers, saying that then nothing would be easier than to starve Toussaint into subjection.

On January 29, 1802, the Leclerc expedition anchored off Samaná Bay in eastern Hispaniola. Leclerc's troops occupied the burned out remains of Cap François not long after. The black troops of Saint Domingue had torched the city and taken defensive positions in the mountainous interior. But Bonaparte resorted to treachery, which was one of his most effective weapons. He had initially sent more than 20,000 troops against the black rebels, but he had hoped to divide the black generals against one another as a means to avoiding a bloody fight with the black soldiers and cultivators. He had promised the black generals places of command in the French army and guaranteed them their freedom. Two of Toussaint's most trusted allies, **Jean-Jacques Dessalines** and Henri Christophe, deserted Toussaint for the French. On May 1, 1802, Toussaint surrendered to Leclerc under a flag of truce. Dreading Toussaint's power over the black troops, Leclerc had Toussaint kidnapped and shipped off to Europe, where the martyr for freedom died in a dank prison in the Jura Mountains. The convenient fiction adopted by the French leaders and black generals was that the conflict with France had only been occasioned by a misunderstanding. Learning of French treachery against Toussaint, the black soldiers and cultivators remained passive, hoping to avoid a war to the death with the French, by not reacting to the seizure of Toussaint and his forced departure from the island.

The **Haitian Revolution**, 1791–1804, appeared to have been stopped dead in its tracks. But in mid-1802, a fateful French decision provoked a general uprising against the Leclerc expedition. Napoleon was under the influence of the former slaveholders of Saint Domingue and they insisted that the profitability of the plantations could only be restored if slavery were restored throughout the French islands. In mid-1802, the news arrived in Saint Domingue from the French colony of Martinique of French efforts to implement Bonaparte's decision to restore slavery, forced labor, and the old regime as it had existed before 1791. The news from Guadeloupe provoked a near universal movement for independence among the black and free colored of Saint Domingue; the movement began first among the mid-level officers in the black army and then spread to the remainder of the black troops and cultivators. It later drew in the black generals and black and colored elites of Saint Domingue. It also solidified an alliance between the blacks and free colored troops, who were led by Alexander Pétion and others. Bonaparte's objective had been the restoration of pre-1791 settlement of Saint Domingue. But neither the blacks nor free colored elites, nor the mass of black workers and cultivators, were willing to accept Bonaparte's reactionary vision.

By 1802, black soldiers had been fighting against foreign domination for more than a decade, and had finely honed skills. Now the blacks and coloreds moved in unison against the invasion. However, the black-mulatto soldiers needed arms and ammunition from outside the island to pursue their struggle for freedom, and in this regard they secured assistance from an unlikely ally, the Jefferson administration.

The United States was unwilling to see the expansion of French power in the Caribbean. Jefferson and Madison now preferred a weak black-colored regime under the control of indigenous elites to a powerful government controlled by Bonaparte. Shortly after the arrival of French troops in Saint Domingue in 1802, Pichon asked President Jefferson to embargo American trade with the insurgent blacks and free colored of Saint Domingue, but Jefferson had changed his mind about helping the French. Even though Jefferson's policy would result in the independence of Saint Domingue under black domination, Jefferson turned a cold shoulder to Pichon's entreaties, asking the French chargé why Bonaparte had decided to send such a large expedition to Saint Domingue. By early 1802, rumors of French treachery circulated in the Atlantic World, saying that the French had sent such a large expedition so that the French could seize control of Louisiana and restore the French colonies of Martinique and Guadeloupe. Others speculated that the large French army would be used to conquer the rich English colony of Jamaica, while still others insisted that the French intended the conquest of the Mississippi valley and that the French had secured the retrocession of Louisiana from Spain to France. The upshot was that American merchants refused to trade with the French, but they traded freely with the black and colored elites and their leaders. So it was the French who found themselves starving in Saint Domingue while the black revolution received everything it needed to prosecute the war against France.

President Jefferson went further, threatening use of American troops against the French. He told the French directly that if they attempted to seize New Orleans, the United States would negotiate an alliance with England and declare war on France. Jefferson's moves contributed to the black victory over the Leclerc expedition in 1803, but it was the English who assumed the role of protector of black Saint Domingue. British agents met with **Jean-Jacques Dessalines** at Gonaives in early 1803, offering assistance against France. The British also blockaded the French held ports of Saint Domingue. General Leclerc himself died of yellow fever in 1803, but General Rochambeau continued the fight. Rochambeau sent several dispatches to Pichon in the United States, calling on Pichon to feed the French army. On November 19, Rochambeau and General Dessalines signed an agreement involving the French evacuation of Saint Domingue, and a few days later Rochambeau sailed from Cap François to surrender to the British. On January 1, 1804, Dessalines declared the independence of the former colony, restoring to the island the Indian name of Haiti and asserting the indivisibility of eastern and western Hispaniola.

Bonaparte's army had suffered devastating losses in Saint Domingue; only 7,000 troops evacuated the island in 1803. Their defeat had momentous consequences for the Atlantic World. For Afro-America, Haiti assumed the role of beacon of hope and symbol of freedom and served as a magnet for free blacks and colored elites in the Americas who had the means to escape to "free soil." For the United States, it provided the Jefferson administration with the opportunity to take Louisiana, which Jefferson purchased from the French on April 30, 1803, thus sending the most important part of the French empire in the Americas.

For the English, it led to a fundamental shift on slavery. The English anti-slavery movement had grown dramatically during the war with France; anti-slavery leaders, such as the "saints" **William Wilberforce** and James Stephen, mobilized middle-class and even working-class support against the slave trade, and the saints secured the termination of the international slave trade to the Americas. Over the next century, England conducted an international crusade against the slave trade, a policy that grew out of the collapse of French power in Saint Domingue. English abolitionists seized on the termination of French competition in the slave trade to call for its abolition and the English Parliament agreed. From the perspective of the "saints" it was a moral obligation to end the slave trade and slavery. But the members of Parliament decided to end the slave trade as a war measure against the enemies of England. Parliament realized that the French had mobilized thousands of Africans as troops against England, and terminating the slave trade undercut France's ability to continue to do so.

Following the creation of independent Haiti, Jefferson shifted his policy toward Saint Domingue once again. He had first volunteered to help the French against Toussaint, but he grew alarmed at the enormous size of the French expedition. Deciding to assist the rebels against France, once Generals Dessalines and Henri Christophe had driven Rochambeau from the island, he reversed himself again. Alarmed by black revolution in the United States following the Gabriel rebellion of 1800 in Virginia, President Jefferson responded to Southern calls for protection against black rebels. In 1805, Jefferson embargoed American trade with Haiti, a policy that France also sought. This policy remained in effect until 1862 when it was reversed by the **Lincoln** administration. President Jefferson helped seal the fate of French slavery in the Americas, but his imperial expansion of American power in Louisiana reinvigorated slavery in the Old Southwest and the Louisiana territories and led Jefferson to reverse his earlier opposition to the expansion of slavery in the west. *See also* French Colonies, Emancipation of.

Further Readings: Auguste, Claude B. and Marcel B. Auguste, *L'expedition Leclerc, 1801–1803*. Port-au-Prince, Haiti: Impr. H. Deschamps, 1985; DeConde, Alexander. *This Affair of Louisiana*. New York: Scribner, 1976; Matthewson, Tim.

A Proslavery Foreign Policy: Haitian-American Relations during the Early Republic. Westport, CT: Praeger, 2003; Ott, Thomas O. *The Haitian Revolution, 1789–1804.* Knoxville, TN: University of Tennessee Press, 1973; Pluchon, Pierre. *Toussaint L'ouverture: de l'esclavage au pouvoir.* Paris: l'École, 1979; Wilson, Ruel K. et al., *Poland's Caribbean Tragedy: A Study of Polish Legions in the Haitian War of Independence, 1802–1803.* New York: Distributed by Columbia University Press, 1986.

Tim Matthewson

Sandoval, Alonso de, S.J. (1576–1652)

Alonso de Sandoval was a Catholic priest, a member of the Society of Jesus, commonly referred to as the Jesuits, who worked among the African slaves in Spanish America, seeking to convert them to Christianity. Although he never denounced slavery directly, his writings vividly described the sufferings of the black populations enslaved in the Spanish colonies of the New World.

Sandoval was born in Seville, Spain, in 1576. During his childhood, his parents emigrated with his other six brothers and sisters to Lima, Peru, at that time a large viceroyalty in the Spanish Empire. He matriculated to the San Martin Seminar in Lima in 1591 and in 1593, he entered the Society of Jesus as a novice. From 1605 until his death in 1652, he lived and worked in Cartagena de Indias, now in Colombia, in the College that the Jesuits had opened there in 1605.

Cartagena de Indias was an important harbor in the Spanish commercial system when Sandoval lived there, and it served as one of the main harbors for ships arriving from Africa with people captured for sale as slaves. An important task for the Catholics priests there was to meet the ships and provide "spiritual" care for the Africans. Alonso de Sandoval dedicated his life in Cartagena to this ministration.

Sandoval was dedicated to Christianizing these slaves. He gathered together a number of Africans who served as interpreters, and for years he baptized and cared for the Africans who had just completed the grueling Middle Passage. Concerned to know more about the life of these Africans so he might minister to the arrivals more effectively, he began to collect a great amount of information about Africa. From 1617 to 1619, he returned to Lima to study Africa in the Jesuit Library. He even wrote letters to other Jesuits working in Africa seeking details not only of their spiritual work, but also about the life and customs of the African population.

By 1627, he published in Seville *De Instauranda Aethiopum Salute*, a lengthy compilation of all that he had learned about the continent. This book was actually influenced by the work, *De Procuramdam Indorum Salute* (1588), of another famous Jesuit, José de Acosta, who had a similar concern about the "spiritual life" of the indigenous population in the Hispanic colonies. Sandoval's book offered an historical and geographical description of the known world, a vivid account of the suffering of the African slaves, and a practical guide for Jesuit missionaries. In many ways, the work denounced African slavery in the Americas. However, because African slavery was perceived as a "natural" institution in the colonial period—even the Jesuits had slaves and sugar estates, many theologians justified the enslavement of "infidels," and the Inquisition was still active—Sandoval did not publicly call for a frontal assault on slavery.

Yet, this seminal work of Alonso de Sandoval was well-known among priests who ministered to the black population. Moreover, it was one of the first "ethno-historical" treatments of the black population in the Americas. Pedro Claver, one of Sandoval's closest disciples, would receive the formal recognition never accorded Sandoval when he was proclaimed a saint in 1888. *See also* Las Casas, Bartolomé de; Roman Catholic Church and Antislavery and Abolitionism; Spanish Empire, Antislavery and Abolition in.

Further Readings: Olsen, Margaret. *Slavery and Salvation in Colonial Cartagena de Indias*. Gainesville: University Press of Florida, 2004; Vilar, Enriqueta Vila, ed. *Un tratado sobre la esclavitud*. Madrid: Alianza Editorial, 1987.

Luis Gomez

Saudi Arabia and Abolition

From ancient times through the 1960s, slavery was a fact of life in Arabia. African captives were imported into the Arabian Peninsula to be sold as slaves until the late-nineteenth century. While some may have served as soldiers, sailors, and commercial workers, the vast majority were destined to become domestic slaves who provided various services in rich households in urban centers. The practice of confining women to certain quarters of the house—common among the upper class—created a need to acquire domestic servants to perform their domestic chores. This work is now undertaken by maids from south and southeast Asia.

Why did slavery persist for so long in Saudi Arabia despite Quranic teachings encouraging manumission as an act of penance and as a sign of piety? First, slavery was recognized as a right that was permitted by law. Second, readily available slaves from across the Red Sea were relied upon for labor, especially in the households of mercantile families. Well into the twentieth century, slavery was understood as both an economic necessity and a critical component of the country's system of social stratification. Moreover, the royal family itself owned many slaves, and King Ibn Saud saw nothing wrong with slavery especially since existing slaves were believed generally to be well treated.

After World War I and the dissolution of the Ottoman Empire, Britain was increasingly involved in the affairs of the Middle East and attempted to circumscribe the widespread practice of slavery. In 1927, Britain and Saudi Arabia signed the Treaty of Jeddah, which granted Britain rights of manumission within the country in return for recognizing the independence of the Saudi king's realm. Thus, in the late 1920s and 1930s, Britain freed and repatriated hundreds of runaway slaves. This right of manumission, however, was revoked in 1936, the year that King Abdul Aziz al-Saud (r. 1902–1953) established new slave regulations. King al-Saud had issued a decree—an outcome of yet another treaty with Britain—ending the importation of new slaves into the country, regulating the conditions of slaves, and providing for manumission under some conditions. Nevertheless, British records show clearly that these regulations were not being enforced and the number of slaves who continued to run away attested to their masters' poor treatment of them. In fact, the policy of consular manumission was pursued even as the British attempted not to meddle in the internal affairs of the kingdom. The Saudis appeared unwilling even to ameliorate slavery, let alone abolish it.

Although Ibn Saudi's imposition of peace and order helped restore some stability to the Kingdom and pilgrimages to Mecca resumed, slave imports, while declining, continued and the king profited from customs duties assessed on them. Slaves were now being sold, not openly, but in informal or disguised markets. In 1928, West Africans, called Takruni, were still being imported illegally to Saudi Arabia during the pilgrimage season—but not at the levels they had in decades past because closer control of the pilgrimage by European colonial powers ensured that unscrupulous dealers did not bring in people to Saudi Arabia under false pretexts. Declining demand for slaves further unsettled the institution of slavery. The increasing use of cars to replace slave camel drivers undermined the economic interests of Hijazi dealers who gained most from this trade. Demand for slave soldiers was drying up. Thus, by the end of the 1950s, slave markets had been significantly curtailed as had been slavery itself.

In November 1962, Prince Faisal, appointed prime minister by his brother, King Saud, issued a Ten-Point Program to abolish slavery. This was a bold and revolutionary move on the part of conservative Saudi Arabia which was increasingly vulnerable to the criticism of progressive Arab leaders such as Egypt's outspoken Jamal Abdel Nasser. Prince Faisal officially abolished slavery on the grounds that it was difficult to guarantee the Islamic stipulation that kindness ever be shown to one's slaves. Yet, it is doubtful that slavery came to an end at once. Several more years were required to make it an obsolete practice. The emergence of the lucrative oil industry, gradual modernization of the Saudi economy, and outside pressure from the West eventually made slavery no longer respectable or acceptable. In 1964, the sixth World Muslim Congress, which has Consultative Status with the **United Nations** and Observer status with the Organization of Islamic Countries, pledged support for all antislavery movements. *See also* Arabia and Nineteenth- and Twentieth-Century Slavery; Islam and Antislavery; Ottoman Empire, Decline of Slavery in.

Further Readings: Hutson, Alaine. "Enslavement and Manumission in Saudi Arabia, 1926–38." *Critique: Critical Middle Eastern Studies* 11, 1 (Spring 2002): 49–70; Miers, Suzanne. *Slavery in the Twentieth Century: The Evolution of a Global Problem.* New York and Oxford: Altamira Press, 2003.

Abdin Chande

Schoelcher, Victor (1804–1893)

Victor Schoelcher was the most important French abolitionist of the nineteenth century. The son of a wealthy French merchant and industrialist, Schoelcher early became an active participant in Parisian intellectual, artistic, and literary life. He inherited enough money to devote himself to travel and to writing. In 1829, he made the first of several trips to the Americas, visiting Mexico, Cuba, and the Southern United States where he discovered the issue to which he was to devote the rest of his life, slavery. He wrote about the issue in Parisian journals and in 1833, published *De l'esclavage des noirs et de la legislation coloniale*. In the course of a long life, he wrote about twenty books, almost half of them on slavery and on race prejudice. He also published regularly in Parisian journals. In 1840 and 1841, he toured the West Indies, and in 1847, he visited Senegal. By 1848, he was well-known in progressive circles in Paris.

When the revolution of 1848 took place, he entered the provisional government as undersecretary of state for the colonies and wrote the law abolishing slavery in all French colonies. It went into effect on April 27, 1848, and provided for total and immediate emancipation everywhere in the French empire. Slaveowners were to be reimbursed for their losses. That summer, he was elected to the National Assembly from both Martinique and Guadeloupe, where he was regarded as the liberator. When Louis Napoleon seized power in 1852, Schoelcher went into exile. He remained in exile until the fall of Napoleon after France's defeat in 1871 in the Franco-Prussian War. When elections were held in 1871, he was elected once again from the island of Martinique. In 1875, he was elected to the Senate.

As a deputy and a senator, Schoelcher defended the interests of his West Indian constituents and in particular, the interests of the former slaves. He was also involved in slavery issues elsewhere. Under Napoleon, and again during the early years of the Third Republic, France was extending its control over various African territories. Starting in the first African colonies, France's colonial proconsuls found ways of avoiding the abolition law of 1848 so as not to disturb trading partners. Schoelcher had correspondents in Senegal and elsewhere and used his position in the assembly and then the Senate to alert French public opinion about compromises of French political principals. Particularly important was a speech he gave in 1880, attacking the conduct of the colonial administration in Senegal. It forced the colonial regime to change many of its policies, in particular, the expulsion of runaway slaves from French towns in a way that made it easy for masters to seize their slaves.

In 1882, he founded *Le Moniteur des Colonies*, which became a progressive voice on colonial issues. He also worked for abolition of the death penalty, for prison reform, and for the rights of women and children. In 1889, he published a biography of **Toussaint L'Ouverture**, the leader of the successful **Haitian Revolution** in the 1790s.

Further Reading: Schmidt, Nelly. *Victor Schoelcher*. Paris: Fayard, 1994.

Martin A. Klein

Scotland, Antislavery in

Scottish philosophers including Francis Hutcheson, **Adam Smith**, James Beattie, and John Millar developed some of the eighteenth century's most influential arguments against slavery. Yet for a country of its size, Scotland was also disproportionately involved in the slave trade. This contradiction between Scottish theory and practice may have stemmed in part from Scotland's economic and political disempowerment relative to England following the Anglo-Scottish Union of 1707. Britain's colonies in America and in the West Indies offered Scots economic and political opportunities that they were denied at home. Accordingly, Scotland's economy relied heavily upon the tobacco and sugar trades, which in turn relied on slave labor. Scottish influence on the British Emancipation Act (1834) thus followed the circuitous route of Scottish emigration to the colonies: American antislavery pamphleteers appropriated the theoretical arguments of **Enlightenment** philosophers to protest the practice of slavery in the American colonies, and their pamphlets in turn influenced Evangelical abolitionists in early-nineteenth-century England.

Scottish intellectuals developed moral and economic arguments against slavery, both of which were governed by the principle of utility, and both of which will seem familiar from their reiteration in antebellum America. Together, these arguments demonstrated that slavery was not simply unnecessary to the happiness of any given society, but also detrimental to its prosperity. Moralists asserted that slavery corrupted our natural propensities to sympathy and benevolence while economists argued that all individuals work more efficiently when motivated by the prospect of personal profit. Thus, when Adam Smith declared in *The Wealth of Nations* (1776) that "the work done by slaves, though it appears to cost only their maintenance, is in the end the dearest of all," he referred to both the economic and moral price of slavery. Edinburgh lawyer George Wallace added a more radical claim based on natural law to these economic and moral arguments; he asserted in his *System of the Principles of the Law of Scotland* (1760) that each person's inherent right to liberty is legally inalienable.

The theoretical arguments against slavery developed by Scotland's intellectual elite reached a broad audience through university classes and debating clubs in Glasgow, Edinburgh, and Aberdeen; through regional branches of London-based groups including the Society for the Mitigation and Gradual Abolition of Slavery throughout the British Dominions; and through widely-read periodicals like the *Aberdeen Journal* and the *Edinburgh Review*. Directed towards a middle-class reading public, these periodicals featured polemical articles like "The Horrors of Negro Slavery existing in our West India Islands" (*Edinburgh Review*, 1805) and excerpts from longer antislavery works like **Thomas Clarkson**'s *History of the Abolition of the Slave Trade* (*Edinburgh Review*, 1808). Two court cases in the latter half of the eighteenth century illustrate the practical impact of popular antislavery sentiment in Scotland. In Fife in 1777, a group of miners raised money for the legal defense of David Spens, a slave who resisted his master's attempts to return him to the West Indian plantation from whence he came. The miners who supported his case were probably motivated less by abstract philosophical arguments against slavery than by the sympathies arising from their own status as indentured servants—until 1799, Scotland's municipal law dictated that miners could be hereditarily bound to their occupation, and many wore collars engraved with their master's name. Spens won his case and his freedom, and worked in Scotland as a farm laborer for the rest of his life. A similar case arose in 1778, when John Wedderburn brought a slave named Joseph Knight to Scotland as his personal servant. When Knight requested permission to leave his master's service, the Scottish Court of Sessions ruled that the municipal law of the British colonies had no authority in Scotland. Invoking George Wallace's arguments concerning natural law, the court claimed that the "unjust dominion" supported by Jamaican law "is repugnant to the first principles of morality and justice" which dictate that no person can alienate his or her right to liberty.

Following the case of Joseph Knight, the Court of Sessions ruled that any slave who set foot in Scotland automatically became free. However, Scots remained heavily involved in the slave trade—as private traders, managers of trading companies, factories, and plantation owners—in Africa, the West Indies, and the United States. Their involvement suggests that antislavery movements in Scotland must be situated in the broader context of Scotland's prominent role in British colonialism. *See also* Antislavery Evangelical Protestantism; Atlantic Slave Trade and British Abolition; Scottish Churches and Antislavery.

Further Readings: Fry, Michael. *The Scottish Empire.* Edinburgh: Birlinn, 2001; Hancock, David. "Scots in the Slave Trade." In Ned C. Landsman, ed., *Nation and Province in the First British Empire: Scotland and the Americas, 1600–1800.* Lewisburg, PA: Bucknell University Press, 2001, pp. 60–93; Hargreaves, John D. *Aberdeenshire to Africa: Northeast Scots and British Overseas Expansion.* Aberdeen: Aberdeen University Press, 1981; Rice, C. Duncan. *The Rise and Fall of Black Slavery.* New York: Harper, 1975.

Juliet Shields

Scottish Churches and Antislavery

Scotland in the eighteenth and nineteenth centuries had considerable involvement in the slave trade and Caribbean slavery, but the nation also made a significant contribution to the campaign for emancipation. In an age and culture that took religion very seriously, Scottish churchmen provided theological and practical tools to mount an effective attack on slavery.

The influence of the Church was evident when Scottish courts considered slaves on Scottish soil. In 1756, Jamie Montgomery was given a "Certificate of Christian Conduct" in Ayrshire by his minister John Witherspoon, but his bid for freedom ended in his death while awaiting trial. David Spens took his minister's surname at his baptism in 1760, but was only freed when his master died the next year. Although baptism was regarded by English courts as having no standing in law, biblical arguments were fiercely debated in three cases before the Scottish Court of Session in Edinburgh. A majority of judges found that slavery was incompatible with the Christian nation of Scotland and freed the Jamaican slave, Joseph Knight, in 1778.

In 1788 and 1792, the national Church of Scotland provided by far the majority of Scottish petitions to the House of Commons against the slave trade, mainly through the widely representative Presbyteries and Synods. William Dickson toured the country for three months in 1792 on behalf of the London Abolition Committee, and it was mainly due to his contacts with church ministers from Inverness to Galloway that 185 petitions came from Scotland out of a British total of 519. In addition, community and civic petitions often followed public meetings held in churches and chaired by ministers. Although the General Assembly never petitioned, its condemnation of the slave trade was heard with approval by the celebrated ex-slave **Olaudah Equiano** and featured in the Church's annual address to the king.

Presbyterian secessionist churches and other independents became more prominent in the campaign against slavery after 1823. John Ritchie, a United Secessionist minister in Edinburgh, distributed leaflets and persuaded over 150 congregations to petition in 1830–1831. The cluster of twelve Roxburgh villages that sent resolutions to parliament in 1833 reflected the enthusiasm of a Congregational evangelist, James Douglas of Cavers. Eight Methodist congregations in Shetland and Baptists in Stirling, Perth, and Dunfermline also petitioned.

The public impatience with the failure of effective improvements in West Indian slavery was voiced in October 1830 by a leading Church of Scotland minister, Andrew Thomson of Edinburgh. Thomson argued that there could be no mitigation of evil, or gradual abolition of sin, and he compared slavery to the poisonous Upas tree that must be immediately uprooted. This uncompromising stance not only spurred change in the Scottish and British movement, but also inspired abolitionists in the United States. Thomson died in 1831, but not before the *Christian Observer*, which he edited, carried vigorous theological debate on "immediatism," the "gradualist" position being expounded by Henry Duncan, minister of Ruthven near Dumfries.

From 1834 until the end of the Apprenticeship Scheme in 1838, the main locus of Scottish antislavery moved from Edinburgh to Glasgow. Ralph Wardlaw, a leading Congregationalist, chaired the Glasgow Emancipation Society, whose attention later moved to abolition in the United States and throughout the world. Before long, Scottish abolitionists were drawn into American abolitionist disputes, but the fieriest controversy was over money sent from the Southern States to support congregations of the Free Church that had split from the Church of Scotland in 1843. In 1845 the runaway American slave **Frederick Douglass** toured Scotland and denounced this acceptance of "blood money." The "Send Back the Money" campaign divided the nation and weakened the emancipation societies, who lost Free Church supporters whilst never achieving the return of the money.

The final chapter of Scottish church support for antislavery was written in the late-nineteenth century by missionaries in different parts of Africa. **David Livingstone**'s lifelong passion for "Commerce and Christianity" as a weapon to kill the central African slave trade was first inspired by attending Wardlaw's antislavery sermons in Glasgow. In 1841, Livingstone was encouraged to hear fellow Scottish missionary John Phillip describe his struggle to free the Khoi people of South Africa from slavery. Thirty years later, John Kirk, a doctor from Dundee, persuaded the Sultan of Zanzibar to outlaw the slave trade on the island. It was another milestone in over a century of campaigning, starting from the baptism of Jamie

Montgomery by a man who was later to sign another freedom document, the **Declaration of Independence**, in America in 1776. *See also* Scotland, Antislavery in.

Further Readings: Rice, C. Duncan. *The Scots Abolitionists 1833–1861*. Baton Rouge: Louisiana State University Press, 1981; Whyte, Iain. *Scotland and the Abolition of Black Slavery 1756–1838*. Edinburgh: Edinburgh University Press, 2006.

Iain Whyte

Secession Crisis and Abolitionists

Between **Abraham Lincoln**'s election on November 6, 1860, and the attack on Fort Sumter in mid-April 1861, seven Southern states left the Union, and four more would join them in the spring and early summer, making up the Confederate States of America. For many Southerners, particularly slaveholders, this moment was the culmination of a long, tortuous process of anxious negotiation. By balancing a desire for independence with an attention to the fragile regional unity that created the Confederacy, Southerners built a society on the understanding that slavery was right and just, and that the white man was intended by Scripture and nature to rule over the black.

Several moments in earlier decades of the nineteenth century suggested that secession might be an option that would allow Southerners to protect slavery. During one of the first options—South Carolina's 1832 Nullification Controversy with the federal government—the citizens of the state proved

The first flag of independence raised in the South, by the citizens of Savannah, Georgia, 1860. Courtesy of the Library of Congress.

unwilling to declare independence. By the 1850s, what had earlier seemed a dim possibility became a growing reality. The efforts of Northern abolitionists by then were important to the development of a common perception among many Southerners that secession was the only option for protecting slavery, their key labor source. Important turning points were the eruption in Kansas of a bloody conflict between slaveholders and free soilers in the mid-1850s and John Brown's raid into Harpers Ferry, Virginia, in 1859. Events in Kansas showed Southerners the lengths to which abolitionists were willing to go to thwart the slaveholder's right to human property. Brown's raid in 1859 exposed the efforts of a few radical abolitionists to topple slaveholder power by storming a military battery and potentially spurring slaves into rebellion.

Though these incidents proved especially powerful in setting Southern opinion in favor of secession, it was Lincoln's election that proved the central catalyst. Secessionist "fire eaters" painted a picture of manipulation and abolitionist control of the central government that they elaborated into an 1860 campaign filled with images of racial mixing, intermarriage, and the overturn of white supremacy. "Black Republican" became a watchword for a national political party firmly in the control of a radical group bent on the destruction of the South. Despite the Republicans' best efforts to show that a Lincoln administration would check the growth of slavery in western territories, and not the institution's eradication, most Southern slaveholders fervently believed that any attempt to abrogate their right to own slaves would propel the South into a subservient position to the industrializing North. However, as each Southern state deliberated on its future, deep and important divisions emerged which threatened a new Southern nation from the beginning. Secession in Mississippi and Alabama passed, respectively, on January 9 and 11, 1861, but not before exposing divisions between slaveholding southern counties and non-slaveholding northern counties in each state. Georgia seceded from the Union on January 19, 1861, but not before a protracted deliberation that revealed the fragility of slaveholder control over politics in the state; non-slaveholding counties which had long supported the **Democratic Party** shifted their support in the secession election against slaveholders who wished to join the Confederacy, creating anxiety among secession leaders that they were losing an assumed base of support. There were also constant concerns in the Deep South over the loyalties of the Upper South. Virginia, Arkansas, North Carolina, Tennessee, and Kentucky were all initially cool to secession, but the Confederate attack on Fort Sumter on April 14, 1861, and Lincoln's call for 75,000 troops the following day to put down the Southern "insurrection," brought all the reluctant states, save for Kentucky, into the Confederacy by the following June. *See also* Bible and Slavery; Bleeding Kansas; Radical Republicans.

Further Readings: Barney, William. *The Secessionist Impulse: Alabama and Mississippi in 1860*. Princeton, NJ: Princeton University Press, 1974; Crofts, Daniel W. *Reluctant Confederates: Upper South Unionists in the Secession Crisis*. Chapel Hill: University of North Carolina Press, 1989; Johnson, Michael. *Toward a Patriarchal Republic: The Secession of Georgia*. Baton Rouge: Louisiana State University

Press, 1977; Potter, David M. *The Impending Crisis, 1848–1861*. Completed by Don E. Fehrenbacher. New York: Harper & Row, 1976.

Erik Mathisen

Secondat, Charles de, Baron de Montesquieu. *See* Montesquieu, Charles de Secondat, Baron de

Second Confiscation Act. *See* Confiscation Acts

The Secret Six

"The Secret Six" were the six Northern abolitionists who helped to finance John Brown's antislavery violence in Kansas and his raid on the federal arsenal at Harpers Ferry, Virginia in October 1859. They comprised Thomas Wentworth Higginson, Samuel Gridley Howe, Theodore Parker, Franklin Sanborn, **Gerrit Smith**, and George Luther Stearns. Their identities became public after the failed raid at Harpers Ferry, when federal troops discovered papers abandoned by several of Brown's cohorts in a farmhouse near Harpers Ferry. Two of the men, Howe and Stearns, appeared before a U.S. Senate committee, chaired by Senator James Mason of Virginia, that investigated the raid at Harpers Ferry. The committee failed to prove decisively that Howe and Stearns had advance knowledge of Brown's plans.

"The Secret Six" were fortunate the Mason Committee was unable to link them in any conclusive way to Brown's raid, because their support was incontrovertible. They had raised money for Brown from contacts within their social and ideological circles, given him money themselves, hosted him in their homes, introduced him to local notables such as Ralph Waldo Emerson and Henry David Thoreau, and shipped rifles to him in Kansas. Two of the six, Higginson and Smith, were fanatical in their support of

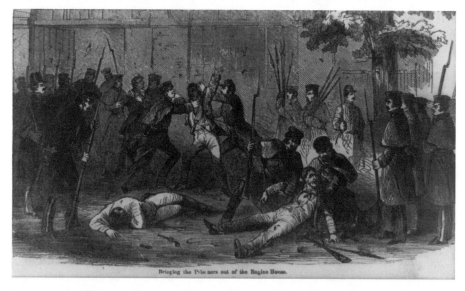

Bringing the Prisoners out of the Engine House.

John Brown and other prisoners coming out of the engine room during his attempt to free the slaves of Virginia (Harpers Ferry Raid). Courtesy of the Library of Congress.

Brown's violent attacks on slaveholders and their followers. Higginson would go on to lead a regiment of African American soldiers in the Union Army during the Civil War.

These men who became the "Secret Six" were pillars of their communities. They were the descendants of some of the most prominent families in the northeastern United States. Higginson, who had begun studies at Harvard at age thirteen, was a well-respected author, editor, and minister, who also supported disunion abolitionism in the 1850s. He believed that the Constitution was a proslavery document, and believed that slavery had corrupted American politics. The best thing that could happen would be a separation of North and South. Howe was a medical doctor whose wife, Julia Ward Howe, would gain fame for writing the "Battle Hymn of the Republic" during the Civil War. This song was based on "John Brown's Body," a song written to commemorate Brown's execution by Virginia authorities and which helped him achieve martyr status in many parts of the North. Howe's relatives had participated in major events in the American Revolution, such as the Boston Tea Party and the building of fortifications for the Battle of Bunker Hill. Howe had also supported republican revolutions in Greece, France, and Prussia in the late 1820s and early 1830s.

Sanborn instructed the sons of prominent families from both North and South at his school. Some of his students, in fact, prevented federal marshals from seizing Sanborn in a late night raid. They sought to bring him to Washington to testify before the Mason Committee. Not surprisingly, parents of Southern boys withdrew their sons from his school as sectional tensions escalated after Brown's raid and the revelation of Sanborn's involvement. Parker was a well-respected Unitarian minister whose failing health forced him to leave the United States before Brown's raid. Parker died in Florence, Italy, on May 10, 1860, roughly six months after the raid on the federal arsenal. Smith was a wealthy landowner who lived near Syracuse, New York. He had supported **Frederick Douglass**'s newspaper, *The North Star*, and had set aside 120,000 acres of land in upstate New York, near Lake Placid, for black freedmen. Smith also was one of the founders of the **Liberty Party** in 1840, a party that promoted abolition and ran candidates on its antislavery ticket.

Members of the "Secret Six" became radicalized by two important events of the 1850s, the passage of the **Fugitive Slave Law** of 1850 and the Kansas-Nebraska Act of 1854. Gerrit Smith led an armed rescue of a fugitive slave, Jerry McHenry, from a Syracuse jail in the autumn of 1852. Thomas Wentworth Higginson led a raid that attempted, but failed, to free a fugitive slave, **Anthony Burns**, from prison in Boston in 1854. Higginson and Parker condemned the Fugitive Slave Law in sermons, while George Luther Stearns, who was a wealthy businessman, joined the antislavery effort because the same law was anathema to him.

The Kansas-Nebraska Act of 1854 led to the overturning of the **Missouri Compromise** of 1820, which had banned slavery north of 36° 30', with the exception of Missouri. The 1854 act allowed settlers to decide if slavery would exist in the two new territories. Wealthy men from Boston established the New England Emigrant Aid Company to help settlers move west and populate Kansas with enough free-state settlers to gain control of the territory and form a government opposed to slavery. When "border ruffians" from Missouri began raiding free-state settlements, Parker began buying guns and bullets for the migrants from New England.

Their hatred of slavery, the "Slave Power," and the perceived injustice of the Fugitive Slave Law, led the "Secret Six" to support John Brown. He was a man willing to wage war on slavery, as he proved in Kansas, most notoriously in the Pottawatomie Creek massacre in 1856, and he believed that he could launch a massive slave rebellion in the valley of northwestern Virginia. The idea of provoking civil war between North and South appealed to members of the "Secret Six," especially Smith and Higginson. Not all of the six believed this idea was prudent, a sentiment shared by Frederick Douglass. None of the six abolitionists faced prosecution for their actions, though they suffered ignominy from their conservative friends and associates for a time. Some of the six, such as Sanborn, continued to defend Brown from critics for as long as he lived. The episode of the "Secret Six" revealed the depth of passion aroused by slavery and the events of the 1850s. *See also* Bleeding Kansas; Jerry Rescue (1851).

Further Readings: Renehan, Edward J., Jr. *The Secret Six: The True Tale of the Men Who Conspired with John Brown.* New York: Crown Publishers, Inc., 1995; Reynolds, David S. *John Brown, Abolitionist: The Man Who Killed Slavery, Sparked the Civil War, and Seeded Civil Rights.* New York: Alfred A. Knopf, 2005.

James C. Foley

Segregation and Disenfranchisement in the American South

The segregated or "Jim Crow" South developed amid the social and political turmoil of the late-nineteenth century, when economic depression, a growing disparity of wealth, increased tenancy (sharecropping), and rural indebtedness created an environment of political radicalism and growing racial animosity. By the 1880s, repressive measures written into law and supported by violent white reprisal carefully circumscribed the actions of black Southerners, blocking their ability to vote, and keeping political control in the hands of a coterie of elite white Southerners. In 1896, the United States Supreme Court enshrined the prevailing ethos of racial segregation with the decision on *Plessy v. Ferguson.* With the backing of progressive reformers and the sanction of scientific racism, the Court's decision deemed African Americans "separate but equal"—a slogan that legitimated violence, intimidation, lynching, segregated public space, unequal access to state services, and an unwritten code of racial conduct that prevailed for over half a century.

Both segregation and disenfranchisement drew inspiration from a desire to control blacks and limit their access to political representation in Southern politics. Disenfranchisement was the pivotal feature of white supremacy; by neutralizing African Americans as a force in politics, white legislators put wider segregation measures in place. Beginning in 1890 with

A young boy drinks from the "colored" water fountain on the county courthouse lawn, Halifax, North Carolina, April 1938. Getty Images.

what became known as "The Mississippi Plan," the state passed laws requiring literacy and "understanding tests," poll taxes and grandfather clauses—all designed to bar blacks from the polls. By 1908, six Southern states had followed Mississippi in passing similar laws. Trumpeted by many white Southern progressives as an effort to cleanse the electorate of the greed and graft which, they charged, characterized Southern politics as far back as Reconstruction, disenfranchisement excluded the vast majority of blacks and many poorer white Southerners from the ballot box.

While disenfranchisement excluded them from the nation's body politic, segregation limited blacks in public space. Segregation was a largely urban phenomenon, designed to ensure that African Americans intruded as little as possible into white New South towns and cities. Public transportation was one of the early efforts to erect a code of separation. Between 1887 and 1907, every state in the former Confederacy designed laws to segregate passengers on railways. Black access to state services like health care and education were also severely limited, and when blacks did have access to them, those services were severely under funded. Whites segregated virtually every area of Southern public life in which the races interacted, both by law and by custom that varied from city to city. White Southerners also supported segregation with violence. Between 1880 and 1930, whites lynched approximately 3,220 African Americans (and 723 whites), many in public demonstrations meant to unify whites and terrify blacks into accepting the status quo.

African Americans responded to this widespread social and political repression throughout the nation. The formation of the National Association for the Advancement of Colored People (NAACP) in 1909 was but one of many black organizational efforts to combat a system of repression. Many black Southerners also sought relief from Jim Crow by leaving the region; over one million African Americans left the South between 1910 and 1930. While white Southerners supported their control over blacks with ceaseless effort, African Americans throughout the South and the nation campaigned for several more decades to overturn the codes of southern segregation and disenfranchisement.

Further Readings: Brundage, W. Fitzhugh. *Lynching in the New South: Georgia and Virginia, 1880–1930*. Urbana: University of Illinois Press, 1993; McMillen, Neil R. *Dark Journey: Black Mississippians in the Age of Jim Crow*. Urbana: University of Illinois Press, 1989; Rabinowitz, Howard N. *Race Relations in the Urban South, 1865–1890*. Athens: University of Georgia Press, 1996. Reprint, 1978; Woodward, C. Vann. *The Strange Career of Jim Crow*. 3rd rev. ed. Oxford and New York: Oxford University Press, 1974.

Erik Mathisen

"The Selling of Joseph" (Sewall, 1700)

In 1700, Samuel Sewall (1652–1730), an affluent judge and merchant in Newbury, Massachusetts, published one of the earliest American antislavery tracts, "The Selling of Joseph, A Memorial." Sewall's pamphlet helped spur a debate in New England over the appropriateness of slavery in their society that would continue through the eighteenth century. Sewall's nephew, Jonathan Sewall, would in fact lead the fight for slave emancipation in Massachusetts courts in the late 1760s and 1770s.

An ongoing feud with John Saffin, a local merchant and slave trader, motivated Sewall to write the pamphlet. In 1694, Saffin had promised his slave, Adam, freedom, but then failed to manumit him when the designated time arrived. Adam then sought his freedom through the courts and engaged Sewall to provide legal assistance. In the process of assisting Adam in his legal battle, Sewall wrote "The Selling of Joseph" specifically to attack Saffin and defend Adam, but more broadly as a probing inquiry into the leading justifications of Atlantic World slavery. "The Selling of Joseph" highlighted two key arguments against slavery and the slave trade. Establishing the common ancestry of all human beings through Adam, Sewall then used biblical exegesis to prove the immorality of the selling of humans. He delineated a more practical argument that urged his peers to use white indentured servants rather than black slaves who, he argued, because of their racial inferiority, could never become fully accepted members of New England society and would pollute white bloodlines if, as they well might, intermarried with whites. He concluded the pamphlet by countering some other common arguments used to support slavery including the contention that Africans were the cursed descendants of Cham, that the Christianization of the pagan Africans justified their enslavement, and that the Africans imported into the colonies had been justifiably sold as captives from just wars. Saffin responded to "The Selling of Joseph" with his own pamphlet, "A Brief and Candid Answer to 'The Selling of Joseph,'" in which he defended slavery and the slave trade. Adam was eventually freed in 1703.

Further Readings: Towner, Lawrence W. "The Sewall-Saffin Dialogue on Slavery." *William and Mary Quarterly*, 3d ser. 21 (1964): 40–52.

Emily V. Blanck

Seminole Wars

The Seminole Wars comprised the three wars fought between the United States and the Seminole Indians during the first half of the nineteenth century. They resulted from Indian slavery and the desire for Indian removal. An increasing number of escaped black slaves took refuge among Seminoles in Florida, a practice the United States government refused to tolerate. During the fighting, hundreds of slaves and former slaves fought for their own freedom. The wars ended without a formal surrender by the Seminoles. Nevertheless, the wars effectively removed most of the Seminoles to Indian Territory in Oklahoma and terminated the ability of African Americans to find freedom in Florida.

The first Seminole War occurred in the aftermath of the War of 1812, when the Spanish government in Florida turned a deaf ear to American complaints about the Negro Fort, a hideaway for runaway slaves in the Florida panhandle. The United States Army, under the command of Major General Edmund P. Gaines, attacked and destroyed the fort on July 27, 1816. Most of the 300 African American inhabitants were killed, and Gaines returned any survivors to slavery.

Despite Gaines's success, African Americans continued to find freedom by crossing the permeable Florida-Georgia border. In Florida, a colony that Spain struggled to control, blacks allied and sometime intermarried with Seminole Indians who had their own tensions with white Georgians. Many of these African Americans lived in villages that existed autonomously from their Indian allies, while others lived as members of Seminole villages.

After a series of skirmishes with the Seminoles, the United States authorized General Andrew Jackson to capture or kill the Seminole warriors. Jackson pursued the Indians and their African American allies into Florida, burning villages and agricultural fields as they went. Ignoring orders that forbade him from attacking the Spanish, Jackson also captured the Florida towns of St. Marks on April 7, 1818 and Pensacola on May 24, 1818. Soon after, the United States arranged to take possession of Florida.

Nevertheless, African Americans continued to seek refuge in Florida after the United States occupied the territory. As cotton agriculture spread in northern Florida, slaveowners sought to end the Seminole harboring of runaway slaves. In the 1823 Treaty of Moultrie Creek, the Seminoles agreed to return these fugitives and move onto reserved lands to the south in return for protection and cash payments. Although the Seminoles relocated, the protection and payments promised by the United States government did not follow. None of that inhibited runaway blacks from relentlessly pursuing refuge among the Seminoles in the Florida interior. With the treaty widely considered a failure, the U.S. government demanded the complete removal of Indians from Florida. In 1832, seven Seminole chiefs agreed to this demand in the Treaty of Payne's Landing. Most Seminoles were outraged, and they responded by assassinating Charley Emathla, the chief largely blamed for agreeing to the land cession. In adherence with the treaty, nearly 4,000 Seminoles moved to Indian Territory. The rest of the Seminoles, led by Osceola and supported by hundreds of African Americans, went to war with the United States.

From 1835 to 1842, the U.S. government repeatedly tried to subdue the Indians in Florida. The Second Seminole War, as it was later called, provided the opportunity for hundreds of African Americans in Florida and Georgia to fight for their freedom. In many of the battles, American soldiers were struck by the presence and bravery of "black Seminoles." At the Battle of Lake Okeechobee on Christmas Day 1837, the actions of John Horse led the United States to change its policy regarding blacks in Florida. Rather than insisting on their reenslavement, in 1838 the United States offered them freedom if they agreed to move to Indian Territory. Over the next few years, more than 500 African Americans took this option, thus curtailing the ability of the Seminoles to launch large-scale resistance.

When the fighting finally ended in 1842, the U.S. government removed another 4,400 Seminoles to Indian Territory. A few hundred Seminoles moved even further from American settlements and remained in Florida. In the following years, only a few African Americans found refuge in the swamps of Florida and among the Seminoles.

While the Seminoles served as an ally to runaway blacks, they also enslaved them at times. Indeed, at the conclusion of the Civil War, the U.S. government insisted that the Seminoles provide for black slaves on their land. Section Two of the March 21, 1866, treaty with the Seminoles stated: "And inasmuch as there are among the Seminoles many persons of African descent and blood, who have no interest or property in the soil, and no recognized civil rights it is stipulated that hereafter these persons and their descendants, and such other of the same race as shall be permitted by said nation to settle there, shall have and enjoy all the rights of native citizens."

Further Readings: Heidler, David, and Jeanne Heidler. *Old Hickory's War: Andrew Jackson and the Quest for Empire*. Mechanicsburg, PA: Stackpole Books, 1996; Kappler, Charles J., ed., *Indian Affairs: Laws and Treaties. Vol. 2 (Treaties)*. Washington, D.C.: Government Printing Office, 1904; Mahon, John K. *History of the Second Seminole War, 1835–1842*. Gainesville: University Press of Florida, 1992; Miller, Susan A. *Coacoochee's Bones: A Seminole Saga*. Lawrence: University Press of Kansas, 2003; Rivers, Larry Eugene. *Slavery in Florida: Territorial Days to Emancipation*. Gainesville: University Press of Florida, 2000.

Andrew K. Frank

Seneca Falls Convention (1848)

On July 19–20, 1848, about 300 people met in the Wesleyan Chapel in Seneca Falls, New York, in the first woman's rights convention held in the

United States. One hundred of them (sixty-eight women and thirty-two men) signed a Declaration of Sentiments, patterned after the **Declaration of Independence**, asserting that "all men and women are created equal" and listing grievances of women against the patriarchal establishment of the United States, which included inequalities in political rights and suffrage, legal rights, economic opportunities, education, religion, sexual morality and personal self-respect. Although the Declaration itself made no mention of slavery, all the identifiable signers were from one of two abolitionist groups. More than one third of the signers came from political abolitionist households in Seneca Falls that supported the new Free Soil Party. At least one quarter of the signers were Garrisonian Quaker abolitionists from nearby areas who were in the process of forming a new, egalitarian group called the Congregational Friends (later the Progressive Friends or Friends of Human Progress). **Elizabeth Cady Stanton**, the convention's main organizer, had friends in both groups and acted as a catalyst for the convention. Without an antislavery movement, there would have been no Seneca Falls woman's rights convention.

The convention touched off the organized woman's rights movement. From 1850 until the Civil War, national woman's rights conventions met every year except one. Women's rights activists continued to draw extensively on the antislavery movement for inspiration and support, and many black women and men including **Frederick Douglass**, William C. Nell, **Sojourner Truth**, and Jermain Loguen became key woman's rights supporters. In 1866, supporters of equal rights formed the American Equal Rights Association. This division occurred in 1869 when the Fifteenth Amendment gave the vote to African American men, but not to women of any color. Supporters of the Amendment including Lucy Stone formed the American Woman Suffrage Association. Opponents, including Elizabeth Cady Stanton and Susan B. Anthony, formed the National Woman Suffrage Association. In 1890, these groups merged into the National American Woman Suffrage Association. *See also* Garrisonians; Gender and Slave Emancipation; Gender Relations within Abolitionism; Quakers and Antislavery; Women's Antislavery Societies.

Further Readings: Bacon, Margaret Hope. *Valiant Friend: The Life of Lucretia Mott*. New York: Walker and Company, 1980; Livingston, James, and Sherry H. Penney. *A Very Dangerous Woman: Martha Wright and Women's Rights*. Amherst: University of Massachusetts Press, 2004; Wellman, Judith. *The Road to Seneca Falls: Elizabeth Cady Stanton and the First Woman's Rights Convention*. Urbana: University of Illinois Press, 2004.

Judith Wellman

Sewall, Samuel. *See* "The Selling of Joseph"

Seward, William Henry (1801–1872)

William Henry Seward was one of the most important American politicians of the nineteenth century. His political career began in the early 1820s with **John Quincy Adams** and continued through Andrew Johnson

William Henry Seward. Courtesy of the Library of Congress.

and Reconstruction. Seward rose from state senator in New York to become governor, U.S. senator, and finally secretary of state under Presidents **Abraham Lincoln** and Andrew Johnson. His political affiliation was almost as complex. He began as a National Republican, became an Anti-Mason, then a Whig, and finally, a Republican.

Seward was both a man of his time and a man ahead of his time. His racial and ethnic attitudes confirm this characterization. Seward rejected the nativism, the hatred and fear of foreigners, embraced by many of his contemporaries. He supported Irish independence and educational opportunities for Catholic immigrants. His views of African Americans were more nuanced. Seward believed African Americans to be inferior to whites, yet he vehemently opposed slavery. He believed African Americans deserved freedom and the opportunity to improve themselves through education, and supported suffrage for all qualified residents of New York State. Seward and his wife even raised their children in a household where racial prejudice was not tolerated. Seward also opposed slavery because it hindered economic growth, an argument made popular first by the Free Soil Party and then the Republicans. Most importantly, Seward opposed slavery because it besmirched American claims to be the asylum for liberty. A nation devoted to freedom could not also have slavery. In 1839, as governor of New York he opposed returning a fugitive slave to Virginia, asserting that it was impossible for a human being to be considered the property of another. As a U.S. senator he supported resolutions that called for compensated emancipation.

Seward's dislike for slavery often put him at odds with the South and conservative Northerners. His election to the United States Senate in 1849 gave him more prominence in the growing controversy over the westward expansion of slavery. From 1849 to1861, Seward was often in the middle of this political crisis. His first speech in the Senate opposed Henry Clay's compromise plan for the admission of California without recognizing it as a free state. Seward's speech of March 11, 1850, has come to be known as the "**higher law**" speech. Seward rejected compromise over slavery, because he viewed it as a transitory institution while freedom was a perpetual institution, even in the South. He asserted that the public lands of the West were the "common heritage of mankind, bestowed upon them by the Creator of the universe. We are his stewards, and must so discharge our trust as to secure, in the highest attainable degree, their happiness." Seward rejected arguments that politicians only had recourse to the Constitution for guidance on this issue. "But there is a higher law than the Constitution, which regulates our authority over the domain, and devotes it to the same noble purposes." This law was God's law.

Seward opposed the Kansas-Nebraska Act and wrote an "Address to the People of the United States," which detailed the growth of the Slave Power. He supported the Free State settlers in Kansas and denounced the policies of the administrations of Presidents Pierce and Buchanan. Seward denounced Buchanan and Chief Justice Roger Taney for their roles in the Dred Scott decision, accusing them of destroying American liberty in the interests of preserving slavery. In 1858, while campaigning for the Republican gubernatorial candidate in New York, Seward gave his famous "irrepressible conflict" speech. Seward asserted that the United States had two political systems, and what divided them was the conflict between slavery and free labor. As the country grew in size, the two systems came into contact and conflict, and the result was an "irrepressible conflict," meaning that one of the two antagonists, slavery or free labor, must give way. Slavery could only win through the support of the Democratic Party and violation of the Constitution; therefore, Seward urged American voters to reject Democratic candidates for political office. Seward's belief in the superiority of free labor was grounded in his idea of a permanent American union bound together by the ideals of the **Declaration of Independence** and the Constitution, as well as by geographic features, immigration, education, national pride, transportation, and trade.

Seward's speeches often hurt him politically. He was a conservative, but the rhetoric in his major speeches was often radical. As a result, other politicians and political leaders often did not trust him. Was he a statesman or an office seeker? His strong views cost him some political friends and support, a fact that became evident in 1856 and 1860, when the Republican Party rejected him to nominate, instead, John Frémont and Abraham Lincoln, respectively. These rejections wounded Seward, who felt particularly bitter in 1860 because he believed that his time had come as a presidential candidate and other Republicans had told him so as well.

Despite his disappointment, Seward agreed to serve as Lincoln's Secretary of State. Seward wielded considerable influence in the cabinet and with Lincoln early in his presidency. Lincoln supported Seward when other cabinet members called for his ouster. Seward and Lincoln worked well together during the secession crisis and the Civil War. Seward's diplomatic skill during the war helped the United States avoid conflict with Great Britain and France. Seward helped to smooth over relations with Great Britain during the "*Trent* affair," when a U.S. Navy vessel removed two Confederate diplomats from a British vessel and successfully pressured Great Britain not to build warships for the Confederacy. Seward's advice to Lincoln on the Emancipation Proclamation was critical. He encouraged Lincoln not to issue the preliminary document until the Union enjoyed a victory, lest foreign powers perceive its issuance as an act of desperation. Lincoln heeded this advice and waited until after the victory at Antietam in September, 1862, to issue the preliminary Emancipation Proclamation.

Seward survived an assassination attempt on the night Lincoln was assassinated, April 14, 1865. He recovered from those wounds, and earlier wounds from a carriage accident, and served Andrew Johnson as secretary of state. In terms of domestic policy, Seward's ideas about Reconstruction were much the same as Johnson's, a quick reunion with little support for freedmen's rights. Seward believed that restoring the Union was more important than assuring rights for the freedmen, whom he viewed as inferior and whose improvement would take many years. For his support of Johnson's policies, Seward received the scorn of many **Radical Republicans**. As for foreign policy, Seward remained an ardent expansionist, encouraging the purchase of Alaska from Russia in 1867, and attempting to purchase islands in both the Atlantic and Pacific Oceans for naval bases. Seward left office on March 4, 1869, and began his retirement from public life. He died on October 10, 1872. *See also* Compromise of 1850; Democratic Party and Antislavery; Radical Republicans; Whig Party and Antislavery; United States Constitution and Antislavery.

Further Readings: Gienapp, William E. *The Origins of the Republican Party, 1852–1856*. New York: Oxford University Press, 1987; Holt, Michael F. *The Rise and Fall of the American Whig Party: Jacksonian Politics and the Onset of the Civil War*. New York: Oxford University Press, 1999; Sewell, Richard H. *Ballots for Freedom: Antislavery Politics in the United States, 1837–1860*. New York: Oxford University Press, 1976; Van Deusen, Glyndon G. *William Henry Seward*. New York: Oxford University Press, 1967.

James C. Foley

Sherman, William T. *See* Field Order No. 15

Sierra Leone

Known as the "Province of Freedom," Sierra Leone was the first established settlement for repatriated freed slaves. Between 1787 and 1850, four waves of settlers arrived—free blacks from London, black Loyalists from Nova Scotia, exiled Jamaican **Maroons**, and Africans released from captured slave ships. Descendants of these settlers are known in Sierra Leone as Creoles.

After the end of the American Revolution, hundreds of African Americans went to London, after having been wooed to support the unsuccessful British cause by promises of freedom and land. Unfortunately, these promises were not kept, and without access to land or work, the majority of the newly freed blacks lived in poverty. Their situation elicited sympathy from philanthropists, who began to consider resettlement as a solution to both help poor blacks and relieve the burden on city government.

The selection of Sierra Leone was inspired by British entomologist-turned-abolitionist Henry Smeathman who had spent three years studying insects on the Banana Islands, off the coast of Sierra Leone. His idea was taken up with great enthusiasm by abolitionist Granville Sharp, who became the chief architect of the resettlement scheme. There was not unanimous support for the plan; black leaders such as **Ottobah Cugoano** and **Olaudah Equiano** withdrew their support, accusing the organizers of not having the best interests of blacks in mind.

The first group of 356 settlers arrived in Sierra Leone in 1787 and established their settlement, Granville Town, on land purchased from the local Temne ruler, King Tom. As a result of harsh rains, malaria, tensions with the local population, and lack of food to plant and eat, the majority of these first settlers succumbed to illness.

The second migration came from black Loyalists in Nova Scotia, individuals who had been promised land in **Canada** in exchange for serving with the British. Approximately 3,500 had settled in Nova Scotia, only to be cheated out of land and employment opportunities. Black Loyalists petitioned the British government for resettlement, and approximately 1,000 chose to make the move to Sierra Leone. Upon arrival in 1792, they built a settlement entitled Freetown, the name of the present-day capital.

The third wave of settlers came from Jamaica. These were the **Maroons**, named after the Spanish word for wild, *cimaron*. Maroons had been released by Spanish slave owners in the 1650s, and had maintained their independence through agreements with the British to help capture any newly escaped plantation slaves. A Maroon rebellion against the British led to the dissolution of all past agreements and their exile to Nova Scotia. Similar to the Loyalists, the Maroons petitioned the British government for resettlement, and approximately 550 Maroons arrived in 1800.

The largest wave of settlers, known as "Recaptives" and "Liberated Africans," came from captured slave ships. In 1808, when the British government took responsibility for the settlement and it became the colony of Sierra Leone, the British Navy began suppressing the Atlantic slave trade and releasing the liberated slaves in Freetown. Approximately 40,000 liberated slaves settled in Sierra Leone between 1808 and 1850. *See also* Atlantic Slave Trade and British Abolition; Liberia.

Further Readings: Equiano, Olaudah. *The Interesting Narrative and Other Writings*. New York: Penguin Books USA, 1995; Grant, John N. *The Maroons in Nova Scotia*. Halifax, Nova Scotia: Formac Publishing Company, 2002; Hochschild, Adam. *Bury the Chains: Prophets and Rebels in the Fight to Free the Empire's Slaves*. New York: Houghton Mifflin, 2005; Wyse, Akintola. *The Krio of Sierra Leone: An Interpretive History*. Washington, D.C.: Howard University Press, 1991.

Chitra Aiyar

Slave Narratives

Slave narratives were autobiographies written by ex-slaves. There were two major periods in which slave narratives were published, 1760–1807 and 1831–1865. During the initial period, slave narratives described the authors' lives as slaves. In the later period, authors provided more brutal descriptions of slavery, overtly agitating for the abolition of slavery.

In the early period, slave narratives were part of the larger genre of colonial autobiography and narrated the adventures of Africans who became enslaved. Authors portrayed slavery as the absence of physical freedom, with the dehumanizing elements of slavery rarely emphasized. Rather, the focus was on the protagonist who usually assimilated into western culture and converted to Christianity, with freedom offered as a reward. Some of the most noteworthy examples of this genre are Venture Smith, *A Narrative of the Life and Adventures of Venture, a Native of Africa* (1798); Boston King, *Memoirs of the Life of Boston King, a Black Preacher* (1798); Quobna Ottobah Cugoano, *Thoughts and Sentiments on the Evil and Wicked Traffic of the Slavery . . .* (1787); and Olaudah Equiano, *The Interesting Narrative of the Life of Olaudah Equiano, or Gustavus Vassa, the African* (1789).

While a handful of slave narratives appeared in the early decades of the nineteenth century, the growth of the American abolitionist movement in the 1830s renewed interest in publishing slave narratives. White abolitionists understood that slave narratives could serve as a powerful propaganda tool for their cause. Often ex-slaves were aided by sympathetic abolitionist editors in writing their autobiographies. Many narratives also included testimonials about the author, generally written by white abolitionists or ministers, to authenticate the author's good character and the truth of his story. With slavery becoming increasingly controversial during the antebellum period, many Northern whites became interested in the lives of slaves. Reflecting the power of these first-hand accounts of slavery, several slave narratives went through multiple editions.

Antebellum slave narratives provided much more graphic descriptions of slavery than their eighteenth-century counterparts. The physical hardship and brutality of slavery were narrated in detail. The emotional, intellectual, and spiritual deprivations were also provided, revealing the human side of the slave experience. Many of the most popular slave narratives, such as Frederick Douglass's *Narrative of the Life of Frederick Douglass, an American Slave* and Harriet Jacobs' *Incidents in the Life of a Slave Girl*, emphasized the authors' pursuit of individual freedom and their perseverance through slavery, gross exploitation, and the dangerous flight to freedom. Slave narratives often adopted the sensational and sentimental literary styles of the nineteenth-century United States. To speak effectively to a highly religious audience, the religious contradictions of slavery were also exposed.

While slave narratives have been extremely useful to historians because of their first-hand accounts of slavery, they are not fully representative of the antebellum slave experience. Less than 15 percent of the antebellum slave narratives were written by women, and most of the slave narratives describe slavery in the upper South, leaving few accounts of slavery in the lower South. In their ability to escape from slavery and subsequently write perceptively about it, the authors of slave narratives were also exceptional and, not infrequently, privileged slaves with the occupational and geographical mobility to enhance success at flight.

Further Readings: Davis, Charles T., and Henry Louis Gates, Jr., eds. *The Slave's Narrative*. New York: Oxford University Press, 1985; Foster, Francis Smith. *Witnessing Slavery: The Development of Antebellum Slave Narratives*. Madison: University of Wisconsin Press, 1979.

Daniel P. Kotzin

Slave Power Argument

The three-fifths clause in the **United States Constitution** called for three-fifths of the Southern slave population to count in the total population of the slave states, both for tax purposes and for representation in the United States House of Representatives, and therefore in the electoral college as well. Thus, the slave states increased their representation in Congress; in fact, they continuously had one-third more seats than if only their free populations had counted for representative purposes. In 1793, the slave states (not including those Northern states such as New Jersey and New York that enacted plans of gradual emancipation after 1793) had forty-seven seats as opposed to the thirty-three that their free population warranted. In 1812, they had seventy-six instead of fifty-nine, and in 1833, they had ninety-eight instead of seventy-three. This inflated representation for proslavery Southerners formed the basis of the Slave Power.

Due to their inflated congressional representation and incredible unity, the slave states needed only to sway a few Northern voters in order to enact their policies in the House of Representatives, while the balance of free and slave states meant only one Northern vote was necessary for the Slave Power to succeed in the Senate. This magnified representation also helped in presidential elections, as it was only necessary for a Southern candidate to carry a small portion of the Northern electoral votes to win the election. With the exception of the two single-term Adams presidencies, from 1797–1801 and 1825–1829, the president hailed from a slave state for the entire first half of the nineteenth century. Therefore, between the election of George Washington and **Abraham Lincoln**, at least nineteen of the thirty-four appointees to the Supreme Court were slaveholders. Due to this power, a string of proslavery laws and court decisions were put into effect. For example, the Slave Power defeated the Tallmadge Amendment to the Missouri statehood bill in 1819, which proposed banning the further introduction of slavery into Missouri and gradual emancipation to manumit slaves born there. The Slave Power also crushed the Wilmot Proviso, which proposed banning slavery in all territory taken from Mexico. The same forces were behind the admission of Texas into the Union as a slave state, the **Fugitive Slave Law**, and the Kansas-Nebraska Act that repealed the **Missouri Compromise**. The Taney Court's 1857 Dred Scott decision—which ruled against the power of Congress to regulate slavery in the territories—was decided by a staunchly pro-South Court. These laws and decisions greatly alarmed antislavery Northerners. Concerned about this slave oligarchy extending slavery at the expense of the rights and liberty of Northern whites, antislavery fervor increased, culminating with the rise of the Republican Party in the North. The Whig Party disintegrated, and the Northern Democrats sustained irreparable damage. Increasing numbers of immigrants had substantially swung the representative balance of power back to the North, so with the elections of 1858 and 1860, the Republicans seized control of Congress and the White House, crushing the Slave Power. *See also* Adams, John Quincy; Democratic Party and Antislavery; Radical Republicans; Texas, Annexation of; Whig Party and Antislavery.

Further Readings: Richards, Leonard L. *The Slave Power: The Free North and Southern Domination, 1780–1860.* Baton Rouge: Louisiana State University Press, 2000; Gara, Larry. "Slavery and the Slave Power: A Crucial Distinction." In John R. McKivigan, ed. *History of the American Abolitionist Movement.* New York: Garland Publishing, Inc., 1999, pp. 203–217.

John French

Slavery and Abolition in the Twentieth Century

By the beginning of the twentieth century, chattel slavery was no longer legal in most of the world outside of the Arabian Peninsula and Ethiopia. A chattel slave was a possession, who could be bought, sold, or transferred, at the will of his or her owner. Such slaves owned nothing, and had no control over their lives or families. Their subjection was complete, lifelong, and hereditary. This type of slavery had existed since ancient times and was widespread and legal in much of the world until the later nineteenth century. Although by definition chattel slaves were simply commodities, their worldly status and lifestyle varied considerably. Many were agricultural laborers or domestic servants, often harshly treated. However, some were respected retainers, trusted soldiers, and even, particularly in the Muslim world, high officials of state. The most fortunate of the women were beloved concubines, or even the powerful mothers of rulers. Some of the males were eunuchs, particularly valued by rulers as soldiers and officials because they could not father rival dynasties. They also served in harems and tended mosques.

Chattel slavery came under growing attack in the western world during the eighteenth century and was gradually eliminated in many European possessions, in the United States of America, Latin America, and various other areas in the nineteenth century. The last western country to outlaw it was Brazil in 1888. The abolitionist movement had a number of roots. The most vocal protagonists were evangelical Christians who thought slavery was a sin. Moreover, the various missionary societies who worked among slave-owning peoples thought it impeded the spread of Christianity. Philosophers and activists regarded it as incompatible with human rights. Economists believed it was less profitable than wage labor. The working classes, particularly in twentieth century Britain and the United States, increasingly saw it as a threat to free wage labor.

In the early twentieth century, chattel slavery was still legal in Arabia, then mainly under Ottoman rule, and in the small enclaves claimed, but not ruled, by the British—notably the Aden Protectorate and the sheikhdoms on the Persian Gulf. It was widely practiced in much of Africa, particularly in the remoter areas barely occupied by the European colonial powers, such as Niger and Mauritania, parts of Assam and Burma. It was also legal in some independent states such as Thailand (Siam) and Nepal. It was practiced in parts of the Philippines and Baluchistan. Remnants of it were to be found in Korea. In Ethiopia, it was legal and widespread, slave raiding was endemic in some areas, and slave trading was a fact of life.

As long as there was a demand for slaves, slave raids, the slave trade, and the export of slaves, particularly from Africa, continued. They were gradually reduced as the colonial powers gained control of the coastal areas during the late-nineteenth and early twentieth centuries and later occupied most of the interior. However, a small-scale slave traffic across the Red Sea and Indian Ocean continued as an illegal smuggling trade from the East African coast, parts of India, Baluchistan, Southeast Asia, and even China. Muslim pilgrims on their way to Mecca from all over the world, traveling overland or by sea, were also often enslaved on their way to, or in, Arabia itself.

On the African continent, in the early twentieth century, slave raids were slowly eliminated, and slave trading was gradually reduced to a small smuggling trade as new areas were brought under European control. They continued in remote areas such as Mauritania and the Sahara fringe, on a diminishing scale throughout the colonial era. Small-scale trading, particularly in children, was also endemic in much of Africa.

During the period of conquest, it was as much in the interests of the colonial rulers to keep slaves in place and working as it was in the interests of their owners. Each colonial power dealt with the question in its own way. Their aim was to end or modify slavery slowly so as not to disrupt the existing economies by provoking resistance on the part of the owners or wholesale flight by the slaves. The British, whose empire was the most extensive, outlawed slavery in very small areas designated as colonies. The greater parts of their territories were designated "protectorates," in which slavery was not initially under attack. They introduced a system worked out in India in the nineteenth century, simply announcing that slavery no longer had any legal status. Slaves could stay with or leave their owners as they wished. The theory was that slavery would gradually die out with minimal disruption as, on the one hand, the supply of new slaves was cut off and on the other, job opportunities or access to land became available to former slaves, and economic development allowed masters to hire free labor or turn to other forms of investment.

Other powers developed their own policies for ostensibly ending slavery, but often tacitly allowing it to continue or finding means of using slaves for their own projects. The Portuguese declared slavery illegal, but in practice it simply continued under another name and in another form. The Belgians virtually ignored it. The French, however, outlawed it in West Africa after failing to stop the wholesale exodus of slaves from one area in 1905–1906. In time, as European control increased, the end of raids and wars curtailed the supply of slaves. Moreover, large numbers of followers ceased to be the main requisite for power and prestige, and where poll or hut taxes were imposed on owners, slaves became an expense and not a source of wealth. However, in Africa many slaves, having little alternative, simply stayed with their erstwhile owners. Where possible they renegotiated their terms of service. Some became share croppers. Others performed various services for their owners, or paid them part of any wages they earned. In many areas, such services eventually became largely symbolic, but social discrimination continued right through the century, particularly when it came to questions of marriage, inheritance, rights to land, and religious ceremonies.

In the 1920s, particularly in the Arabian Peninsula and in Ethiopia, slavery was both legal and widely practiced. Arabia was the main importer of slaves. Their fate varied. They might be servants of poor Bedouins, pearl divers, dockers, camel drivers, domestic servants, concubines, or eunuchs. Many were illegally imported from eastern Africa, Baluchistan, India, South East Asia, and even China. Ethiopia was a ready source of supply as raiding continued on the frontiers, and slaves were seized by unpaid soldiers and officials, or sent as tribute to the rulers. Pilgrims on their way to or from Mecca were enslaved in spite of the fact that Islamic law forbade the enslavement of Muslims.

In areas where the colonial rulers had ended the legal status of slavery, they had a desperate need for labor to develop their new territories. Hence they used various means of coercion to force indigenous peoples into the labor force. These devices became known as "new forms of slavery." Some of the worst cases were in Africa. Thus, in King Leopold's Congo Independent State, French Equatorial Africa, and Portuguese Africa, concessionaire companies were given exclusive rights to certain products such as rubber or other forest products in a particular area. Some also had administrative powers. The result was that unscrupulous employees determined to meet targets simply forced the inhabitants to collect these products, taking no account of the Africans' own agricultural cycle and often committing atrocities. Africans were killed, mutilated, beaten, or fined and their wives and children were held as hostages until arbitrary quotas were met. The colonial powers also conscripted Africans as forced labor, often performed far from home with great loss of life, due to ill-treatment and undernourishment, but also to exposure to new disease environments and unfamiliar foods. Thousands died during the First World War in the British East African Carrier Corps. Between 1921 and 1934, 14,000 to 20,000 conscripts died building the French Congo railway. The Portuguese ran a virtual slave trade in so called "contract" workers to their islands of São Tomé and Principe, and on the mainland, Africans were forced to work for Portuguese companies or other European enterprises for six months of the year for a pittance. In settler colonies, large areas were alienated for European settlers and Africans were only allowed to live in increasingly inadequate and underdeveloped reserves, forcing the men and some women to work for low wages in the colonial economy. Wages could be kept at a minimum because families produced their own food in the reserves. Africans were also driven onto European estates as squatters, forced to work for the landowners in return for the right to grow some crops but without security of tenure. Another device was to make people grow export crops such as cotton on their own land, in often unsuitable soils. In other parts of the world, notably Latin America and the Southern United States, former slaves became sharecroppers and peons—and formed a poverty stricken underclass. Some indigenous peoples, as in Putamayo, were virtually enslaved by rubber producing companies. In the Indian sub-continent, whole families fell into debt bondage. This was virtual slavery as the debts could never be repaid and were sometime hereditary.

All of these abuses were attacked in the metropoles, by various groups of abolitionists vying for funds for their causes. Prominent amongst them were missionary societies, who believed that these practices impeded the spread of Christianity and who called on church groups to denounce slavery. A minority were activists, such as E.D. Morel, who founded the Congo Reform Association and believed that human rights included recognizing indigenous peoples' rights to their land and their right to live by their own creeds and customs. The most prominent organization was the British **Anti-Slavery Society**, which in 1909 amalgamated with the Aborigines Protection Society, to form the Anti-Slavery and Aborigines Protection Society. The purpose of the society was to use peaceful means to protect colonial peoples from both chattel slavery and various forms of "new slavery." In spite of its tiny budget and small membership, this society, called Anti-Slavery International from 1990, was, and remained, the acknowledged world leader of the anti-slavery movement. The main abolitionist struggles of the early twentieth century were fought out in the metropoles by these groups, who tried to muster public support against governments anxious to make their colonial possessions pay and businessmen determined to make profits.

At the end of World War I, the victorious allies decided that the slave trade and slave raids had virtually ended. They abrogated the **Brussels Act**, which they wished to end for other reasons. However, article 23 of the Covenant of the League of Nations bound members to secure "fair and humane" conditions for labor in all countries with which they had commercial dealings. Former German and Ottoman territories were shared out among the victorious colonial powers as mandates to be ruled in the interest of their populations until they were "ready" for self-government. In the mandates, slavery was to be ended as soon as social conditions allowed it. In 1919, a treaty signed at St. Germain replaced the Brussels Act and bound signatories to suppress slavery in all its forms. These were vague commitments without time limits. There the matter would probably have rested had not news arrived of widespread slave-raiding and slave-trading in Ethiopia. This was quickly followed by evidence of an active slave traffic across the Red Sea, particularly to the new kingdom of Hijaz, founded when the Ottoman Empire was broken up at the end of the war.

Finding the British government unwilling to take action, the secretary of the Anti-Slavery and Aborigines Protection Society, John Harris, waged an active press campaign and persuaded the delegate from New Zealand to raise the question at the League of Nations. Dramatic proof that the slave trade was active was furnished by the capture in 1922 of a slaver carrying victims from Ethiopia to Arabia. The result of this humanitarian campaign was that, in spite of the opposition of the colonial powers, the League appointed a Temporary Slavery Commission in 1924 to inquire into slavery in all its forms. This had been the aim of the antislavery society from its formation in 1839. It enabled the commission, which was composed of seven independent members, including former colonial governors and officials and a representative of the International Labor Organization, to discuss questions not previously considered forms of slavery. The colonial powers did what they could to hamstring the commission, restricting its sources and limiting its range of inquiries, particularly in the case of forced labor which was, as has been seen, widely practiced in all their territories in various forms.

However, in its report this commission extended the definition of slavery to include pawning (the pledging of a person as collateral for debt), forced marriage, child marriage, the transfer or adoption of children to exploit them, debt bondage and peonage, serfdom, forced crop growing, and, most controversial of all, forced labor. The British member, Lord Lugard, forced the hand of his government by sending it a draft convention against slavery. The British felt bound to negotiate a treaty based on this report, but they watered it down to protect their own interests before presenting it to the **League of Nations**. The result, after much haggling by the colonial powers each trying to defend their own practices, was the **Slavery Convention of 1926**, which was still in force at the beginning of the twenty-first century.

This convention defined slavery as "the status or condition of a person over whom any or all of the powers attaching to the right of ownership were exercised." It thus went far beyond the chattel slavery hitherto under attack, but it was vague and the various forms of ownership identified by the commission were not listed in the convention. Moreover, signatories were merely bound to secure the "progressive" disappearance of the various forms of servitude under attack, and no time limit was set. Forced labor was always to be paid and performed near home and was only to be used "exceptionally" and for "public purposes." These purposes were not defined, nor were the terms of service. Finally, signatories were only bound to end it "progressively and as soon as possible."

The convention was weakened by the fact that no monitoring system or means of enforcement was established. The League, it was held, could not interfere in the internal affairs of states. Clauses against the maritime slave trade proposed by the British were rejected. Instead the powers with territories in areas where the slave trade was still active agreed to sign a further agreement against it, but this was never done. Moreover, signatories of the convention could exclude any of their territories to which they did not want to apply it. The British, for instance, excluded the Indian princely states as well as unadministered tracts in India and Burma. The French excluded Tunisia and Morocco. There was also no means of forcing countries like Saudi Arabia, where slavery was rife, to sign the convention.

Although the convention had these serious weaknesses, it was the first international legal document to establish a moral position condemning slavery, the slave trade, and a range of practices previously not considered forms of slavery. It thus marked the beginning of the international attack on them. One of the most significant results was that the forced labor question was taken up by the International Labor Organization (ILO), which negotiated the Forced Labor Convention of 1930.

Although chattel slavery had now been condemned in an international instrument, it only died out slowly. The Anti-Slavery and Aborigines Protection Society continued to press for its abolition worldwide and was joined by various other non-governmental organizations, as well as dedicated individuals. It was they who called public attention to the continuing plight of certain chattel slaves, shaming governments into action. Thus the first serious steps against slavery in the Sudan, for instance, were taken by the

British only in the late 1920s. Attitudes changed slowly, however, and ending the legal status of slavery was only the first step. Slaves anxious to leave their owners had to assess their chances, in the case of men, of finding other means of livelihood. For women it was even more difficult unless they could find a male protector. Some women, particularly in rural areas, were still under their masters' control in Sudan thirty years later. In Ethiopia horrendous reports were still being received of slaving on the frontiers right up to the Italian occupation in the mid 1930s. In Sierra Leone, although slaves were told they were free and officials were forbidden to recognize slavery in the late 1920s, in practice little changed. Many former slaves, now called "cousins," continued to work for their former owners without pay in return for access to land, lodging, and food as late as 1956. In French ruled Mauritania, women and children in particular were retained as slaves in spite of the outlawing of slavery. Similarly, slavery continued in Niger through the twentieth century.

In the 1930s, as the result of continuing humanitarian pressure, a second slavery committee was formed by the League of Nations, the main result of which was the establishment of a permanent committee, the Advisory Committee of Experts on Slavery, which met from 1935–1938. Due to its British member, this committee continued the attack begun by the first committee on the various practices that it had designated as slavery. These included particularly the Chinese practice of "adopting" children, mainly little girls who were called *Mui Tsai* ("little sister" in Cantonese). Ostensibly adopted, usually because their parents could not afford to keep them, many ended up as unpaid ill-treated domestic drudges. Unknown numbers were brought to the island of Hong Kong and other British possessions in southeast Asia, as well as to French and Dutch territories. The committee also discussed other forms of child labor, as well as debt bondage, peonage, serfdom, pawning, and slavery in the Muslim world. In 1935, in the midst of the committee's proceedings, the Italians conquered Ethiopia using the suppression of slavery as one excuse for their unprovoked attack.

The Advisory Committee collected a great deal of information, and by the outbreak of the Second World War, some progress had been made by the colonial powers, particularly Britain and France, who demanded reports from colonial governors and in some cases, reviewed and reenacted some of their antislavery laws. The Italians claimed to have outlawed slavery in Ethiopia. The committee, however, died of attrition as the result of events leading to the Second World War.

The 1920s and, more particularly, the 1930s had been notable for the emergence of new forms of servitude. From the early 1920s, the Russians were using political and other prisoners as forced labor in so-called gulags. Victims were worked, often to death, in horrendous circumstances, producing gold, timber, and other export goods, and building dams and roads. Capitalist firms in the western world feared they would be undercut and western trade unions believed that free labor was threatened. The basic facts were known by the 1930s. But these gulags were not discussed by the League committees. They fell into the realm of forced labor. In any case, the Soviet Union was not a member of the League of Nations, and thus beyond the reach of its committees. Moreover, the full development of the gulags occurred only during and after World War II.

In the 1930s, Nazi Germany instituted concentration camps in which Jews and gypsies, together with political prisoners, and other persons considered undesirable were worked to death. Inmates incapable of work were killed on arrival. During the war itself, the Germans expanded these camps and also forced thousands of workers from all over occupied Europe to work as virtual slaves, producing arms and other goods for the German war effort. The concentration camps were not discussed by the League slavery committees, although much was known about them by 1938. Germany had by then withdrawn from the League. The recruitment of foreign slave laborers only took place during the war after the committee had ceased to meet.

After the end of the war in 1945, many of the prewar concerns discussed by the Advisory Committee on Slavery no longer existed. Slavery had been outlawed in Ethiopia in 1943, as the result of the British expulsion of the Italians and the restoration of the emperor. In 1946, the French ended the use of forced labor. In the 1950s, the communist conquest of China cut off the supply of new *mui tsai*, which Britain had already done much to suppress in its own colonies. Chattel slavery, however, remained legal in Saudi Arabia, Oman, and the British satellites on the Persian Gulf. It also continued illegally in Mauritania and Niger and other areas on the Sahara fringe. Forced labor in various forms still continued in, for instance, Portuguese African possessions, where labor laws required people to work in the colonial economy for half the year, for a pittance. Moreover, debt bondage remained widespread particularly on the Indian subcontinent.

As early as 1946, the Anti-Slavery Society, now led by Charles Greenidge, began agitating for the appointment of a UN permanent committee against slavery on the lines of the last League committee. The Charter of the **United Nations** issued in 1945 stated that one of its aims was to promote respect for the observance of human rights and to ensure fundamental freedoms for all without respect to race, sex, language, or religion. Slavery was not specifically mentioned, but its eradication was clearly implied. However, like the League, the United Nations was hamstrung by the same inability to enforce its treaties or interfere in the internal affairs of member states. It was also deeply divided on what constituted human rights. It was dominated, on the one hand by the United States and its democratic allies, and on the other by the Soviet Union which now led the much expanded communist world. Their concepts of freedom were different. The United States and its allies stressed political rights, freedom of expression, of information, of religion, freedom from arbitrary arrest, the right to a fair trial, and other components of the rule of law. The communist world stressed economic and social rights, equal opportunity, and the right to education. It condemned racial discrimination. This was a weak point for the United States because of its treatment of non-whites, and for the colonial empires, which discriminated against their indigenous subjects. The slavery question became a pawn in the struggle for the hearts and minds of the so-called non-aligned states, former colonies such as India, Pakistan, Indonesia, Ghana, and many others which, as they became independent, took their places at the United Nations.

The Anti-Slavery Society persuaded the Belgian delegate to raise the issue of slavery at the United Nations. There was a fatal division between the Socialist "eastern bloc" and the Democratic "western" bloc as to what constituted slavery. The Russians thought of it as the chattel slavery of old and the various other practices condemned by the League committees. The British, anxious to divert attention from the chattel slavery in their South Arabian protectorate and their satellites on the Persian Gulf, claimed that it included forced labor, peonage, and mui tsai which still continued in China. In 1949, the United States proposed an inquiry into forced labor everywhere.

A UN committee was finally established to deal with slavery only. Forced labor was once more the province of the ILO. This ad hoc committee was appointed in 1949 to "survey the field of slavery and other institutions or customs resembling slavery." Its four members met in 1950 and included Charles Greenidge, the secretary of the Anti-Slavery Society. It had more leeway than the League committees had had to solicit and collect information. However, it broke up early and in disorder, largely because it was attacked by Peru, Colombia, and Chile for discussing peonage.

However, it had important results. The United Nations took over the 1926 Slavery Convention and Greenidge presented the British government with a new convention to include the practices defined as slavery in the report of the Temporary Slavery Commission but not formally incorporated in the 1926 treaty. These were debt bondage, serfdom, forced marriage, and the adoption of children for their exploitation. He also suggested treating the maritime slave trade as piracy. The British felt bound to present a watered-down version of this to the United Nations, and the result after much wrangling was the negotiation of the **Supplementary Convention on the Abolition of Slavery** of 1956. This convention had an unexpected result. It ended all of Britain's treaty rights to search shipping on the high seas. These were now resented by rising powers such as Iran and Pakistan, and had barely been used by the scaled down British navy after World War II. A step forward was the condemnation in the convention of peonage, debt bondage, forced marriage, and adoption for exploitation. This was followed by the negotiation by the ILO of the Abolition of Forced Labor Convention of 1957. This outlawed forced labor for economic advantage, political repression and labor discipline—a clear attack on the gulags. These were being dismantled in the Soviet Union after the death of Stalin, but were being introduced in China and other communist powers to suppress dissent and to produce goods for export.

The long struggle for the supplementary convention focused attention on Arabia, which became the center of the antislavery struggle for the next few years. There was still no means of forcing states to sign or carry out the two antislavery treaties. However, the British began to pressure the sheikhs in Qatar and the Trucial Coast to end slavery. As oil revenues mounted, Qatar did so in 1952, paying compensation to slave owners. Britain also formed a special force ostensibly to suppress the trade on land in the Trucial States and Oman, and to drive out the Saudis from the Buraimi Oasis, where they were accused of slave dealing. The next few years were a period of turmoil in the Middle East, as Gamal abd el-Nassr nationalized the Suez Canal and launched a campaign of revolutionary socialism aimed at ousting colonialism from the Arab world together with all the "feudal rulers." The development of the oil industry enabled fugitive slaves to find jobs and opened up new avenues of investment for their owners. Much publicity was given in the western press to the enslavement of pilgrims to Saudi Arabia coming from as far away as West Africa. In 1962, pressure on the Saudi rulers mounted as Egypt sent a force to support a military coup in Yemen, where the new government declared an end to slavery. Soon after, Saudi Arabia declared slavery abolished and offered compensation to owners. This led to the announcement by the Trucial sheikhs, under British pressure, that slavery had long been illegal in their territories. In the Aden Protectorate, the British, faced with rebellion, left in 1967 without having officially ended slavery, but their left-wing successors soon outlawed it. Finally in 1970, a British supported coup in Oman led to its abolition by the new sultan. Chattel slavery was now illegal everywhere.

This, however, does not mean that it had ended everywhere. Evidence of its persistence in Mauritania surfaced in the 1980s and new laws against it were issued by Niger in 2005. Moreover, many ties between former slaves and their former owners or their descendants were still active at the end of the century, even among members of both groups who had immigrated to France.

If slavery was now illegal everywhere, the demand for cheap and subservient labor was growing rapidly with globalization, and the last years of the twentieth century saw an enormous increase in the "new" forms of slavery now called "slavery-like practices." The abolitionists, led by the Anti-Slavery Society, focused full attention on them and encouraged the formation of local non-governmental organizations (NGOs) to attack them. After a long struggle led by the society and a series of UN-commissioned reports, the United Nations finally formed a working group on slavery, later called the Working Group on Contemporary Forms of Slavery. It consisted of five members of the Sub-Commission on the Prevention of Discrimination and the Protection of Minorities. Its first meeting was in 1975, and with one exception it met annually until the end of the century. It consisted of one member from each of the five areas into which the United Nations divided the world—the western democracies, the eastern (originally communist) bloc, Africa, Latin America, and Asia.

This committee had no powers of investigation and no way of enforcing its resolutions. In its early years it was divided by the Cold War and by the issue of apartheid in South Africa. Only after these issues were settled was it able to conduct its meetings with less desire to score political points against adversaries and more willingness to listen to the cases brought to its notice by NGOs, international non-governmental organizations (INGOs), UN organizations such as UNESCO, UNICEF, UNDP and others, including Interpol. The work of this virtually powerless committee, together with that of the much more effective International Labor Organization (ILO), publicized the many and varied forms of servitude which existed at the end of the twentieth century. Many of them were as old, or older than, slavery. Some, such as forced prostitution, had been considered by various committees of the League. By the end of the twentieth century, however, they were all brought to the Working Group, which changed its name to bring it into line with its work. It thus became the Working Group on Contemporary Forms of Slavery. A separate group was formed to deal with the exploitation of indigenous peoples.

By 1975 chattel slavery and the slave trade were only practiced in a few remote areas. Many more people were affected by contemporary forms of slavery. As the colonial empires disintegrated, some states became richer as they developed their resources, while others sank into greater poverty. As globalization intensified, so labor began to be organized in different ways and flowed under different guises in ever increasing numbers from poor areas to richer or "developing" areas, often, but not always, in foreign countries. These changes had begun earlier, but were intensified in the last quarter of the century by attempts at globalization, by the growth of the arms and drugs trades and the ever-rising organized crime, assisted by the Internet and the ease of laundering money.

One of the most widespread abuses considered a contemporary form of slavery was debt bondage. This possibly predates slavery itself. It was widespread among the rural population of the Indian sub-continent, but also took root in factories and other industries, and by the end of the century was a worldwide problem. People borrowed money for a variety of reasons—for the use of land, to buy tools, to pay for medical treatment, to pay their fares to get to a promised but non-existent job—only to find themselves bound by debts they could never repay. In some cases, notably South Asia and Latin America, the debt was hereditary. In others it was continually being extended. Thus, Chinese triads smuggled illegal aliens into Britain, and then demanded more money from the workers under threat of harming not just the workers, but also their families in China. By the year 2000, victims might find themselves working anywhere in the world in restaurants, gold mines, garment factories, farms, brick factories, and so on. Some were imported as servants by diplomats and kept locked up, isolated in homes, unable to speak the local language, and with their passports taken from them. Many were the easy victims of brutal treatment.

Forced prostitution was another form of contemporary slavery, flourishing at the end of the twentieth century. Unknown numbers of girls and some boys were tricked or lured into being trafficked to various countries, or forced to work on the streets or in brothels in their own countries. By the late 1990s, an estimated forty to fifty thousand women and children were believed to be trafficked annually to the United States alone, many of them victims of poverty from Eastern Europe and the former Soviet Union. The traffic was worldwide, and the propagators of this form of slavery did not hesitate to use force. Victims who resisted faced mutilation or death. All faced the threat of contracting HIV-AIDS or other infections in which case they might be simply thrown out on the streets.

Children in particular were victims of contemporary forms of slavery. Child labor was the subject of special UN reports in the 1980s and 1990s.

Children are cheap and defenseless, hence easily exploited. The problem was world wide but worse in poorer countries. In Thailand in the 1980s, poverty stricken parents in the north sold their children to work in sweatshops in Bangkok in appalling conditions. In India parents in debt-bondage sent their children to toil long hours in carpet factories where they were often tied to looms, sometimes to the point of being crippled. Others were deliberately mutilated in order to send them out to beg in the streets. In Pakistan whole families worked in brick factories. In El Salvador children were forced by poverty-stricken parents to wade in swamps for fourteen hours a day searching for mollusks, smoking cigars to keep off the mosquitoes, and taking amphetamines to keep awake. In West Africa boys in search of jobs ended up as prisoners working as slave labor on cocoa plantations.

Most dangerous was the use of children in armed combat. Boys between twelve and seventeen were forcibly recruited as soldiers, usually in rebel armies. Others joined as a survival strategy. In some cases, such as Sierra Leone, they were forced to mutilate civilians. Renamo in Mozambique made them kill their parents and then recruited them to fight. The Lords Army in Sudan kidnapped school children, forcing the boys to serve as soldiers and the girls as sex slaves.

Most pitiable were the children of both sexes, but mainly girls, forced into sexual slavery. In India thousands were trafficked around the country to meet the growing demand for young virgins. Many were Indian or Nepalese, but some came from China, Russia, or Latin America. Sex tourism involving children was a growing industry in the last decades of the twentieth century. Tour agencies advertised sex tours as package deals involving a range of deviant practices. Men fearful of contracting AIDS were demanding younger and younger children. In 1989, Interpol reported to the Working Group that there was a growing demand for child pornography, encouraged by the development of the Internet.

In 1988, the Working Group was told by a Thai NGO that some 10,000 babies a year were kidnapped or bought for adoption in Malaysia. Similarly, children were kidnapped or bought in South America and Romania for adoption in Europe or North America. In China baby girls could be bought from orphanages for some $20,000 or more.

In the early 1990s, the Anti-Slavery Society, now called Anti-Slavery International, turned its attention to "servile marriage"—marriage in which women did not have the same rights to property, or to their children, or to divorce as men, and in which men might have more then one wife. In many countries children were betrothed without the right of refusal. In some countries widows were inherited by their husband's kinsmen. Although in the latter case the intention was to provide the widow with a male protector, it could also condemn her to an unhappy marriage. Some children were also dedicated to a deity, often to expiate the sin of some relative. They became, in effect, the wives or servants of the priest—a hereditary situation from which they could not escape.

Forced labor was another form of contemporary slavery reported to the Working Group. Sometimes it was, as in the past, practiced by governments like the government of Myanmar, which forced dissident peoples to work in harsh and often dangerous conditions. China sentenced dissidents to gulags, where many were used to produce goods for export or as cheap labor for agriculture or domestic construction. Some forms of forced labor were to be found in the private sector. In 1999, for instance, some 40,000 young Asian women were found on the American island of Saipan, imprisoned in compounds, threatened with violence, and forced to work twelve hours a day, seven days a week, producing goods for well-known U.S. firms. Migrant laborers are particularly vulnerable to forced labor and some have been found working as virtual prisoners on farms and garment factories in the United States, and in sweat shops in Europe.

It remains here to discuss what steps had been taken by the end of the century to stop these abuses which were well-known as they were reported to the Working Group on Contemporary Forms of Slavery, and to the ILO, and were exposed by the media. In theory much had been gained. Reports had been commissioned and conventions negotiated on a whole range of questions, including slavery, forced labor, and debt bondage. There followed conventions for the suppression of the traffic in persons and the exploitation of prostitution, and the convention on consent to marriage, the minimum age for marriage and the registration of marriages. There was also a declaration on the elimination of discrimination against women. To protect children, a convention was passed on the rights of the child, followed by an ILO convention against the worst forms of child labor. There was also a

Henry, a teenage Revolutionary United Force rebel solider, brandishes his weapon in the town of Koindu, Sierra Leone, 2001. Chris Hondros/Getty Images.

declaration to protect women and children in emergencies and armed conflict. Added to these were treaties against trafficking and a convention to protect migrant workers and their families. Thus, by the end of the century a whole range of conventions and agreements were in existence to protect the most vulnerable from abuse.

The remnants of chattel slavery were under attack in Mauritania and Niger. Public opinion was being mobilized, not just in the developed world, but also in the areas from which most victims came or where they lived. The Working Group which had gathered so much information was still not able to do more than advise on action, but the problems were now becoming known all over the world and attempts were being made to alert potential victims to the dangers they might face. Moreover, NGOs proliferated and did their best to make abuses known, and often took action themselves to combat them, sometimes at risk of members' own lives.

However, the basic problem which generated so many vulnerable workers remained untouched—the huge gap between rich and poor countries which drew thousands of potential victims into the hands of international criminal networks. Moreover, the numerous treaties, conventions, and declarations could only be enforced by governments, and many of them were too poor or too corrupt to take the steps needed to end particular abuses. Added to these difficulties was the proliferation of small wars, which dislocated economies and flung thousands of economic refugees on the market. Similarly, the disintegration of the Soviet Union sent unknown numbers of poverty-stricken people into one form or another of contemporary slavery. At the heart of the problem was the weakness of the United Nations and the lack of a concerted and determined attempt to carry out its many conventions. *See also* Arabia and Nineteenth- and Twentieth-Century Slavery; Ethiopia, Haile Selassie and Abolition in; Muscat and Oman, Abolition of Slavery in.

Further Readings: Bales, Kevin. *Disposable People: New Slavery in the Global Economy.* Berkeley: University of California Press, 1999; Miers, Suzanne. *Slavery in the Twentieth Century: The Evolution of a Global Problem.* Walnut Creek, CA: Altamira Press, 2003; *Reports of the Working Group on Contemporary Forms of Slavery.*

Suzanne Miers

Slavery Convention of 1926

The Slavery Convention of 1926 was the first international treaty against both slavery as well as the slave trade. It defined slavery as "the status or condition of a person over whom all or any of the powers attaching to the rights of ownership are exercised." It bound signatories "to prevent and suppress the slave trade" and to "bring about progressively and as soon as possible the complete abolition of slavery in all its forms." Moreover, signatories undertook to take "all necessary measures to prevent compulsory or forced labor from developing into conditions analogous to slavery."

This treaty was recommended to the League of Nations by the Temporary Slavery Commission of 1924–25. This commission had recommended a treaty for the immediate abolition of the legal status of slavery "in all its forms." It had defined the forms to include chattel slavery and serfdom, debt bondage and peonage, forced marriage of women, girls and widows, and the exploitation of children. It thus began the process of changing the meaning of slavery at the international level. It had suggested that slave traders at sea should be treated as pirates, that signatories should grant each other rights to pursue slavers over land frontiers and in territorial waters, and that severe penalties should be imposed for slave raiding and trading. Most controversial of all, it urged that forced labor, which was widely used by the colonial powers, should be abolished except for essential public works.

Neither the British nor the other colonial governments had any desire for such a treaty, but the Anti-Slavery and Aborigines Protection Society advocated it, and the British government had recently assured Parliament that it was still committed to leading the antislavery campaign, which commanded wide public support. Therefore, the British drew up an emasculated version of the commission's proposals and presented them to the Sixth Commission of the League Assembly in September 1925. It caused consternation among the colonial powers, each of which set out to protect its own practices and interests.

The French refused to allow slave trading at sea to be treated as piracy or to allow the British or any other nation the right to search ships flying their flag. This impasse was solved by a clause stating that powers in whose areas the slave trade was active would take all possible measures to end slaving under their flags and would negotiate agreements giving each other special rights to search their ships. Moreover, the French hinted that searches could be made ostensibly for arms, and if slaves were found on board, the vessel could be arrested and taken to the nearest port of the nation whose flag it was flying. All Britain's existing maritime treaties remained in force.

The convention was weakened because signatories were only bound to end slavery progressively, and the powers in whose territories and on whose waters the traffic flourished never negotiated the special agreements necessary to help each other track down slavers.

Forced labor was used by all the colonial powers in varying degrees for projects, such as providing labor for concessionaire companies, for building public works, for the growing of export crops, to provide labor for private companies and individuals, for porterage, and for the army. It might last from a few days to a lifetime, and at its worst included men, women, and children. After long discussions, the treaty stipulated that forced labor could only be used for "public purposes" in exceptional circumstances, and that it must be paid, and employed near home. However, neither the exceptional circumstances, the public purposes, nor the terms of service were defined.

The convention was signed on September 26, 1926, by thirty-six members of the League and acceded to by the United States, which was not a member. Other powers also gradually signed or ratified it. Exceptions included the Soviet Union, which also did not belong to the League, and more important at the time, Saudi Arabia and Yemen, in both of which slavery was still legal. The convention had serious weaknesses. It fixed no date for the end of slavery, and its definition of slavery based on degrees of ownership did not stand the test of time. The maritime powers in the slaving zones never signed the agreements stipulated. There was no monitoring system and no way to enforce the provisions of the convention, many of which were ignored for years. Moreover, signatories were allowed to exempt some of their territories from it provisions.

Nevertheless, as the first international treaty against slavery it was an important landmark in the abolition movement. The signatories had at least agreed to end slavery as a legal status—albeit in their own time. By calling attention to the fact that forced labor could be a form of slavery, the treaty played a part in opening the way to the negotiation of the International Labor Organization's Convention against forced labor. Finally, the definition of slavery as forms of ownership, together with the recommendations of the Temporary Slavery Commission, began the international attack on other forms of exploitation, such as peonage, debt bondage, servile marriage, and the exploitation of children—all subjects of later treaties.

The 1926 Convention is still in force. It was taken over by the United Nations in 1953 and extended, but not replaced, by the United Nations Slavery Convention of 1956. It now stands at the center of a network of later treaties for which it laid the groundwork. *See also* League of Nations and Antislavery and Abolition; Supplementary Convention on the Abolition of Slavery, the Slave Trade and Institutions and Practices Similar to Slavery; United Nations and Antislavery.

Further Readings: Brownlie, Ian, ed. *Basic Documents on Human Rights*. 3rd ed. Oxford: Clarendon Press, 1998; Miers, Suzanne. *Slavery in the Twentieth Century: The Evolution of a Global Problem*. Walnut Creek, CA: Altamira Press, 2003.

Suzanne Miers

Smith, Adam (1723–1790)

Adam Smith was a Scottish political economist concerned with global economics. *The Wealth of Nations* (1776) is Smith's great book and remains an important contribution to the foundations of the study of political economy. Smith favored capitalism and political liberalism, believing that the role of government was to legislate and that government ought not to interfere in the machinery of capitalism. Smith opposed strict government regulation of human behavior and the economy, especially trade. He sought to expand the sphere in which rational individuals pursuing their own best interests might act as freely as possible in the economy. Such a dynamic, he argued, would lead to that society's increased productivity and wealth.

Slavery was not a principal concern for Smith. In the *Wealth of Nations*, he devoted relatively little space to the topic. Rather, he was more concerned with the economic impact of wage labor. For Smith, slavery was not as economically sensible as wage labor. Wages for labor were driven by the market and wage laborers were interchangeable—one could be substituted for another and at the same wage. Slavery, however, was more substantially an investment. No wage attached to the labor of the slave, and the return on the investment in the slave was wholly dependent on the slave's longevity and regularity of labor. For Smith, wage labor made more sense than slavery: "The wear and tear of a slave, it has been said, is at the expense of his master; but that of a free servant is at his own expense" (Smith 1989: 85). The actual costs of "replacing or repairing" (Smith 1989: 85) a slave are not present when one pays a laborer a fixed wage.

As with Rousseau and other social contract theorists of the **Enlightenment**, Smith imagined a sort of pre-economic social organization that had been drastically altered with the arrival of private property and formal political organization.

> In the original state of things, which precedes both the appropriation of land and the accumulation of stock, the whole produce of the labour belongs to the labourer. He has neither landlord nor master to share with.... . But this original state of things, in which the labourer enjoyed the whole produce of his own labour, could not last beyond the first introduction of the appropriation of land and the accumulation of stock. (Smith 1989: 68, 69).

Thus, for Smith, slavery was one form, but not the only form, of the alienation of laborers from the product of their labor. *See also* Literature and Abolition.

Further Reading: Smith, Adam. *The Wealth of Nations*. Amherst, NY: Prometheus Books, 1989 [1776].

Noah Butler

Smith, Gerrit (1797–1874)

Among the most renowned abolitionists and nineteenth-century philanthropists, Gerrit Smith devoted his life and most of his great wealth to the cause of equal rights for all men and women. Over a twenty-year period, from 1838 until the Civil War, the immediate abolition of every sin was his most passionate desire, and he went to great lengths to effect it. Smith, along with his close friend, John Brown, was virtually unique among white reformers in his efforts to overcome enormous class and racial barriers and to establish close affinities with other blacks. But following John Brown's raid on Harpers Ferry in 1859, Smith suffered a crisis of faith that resulted in his support for more conservative reform measures during the Civil War and Reconstruction; he supported Lincoln and the Republican Party, emphasized the suppression of the Rebellion over emancipation, and after the war advocated clemency to former rebels.

Smith was born in Utica, New York on March 6, 1797, into one of the wealthiest families in the country. In 1806, his parents, Peter and

Gerrit Smith. Courtesy of the Library of Congress.

Elizabeth Livingston Smith, moved the family to Peterboro, a village they founded in Madison County, part of the "**Burned-Over District**" of western New York, where Gerrit lived for the rest of his life. As a young patriarch, Smith had visions of becoming a man of letters, an eminent lawyer, a respected minister, or a statesman. But immediately after graduating as vale-dictorian from Hamilton College in 1818, a series of incidents occurred which precipitated his turn to reform work including the death of his mother, the death of his new bride, and the retirement of his father, who requested that Gerrit manage his vast property concerns. In little more than a year after reaching "manhood," he found himself back in the family mansion house overlooking the village green of Peterboro, bound to his ledger books and land office, with his dreams shattered and the two most important people in his life dead.

In 1823, he married Ann Carroll Fitzhugh Smith, a cousin of **George Fitzhugh** and a fervent evangelical. She was instrumental in fueling her husband's religious zeal and spawning his vision of a broad sacralization of the world. He soon became an avid temperance reformer, and in 1827 he joined the **American Colonization Society**, whose efforts to colonize blacks in Africa represented for him the most effective way to bring about gradual emancipation and an end to the degradation of free blacks. His complete break with colonization and whole-hearted embrace of immediate abolition occurred in 1837, and it corresponded to a fundamental shift in the source of his values; he became a self-described "outsider" and "fanatic," rejected existing social conventions and authority, and turned inward by affirming his spiritual instincts and passions of the "heart." His belief in the preservation of the social order and distinct hierarchies—values on which the principles of colonization were based—had crumbled. This profound shift was due in part to the Panic of 1837, which brought him to the brink of bankruptcy; to the deaths of two children, one in 1835 and the other in 1836; and to his newfound reliance on "sacred self-sovereignty."

One of the most important applications of Smith's religious vision was his reinterpretation of the Golden Rule as empathy. He continually sought to participate in the feelings and sufferings of his black brethren and to see himself as a black man. "To recognize in every man my brother—ay, another self" was his wish, and he often described his efforts "to make myself a colored man." His empathic awareness and black identification had tangible results: He was instrumental in turning Madison County into the most fervent abolition county in the country; his own village of Peterboro, which the black leader **Henry Highland Garnet** likened to "Heaven," became an antebellum model of interracial harmony; and in 1846, he gave to each of some 3,000 poor blacks from New York roughly 50 acres of land in the Adirondacks (where John Brown eventually settled) as a way for them to attain the franchise, become self-sufficient, and remain isolated from the virulent racism in the cities. Black leaders throughout the North, from Garnet and **Frederick Douglass** to **James McCune Smith** and Samuel Ringgold Ward, became respected friends and allies; and the black abolitionist paper, *The Ram's Horn*, went so far as to say, "Gerrit Smith is a colored man!"

Smith's radical reform efforts from 1840 to the Civil War closely para-lleled those of black leaders in New York, who overwhelmingly embraced political abolitionism and lost patience with peaceful means of abolishing slavery, especially following the **Fugitive Slave Law** of 1850. Smith helped found the **Liberty Party** in 1840, which interpreted the Constitution as an antislavery document, and in 1852 he was elected to the House of Repre-sentatives on an abolition ticket that advocated immediate abolition, univer-sal suffrage for men and women, and land grants to the landless. He never completed his term in Congress, however. Immediately following the pas-sage of the Kansas Nebraska Act in 1854, Smith resigned out of disgust with Congress and the white laws perpetuating slavery, and became a revolution-ary. The tension between his boundless reform visions and the present, sin-ful reality had reached a breaking point; he began to see himself as a prophet and accepted blood atonement as a necessary means for vanquish-ing the forces of evil. He donated over $16,000 in "emigrant aid" that sent fighting men and munitions to "save" Kansas from slavery; and he became a lead conspirator in John Brown's efforts to liberate slaves that culminated with the attack on the federal arsenal at Harpers Ferry in October 1859.

The Harpers Ferry raid profoundly affected Smith's world views and reform visions. He was the only conspirator who, in the aftermath of the raid, considered it wrong and experienced profound guilt over his participa-tion in it. He believed himself culpable for all the lives lost in the incursion, and suffered a complete, but brief, emotional collapse. Following his recov-ery in early 1860, he distanced himself from blacks, and viewed his black identification and close friendship with blacks, as well as his acceptance of prophecy belief and blood atonement, as the dark sources of violence. In May 1860, he acknowledged that "much of the year 1859," his most active period of pursuing violent remedies for ending slavery, was "a black dream," and he described the link between his black identification and his descent to violence in a short story called "The Ruinous Visit to Monkeyville." He never again identified so closely with blacks, became considerably more moderate in his reform efforts, and for the rest of his life denied his com-plicity in the Harpers Ferry raid. Before the Civil War officially began, Smith became a casualty in his own civil war, and he lost faith in the power of empathy and sacred self-sovereignty.

Shortly after the election of 1860, Smith began to support **Abraham Lin-coln** and the Republican administration. Although he was himself nomi-nated for president on a Radical Abolition ticket, he did not take his candidacy seriously, and felt that Lincoln was "in his heart an abolitionist." As the Southern states seceded, he advocated the compromise measures of a lower tariff and compensated emancipation to lure the South back into the Union without bloodshed. But following the firing on Fort Sumter, he fervently embraced the war efforts of the administration to "put down the Rebellion," and believed that its suppression would be the means for ending slavery. The war had dissolved all party distinctions, he argued, and he viewed all Northerners as either Unionists or disloyal Rebels who must be crushed: "We are assembled... not as Republicans, nor Democrats, nor Abo-litionists—but as Americans," he said in the first of many speeches to raise money and troops for the war effort; "we are all on the side of the Government," which "must be upheld at whatever expense to friend or foe." The Rebellion was "simply slavery in arms."

Smith's primary role in the war was to lend his support to the Lincoln administration by urging unified support to the Union cause. He published numerous speeches to this effect, and campaigned for Lincoln in 1864. He spent over $10,000 of his own money and raised thousands more for troops, equipment, and the relief of afflicted families, and he urged a stiff income tax on the wealthy to help fund the war. For the first time since becoming a radical abolitionist in 1838, he was no longer considered an "outsider" and "fanatic," but a respected, though eccentric, elder statesman.

Smith's attitude toward the use of black troops highlights the enormous shift that occurred in his attitude toward blacks following the Harpers Ferry raid. He urged black participation as early as August 1861, but primarily as a tactical measure: "The party that gets the blacks to fight for it gets the victory." Although he believed that arming blacks would facilitate the cause of equal rights, in 1863 he also compared blacks (and Indians) to devils and suggested that putting "down a base, brutal, abominable, causeless, accursed Rebellion" required the use of dark-skinned, base, and brutal savages: "Common-sense teaches us that we should get the negro to help us if we can; and the Indian also if we can; and the devil himself if we can. I would that we could succeed in getting our harness upon his back and in making him work for us. It would by the way, be doing a great favor to the old rascal to make him serve a good cause once in his life." While he never abandoned his quest for equal rights, he now considered blacks to be potentially dangerous and by nature less civilized than whites. His first utterance that betrayed a belief in the prevailing pseudo-scientific arguments for innate black inferiority occurred in late 1861, when he admitted, "were the laws of nature allowed free play, the dark-skinned races would find their homes within and the light-skinned races without the tropics." Simultaneously he renewed his faith in colonization—after having denounced it for twenty years as inherently racist—as the most effective way to solve the race problem, so long as the decision to colonize rested with blacks themselves.

As Smith moved into the mainstream role of elder statesman and "insider," his racial views became increasingly conservative, and his position during Reconstruction was one of moderation. Initially he refused to support the **Thirteenth Amendment** because of his long-held belief that the Constitution was already an antislavery document and because he felt it would detract from the war effort, but he eventually endorsed it. Similarly, he initially advocated literacy as a condition of voting for both blacks and whites before accepting universal black suffrage. Throughout Reconstruction he sought amnesty for rebels, and in 1867, he alienated himself from most Northern radicals by signing Jefferson Davis's bail bond—along with mainstream leaders Horace Greeley and Cornelius Vanderbilt.

Smith's declension from his perfectionist vision and close identification with blacks in the 1840s and 1850s did not go unnoticed by black leaders. His correspondence with them, which surpassed that of all other white reformers combined before the war, waned considerably following Harpers Ferry. Some former friends and allies harshly rebuked him; the black physician and intellectual, James McCune Smith, began criticizing Gerrit as early as August 1861: "I charge you... with being unequal to the exigency of the hour. After lives spent in signal devotion to the cause of the slave you fairly abandon that cause in the hour of its trial and triumph." But black leaders never forgot the great lengths Smith went to for the cause of equal rights in the twenty years before the war. In 1873, a year before Gerrit's death, Henry Highland Garnet summed up the feelings of many black reformers by saying: "Among the hosts of great defenders of man's fights who in years past fought so gallantly for equal rights for all men," Smith was "the most affectionately remembered and loved." *See also* Bleeding Kansas; Radical Republicans.

Further Reading: Stauffer, John, *The Black Hearts of Men: Radical Abolitionists and the Transformation of Race*. Cambridge, MA: Harvard University Press, 2002.

John Stauffer

Smith, James McCune (1813–1865)

James McCune Smith, black abolitionist and physician, was born in New York City, the son of slaves. All that is known of his parents is that his mother was, in his words, "a self-emancipated bond-woman." His own liberty came on July 4, 1827, when the Emancipation Act of the state of New York officially freed its remaining slaves. Smith was fourteen at the time, a student at the African Free School no. 2, and he greeted the day as a "real full-souled, full-voiced shouting for joy" that brought him from "the gloom of midnight" into "the joyful light of day." He graduated with honors from the African Free School, but was denied admission from Columbia College and Geneva, New York medical schools on account of his race. With assistance from the black minister Peter Williams, Jr., he entered the University of Glasgow, Scotland in 1832, at the age of nineteen, and earned the degrees of B.A. (1835), M.A. (1836), and M.D. (1837). He returned to America in 1837 as the first professionally trained black physician in the country.

Smith resettled in New York City, married Malvina Barnett, who bore him five children, and established himself as a successful physician. He set up practice in Manhattan as a surgeon and general practitioner for both blacks and whites, became the staff physician for the New York Colored Orphan Asylum, and opened a pharmacy on West Broadway, one of the first in the country owned by a black.

It was his activities as a radical abolitionist and reformer, however, that secured his reputation as one of the leading black intellectuals of the antebellum era. As soon as he returned to America, he became an active member of the **American Anti-Slavery Society**, which sought immediate abolition by morally persuading slaveholders to renounce the sin of slavery and emancipate their slaves. By the late 1840s, he had abandoned the policies of non-resistance and non-voting set forth by **William Lloyd Garrison** and his followers in the Society, for political abolitionism, which interpreted the Constitution as an antislavery document and advocated political, and ultimately violent, intervention to end slavery. In 1846, Smith championed the campaign for unrestricted black suffrage in New York state; that same year he became an associate and good friend of **Gerrit Smith**, a wealthy white abolitionist and philanthropist, and served as one of three black administrators for his friend's donation of roughly fifty acres to each of some three thousand New York blacks on a vast tract of land in the Adirondacks. He became affiliated with the **Liberty Party** in the late 1840s, which was devoted to immediate and unconditional emancipation, unrestricted suffrage for all men and women, and land reform. In 1855, he helped found the New York City Abolition Society, which was organized, as he put it, "to Abolish Slavery by means of the Constitution; *or otherwise*," by which he meant violent intervention in the event that peaceful efforts failed (though there is no indication that he resorted to violence). When the Radical Abolition Party, the successor to the Liberty Party, nominated him for New York Secretary of State in 1857, he became the first black in the country to run for a political office.

In his writings Smith was a central force in helping to shape and give direction to the black abolition movement. He contributed frequently to the *Weekly Anglo-African* and the *Anglo African Magazine*, and wrote a semi-regular column for *Frederick Douglass' Paper* under the pseudonym "Communipaw," an Indian name that referred to a charmed and honored black settlement in Jersey City, New Jersey. He also wrote the introduction to **Douglass**'s 1855 autobiography, *My Bondage My Freedom*, and he often expressed his wish that Douglass relocate his paper from Rochester to New York City. Douglass considered Smith the "foremost" black leader to have influenced his reform vision.

Smith's writings focused primarily on black education and self-help, citizenship, and the fight against racism; and these themes represented for him the most effective means through which to end slavery and effect full legal and civil rights. He was a life-long opponent of attempts among whites to colonize blacks in Liberia and elsewhere, and a harsh critic of black nationalists who, beginning in the 1850s, encouraged emigration to Haiti and West Africa rather than continuing to fight for citizenship and equal rights. Although he defended integration, he also encouraged blacks to establish their own presses, initiatives, and organizations. "It is emphatically our battle," he wrote in 1855. "Others may aid and assist if they will, but the moving power rests with us." His embrace of black self-reliance in the late 1840s paralleled his departure from Garrisonian doctrines and the American Anti-Slavery Society, which largely ignored black oppression in the North— even among abolitionists—by focusing on the evils of slavery in the South. Black education in particular, he concluded, led directly to self-reliance and moral uplift, and these values in turn provided the most powerful critique against racism. He called the schoolhouse the "great caste abolisher," and vowed to "fling whatever I have into the cause of colored children, that they may be better and more thoroughly taught than their parents are."

The racist belief in innate black inferiority was for Smith the single greatest and most insidious obstacle to equality. In 1846, he became despondent over the racial "hate deeper than I had imagined" among the vast majority of whites; fourteen years later he continued to lament that "our white countrymen do not know us"; "they are strangers to our characters, ignorant of our capacity, oblivious to our history." He hoped his own distinguished career and writings would serve as both a role model for uneducated blacks and as a powerful rebuttal against racist attacks. And as a black physician he was uniquely suited to combat the pseudo-scientific theories of innate black inferiority. In two important and brilliantly argued essays—"Civilization" (1844) and "On the Fourteenth Query of Thomas Jefferson's Notes on Virginia" (1859)—he incorporated his extensive knowledge of biology and anatomy to directly refute scientific arguments of innate black inferiority.

The driving force behind Smith's reform vision and sustained hope for equality was his supreme "confidence in God, that firm reliance in the saving power of the Redeemer's Love." Much like other radical abolitionists such as Douglass and Gerrit Smith, he viewed the abolition movement and the Civil War in millennialist terms; slavery and black oppression were the most egregious of a plethora of sins ranging from tobacco and alcohol to apathy and laziness that needed to be abolished in order to pave the way for a sacred society governed by "Bible Politics," as he envisioned God's eventual reign on earth. He strove to follow his Savior's example by embracing the doctrine of "equal love to all mankind" and at the same time remaining humble before Him; he likened himself to "a coral insect... loving to work beneath the tide in a superstructure, that some day when the labourer is long dead and forgotten, may rear itself above the waves and afford rest and habitation for the creatures of his Good, Good Father of All." Following his death in 1865 from heart failure, his writings and memories remained a powerful source of inspiration, "rest and habitation" to future generations of reformers.

Further Readings: Blight, David W. "In Search of Learning, Liberty, and Self Definition: James McCune Smith and the Ordeal of the Antebellum Black Intellectual," *Afro-Americans in New York Life and History* 9, 2 (July 1985): 7–25; Dain, Bruce. *A Hideous Monster of the Mind: American Race Theory in the Early Republic*, 2002; Rael, Patrick. *Black Identity and Black Protest in the Antebellum North*, 2002; Stauffer, John. *The Black Hearts of Men: Radical Abolitionists and the Transformation of Race*. Cambridge, MA: Harvard University Press, 2002.

John Stauffer

Society for the Propagation of the Gospel (SPG)

The Society for the Propagation of the Gospel (SPG) was an Anglican missionary organization established in 1701 by Thomas Bray, commissary for the Bishop of London. It was designed to spread the "word" of the Church of England and to promote Christianity in the North American colonies. The Society provided clergymen for Anglican parishes in the colonies and the Caribbean. By the time of the American Revolution, they had sent over 600 ministers to the colonies and solicited support for local and parish libraries. In 1760, the Quaker **Anthony Benezet** wrote asking **Quakers** to aid the

SPG so that, "books might be provided, as they were scarce in those Parts [the South] except sent by ye society."

One man who deeply inspired their work was **Morgan Godwyn**, who had been an early supporter of the conversion and baptism of blacks without freeing them. Serving as a minister in Virginia in the late 1660s, he also traveled to Barbados to begin laying ground for the Society's later work there. He wrote in a pamphlet in 1680, quoting from Acts 17:26, "That God had made (of one Blood) all nations of Men, for to dwell on the face of the earth."

In 1711, Bishop William Fleetwood gave a sermon at the annual SPG meeting in London, calling for the baptism of slaves but maintaining that "we are a people who live and maintain ourselves by *Trade;* and that if *Trade* be lost, or overmuch discouraged, we are a ruined nation." Later in 1727, the Bishop of London told American slaveowners that if they converted their slaves, the enslaved Africans would be under "stronger Obligations to perform those Duties with the greatest Diligence and Fidelity, not only from the Fear of Men, but a Sense of Duty to God." The conversion of slaves need not also require their manumission argued the SPG. The SPG actually owned several large plantations in Barbados, and hundreds of slaves.

The SPG sent its first missionary, Samuel Thomas, to South Carolina in 1703. By 1706, he had begun to convert some Africans and Native Americans, all of whom he believed were just like so many whites—"sheep without a shepherd." The Society also opened schools for blacks, most notably in South Carolina and New Jersey, a program later taken up more substantially by Anthony Benezet. The SPG, while advocating the baptism of blacks and priding itself in teaching slaves, young and old, to read and write and to learn the scriptures, simultaneously supported newly established laws guaranteeing that baptism did nothing to alter the state of their slavery.

On April 26, 1767, Anthony Benezet sent the SPG a letter with a copy of his *A Caution and a Warning to Great Britain* in which he requested that the SPG "seriously consider" opposing the Atlantic slave trade. In early 1768, the SPG replied to Benezet by praising his work among the enslaved and admonishing him not to jeopardize it by alienating masters from the SPG with his opposition to the slave trade and, more fundamentally, to slavery itself. His correspondent urged him "not to go further in publishing your Notions, but rather to retract them."

As the American Revolution approached in the colonies, The SPG's labors continued, but its authority and mandate were weakening. All the American colonies would come to prohibit the slave trade by 1775 and the Anglican SPG was increasingly suspect. After the American Revolution, the SPG ended its activities in the United States. *See also* Associates of Dr. Thomas Bray; Atlantic Slave Trade and British Abolition; Bible and Slavery.

Further Readings: Bennett, J. Harry. *Bondsmen and Bishops: Slavery and Apprenticeship on the Codrington Plantations of Barbados, 1710–1838.* London, 1958; Van Horne, John C., ed. *Religious Philanthropy and Colonial Slavery: The American Correspondence of the Associates of Dr. Bray, 1717–1777.* Urbana: University of Illinois Press, 1985.

Maurice Jackson

Somerset Decision (1772)

The Somerset case, decided in 1772 by Lord Mansfield (William Murray), helped launch the movements to abolish slavery in England and the United States, and became a significant part of the common law of slavery in the English-speaking world.

James Somerset was born in Africa, sold into the slave trade, and then taken to Virginia where Charles Stewart purchased him. Stewart took Somerset to England in 1769. In October 1771, Somerset escaped, and when Stewart recaptured him, he immediately imprisoned Somerset on a boat headed to Jamaica where he planned to sell him. Three abolitionists, Thomas Watkins, Elizabeth Cade, and John Marlow, came to Somerset's aid and submitted affidavits to the court for a writ of *habeas corpus*. Mansfield agreed to hear the plea and summoned Thomas Knowles, the owner of the ship, to bring himself and Somerset to court on December 9, 1771.

Knowles testified that Somerset belonged to Charles Stewart, that he had never been "manumitted, enfranchised, set free or discharged," and that Somerset had "departed and absented himself" from service without permission from Stewart. Mansfield believed the case had merit and arranged court dates in February and in April 1772 to hear arguments from both sides.

The two lead lawyers, Francis Hargrave and John Dunning, gave sophisticated arguments before the court. The primary question confronting the court was whether an owner could remove a slave from England. Although Hargrave had never argued before the bar, he presented a subtle and compelling case that slavery was contrary to English common law. Seeming to anticipate almost every counterargument, Hargrave admitted that *villenage*, or conditions pertaining to feudal serfs, and colonial slavery were legal, but forced the court to recognize the way that English common law had steadily progressed *in favorem libertatis* or in favor of liberty. He argued that if England accepted American racial slavery, it would be forcing the law to regress rather than progress. Furthermore, English law required consent in all service relationships, and Hargrave contended that "no man can by compact enslave himself." His arguments were published in the United States and England and were widely used by abolitionists.

John Dunning, a well-respected lawyer who had argued just a year before that no one could be detained as a slave in England, defended Knowles and Stewart's right to imprison and sell Somerset. He tried to argue from fact and law to unsettle the emotional strength of Somerset's case. He contended that the emancipation of Somerset would undermine the respect that the court should hold for the law of Virginia where Somerset was purchased, and where slavery was legal. More effectively, he argued that the emancipation of Somerset could precipitate the emancipation of all enslaved blacks in England, a scenario that would divorce men from their property and place a great burden on England's poorhouses.

Mansfield did not feel compelled to write the decision in this case, but Somerset's unwillingness to settle out of court forced him to do so. Mansfield's greatest contribution finally to English law was not the Somerset decision, but his promotion of commercial law, which helped England's emerging capitalism to flourish. His brief decision reflected the tenuous relationship between capitalism and slavery. He recognized that his decision could disrupt the property rights of thousands of slave owners, but concluded, *"fiat Justitia, ruat coelumtet"* (let justice be done whatever the consequences). Slavery, he argued, was different in each locality and "so odious, that nothing can be suffered to support it, but positive law." The case, as Mansfield made clear, did not end slavery in any of the British colonies, nor, as he showed in subsequent cases, did it end slavery in England; however, it did prevent owners from forcibly detaining slaves and deporting them for sale. This careful decision, historian David Brion Davis notes, preserved the service of the slaves to their masters, but at the same time established an important precedent that labor is voluntary, an important legal foundation for a capitalist society.

Whatever Mansfield's intention, the case had a much wider influence. It was the first step toward the emancipation of blacks in England. In America, some slaves and abolitionists incorrectly used the case to support the end of slavery. Other opponents of slavery more correctly used the case as support to end slavery in only parts of the United States, requiring positive law to maintain slavery and contending that slavery could be upheld in one locality but not another. This understanding of slave law, as requiring positive law, became the common law in the United States and is reflected in the Constitution's support of slavery without mentioning slavery by name. Slavery became a local (state) issue, not a national one and required positive law to be upheld in each locality. Somerset was almost immediately cited in court cases and petitions in Massachusetts. Likewise, throughout the antebellum era, judges and legal commentaries on slavery used the case as the foundation of opposition to slavery in America.

Further Readings: Davis, David Brion. *The Problem of Slavery in the Age of Revolution 1770–1823*. 2nd ed. Oxford: Oxford University Press, 1999; Hargrave, Francis. *An Argument in the Case of James Sommersett a Negro*. 1774; Higginbotham, A. Leon. *In the Matter of Color: Race and the American Legal Process, The Colonial Period*. 1978; Hall, Kermit L. *The Magic Mirror: Law in American History*. 1989; *Somerset v Stewart*, Lofft 1–18; 20 Howell's State Trials 1, 79–82; 98 Eng Rep 499–510 (King's Bench, 22 June 1772).

Emily V. Blanck

Sonthonax, Léger Félicité (1763–1813)

Léger Félicité Sonthonax was a dynamic Jacobin and zealous antislavery advocate, who arrived in Saint Domingue in September 1793. He had been sent to Saint Domingue as the head of a Civil Commission whose goal was to restore peace between the contending factions in the island and to prepare the French colony to repel an English assault. A prosperous son of a French merchant and Revolutionary, he rose in the ranks during the French Revolution and in 1792, was sent to Saint Domingue as part of the Second Civil Commission, a group of three men sent to defend the interests of France there.

Sonthonax conceived of his mission as having two primary objectives: enforce the law of April 4, 1792, which granted full citizenship to the colony's free men of color, and save Saint Domingue for France. He recognized that the slaves had revolted in the north province and held most of the north plain, but he was most concerned about the French royalist planters. He distrusted the white planters, who resisted full citizenship for the free men of color and talked of declaring independence from France and welcoming an English intervention. Sonthonax's aims were to restore plantation production in Saint Domingue and defend it against subversion.

Sonthonax recognized that French authority had disintegrated on Saint Domingue. He allied himself to the free men of color who he believed would be fiercely loyal to France. But by aiding the free coloreds, he antagonized the white planters still further. He exiled many royalist whites, which attached the men of color to him all the more. He did not defeat the black insurgency, but he was able to confine it largely to the northern plain.

By early 1793, Sonthonax had achieved his primary objectives. But in February 1793, France declared war on Britain. The war highlighted two major problems for France and Saint Domingue—French preoccupation with European affairs and French naval weakness in the Caribbean. Owing to the French declaration of war on England, Sonthonax set about building defenses against impending English and Spanish assaults. His most famous act, however, was related to his republican ideals and zealous commitment to antislavery. On August 29, 1793, Sonthonax issued a proclamation extending freedom to the slave insurgents, one of the most radical steps in the French and Haitian Revolutions.

War and emancipation had always been linked in history. By forming an alliance with the African slaves against England and Spain, Sonthonax's motivations were clear enough: they included a genuine belief that the principles of the French Revolution—liberty, equality and fraternity—required an end to slavery and racism in any form; a desire to expand the French Revolution and bring Saint Domingue under its banner; and solidification of an alliance with the freedmen against Britons and Spaniards.

But even facing the British and Spanish invasions of the island, unity in Saint Domingue remained elusive. White colonists continued their fight against Sonthonax; they wanted the restoration of the French monarchy and slavery. Even some free men of color joined the white planters, for they desired their own citizenship, but they were reluctant to extend freedom to the African slaves, and indeed some wanted the restoration of slavery. Neither did the African slaves trust Sonthonax completely, for it was not until February 4, 1794 that the French National Convention ratified Sonthonax's general proclamation of freedom to the slaves, thus formally ending the 300-year history of slavery in Saint Domingue.

Meanwhile, the French National Convention recalled Sonthonax to France to defend his proclamation of freedom. He did return to Saint Domingue during spring 1796 at the head of the Third Civil Commission, but Sonthonax's moment in history had passed. Both the free men of color and freed slaves had turned against Sonthonax. As during his previous mission to Saint Domingue, his goals were to save Saint Domingue for France and extend full citizenship to the freed slaves, but he lost out in the struggle for power in Saint Domingue.

By 1796, the African leader **Toussaint L'Ouverture** had seized the leadership of the northern free blacks, who were now called "cultivators." Regardless of his emancipation act of August 29, 1793, African slaves feared that Sonthonax had been sent to Saint Domingue to restore slavery, which was a persistent dread among the slaves. Toussaint L'Ouverture exploited that African dread and forced Sonthonax to flee to France. By August 24, 1797, when Sonthonax boarded a ship for France, Toussaint and the black cultivators had developed their own agenda and their own consciousness, and they would accept no settlement to the black revolution that failed to include complete emancipation.

Even during the intervening 200 years, Léger Félicité Sonthonax has remained a controversial figure of the Haitian Revolution. His critics have denounced him as vain, power hungry, and duplicitous. Still, a leading Haitian historian, Thomas Madiou, wrote that the people of Haiti spoke well of Sonthonax as a defender of their freedom. Another historian, Robert Stein, presented Sonthonax as a dedicated French Republican, a patriot who wanted to preserve French sovereignty over Saint Domingue, and a principled advocate of the Rights of Man. *See also* Dessalines, Jean-Jacques; French Colonies, Emancipation of; Haitian Revolution; Saint Domingue, French Defeat in.

Further Readings: Fick, Carolyn. *The Making of Haiti: The Saint Domingue Revolution from Below.* Knoxville: University of Tennessee Press, 1990; Geggus, David P. *Haitian Revolutionary Studies.* Bloomington: Indiana University Press, 2002; Geggus, David P. *Slavery, War and Revolution: The British Occupation of Saint Domingue, 1793–1798.* Oxford: Oxford University Press, 1982; James, C.L.R. *The Black Jacobins: Toussaint L'Ouverture and the San Domingo Revolution.* 1938. 2nd ed., New York: Vintage, 1963; Ott, Thomas O. *The Haitian Revolution, 1789–1804.* Knoxville: University of Tennessee Press, 1973; Scott, Julius S. "The Common Wind: Currents of Afro-American Communication in the Era of the Haitian Revolution," Ph.D. dissertation, Duke University, 1986; Stein, Robert L. *Léger Félicité Sonthonax.* Rutherford, NJ: Fairleigh Dickinson University Press, 1985.

Tim Matthewson

Spanish Empire, Antislavery and Abolition in

Beginning with Christopher Columbus's voyages in the 1490s, Spain began a conquest of a vast colonial empire in the Americas. It soon also expanded the African slave trade into an Atlantic slave trade that helped to provide slave labor for Spain's growing American colonies. Its slave trade remained a closely controlled monopoly enterprise until 1789, when Spain removed some of the monopoly restrictions and broadened the slave trade to Spanish colonies by permitting foreigners to participate legally. Opponents of African slavery and the slave trade did not begin to surface within Spain or its colonial empire until the nineteenth century, and even then there was no concerted abolitionist movement in Spain until the latter half of the nineteenth century. **Bartolomé de las Casas** and a handful of other Catholic clerics had spoken and written forcefully on behalf of enslaved Indians in the sixteenth century, but the enslaved Africans had no similar champion in Spain or its colonies.

The summoning of a Cortes or Parliament in Cadiz from 1810 with members from Spain's overseas colonies enabled colonial questions to be debated publicly. Two of the most important were the slave trade and slavery. The rise of a powerful abolitionist movement since the 1790s had led to the prohibition of the slave trade in the British Empire and in the United States. British diplomats at Cadiz were instructed to do whatever they could to persuade the Spanish government and deputies to follow Britain's example and pass legislation against the slave trade. A small number of Spanish and colonial liberals wanted to join Britain in this campaign. Miguel Guridi y Alcócer, a deputy from New Spain (later Mexico), introduced a motion into the Cortes on March 26, 1811 to abolish the slave trade. The actual Cortes debate in April, 1811, took place on resolutions introduced by the Spanish liberal, Agustín Arguelles, also against the slave trade, but at the end of this debate Alcócer steered it toward the abolition of slavery. The Cortes did not pass any of the resolutions, but instead turned them over to a commission to examine them. Here Cuban planters were able to exercise their considerable economic and political influence to defeat any further action by the metropolis against the source of their plantation labor.

Another isolated sign of Spanish liberal opposition to slavery had come much earlier in 1802, when Isidoro de Antillón y Marzo read a dissertation against slavery to the Real Academia Matritense de Derecho. In 1813, he tried again to bring up the subject of slavery in Spain's empire, but without success. When the Cortes was reconvened in 1820 for another three-year period, the Cuban cleric and philosopher, Padre Félix Varela y Morales, a Cuban delegate to the Cortes, presented his own plan of slave abolition to the Cortes. The Cortes took no action on this plan, but it represented the one occasion during the brief periods of Spanish liberalism at the beginning of the nineteenth century when a prominent clergyman took a stand against slavery in the Spanish Empire.

Following the independence of Spain's mainland Latin American colonies, Spain and the colonial elites in Cuba and Puerto Rico refashioned a second colonial empire based on plantation slavery in these islands. Opportunities for public debate on such a politically sensitive topic as slavery were rare in the colonies until the latter part of the nineteenth century because of the censorship Spain imposed, but in the metropolis itself the public sphere expanded at the same time as metropolitan and colonial politics became more closely intertwined. Slave labor provided the basis of the wealth of Spain's colonies upon which Spain depended. Yet the institution was coming under increasing attack principally from the abolitionist movement in Britain, but also from the United States and fledgling abolitionists in Spain itself.

The Abolitionist Society of Spain was not formally founded until 1865 when the abolition of slavery in the United States forced a radical rethinking of Spanish colonial policy. In the middle of the nineteenth century, however, public institutions began to proliferate in Madrid, giving rise to a growing number of debates on public policy. As Christopher Schmidt-Nowara has pointed out, the debate over free trade presaged the debate on abolition: free traders would support abolitionism while defenders of protection upheld colonial slavery because of the wealth that labor produced. The debates over slavery became inextricably entangled with the complexities of Spanish colonial policy towards Cuba and Puerto Rico.

A Puerto Rican intellectual, Julio de Vizcarrondo, was one of the key founders of the Spanish Abolitionist Society, although the Spanish politician, Rafael María de Labra, soon emerged as Spain's leading abolitionist. Puerto Rican abolitionists tended to favor immediate abolition while the Cuban reformers favored a gradualist approach. The gradualists feared both the impact of immediate abolition and its denial of the property rights of the slaveholders. Thus they favored compensation to the owners of slaves in return for their accepting abolition.

Following the passage of the law of free birth in 1870, the Moret Law, Spanish abolitionism fused with Spanish politics and mobilized a steadily expanding middle-class opposition. In 1873, an estimated 10,000 people marched in Madrid in favor of Puerto Rican emancipation. This public protest, along with others in major Spanish cities, marked a high point of Spanish abolitionism. When Spain became a republic in 1873, one of the first acts of the republican government was to abolish slavery in Puerto Rico, freeing the island's 29,000 slaves with indemnities for the slave owners and a contract for the slaves to work for a further three years for their former masters. Cuba, however, was not included.

The ten-year civil war that broke out in Cuba in 1868 took the question of Cuban abolition out of the hands of the metropolitan abolitionists in Spain. Slavery in Cuba began to erode first in the east as slaves took advantage of the wartime conditions to find freedom and planters promised freedom to those slaves who would fight alongside them. Then, following the end of the Ten Years War, the metropolitan government promised a gradual emancipation in 1880, but was forced to accelerate it and enact a complete abolition law in 1886. The conditions in Cuba, including the dynamic efforts of the slaves themselves to seize their own freedom, determined the pace of Spanish abolition in Spain's most important overseas colony. In contrast, the Spanish abolitionists played a relatively minor role in the final emancipation of slavery in Spain's overseas empire. The emergence of Spanish abolitionists and Spanish abolitionism as a political force in the metropolis in the second half of the nineteenth century, however, is one of the elements behind the final success of the long and protracted emancipation struggle in Puerto Rico and Cuba. *See also* Cuba, Emancipation in; Latin America, Antislavery and Abolition in; Roman Catholic Church and Antislavery and Abolitionism.

Further Readings: Schmidt-Nowara, Christopher. *Empire and Antislavery: Spain, Cuba and Puerto Rico, 1833–1874.* Pittsburgh: University of Pittsburgh Press, 1999.

David Murray

Spartacus Revolt (73–71 B.C.E.)

The revolt led by the slave Spartacus was the last in a series of three great slave rebellions that shook the Roman world during the second half of the

Death of Spartacus, a slave who led a gladiators' revolt in ancient Rome, 71 B.C.E. Courtesy of the North Wind Picture Archives.

first century B.C.E. The first two uprisings occurred in Sicily, in 135 to 132 B.C.E. and from 104 to 100 B.C.E. In the first Sicilian war, the rebel slaves, who were led by a Syrian slave called Eunus and were comprised principally of herdsmen, took the city of Enna. Another group led by the slave Cleon later joined them. The slaves gained control of several cities in Sicily, but were ultimately defeated by the Romans. The second Sicilian slave war was a consequence of a law that ordained that no free citizen of an allied state could be enslaved in a Roman province. The governor of Sicily then freed 800 slaves but encountered the opposition of the slaveowners. When the governor decided to abrogate the law, a slave revolt ensued. The slaves chose Salvius as their leader and he established a kind of monarchy at the city of Triokala. A second group of slaves, led by the Cilician Athenion, also joined Salvius, and together they resisted the Roman forces until the final defeat.

These three slave revolts can be interpreted as a result of the political and economic transformations that had affected the Mediterranean area since the second century B.C.E. The Roman victory over Carthage and its hegemony in the Italian peninsula led to a concentration of wealth, particularly lands and captives, in the hands of the Roman aristocracy. In the territories of southern Italy and Sicily, as well as in North Africa, an agrarian economy developed that employed large numbers of slaves, although a free peasant economy never completely disappeared. War and piracy provided slaves particularly from the eastern Mediterranean and introduced into Italy men and women of common ethnic and cultural origins. In southern Italy and Sicily the slaves were employed in rural properties that combined market-oriented agriculture with the raising of cattle and sheep. Spartacus' revolt differed from the Sicilian wars in two aspects: it occurred in southern Italy and not Sicily, and it was composed of gladiators, a role commonly assigned to slaves in the Roman world.

Spartacus, a Thracian by birth, was a gladiator in Capua. In 73 B.C.E., about seventy gladiators escaped from their training school and, led by Spartacus, started a revolt that ended only in 71 B.C.E. The revolt soon gathered broad popular support—it is estimated that 90,000 enslaved and free poor men joined—and spread to the Italian peninsula south of Rome. Rome's first response was to send out a pretor, Gaius Claudius Glaber, with 3,000 men. This army was defeated by Spartacus on Mount Vesuvius. A second force was then sent out, under the command of another pretor, Publius Varinius. Spartacus also defeated this army and even took the Roman lictors—symbols of magisterial authority—and Varinius's horse. In 72 B.C.E., two consuls, Lucius Gellius Publicola and Gnaeus Cornelius Lentulus, were sent out with two legions against Spartacus' troops. Both consular armies were defeated and the slaves took their supplies of food and weapons, which were divided among the followers. By late 72 B.C.E., the Senate assigned Marcus Licinius Crassus, a Roman noble, the command of almost 40,000 men to suppress Spartacus' revolt. After six months, the slave army was defeated in Lucania and Spartacus was killed. Crassus pursued the remnant that survived and killed 6,000 of them. They were crucified along the Via Apia, from Capua to Rome. Another 5,000 survivors were crushed by Pompey's army that was returning from Spain.

Spartacus' Revolt never faded from Roman memory. The historian, Tacitus, mentioned the Revolt in the second century C.E. in his *Annals*, as did the Christian writer, Orosius, in the fifth century C.E. in *History against the Pagans*. Spartacus was upheld as a paradigm of social unrest precisely because he threatened so fundamentally the slave-holding ideology of Roman society. Nevertheless, Latin and Greek sources on the revolt extolled its justice and discipline. They criticized the unjust behavior of owners that led the slaves to revolt; they contrasted the discipline of Spartacus' army with the lack of proper command in the Roman forces. It was just after Cassius restored the army discipline that victory was finally achieved; but they also emphasized the lack of honor in a Roman fighting such a war for slaves who were deemed incapable of waging war. According to Plutarch, Crassus "did not even attempt to ask for a great triumph for himself. Indeed, it seemed ignoble for him to celebrate even the lesser triumph ... that the Romans call an *ovatio* for a war fought against slaves."

Yet neither Spartacus' revolt nor earlier slave rebellions in Sicily offered any critique of slavery as a social institution. The rebels led by Spartacus desired to leave Italy and return to their homelands. It was only in Europe in the eighteenth century as slave revolts erupted in European overseas colonies that Spartacus acquired the image of a revolutionary who had fought for universal freedom. Although **Toussaint L'Ouverture**, the leader of the

1791 slave revolt in the French colony of Saint Domingue, was called "the black Spartacus" by an admirer, Spartacus himself was no Toussaint *avant la lettre*. His aim as a rebel slave-leader was not to abolish slavery, but to struggle to escape the life of a slave. *See also* Cicero; Classical Rome and Antislavery.

Further Readings: Bradley, Keith R. *Slavery and Rebellion in the Roman World, 140BC–70BC*. London: B.T. Batsford, 1989; Shaw, Brent D. *Spartacus and the Slave Wars: A Brief History with Documents*. Boston/New York: Bedford/St. Martin's, 2001; Urbainczyk, Theresa. *Spartacus*. London: Bristol Classical Press, 2004; Vogt, Joseph. "The Structure of Ancient Slave Wars." In Thomas Wiedemann, trans. *Ancient Slavery and the Ideal of Man*. Cambridge, MA: Harvard University Press, 1975, pp. 39–92.

Fábio Duarte Joly

Spooner, Lysander (1808–1887)

Lysander Spooner was an American legal theorist who became a prominent member of the radical abolitionist community in the 1840s when he wrote *The Unconstitutionality of Slavery*. His argument that the United States Constitution did not sanction slavery was made two decades before the ratification of the **Thirteenth Amendment**. Spooner's theory challenged the view, held by **William Lloyd Garrison** and **Wendell Phillips**, that the Constitution was a "covenant with death, and an agreement with hell" that permitted and protected slavery. In later life, Spooner wrote about anarchism, but his abolitionist writings were his most influential; both the **Liberty Party** and **Frederick Douglass** embraced his theory.

Whether the subject matter was deism, economics, jury trials, or slavery, Spooner always made legalistic arguments based on individuals' natural rights. In his most famous abolitionist work, *The Unconstitutionality of Slavery*, published in two parts in 1845 and 1847, Spooner said that written laws violating these natural rights were not legitimate and that people were not legally obliged to obey them. The only permissible exception was when a law specifically stated, in unequivocal language, that the government was permitted to infringe on these rights. The Constitution was not such a law; it did not mention "slavery" or "slaves."

This interpretation is based on an understanding of the original meaning of the language used by the Framers of the Constitution, and directly challenged the arguments made by Wendell Phillips. Phillips used historical documents (such as James Madison's notes from the Constitutional Convention in 1787) to show that the original *intent* of the Framers had been to build into the Constitution a series of compromises that protected slavery. Spooner rejected the legal relevance of these documents, because he believed that a law could only be legally binding as it was specifically written down.

Spooner was not the first to argue that slavery was unconstitutional, or to reach this conclusion using natural rights arguments. The intellectual ancestry of his theory is seen in the 1830s works of, for example, Alvan Stewart and William Goodell. His was, however, the most comprehensive and legalistic of these analyses of the relationship between slavery and the United States Constitution.

Although he never again reached an audience matching that of the 1840s, Spooner continued to write antislavery works. In 1850, in *A Defence for Fugitive Slaves*, he challenged the legality of the fugitive slave acts of 1793 and 1850. Consistent with his lifelong distrust of government officials, he encouraged people to facilitate the escape of fugitive slaves. If this resulted in their arrest, Spooner believed that the best course of action was to challenge the constitutionality of the fugitive slave laws. He combined the natural rights theory of *The Unconstitutionality of Slavery* with the elements of judicial process that formed the core of his later work on jury trial. While his argument was radical, the civil disobedience that he advocated was a strategy widely adopted by opponents of the 1793 and 1850 laws.

Spooner enjoyed less support for the views expressed in *A Plan for The Abolition of Slavery (and) To the Non-Slaveholders of the South*, an 1858 pamphlet responding to the Supreme Court's Dred Scott decision (1857). His radicalism continued to increase, as he saw no hope for a political end to slavery. He now advocated, if necessary, violent rather than merely legal challenges to laws. Illustrating his argument by using examples from the American and French Revolutions, Spooner called upon whites and blacks alike to engage in a revolutionary uprising in the South to liberate slaves. This ignited a wellspring of criticism, and most abolitionists were unwilling to condone this plan at a time of increasingly volatile sectional divisions. Spooner initially sought to ensure widespread distribution of his pamphlet, but John Brown persuaded him to suppress the publication because Brown feared it would jeopardize his planned raid at Harpers Ferry in 1859. Their ideas were similar, but consistent with his other writings Spooner focused on the theory of a revolution, whereas Brown intended to put ideas into practice.

Overall, during his lifetime the influence of Spooner's work was limited; he never achieved the fame he expected his writings to bring. He lacked the social benefits of a college or law school education, having learned the law as an apprentice to several prominent Massachusetts lawyers (including Governor, and later Senator, John Davis). His status as a serious legal scholar was undermined by some of the radical positions that he adopted, and, as a result, history has generally regarded him as an abolitionist whose writings, while voluminous, were of limited legal or theoretical importance. *See also* Fugitive Slave Law; Garrisonians; United States Constitution and Antislavery.

Further Readings: Cover, Robert M. *Justice Accused: Antislavery and the Judicial Process*. New Haven, CT: Yale University Press, 1975; Spooner, Lysander. "The Unconstitutionality of Slavery." In Charles Shively, ed. *The Collected Works of Lysander Spooner*. Vol. 4: *Anti-Slavery Writings*. Weston, MA: M&S Press, 1971; Wiecek, William M. *The Sources of Antislavery Constitutionalism in America, 1760—1848*. Ithaca, NY: Cornell University Press, 1977; Lysander Spooner Web site: www.lysanderspooner.org.

Helen J. Knowles

Sri Lanka, Antislavery in

Portuguese (1505–1658) and Dutch (1658–1796) colonial Sri Lanka— until 1972, named Ceylon—imported chattel slaves as domestic servants. After the British replaced the Dutch in 1796, they considered two other forms of involuntary labor in Sri Lanka to be "slavery." These were the "slave castes" of the Tamil north and slaves held in the Kandyan Kingdom in the interior of the island, which was annexed in 1815. Their gradual abolition became an important part of British triumphalist accounts of the benefits they brought to the colony. Other forms of coerced labor continued, however, and the plantation economy they created condemned millions of laborers to poverty and servility.

The British had guaranteed the property rights, including slaves, of Dutch subjects, and they also purchased slaves in India as soldiers ("Kaffir Corps") and road laborers ("Pioneer Corps"). Once the Colonial Office assumed control from the English East India Company in 1802, the Government of Ceylon began to take steps to abolish slavery. Most chattel slaves were owned by Dutch descendants and by a few Sri Lankan elites who emulated them. The British ended the slave trade with India and began to compile slave registers to facilitate a gradual abolition. The first governor, Lord Frederick North (1798–1805), unsuccessfully attempted to abolish slavery by proclamation, but his successor, General Thomas Maitland (1805–10) defended the rights of slaveowners. Alexander Johnston, Chief Justice of the Supreme Court, convinced slaveowners to liberate the children of their slaves voluntarily in 1816, and this was implemented by legislation in 1818. After 1821, the government emancipated the children of slaves in the southwest of the island by purchasing them at birth. Government slaves were liberated and served under indenture.

The "slave castes" of Jaffna proved to be an intractable problem. Three castes—*k∩viyar, nallavar,* and *pallar*—historically were bonded as laborers to members of the dominant *veëë~ëa* caste. Because they produced agricultural commodities valuable to the export trade, the Dutch considered them in law to be chattel slaves. In 1806, the *veëë~ëa*s were required to register their dependent laborers on penalty of forfeiture. This was never enforced. Ownership of slaves in Jaffna was made illegal after August 12, 1819, but no action was taken to relieve the disabilities of the bonded laborers.

Under Kandyan law, people of all castes could be enslaved temporarily in several ways: sold by poor parents, entering into debt peonage, as compensation for a crime, or (for women) as a result of sexual offenses. Keeping slaves as domestic servants and personal attendants was an important symbol of high status for royalty and chieftains. The government of Ceylon emancipated the slaves of the royal household when they deposed the last king, but they were reluctant to interfere with the privileges of their allies among the chieftains. They considered it a benign form of servitude, preferable to alternative punishments, and did not act against it.

Sri Lanka was exempted from the British Emancipation Act of 1833, but it stimulated interest in the remnants of slavery in the colony. The Act's extravagant compensation to British West Indian slaveholders encouraged

Jaffna slave owners, especially in the coastal areas, to register their dependents in vain hope of receiving similarly generous compensation. Under scrutiny from the antislavery movement in England, the Colonial Office insisted in 1837 that all slaves be registered. Kandyans in the interior of Sri Lanka resisted the expensive and unwieldy provisions of this Act, and when the government failed to enforce it, the Colonial Office demanded the total abolition of slavery in 1841. The colonial government temporized, passing yet another slave registration act, which outraged the Colonial Office since all slaves could have been liberated for non-registration under earlier acts. When no slaves were registered, the governor proclaimed that slavery had ended, although a few hundred Kandyans continued to serve their chieftains. Ordinance No. 20 of 1844 finally made slavery illegal.

Although the formal abolition of slavery is usually listed as one of the great accomplishments of British colonial rule, the government of Ceylon only reluctantly yielded to British demands for abolition. Missionaries showed little interest in the antislavery movement, since their proselytizing was aimed at the higher castes. The government did little to improve the conditions of the people who were liberated: the "slave castes" of Jaffna remained depressed, and the Kandyan chieftains continued to behave as if they were a feudal aristocracy.

The government did not intervene in the forced labor of the lower grades of the Sinhalese *sal~gama* caste who had been required since pre-colonial days to peel cinnamon bark for export. Only the collapse of the cinnamon industry ended this practice. The British colonial government relied on universal corvée labor (*r~jak~riya*), primarily for opening roads, until 1833, when it was replaced by a road tax.

The emergence of a plantation economy in the 1830s resulted in a new form of servitude. The coffee plantations of Sri Lanka were modeled directly on the slave plantations of the Caribbean, substituting poor immigrant labor from south India for slaves. These "Plantation Tamils" were isolated in "cooly lines" on the plantations, ethnically distinct from the local population, and tied by indebtedness to the plantation. Labor laws made it difficult to leave the plantations. Ironically, these laborers were called "free laborers" because they were unindentured.

The Colonial Office rejected labor legislation based on archaic English "Master and Servant" laws in 1837 and 1840 on the grounds that they set out severe penalties for laborers, on the word of the employers, but offenses of employers against their workers were not made punishable. The government of Ceylon added provisions to make employers who failed to honor contracts liable to a fine of £10, and this took effect as Ordinance No. 5 of 1841. Under this act, all laborers were under contracts that remained in effect until the laborer gave one month's notice. The planters put every possible obstacle in the way of a laborer who attempted to give notice against their wishes. Laborers were not allowed to exercise their right to break a contract for non-payment of the previous month's wages on the grounds that they had entered into a fresh contract by accepting food and lodging on the plantation, something that was unavoidable.

The living and working conditions of Plantation Tamils were improved only from pressure from the Colonial Office, most famously after 1861 when Florence Nightingale questioned the government about the high mortality rates of plantation laborers. Some laborers also managed to leave the plantations illegally. Gradually, the living and working conditions of the Plantation Tamils improved, but they remain the poorest people on the island. *See also* Indian Sub-Continent, Antislavery in.

Further Readings: Caplan, Lionel. "Power and Status in South Asian Slavery." In James L. Watson, ed. *Asian and African Systems of Slavery.* Oxford: Blackwell, 1980, pp. 169–194; de Silva, Colvin R. *Ceylon under the British Occupation, 1795–1833. Its Political, Administrative and Economic Development.* 2 vols. Colombo: Colombo Apothecaries, 1953; de Silva, K.M. *Social Policy and Missionary Organizations in Ceylon, 1840–1855.* London: Longmans, Green and Co., 1965; Hayley, Frederick Austin. *A Treatise on the Laws and Customs of the Sinhalese, Including the Portions Still Surviving under the Name of Kandyan Law.* Colombo: H.W. Cave, 1923. [Reprinted Navrang, New Delhi, 1993.] Peebles, Patrick. *Plantation Tamils of Ceylon.* London: Leicester University Press, 2001.

Patrick Peebles

Stanton, Elizabeth Cady (1815–1902)

Elizabeth Cady Stanton was best known as a leader of the woman's rights movement in the United States, but she found inspiration and allies through her early identification as an abolitionist. She converted to abolitionism at her cousin **Gerrit Smith**'s home in the mid-1830s, where "the anti-slavery platform," she remembered, "was the best school the American people ever had on which to learn republican principles and ethics." She married Henry B. Stanton, political abolitionist leader, on May 1, 1840. On their honeymoon, the Stantons visited the Weld-Grimké family and attended the **World's Anti-Slavery Convention** in London, where Elizabeth met **James G. Birney**, **William Lloyd Garrison**, and **Lucretia Mott**, who became her lifelong mentor. When the London meeting refused to seat U.S. women, Stanton and Mott resolved to call a convention solely to discuss the rights of women. Eight years later, in 1848, they organized such a convention at Seneca Falls, New York. There, 100 women and men signed a Declaration of Sentiments (drafted in part by Stanton), asserting that "all men and women are created equal."

Although a lifelong sympathizer of Garrisonian abolitionists, Stanton also had learned from political abolitionists the importance of the vote. Supported by **Frederick Douglass**, she introduced the demand for woman's suffrage at the **Seneca**

Elizabeth Cady Stanton. Courtesy of the Library of Congress.

Falls Convention. Throughout the 1850s, Stanton worked with Susan B. Anthony, drawing on a network of abolitionist allies to promote women's right to vote, keep their children in case of divorce, and control their own wages. During the Civil War, Elizabeth Cady Stanton and Susan B. Anthony formed the Women's Loyal National League, which generated petitions with 400,000 signatures in support of abolitionism. In 1866, Stanton helped to "bury the woman in the citizen," turning the Eleventh National Woman's Rights Convention into the American Equal Rights Association to work for voting rights for African American men and women of all races. She and Anthony spoke throughout Kansas in 1867, on behalf of a state constitution that would grant equal suffrage for all. When Congress passed the Fifteenth Amendment, giving voting rights to African American men but not to women, Stanton and Anthony formed the National Woman Suffrage Association to work for woman suffrage. *See also* Gender and Slave Emancipation; Gender Relations within Abolitionism; Grimké, Angelina; Grimké, Charlotte Forten; Weld, Dwight Theodore; Women and Antislavery; Women's Antislavery Societies.

Further Readings: Gordon, Ann D., ed. *The Selected Papers of Elizabeth Cady Stanton and Susan B. Anthony*. Vol. 1: *In the School of Anti-Slavery, 1840–1866*. New Brunswick, NJ: Rutgers University Press, 1997; Griffiths, Elisabeth. *In Her Own Right: The Life of Elizabeth Cady Stanton*. New York: Oxford, 1984; Stanton, Elizabeth Cady. *Eighty Years and More: Reminiscences, 1815–1897*. Reprint: Boston: Northeastern University Press, 1993; Wellman, Judith. *The Road to Seneca Falls: Elizabeth Cady Stanton and the First Woman's Rights Convention*. Champagne-Urbana: University of Illinois Press, 2004.

Judith Wellman

Stewart, Maria Miller (1803–1879)

Black abolitionist writer and speaker, Maria Stewart, is most often cited as the first recorded American-born woman to give a public political speech in the United States, when she addressed a "promiscuous audience" of male and female, black and white, in Boston's Franklin Hall, on September 21, 1832.

Maria Miller was born a free black woman in 1803 in Hartford, Connecticut. After being orphaned at a young age, she was raised in a clergyman's family as a servant. She was a domestic worker from the age of fifteen until her marriage. It is not known exactly when she moved to Boston, where she became part of the small but active black community there in the 1820s. In 1826, she married a black veteran of the War of 1812, James Stewart. James Stewart worked as a ship's outfitter, which, together with shared attendance at the African Baptist Church, brought the couple into regular contact with the used clothing merchant and black antislavery activist, David Walker. His famous *Appeal* (1829) proved a major intellectual influence on Maria Stewart.

Following the publication of Walker's *Appeal*, a rapid sequence of tragedies struck Maria Stewart. First, her husband James died in December 1829; then David Walker died of consumption in August 1830. Dishonest white lawyers compounded Stewart's sorrows by cheating her of her late husband's pension, which meant she had to return to domestic labor.

Stewart was among those who supported *The Liberator*, a pioneering abolitionist newspaper published by **William Lloyd Garrison**, when it commenced in 1831. She brought her first essay for publication to Garrison's office in September of that year. The significance of this essay, "Religion and the Pure Principles of Morality, the Sure Foundation on which We Must Build," resides in both its occasion and its content. Published soon after **Nat Turner**'s revolt in Southampton, Virginia in August 1831, but while Turner was still hiding, Stewart boldly extended Walker's critique of American slavery and racism to new circumstances, and as a woman. Stewart pointedly argued that "if blacks are spiritually equal to whites, then social equality must follow." Noting the sexual abuse that accompanied slavery, she taunts the slaveholders that they have already created a multiracial nation, in which "our souls are fired with the same love of liberty and independence with which your souls are fired." Recognizing the singularity of Stewart's voice and perspective, Garrison became an outspoken supporter of hers, and published the essay as a free-standing pamphlet.

In 1832 and 1833, Stewart gave a series of four public talks, the texts of which were all published in *The Liberator*. Three years before the white Grimké sisters roused controversy by speaking in public, Stewart experienced both the self-empowerment and the vitriol visited upon women who dared to defy their traditionally enforced silence. The criticisms eventually discouraged her enough that she abandoned her speaking career, leaving Boston to resettle in the Brooklyn, New York area in late 1833.

Her speeches and writings developed four important themes. The first was black self-reliance; she consistently called on the free black community to build its own schools, stores, and other institutions. Secondly, she stressed the nexus of religion and respectability; Stewart closely linked piety with sobriety, education, and black progress. She often employed evangelical language, and, following Walker, denounced American racial hypocrisy as the most perilous of sins.

Politically, Stewart focused more on Northern racism than on Southern slavery. She denounced rampant discrimination in employment, the consignment of blacks to manual labor, and vociferously opposed the plan of the **American Colonization Society** to return free blacks to Africa. Finally, her feminism grew over her brief public career; in her farewell speech given in Boston in September 1833, she vigorously defended her public speaking by dismantling apparent biblical mandates proscribing women's public voice, especially those pronounced by Paul in his New Testament Letters.

After moving to Brooklyn, Stewart remained involved in abolitionist activity. She attended the 1837 Women's Antislavery Convention, and participated in a black women's literary society. She sent letters to **Frederick Douglass**'s paper, *The North Star*. In the 1840s, Stewart became a schoolteacher in Brooklyn. In 1852, she moved to Baltimore, where she started her own school. During the Civil War, she relocated to Washington D.C., where she continued her teaching. In 1872, she served as matron of the Freedman's Hospital in Washington. In her last years, she recovered her husband's stolen pension; she used the funds to reissue her writings in 1879. Stewart died in Washington, D.C., in December of that same year.

Maria Stewart has unjustly remained a footnote in women's and abolitionist history. Stewart was a self-educated and sophisticated thinker whose writings pioneered the exploration of intersections of gender, class, labor, privilege, and race that are still debated today. Inspired by the insights and passion of David Walker, she, too, united evangelical language with an incisive analysis of the situation of free blacks to array the religious hypocrisies and gross racial injustice of antebellum America. Though her public career was brief, her commitment to attaining freedom and self-development for her people never wavered. While the recognition of her importance to feminist thought has grown over the past few decades, Maria Stewart's significance has yet to be fully plumbed. *See also* Gender and Slave Emancipation; Gender Relations within Abolitionism; Grimké, Angelina Emily; Women's Antislavery Societies.

Further Readings: Collins, Patricia Hill. *Black Feminist Thought: Knowledge, Consciousness, and the Politics of Empowerment.* New York: Routledge, 1990; Garcia, Jennifer Anne. *Maria W. Stewart: America's First Black Feminist.* Master's Thesis: Florida International University, 1998; Hinks, Peter P. *"To Awaken My Afflicted Brethren": David Walker and the Problem of Antebellum Slave Resistance.* University Park, Pennsylvania: Pennsylvania State Press, 1997; Horton, James Oliver and Lois E. Horton. *Black Bostonians: Family Life and Community Struggle in the Antebellum North.* New York: Holmes and Meier, 1979; Houchins, Sue, ed. *Spiritual Narratives.* New York: Oxford, 1988; Porter, Dorothy B. "The Organized Educational Activities of Negro Literary Societies 1828–46," *Journal of Negro Education* 5 (1936): 555–576; Richardson, Marilyn, ed. *Maria Stewart: America's First Black Woman Political Writer.* Bloomington, Indiana: Indiana University Press, 1987; Rycenga, Jennifer. "Maria Stewart, Black Abolitionist, and the Idea of Freedom." In Marguerite Waller and Jennifer Rycenga, eds., *Frontline Feminisms: Women, War and Conflict.* New York: Garland, 2000, pp. 297–324; Sterling, Dorothy. *We Are Your Sisters: Black Women in the Nineteenth Century.* New York: W.W. Norton and Company, 1984; Yellin, Jean Fagan, *Women and Sisters: The Antislavery Feminists in American Culture.* New Haven: Yale University Press, 1989.

Jennifer Rycenga

Stipendiary Magistrates

In 1833, the Emancipation Act was passed in England, ending 300 years of slavery in the British-colonized Caribbean. Among the clauses of the Act, designed to be implemented on August 1, 1834, was the provision for the introduction of stipendiary magistrates.

These men, sent out from England, were appointed to visit the plantations and settle disputes between employers and apprentices, and generally to make sure that the labor system ran properly. They worked on two-year contracts and could be dismissed if they were inefficient. But there were not enough stipendiary magistrates in each territory to make the system work well. There were only 150 in all for the British-controlled Caribbean territories, with sixty of these stationed in Jamaica. In the Bahamas, three were appointed in 1834 for New Providence, Eleuthera and Turks Islands.

By 1838, three more were appointed and the system was described as working fairly well in the Bahamas. In fact, there were fewer complaints in the Bahamas and the British Virgin Islands over how the system worked.

In some territories, the local Justices of the Peace (JPs) assisted stipendiary magistrates. Some of these JPs were of mixed race (coloreds), like Richard Hill of Jamaica. This complicated arrangements because some white employers did not wish to relate to colored people in this way. Some white JPs themselves also used apprentice labor and did not want colored people employed as JPs.

Many magistrates came from the planter class or were proplanter in their thinking and so could not function as objective and neutral negotiators in disputes. Some found the task of visiting the numerous estates difficult, especially in a large island like Jamaica. Many died from health-related illnesses during the first year of their service. They considered the initial salary of £300 grossly inadequate. This was later increased to £450. It was widely understood that this low salary made them likely to accept bribes from employers. In addition, as the magistrates did not have any control over plantation discipline, the owners could quite freely administer punishments. If the apprentices refused to work and had to be brought before the courts, then the magistrates had no control over the legal process. The result was that apprentices were systematically victimized by the legal system. *See also* Apprenticeship.

Further Readings: Beckles, Hilary & Verene Shepherd, eds. *Caribbean Freedom.* Kingston: Ian Randle Pubs., 1993; Beckles, Hilary and Verene Shepherd, eds. *Freedoms Won.* Capetown: Cambridge University Press, 2004; Holt, Thomas. *The Problem of Freedom.* Kingston: Ian Randle Pubs., 1992.

Verene Shepherd

Story of Joseph (Genesis 30:22−24, 37−50)

The earliest Anglo-American abolitionism, both black and white, was informed by Christianity. Abolitionists scanned the Bible for arguments against the slave trade and slavery, and they relied on the superiority of the New over the Old Testament to dismiss the common claim that Jewish slaveholding authorized the modern institution among Christians. Furthermore, abolitionists drew on biblical narratives to support their arguments. The deliverance of Israel from Egypt through Moses (Exodus 1−15) has often been considered the foundational biblical narrative of African American writing, both creative and religious, but early black writers were far more interested in Joseph than in Moses. The story of Joseph provided a narrative foundation on which books like **Olaudah Equiano**'s *Interesting Narrative* (1789) were built. Joseph provided a model of a righteous slave who became the savior of his family—a useful paradigm for black men who were acting as abolitionists. Several points of convergence between the ancient and the modern lines of events seemed obvious. Joseph was betrayed by his brothers and seized by slave traders traveling into Egypt: this corresponded to the West African slave trade. He was made a slave, pushed toward dangerous sexual activity, and sent to prison: these corresponded to the hardships, vulnerabilities, and humiliations of American slavery. His ability to interpret dreams secured his release from prison: this corresponded to an African religious background shared by many slaves, as well as probably to African American folk practices. And he ultimately came to understand that God's hand had been at work in all his trials, leading him to be the savior of his family as he provided them food and arranged for their pasture lands in a time of drought: this corresponded to the Calvinist predestinarianism that was common among Equiano's peers, as well as to their sense that they were serving blacks by opposing the slave trade and slavery. In general, thus, when the biblicism of the abolitionists is considered, we should be aware of the ways the scriptures were deployed. The Bible provided material for antislavery arguments (such as the mandate to love others), personae who triumphed because of righteousness or faith (such as Moses, Job, Daniel, and Jesus), and narratives useful to the self-understanding of abolitionists (such as the story of Joseph). *See also* Bible and Slavery; Book of Exodus.

Further Reading: Richards, Phillip. "The 'Joseph Story' as Slave Narrative: On Genesis and Exodus as Prototypes for Early Black Anglophone Writing." In Vincent L. Wimbush, ed., *African Americans and the Bible: Sacred Texts and Social Textures*. New York: Continuum International Publishing, 2000, pp. 221–235.

John Saillant

Stowe, Harriet Beecher (1811–1896)

Harriet Beecher Stowe. Courtesy of the Library of Congress.

Harriet Beecher Stowe's contribution to the antislavery movement centers upon her novel, **Uncle Tom's Cabin**, which rapidly attracted worldwide attention, above all along a transatlantic axis running between the United States and the United Kingdom and Europe. *Uncle Tom* concentrates upon the stories of two families of slaves "owned" by a Southern planter family, the Shelbys, and on the fates of Uncle Tom on the one hand and George and Liza Harris on the other. The novel first appeared in serial form in the abolitionist newspaper, *The National Era*, during 1851–1852, and immediately afterward as a book published by John P. Jewett, entitled *Uncle Tom's Cabin; or, The Man That Was a Thing*.

Stowe, from late adolescence onwards, had developed growing antislavery sympathies, first in New England and, after 1832, in Ohio. But she had almost no direct experience with slavery in the American South save for one brief visit to Kentucky in 1834. Thus she largely relied upon anecdotes related by others, for example, the stories told to her by escaped slaves, including her own servant, Eliza Buck, when she was living in Cincinnati from 1832 to 1850. Stowe also drew upon antislavery publications, such as the pamphlet written by **Theodore Dwight Weld**, **Angelina Grimké** Weld, and Sarah Grimké, *American Slavery as It Is: Testimony of a Thousand Witnesses* (1839). The pamphlet drew on a mélange of sources, including escaped slaves' stories, but chiefly on newspaper reports, particularly accounts in numerous Southern newspapers. Stowe also spoke to an escaped slave, Josiah Henson, and read his 1849 autobiography. In the subtitle of later editions of his book, Henson claimed to be "Mrs. Harriet Beecher Stowe's 'Uncle Tom.'" However, Stowe never accepted this claim, and, though there are similarities with Henson, Tom is substantially a fictional character—the creation of a white female writer seeking to stir up active resistance to the continuation of slavery in the United States, and especially to the 1850 **Fugitive Slave Law**.

Stowe succeeded in her aim. **Abraham Lincoln**, on meeting her in 1862, is said to have exclaimed, "So you're the little woman who wrote the book that started this great war?" The persistence of this apocryphal story provides an indication of the scale of *Uncle Tom's* success. The first printing of the book (5,000 copies) sold out in a few days, and it was to be constantly reprinted in the United States and the United Kingdom and across Europe (in translation). Over 300,000 issues were sold in the first year in the United States, a figure still dwarfed by British sales, which soared over 1.5 million. Voyaging abroad to receive an antislavery petition composed by the duchess of Sutherland, the earl of Shaftesbury, and the earl of Carlisle, and signed by half a million women inspired by *Uncle Tom's Cabin*, Stowe discovered how much of an international antislavery celebrity she had become. She subsequently traveled widely in Europe, particularly in Britain and Ireland, rallying support for American antislavery efforts.

Yet, *Uncle Tom*'s reliance on anecdote, its force as an antislavery polemic, and its targeting of a white audience have given the book a controversial history. White Southerners were incensed, claiming the book distorted the workings of the institution of slavery. Faced with such criticism, Stowe rushed out *A Key to Uncle Tom's Cabin Presenting the Original Facts and Documents Upon Which the Story Is Founded* in 1853. African Americans, for very different reasons, were also uneasy, particularly about the book's portraits of black slaves. For example, the portrayal of Topsy, the young slave girl, as a naïve, mischievous, capering, dishonest self-hater, came in for heavy criticism—Stowe's unthinking reliance on blackface minstrelsy's excesses were all too clear. But Uncle Tom himself attracted the heaviest criticism. As early as 1852, William C. Nell criticized Tom for his passive reliance on the efficacy of Christian forgiveness. By 1865, **Frederick Douglass**, despite his *Paper*'s initial enthusiasm, in a speech to the Annual Meeting of the Massachusetts Anti-Slavery Society, expressed concern about Tom's readiness "to take off his Coat whenever required, fold his hands, and be whipped by anybody who wanted to whip him." By 1926, William Stanley Braithwaite observed in *The Negro in American Literature* that "the moral gain and historical effect of Uncle Tom have been artistic loss and setback." In 1956, J.C. Furnas, in his *Goodbye to Uncle Tom*, described the "theological terror" that the book invoked as comparable to the "terror" upon which the Southern States' "lynch mob[s]" had relied. Consequently, Furnas claimed, "American Negroes have made ... ["Uncle Tom"] a hissing and a byword." Or, as James Baldwin put it in his *Partisan Review* essay of 1949, "Tom ... has been robbed of his humanity and divested of his sex."

In contrast, outside the South, the white reception of the book was generally characterized by respect, if not admiration. Initial reviews from antislavery sympathizers on both sides of the Atlantic were eulogistic, although some advocates of "immediate" or "ultra" abolition found Stowe's message too conservative. Those unconvinced about abolition's desirability were even more wary, if compelled, to recognize the book's power. For example, on September 3, 1852, a London *Times* reviewer wrote that "with the instincts of her sex, the clever authoress takes the shortest road to her purpose, and strikes at the convictions of her readers by assailing their hearts." As this passage implies, Stowe's novel is carefully contrived, strategically aiming to appeal as widely as possible to its audiences, be they antislavery converts, the unconverted or—perhaps above all—agnostics. Part of the problem would seem to be Stowe's relative naiveté concerning abolitionist politics. Before the publication of Uncle Tom's Cabin, Stowe was only a sympathizer, not an active abolitionist; she only learned to negotiate with confidence the politics of abolition—the competing claims of **Garrisonian** advocates of immediate abolition on the one hand and gradualists on the other—after being thrust into the international limelight.

Yet Stowe's naiveté can be overstated. Acknowledging this provides a way of analyzing why *Uncle Tom*'s narrative splits into two stories. As the fugitive slaves George and Eliza Harris escape North, Tom, however, progresses southwards, deeper into servitude and suffering. As George and Eliza travel North, their story increasingly engages with the public politics of abolitionism and the solutions posited by those abolitionists, political abolitionists, who saw the remedy for slavery as primarily residing in political change. The passage of the Fugitive Slave Act marked a significant defeat for these political abolitionists, by dramatically *extending* slavery's impact. Stowe traces the Act's consequences for Eliza and George during their northward journey. Bounty hunters strive to recapture the Harrises during their journey; Senator Bird and his wife debate the Act's rectitude; George makes his "Declaration of Independence" in an armed stand-off; and the British colony of Canada is ironically identified as the runaways' blessed land of freedom. The repeated sense is that in the public domain of politics, insuperable institutional impediments block the achievement of perfect Christian charity. Indeed doubt is shed upon the idea that any public human institution can deliver the necessary reform.

In counterpoint with this political, Northward plotline, Tom's involuntary progress South effectively takes up the arguments of those abolitionists who saw a resolution to the issue of slavery residing not in the political arena, since even the **United States Constitution** itself countenanced slavery but in the persuasive efficacy of the moral arguments against both slavery—as when the saintly Little Eva disputes with the slave-owning St. Clare—and racism—as when St. Clare shows Ophelia how she dreads "touching" Topsy. This sort of moral persuasion is climactically advanced by Tom's Christ-like death and final words: "Ye poor miserable critter [Legree]! . . . I forgive ye, with all my soul!" (II: 275). The focus of the political plot-strand centering on Eliza and George is primarily external/public, demanding political action and resistance, while the moral suasionist strand of Tom's story is primarily internal/domestic. Tom practices perfectionism in his faith, residing in his belief that, even unto death, God's justice will prevail.

Focusing upon this narrative division and the implicit support it provides to moral suasionists provides a way of understanding how some feminist critics came to take *Uncle Tom* as highly significant in its advocacy of moral nurturing, archetypally depicted in the Quaker matriarch, Hannah's harmoniously-organized Christian kitchen. More significantly, the novel's double plotline also, at least apparently, provides a way of rebutting those critics dismayed by Tom's passivity: George, unlike Tom, actively fights his persecutors. Though George is a light-skinned quadroon, so raising the issue of how skin color ranks high in many abolitionists' calculations of "worth" (as in Richard Hildreth's *The White Slave* (1836) and its use of a "white" hero to stir up antislavery anger), vigorous resistance is also offered in Stowe's novel by the dark-skinned Jim Selden. This surely contradicts Baldwin's 1949 suggestion that Tom is Stowe's "only black man." Yet it is clear why Baldwin errs; Selden appears only briefly, and elsewhere St. Clare ponders how, since "there is a pretty fair infusion of Anglo-Saxon blood among our slaves now . . . with all our haughty feelings burning in their veins," they "will not always be bought and sold" (II: 76). African Americans' unease with this novel's color politics cannot be dismissed.

Yet it is important to distinguish between the novel itself and variations that have constantly flourished in popular culture. The illustrations to the novel have often emphasized a sentimentalized Uncle Tom, or brought out the blackface traces in Stowe's characterizations. Much more damagingly, Southern racist popularizations, as in the staging of *Uncle Tom's Cabin as It Is* in Baltimore in 1852, or in *Aunt Phillis's Cabin; or Southern Life As It Is* by Mary Henderson Eastman in 1852, portrayed Southern slavery as a pastoral idyll overseen by paternalistic planters and "Uncle Tom" suffering racism in the North and gladly returning South to his cabin. Such deformations explain well just why "Uncle Tom" became so much of a "hissing and a byword," in J.C. Furnas's 1956 verdict. As a tentative counter-balance to this emphasis, reference needs to be made to Stowe's other antislavery novel from 1856, *Dred; a Tale of the Great Dismal Swamp*, which offers a messianic portrait of a runaway maroon. Concealed in the swamps, Dred resists white attempts at recapture, while denouncing slavery—if in an overly melodramatic and apocalyptic fashion. However, Stowe has always primarily entered public consciousness as Uncle Tom's creator, and, in her depiction of George and Eliza resolving to travel to Africa in line with **American Colonization Society** propaganda, as a colonizationist. One sign of the resulting problem of this legacy is how, in the late 1960s, Tom once again needed reinventing—this time, in the wake of the rise of black power—as a resistant hero quite unlike the original. Stowe's Uncle Tom remains deeply discomforting. *See also* Literature and Abolition.

Further Readings: Hedrick, Joan D. *Harriet Beecher Stowe: A Life*. New York: Oxford University Press, 1994; Weinstein, Cindy. *The Cambridge Companion to Harriet Beecher Stowe*. Cambridge: Cambridge University Press, 2004.

Richard J. Ellis

Sturge, Joseph (1793–1859)

Joseph Sturge was an English corn factor, abolitionist, and political reformer. A member of the Society of Friends, or **Quakers**, Sturge's life-long political activism was characterized by an uncompromising moral certitude informed by his evangelical religious faith. Sturge devoted much of his life to the struggle to emancipate all slaves and end the system of apprenticeship that followed slavery in parts of the West Indies. He also contributed his considerable energies to expanding the franchise and to promoting pacifism, free trade, education reform, church disestablishment, and temperance. His life-long unwillingness to compromise moral principle for political expedience can be seen in his commitment to the temperance movement. Despite the importance of the trade in alcohol for most corn factors, Sturge steadfastly refused to sell malting barley to distilleries or rent his warehouses to spirit merchants. Such uncompromising stances characterized his activism in the antislavery movement as well.

Joseph Sturge was born August 2, 1793 in Elberton. At the age of twenty-one, Sturge became a partner in a corn factor business in Bewdley. In 1823, he relocated to Birmingham, a move that marked both the beginning of his ascent in the world of business and his entry into popular political agitation. In 1834, he married Eliza Cropper, who died in childbirth less than a year later, and in 1846 remarried to Hannah Dickinson, with whom he had five children.

Shortly after moving to Birmingham, Sturge began organizing and attending public meetings advocating the gradual emancipation of slaves throughout the British Empire, and by 1826 he was secretary of the Birmingham Anti-Slavery Society. By 1830, Sturge was calling for immediate abolition, and pursuing more aggressive grassroots strategies for achieving this end. His conversion to immediate abolition is representative of a wider conflict within the abolitionist movement between many in the rank-and-file, who were losing patience with London-based leaders advocating gradual and conditional, rather than immediate and entire, abolition.

In 1831, Sturge contributed to the formation of the Agency Committee, which paid lecturers to travel the country and speak at public meetings about the merits of immediate abolition within the British Empire. These lecturers also worked to coordinate the petitioning and other activities of local antislavery societies, particularly the large number of women's antislavery societies, which had been in existence for some time. This created a swell of grass-roots pressure that often ran ahead of the movement's London leadership. After the passage of the 1832 Reform Act, Agency Societies worked to extract pledges from parliamentary candidates in favor of immediate emancipation, which Sturge published to encourage supporters to vote only for pledged candidates. In 1833, voters returned a Parliament with over 100 pledged members and in the same year Sturge participated in an antislavery delegate conference in London to keep the pressure on the government to act.

Lord Stanley's 1833 Act abolishing slavery in the British Empire, with its provisions for a period of unpaid apprenticeship for former slaves and compensation for slave owners, was a bitter disappointment for Sturge. He believed that the apprenticeship system was de facto slavery, and felt that it was the slaves themselves, rather than the owners, who deserved to be compensated. Sturge personally communicated these feelings to Lord Stanley himself, and the strength of his anger over the provisions of this act put him at odds with many parliamentarians, as well as much of the leadership of the London **Anti-Slavery Society.**

As Sturge began to hear reports of ill-treatment of apprentices in the Caribbean, he and others attempted to reenergize the rank-and-file of the abolitionist movement. In November of 1836, Sturge traveled to the West Indies with Thomas Harvey, Reverend John Scoble, and William Lloyd in order to collect information about the apprenticeship system first-hand. They interviewed apprentices, magistrates, and plantation owners, and uncovered abundant evidence of cruelty and injustice. Sturge and Harvey laid out their findings in *The West Indies in 1837*. Sturge also purchased a Jamaican apprentice named James Williams, freed him, brought him to Britain, and published an account of the violent and inhumane treatment he suffered as an apprentice in *The Narrative of James Williams*.

Upon his return in May of 1837, Sturge traveled across England delivering public speeches about his experiences in the West Indies and the brutality of post-abolition apprenticeship. The Colonial Office was forced to investigate his allegations, and Sturge was called to testify before the reconvened Parliamentary Select Committee on Apprenticeship. In November 1837, he called a meeting of delegates in London to coordinate the activities of local antislavery societies for exerting pressure on Parliament to end apprenticeship. At this meeting, the Central Negro Emancipation Committee was founded, and soon Parliament was besieged with petitions from all corners of Britain. By act of Parliament, all apprentices were emancipated on August 1, 1838.

Next, Sturge focused on the conditions and rights of recently freed slaves, as well as the abolition of slavery worldwide. In April 1839, the **British and Foreign Anti-Slavery Society** was formed, and Sturge was made an honorary member. In June of 1840, a **World's Anti-Slavery Convention** was held in London. Although many countries were represented, most of the delegates came from Britain. The conference bitterly divided over the issue of whether female attendees would have the full rights of participants or would be treated merely as "visitors," with Sturge taking the latter side of the debate. The conference achieved little. In 1841, Sturge traveled to the United States, where he met with many American abolitionists and politicians, and also engaged in some dangerous confrontations with slave owners and traders. He participated in a variety of antislavery protests, including the illegal distribution of antislavery literature in slave states. He wrote about his experiences in *A Visit to the United States in 1841*. Sturge was involved with the international antislavery movement for the remainder of his life.

During the period in which Sturge was active in abolitionism, he was aware of the growing use of rhetoric comparing the denial of political rights to British male workers at home to slavery. Although Sturge disapproved of physical force used by some supporters of Chartism, and personally disliked Feargus O'Connor, he was sympathetic to the cause of universal suffrage. As a Birmingham alderman, he forcefully argued against the importation of a small contingent of the Metropolitan Police Force to suppress Chartist meetings in 1839. Sturge, who had many friends among "new move" and "church chartists," gradually became more vocal in support of universal male suffrage. In November 1841, Sturge suggested the Anti-Corn Law League work toward expanding the franchise. Despite the cold reception he received, Sturge continued to work for a middle class alliance between supporters of the Anti-Corn Law League and Chartists in order to gain universal suffrage. This Alliance was realized in April 1842 at a Birmingham conference that led to the formation of the National Complete Suffrage Union (NCSU). Complete Suffrage Union branches were formed in many parts of the country. The proposed alliance ultimately foundered due to the unwillingness of Chartists to abandon the full Charter, or even the Charter in name, which some members of the NCSU felt had been tainted with sedition and violence. The alliance was further undermined by leaders of the National Charter Association, who felt that the NCSU distracted Chartists from the primary goals of the movement, and expressed doubts about whether the repeal of the Corn Laws would result in benefits for the working class. Additionally, the strikes and disorder of August of 1842, as well as the failure of the second Chartist petition, frightened away many potential middle class supporters. In 1842, Sturge stood for Parliament in Nottingham, but lost to John Walter, the owner of *The Times*.

Joseph Sturge died on May 14, 1859 in Birmingham. Three years after his death, a crowd of nearly 12,000 people came out to witness the unveiling of a statue of Sturge created by sculptor John Thomas. The statue recognized the very important contributions that Joseph Sturge made in the abolition movement and to the ending of apprenticeship. *See also* Atlantic Slave Trade and British Abolition; Immediate Emancipation.

Further Readings: Fladeland, Betty. *Men and Brothers: Anglo-American Anti-Slavery Cooperation*. Urbana: University of Illinois Press, 1972; Fladeland, Betty. "Our Cause Being One and the Same: Abolitionists and Chartism." In James Walvin, ed. *Slavery and British Society, 1776–1846*. Baton Rouge: Louisiana State University Press, 1982; Hobhouse, Stephen. *Joseph Sturge: His Life and Work*. London: J.M. Dent and Sons, 1919; Richard, Henry. *Memoirs of Joseph Sturge*. London, 1864; Sturge, Joseph. *The United States in 1841*. London, 1841; Sturge, Joseph, and Thomas Harvey. *The West Indies in 1837*. London, 1837; Tyrrell, Alex. *Joseph Sturge and the Moral Radical Party in Early Victorian Britain*. London: Christopher Helm, 1987.

Christopher Frank

Supplementary Convention on the Abolition of Slavery, the Slave Trade, and Institutions and Practices Similar to Slavery (1956)

The Supplementary Slavery Convention of 1956 complemented but did not replace the **Slavery Convention of 1926**. The Second World War had seen Nazi concentration camps in which inmates were either killed or worked to death, and the forced recruitment of thousands of Europeans from German-occupied countries to work as slave labor for the Germans. The gulags or forced labor camps in the Soviet Union, to which dissenters, kulaks, criminals, prisoners of war, and many innocent people were sentenced, were now known to be huge enterprises, producing goods for export on an unprecedented scale. The slave trade had been reduced to a small smuggling traffic and chattel slavery was still legal in the Arabian Peninsula, including the British-protected emirates on the Persian Gulf and in the Aden Protectorate. Servile and forced marriage and the exploitation of children continued.

The colonial powers, as the result of the war, had been supplanted as great powers by the United States and the Soviet Union. The **United Nations**, which had replaced the defunct League of Nations, was torn by permanent rivalry between the communist states and their supporters and the western powers and their allies. In 1948, the United Nations issued the Universal Declaration of Human Rights. The Soviets, who considered slavery to be merely the chattel slavery practiced in Arabia and in some British territories, were responsible for article four of the declaration which said that no one should be held in slavery or servitude and that the slave trade should be prohibited "in all its forms." The United States and its allies considered that "slavery in all its forms" included the gulags and other Soviet labor practices. The declaration, however, was a mere statement of principle requiring the drafting of conventions to give it force.

Against this background of growing tension between the Soviets and their allies, and the democratic powers and their supporters, the British Anti-Slavery and Aborigines Protection Society, led by Charles Greenidge, came to New York to rally support at the United Nations for a new and more effective treaty against chattel slavery and the range of practices similar to it, that had been described in the Report of the Temporary Slavery Commission in 1925.

Greenidge persuaded the Belgian delegate to the United Nations Economic and Social Council (ECOSOC) to propose that the United Nations establish a committee to inquire into slavery in all its forms. This became inextricably mixed up with British and United States' efforts to include the slave labor camps of the Soviet Union, and with the Soviet attacks on the labor practices of the capitalist states and colonial powers. After much wrangling, an ad hoc committee on slavery finally met in 1950 and 1951. It was supposed to consist of five members—one from each of the areas into which the United States had divided the world—the Soviet or Eastern Bloc, the Western bloc, Latin America, Asia, and Africa. But suitable members could not be found for all areas. The committee eventually broke up in disorder, its members at loggerheads, and its time cut short by ECOSOC because Chile, Peru, and Colombia objected to the inclusion of peonage in its discussions. The United States also decided that forced labor should be the subject of a separate committee.

However, the slavery committee's recommendation that the United Nations should take over the 1926 Slavery Convention was accepted in 1953. Then Greenidge took the decisive step of submitting a draft supplementary convention to ECOSOC. Eventually after more discussions and reports, ECOSOC appointed a small drafting committee to draw up the convention. It met in Geneva in January 1956. It consisted of the colonial powers and their supporters, five in all, and of an anticolonial block of India, Ecuador, Egypt, Yugoslavia, and Soviet Russia. Agreement was thus hard to get and interest ran high. When the draft was finally discussed in ECOSOC, the delegates of more than fifty states attended. The communist bloc and Latin American states came in force, and the discussions took place in the highly charged atmosphere that followed the Suez Canal crisis. Decisions were made for political, rather than humanitarian, reasons.

Nevertheless, the Supplementary Convention was signed in 1956. Unlike the 1926 convention, it clearly stated that slavery included debt-bondage, serfdom, forced marriage, early marriage, transfers of and the inheritance of women, and the adoption of children for their exploitation. It also defined these practices and stated that they should be eliminated, together with the slave trade. Enslavement and enticement into slavery were to be criminal offences, as were branding and mutilation. Signatories were to cooperate and to supply the Secretary General with copies of their laws and the measures they were taking to end all these forms of slavery. However, there were no means for enforcement, and many of the practices were embedded in the cultures of the former colonial states, which had gained or were just gaining their independence.

The treaty marked the beginning of the end of Britain's leadership of the antislavery movement. It had to give up its long held rights to search shipping even in the slave trade zone in response to protests from Saudi Arabia, Sudan, Pakistan, and Iran, and in order to gain other concessions over applying the treaty to those parts of the British Empire in various stages of dependence over which it no longer had full control.

The convention continued the ever-widening definition of slavery, or "slavery like practices" begun in 1926 and which continued for the rest of the twentieth century. It also convinced the Anti-Slavery Society of the need for a permanent United Nations Slavery Committee. *See also* Brussels Act; League of Nations and Antislavery and Abolition.

Further Readings: Brownlie, Iain. *Basic Documents on Human Rights*. 3rd ed. Oxford: Clarendon Press, 1998; Greenidge, Charles W.W. *Slavery*. London: Allen and Unwin, 1958; Miers, Suzanne. *Slavery in the Twentieth Century: The Evolution of a Global Problem*, Walnut Creek, CA: Altamira Press, 2003.

Suzanne Miers

Swisshelm, Jane Grey (1815–1884)

Jane Swisshelm enjoyed considerable attention as an American antislavery newspaper editor and writer, especially in the late 1840s and early 1850s.

She also endorsed other social reform movements, including women's rights and temperance.

Born into a Scottish-Irish family in Pittsburgh, Pennsylvania, Swisshelm's life was in many ways shaped by her Covenanter faith, a branch of the Presbyterian Church that often preached opposition to slavery. Taught by her religion to dislike slavery in theory, Swisshelm's brief residence with her husband, James Swisshelm, in Louisville in the late 1830s convinced her to dislike it in practice. Her experiences there, including her conversations with enslaved women and men and their owners, formed much of the material she would later use in her editorials and public addresses.

By the 1840s, the couple had returned to the Pittsburgh area, and Jane Swisshelm began to write for the local **Liberty Party** paper, the *Spirit of Liberty*. When that paper went bankrupt, in December 1847, Swisshelm started her own paper for the Liberty Party, the *Pittsburgh Saturday Visiter*. She soon gained notoriety because of her willingness to engage male editors in heated debates over slavery and women's rights. Swisshelm opposed slavery on the grounds that slaves, especially women, were poorly and immorally treated, and she sited anecdotes from her stay in Louisville to illustrate her points. Although her newspapers consistently endorsed the Free Soil and Republican parties that called only for halting the spread of slavery into the Territories, Swisshelm held that the Constitution would allow immediate abolition everywhere. Further, immediate abolition was necessitated by the extent of slavery's moral crimes.

Her editorials were reprinted in a wide variety of newspapers because of her flare for language and personal invective, and Swisshelm quickly became a leading American journalist. Horace Greeley, editor of the *New York Tribune*, hired her to cover Washington politics in 1850, where she was the first female reporter to sit in a congressional press box. However, she soon lost her position when she unleashed her penchant for personal attack on Senator Daniel Webster, who had just infuriated the antislavery community by supporting the **Fugitive Slave Law**. Reporting that Webster had a large family by a black mistress, Swisshelm spread a current rumor but was unable to back up her story. While fired by Greeley, Swisshelm's continued work for abolition won the praise of **Frederick Douglass**. By 1853, her paper had a circulation estimated at approximately 6,000. She also serialized her own fiction (under both her own name and the pseudonym Jeannie Deans) in the *Pittsburgh Saturday Visiter*, including her prodivorce reform novel *The Locust's Song*. In addition, she wrote an advice book, *Letters to Country Girls*, in 1853.

By the mid-1850s, however, Swisshelm struggled to keep her paper afloat in the face of a lack of party financial support and the need to spend time with her daughter, Zo. She sold the *Saturday Visiter* in 1854. In addition, her always tempestuous marriage was collapsing. In 1857, she deserted her husband and moved to St. Cloud, Minnesota, to live with her sister. There she founded another newspaper, the *St. Cloud Saturday Visiter*, which was soon embroiled in verbal combat with the powerful local **Democratic Party** leader, Sylvanus Lowry. In March 1858, Lowry and others destroyed Swisshelm's printing press. Swisshelm thrived on conflict, however, and she soon had a new paper, the *St. Cloud Democrat*, up and running. Once again in the forefront of the news, Swisshelm embarked for the first time on a speaking tour, traveling throughout Minnesota giving rousing and often satiric speeches in favor of abolition and women's rights.

The *St. Cloud Democrat* endorsed **Abraham Lincoln** for the presidency in 1860, and Swisshelm moved to Washington, D.C., during the Civil War to claim a job at the War Department. While there, she became a close friend of Mary Todd Lincoln. Selling her St. Cloud newspaper in 1863, she threw herself into her clerkship, occasionally nursed Union soldiers, and eventually started another newspaper, the *Reconstructionist*, in December 1865. That paper soon folded, and she returned to Swissvale, outside Pittsburgh, to live on land won in a lawsuit against her husband's estate. There she worked as a columnist and a public lecturer. She also wrote her caustic and entertaining autobiography, *Half a Century* (1880).

Swisshelm is remembered for her satiric, often contemptuous exchanges with her opponents and for her courage in facing down both her conservative antiabolitionist opponents and also the many fellow reformers with whom she disagreed. Because of her dislike of conventions as a reform tactic, she fell out of favor with the leadership of the women's rights movement despite her early support for female suffrage, married women's property laws, and equal educational and vocational access for women. Likewise, she often disagreed with people in her own antislavery parties because they moved too slowly for her tastes. Seemingly a loner by temperament, she wrote best when on the attack, and these attributes caused gulfs to develop not only between her and her enemies but also between her and people she probably ought to have befriended. As a result, she faded into relative historical obscurity. Nevertheless, she was a pioneer in women's journalism both as an editor and reporter and was one of the better-known abolitionist writers in the United States, especially in the early 1850s. *See also* Gender and Slave Emancipation; Gender Relations within Abolitionism; Radical Republicans; Women's Antislavery Societies.

Further Readings: Klement, Frank. "The Abolition Movement in Minnesota." *Minnesota History* 32 (1951): 15–33; Painter, Nell Irvin. *Sojourner Truth: A Life, A Symbol*. New York: W.W. Norton & Co., 1996.

Michael D. Pierson

T

Tacky Rebellion. *See* Maroons of Jamaica/Tacky Rebellion

Tappan, Arthur (1786–1865)

Arthur Tappan, with his younger brother, **Lewis Tappan,** became one of the most famous abolitionists in the United States. The brothers helped establish the **American Anti-Slavery Society** in 1833 and led the fight against slavery throughout the antebellum period. Together, the brothers made millions in business and used their wealth to fund abolitionist and other social reform organizations. Less well-remembered than his brother because of Lewis's role in the famous ***Amistad*** case, Tappan's influential leadership helped create and shape the direction of abolitionism.

Born in 1786 in Massachusetts, Tappan's early life was directed by his mother, Sarah. More forceful than her husband, Benjamin, Sarah instructed her children in a strict, yet loving, way that emphasized a Calvinistic interpretation of the Christian religion. While Lewis often required his mother's reproof and punishment, Tappan was a submissive boy who rarely needed discipline. As Lewis put it in his biography of his brother, Tappan "had the good fortune to escape much chastisement at home, or in school." His submission was rooted, no doubt, in his introspective personality, but may also have stemmed from his mother's constant reminders of the uncertainty of life. She often told him how he had nearly died on several occasions. When combined with his reserved nature, his mother's interpretation that he was alive only by the miracle of God made Tappan an obedient boy. Her influence was so strong that Tappan apparently did not experience an emotional conversion to Christianity. It was as if he had always been saved, and there was no room for doubting this. While his brother briefly became a Unitarian, Lewis's return to orthodoxy was treated with the kind of celebration that often accompanied conversion in evangelical Christian circles. But Tappan inherited his mother's sense of religious mystery and alternating feelings of guilt and gratefulness for being alive.

Tappan entered into business as a teenager, working as a merchant apprentice in Boston. Later he went to Montreal to sell blankets for trade with the

Arthur Tappan. Courtesy of the Library of Congress.

Indians. The War of 1812 interrupted his business, and he lost money in the venture. Upon his return, he borrowed money from Lewis to start an importing business in New York City. He was successful, especially as a silk merchant, and his firm flourished. Located on Pearl Street, his store was a center of fashion, with the latest styles of hats and umbrellas and ladies' apparel. As his business and wealth expanded, Arthur became involved in social and religious reform. Like many other Calvinists in the early nineteenth century, he became an evangelical and joined with other Christians to improve society and save souls. He was one of the founders of the American Tract Society in 1825, gave liberally to the American Sunday School Union, and worked hard to promote education, help prostitutes get off the streets, stop the evils of alcohol, and pass Sabbatarian legislation. His reserved personality and aversion to the urban environment took its toll, however, and he invited his brother to join him in business in 1828. Not long after Lewis arrived, Tappan moved his family to the quieter atmosphere of New Haven, Connecticut.

Even as he struggled with his own guilt, Tappan became convinced of the nation's sin. Urged on by the great revivalist, **Charles Grandison Finney,** Tappan and his brother had become part of a circle of wealthy Christian philanthropists who funded various benevolence organizations, founded colleges, and promoted reform. This included Tappan's generous contributions to Oberlin College in Ohio, a school that became a hotbed of Christian **perfectionism** and abolitionist activity. Convinced of the abolitionist position in the mid-to-late 1820s, Tappan founded an antislavery newspaper, but was hesitant to embrace what he perceived to be the radicalism of outspoken abolitionists such as **William Lloyd Garrison.** This changed by the early 1830s when he helped organize the American Anti-Slavery Society, which came to lead to national movement for abolitionism.

His activism made Tappan very unpopular, and he became the target of mobs and was lampooned in songs and newspapers across the country. When the brothers experienced financial setbacks in the late 1830s after a fire destroyed their warehouses, followed by the Panic of 1837, the Tappans did not despair. They struggled on, honoring their debts and rebuilding their business empire. Tappan responded to all adversity with stoicism and a dogged determination to do his duty. Along with Lewis, he founded the Mercantile Agency, the country's first credit-rating service, to help stabilize the economy in the wake of the Panic of 1837.

Elected president of the American Anti-Slavery Society when it was founded, Tappan soon became known as a conservative influence in the organization. Although a devoted abolitionist, he also wanted to remain respectable and was suspicious of the methods of radicals like Garrison. His quiet personality made him an unlikely choice for top leadership and, although other abolitionists appreciated his financial donations, they doubted his abilities to bring about real change. In the movement, as in his own business, Tappan followed a strict, cautious line of financial responsibility. While this worked well in keeping the society solvent, it was unpopular with those who wanted to move more quickly and use dramatic methods. His cautious nature also led him to move briefly toward gradual emancipation, rather than the more radical immediatism called for by Garrison. This brought widespread criticism, and Garrison used it to ask Tappan to step aside. Instead, Tappan recanted his heresy, returned to supporting **immediate emancipation,** and donated a large sum of money to buy the forgiveness of the radicals.

Tappan made many mistakes and often seemed reluctant to support the radical abolitionists completely. From the perspective of later generations, he was not a saint and not a great hero. In part this was due to his personality and the fact that he left very few papers and made very few public speeches. His brother, Lewis, was by far the more popular candidate for abolitionist sainthood, as he remained active in the movement up to the Civil War, pushed for the most radical methods, and supported the *Amistad* slaves in their famous case. Eventually, Lewis himself tried to restore Tappan to his proper place in the history of abolition by publishing a biography of his brother, but even that was not enough. Some scholars believe that Lewis was too modest and attributed some of his own work to his older brother. Despite his flaws and his somewhat ambivalent record, Tappan was an important leader of the abolitionist movement and his contributions were more than just financial in nature. In the context of the 1830s, he was at the forefront of the fight against slavery and deserves to be remembered for his efforts. *See also* Garrisonians; Unitarianism and Antislavery.

Further Readings: Tappan, Lewis. *The Life of Arthur Tappan.* 1870. Westport, CT: Negro Universities Press, 1970; Wyatt-Brown, Bertram. *Lewis Tappan and the Evangelical War against Slavery.* 1969. Baton Rouge: Louisiana State University Press, 1997.

A. James Fuller

Tappan, Lewis (1788–1873)

Lewis Tappan, Christian reformer, businessman, and philanthropist, epitomized evangelical abolitionism in nineteenth-century America. A signal leader in numerous benevolent associations, Tappan believed in antislavery as a righteous cause. No American abolitionist had a longer or more dedicated career.

Raised in Massachusetts by devout Congregational parents, Benjamin and Sarah Tappan, Lewis retained a lifelong dedication to piety and social conscience. After a short-lived youthful embrace of **Unitarianism** in Massachusetts, Tappan joined the New York silk merchandising firm of wealthy older brother **Arthur Tappan** in 1827, where he not only managed operations but also entered Arthur's world of orthodox evangelicalism. Together with other pious New York businessmen, they founded the *Evangelist* in 1827 and hired Joshua Leavitt to edit the new journal. The Tappans supported the Free Church movement to make seating and membership in a church not contingent upon payment of a fee. Combining this policy with their new dedication to popular enthusiastic preaching associated with the Second Great Awakening, they helped organize the Chatham Street Chapel as a part-time home for fiery revivalist **Charles G. Finney**.

The Tappan brothers' conversions to abolitionism came gradually, but by 1833 Arthur had helped launch the *Emancipator*, hiring Elizur Wright, Jr., as secretary. Conversations with **Theodore Dwight Weld** turned Lewis to **immediate emancipation,** and in 1833 the Tappans, staying just ahead of an antiabolitionist mob, inaugurated the New York Anti-Slavery Society at the Chatham Street Chapel. That December the first national antislavery convention witnessed Lewis bridging the interests of the New York organization and the more liberal Boston-based **Garrisonians**. Both Tappan brothers held high positions in the **American Anti-Slavery Society (AASS)** that issued from that meeting, and helped author its declaration that slavery was both a crime and a sin. To promote Christian abolitionism's westward expansion, they supported Lyman Beecher and Lane Seminary in Cincinnati; later, Arthur put his substantial fortune behind founding the more radically antislavery Oberlin College in northeastern Ohio.

Lewis Tappan's talents as an editor, fundraiser, and administrator were tremendously useful in the war against slavery. Belief that moral suasion could produce manumissions led him to mount a massive **postal campaign** in 1835 directed at Southern slaveholders. The South's furious reaction against this campaign earned the antislavery movement national attention and chastened Lewis's confidence that moral suasion alone would convert the South to abolition.

William Lloyd Garrison's growing radicalism only increased the Tappan brothers' discomfort with non-evangelical abolitionists, and contributed to a schism in the national organization in 1841 and the Garrisonians gaining control of the AASS. Lewis immediately led a handful of men centered in New York City to form the **American and Foreign Anti-Slavery Society (AFASS)** that, like its British model, stressed international cooperation among antislavery reformers. Their numbers were small: internecine bickering and the challenges of conducting business in a climate of notoriety had recently led Arthur to retrench from visible antislavery activity, while other former cohorts stayed with Garrison in the AASS, retired, or sought political solutions through participation in the newly formed **Liberty Party.**

In 1839, Lewis Tappan formed a committee to free jailed Africans who had recently mutinied and murdered some crew members on the Cuban slaving schooner *Amistad*. The case, which attracted national attention, provided a ready outlet for Tappan's talents as administrator, publicist, religious teacher, and legal advisor. A few years later, the crisis over Texas annexation inspired Tappan to travel to England, where he failed to convince British leaders to acquire Texas for the empire and concurrently block the spread of American slavery.

In England, Tappan witnessed the potential value of third-party political action. Upon his return, he began to support the Liberty Party, and founded their popular journal, the *National Era*, under the editorship of the dynamic **Gamaliel Bailey**. Politically, antislavery's propensity for pragmatism and compromise disquieted Tappan, however, and when its various factions combined with assorted disaffected partisans to form the Free Soil Party in 1848, Tappan, shocked and wounded, refused to join.

Political interest soon gave way to pursuits more suited to a pious evangelical whose primary objection to slavery had always been its spiritually destructive effects. Tappan refocused his efforts on Christian abolitionism. In 1842, his *Amistad* committee had merged with the black-founded Union Mission, an alliance that within a few years expanded into a reconstituted **American Missionary Association** (AMA), an officially nonsectarian organization that nonetheless drew heavily from Congregationalist support. Largely in pursuit of Tappan's dream of an interracial Christian fellowship, the AMA by 1860 had spent over one million dollars on antislavery missions worldwide.

Tappan's visibility as an antislavery reformer waned, yet sectional violence in the 1850s led him to resurrect the AFASS as the American Abolition Society and renew his condemnation of bondage as criminal and unconstitutional. During this period, he also challenged evangelicals who continued to tolerate slavery, an effort that climaxed in a dramatic clash at the American Tract Society's convention in 1856. Although best remembered for his evangelical abolitionism, Tappan was also the founder in 1827 of the *Journal of Commerce* and in 1841 of the Mercantile Agency (later Dun and Bradstreet), the country's first credit reporting agency.

Further Readings: McKivigan, John R. *The War against Proslavery Religion: Abolitionism and the Northern Churches, 1830–1865*. Ithaca, NY: Cornell University Press, 1984; Wyatt-Brown, Bertram. *Lewis Tappan and the Evangelical War against Slavery*. Baton Rouge: Louisiana State University Press, 1969.

Cathy Rodabaugh

Texas, Annexation of (1845)

The annexation of Texas was the central issue in the expansion of slavery into new territories, and the various factions of the antislavery movement united in opposition to it.

In the 1820s, the Mexican government encouraged Americans to migrate to the very sparsely settled lands of Mexico's most northern province, Texas. Many came from the Southern states, and brought their slaves with them. But having abolished slavery in 1829, Mexico reversed its settlement policy in 1830 and prohibited both further American immigration and the importation of slaves. In 1835, Texas revolted against Mexican rule, winning its independence in 1836 and establishing the Republic of Texas. Immediately after and for the next nine years, Texas nevertheless actively sought annexation to the United States.

In 1835, the abolitionist **Benjamin Lundy** wrote two pamphlets denouncing the Texas revolution as an effort to restore slavery where it had been abolished and create the opportunity for the United States to annex it. Most opponents of annexation followed his lead. **John Quincy Adams** delivered lengthy speeches in 1836 and 1838 opposing the annexation of Texas, casting the measure as risking war for the benefit of slavery. Texas was a key component in what antislavery forces saw as a Slave Power conspiracy. On March 3, 1843, Adams and several other antislavery congressmen issued an address depicting the annexation of Texas as a measure to insure the permanent rule of the slave states over the free states.

The antislavery furor prevented Jackson and Van Buren from annexing Texas. In 1843, John Tyler actively revived the project. He sent Duff Green as his personal representative in Great Britain to speak to Texas officials there and to ascertain British intentions in Texas. Green concluded that British abolitionists wanted to use the promise of guaranteed loans to force Texas to abolish slavery, which would serve as a prelude to attacking the institution in the United States, in part by encircling the Southern states with colonies and nations where slavery had been outlawed. Tyler and his allies tried to portray the annexation of a slave state as a benefit to the North. In January 1844, Senator Robert J. Walker put forth the theory that a slave Texas would tend to draw slavery further south, and prevent the migration of escaped slaves to the north. Walker cited statistics from the 1840 census, which purported to show a high incidence of insanity among free blacks. The effort failed, and the Senate rejected an annexation treaty in June 1844. In the closing days of his administration, Tyler achieved the annexation of Texas through a joint resolution of Congress. Opponents of annexation considered the joint resolution as the triumph of the Slave Power over the **United States Constitution.** It certainly helped prompt the United States' war with Mexico. *See also* Slave Power Argument.

Further Readings: Hietala, Thomas R. *Manifest Design: Anxious Aggrandizement in Late Jacksonian America.* Ithaca, NY: Cornell University Press, 1985; Merk, Frederick. *Slavery and the Annexation of Texas.* New York: Alfred A. Knopf, 1972; Pletcher, David. *The Diplomacy of Annexation: Texas, Oregon and the Mexican War.* Columbia: University of Missouri Press, 1973.

Robert W. Smith

Thirteenth Amendment (1865)

The Thirteenth Amendment abolished slavery and involuntary servitude in the United States. Adopted by two-thirds of Congress in January 1865, and declared ratified by three-fourths of the states in December of that year, the measure declared in its first clause that "Neither slavery nor involuntary servitude, except as a punishment for crime whereof the party shall have been duly convicted, shall exist within the United States, or any place subject to their jurisdiction." In its second clause, the amendment added that "Congress shall have power to enforce this article by appropriate legislation."

The amendment represented a monumental, if largely unanticipated, consequence of the Civil War. In the first year of the war, political leaders of the Union promised not to interfere with slavery where it already existed, a promise that **Abraham Lincoln** and others of the Republican Party had

Reading the Emancipation Proclamation. Courtesy of the Library of Congress.

made in the 1860 election campaign. Lincoln even supported a constitutional amendment, sometimes called the "first Thirteenth Amendment," adopted by Congress in March 1861, which prohibited federal interference with slavery where it existed. The proposed amendment was signed by President Lincoln, on the day of his inauguration (March 4, 1861)—the only amendment ever signed by a president—and later that day was sent to all states for ratification. Three states actually ratified it and more might have had it not been for events unfolding in the South.

As the war continued beyond the first year, more Northern whites accepted, if not encouraged, the use of emancipation as a war measure against the Confederacy. Union commanders, who during the first year of the war had been instructed by the Lincoln administration to return escaped slaves to their owners, began to follow the lead of General Benjamin Butler, who from the beginning of the war had refused to return African Americans and instead declared them "**contraband**" of war. Congress endorsed the contraband policy by passing **Confiscation Acts** in 1861 and 1862, which declared that all rebel property, including slaves, would be seized by the Union. The initiative taken by runaway slaves, by military commanders, and by Congress ultimately led President Lincoln to issue the Emancipation Proclamation, which declared "forever free" all slaves in rebellious areas. However, the Proclamation exempted those slaves in Union-controlled regions of the South and Border States. Lincoln signed the final Emancipation Proclamation on January 1, 1863.

After Lincoln signed the Proclamation, abolitionists used petition drives to press for a broader act of emancipation. In April 1864, the U.S. Senate adopted a resolution for an antislavery amendment, but the House of Representatives failed to carry it in June. Lincoln ensured that the amendment was on the national platform of the Republican Party that summer. Lincoln and the Republicans scored victories in the fall elections, and the president claimed the vote as a popular endorsement of the amendment. He urged the House of Representatives to take up the measure again. Using informal cajoling as well as offers of patronage, Lincoln applied pressure to lame-duck Democratic congressmen to win their votes. Rumors floated through Washington that Lincoln's agents were bribing congressmen on behalf of the amendment, but no evidence of bribery has ever been uncovered. Enough Democrats changed their vote or absented themselves so that on January 31, 1865, the House of Representatives carried the amendment. States across the North immediately began to ratify the amendment, though some such as New Jersey initially voted against ratification. After Lincoln's assassination and the end of the war, President Andrew Johnson made ratification a condition of Southern states' readmission to the Union. On December 18, 1865, Secretary of State **William Henry Seward** issued a proclamation that the amendment had been ratified by three fourths of the states.

Almost immediately, Congress began to debate the meaning of the amendment. While Democrats and conservative Republicans argued that it merely abolished chattel slavery and secured no rights to the freed people, moderate and **Radical Republicans** claimed that the measure guaranteed equal rights for African Americans. The argument for equality won the day: Republican congressmen used the amendment's enforcement clause to create the Civil Rights Act of 1866, the first clause of which guaranteed "full and equal benefit of all laws and proceedings" to African Americans. They also invoked the amendment to renew the **Freedmen's Bureau,** which had been created in 1865. Congress carried both the act renewing the Freedmen's Bureau and the Civil Rights Act of 1866 over the veto of President Andrew Johnson, who had begun to court the support of conservatives. Ultimately, the Thirteenth Amendment was eclipsed by the Fourteenth Amendment, which was adopted in 1868 and added specificity to freedom by setting the terms of citizenship and explicitly prohibiting states from denying "due process" and equality before the law.

The long-term effects of the Thirteenth Amendment were limited. The measure became an important weapon against various forms of involuntary servitude, but its phrasing allowed peonage, or debt slavery, to persist into the twentieth century. The most common victims of this form of servitude were African Americans, the very people meant to benefit from the Thirteenth Amendment.

Although the Thirteenth Amendment is overshadowed by the Fourteenth, the measure retains great significance. Civil rights lawyers still use the amendment, sometimes with success. In the Supreme Court case of *Jones v. Mayer* of 1968, for example, the Court accepted the Thirteenth Amendment as the basis for overturning discriminatory housing practices. The amendment remains a perpetual monument to the cause of freedom in the

United States. Slavery, a word not used in the original Constitution, had long been protected by it. With the Thirteenth Amendment, slavery was officially abolished. *See also* Democratic Party and Antislavery; Radical Republicans; United States Constitution and Antislavery.

Further Readings: Hyman, Harold M., and William M. Wiecek. *Equal Justice Under Law: Constitutional Development, 1835–1875.* New York: Harper and Row, 1982; Tsesis, Alexander. *The Thirteenth Amendment and American Freedom.* New York: New York University Press, 2004; Vorenberg, Michael. *Final Freedom: The Civil War, the Abolition of Slavery, and the Thirteenth Amendment.* Cambridge: Cambridge University Press, 2001.

Michael Vorenberg

Thompson, George (1804–1878)

George Thompson was a British abolitionist and wide-ranging reformer whose chief importance was his leadership of **Garrisonians** in the United Kingdom. Thompson began his professional career as a reformer in 1831, when he became a salaried lecturer for the Agency Committee and participated extensively in the popular campaign that culminated in the emancipation bill of 1833. In that same year, when **William Lloyd Garrison** traveled to England, he began a lifelong friendship with Thompson, whose eclectic radicalism and commitment to reform by moral suasion affirmed Garrison's views. The following year, at Garrison's invitation, Thompson visited the United States for a lecturing tour that became the defining moment of his abolitionist career.

Before leaving for the United States, Thompson helped to organize antislavery societies in Glasgow and Edinburgh; his influence among Scottish abolitionists remained strong throughout his life. Embryonic though they were, these societies funded Thompson's 1834 Atlantic crossing. Thompson arrived in New England in October and remained for a year, lecturing from Massachusetts to Maine on the virtues of **immediate emancipation** and the viability of Anglo-American cooperation in the antislavery struggle. But where Thompson saw cooperation, his enemies sensed conspiracy. Thompson's visit fueled antiabolitionist paranoia that English support was behind radical Garrisonianism; he was routinely tarred with accusations of "foreign interference." In 1835, as antiabolitionism moved rapidly from verbal abuse to violence, Thompson's lectures were sometimes disrupted or threatened by rioters. The great Boston mob that nearly lynched Garrison on October 21 formed in part because of rumors that Thompson would be speaking before a meeting of the Boston Female Anti-Slavery Society. A month later, Thompson returned to Britain and broadcast news of his violent reception, thus contributing to a growing belief in England that American abolitionists were martyrs.

Thompson continued as an advocate of Garrisonian abolitionism in Britain even after the 1840 schism in the **American Anti-Slavery Society,** during which most British abolitionists sympathized with **Lewis Tappan** and **James Birney**. In the 1840s, he allied himself with a variety of British reforms, including the Anti-Corn Law League and moral-force Chartism. Thompson turned most of his attention, however, to land reform in British

India, serving as an agent of the Aborigines' Protection Society and a lecturer for the British India Society. He agreed with some other British abolitionists that the cultivation of Indian cotton by free labor, combined with free trade policies, would deprive slave-grown American cotton of its European markets, thus hastening the end of slavery. In 1843 and 1844, Thompson made his first visit to India to investigate land tenure policies, but was distracted by his defense of the Rajah of Satara, who claimed to have been unjustly deposed by British officials. In subsequent years, Thompson took up the Rajah's cause in England.

In the general election of 1847, Thompson was elected to Parliament by the London district that Stephen Lushington, a distinguished jurist and abolitionist, had represented. But when he toured America again in 1850 and 1851, this time as a member of the British government, cries about the impropriety of his "foreign interference" were raised both by enemies abroad and constituents at home. In 1852, Thompson lost his seat in the House of Commons. After his defeat in 1852, Thompson became involved in scattered enterprises, but his activity and influence waned. Financial difficulties hounded the last quarter-century of his life. He remained close friends with American Garrisonians, who on occasion tried to raise funds to support him. From 1863 to 1867, Thompson even lived in Roxbury, Massachusetts, near Garrison, and witnessed the final throes of the Civil War. He joined Garrison in supporting **Abraham Lincoln**'s reelection in 1864, and in 1865, he introduced Garrison at the flag-raising ceremony at Fort Sumter that symbolized the end of the conflict. Returning to England in 1867, he died in Leeds in 1878.

Although a consistent ally of the Garrisonians, Thompson was hardly controlled by them. At the **World's Antislavery Convention (1840),** he disappointed Garrisonians by not denouncing the exclusion of women. He often frustrated his allies by his interest in other reform causes and his lack of financial acumen. His brief stint as a Member of Parliament also concerned Garrisonians, who opposed politics on principle. But despite these occasional disagreements, Thompson was one of the few nationally renowned British abolitionists whom Garrisonians could always count on as an ally. He served as an important liaison between British and American antislavery radicals, introducing many in the United Kingdom to the Garrisonians' ideas, and his transatlantic trips impacted the course of the American movement at key junctures in its history. *See also* British Slavery, Abolition of; Scotland, Antislavery in.

Further Readings: Rice, C. Duncan. "The Anti-Slavery Mission of George Thompson to the United States, 1834–1835." *Journal of American Studies* 2 (1968): 13–31; Rice, C. Duncan. *The Scots Abolitionists, 1833–1861.* Baton Rouge: Louisiana State University Press, 1981; Temperley, Howard. *British Antislavery, 1833–1870.* London: Longman, 1972.

W. Caleb McDaniel

Tocqueville, Alexis de (1805–1859)

French historian, political theorist, and statesman, Tocqueville was born Alexis Charles Henri Maurice Clerel de Tocqueville in Paris. Throughout his public life, he opposed slavery on Christian principles, the philosophy of the rights of man, and the pragmatic concerns of the French colonies.

The child of an aristocratic family, Tocqueville studied law and became an assistant magistrate in 1825. In 1831, Tocqueville and his friend, Gustave de Beaumont, traveled around the United States for nine months with a commission to study the American penal system. Tocqueville also had a larger interest in understanding how democracy worked in the United States. His observations were published in a two-volume tour-de-force entitled *Democracy in America* (1835). While Beaumont would publish a book specifically about slavery, Tocqueville also expressed concern about the institution in *Democracy in America*, calling it "evil." Yet he recognized the problems for a fuller black inclusion in American society because the vicious racism toward free blacks in the North largely barred them from civic life.

In 1835, after his return to France, he became a charter member of the Society for the Abolition of Slavery. After being elected to the Chamber of Deputies in 1839, he served as reporter on a commission to investigate the abolitionist proposal of Destutt de Tracy. Tocqueville's report, critical of the policy of gradual emancipation as impractical, advocated for the **immediate emancipation** of slaves in the French colonies as in the best economic interest of both slaves and planters. Although the Chamber of Deputies never discussed the report, Tocqueville sent it to friends in the United States who published and circulated it widely. Concerned about the inaction of the French government, in 1843 he published anonymously a series of articles for the opposition newspaper, *La Siècle*, arguing for the necessity of emancipation. The honor of France, he insisted, was at stake. Moreover, with slavery ended in Britain's Caribbean colonies, French slaves on Caribbean islands would surely flee to the British. The French colonies were thus in jeopardy of losing their labor force unless the slaves were emancipated.

Tocqueville's final public discussion of slavery occurred in 1845 during a series of debates in the Chamber of Deputies where he argued for establishing laws to improve the conditions of slavery in the French colonies. He maintained that they would establish France's, rather than the colonies', authority over slavery and thus lay the foundation for the French government to abolish slavery in the near future. *See also* Literature and Abolition.

Further Readings: Gershman, Sally. "Alexis de Tocqueville and Slavery." *French Historical Studies* 9 (Spring 1976): 467–483; Jardin, Andre. *Tocqueville: A Biography.* Lydia Davis with Robert Hemenway, trans. New York: Farrar Straus Giroux, 1988; Tocqueville, Alexis de. *Democracy in America.* George Lawrence, trans. J. P. Mayer, ed. Garden City, NY: Anchor Books, 1969.

Daniel P. Kotzin

Truth, Sojourner (c. 1797–1883)

Sojourner Truth was born Isabella Van Wagenen in about 1797 as a slave in Hurley, New York. During her life as a slave, she allegedly bore thirteen

I SELL THE SHADOW TO SUPPORT THE SUBSTANCE. SOJOURNER TRUTH,

Sojourner Truth. Courtesy of the Library of Congress.

children, of which three were sold into slavery. She served five masters until slavery was abolished in the state of New York on July 4, 1827. After experiencing a religious epiphany, the ex-slave Isabella changed her name to Sojourner Truth and became a singing preacher traveling throughout New York and Connecticut.

In 1847, Sojourner Truth became associated with the Northampton Association of Education and Industry, which was founded in 1841 as a community dedicated to abolitionism, pacifism, equality, and the betterment of human life. It was there at Northampton that she became immersed in the abolitionist movement and began working with many of the movement's leaders including **William Lloyd Garrison** and **Frederick Douglass**.

Although illiterate, Sojourner Truth's memoirs were published in 1850 with the assistance of Oliver Gilbert (a fellow abolitionist) as *The Narrative of Sojourner Truth: A Northern Slave*. Her book, along with her speaking skills, propelled her to the front of both the abolitionist and women's rights movements and she spoke broadly in the lyceum circuit. Her most famous speech—"Ar'n't I a Woman?"—was made at a women's convention in Ohio in 1851.

In 1857, Sojourner Truth moved to Battle Creek, Michigan and after the **Emancipation Proclamation** she relocated to Washington, D.C., where she worked to gain support for a land distribution program for former slaves. This effort failed when Congress refused to enact the bill. Afterward, she returned to her home in Battle Creek. All in all, she dedicated over forty years of her life to denouncing slavery, promoting women's equality, and later, after slavery ended, to promoting equality for blacks and providing assistance to ex-slaves in need. Surrounded by family and friends, this influential icon died in 1883. *See also* Gender and Slave Emancipation; Gender Relations within Abolitionism.

Further Reading: Painter, Nell Irvin. *Sojourner Truth: A Life, A Symbol.* New York: W.W. Norton & Co., 1996.

Iris Hunter

Tubman, Harriet (c. 1825–1913)

Born into slavery as Araminta Ross, Harriet Tubman was a self-emancipated woman, conductor of the **Underground Railroad,** abolitionist, feminist, soldier, and philanthropist. As a multi-faceted person, her family, friends, and acquaintances also knew her as Moses, Aunt Harriet, Minty, and

General Tubman. Tubman fought to eradicate slavery in the United States by rescuing enslaved Africans and their families from a life of anguish.

Tubman was born near Bucktown in Dorchester County, Maryland, to Harriet (Rittia) Green and Benjamin Ross. As an enslaved child, Tubman was hired out to several families, working as a muskrat trapper, nursemaid, and domestic. In her adolescent years, she was assigned to manual labor. In 1844, Tubman married a free black, John Tubman. In 1849, she escaped the bonds of slavery, leaving her former slave life and moving to Philadelphia, where she initiated contacts and networks with local abolitionists. Tubman's marriage ended shortly after her escape.

In 1850, she returned to Maryland as a conductor of the Underground Railroad and made her first rescue. Initially, Tubman focused her efforts on relocating her siblings and their families to St. Catherine's, Upper **Canada** (present day Ontario, Canada) via Underground Railroad networks in Maryland, Pennsylvania, and New York. However, her fight against slavery expanded to include non-family members from the Dorchester county area. She confidently rescued and directed approximately 120 enslaved Africans and their families to free states in the North and to Upper Canada.

Harriet was not formally educated and relied on her impeccable memory, her astute Christian

Harriet Tubman. Courtesy of the Library of Congress.

beliefs, her prophetic abilities, and use of pictographs to complete successful Underground Railroad journeys. Her successful career as an Underground Railroad conductor was extraordinary, since she was one of the most famous and most wanted runaways in the United States. Several slaveholders and planters in the Maryland area offered large bounties for Tubman's arrest or her head.

As General Tubman, she participated in fundraising efforts for John Brown's unsuccessful war against the United States government to end slavery. She recruited African American soldiers for Brown's war and for the Union army during the Civil War. She served in the South Carolina branch of the Union army, working as a laundress, cook, nurse, and spy. During Reconstruction, she directed her attention to women's suffrage movements and dedicated her life to the betterment of African Americans. In 1869, Tubman wedded Civil War veteran, Charles Nelson Davis. Davis and Tubman spent the rest of their lives committed to improving the lives of African Americans in Auburn, New York.

In 1897, Tubman was recognized by Britain's Queen Victoria and awarded the Silver medal for her fight against slavery. In 1990, President

George H.W. Bush declared March 10 as Harriet Tubman Day, acknowledging her passion and dedication to ending slavery in the United States.

Further Readings: Clinton, Catherine. *Harriet Tubman: The Road to Freedom.* New York: Little, Brown and Co., 2004; Humez, Jean. *Harriet Tubman: The Life and the Life Stories.* Madison: University of Wisconsin Press, 2003; Larson, Kate Clifford. *Bound for the Promised Land: Harriet Tubman, Portrait of an American Hero.* New York: Ballantine, 2004; Harriet Tubman Historical Society [Online, August 2005]. www.harriettubman.com; Underground Railroad Web links [Online, August 2005]. Harriet Tubman Resource Centre on the African Diaspora www.yorku.ca/nhp.

Nadine Hunt

Tucker, St. George (1752–1827)

St. George Tucker was a Virginia lawyer, judge, law professor, and legal scholar. He was born in Bermuda and raised in that slaveholding society. His father, Henry Tucker, was a successful merchant, whose holdings included land and slaves. St. George was comfortable with slaves and slavery. It was part of his life on an island where half the population was enslaved. In 1771, at age nineteen, he migrated to the Virginia colony to attend the College of William and Mary, studying law with George Wythe, the first true professor of law in America, and the same man who had taught Thomas Jefferson a decade earlier. Here he was once again immersed in a culture of slavery. His mentor, Wythe, was a slaveholder but also a critic of the institution. Wythe ultimately took a strong stand against slavery, emancipating his own slaves and bravely attempting to strike down slavery by judicial fiat in the case of *Hudgins v. Wrights* (1803), where as a trial court judge, Wythe declared slavery to be in violation of the Virginia Declaration of Rights.

After studying at William and Mary, Tucker was admitted to the Virginia bar in 1774 and then returned to Bermuda. When the American Revolution began, Tucker returned to Virginia as a merchant, bringing gunpowder and salt for the patriot cause from his native Bermuda to his adopted homeland. He subsequently joined the militia, rising to the rank of Lt. Colonel and being wounded at Yorktown. As the war wound down, Tucker began to practice law in his now adopted country, served on the Board of Visitors of his alma mater, and rose rapidly in the legal/political world of post-war Virginia, arguing cases before the state's highest courts, publishing political tracts, and serving as a delegate to the failed Annapolis Convention. Tucker served as a judge in 1788 and in 1790 succeeded Wythe to the chair in law at William and Mary.

Like many elite Virginians of the immediate post-Revolutionary era, Tucker understood that slavery was a danger to society and incompatible with Republican institutions. He told his students at William and Mary that it was "hard to determine" just "how far" was "the condition of these unfortunate people . . . reconcilable to the principles of our government." In the aftermath of the Revolution he wondered "whether there is a due consistency between our avowed principles and our practice."

Unlike other Virginians who were troubled by the inconsistencies of proclaiming liberty and owning slaves, Tucker set his mind to figuring out how to deal with the issue. He did not focus on his personal status as a slave-owner. Nor did he agonize about slavery, becoming paralyzed by the enormity of the problem as his friend Jefferson did. Rather, he focused on the public policy question. He asked the activist's question: how do we end this institution? More to the point, he framed it with the mind of the practical lawyer: how do we end this institution safely and with as little social dislocation as possible? Tucker, the law professor, also asked the scholar's question: how have other societies, other states in the new Union, eliminated the problem?

This led him to write *A Dissertation on Slavery: With a Proposal For the Gradual Abolition of It, in the State of Virginia*, which he published in 1796. This was the only serious proposal to end slavery written by a Southerner in this period. The dissertation contains a short history of slavery in Virginia, and a reasonably good summary of all legislation on slavery in Virginia. The heart of the *Dissertation* was a plan to end slavery gradually, through a complicated and convoluted system of partial emancipation over many years. Under Tucker's plan, the daughters of all slave women born in Virginia, but not the sons, would be born free. Those daughters would have been kept as servants of their mother's master until they turned twenty-eight, at which time they would be completely free. Their children, however, would be bound out as apprentices until age twenty-one. Meanwhile, the sons of all slave women would be born as slaves for life. This meant that for at least twenty-eight years after the plan went into effect *all* blacks in the state, except those already free, would remain in some form of bondage. At that point, twenty-eight-year-old women would start to become free. Their children, male and female, would be born free, but would be indentured until age twenty-one. Tucker estimated that this system would keep some blacks in bondage for more than a century.

In addition to regulating black labor, Tucker would have prohibited free blacks from owning land, inheriting property, or participating in civic life at all. Tucker believed his system would allow planters to control black labor, while gradually ending slavery. He thought that in a century-long process blacks and whites could learn to live together in this new environment, or else blacks would gradually leave the state.

Tucker addressed his dissertation to the state legislature, which completely ignored it. He distributed it as a pamphlet and reprinted it in 1803 as an appendix to his five-volume edition of *Blackstone's Commentaries*. By the time he published the *Commentaries*, there was no support at all for his proposal. Even Tucker himself seemed to realize it was a proposal that would go nowhere.

Tucker was no abolitionist. He realized that a speedy emancipation would be unacceptable to Virginia's white majority and that it would have led to great social disruption. He offered a gradual solution to the problem of slavery, but his plan was so convoluted and complex that it is unlikely very many Virginians even understood it, much less endorsed it. Nevertheless, it was the *only* attempt by an elite Southerner to deal with the problem of slavery in the new state. Tucker's effort might have led to further debate and perhaps a more refined and practical answer to the problem if other Virginians, especially his friend Thomas Jefferson, had entered the debate. But, Jefferson chose to keep his comments on slavery private, and never took a public stand against the institution.

A few years after publishing his edition of the *Commentaries*, Tucker wrote the opinion of Virginia's highest court in the case of *Hudgins v. Wrights* (1806). The case involved the Wright family, which claimed to be free on the grounds that their maternal ancestor was not a black slave, but an American Indian. In the lower court, Chancellor George Wythe had ruled the Wrights were free since they were not black, but also because the Virginia Declaration of Rights declared that "all men are by nature equally free and independent and have certain inherent rights, of which, when they enter into a state of society, they cannot by any compact, deprive or divest their posterity; namely the enjoyment of life and liberty, with the means of acquiring and possessing property, and pursuing and obtaining happiness and safety." Tucker upheld the freedom of the Wrights on racial grounds, and indeed, set out a standard based on race for determining who was a slave and who was not, but he flatly rejected Wythe's assertion that the Virginia Declaration of Rights affected the status of slaves in the state. Tucker wrote: "I do not concur with the Chancellor in his reasoning on the operation of the first clause of the Bill of Rights, which was notoriously framed with a cautious eye to this subject, and was meant to embrace the case of free citizens or aliens only; and not by a side wind to overturn the rights of property." Thus,. despite the opportunity, Tucker declined to strike a blow against all bondage in Virginia. His antislavery notions were limited to a slow and agonizingly gradual end to slavery. It seems anything else was too dangerous to contemplate for this slaveholding Virginian who, more than any of his neighbors and friends, understood the dangers slavery posed for his society. Though unable to devise a practical solution to slavery, Tucker remains the only Virginian to offer any plan to end slavery in that state.

Further Readings: Finkelman, Paul. *Slavery and the Founders: Race and Liberty in the Age of Jefferson.* 2nd ed. Armonk, NY: M.E. Sharpe, 2001; Finkelman, Paul. "The Dragon St. George Could Not Slay: Tucker's Plan to End Slavery." *William and Mary Law Review* 47 (2006): 1213–1243.

Paul Finkelman

Tupac Amaru II (1738–1781)

A famous indigenous leader in colonial Peru, Tupac Amaru II was born Jose Gabriel Condorcanqui in a small town called Surimana, about sixty miles from Cuzco, the former capital of the pre-Columbian Inca Empire. He was descended from Felipe Tupac Amaru, the last Inca to resist the siege of Spanish conquerors at Vilcabamba. Tupac Amaru II was a *curaca*—or indigenous leader—of the towns of Tungasuca, Surimana and Pampamarca. As with all indigenous leaders in Colonial Peru, he was exempted from paying the tribute, spoke Spanish and Quechua (an important indigenous language in the Central Andes) and attended the school that the Jesuit Congregation had in colonial Cuzco for the sons of the *curacas*. His descent from an Inca royal family also entitled him to use his royal last name, *Tupac Amaru*. Although he became a prosperous merchant, he had many concerns about the life and social conditions of the common indigenous population. He asked for the colonial rulers to liberate the indigenous population from forced labor in the mines, but they refused.

Deeply disillusioned and supported by his relatives and other indigenous people, Tupac Amaru II organized the most important rebellion in late colonial Peru. The rebellion began in Tinta on November 4, 1780, when the rebels executed the regional governor of Tinta, Antonio de Arriaga. Failing to secure an end to abuses by the regional governors (*corregidores*) and improvements in the life of the indigenous population, the rebellion spread quickly from Tinta to the entire Andean region around Lake Titicaca. The rebels laid siege to Cuzco but never actually entered the city. Seeking further support, Jose Gabriel Tupac Amaru declared that all the black slaves who joined with him would be free. As it unfolded, the rebellion increasingly became more radical, more anti-Hispanic, and more antislavery. Finally, the rebels were defeated and Jose Gabriel Tupac Amaru was tortured and then killed in Cuzco's main square in 1781. Almost all of his family, including his wife, Micaela Bastidas, suffered the same fate. Only one of the members of the Tupac Amaru family survived, his little son, Fernando.

After his death, the rebellion continued, but only for a brief period of time. Although all traditions identified as "Inca" were now outlawed, the *curacas* who had helped to destroy the rebellion remained in their posts. Hated by the colonial rulers, Jose Gabriel Tupac Amaru became an icon during the period when Peru gained its independence. He has been reclaimed as a patriotic champion by twentieth century political groups ranging from the right wing to the more radical leftist organizations such as *Movimiento Revolucionario Tupac Amaru*. Jose Gabriel Tupac Amaru remains heralded nationally because of his defense of native Peruvians, his opposition to the colonial rulers, and his bold call for the emancipation of the enslaved population. *See also* Spanish Empire, Antislavery and Abolition in.

Further Readings: Duthurburu, Jose Antonio del Busto. *José Gabriel Túpac Amaru antes de su rebellion*. Lima: Pontificia Universidad Católica del Perú, 1981; O'Phelan, Scarlett. *Rebellions and Revolts in Eighteenth Century Peru and Upper Peru*. Koln: Böhlau Verlag, 1985; Stavig, Ward. *The World of Túpac Amaru*. Lincoln: University of Nebraska Press, 1999.

Luis Gomez

Turner, Nat (1800–1831)

Nat Turner is best known for the 1831 slave revolt he led in plantation-dotted Southampton County, Virginia. A decade before his eponymous revolt, Turner had a vision that he would lead a slave rebellion. Despite having escaped from slavery in 1821, Turner's vision compelled him to return voluntarily to his former plantation, where he would bide his time until the moment for rebellion was nigh. In the late 1820s, Turner began preaching to slave congregations. His sermons focused on themes like freedom,

Capture of Nat Turner, leader of slave revolt in 1831. Courtesy of the North Wind Picture Archives.

liberation, and redemption. His powerful exhortations attracted many followers, some of whom would refer to Turner as "The Prophet." As a preacher, Turner had the liberty to travel to different plantations, which was ideal for reconnaissance and rallying support from local slaves.

Turner interpreted a solar eclipse in February 1831 as a sign to begin his rebellion. He planned to launch it on July 4; the date was chosen intentionally for its symbolic importance. However, Turner fell ill, so the revolt was postponed until August 22. (This was the anniversary of the 1791 slave uprising in Saint Domingue, which probably inspired Turner and his coconspirators.) The revolt began at the home of Joseph Travis (Turner's owner), where the rebels killed everyone in the household. Turner planned to move from plantation to plantation, killing all the whites. He made it clear that this strategy was only a means of intimidating whites and inspiring other slaves to join his cause. Once the rebellion had achieved critical mass, Turner expected the indiscriminate violence to abate.

Turner turned his insurgents towards an arsenal in Jerusalem, Virginia. However, as more supporters joined the rebellion, Turner had to contend with collapsing organization in his ranks. After three days, the rebels were dispersed by militiamen, who killed more than 100 slaves while suppressing the revolt. Turner survived as a fugitive until he was captured on October 30, 1831. He was tried, sentenced to death, and hanged on November 11, 1831. While awaiting execution, Turner recounted his hopes and plans to his attorney, Thomas Gray. Gray later published *Nat Turner's Confessions*.

Nat Turner's revolt was the most violent slave uprising in American history. The brief rebellion and its brutal repression left almost 200 people dead on the plantations of Southampton County, Virginia. Later, more than 100 slaves were executed for their involvement in the uprising. Eugene Genovese, the noted historian of American slavery, has suggested that Turner's revolt was a turning point in the movement towards the United States Civil War because it stiffened the resolve of both abolitionists and proslavery advocates. It seemed to vindicate the position of those abolitionists who believed that slaves would fight for their freedom if they were organized and armed from without. (This attitude would have significant implications for someone like John Brown.) As with previous slave revolts, Turner's rebellion encouraged many Southerners to demand harsher restrictions on slaves. After 1831, American abolitionists became more radical in their demands and plantation owners became more bellicose in their support for slavery. The myth of the happy slave died with Nat Turner. *See also* Gabriel's Conspiracy; Haitian Revolution; Literature and Abolition; St. Domingue, French Defeat in; Vesey's Conspiracy.

Further Readings: Genovese, Eugene. *From Rebellion to Revolution: Afro-American Slave Revolts in the Making of the Modern World*. Baton Rouge: Louisiana State University Press, 1979; Greenberg, Kenneth S. *Nat Turner: A Slave Rebellion in History and Memory*. Oxford and New York: Oxford University Press, 2003.

Jennifer J. Pierce

U

Uncle Tom's Cabin (1852)

In 1852, **Harriet Beecher Stowe** took the nation by storm with her anti-slavery novel, *Uncle Tom's Cabin*. A cultural phenomenon rather than a mere book, *Uncle Tom's Cabin* sold some 300,000 copies within a year of its release and went on to become, after the **Bible**, the second-best selling book in the world during the nineteenth century. *Uncle Tom's Cabin* almost immediately gave rise to a number of dramatic productions and spawned a cottage industry in figurines, collectors' plates, and other decorative items that represented popular scenes and characters from Stowe's story. As late as the 1930s, some eighty years after the novel's publication, "Tom shows" toured the United States, making Uncle Tom, Eliza, Topsy, Little Eva, and Simon Legree some of the most recognized literary figures in the nation.

Originally serialized in the *National Era, Uncle Tom's Cabin* emerged out of Harriet Beecher Stowe's anger over the **Fugitive Slave Law** of 1850. Like many white Northerners at the time, Stowe was not an abolitionist. But as a former resident of Cincinnati, gateway to the free North for many slaves, she felt outraged at the cruelty the system inflicted, and was particularly appalled at its destruction of slave families. Prompted by her sister-in-law to "write something" on the subject, Stowe designed a novel that would tug at the heartstrings of men, women, and children who had previously felt little personal connection with, or individual responsibility for, Southern slavery. She also hoped to effect the conversion of slaveholders with her sentimental portrayal of the suffering that

Uncle Tom and Eva from *Uncle Tom's Cabin*. Courtesy of the Library of Congress.

Like the majority of late-nineteenth-century popular editions of Stowe's novel, this "Young Folk's Edition" prominently features what had become the novel's iconographic image, Uncle Tom and Little Eva close together. Anon, cover illustration, Harriet Beecher Stowe, *Uncle Tom's Cabin*, Young Folk's Edition, New York: A. Donahue and Co., n.d. [c. 1890].

slaves endured regardless of the kindness or cruelty of any individual master. As Stowe suggested in *Uncle Tom's Cabin*, even when a slave was owned by an indulgent or compassionate slaveholder, the laws that supported slavery made the existence of all slaves precarious, and likely to be rendered unbearable at a moment's notice.

While Stowe's fictional portrayal of Southern slavery attracted an unprecedented following among white Americans, it also drew considerable criticism. Many Northerners and Southerners alike viewed *Uncle Tom's Cabin* as an affront to slaveholders and a threat to the Union, prompting the publication of both angry reviews and over two dozen "anti-Tom" novels intended to discredit Stowe's representation of slavery. Some abolitionists, on the other hand, pointed out that *Uncle Tom's Cabin* reinforced negative stereotypes of African Americans. Stowe allowed the light-skinned slaves George and Eliza Harris to escape to Canada, even depicting the highly capable George shooting and wounding a white slave catcher along the way. Yet the much blacker, more simple-minded Uncle Tom died a martyr on a Louisiana plantation, rejecting violence to the very end as a legitimate means of gaining freedom. Scholars have long debated whether Tom's choices represent resistance to slavery and loyalty to the slave community or submissiveness to, and even a complicity in, white power. Finally, Stowe's conclusion, in which the entire Harris family relocated to Africa rather than becoming integrated into American society, troubled abolitionists who regarded colonization as a racist policy that worked against black equality. *See also* Literature and Abolition.

Further Reading: Sundquist, Eric, ed. *New Essays on Uncle Tom's Cabin*. New York: Cambridge University Press, 1986.

Sarah N. Roth

Underground Railroad

The essence of the Underground Railroad, to use the National Park Service's Network to Freedom's definition, was "the effort of enslaved African Americans to gain their freedom by escaping bondage." The origin of the term "Underground Railroad" is not known, but it appears to have come into use by the 1830s. As **Frederick Douglass** noted, "secrecy and concealment were necessary conditions to the successful operation of this

A group of slaves escaping in the night. Courtesy of the North Wind Picture Archives.

railroad, and hence its prefix 'underground.'" Several different stories explain the origin of the term. One of the best-known relates to Tice Davids, a freedom seeker who swam the Ohio River from Kentucky to Ripley, Ohio, and disappeared so quickly that his master thought he must have "gone off on an underground road."

Freedom seekers (generally known as fugitives) traveled alone or in groups, with or without help. Usually they were young men, but many women and children also escaped, often as families. Fear of imminent sale was a common motivation. They walked, used horses, boats, ships, wagons, or railroads. Most often, they escaped from the upper South (Maryland, Virginia, Kentucky, or Tennessee), but sometimes people escaped from port cities along the Mississippi River, the Gulf, or the Atlantic. Sometimes they escaped for only a few days to nearby woods or to maroon communities. Often, however, they left permanently. Many headed for **Canada**. A few went to Mexico or the Caribbean, but many also settled in Northern free states. By the late 1830s, Vigilance Committees—the first of them started by David Ruggles and other black abolitionists in New York City in 1835— were quickly organized by black and white Underground Railroad supporters throughout the North, and they openly assisted freedom seekers.

Both African Americans and white Americans kept safe houses. In Wilmington, Delaware, **Quaker** Thomas Garrett, friend of **Harriet Tubman**, noted that he had helped 2,038 fugitives by 1856. In many Northern cities, African Americans kept the major safe houses, sustained by a wide biracial network. Robert Purvis and William Still, both African Americans, worked with whites J. Miller McKim and **Lucretia Mott** in Philadelphia. Oliver

Johnson and Sydney Howard Gay assisted African Americans **David Ruggles** and Theodore Wright in New York City. **Stephen Myers**, Reverend Jermain Loguen (known as "the king" or "the prince" of the Underground Railroad, probably for his central location, his importance, and his size), and John Jones, all African Americans, kept the main safe houses in Albany, Syracuse, and Elmira, New York. In Newport, Indiana, and later Cincinnati, Ohio, Quaker Levi Coffin kept a major safe house. In Detroit, William Lambert and George DeBaptiste, African Americans, worked with Seymour Finney, a white hotel operator.

While it is impossible to know how many people escaped on the Underground Railroad, 1,500 per year is a generally accepted estimate. Certainly, enough people escaped to make passage of a **Fugitive Slave Law** a top priority for white Southerners as part of the **Compromise of 1850**. The Fugitive Slave Act required federal marshals to assist slave-catchers to capture accused fugitives. Freedom seekers had no right to testify on their own behalf. Underground Railroad helpers could be jailed for six months and fined $1,000 for each person they helped. Commissioners received $10 for ruling on behalf of slave-catchers and $5 for ruling on behalf of the freedom seeker. Fearing recapture, many freedom seekers who had settled in the Northern United States fled to Canada. Others, including Shadrach Minkins in Boston and William "Jerry" Henry in Syracuse, successfully escaped federal agents. The federal government did capture **Anthony Burns** in Boston, however, and returned him to slavery under the terms of the Fugitive Slave Act.

William Still's extensive notes formed the basis for his 1872 book, *The Underground Railroad*. Memoirs of people such as Quaker Levi Coffin, Harriet Tubman, and **John Parker**, themselves freedom seekers, offer important primary source evidence. Historians in the late twentieth century generally ignored the history of the Underground Railroad, citing the unreliability of oral traditions and the lack of written primary evidence. A closer look at both oral traditions and written evidence, however, has led to a rejuvenation of interest in this field. *See also* Jerry Rescue; Rankin, John.

Further Readings: Bordewich, Fergus. *Bound for Canaan: The Underground Railroad and the War for the Soul of America*. New York: HarperCollins, Amistad Press, 2005; Bradford, Sarah. *Scenes in the Life of Harriet Tubman*. Auburn, NY: W.H. Moses, 1869; Hagedorn, Ann. *Beyond the River: The Untold Story of the Heroes of the Underground Railroad*. New York: Simon and Schuster, 2002; Gara, Larry. *The Liberty Line: The Legend of the Underground Railroad*. Lexington: University of Kentucky, 1961; Griffler, Keith P. *Front Line of Freedom: African Americans and the Forging of the Underground Railroad in the Ohio Valley*. Lexington: University Press of Kentucky, 2004; Grover, Kathryn. *The Fugitive's Gibraltar: Escaping Slaves and Abolitionism in New Bedford, Massachusetts*. Amherst: University of Massachusetts Press, 2001; Hudson, J. Blaine. *Fugitive Slaves and the Underground Railroad in the Kentucky Borderland*. Jefferson, NC: McFarland and Company, 2002; John Parker, *His Promised Land: The Autobiography of John P. Parker, Former Slave and Conductor on the Underground Railroad*. Stuart Seely Sprague, ed. New York: W.W. Norton, 1996; Sernett, Milton. *North Star Country: Upstate New York and the Crusade for African American Freedom*. Syracuse, NY: Syracuse University Press, 2002; Siebert, Wilbur. *The Underground Railroad from*

Slavery to Freedom. New York: Macmillan, 1898; Still, William. *The Underground Railroad*. Philadelphia, 1872.

Judith Wellman

Unitarianism and Antislavery

It is difficult to summarize the relationship of Unitarians to the antislavery movement. Most Unitarians, it appears, were opposed in principle to slavery. Many Unitarians tacitly, if not actively, supported the moderate antislavery movement and its agenda of **gradual emancipation**, slaveholder compensation, and African colonization. With the emergence of **William Lloyd Garrison** and the abolitionist movement in the 1830s, however, leading members of the Unitarian clergy publicly chastised the **Garrisonians** for their advocacy of **immediate emancipation** and for their confrontational, socially disruptive tactics. Still other Unitarians emerged in the 1850s as spokespersons for the radical vanguard of the abolitionist movement. While it is difficult, therefore, to generalize about Unitarianism and antislavery, it is possible to identify the socio-economic and cultural factors behind their initial conservatism, and to chart the relationship between their evolving radicalism and the major political events of the day.

Reverend William Ellery Channing, (1780–1842), the leading Unitarian minister of his generation, lamented privately to a friend, that "no sect in this country has taken less interest in the slavery question" than the Unitarians. As a small sect of liberal Congregationalist ministers located initially in and around Boston, the Unitarians were closely associated with the city's wealthy mercantile families and elite cultural institutions. Many Boston merchants had long-established relationships with Southern slaveholders, first as owners of the merchant ships that trafficked in African slaves, and later as owners of and investors in New England's growing textile industry, which depended on a regular supply of Southern cotton. Economic self-interest, compounded by a social conservatism and cultural elitism shared by Boston's merchants and Unitarian clergy, sanctioned expression of only the most moderate antislavery sentiments. Reverend Henry Ware, Jr., a professor at Harvard Divinity School, was pressured in 1834 by Harvard administrators, Boston newspapers, and members of his own congregation, to renounce his affiliation with the Cambridge Anti-Slavery Society, a moderate antislavery association. Another member of Harvard's faculty, Carl Follen, a distinguished German scholar, was dismissed for publicly voicing antislavery views. By the early 1850s, one-third of Harvard's undergraduates were the sons of Southern planters, and with the outbreak of Civil War in 1861, Harvard could claim the dubious honor of counting seventeen Confederate generals among its alumni.

William Ellery Channing typifies the relationship of many Unitarian ministers to the antislavery movement. Channing was born and raised in Newport, Rhode Island, a town still referred to in the late-eighteenth century as "the slave market of America." After graduating from Harvard in 1798, Channing spent two years in Virginia tutoring the children of a prominent Richmond slaveholder. Channing married into a wealthy Newport mercantile family whose fortune had been earned in part by selling rum to slave-traders, who occasionally settled their debts in slaves. In 1830, troubled by poor health, Channing vacationed on a slave plantation on the Caribbean island of St. Croix, where he once again witnessed first-hand the harsh realities of the plantation system.

Despite these experiences, or perhaps more accurately, due largely to these experiences, Channing refrained from commenting publicly on or participating in the antislavery movement until the last years of his life. Criticized by Maria Weston Chapman, a radical member of his congregation, and by the Reverend Samuel J. May, a young Unitarian minister converted to abolitionism, Channing admitted in 1834 that he had been "silent too long" on the subject of slavery. *Slavery*, Channing's first public statement in support of antislavery, was published in 1835. From that year onward until his death, Channing took an increasingly public stance against slavery. In 1837, Channing organized a memorial service for the murdered Illinois abolitionist, **Elijah P. Lovejoy**, over the protests of Andrews Norton, another leading Unitarian minister, and despite increasingly hostile condemnations by members of his Federal Street congregation and other prominent Bostonians. A cursory reading of *Slavery* and Channing's other published antislavery works reveals, however, that despite his heightened political activism, Channing's views never evolved beyond a moderate antislavery position. Even as he proclaimed his devotion to the antislavery cause, in nearly every work Channing reserved his harshest criticism for the abolitionists, whom he criticized repeatedly as irresponsible, if well intentioned, extremists.

Channing's evolving views on slavery are significant only in comparison to the intransigent and often intemperate condemnations of the antislavery movement voiced throughout the 1830s and 1840s by Andrews Norton, Ezra Stiles Gannet, and other leading Unitarians. Despite the social conservatism of Channing's generation, by the 1850s younger Unitarian ministers like Thomas Wentworth Higginson and Theodore Parker had repudiated their elders' views on antislavery and achieved prominence as leading spokespersons in the vanguard of the abolitionist movement. The radicalism of these younger Unitarians achieved its fullest expression in the abolitionist activism of Reverend Theodore Parker.

Parker's radicalism had several sources. Parker was particularly proud of the fact that his grandfather led the local militia in the Battle of Lexington, and references to the American Revolution recur throughout his antislavery writings. Like many New Englanders, Parker was also outraged by passage of the **Fugitive Slave Law** and by the outcome of the case of **Anthony Burns**. The failed efforts to prevent Burns's reenslavement, compounded by news of the outrages committed in Kansas by proslavery forces, compelled Parker and many other Unitarians to accept violence as a legitimate tactic in the war against slavery. Parker took to carrying loaded pistols, and supported the movement to arm Kansas free-state settlers, including the militant abolitionist John Brown. Parker's support for Brown continued even after Brown's massacre of unarmed, proslavery settlers at Pottawatomie Creek. In 1859, Parker, along with Higginson, became a member of the **Secret Six**, a group of prominent, proviolence abolitionists who provided

Brown with funds for his intended, and ultimately unsuccessful, slave insurrection at Harpers Ferry, Virginia. By the time Brown's ill-fated raid came undone in October 1859, Parker lay dying in Rome, Italy, where he had hoped to recuperate from tuberculosis. Nevertheless, upon learning of Brown's indictment and pending execution, Parker used "what poor remnant of power is left to me," to celebrate Brown as a martyr and a saint, and to assert that the slave "has a natural right to kill every one who seeks to prevent his enjoyment of liberty." *See also* Bleeding Kansas.

Further Readings: Commager, Henry Steele, ed. *Theodore Parker: An Anthology.* Boston, Beacon Press, 1960; Howe, Daniel Walker. *The Unitarian Conscience: Harvard Moral Philosophy, 1805–1861.* Middleton, CT: Wesleyan University Press, 1988; Pease, Jane H. and William H. Pease. "Confrontation and Abolition in the 1850s." In John R. McKivigan, ed., *History of the American Abolitionist Movement: A Bibliography of Scholarly Articles.* New York: Garland Publishing, 1999, pp. 293–307; Stange, Douglas C. "Abolitionism as Treason: The Unitarian Elite Defends Law, Order, and the Union. *Harvard Library Bulletin* 28 (1980): 152–170; Stange, Douglas C. *Patterns of Antislavery among American Unitarians, 1831–1860.* Rutherford, NJ: Associated Universities Press, 1977.

Neil Brody Miller

United Nations and Antislavery

The United Nations (UN) was formed immediately after the end of the Second World War. Like its predecessor, the League of Nations, its purpose was to ensure peace by preventing wars and promoting human welfare. Its charter issued in 1945 stated that one of its aims was to promote "universal respect for, and observance of, human rights and fundamental freedoms for all without distinction as to race, sex or language or religion." Although slavery was not specifically mentioned, its eradication was clearly implied. However, like the League, it ruled out interference in the domestic affairs of member states. Hence, it could negotiate covenants but had no means of enforcing them even in the case of members that had signed and ratified them.

In the late 1940s and early 1950s, its subsidiary bodies were formed in an atmosphere of rising tension created by the Cold War—the intense hostility between the communist bloc led by the Soviet Union and the western democracies led by the United States. These were the only remaining great powers, as one by one, the European colonial empires disintegrated and the newly independent states took their places at the United Nations. To the Western Bloc, human rights included freedom of expression, of assembly, of information, of religion, and freedom from arbitrary arrest and other components of the rule of law, while the Soviet Bloc stressed freedom from want and discrimination, the right to education, equal opportunity, and other economic and social rights.

The abolition of slavery became a pawn in the battle between the western democracies and the Soviet Union and its allies to win over world public opinion. The Commission on Human Rights (CHR), a subsidiary of the

United Nations Economic and Social Council (ECOSOC), drafted the Universal Declaration of Human Rights in 1948. The Russians maintained that slavery meant only the chattel slavery which was still legal only in the Aden Protectorate and the small sheikdoms on the Persian Gulf under British protection, and in the independent states of Saudi Arabia and Yemen. Hence, they proposed that article four of the Universal Declaration should declare that "no one shall be held in slavery or servitude: and the slave trade shall be prohibited in all their forms." To the Western Bloc, however, "slavery in all its forms" included the forced labor practiced in the gulags of the Soviet Union and the other practices included in the report of the League of Nations Temporary Slavery Commission and referred to in the **Slavery Convention of 1926**. The Universal Declaration, however, was simply a declaration of principles. Covenants were needed to implement it and these were many years in coming.

The Secretary of the British Antislavery Society began to pressure the United Nations to appoint a permanent slavery committee as early as 1946. The result, after much disagreement and discussion, was the appointment of the Ad Hoc Committee on Slavery 1950–51. Two years later, the UN took over the Slavery Convention of 1926, including its unsatisfactory definition of slavery. This in turn led to the negotiation of the **Supplementary Convention on the Abolition of Slavery, the Slave Trade and Institutions and Practices Similar to Slavery** in 1956. This treaty confirmed that these practices included debt-bondage, serfdom, forced labor, the adoption of children under 18 in order to exploit them, as well as forced marriage, the forced transfer of married women, and the inheritance of widows. To prevent child marriage, signatories undertook to set a minimum age for marriages, to register them, and to ensure that consent should be freely expressed by both parties before competent authorities. These provisions were incorporated into the Convention on Consent to Marriage, Minimum Age for Marriage and Registration of Marriages of 1962. This was followed by a recommendation of the UN General Assembly in 1965, which suggested that fifteen should be the minimum age for marriage.

Similarly, the UN General Assembly issued the Declaration on the Rights of the Child in 1959, proclaiming that children must be assured a "happy childhood" free from discrimination, and insecurity. They had a right to free and compulsory education, and must be allowed time for recreation. They should not be employed below a minimum age, or engaged in any occupation dangerous to their health and development.

Thus by the 1960s, the United Nations had negotiated important human rights covenants and declarations but it had no means of enforcing them. During the next few years, the antislavery campaign must be seen against the background of increasing tension as each side in the Cold War sought support from the newly independent unaligned former European colonies. The revulsion of these new countries against colonialism increased as South Africa's policy of apartheid became ever more brutal, as Rhodesia declared independence from Britain and tightened its racial policies, and as Africans turned to guerrilla warfare against South Africa, Rhodesia, and the Portuguese colonies. Fuel was added to the fire by the United States' embroilment in war between South Vietnam and the communist North Vietnam, and by Israel's humiliating victory in the 1967 war against its Arab neighbors.

The slavery question at the United Nations was put on the agenda of ECOSOC in 1960 by a group of closely allied non-governmental organizations (NGOs) led by the Anti-Slavery Society and including women's organizations. They demanded the establishment of a UN commission of inquiry or a committee of experts on slavery. The slavery question assumed political importance when President Nasser of Egypt emerged as a leading abolitionist denouncing chattel slavery in Arabia. Saudi Arabia and Yemen outlawed it in 1962. Thus, the only areas in which chattel slavery was legal were the Aden Protectorate and the Trucial States, both under forms of British protection, and Oman, whose sultan was a close ally of Britain. However, many of the practices designated forms of slavery in the 1956 and subsequent treaties were still practiced in the newly independent former colonies.

By the end of 1962, only 44 of the 104 members of the UN had acceded to the 1956 treaty. A compromise was reached at the UN with the appointment of a special rapporteur on slavery, rather than the committee wanted by the NGOs. The rapporteur, Dr. Mohammed Awad, an Egyptian scholar, began work in 1964, sending out questionnaires asking governments to report on the situation in their countries. Most of the replies were less than honest. In his report, discussed in the social committee of ECOSOC in 1966, Awad advocated the appointment of a UN slavery committee with its own secretariat. He wanted it to have the power to promote and supervise the activities of specialized agencies and NGOs, as well as to cooperate with, and advise, governments on action they might take. He even hinted that the committee might send experts to investigate conditions and offer advice to countries needing help.

The proposal was strongly opposed. The USSR claimed it was unnecessary. The United States objected to the expense. Many of the newly independent states had no desire for investigations into questions such as marriage customs, cult slavery, child labor, debt bondage, and so forth. The Latin American nations had no wish to tackle peonage or the plight of their indigenous minorities. The British, to placate Parliament, the Anti-Slavery Society and the public, were reluctantly prepared to support such a committee, but suggested that it should be purely advisory. However, the coup de grace came when Tanzania and other former colonies succeeded in passing a resolution which included the "slavery-like practices of apartheid and colonialism" as forms of servitude and called on the Commission on Human Rights to consider ways to end them, effectively and immediately. This was opposed by Britain, and the proposal for the committee died.

In the years that followed, the slavery issue was kept alive by NGOs led by the Anti-Slavery Society. In 1967, the Commission on Human Rights (CHR), to whom ECOSOC had referred the question, passed it on to its Sub-Commission on the Prevention of Discrimination and the Protection of Minorities (SPDPM). This was a committee of so-called independent experts appointed by the CHR but approved by their governments. How independent they were depended on their governments. Originally most were lawyers, sociologists, and other academics, but from 1969, as their numbers were enlarged to give more representation to Africans, Asians, and Latin Americans, more diplomats and civil servants were appointed and the appointments became more politicized. The members represented the five areas into which the UN divided the world. They had a large mandate—to protect minorities and prevent discrimination and other infringements of human rights. Henceforth this was the body that dealt with slavery questions.

Although the appointment of a special committee to deal with slavery was for the time being a dead issue, the UN issued a number of declarations and negotiated conventions dealing with various forms of servitude. In 1968, for instance, ECOSOC declared trafficking in persons for prostitution to be a form of slavery, and called on the specialized agencies such as the International Labor Organization (ILO), the UN Educational, Scientific and Cultural Organization (UNESCO), the World Health Organization (WHO), and the UN Food and Agriculture Organization (FAO) to rehabilitate the women and girls who were freed. The Convention for the Suppression of the Traffic in Persons and the Exploitation of Others had replaced earlier treaties in 1949, but for legal and other reasons, its provisions could not be effectively implemented.

In 1969, a further Awad report was commissioned. Awad was particularly urged to seek information from the specialized agencies as well as NGOs and Intergovernmental Organizations (IGOs) such as the Organization of African Unity (OAU), the Arab League, and the Organization of American Unity (OAS). He was also asked to investigate specific manifestations of apartheid, such as sweated labor and the denial of trade union rights to Africans.

Meanwhile, the Anti-Slavery Society formed an All Party Group in the British Parliament to pressure the government into taking stronger action at the UN. The group, however, was particularly interested in the welfare of indigenous peoples such as "Amerindians" in South America and the "Bushmen" in Southern Africa.

The definition of slavery was constantly expanding. Various agencies and increasing numbers of NGOs were being drawn into the abolition struggle, but there was no organization to oversee their efforts, and action depended entirely on government cooperation. Moreover, when Awad presented his final report in 1970, it was disappointing. The UN special agencies who relied on the cooperation of governments for their work, had not wanted to be drawn into the antislavery campaign, and many governments had still ignored or failed to ratify the conventions. In many cases they had outlawed slavery and denied that it existed; hence they were reluctant now to admit that their laws were not being carried out.

Britain's dilemma over chattel slavery was reduced when the rulers of the Trucial states were induced to sign a decree stating that it had long been forbidden in their territories. In the Aden Protectorate, where British control was non-existent in some areas, slavery was still practiced to an unknown extent. This problem was solved when Britain withdrew from

Aden in disarray late in 1967, and the extreme socialist government that took over outlawed slavery. In Oman, closely allied to Britain, slavery ended when a British-supported coup replaced the existing ruler with his son in 1970. By this time, South Africa had left the British Commonwealth on the issue of apartheid, and the only colonies remaining under British rule continued to do so by their own choice. Henceforth, Britain had no difficulty submitting to the demands of the Anti-Slavery Society and its supporters, who urged the government to pressure the UN to establish some mechanism to foster and supervise action against slavery.

At the UN, pressure from more than twenty NGOs and revelations that a number of Africans were being smuggled into Europe and ill-treated, led to the appointment of the Working Group on Slavery in 1974. It consisted of five members of the sub-commission, one from each of the areas into which the United Nations had divided the world. The Soviets, however, stipulated that it was only to meet for three days every other year. It could not carry out investigations and it had no authority to see that the advice it was expected to provide was carried out. Its membership, constantly changing, was unlikely to produce any experts on slavery. It was thus a small toothless committee established to end contemporary forms of slavery that in the last years of the twentieth and early ones of the twenty-first centuries were constantly taking new forms.

Some of the Group's early defects were remedied in the next few years due to intense NGO pressure. It became a permanent body, meeting annually first for five days and then for eight. Most importantly, its meetings were held in public with simultaneous translation into English, French, Russian, and Spanish. Moreover, NGOs and specialized agencies were invited to attend and give evidence. By 1992, its meetings were held long enough before the meeting of the sub-commission for the latter to have time to read its reports and act upon them. However, it lacked secretarial support and could not conduct its own investigations on the ground or enforce its recommendations. It was thus dependent on the information which was brought to it by the UN Secretariat and NGOs, as well as the UN special agencies, many of which did not attend its meetings regularly.

Its early meetings were highly politicized as members defended their own regions. The Cold War introduced a competitive atmosphere in which the Soviet and Asian Blocs in particular flatly denied the various charges brought against them. The communists, for instance, claimed there was no prostitution in their countries. When Ethiopia was accused of hijacking people off the streets of Addis Ababa to work in the sesame fields as forced labor, a Russian representative claimed that the accusation was untrue and that the evidence was produced by the Western Bloc to embarrass the Ethiopian communist government. When debt bondage in India was denounced, the chairman complained that his area of the world was being "picked on." Members wandered in and out of the meetings and appeared to have little interest in the proceedings. Moreover, there was rarely any press coverage, which was what hard pressed, under funded NGOs craved.

With the end of the Cold War and of apartheid in South Africa, following the dissolution of the European colonial empires, the atmosphere at the

Working Group became less politicized. Another big change was that public awareness of the various forms of modern servitude heightened as these abuses attracted more attention in the press. By the last decade of the twentieth century, the number of NGOs had proliferated and more and more of them came to the meetings of the Group. It was one institution at which they were sure of being heard. Although its powers were extremely limited, the Group was responsible for the appointment of several special rapporteurs, particularly on the exploitation of children. It also initiated the establishment of the UN Trust Fund on Contemporary Forms of Slavery, financed by government donations. This fund brought local NGOs and sometimes victims of contemporary slavery to Geneva to provide first hand accounts of abuse.

By the end of the twentieth century, chattel slavery had almost disappeared. It still existed illegally in Mauritania and in some of the neighboring countries in the Sahel. The Sub-Commission sent out a committee to investigate the situation in Mauritania in 1984. Progress was slow; in the 1990s, many slaves, especially men, had been freed, but owners were still trying to keep women and children. Slave-raiding and slave-holding also revived in Sudan as the result of the war between the North and the South. A special rapporteur was sent out by the UN, and agencies such as UNICEF, tried to trace abducted women and children in order to rehabilitate them. The UN was involved in trying to broker peace in the Sudan.

In most of its sessions, however, the Working Group found itself hearing about more and more practices that had not in the past been defined as slavery, or had been called "slavery-like practices." After much discussion, it decided in 1987 to change its name to the Working Group on Contemporary forms of Slavery. The sub-commission defined slavery as the "exploitation of man by man," and maintained that, as this was constantly changing its forms, the definition of slavery could not be a static concept.

Under this rubric, the Group collected more and more information on practices that differed from chattel slavery in certain important features. The emphasis changed from ownership to control, and often to temporary control, as for instance, slave children grew up and forced prostitutes grew old or ill. Moreover, slaves were no longer acquired by raids. Some were still kidnapped, but many came willingly in search of jobs and on arrival found the job they had been promised did not exist and were then forced into various forms of servitude through debt bondage or brutalization or threats. Thus, people were recruited in the slums of Brazil to work in Amazonia, only to find on arrival that they were in debt to the people who had transported them. The debts could not be repaid, and hence they were forced to work in gold mines or other jobs. Women and girls found themselves forced into prostitution. Similar scams were practiced in areas as different as Eastern Europe and West Africa. Parents sold their children on the promise of a good job or an education, only to find that they were worked like slaves on plantations and quarries, or as domestic servants, or prostitutes in their own countries or abroad. Debt-bondage was an old form of servitude, particularly in South Asia, where it was often hereditary. It took the form of peonage in the Americas. It now increasingly spread to new areas and played an intrinsic part in the rising flow of labor from the poor areas of the world to the rich ones.

The exploitation of child labor was the subject of special UN reports in the 1980s and 1990s. Children were especially vulnerable to exploitation, and the problem was world-wide but particularly widespread in poor countries. Children worked in mines, factories, cottage industries, stone quarries, brick kilns, agriculture, and domestic service. Small boys from South Asia were recruited to ride as camel jockeys in the United Arab Emirates (formerly the Trucial States). Some children worked with their parents, others worked away from home. Criminal gangs used "street" children for prostitution, drug trafficking, and theft, and even mutilated them to turn them into beggars. Many were victims of sex tourism, forced prostitution, and child pornography. Child soldiers were widely recruited, mostly in rebel armies, and in some cases were forced to commit atrocities, killing or mutilating even children, as in Sierra Leone.

Much information on these iniquities was brought to the Working Group, before and after the signing of the Convention on the Rights of the Child of 1989. In the 1990s, the Group drew up a plan of action to be sent to governments. The Commission on Human Rights appointed special rapporteurs to deal with the child slavery. Finally, the ILO established the International Program on the Elimination of Child Labor (IPEC) and in 1999, negotiated the Convention against the Worst Forms of Child Labor (no. 182).

Some of the many cases brought before the Working Group bore little or no relation to slavery as generally conceived. These cases included female genital excision (also called cutting or circumcision), the honor killings of Muslim girls by their relatives in the belief that they had disgraced them, the murder of persons to use their organs in transplants, as well as incest, and other iniquities. As a result by the late 1990s, the Working Group was in danger of losing its focus.

Some forms of servitude, however, were transferred to other UN working groups. Legal foreign migrant laborers were often denied the benefits due to citizen workers. Moreover, they lived away from their families, and faced violence and racism. Illegal alien migrants were particularly vulnerable to abuses such as extortion by the criminal groups who smuggled them into the richer nations. Thus, Chinese triads extorted money from them as well as their families under threat of violence. Some illegal aliens were forced into sweatshops which were virtual prisons. At best these economic refugees faced resentment from local workers, fearful of losing their jobs. To protect them, the Convention on the Protection of the Rights of all Migrant Workers and their Families was signed in 1990. Seven years later, the Commission on Human Rights established a working group to consider the protection of migrants.

Similarly, the Working Group on the Protection of Indigenous Populations (WGIP) was established in order to protect their rights to lands, and ensure they did not become victims of serfdom, debt bondage, forced labor, and discrimination. This UN Group attracted wide support. It drafted a Universal Declaration on the rights of indigenous minorities and helped establish the Permanent Indigenous Forum under ECOSOC. It also established a Trust

Fund to bring spokesmen to meetings at which governments exchanged information on indigenous peoples.

In sum, the United Nations through its various committees, working groups, and specialized agencies was actively involved in the suppression of the various forms of slavery which evolved in the twentieth century, as well as in ending the remaining vestiges of chattel slavery. It remains to be seen how successful it has been. The Working Group on Contemporary Forms of Slavery plans to review its work and its impact in 2005 and to meet together with the more powerful ILO to consider plans for the future. The distinction between forced labor and slavery has not been clear-cut since forced labor was included in the definition of slavery by the League of Nations Temporary Slavery Commission. However, although the Working Group has heard evidence on the question, it was the ILO which negotiated the various forced labor conventions.

Many of the problems the United Nations has attacked are almost intractable as they are the result of dire poverty in some regions of the world in contrast to the great wealth of others. The result has been a steady flow of migrants, both free and in servitude, from the poor areas to the rich areas. Globalization is still in its infancy. The problem of protecting the vulnerable from exploitation by employers and criminal gangs became more difficult with the increasing ease of communications, with money laundering, and widespread official corruption, as well as the growth of organized crime. On paper much has been achieved. Conventions have been signed. Wide publicity has been given to various forms of contemporary slavery. However, some serious problems remain. Governments do not have to sign or ratify the conventions. If they do sign them, and if they pass the laws needed to implement them, they are often too poor or too corrupt to enforce them. Moreover, if treaties are to be carried out, an up-to-date definition of slavery is needed. At present it is still defined as in 1926 as a question of ownership. Thus, in spite of considerable UN efforts, many forms of contemporary slavery have continued into the early twenty-first century. *See also* League of Nations and Slavery; Muscat and Oman, Abolition of Slavery in; Slavery and Abolition in the Twentieth Century.

Further Readings: *Anti-Slavery Reporter and Aborigines Friend* 1946–80, and thereafter published as *Anti-Slavery Reporter*, published by Anti-Slavery International, London; Korey, William. *NGOs and the Universal Declaration of Human Rights: a Curious Grapevine.* St. Martin's Press, New York, 1998; Miers, Suzanne. *Slavery in the Twentieth Century: the Evolution of a Global Problem.* Walnut Creek, CA: Altamira Press, 2003; *Reports of the Working Group on Contemporary Forms of Slavery,* published annually by the United Nations together with other United Nations Reports and Human Rights Conventions.

Suzanne Miers

United States, Antislavery in

Organized antislavery in the United States has a long history that can be roughly divided into four somewhat overlapping phases. The movement began during the American Revolution and for the most part ended with the adoption of the **Thirteenth Amendment**, which abolished slavery in the United States. However, some opponents of slavery and a few organizations continued to be active in the United States well after slavery was abolished in the nation. One of the earliest antislavery organizations, the Pennsylvania Society for the Abolition of Slavery, never disbanded and continues to work for better race relations.

Early Abolition Societies

During the American Revolution, opponents of slavery in most of the Northern states, and a few states of the upper South, organized what were known at the time as abolition societies. The most important was the Pennsylvania Society for Promoting the Abolition of Slavery, the Relief of Free Negroes Unlawfully Held in Bondage, and for Improving the Condition of the African Race, more commonly known as the **Pennsylvania Abolition Society**, or the PAS. The PAS was first organized in 1775, but became moribund during the British occupation of Philadelphia. A revived society reemerged in 1784. However, members and future members of the Society helped work for the passage of the Pennsylvania Gradual Abolition Act of 1780, the first American legislative act to begin the process of dismantling slavery. Similar organizations in other states successfully worked for gradual abolition acts in Rhode Island (1784), Connecticut (1784), New York (1799), and New Jersey (1804). Societies in Delaware, Maryland, Virginia, and Kentucky were unsuccessful in moving those states toward abolition, and by 1810, the Southern societies were moribund or simply no longer functioning. Many of the leaders of these societies were leaders of the new nation itself. **Benjamin Franklin** and Dr. **Benjamin Rush**, a signer of the Declaration of Independence along with Franklin, served as presidents of the Pennsylvania Society. The president of the New York Society was **John Jay**, the diplomat and future chief justice of the United States. Another key member was Alexander Hamilton, who coauthored the *Federalist Papers* with Jay and then served as secretary of the treasury. James Wood, who served as governor of Virginia from 1796 to 1799, was also the vice president of the Virginia Abolition Society. Other members of these societies included **Thomas Paine**; James Otis; James Pemberton, a **Quaker** merchant; Philadelphia mayor, Hilary Baker; Rufus King, a signer of the U.S. Constitution; Judge James Duane; and Daniel D. Tompkins, a future governor of New York.

The Northern abolition societies had four general goals. The first was to abolish slavery in their own states. In this they were remarkably successful. In addition to those Northern states which ended slavery through gradual abolition acts, Massachusetts, New Hampshire, and Vermont (the fourteenth state) abolished slavery through constitutional provisions. By 1804, all of the Northern states had either ended slavery outright or were in the process of gradually destroying it. The slave population in the North dropped precipitously, while the free black populations grew rapidly. For example, in Pennsylvania the slave population dropped from 6,855 in 1780 to 211 in 1820. In New York there were 21,324 slaves in 1790 and just over 10,000 in 1820. In 1827, the state freed all remaining slaves. New England had 3,870 slaves in 1790 and 145 by 1820.

Second, the societies agitated for an end to the African Slave Trade. In the first session of Congress, the Pennsylvania Society petitioned Congress to end the commerce. The Constitution prohibited an absolute ban on the trade at that time. Nevertheless, the Society petitioned Congress to end the trade, which led to an astounding attack on abolitionists by Southern members of Congress. Benjamin Franklin responded, in his last published essay before he died, with a brilliant satirical attack on the slave trade. In this essay, Franklin took on the voice of a North African Moslem, praising the virtue of enslaving Christians. Even though Congress could not yet ban the trade, the individual states could. Thus, the Northern states and a number of Southern states, prohibited their citizens from participating in the trade. The abolition societies worked to make sure these laws were enforced.

Third, the societies fought to protect free blacks. The PAS, for example, agitated for legislation to protect free blacks from kidnapping and reenslavement. This led, in 1788, to an elaborate amendment strengthening the 1780 gradual abolition act. The PAS, as well as other societies, also used litigation to protect free blacks, help emancipate slaves, and make life miserable for slaveowners. At one point, President George Washington complained to political leaders in Pennsylvania that the PAS was harassing too many Southern masters. The PAS and its New York counterpart also initiated litigation to secure the liberty of blacks who had a legal claim to freedom. The threat of a lawsuit was probably the reason **Thomas Jefferson** reluctantly signed a paper agreeing to free his slave James Hemings, after he brought him to Philadelphia. Ironically, intervention by the PAS on behalf of a kidnapped free black ultimately led to the adoption of the 1793 fugitive slave law. However, despite that outcome, the abolition societies throughout the North used the legal talent of their members to secure the freedom of a number of blacks. In many ways, these societies were the first public interest organization to use litigation to achieve social reform. They can be seen as the precursors of the NAACP Legal Defense Fund or the American Civil Liberties Union.

Fourth, the societies worked to enhance the social conditions of blacks. They built schools for blacks, helped raise money for black education, black churches, orphanages, and other social institutions. In an age before public education and a social safety net, the abolition societies provided significant material aid to black communities.

The abolition societies continued to function into the early part of the nineteenth century. With immediate abolition in northern New England and the last gradual abolition act passed in New Jersey in 1804, the mission of the societies evolved to protecting free blacks from kidnapping and helping black communities provide education for their children. Except for the African slave trade, the societies were mostly focused on local issues. Their purpose was to end slavery in their own backyard and end the African slave trade. By 1808, they had accomplished both. By the 1820s, they had ceased having national conventions as they had done in the 1790s and generally disbanded or, like the PAS, faded into obscurity, continuing to help runaway slaves and black schools, but otherwise not participating in the emerging new attack on slavery in the 1830s.

American Colonization Society

In 1816, a diverse collection of humanitarians, opponents of slavery, slaveowners fearful of free blacks, and various politicians, organized the American Society for Colonizing the Free People of Color, better known as the **American Colonization Society** (ACS). The early leaders of the ACS included **Henry Clay**, the speaker of the House of Representatives; Congressman Charles Fenton Mercer of Virginia; Maryland lawyer and author of the *Star Spangled Banner*, Francis Scott Key; and James Monroe, who would become the fifth president of the United States. The first president of the Society was Supreme Court Justice Bushrod Washington, the nephew of President George Washington. The ACS transported free blacks and recently manumitted slaves to Africa, where they established colonies and settlements and eventually the country of **Liberia**. The goals of the Society were mixed. Many of the slaveholding Southern members saw the Society as a vehicle for removing free blacks from the United States. They believed free blacks were subversive to slavery. Other members, such as the Massachusetts politician Daniel Webster, believed the ACS would encourage masters to free their slaves by providing a safe place to send them. Thus, the ACS combined proslavery racism with antislavery humanitarianism. Over the years, some masters took advantage of the ACS to emancipate their slaves. This was particularly applied in states like Virginia and North Carolina, which had made manumission without also removal from the state extremely difficult. Some free blacks supported the ACS because they felt Africa offered them more opportunity than the United States.

Most free blacks, however, saw the ACS as a threat to their liberty. In Philadelphia, the Reverend **Richard Allen** led a huge protest against the ACS. The black revolutionary **David Walker** vigorously attacked colonization in his pamphlet, *An Appeal to the Colored Citizens of the World* (1829). The free black opponents of the ACS understood that its slave-owning leaders and proslavery supporters, such as the Virginians John Tyler and Abel Upshur, were hardly friends of emancipation or free blacks. These Southerners wanted the ACS to remove free blacks, not slaves, from American shores. In the 1830s, the new antislavery movement attacked the ACS as a friend of slavery, not of blacks. In fact, it was a friend of slavery, but at the same time, the ACS facilitated the private manumission of a few thousand or so slaves.

The Emergence of Immediatism

Opponents of slavery objected to colonization because the colonizationists were not, ultimately, interested in ending slavery. At best, the ACS facilitated liberty for a few slaves through private manumission. But, the cost of this private manumission for the African Americans was high; to gain freedom they had to leave the land they knew, the United States, and relocate to another land where they had never been, Africa. They had to leave friends and relatives behind and venture to an unknown place. Most of all, however, colonization retarded any direct assault on slavery.

Blacks like David Walker and Richard Allen were the first to condemn colonization, but in the early 1830s, white opponents of slavery also attacked the ACS. The most important of these—indeed, the most important opponent of slavery for the next three decades—was **William Lloyd Garrison**, a native of Newburyport, Massachusetts and a printer by trade. In 1831, Garrison began publishing *The Liberator*, which became the nation's leading antislavery paper. Garrison, along with other early white abolitionists including **Arthur** and **Lewis Tappan**, had been deeply influenced by the intensity of black opposition to colonization, their increasing attacks on slavery, and their dedication to faith and self-improvement. This influence was critical in moving the previously procolonization Garrison and the brothers Arthur and Lewis Tappan out of the fold and toward a demand for total and immediate abolition. Quoting the nation's founding document in the inaugural issue of *The Liberator*, Garrison asserted his support for "the 'self-evident truth' maintained in the American Declaration of Independence, 'that all men are created equal, and endowed by their Creator with certain inalienable rights—among which are life, liberty and the pursuit of happiness.'" Garrison proclaimed, "I shall strenuously contend for the immediate enfranchisement of our slave population." Setting the tone for the next three decades, Garrison declared the following in his newspaper:

> I am aware that many object to the severity of my language; but is there not cause for severity? I will be as harsh as truth, and as uncompromising as justice. On this subject, I do not wish to think, or to speak, or write, with moderation. No! no! Tell a man whose house is on fire to give a moderate alarm; tell him to moderately rescue his wife from the hands of the ravisher; tell the mother to gradually extricate her babe from the fire into which it has fallen; but urge me not to use moderation in a cause like the present. I am in earnest—I will not equivocate—I will not excuse—I will not retreat a single inch– AND I WILL BE HEARD. The apathy of the people is enough to make every statue leap from its pedestal, and to hasten the resurrection of the dead.

A year later, in 1832, Garrison helped found the **New England Anti-Slavery Society**, which advocated immediate abolition. In December 1833, sixty-two opponents of slavery met in Philadelphia to form the **American Anti-Slavery Society** (AASS). The delegates included three blacks and four women, in an age when men and women rarely gathered in public meetings and blacks and whites rarely worked together. Most of the delegates were religiously motivated and saw their movement as part of a moral crusade to rid America of sin. Many came out of the temperance movement. The abolitionists demanded the "immediate, unconditional, uncompensated emancipation" of the nation's slaves. They rejected the gradualism of the earlier abolition societies and the absurd position of the ACS that free blacks had to be removed from the nation. Such a position was unfair to blacks and at the same time made ending slavery impossible, because the prerequisite for emancipation—moving the former slaves to Africa—was impossible. There were simply not enough ships or resources to move American slaves to Africa or anywhere else, assuming they wanted to go.

The new "immediate" abolitionists believed that they could accomplish their goals through moral suasion—that is, by persuading slaveowners that they should free their slaves because it was their Christian duty to do so. Their tactics included flooding the mails with pamphlets and letters and trying to convince leading Southerners, especially churchmen and lay leaders, to take a stand against slavery. Later, the abolitionists would flood Congress with petitions against slavery. The AASS developed local and state organizations throughout the North. While women continued to work within the men's organizations, they also formed their own groups, such as the Boston Female Anti-Slavery Society. Members of this group found an attorney to petition for a writ of *habeas corpus* to test whether a visitor could bring a slave into Massachusetts. In *Commonwealth v. Aves* (1836), they succeeded in getting the Massachusetts Supreme Judicial Court to hold that slaves brought into the state immediately became free.

Abolitionists were trapped by their own language—immediate emancipation—because no one believed this was either possible or desirable. Almost all whites, even those opposed to slavery, believed that most of the two million or so slaves in the nation were not ready for immediate freedom. Furthermore, even opponents of slavery understood that the overwhelming majority of whites in the North as well as the South were not prepared to accept so many free blacks living among them. This led to the complicated explanation that the new abolitionists favored "immediate abolition, gradually achieved." They believed the ending of slavery must start immediately, and the Americans, especially slaveholders, had to commit to emancipation to save the very soul of the nation. This led to the tactics of moral suasion.

These early abolitionists met with little success. In the North they were mobbed and in the South they were ignored or banned. Between 1833 and 1835, citizens in Canterbury, Connecticut repeatedly attacked a boarding school for black girls run by a **Quaker** abolitionist, **Prudence Crandall**. In 1835, a mob in Boston threatened to lynch **William Lloyd Garrison**, dragging him through the streets with a rope around his neck. In 1837, an abolitionist printer, the Reverend **Elijah P. Lovejoy** was killed as he tried to defend his business and printing press from a proslavery mob attempting to throw his press into the Mississippi River. Mobs in Utica, New York City, Philadelphia, and elsewhere broke up antislavery meetings and even burned buildings. Some abolitionist speakers were beaten up and chased out of towns in the North. Congress passed a "gag" rule to prevent the reading of abolitionist petitions, and relatively few Northerners joined antislavery organizations.

Abolitionists also struggled with each other over a variety of issues. Garrison and his allies were not content with focusing on antislavery. Garrison campaigned for women's rights, world peace, pacifism, and temperance. He attacked the organized churches and became increasingly disaffected with politics. By the end of the 1830s, he was moving to the position that abolitionists should reject political activity altogether. Declaring the Constitution to be a "covenant with death and an agreement in hell," he adopted as a slogan for his newspaper, "No Union with Slaveholders." This radical dis-unionism made him even less popular among most white Northerners. Most of the subscribers to his newspaper were blacks. However, despite his personal unpopularity, and the small number of whites or blacks who joined the AASS, Garrison's message began to take hold. Northerners who had never thought about slavery could no longer avoid the issue. In addition, **Garrisonians** used the courts in Massachusetts and elsewhere to challenge slavery where they could. Members of the Boston Female Anti-Slavery Society brought the issue of visiting slaves before the Massachusetts Supreme Judicial Court in *Commonwealth v. Aves* (1836). The conservative chief justice, Lemuel Shaw, sided with the abolitionists, holding that a slave became free the moment he or she entered the state, unless as a fugitive slave. Within a decade, most other Northern states had followed this rule. The AASS also provided legal help to fugitive slaves. The AASS continued to operate until the end of the Civil War. Small in numbers, the society had powerful speakers, including **Wendell Phillips** who was perhaps the greatest orator of the age. **Frederick Douglass** began his career as a Garrisonian, and as an agent for the Massachusetts Anti-Slavery Society. Women speakers like **Abby Kelley Foster** were also important in spreading the gospel of strong antislavery ideas. The AASS served as a powerful force for changing opinion, even if it lacked members and convinced few to accept all of its goals. Northerners introduced to abolitionist ideas by AASS pamphlets, books, and its many speakers might not have become immediate abolitionists, but many became strongly antislavery, and those sentiments eventually affected politics, law, and social relations.

Political Antislavery

Garrison's increasing radicalism led to a split within the movement. In 1840, moderate abolitionists, led by **James G. Birney** and Lewis and Arthur Tappan, formed the **American and Foreign Anti-Slavery Society**. The AFASS rejected women's rights, pacifism, and other causes and focused only on slavery. The election of Abby Kelley to the AASS board precipitated the creation of the new organization, but this was not the only cause of the schism. Garrison and other leaders of the AASS had mounted an unrelenting campaign against the organized churches—"synagogues of Satan" and "cages of unclean birds" as one Garrisonian called them. But other abolitionists, evangelicals such as Arthur and Lewis Tappan, James G. Birney, and **William Jay** (the son of former Chief Justice **John Jay**) were more orthodox in their religious beliefs and support for existing churches. They were also not ready to mix antislavery with support for women's rights and other issues. Thus, in 1840 a number of key AASS members, led by the Tappans and Birney, formed the AFASS. The organization would continue to operate until the mid-1850s, when it faded from the scene. The split between the two antislavery societies left both of them weaker. But, by competing with each other, they probably increased the total number of antislavery books, pamphlets, and newspapers in circulation, and gave more people access to antislavery ideas.

Initially, the new organization ignored politics, but shortly after the schism, the Tappans and Birney help form the **Liberty Party**, with Birney as its first presidential candidate in 1840. The Liberty Party was the first political party in the nation's history to openly oppose slavery. By this time, the antislavery movement was beginning to have an effect on electoral politics. Antislavery sentiment was particularly strong in northern New England, northern and central New York, much of Massachusetts, northern Ohio, and the new state of Michigan. Some Whig members of Congress, such as **John Quincy Adams** of Massachusetts, Seth Gates of New York, Joshua Giddings of Ohio, and William Slade of Vermont, were openly sympathetic to antislavery. So too were some important state politicians, like Governor **William H. Seward** of New York. But antislavery Whigs were a minority in their party. While a few Democrats also opposed slavery, for the most part the office holders and rank and file of the Democracy were deeply hostile to antislavery. The national **Democratic Party** was dominated by Southerners, and most Northern Democrats followed their lead on issues of slavery and race. The Liberty Party offered antislavery voters an opportunity to express their opposition to slavery and their disgust that neither of the two major parties was willing to take a stand against slavery. In 1840, the new party won only 7,000 votes nationally, and had no effect on the election.

In 1844, Birney again ran for president on the Liberty ticket. This time he won slightly over 62,000 votes. The party won no electoral votes, but may have taken enough votes from the Whig candidate, Henry Clay, to give the election to the Democrat, James K. Polk. In the popular vote, Polk beat Clay by just over 38,000 votes. In New York, Clay lost to Polk by fewer than 5,000 votes, while the Liberty Party won about three times that many votes. Clay believed the Liberty Party cost him New York, and the election. He was certain that he would have won most of the votes going to Birney had there been no Liberty Party, and thus but for the third party would have been elected president. But, this analysis, supported by some historians, assumes that the antislavery voters who supported Birney would have been willing, in the absence of an antislavery party, to vote for the slave-holding Clay. This is at least debatable. It is just as likely they would have stayed home and refused to vote for either slave-holding candidate.

In 1848, another antislavery party emerged, the Free Soil Party. In the wake of the war with Mexico, the Free Soilers insisted on preventing the spread of slavery into the west. Unlike the Liberty Party, the Free Soilers were not dedicated to ending slavery where it existed. The new party nominated Martin Van Buren, the former Democratic president, who had great popularity among Northern Democrats, particularly in his home state of New York. Despite the Party's refusal to attack the existence of slavery, the Free Soilers' commitment to stopping the spread of slavery made their organization an important and powerful alternative to the Whigs and Democrats for those voters who opposed slavery. Before 1848, mainstream antislavery politicians had generally been Whigs. But in 1848, the Democrats faced the problem of a rank and file revolt against allowing slavery to exist in the newly acquired territories. This was perhaps a testament to the success of the abolitionists. While neither of the two major antislavery societies had gained very many members, together they had helped usher in a sea change in Northern opinion. Thus, many Northern Democrats now had to offer some antislavery sentiments to their constituents. The Free Soil Party appealed to these Democrats, as well as to the Liberty Party voters.

The Free Soil Party's candidate, former Democratic president, Martin Van Buren, gained over 290,000 votes. Van Buren clearly took votes away from the Democratic candidate, Lewis Cass, setting the stage for the Whig candidate to win the election. Meanwhile, other Free Soilers were elected to state legislatures and Congress. In Ohio, a small group of Free Soilers held the balance of power between the Democrats and Whigs. They leveraged this position to gain repeal of most of Ohio's black laws and to send an abolitionist, Democrat **Salmon P. Chase**, to the U.S. Senate. Joining him that term was the Whig abolitionist, William Henry Seward of New York. Scores of others in the House and Senate were now adamantly opposed to slavery in one form or another. Few came close to the Garrisonian position of immediate abolition. Almost all believed the federal government had no power to end slavery in the states. However, the antislavery men in the House and Senate were determined to prevent the spread of slavery into new territories and states, and were willing to fight to chip away at slavery where they could—such as in the District of Columbia, the federal territories—and by more effectively enforcing the ban on the African Slave trade. They unsuccessfully opposed the stringent **Fugitive Slave Law** of 1850, but its repeal would be part of the political agenda of antislavery activists for the rest of the decade.

By the 1850s, antislavery was part of mainstream politics in the North. The AASS and the AFASS continued to agitate, send out speakers, publish attacks on slavery, aid fugitive slaves, and fight segregation and racism. William C. Nell, a black Garrisonian, spearheaded a drive to integrate Boston's schools. His work led to the first school desegregation case, *Roberts v. Boston* (1850), which was argued by Charles Sumner, the soon-to-be abolitionist U.S. Senator, and Robert Morris, one of the first black attorneys in the nation. The plaintiffs lost before the Massachusetts Supreme Judicial Court, but Nell did not stop there. Despite the Garrisonian rejection of voting, Nell persistently petitioned the state legislature, ultimately succeeding with a law in 1855 that banned segregation in the state's public schools.

Informal and small antislavery groups helped fugitive slaves evade capture and aided them in seeking shelter in the United States or in **Canada**. They included some groups that were exclusively black and some that were integrated. In the 1830s, the black leader, **David Ruggles**, organized the **New York Committee of Vigilance** in New York City. The Committee helped hide fugitive slaves and helped expose professional slave catchers. After the adoption of the 1850 Fugitive Slave Law, blacks, sometimes working with whites, organized more vigilance committees to help protect themselves from slave catchers. In 1851, at Christiana, Pennsylvania, scores of blacks and whites showed up when horns were blown because a master was trying to recover his fugitive slave. The abolitionists tried to talk the master out of seeking his slave, and when this failed, gunfire broke out.

The master was killed, the slaves escaped, and the government indicted numerous bystanders for treason. Abolitionist lawyers, including the Whig congressman Thaddeus Stevens, defended those indicted, all of whom were acquitted.

The major antislavery organizations persistently denounced the fugitive slave laws and helped raise money for fugitives in Canada. Attorneys who were members of the AASS and AFASS often represented fugitive slaves or those charged with helping them escape. In New York City, for example, William Jay and his son John Jay, Jr., were extremely active in supporting fugitive slaves, as were a number of Liberty Party men. American abolitionists corresponded with members of the Anti-Slavery Society of Canada and other Canadians who were dedicated to helping fugitive slaves. Americans like Frederick Douglass and Wendell Phillips lectured in Canada. John Brown, who operated outside of any organizational structures that were not his own, held a meeting in Ontario to plan his raid on Harpers Ferry.

Most of the antislavery societies were integrated—at least if there were blacks in the area. Many local societies were in the rural North, where few, if any, blacks lived. African Americans organized numerous societies and conventions, focusing on their social, political, and legal rights. Slavery, and especially the protection of fugitive slaves and stopping the kidnapping of free blacks, was always on their agenda. But, these organizations were far broader than the traditional antislavery societies. Overlapping interests led to cooperation between black and white groups on a variety of issues. Indeed, one of the great legacies of antislavery was the development of interracial cooperation. Equally important was the development of separate black groups that provided leadership training and organizational skills that helped develop Northern black communities and set the stage for black leadership in the post-Civil War South.

Mainstream Politics and the End of Slavery

In 1854, the Democratic majority in Congress passed the Kansas-Nebraska Act, opening almost all of the western territories to slavery. This led to the formation of the Republican Party. By 1856, most political abolitionists had become Republicans. The AFASS virtually disappeared, as did what was left of the Liberty Party. The Republicans were not a single-issue party. The party took positions on tariffs, land policy, Mormon polygamy, banking and currency, and foreign policy. But, the party's biggest issue was slavery. The Republican Party captured Northern state legislatures, elected governors, congressmen, and senators. In 1860, it would capture the presidency. The first Republican president, **Abraham Lincoln**, personally hated slavery. He correctly understood the Constitution to protect slavery where it already existed, but he was determined to prevent its spread to new places.

Lincoln's election was an ironic culmination of decades of abolitionist agitation. The Garrisonians sneered at Lincoln. Referring to one case where Lincoln represented a slaveowner (and lost), Wendell Phillips called him "the slave hound of Illinois." Lincoln similarly despised the disunionism of Garrison and Phillips and the violence of their new hero, John Brown. In fact, however,

Lincoln and his party owed much of their success to the organized antislavery movement of the previous three decades. Abolitionists like Phillips, Garrison, Douglass (who voted for Lincoln), **Theodore Dwight Weld, Elizabeth Cady Stanton**, Abby Kelley Foster, **Harriet Beecher Stowe,** and **Gerrit Smith** had convinced the vast majority of Northern whites that slavery was simply wrong, that it was sinful and unnatural, and that it violated the basic principles of American society. Lincoln and his party provided an effective political vehicle for implementing these sentiments.

During the Civil War, the Republican Party and the U.S. Army became the most effective instrument of antislavery philosophy and politics. Abolitionists like Chase and Seward entered Lincoln's cabinet. Other abolitionists were military officers, including Reverend Thomas Wentworth Higginson. In the 1840s, he was a member of the Essex County Antislavery Society. He later ran for Congress as a Free Soiler. At the same time he worked with Garrison and supported women's rights. In 1854, Higginson had helped storm a Boston jail in an unsuccessful attempt to rescue the fugitive slave **Anthony Burns**. He was allied with Garrison intellectually, on some issues, but rejected non-resistance and pacifism. In 1854, Higginson also helped organize the Massachusetts Kansas Aid Committee, which worked with the Kansas Emigrant Aid Society. Higginson's "aid" to settlers in Kansas often took the form of rifles known as "Beecher's Bibles." In 1857, he organized a "disunion" convention in Worcester, Massachusetts. In 1858 and 1859, he was one of the "secret six" who backed John Brown in his abortive raid on Harpers Ferry. In 1862, he accepted a commission as a Colonel in the First South Carolina Volunteers, a regiment made up of former slaves who enlisted on the South Carolina Sea Islands. He spent the next two years fighting slavery as a soldier and a commander of black troops. In 1864, he left the army because of illness.

Meanwhile, other abolitionists moved to the South to set up schools for former slaves and in other ways to help them adjust to freedom. In 1862, for example, James Miller McKim organized the Philadelphia Port Royal Relief Committee, which later became known as the Pennsylvania Freedmen's Relief Association. Before the war, McKim had been the general agent for the Pennsylvania Anti-Slavery Society. McKim illustrates the flexibility of abolitionists. He was Garrisonian in his view that the Constitution was proslavery, but he worked closely with legislators in Pennsylvania and also supported John Brown. And, when the war began he worked with former slaves. He was also a member of the Union League of Philadelphia and helped recruit black regiments in the state. He remained involved in helping former slaves until 1869. He also fought for a ban on segregation in public transportation in Pennsylvania.

Unlike McKim, Garrison thought his work was done in 1865 when he dissolved the American Anti-Slavery Society, believing that the adoption of the **Thirteenth Amendment** had rendered his organization no longer necessary. In retrospect, we know that conclusion was a mistake. After slavery, blacks needed support, education, and activist allies. Some white abolitionists like McKim stayed longer. Wendell Phillips continued to be concerned about the plight of blacks, but also focused on labor reform after the war.

Black abolitionists like Frederick Douglass continued their work until the end of their lives.

In the end, the antislavery movement set the moral tone for the nation. The leaders of the movement developed organizing skills and propaganda techniques. Despite intramural disputes and disagreements over tactics and theories, in retrospect the antislavery movement was surprisingly coherent. The schisms and internal disputes mask the diversity of opinions and the ability of abolitionists to accept a variety of tactics and goals. Garrison, Phillips, or McKim may not have voted, but they worked well with politicians in their own states and many of their followers did vote. The non-voting abolitionists helped create a huge constituency of fellow travelers who did vote, and who would ultimately only vote for opponents of slavery. At the social level, not all abolitionists were integrationists, or even racial egalitarians. But, the organizations almost universally opposed discrimination and emphatically supported black rights. Abolitionists fought for integrated education, antidiscrimination laws, and black suffrage. Abolitionist women in Massachusetts successfully petitioned the legislature to repeal the state's ban on interracial marriage, because they believed the state should have no laws that sanctioned racial discrimination. Even non-political Garrisonians agitated for blacks to have the same right to vote as whites. Interracial cooperation within the movement was never perfect. But, nowhere else in the United States was there as much cooperation and interracial opportunity. Much of the post-war black leadership came out of the antislavery movement. Similarly, women in the movement gained valuable experience, which they applied to their fight for legal equality after the war. The top leaders of the women's movement—Elizabeth Cady Stanton, **Lucretia Mott**, and Susan B. Anthony—had all been active abolitionists before the war. A final legacy of organized antislavery was its persistence and staying power. For more than three decades abolitionists labored against the monstrous injustice of slavery. They provide a model of how to keep an eye on the prize through decades of struggle and discouragement. *See also* Immediate Emancipation; Mexican War and Antislavery; Postal Campaign; Whig Party and Antislavery.

Further Readings: Finkelman, Paul. *Slavery and the Founders: Race and Liberty in the Age of Jefferson.* Armonk, NY: M.E. Sharpe, 1996; Foner, Eric. *Free Soil, Free Labor, Free Men: The Ideology of the Republican Party before the Civil War.* Reprint ed. New York: Oxford University Press, 1995; Stewart, James Brewer. *Holy Warriors: The Abolitionists and American Slavery.* 2nd ed. New York: Hill and Wang, 1997; Walters, Ronald. *The Antislavery Appeal: American Abolitionism After 1830.* New York: W.W. Norton and Company, 1985.

Paul Finkelman

United States Constitution and Antislavery

The United States Constitution protected slavery in a variety of ways. Article I, Sec. 2. Par. 3, contained the three-fifths clause, which counted three fifths of all slaves for purposes of representation in Congress. That provision vastly increased the power of the South in Congress. The three-fifths clause also gave the South extra power in electing the president because the allocation of presidential electors was based on the number of representatives in Congress. **Thomas Jefferson**, who owned nearly 200 slaves, would not have been elected president in 1800 without the extra electors produced by the three-fifths clause. Article I, Sec. 8, Par. 15, known as the domestic insurrections clause, empowered Congress to call "forth the Militia" to "suppress Insurrections," including slave rebellions. Southerners were delighted by this provision, as well as one in Article IV, Sec. 4, known as the domestic violence provision guaranteeing that the U.S. government would protect states from "domestic violence," including slave rebellions. Article I, Sec. 9, Par. 1, popularly known as the "slave trade clause," prohibited Congress from banning the African slave trade before 1808. Under this clause, more Southerners imported about 100,000 Africans into the United States in the early nineteenth century. The amendment provisions of Article V further protected the slave trade by specifically prohibiting any modification of that provision before 1808. Article I, Section 9 and Section 10 prohibited taxes on exports, which Southerners demanded as a way of prohibiting an indirect tax on slavery and slave produced products. Article IV, Sec. 2, Par. 3, the fugitive slave clause, prohibited the states from emancipating fugitive slaves and required that runaways be returned to their owners "on demand."

Besides specific clauses of the Constitution, the structure of the entire document ensured against emancipation by the new federal government. Because the Constitution created a government of limited powers, Congress lacked the power to interfere in the domestic institutions of the states. Thus, during the ratification debates, only the most fearful Southern antifederalists opposed the Constitution on the grounds that it threatened slavery. But most Southerners agreed with the federalists, who argued that the Constitution created a limited government that could not harm slavery. For example, General Charles Cotesworth Pinckney of South Carolina, crowed to his state's house of representatives, "We have a security that the general government can never emancipate them, for no such authority is granted and it is admitted, on all hands, that the general government has no powers but what are expressly granted by the Constitution, and that all rights not expressed were reserved by the several states." Similarly, at the Virginia ratification convention, Edmund Randolph asserted, "Were it right here to mention what passed in [the Philadelphia] convention... I might tell you *that the Southern States, even South Carolina herself, conceived this property to be secure*" and that "there was not a member of the Virginia delegation who had *the smallest suspicion of the abolition of slavery*."

The amendment process, set out in Article V, further secured slavery. Under Article V, an amendment required the ratification of three-fourths of the states. As long as the slave states voted against an amendment, it could not pass. In 1860, for example, there were thirty-three states, of which fifteen were slave states, thereby eliminating the possibility of twenty-five states (three-fourths of all the states) voting against Southern interests. Voting as a block, these states can still prevent any amendment to the Constitution, even in the modern fifty-state nation.

Because of these many proslavery provisions and compromises with slavery, and the impossibility of ending slavery through a constitutional process,

William Lloyd Garrison, the great nineteenth-century abolitionist, called the Constitution a "covenant with death" and "an agreement with Hell." Garrison and his followers refused to participate in American electoral politics, arguing that if they did so, they would be supporting "the pro-slavery, war sanctioning Constitution of the United States." Instead, under the slogan "No Union with Slaveholders," the **Garrisonians** repeatedly argued for dissolution of the Union.

Part of Garrisonian opposition to the Union stemmed from their desire to avoid the corruption that came from participating in a government created by what they considered a proslavery Constitution. But their position was also at least theoretically pragmatic. The Garrisonians were convinced that the legal protection of slavery in the Constitution made political activity not only futile, but actually counterproductive. They believed that traditional political activity created popular support for the constitutional order, which in turn strengthened the stranglehold slavery had on America. In his pamphlet, *Can Abolitionists Vote or Take Office Under the United States Constitution* (1845), **Wendell Phillips** pointed out that in the years since the adoption of the Constitution, Americans had witnessed "the slaves trebling in numbers—slaveholders monopolizing the offices and dictating the policy of the Government—prostituting the strength and influence of the Nation to the support of slavery here and elsewhere—trampling on the rights of the free States, and making the courts of the country their tools." Phillips argued that this experience proved "that it is impossible for free and slave States to unite on any terms, without all becoming partners in the guilt and responsible for the sin of slavery."

The Garrisonians ultimately argued that since the political system and the Constitution were stacked in favor of slavery, it was a pointless waste of their time and money to try to fight slavery through electoral politics. The Garrisonian critique of the Constitution logically led to the conclusion that the free states should secede from the union. Garrisonians thus rallied to the slogan "No Union with Slaveholders."

Other nineteenth-century antislavery leaders disagreed with the Garrisonians. **Salmon P. Chase**, the most successful antislavery politician of the period, fought throughout the antebellum period to convince his colleagues in Congress, the judiciary, and Northern voters that the Constitution was really antislavery. Chase argued that abolitionists should use the political process to prevent the expansion of slavery and the addition of new slave states. He believed repeal of the fugitive slave laws and other laws protecting slavery were ways in which the Constitution could be used to fight bondage. **Frederick Douglass**, who began his career as a Garrisonian, eventually came to accept the idea that the Constitution could be used to fight slavery. He went so far as to argue that the "three-fifths clause" leaned toward freedom. This analysis ignored the fact that the clause gave extra representation in Congress to the South for its slaves, but of course did not give the slaves any particular power. If the clause leaned toward freedom, it was only because it did not give the South full representation for its slaves.

Despite their creative perseverance, the efforts of Chase, Douglass, **William H. Seward**, and other political abolitionists failed. The United States

Supreme Court almost always protected slavery in the cases it heard. Likewise, almost all American presidents and their cabinet officers protected slavery in foreign and domestic politics. Perhaps most frustrating to the political abolitionists was the fact that some of their most brilliant allies in the crusade against slavery, the Garrisonians, agreed with their enemies on the meaning of the Constitution. Thus, one Ohio **Liberty Party** man, who believed in using politics to fight slavery, expressed his frustration with the Garrisonians after reading Wendell Phillips's pamphlet on the Constitution: "Garrison, Phillips, and Quincy; Calhoun, Rhett, and McDuffie; all harmoniously laboring to prevent such a construction of the Constitution as would abolish slavery."

Once the Civil War began, however, the Lincoln Administration was able to use the Constitution to attack slavery. Lincoln found the necessary authority to issue the **Emancipation Proclamation** in his powers as commander-in-chief. Furthermore, with eleven of the fifteen slave states no longer participating in the government, Congress was free to limit slavery as much as possible. Thus, Congress repealed the Fugitive Slave Laws, banned slavery in the territories, and then ended slavery in the District of Columbia. In 1865, Congress sent the Thirteenth Amendment—ending slavery—to the states. The slave states could come back to the Union only if they ratified this amendment. Thus, in four years of the Civil War, the proslavery Constitution was remade as an antislavery document. Over the next five years, antislavery Republicans would pass two more amendments that further changed the Constitution to give blacks equal political and constitutional rights. *See also* Declaration of Independence; Radical Republicans; Thirteenth Amendment.

Further Readings: Finkelman, Paul. *Slavery and the Founders: Race and Liberty in the Age of Jefferson.* 2nd ed. Armonk, NY: M.E. Sharpe, 2001; Foner, Eric. *Free Soil, Free Labor, Free Men.* New York: Oxford University Press, 1970; Wiecek, William M. *The Sources of Antislavery Constitutionalism in America, 1760–1848.* Ithaca, NY: Cornell University Press, 1977.

Paul Finkelman

United States South, Antislavery in

Long before the dramatic rise of the organized abolitionist movement in the early nineteenth century, slaves themselves commenced resistance and rebellion in the United States South, which had become the heartland of the nation's slave system. In numerous ways slaves signaled their discontent with servitude, by running away, by malingering, sabotage, and arson. Because during the seventeenth and eighteenth centuries parts of the South were still sparsely settled, especially sections of swamps, woods, and mountains, entire small groups hid out as maroons, evading capture for months or even years at a time. While there were no large-scale revolts like those led by **Spartacus** against Rome, there were sporadic uprisings, such as that of a small but determined group of slaves who killed several whites at Stono, South Carolina in 1739, apparently aiming to escape to the colony of free blacks under the Spanish at St. Augustine in Florida.

In addition to actions such as these, the culture and daily life of slaves provided ways to resist as well. Folklore is replete with tales of slaves who outwitted their masters, who like the "trickster" Br'er Rabbit, found their way to safety in the "briar patch." Songs such as "Jimmie Crack Corn," composed by Daniel Emmett with the likely help of African-Americans, made fun of the pomposity of the masters, and took covert satisfaction when they were "accidentally" killed by the Blue Tail Fly.

During the American Revolution, tens of thousands of slaves fled to the British side, having been promised freedom if they did so. All these aspects of early American slave life suggest the constant pressure of slaves themselves against the system.

Small religious groups such as the **Quakers** had long expressed their opposition to slavery, as did figures like the Deist **Thomas Paine**. The Presbyterian leader David Rice made an impassioned plea against slavery at the Constitutional Convention in Kentucky in 1792, but that state was admitted with its "peculiar institution" intact.

In the first two decades of the nineteenth century, the South provided many examples of small groups, mostly of religious leaders, who opposed slavery. In Jonesborough, Tennessee, the Quaker Elihu Embree published seven issues of *The Emancipator* in 1820. After his death that same year, **Benjamin Lundy** started *The Genius of Universal Emancipation* in Greeneville, but moved it to Baltimore in 1824. While it is sometimes claimed that these initiatives represented the beginnings of the abolitionist movement, they usually took a gradualist position, and even supported the "return to Africa" colonization societies. However, **William Lloyd Garrison** was clearly inspired by Lundy's example, and thus there are some valid connections between these isolated and beleaguered Southern antislavery writers and the militant groups that emerged in the 1830s.

The **Nat Turner** Revolt of 1831 led to a complex but open debate about slavery in the Virginia legislature, where opponents tended to come from the western mountain sections, while proponents were from the tidewater and piedmont sections where tobacco produced by slaves was carried out on a large scale. The antislavery forces were defeated, but at least there had been a frank discussion on the issue.

By the middle of the 1830s, Northern abolitionists launched a campaign to saturate the South with their literature, but this only led to violent opposition, including the dramatic burning of U.S. mail by a mob in Charleston in 1835. While the Deist "Founding Fathers" had tended to hope that slavery might eventually and gradually disappear, the 1830s saw a new rigidity on the part of the masters. Gradualism, after all, might be postponed indefinitely, while the immediatism of Garrison and his followers presented them with a more urgent challenge to the entire system. Even though at this time Garrison remained a pacifist or "non resistant," any kind of opposition was met by determined force. As the number of slaves had grown to three million, now almost entirely confined to the South (with emancipation now in effect throughout the North), and their labor was essential to the profitability of the industrialized system of agriculture, the stakes were high indeed.

The tier of Deep South states from South Carolina to Texas was the heart of large scale rice and cotton production, with tobacco predominating in Virginia and North Carolina. The Border States from Maryland to Missouri included mountain areas where poor whites already disliked the predominance of the lowland, tidewater, and river districts, and sometimes assisted escaping slaves. These states provided distinct enclaves of safety and support, both for slaves and abolitionist sympathizers, from the mountains of what would be separated from Virginia to form the new state of West Virginia in 1863, to urban centers like Louisville and St. Louis, where one could hide out at least temporarily.

In spite of this heightened bitterness, Southern figures like **Cassius M. Clay** of Kentucky continued to argue against slavery, though his case emphasized the harmful effects of slavery not so much for its own sake, but because it threatened the well-being of free white labor. In 1845, a mob seized the press of Clay's newspaper *The True American* and shipped it north to Cincinnati. Though Clay courageously continued his struggle, he had little success; while there was a debate about slavery in the Constitution Convention of 1849 in Kentucky, all efforts to abolish it went down to defeat. While Clay remained in the state, many other Southern abolitionists found it necessary to move North in order to avoid assassination. However, their experiences told in books and speeches inflamed Northern opinion. Scores of slave narratives provided vivid details of oppression, brutality and suffering.

The operations of the **Underground Railroad,** as well as less organized individual escapes, meant that by the 1850s, 50,000 slaves per year were attempting to flee. Most of these were captured, but the sheer effort required to try to maintain the system in place was enormous.

By the mid 1850s, a significant component of the antislavery movement included the new immigrants from Germany and other European countries, largely consisting of radical veterans of the Revolutions of 1848. As far west as San Antonio, Adolph Douai published an antislavery German language newspaper until he, too, was forced to leave Texas in 1856. By 1860, things had become so violent in Texas that a peddler who was found with copies of **Hinton Helper's** *The Impending Crisis* in his wagon was suspended from a tree branch, the wagon soaked with oil, and the man burned to death by his own wares.

The sum of this history suggests that the gradualist and colonization tendencies of the emancipation struggle were doomed to be ineffective. Similarly, pacifist and other strategies that emphasized moral persuasion did not succeed. The dynamic convergence of blacks and whites in the Underground Railroad and the broader movement threatened the basis of the slavery system, but in the end it was force in the form of the Union Army that led to the end of slavery in the South.

Further Readings: Aptheker, Herbert. *American Negro Slave Revolts.* 5th ed. New York: International, 1983; Degler, Carl N. *The Other South: Southern Dissenters in the Nineteenth Century.* New York: Harper & Row, 1974; Dillon, Merton L. *Slavery Attacked: Southern Slaves and their Allies 1619–1865.* Baton Rouge: Louisiana State University Press, 1990; Franklin, John Hope, and Loren Schweninger. *Runaway Slaves: Rebels on the Plantation.* New York: Oxford University Press, 1999; Harrold, Stanley. *The Abolitionists and the South, 1831–1861.* Lexington: University Press of Kentucky, 1995; Osofsky, Gilbert, ed. *Puttin' on Ole Massa.* New York: Harper, 1969.

Fred Whitehead

V

Vesey, Denmark. *See* Vesey's Conspiracy

Vesey's Conspiracy (1822)

Perhaps the largest slave conspiracy in North American history, the Charleston, South Carolina, plot was organized by Denmark Vesey, a free black carpenter. Although brought into the city in 1783 as a slave of Captain Joseph Vesey, Telemaque, as he was then known, purchased his freedom in December 1799 with lottery winnings. For the next twenty-two years, Vesey earned his living as a craftsman and, according to white authorities, was "distinguished for [his] great strength and activity," and the black community "always looked up to [him] with awe and respect." His last (and probably third) wife, Susan Vesey, was born a slave but became free prior to his death. But his first wife, Beck, remained a slave, as did Vesey's sons, Polydore, Robert, and Sandy, who was the only one of his children to be implicated in his 1822 conspiracy.

Around 1818, Vesey joined the city's new African Methodist Episcopal congregation. The African Church, as both whites and blacks called it, quickly became the center of Charleston's enslaved community. Sandy Vesey also joined, as did four of Vesey's closest friends: Peter Poyas, a literate and highly skilled ship carpenter; Monday Gell, an African-born Ibo, who labored as a harness maker; Rolla Bennett, the manservant of Governor Thomas Bennett; and "Gullah" Jack Pritchard, an East African priest purchased in Zinguebar in 1806. The temporary closure of the church by city authorities in June 1818, and the arrest of 140 congregants, one of them presumably Vesey himself, only reinforced the determination of black Carolinians to maintain a place of independent worship and established the initial motivation for his conspiracy. The "African Church was the people," Monday Gell insisted. He and Pritchard had considered insurrection in 1818, he swore, "and now they had begun again to try it."

At the age of fifty-one, Vesey resolved to orchestrate a rebellion followed by a mass exodus from Charleston to Haiti. President **Jean-Pierre Boyer** had recently encouraged black Americans to bring their skills and capital to his beleaguered republic. Vesey did not intend to tarry in Charleston long enough for white military power to present an effective counterassault. "As soon as they could get the money from the Banks, and the goods from the stores," Rolla Bennett insisted, "they should hoist sail for Saint Doming[ue]" and live as free men. For all of his acculturation into Euro-American society, Vesey, as a native of St. Thomas, remained a man of the black Atlantic.

Vesey planned the escape for nearly four years. His chief lieutenants included Poyas, Gell, Pritchard, and Rolla Bennett. Although there are no reliable figures for the number of recruits, Charleston alone was home to 12,652 slaves. Pritchard, probably with some exaggeration, boasted that he had 6,600 recruits on the plantations across the Cooper and Ashley Rivers. The plan called for Vesey's followers to rise at midnight on Sunday, July 14— Bastille Day—slay their masters, and sail for Haiti and freedom. As one Southern editor later conceded, "The plot seems to have been well devised, and its operation was extensive."

Those recruited into the plot during the winter of 1822 were directed to arm themselves from their masters' closets. Vesey was also aware that the Charleston Neck militia company stored their 300 muskets and bayonets in the back room of Benjamin Hammet's King Street store, and that Hammet's slave, Bacchus, had a key. But as few slaves had any experience with guns, Vesey encouraged his followers to arm themselves with swords or long daggers, which in any case would make for quieter work as the city bells tolled midnight. Vesey also employed several enslaved blacksmiths to forge "pike heads and bayonets with sockets, to be fixed at the end of long poles."

Considerably easier than stockpiling weapons was the recruitment of willing young men. With Vesey and Pritchard employed about the city as carpenters, it is hardly surprising that so many other craftsmen became involved in the plot. Most of all, Vesey and his lieutenants recruited out of the African Church. As a class leader, Vesey was not only respected by the church membership, but he knew each of them well; he knew whom to trust and whom to avoid. As former Charleston slave Archibald Grimké later wrote, Vesey's nightly classes provided him "with a singularly safe medium for conducting his underground agitation."

The plot unraveled in June 1822 when two slaves, including Rolla's friend, George Wilson, a fellow class leader in the African Church, revealed the plan to their owners. Mayor James Hamilton called up the city militia and convened a special court to try the captured insurgents. Vesey was captured at the home of Beck, his first wife, on June 21 and hanged on the morning of Tuesday, July 2, together with Rolla, Poyas, and three other rebels. According to Hamilton, the six men collectively "met their fate with the heroic fortitude of Martyrs." In all, thirty-five slaves were executed. Forty-two others, including Sandy Vesey, were sold outside the United States; some, if not all, became slaves in Spanish Cuba. Robert Vesey lived to rebuild the African Church in the fall of 1865.

In the aftermath of the conspiracy, Charleston authorities demolished the African Church and banished Morris Brown to Philadelphia. The state Assembly subsequently passed laws prohibiting the reentry of free blacks into the state, and city officials enforced ordinances against teaching African

Americans to read. The City Council also voted to create a permanent force of 150 guardsmen to patrol the streets around the clock at an annual cost of $24,000. To deal with the problem of black mariners bringing information about events around the Atlantic into the state's ports, in December 1822 the legislature passed the Negro Seamen Act, which placed a quarantine on any vessel from another "state or foreign port, having on board any free negroes or persons of color." Although U.S. Circuit Court Judge William Johnson struck the law down as unconstitutional, a defiant Assembly renewed the act in late 1823. It would be no coincidence that many of those who nullified the federal law in 1832—including then-Governor James Hamilton, who resigned his office in 1833 to command troops in defense of his state's right to resist national tariffs—were veterans of the tribunals that tried Vesey and his men a decade before. *See also* Gabriel's Conspiracy; Turner, Nat.

Further Readings: Egerton, Douglas R. *He Shall Go Out Free: The Lives of Denmark Vesey.* Madison, WI: Madison House, 1999; Freehling, William W. *The Reintegration of American History: Slavery and the Civil War.* New York: Oxford University Press, 1994; Lofton, John. *Insurrection in South Carolina: The Turbulent World of Denmark Vesey.* Yellow Springs: Antioch Press, 1964; Paquette, Robert L. "Jacobins of the Lowcountry: The Vesey Plot on Trial." *William and Mary Quarterly,* 59 (January 2002): 185–192.

Douglas R. Egerton

Violence and Non-violence in American Abolitionism

A common assumption shared by historians as well as people generally is that the great majority of American abolitionists were doctrinaire pacifists. Accordingly, John Brown and other antislavery activists who either advocated or engaged in violent tactics were exceptional. Yet, while abolitionists acknowledged the desirability of relying on peaceful tactics, they were not inflexible in regard to violent means. They recognized that white Americans had won freedom from Great Britain through violent means, and they refused to rule out a similar option for African Americans. In January 1842, for example, white abolitionist leader **Gerrit Smith** noted that although "there are ... some persons in our ranks who are opposed to the taking of human life in any circumstances.... the great majority of abolitionists justify their forefathers' bloody resistance to oppression." They could, therefore, oppose slave revolt only on the basis of "expediency." In other words, most abolitionists were ambivalent concerning means. They endorsed violent or non-violent tactics depending on their perception of conditions. Immediate abolitionism arose in the North at a time when black antislavery violence in the South made it expedient for antislavery societies to endorse nonviolence. But, as time passed, abolitionists found violence to be increasingly expedient.

Black Antislavery Violence

During the 1820s and early 1830s, violent black liberators in the South and violent black rhetoric in the North influenced the rise of **immediate**

emancipation. In 1822, a free black carpenter named Denmark Vesey led a slave-revolt conspiracy in Charleston, South Carolina (see Vesey's Conspiracy). The conspiracy collapsed when informants revealed it to their masters. Until recently historians believed the conspiracy, for which Vesey and with thirty-five others were executed, had little impact beyond South Carolina. But historian Peter P. Hinks indicates that unrest within Charleston's black community, if not Vesey himself, directly influenced black abolitionist David Walker. Walker, who had been born free in North Carolina and visited Charleston during the early 1820s, published his *Appeal to the Colored Citizens of the World* in Boston in 1829. The *Appeal* urged black men to assert their masculinity through violent resistance to their masters. It recalled the successful slave revolution in Haiti led by **Toussaint L'Ouverture** and predicted that God would raise up a black warrior to deliver African Americans from oppression.

By relying on black and white seamen, Walker, who died in 1830, was able to circulate his *Appeal* in the South. This, along with **William Lloyd Garrison**'s initiation of his newspaper, *The Liberator*, in January 1831, led many white Southerners to assume that Northern abolitionists encouraged **Nat Turner**'s August 1831 slave revolt in Southampton Country, Virginia. There is no proof that such a linkage existed. But when Turner and his band of more than sixty black men killed approximately fifty-seven white men, women, and children, they convinced white Southerners that a real threat of violent abolitionism existed.

White militia overwhelmed Turner's uprising. He and seventeen of his associates were hanged, and white vigilantes killed at least 100 other African Americans in Virginia and North Carolina. In the North, black and white abolitionists joined in a general revulsion against the bloodshed that Turner had unleashed. Although abolitionists compared Turner to George Washington, L'Ouverture, and other liberators, they emphasized that they did not endorse his violent methods. Instead, they warned that without immediate peaceful abolition, additional slaves would follow his violent example. In other words, they urged a peaceful solution to slavery backed with a violent threat.

Nonviolence

Memories of Turner's revolt and white Southern accusations of abolitionist complicity in it were fresh as immediatists organized in the Northeast during the early 1830s. Invariably they pledged themselves to non-violent means. The New York Anti-Slavery Society at its initial meeting in October 1833 declared, "We have no force but the force of truth." Those assembled promised never to "countenance the oppressed in vindicating their rights by resorting to force." Two months later, the American Anti-Slavery Society's Declaration of Sentiments called on slaves "to reject the use of all carnal weapons for deliverance from bondage."

Sincere Christian morality, including **Quaker** and evangelical strains, influenced these pledges. Non-violence remained a powerful component of immediatism until the Civil War, especially among Garrison and his associates. But circumstances as much as Christianity shaped early immedia-tist rejection of force. A tiny band of abolitionists, already suspect because of its radical views on slavery and race, and accused of involvement in Turner's revolt, dared not put itself beyond the law and outrage public opinion by appearing to justify race war.

Once established as policy, non-violence among abolitionists developed during the 1830s under the influence of a feminized masculinity common among northeastern reformers. Many abolitionist men favored what they regarded as feminine persuasion over male aggressiveness. Conscious of slavery's brutality, a few of them renounced involvement in any system that rested on force. In 1838, Garrison and his friend **Henry C. Wright** formed the Nonresistance Society, which renounced involvement in any form of vi-olence. Members refused to defend themselves. They also became anar-chists because all human government is based ultimately on force. The great majority of abolitionists, including some leading **Garrisonians**, how-ever, opposed non-resistance. They associated it with heretical religion and saw in its rejection of human government a threat to the northern social order. Yet **Lewis Tappan** and other church-oriented abolitionists fervently embraced peaceful means. Tappan and a few other evangelicals approached non-resistance in their refusal to defend themselves or their property against antiabolitionists or to sue in court those who harmed them.

Led by the **American Anti-Slavery Society** (AASS), abolitionists during the 1830s initiated a variety of peaceful strategies (usually referred to as "moral suasion") that continued throughout the following decades. They rapidly formed local antislavery societies across the Northeast and Old Northwest, so that by 1838 the AASS claimed to have 1,350 affiliates and a total of 250,000 members. In 1835, the AASS executive committee, under the leadership of Lewis Tappan, organized an ambitious **postal campaign** designed to send huge amounts of antislavery literature to white Southern-ers. At about the same time, the AASS initiated a gigantic petitioning cam-paign calling on Congress to abolish slavery in the District of Columbia. Abolitionists designed the latter campaign to raise the slavery issue in Con-gress and to bring non-abolitionist Northerners into the antislavery move-ment. Abolitionist women led in circulating the petitions.

As historian Carlton Mabee establishes, abolitionists also engaged in a va-riety of non-violent direct actions. They integrated churches, left churches that did not denounce slavery, and formed new abolitionist churches. They engaged in "ride-ins" in attempting to integrate Northern railroads and worked to integrate Northern schools. Some of them supported boycotts of slave produce sold in Northern markets. They worked peacefully to repeal Northern state laws that discriminated against African Americans. From the mid-1840s through the 1850s, antislavery missionaries, supported by the ab-olitionist **American Missionary Association** and other groups, risked their lives to distribute antislavery literature and provide Bibles to slaves in the Upper South. During the 1840s, many advocates of the abolitionist **Liberty Party** contended that political engagement was a peaceful form of antislavery action, although non-resistants pointed out that politics, like government, rested on force.

In most instances, these peaceful efforts produced disappointing results. Many white Southerners, fearing that abolitionist literature would reach slaves, responded with anger to the postal campaign. A mob in Charleston, South Carolina, burned antislavery publications that reached that city. President Andrew Jackson and several Southern state legislatures called on Northern states to suppress the abolitionist movement. Southern members of the House of Representatives, with considerable Northern help, passed the Gag Rule in 1836, banning the reading of antislavery petitions. Abolitionist speakers, editors, organizers, and missionaries faced mob violence during the 1830s and to a lesser extent during the 1840s and 1850s. It seemed that peaceful moral suasion was not enough to make progress against slavery.

Defensive Violence

From the 1830s into the 1840s, as angry antiblack, antiabolition mobs attacked abolitionists and black communities in the North and Border South, numerous abolitionists forcefully defended themselves and their property. During an antiblack, antiabolitionist riot in New York City in 1834, AASS president **Arthur Tappan** distributed guns to employees at his business. In 1836 in Cincinnati, abolitionist organizer **James G. Birney** and his sons used guns to defend their home against rioters. In Alton, Illinois, abolitionist newspaper editor **Elijah P. Lovejoy** died defending his printing press against a proslavery mob. In the Border South, where abolitionists were more isolated than in the North, organized defensive violence became increasingly common. Kentucky abolitionist **Cassius M. Clay** used a knife in 1849 to kill a proslavery antagonist. During the early 1850s, Clay raised armed bands to defend his non-violent associate John G. Fee. Moral power, Clay contended, had to be supplemented with "cold steel and the flashing blade"—"the pistol and the Bowie knife."

Slave Rebels and a Revolutionary Heritage

Despite their commitment to non-violence and embrace of feminine values, white Northern abolitionists admired slave rebels. Americans, they realized, regarded violent struggles for freedom to be heroic. Although black abolitionists shared their white colleagues' ambivalence toward violent means, a few during the 1830s openly praised Turner. In part this was because a masculine image of a violent Southern black liberator challenged pervasive stereotyping of black men as meek and submissive. By the late 1830s, as well, abolitionists had come to regard slavery as a war of extermination against African Americans. Many of them concluded that Christian morality allowed for black violence in self-defense. The American revolutionary heritage reinforced this point of view. As early as 1837, Garrison observed that the Declaration of Independence "authorized" slaves to "cut their masters' throats." Although outright calls for slave revolt were rare during the 1830s, black and white abolitionists praised such violent black liberators as L'Ouverture, Vesey, and Turner. In December 1841, Liberty Party abolitionists on Long Island, New York, declared that Madison Washington, who a month earlier had led a successful slave revolt aboard the brig *Creole*, "acted in accordance with the principles of the Declaration of Independence." Those attending the meeting hoped that Washington's example would "be imitated by all in similar circumstances."

The Underground Railroad Versus the Fugitive Slave Laws

Garrison argued in 1844 that helping slaves to escape was a non-violent activity, carried out "in the spirit of good will to the oppressed, and without injury to the oppressor." But assisted slave escapes often turned violent. Armed masters used force against escapees, and the escapees sometimes carried weapons to protect themselves. Black and white slave rescuers, ranging from Charles T. Torrey during the early 1840s to **Harriet Tubman** during the 1850s, carried guns and threatened to use them against masters, slave catchers, and law enforcement officials. Black **Underground Railroad** operative **John P. Parker**, who helped slaves escape from Kentucky to Ohio during the 1850s, recalled that there was "real warfare" between antislavery and proslavery forces in the Ohio River Valley. Like Tubman, Parker always carried weapons when he ventured into the South. Also like her, he sometimes threatened to shoot fugitives who endangered the rest of his charges.

The **Fugitive Slave Law** of 1850 pushed northward and widened violent conflict between practical abolitionism and angry masters. Increased numbers of black and white abolitionists aided escapees. Masters enlisted federal marshals to help them recapture their human property. African Americans had violently resisted the earlier Fugitive Slave Law of 1793 since its inception. After 1850, the violence became more biracial and more common as non-abolitionist Northerners joined abolitionists in defying the new law. Influenced by **Harriet Beecher Stowe**'s dramatization of the plight of fugitive slaves in her novel, *Uncle Tom's Cabin*, large numbers of Northerners favored forceful resistance to the law. Although such resistance centered in New England, New York, Ohio, and Pennsylvania, white Southerners believed that militant abolitionists, who used violence against the property rights of masters, pervaded the North.

Although there were numerous instances in which abolitionists violently resisted the Fugitive Slave Law, five cases gained notoriety. In February 1851, a black mob, supported by black and white abolitionists, forcefully rescued fugitive slave Shadrack Minkins from a Boston courtroom. The following September, African Americans, led by underground railroad agent William Parker, killed a master who attempted to recover a fugitive slave at Parker's house in Christiana, Pennsylvania. That November, a biracial mob led by black abolitionist Jermain Wesley Loguen and white abolitionists Gerrit Smith and Samuel Joseph May, stormed the Syracuse, New York police station to rescue William Henry—known as "Jerry." In 1854, black and white abolitionists in Boston unsuccessfully attempted to rescue Anthony Burns from the city courthouse. One of Burns's guards died in the melee. Later, local authorities had to call in state and federal troops to protect those who escorted Burns to a southbound ship in Boston Harbor. Another biracial abolitionist mob composed of faculty and students from Oberlin College forcefully rescued fugitive John Brice from a Wellington, Ohio, tavern where he had been held.

In each of these cases, abolitionist rescuers enjoyed the support of local public opinion. In each case there were indictments and some rescuers went to jail pending trial. But there were few convictions and none at all in the especially violent Christiana and Burns cases. Just as popular opposition had contributed to abolitionist non-violence during the 1830s, awareness of support encouraged abolitionist violence during the 1850s. Prior to the *Jerry* rescue, Smith predicted that the local fugitive slave law commissioner would very likely release the fugitive. "But," Smith advised, "the moral effect of such an acquittal will be as nothing [compared] to a bold and forcible rescue. A forcible rescue will demonstrate the strength of public opinion against the possible legality of slavery and this Fugitive Slave Law in particular."

Bleeding Kansas

Abolitionist participation in violent resistance to the Fugitive Slave Law increased white Southern fear of the movement. Democratic and Whig Party leaders responded by pledging to "crush out" agitation of the slavery issue. The Kansas-Nebraska Act, introduced into Congress in January 1854 and passed the following May, destroyed what chance there was of carrying out such a pledge. The act further divided the two sections of the country and accelerated violent tendencies among abolitionists.

Stephen A. Douglas, a Democratic senator from Illinois, had proposed to organize territorial governments in Kansas and Nebraska chiefly as a means of routing a transcontinental railroad through Kansas. To secure Southern support for his bill, he added a clause repealing the **Missouri Compromise** prohibition of slavery in the two territories and providing that the settlers of each territory vote to decide whether or not to admit slavery. This encouraged Southern leaders to try to make Kansas a slave territory and eventually a slave state. It also outraged most Northerners, who believed Douglas had sold out the interests of free labor, and set the stage for a violent struggle in Kansas Territory between free state and slave state settlers. Free state settlers, who constituted the overwhelming majority in Kansas, battled against "border ruffians" from Missouri, federal officials, and federal troops sent to Kansas by proslavery U.S. President Franklin Pierce. Proslavery aggression in Kansas convinced most abolitionists that force should be used not only on behalf of fugitive slaves but to defend freedom in the territory.

Although few abolitionists went to Kansas, those who did either set out with violent intentions or gave up their commitment to peaceful means after they arrived. Charles B. Stearns, for example, was a non-resistant before he arrived in Kansas in 1855. Shortly thereafter he declared, "These proslavery Missourians are demons from the bottomless pit and may be shot with impunity." A year later, John Henry Kagi, a correspondent of several abolitionist newspapers, killed a proslavery man during a brawl. The most famous abolitionist who fought in Kansas was John Brown. At least since the late 1840s, Brown had advocated violent action on behalf of slaves and against slaveholders. In May 1856, in reprisal for a proslavery attack on the free state town of Lawrence, Brown and several of his sons brutally executed five proslavery settlers at Pottawatomie Creek. Although few, if any, abolitionists knew the details of his actions at Pottawatomie, many of them lionized him and contributed funds to pay for his ambitious plan to assault slavery in the South.

Events in Kansas Territory helped break down what non-violent principles remained among the great mass of abolitionists. Gerrit Smith, Garrison's friend **Wendell Phillips**, and other immediatists contributed money to arm antislavery migrants to Kansas. Smith contended that "the shedding of blood [in Kansas] was unavoidable." Leading abolitionist women, such as **Lydia Maria Child** and **Angelina Grimké** Weld, professed continued preference for peaceful means while recognizing the legitimacy of antislavery violence in Kansas. Weld lamented, "We are compelled to choose between two evils, and all that we can do is take the *least*, and baptize liberty in blood, if it must be so." By the late 1850s, Garrison and Lewis Tappan, who persisted in their formal commitment to peaceful means, represented a distinct minority among immediate abolitionists.

Northern Abolitionists and Slave Revolt

Although abolitionists had long admired slave rebels, before 1850 they rarely called for revolt. Even black abolitionist **Henry Highland Garnet** in his famous Address to the Slaves of August 1843 qualified his demand for resistance with a warning that revolt was inexpedient. But by the late 1850s, amid resistance to the Fugitive Slave Law, guerrilla war in Kansas, and rumors of widespread slave unrest following the Republican Party's first presidential election campaign in 1856, immediatists began forthrightly to call for a slave uprising. That formally non-resistant white Garrisonians often joined black abolitionists in such appeals indicates that the long-term ambivalence among abolitionists concerning peaceful and violent means had decisively shifted in favor of the latter. Sill claiming to be a non-resistant, Wright declared in 1857, "We owe it as our duty to ourselves and to humanity, to excite every slave to *rebellion* against his master."

Traditional notions of masculinity rebounded among abolitionists during the contentious 1850s. Under the racialist assumption that white men were more aggressive than black men, white abolitionists, such as Thomas Wentworth Higginson and Theodore Parker, contended that they had to instruct black men in martial valor. To a degree, black abolitionists shared this view. **Frederick Douglass** declared, "My people can never be elevated until they elevate themselves, by fighting for their freedom, and by the sword obtaining it."

Few prominent abolitionists, however, were willing, prior to the U.S. Civil War, to transform violent rhetoric into action. That was left to Underground Railroad operatives on what historian Keith P. Griffler calls "the front line of freedom" and the few abolitionists who went to Kansas. John Brown belonged to both groups. Emerging from a Garrisonian meeting in 1859, he scoffed, "Talk! talk! talk!—that will never set the slave free." Support from Gerrit Smith, Higginson, and Theodore Parker for Brown's plan to invade the South to launch a black guerrilla war against slavery reflected violent sentiment among abolitionists during the 1850s. But Brown had begun to formulate a plan to lead a slave rebellion during the 1840s. Thirty years of abolitionist admiration for slave rebels and twenty years of abolitionist contacts with slaves in the border South established the context for his plan. Longstanding aggressive tendencies within the antislavery movement contributed as much as the heightened sectionalism of the 1850s to the raid on Harpers Ferry, Virginia, in October 1859.

Brown's raid failed to spark a slave uprising as members of his tiny interracial band were killed, captured, or forced to flee northward. But Brown, who was among those captured, used the month between his trial and his execution to employ a surprising eloquence against what remained of abolitionist pacifism. "I, John Brown, am now quite *certain* that the crimes of this *guilty land* will never be purged away but with *blood*," he declared on the day he died. Although a few Garrisonians, such as Parker Pillsbury, Marius Robinson, and Moncure Conway, continued to disavow violence, most now agreed that black men must follow Brown's example if African Americans were to gain freedom. Garrison declared, "Give me, as a non-resistant, Bunker Hill, and Lexington, and Concord, rather than the cowardice and servility of the southern plantation." On the day of Brown's execution, Garrison proclaimed, "Success to every slave insurrection in the South!" Frederick Douglass suggested that "posterity will owe everlasting thanks to John Brown [because] he has attacked slavery with the weapons precisely adapted to bring it to the death."

Many correctly predicted that Brown's raid would spark civil war between the North and South. When the war began in April 1861, abolitionists became fervent supporters of Union cause, urging from the start that black men be allowed to enlist in Union armies and that emancipation be a war aim. Older abolitionists, including Douglass, helped raise black troops. Younger abolitionists, including sons of Douglass and Garrison, enlisted in what became a successful war against legalized slavery. Several white abolitionists, including Higginson, became officers in segregated black regiments that distinguished themselves in battle. Years later, after the Civil War and Reconstruction had failed to secure equal rights for African Americans, elderly white abolitionists regretted that armed conflict had superseded their peaceful crusade. Violence, they implied, could not end racism. Yet their movement had been rooted in violence, had never been entirely non-violent, and had achieved important objectives through violent means. *See also* Bleeding Kansas; Democratic Party and Antislavery; Jerry Rescue Radical Republicans; Whig Party and Antislavery.

Further Readings: Dillon, Merton L. *Slavery Attacked: Southern Slaves and their Allies 1619–1865.* Baton Rouge: Louisiana State University Press, 1990; Griffler, Keith P. *Front Line of Freedom: African Americans and the Forging of the Underground Railroad in the Ohio Valley.* Lexington: University Press of Kentucky,

2004; Harrold, Stanley. *The Abolitionists and the South 1831–1861*. Lexington: University Press of Kentucky, 1995; Harrold, Stanley. *The Rise of Aggressive Abolitionism: Addresses to the Slaves*. Lexington: University Press of Kentucky, 2004; Hinks, Peter P. *To Awaken My Afflicted Brethren: David Walker and the Problem of Antebellum Slave Resistance*. University Park: Pennsylvania State University Press, 1997; Mabee, Carlton. *Black Freedom: The Nonviolent Abolitionists from 1830 through the Civil War*. London: Macmillan, 1970; McKivigan, John R., and Stanley Harrold, eds. *Antislavery Violence: Sectional, Cultural, and Racial Conflict in Antebellum America*. Knoxville: University of Tennessee Press, 1999; Perry, Lewis. *Radical Abolitionism: Anarchy and the Government of God in Antislavery Thought*. Ithaca, NY: Cornell University Press, 1973.

Stanley Harrold

Von Scholten, Peter (1784–1854)

Peter von Scholten was governor general of the Danish West Indies from 1827–1848. In this position he acted as a reformer who improved the social conditions of free blacks and enslaved laborers. Under pressure from revolting slaves, he abolished slavery in the islands by gubernatorial fiat on July 3, 1848.

Von Scholten began his career of colonial service in the Danish West Indies in 1804. King Frederik VI appointed him to the position of weighmaster in 1814. Frederik VI was historically significant for his liberal reforms, including the abolition of Danish serfdom. Von Scholten shared the king's reformist ideology. From 1814 to 1827, von Scholten held various positions of increasing power, until he was appointed governor general of the Danish West Indies in 1827. As governor general, von Scholten sought to reform the conditions of slavery and to transform the relationships of blacks to whites. To this end, he initiated a social revolution with two goals: changing the social position of free blacks and changing the slave owners' relationships to the enslaved. He orchestrated these changes by increasing the political authority associated with his position and exercising extensive control in regard to the administration of slaves and free blacks.

Von Scholten expanded his role as governor general to realize his plans of ameliorating the social conditions of free blacks and slaves. He placed a considerable number of important political issues and institutions under his exclusive jurisdiction. Consequently, he gained some opponents among slaveowners, Danish officials, and local officials who opposed his omnipotent political power and did not share his racial politics.

Von Scholten's initial reforms were aimed at producing equality for free blacks. There was a large free black population in the Danish West Indies in the early nineteenth century. Despite their "free" designation, they lived under strict regulations that constituted a semi-free status. For example, free blacks were subject to sumptuary laws, could only hold specified jobs, and they were required to carry freedom certificates and to live in houses of specified dimensions in a proscribed area. Von Scholten approached King Frederik VI with proposals to obtain rights for free blacks in 1829 and 1834. The ultimate result of these negotiations was the royal decree of

April 18, 1834 proclaiming complete equality between whites and free blacks, defined as those free by the date of issuance, with a trial period of three years for anyone freed after that date. A new census recording free blacks was also directed by the decree. Von Scholten objected to the lack of distinction of classes for free blacks, the short term of the trial period which he proposed at ten years, and the new census that marked race. He ultimately abolished that designation.

Beyond legislative reforms, von Scholten attempted to change the racialized social climate by placing free blacks in public positions and inviting them to racially integrated dinner parties and official functions. In 1828, Von Scholten began living with his consort, Anna Heegaard, a free mulatto woman, who was sufficiently wealthy to have owned her own property and slaves prior to her relationship with von Scholten. She presided over official meals and entertained at public dinner parties held at their residence. Heegaard undeniably influenced the movement for legal and social equality for free black men and women in the Danish West Indies.

Von Scholten initiated a sequence of reforms in slave conditions in 1828 that eventually came to be regarded as an emancipation plan. He sought approval from the Danish government for some reforms and initiated others independently. As a consequence of von Scholten's reforms in the 1830s, the length of the work day was regulated, slave owners' powers over corporeal punishment were curtailed, public auctions of slaves were banned, slaves gained some property rights, slaves gained the right to change owners if the former owner was compensated, pregnant women were barred from the most demanding field work, and housing improvements were mandated. The governor general gained the right to place a mistreated slave with a new owner. As result of additional reforms in the 1840s, the word *slave* was officially replaced with *unfree*, Saturday became an official day off for all slaves, compensation was required for slaves who worked on Saturday, and elementary schools were established for slave children.

Von Scholten favored gradual emancipation, after a transitional period, rather than **immediate emancipation**. He attempted to control elements that threatened his vision of emancipation. For example, he barred settlement of **Methodists**, **Quakers**, and Baptists because of their disharmonizing effect upon slave societies elsewhere. Von Scholten's 1846 emancipation proposal called for a transitional period of twenty years, which he felt was primarily necessary to prepare slaves for freedom and secondarily to enable planters to benefit from the labor of slaves for the duration period instead of receiving compensation from the Danish government for their freedom. The Royal Rescript of June 28, 1847 regarding emancipation shortened the transitional period to twelve years and, despite von Scholten's advisement against it, ordered that children born to the unfree after the date of the rescript were free from birth. The free birth law was a precipitating cause of the slave revolt that began on July 2, 1848, in Frederiksted, St. Croix.

Enslaved laborers initiated an island-wide work strike on July 2, 1848 and thousands gathered in town on July 3 to demand their freedom. Von Scholten declared emancipation on July 3. He resigned on July 6 and returned to Denmark where he was put on trial for dereliction of duty. Found guilty in 1851, he was acquitted by the Supreme Court upon appeal and granted an honorable discharge in 1852. Former slaves petitioned Denmark for his return to the Danish West Indies after the revolt. He never returned to the islands where his efforts resulted in social transformation and ultimately in emancipation. Von Scholten died in 1854. *See also* Danish West Indies, Abolition and Emancipation in.

Further Readings: Hall, Neville. *Slave Society in the Danish West Indies*. B.W. Higman, ed. Kingston, Jamaica: University of the West Indies Press. 1992; Hall, Neville. "Anna Heegaard—Enigma." *Caribbean Quarterly* 22 (1976): 62–73; Highfield, Arnold, ed. *Emancipation in the U.S. Virgin Islands*. St. Croix: Virgin Islands Humanities Council. 1999; Lawaetz, Hermann. *Peter von Scholten*. Anne-Luise Knudsen, trans. Herning, Denmark: Poul Kristensen Publishing Co. 1999 [1940].

Lori Lee

W

Walker, David (1796/97–1830)

David Walker was born in Wilmington, North Carolina, in the Lower Cape Fear District, in about 1796. His mother was a free black and he thus acquired her status. Slave labor and society was very evident in this region where rice was cultivated and naval stores were produced in the extensive pine barrens. Slaves here proved both very religious and restless. The early Methodist church in Wilmington was overwhelmingly black and probably was the foundation of Walker's lifelong dedication to the denomination. The pervasive swamps of the Lower Cape Fear were commonly refuges for runaways and small maroon encampments, and several incidences of slave rebellion issued from them between 1775 and the early nineteenth century. This black world of religiosity and restlessness likely helped shape David Walker.

Sometime in the 1810s, Walker journeyed to Charleston, South Carolina, which had a much larger free black population than Wilmington, as well as greater employment opportunity. By 1818, Charleston also had one of the earliest congregations of the recently launched African Methodist Episcopal (AME) church, established by **Richard Allen** in Philadelphia in 1817. Vehemently opposed by local white authorities, it was comprised of both free blacks and slaves and quickly became the center of black Charleston. It also was an important nexus for the plotting of a major slave conspiracy led by Denmark Vesey, a free black carpenter who was a member of the church, and a number of other free blacks and slaves in the town. The intensely religious and Methodist Walker likely attended this church and may have been exposed to the conspiring in one form or another. He certainly knew of the plot when it was uncovered in June 1822 and violently crushed by the local magistrates. More than thirty free blacks and slaves were executed and a number of leaders of the church including its minister, Morris Brown, fled the town soon after the plot's exposure. Walker probably left at about the same time and may have roamed along the eastern seaboard of the country. It is very likely that he went to Philadelphia where the seat of the AME church was located and to where most of those blacks fleeing Charleston went. The name David Walker appears in Philadelphia municipal records for 1824. There is even some indication that he may have gone briefly to Haiti when a number of American blacks were emigrating there to accept President **Jean-Pierre Boyer**'s offers of free land and other assistance to settlers.

By 1825, David Walker had settled in Boston, Massachusetts. He soon opened a used-clothing store, married, became an African Mason, bought a house, and joined Reverend Samuel Snowden's black Methodist church. He was the local agent for the first black newspaper, *Freedom's Journal*, and he was a principal in the formation in 1828 of one of the nation's first explicitly black political organizations, the Massachusetts General Colored Association. In December 1828, he addressed the Association and passionately decried slavery, the colonization movement, and racial injustice.

Walker is best known for his publication in September 1829 of his *Appeal to the Colored Citizens of the World*. This booklet was one of the most vivid and incisive denunciations of American slavery, racism, and hypocrisy produced in the country in the nineteenth century. In it, Walker clearly empathized with the suffering, both physical and psychological, endured by the slaves in the South, a people whose world he knew well from his earlier years. But he also chided them for any tendency to succumb to demoralization induced by their brutal treatment and to surrender themselves to slavery and slavishness. He admonished them to refuse to submit to enslavement any further; to do so was to make themselves complicit in the sin of slavery. To whites, he counseled an immediate acknowledgement of their horrible sinning in imposing slavery and degradation upon blacks. They must seek God's forgiveness for their sins and publicly repent. Finally, they must reach out to blacks in Christian fellowship and seek a non-violent path to reconciliation with blacks and the forging of a new free and interracial society in the United States. Walker believed such a reunion was possible, but was also fully aware of the daunting obstacles confronting it. If whites proved unrepentant and continued to enslave blacks, then they had no choice but to reject their enslavement and violently oppose the whites who had in effect rendered themselves Devils. For blacks to do otherwise was the grossest of affronts to God. In the pamphlet, Walker struggled to harness the optimistic activism inherent to evangelical Christianity and revolutionary republicanism to inspire African Americans to a new sense of personal worth and to their capacity to challenge the increasingly systematized ideology and institutions of white supremacy.

By early 1830, Walker had launched a remarkably resourceful circulation of his *Appeal* in Georgia, South, and North Carolina, Virginia, and New Orleans. White authorities throughout the South were enraged and sought to check its influx into their states by monitoring local slaves and free blacks carefully, impeding the movement of Northern white and free black sailors in their ports, and guarding the mails and newspapers from importing any seditious materials. Still, the pamphlet found its way into black hands in the South, especially in North Carolina where an impressive network of runaway slaves, free blacks, and perhaps some white **Quakers** moved it along the state's eastern counties. Walker implored literate slaves and free blacks to read his work to their less educated brethren and apparently some did. The pamphlet failed, however, to spark the wide-scale resistance for which Walker hoped. But his passionate words fired black activism in the North throughout the antebellum era and beyond. **Maria Stewart, Frederick Douglass,** and **Henry Highland Garnet** all looked to Walker as seminal in the movement over which they became so prominent. Even as late as 1940, **W.E.B. Du Bois** lauded the *Appeal* for its "tremendous indictment of slavery" and for being the first "program of organized opposition to the action and attitude of the dominant white group," as well as for its "ceaseless agitation and insistent demand for equality." *See also* Methodists and Antislavery; Vesey's Conspiracy.

Further Reading: Hinks, Peter. *To Awaken My Afflicted Brethren: David Walker and the Problem of Antebellum Slave Resistance.* University Park: Pennsylvania State University Press, 1997.

Peter Hinks

Washington, D.C., Compensated Emancipation in

On April 16, 1862, President **Abraham Lincoln** signed a bill to end slavery in Washington, D.C. The bill, entitled "An Act for the Release of Certain Persons Held to Service or Labor in the District of Columbia," marked the first time that the federal government authorized the emancipation of any slave and the only time that it compensated former owners as part of an emancipation plan.

While compensation was not included in later acts, emancipation in the nation's capital was an early sign of the end of slavery in the United States. The District of Columbia Emancipation Act was received with joy in Washington's African American community and is now remembered in the District's Emancipation Day celebration.

Throughout the antebellum era, ending the slave trade and slavery in Washington, D.C., was a popular cause for abolitionists. They focused on Washington because of the symbolic importance of slavery in the capital of a free republic and because of the ability of the federal government to end it there. Under Article I, Section 8 of the **United States Constitution**, Congress has exclusive power to pass laws for the nation's capital.

On December 16, 1861, Senator Henry Wilson of Massachusetts introduced the District of Columbia Emancipation Act in the Senate. The bill provided for **immediate emancipation** of all slaves in the District of Columbia as well as compensation for their masters and funds for the foreign colonization of slaves who chose to emigrate outside the United States. Wilson's three-point plan linking emancipation with payment to owners and colonization was similar to earlier proposals to end slavery. Supporters reasoned that connecting emancipation with payments to owners and funds to encourage former slaves to emigrate would make the abolition of slavery more palatable to the slaveholding states that had not seceded to join the Confederacy, such as Kentucky and Missouri.

The compensation provision of the District bill, however, divided antislavery members of Congress. Senator Samuel Pomeroy of Kansas criticized compensation for owners on the grounds that it wrongly recognized slaves as property. He argued that if Congress authorized any compensation, it should be paid to former slaves. Senator Charles Sumner of Massachusetts answered Senator Pomeroy, stating that payment to masters was acknowledgement of Congress's responsibility for slavery in Washington and would dull opposition to the bill. Despite this resistance to compensation, it remained in the District of Columbia Emancipation Act.

As passed by Congress and signed by the president, the act appropriated as much as one million dollars to be paid to owners in the District of Columbia, provided that the total amount paid did not exceed an average of $300 per slave. Under the statute, owners could be compensated only if they were loyal to the Union. The act directed the president to appoint three commissioners to receive and investigate petitions and to assess the value of slaves freed by the statute. The act also appropriated $100,000 for voluntary colonization.

After signing the District of Columbia Emancipation Act, President Lincoln appointed commissioners to the three-member board in April 1862. The commissioners met throughout the following three months, receiving claims, determining ownership and loyalty to the Union, and setting compensation for former slaves. Compensation payments were ostensibly based on estimates of the former slaves' intrinsic value to their owners. To determine the intrinsic utility of each, the commissioners began by estimating salable price before the start of the war, relying on the assessments of Bernard Campbell, a slave dealer from Baltimore. As estimated price usually exceeded the average compensation allowed by law, the commissioners granted payments of $300 in most cases.

The loyalty provision prevented only secessionists from recovering compensation. The commissioners interpreted the restriction to apply only upon proof that the "claimants have borne arms against the Government of the United States in the present rebellion or in any way given aid or comfort to the enemy." They justified their interpretation of the statute by noting that its language was similar to the Constitution's treason provision in Article III, Section 3. Since the Constitution defined treason to apply only in specific circumstances with adequate proof, the commissioners accepted claims even of Confederate sympathizers.

The commissioners received 966 petitions, claiming 3,100 former slaves. Of those petitions, the commissioners granted 909 in their entirety and 21 in part, accounting for 2,989 former slaves. The remaining petitions were rejected because former owners had voted for secession or moved south to join the Confederate military or had failed to appear before the board.

On July 12, 1862, a supplemental bill to the District of Columbia Emancipation Act was signed into law. The Supplemental Act allowed slaves and former slaves whose former masters had not filed compensation petitions to assert their own claims to freedom under the April 16 or July 12 statutes. The Act also specified that any slave who had lived or been employed in the District of Columbia with the consent of his or her owner after April 16, 1862, was legally free.

As with the District of Columbia Emancipation Act, the Supplemental Act charged the emancipation commissioners with receiving and investigating petitions. The statute provided that African Americans could not be excluded from testifying. The commissioners received 161 petitions under the Supplemental Act and granted 139.

Further Readings: Fladeland, Betty L. "Compensated Emancipation: A Rejected Alternative." *The Journal of Southern History* 42 (1976): 169–186; Green, Constance. *The Secret City: A History of Race Relations in the Nation's Capital.* Princeton, NJ: Princeton University Press, 1967; Guelzo, Allen C. *Lincoln's Emancipation Proclamation: The End of Slavery in America.* New York: Simon & Schuster, 2004; *H. Exec. Doc. 42*, 38th Cong., 1st Sess. (1864). (Letter from the Secretary of the Treasury, in answer to a resolution of the House of Representatives, of the 11th of January, transmitting the report and tabular statements of the commissioners appointed in relation to emancipated slaves in the District of Columbia.); Kurtz, Michael J. "Emancipation in the Federal City." *Civil War History* 24 (1978): 250–267; Milburn, Page. "The Emancipation of the Slaves in the District of Columbia. *Records of the Columbia Historical Society* 16 (1913): 96–119.

Edward Daniels

The Wealth of Nations. *See* Smith, Adam

Wedderburn, Robert (1762–c. 1831)

An important figure in the radical London underworld and an antislavery activist, Robert Wedderburn was born in Jamaica in 1762. His father was James Wedderburn, a Kingston doctor and plantation owner, his mother a house slave named Rosanna. James Wedderburn sold Rosanna when she was five months pregnant, on the condition that the child should be free from birth. Separated from his mother, the young Robert Wedderburn was raised by his maternal grandmother. He joined the navy at the age of sixteen in 1778, and arrived in London shortly thereafter.

Few details are known about Wedderburn's early years within the underworld community of sailors, former slaves, and radicals in London. He converted to Methodism in 1786, and became a journeyman tailor. He also began to involve himself in radical politics, and eventually converted to Unitarianism. Wedderburn early showed a keen interest in activism. He wrote a theological tract, "Truth Self-Supported," following his conversion to Methodism, and he became a regular participant in radical debating clubs during the first decades of the nineteenth century. Around 1813 he joined the circle of the radical organizer Thomas Spence, embracing the combination of millenarian religion, slave rebellion and emancipation, radical politics, and free thought that characterized Spence's movement. Following Spence's death in 1814, Wedderburn continued to popularize his radical ideas, landing himself in prison on more than one occasion. In 1818, he published *The Axe Laid to the Roots*, which called for **immediate emancipation** and universal suffrage.

Wedderburn's personal history gave him a particular interest in antislavery activities. He spoke out regularly against slavery at his Hopkins Street Unitarian Chapel, and published numerous antislavery tracts. In "A Critical, Historical and Admonitory letter to the Archbishop of Canterbury," he criticized the role of the established church in the perpetuation of the slave system. Wedderburn also authored tracts inciting slaves to rise up and over-throw their masters, smuggling them into the colonies by way of black sailors. His participation in discussions on radicalism and slavery at meetings of the British Forum at Lunts coffee house in London, drew the attention, if not necessarily the full support, of mainstream abolitionists. **William Wilberforce**, who frequently visited jails to evangelize prisoners and encourage their repentance, is known to have visited Wedderburn in prison. Upon his release in 1824, Wedderburn published an antislavery autobiography, entitled "The Horrors of Slavery."

Despite repeated harassment from authorities, Wedderburn continued his political activities. In 1831, at the age of sixty-eight, he was again arrested and returned to prison. The final record of Wedderburn's life is a letter he wrote from the prison to the radical reformer Francis Place. The exact time and circumstances of his death are unknown. *See also* Methodists and Antislavery; Unitarianism and Antislavery.

Further Reading: McCalman, Iain. "Anti-Slavery and Ultra Radicalism in Early Nineteenth Century England." *Slavery and Abolition*, 7 (September 1986): 99–117.

Michael A. Rutz

Weld, Angelina Emily Grimké. *See* Grimké, Angelina Emily

Weld, Theodore Dwight (1803–1895)

Theodore Dwight Weld was an influential abolitionist in the United States during the 1830s and early 1840s. For much of his young life it appeared that Weld, son of a Congregationalist minister, was destined for a career in the ministry. He briefly attended Andover Seminary, but withdrew after experiencing vision impairment, which may have been a psychosomatic manifestation of his dissatisfaction with orthodox Calvinism. In 1826, Weld's religious fervor was renewed after he was converted to evangelicalism by the famed minister **Charles Grandison Finney**. Weld devoted himself to Finney, becoming one of his most trusted aides. His work as a revivalist soon led him into the temperance and manual labor reform movements. As an agent for the Manual Labor Society, he helped establish Lane Seminary in Cincinnati, Ohio, which he entered as a student in 1833 to prepare for the ministry.

Lane instead launched Weld into abolitionism. In 1834, Weld led a revolt amongst the students of Lane against the school's administration over the issue of slavery. In February of that year, Weld helped organize an eighteen-day debate at the seminary where he and his fellow students discussed the duties of Christians regarding slavery, specifically debating the comparative merits of the scheme proposed by colonizationists to end slavery gradually and the demands of radical abolitionists for its immediate abolition. The students emerged from the debate certain of the utter sinfulness of both slavery and racial prejudice, convinced that colonizationism did not offer adequate means to repent those sins, and eager to put their newfound immediatist convictions into practice. They founded an antislavery society at the seminary and, led by Weld, they began to reach out to the local African American community, setting up both secular and religious education programs in

Cincinnati's "Little Africa" district. The activism of the Lane students drew harsh criticism from many in Cincinnati's white community, who called upon the trustees of Lane Seminary to restrain them. In October, the trustees bowed to this pressure, passing resolutions that banned student organizations not directly related to ministerial education and allowing the trustees to expel offending students. Led by Weld, the majority of the students promptly withdrew from the seminary rather than compromise their antislavery beliefs.

This dispute at Lane propelled many of its former students into abolitionist activism, none more so than Weld. Weld spent two years as a full-time agent of the **American Antislavery Society** (AASS) touring Ohio, New York, and other western areas agitating the antislavery cause and helping to establish local abolitionist societies. Despite persistent, sometimes violent, harassment from antislavery mobs, Weld was remarkably successful, helping to establish numerous local societies and converting many who came to hear him speak to abolitionism. In the mid 1830s, Weld's voice was compromised following years of non-stop speaking, and thereafter he assumed a less public role in abolitionism as correspondent, editor, and pamphleteer at the headquarters of the AASS in New York. In 1836, he recruited and trained dozens of abolitionist agents for the AASS including **Angelina** and Sarah **Grimké**. Daughters of an elite South Carolina slaveholding planter, the Grimké sisters had been converted to Quakerism and then to abolitionism. Coached by Weld, the sisters spent much of the following two years touring New England promoting abolitionism. In the midst of this tour, Weld began courting Angelina, and they were married in May 1838.

Collaborating with his wife, Angelina, and sister-in-law, Sarah, Weld produced *American Slavery as It Is: Testimony of a Thousand Witnesses* (1839). In this widely circulated pamphlet, Weld and the Grimkés amassed firsthand accounts of the horrors of slavery compiled from Southern newspapers and personal testimonies solicited from Southerners. The pamphlet documented in grisly detail the violence and cruelty endemic to the institution of slavery. *American Slavery as It Is* ranks as one the most influential works of American antislavery literature. Over 100,000 copies were sold in the first year, and **Harriet Beecher Stowe** later reported that it was an important source for *Uncle Tom's Cabin*.

From 1841 to 1843, Weld labored as a researcher and lobbyist for antislavery Congressmen in Washington. In particular, he helped in the fight against the Gag Rule, which suppressed debate regarding antislavery petitions. This fight was ultimately successful and the Gag Rule was rescinded in 1844. Following his stint in Washington, Weld withdrew from an active role in abolitionism. *See also* Immediate Emancipation.

Further Readings: Abzug, Robert H. *Passionate Liberator: Theodore Dwight Weld & the Dilemma of Reform.* New York: Oxford University Press, 1980; Barnes, Gilbert H. and Dwight L. Dumond, eds. *Letters of Theodore Dwight Weld, Angelina Grimké Weld, and Sarah Grimké, 1822–1844.* Gloucester, MA: Peter Smith, 1965; Nelson, Robert K. "'The Forgetfulness of Sex': Devotion and Desire in the Courtship Letters of Angelina Grimké and Theodore Dwight Weld." *Journal of Social History* 37 (Spring 2004): 663–679.

Robert K. Nelson

Immediate Emancipation in the West Indies, 1838: West Indians rejoice after being emancipated. Courtesy of the Library of Congress.

West Indies Emancipation Day

On August 1, 1834, the emancipation bill of 1833 was promulgated in the British West Indies and placed the former slaves under the transitional system of apprenticeship, which was to last for six years before the enactment of full emancipation. Under apprenticeship, the former slaves were required to labor forty-five hours each week for their master; beyond that time, they could earn wages for themselves. Yet apprenticeship was abolished two years early on August 1, 1838. Both events of August 1 were welcomed by black and white American abolitionists as auspicious signs that success was inevitable in their own country as well, and throughout the remainder of the antebellum period, many commemorated the "First of August" as an antislavery holiday. Although it was also sporadically observed in Great Britain, it became most important as a platform for antislavery agitation in America.

At a time when the Fourth of July was developing into an annual occasion for patriotic effusions about freedom, the First of August was a subversive surrogate for the hypocritical rituals of Independence Day. By celebrating Great Britain's virtue, abolitionists spotlighted America's vice. Simultaneously, they highlighted the path to repentance: by publicizing the perceived peacefulness and profitability of West Indian emancipation, they used the First of August to argue that immediate abolition would be safe and expedient for the American South. In addition to its usefulness as a rhetorical platform, however, the First of August contributed to the movement culture of Northern abolitionists, both black and white, providing them with annual opportunities to congregate, celebrate, and rejuvenate their commitment to reform.

Observances of the First of August clustered around the geographical centers of immediatism, specifically Boston and New England, New York City and upstate New York, Philadelphia, and Ohio. Ceremonies were often held in meeting houses or rustic "groves," and audiences numbered from hundreds to thousands at the largest events. Especially in Massachusetts and New York, assemblies were frequently biracial and composed of both men and women, particularly in the mid- to late-1830s. In the next two decades, however, First of August celebrations were marked by the divisions that plagued the antislavery movement, both among white abolitionist factions and between black and white reform communities. **Garrisonians** in the Massachusetts Anti-Slavery Society and the **American Anti-Slavery Society** consistently observed the day with official "picnics" up to the Civil War, but African American leaders within Boston, New York, and Philadelphia increasingly organized separate celebrations, both to demonstrate the solidarity of black communities and to legitimize their own claims to community leadership.

First of August celebrations drew on many of the cultural traditions that shaped the Fourth of July, but they also manifested the same class tensions that were exhibited on Independence Day. Much like middle-class celebrations of the Fourth, which contrasted with the rowdy celebrations of the urban working class, ceremonies for the First usually emphasized orations and songs. Attending orations allowed abolitionists to display their respectability and temperance, even while espousing radical views; but if the First demonstrated abolitionist decorum, it was also a day for rest and recreation. The resulting tension between recreation, respectability, and radical reform helped produce a diversity of opinions about how the First of August should be observed, just as many contemporaries argued about the proper way to celebrate the Fourth of July.

Recent scholarship has focused on the First of August as a window onto community formation and political mobilization among Northern African Americans. Long before British emancipation in the 1830s, black Northerners had developed holiday alternatives to the Fourth of July, a day on which they were often targeted by racist discourse and dangerous rioters. Many celebrated July 5 (New York state emancipation), instead of the Fourth, or preferred other holidays, like the anniversary of Crispus Attucks's death in March or of the slave trade's abolition later in July. Preexisting traditions were grafted onto West Indian emancipation celebrations by black Northerners, including traditions developed during slavery, when holidays like Pinkster and Negro Election Day served as opportunities for symbolic critique and communal self-expression. Drawing on memories of these events, African American communities often observed the First of August with parades, dances, and militia drills.

These practices were often chastised by white abolitionist leaders, and they were also controversial among black abolitionists. On the one hand, African American leaders wanted to attract people to their First of August celebrations to show numerical strength, and parades and dances were certainly attractive. They also wanted to lay claim to public space as political agents, which parades in particular allowed them to do. But on the other hand, many abolitionist leaders, white and black, stressed the need for "moral uplift" and respectability in black communities, and parades and dances were seen by many as unrespectable. Planners for First of August celebrations attempted to balance the values of group unity, effective political action, and adherence to social conventions. Among black abolitionists, the former two values frequently outweighed the latter. Important as decorum was to African American elites, it was often more important to draw on long-standing festive traditions in African American communities and to draw large crowds to First of August events. *See also* Apprenticeship; Stipendiary Magistrates.

Further Readings: Rael, Patrick. "Besieged by Freedom's Army: Antislavery Celebrations and Black Activism." In *Black Identity & Black Protest in the Antebellum North.* Chapel Hill: University of North Carolina Press, 2002, pp. 54–81;

Kachun, Mitch. *Festivals of Freedom: Memory and Meaning in African American Emancipation Celebrations, 1808–1915*. Amherst: University of Massachusetts, 2003; Gravely, William B. "The Dialectic of Double-Consciousness in Black American Freedom Celebrations, 1808–1863." *Journal of Negro History* 67, 4 (Winter 1982): 302–317.

W. Caleb McDaniel

Whig Party and Antislavery

The Whig Party was an American political party officially formed in 1834 in opposition to Andrew Jackson and the **Democratic Party**. Political descendents of the National Republican Party, the Whigs advocated for "The American System," a nationalistic economic system that featured tariff protection, federally supported internal improvements, and the continuation of the national bank. Drawing much support from New England Congregationalists, Presbyterians, **Quakers**, and evangelical Protestants, the Whig Party endorsed a variety of reform movements, believing government should play a role in the moral behavior of Americans and eliminate sin in the United States. Many Northern Whigs supported abolitionism.

Early on in their party's history, Whigs in Congress split sectionally over slavery issues. In 1836, almost all Northern Whigs in the House of Representatives voted along antislavery lines, while nearly all Southern Whigs voted proslavery. Northern Whigs, however, were unique from their Southern colleagues: Southern Whigs and Southern Democrats generally shared the same position on slavery, whereas the antislavery position of Northern Whigs enabled them to present themselves as unique from Northern Democrats on the issue of slavery. Mutual animosity towards the Democratic Party and a nationalist vision kept the Whig party united in spite of divisions over slavery.

By 1840, Northern Whigs grew in strength as they attracted an increasing number of abolitionists, like **William Seward**. Even with the formation of the abolitionist **Liberty Party** in 1840, Whigs retained the loyal support of abolitionists. As the Liberty Party gained strength between 1840 and 1844, Northern Whigs increasingly attacked slavery to limit defections. With the onset of the annexation of Texas and the Mexican War, Northern "Conscience" Whigs opposed the expansion of slavery into the West, splintering the party further along sectional lines. That a wing of a large national party associated itself so strongly with antislavery, however, helped legitimize the abolitionist movement.

The nomination and election in 1848 of Zachary Taylor, a war hero from the **Mexican War**, helped keep the Whigs united. Taylor's election, however, marked a turning point for the Whig party. The party splintered even further along sectional lines, prefiguring the Civil War. Taylor's effort to avoid the issue of slavery angered some "Conscience" Whigs who joined with members of the Liberty Party to form the Free Soil Party. The defeat of the Whigs in the election of 1852, accompanied by its calls for moderation and union during the struggle over the **Compromise of 1850**, heralded further defections to the Free Soil Party. Southern Whigs fled to the Democratic Party, which appeared to them much more receptive to slave-holding rights. The defections culminated with the formation of the Republican Party in 1854 when numerous Northern Whigs joined the new party. The Whig Party was in such a beleaguered state by 1856 that at its convention it endorsed former President Millard Fillmore, previously a Whig who was now running as the presidential candidate for the anti-immigrant Know-Nothing Party. In 1860, the small number of remaining Whigs reorganized to form the Constitutional Union Party, but they fared poorly in that portentous election. *See also* Antislavery Evangelical Protestantism; Bible and Slavery; Congregationalism and Antislavery; Radical Republicans; Texas, Annexation of.

Further Readings: Holt, Michael F. *The Rise and Fall of the American Whig Party: Jacksonian Politics and the Onset of the Civil War.* New York: Oxford University Press, 1999; Stewart, James Brewer. "Abolitionists, Insurgents, and Third Parties: Sectionalism and Partisan Politics in Northern Whiggery, 1836–1844." In Alan M. Kraut, ed., *Crusaders and Compromisers: Essays on the Relationship of the Antislavery Struggle to the Antebellum Party System.* Westport, CT: Greenwood Press, 1983, pp. 25–43.

Daniel P. Kotzin

Whitefield, George (1714–1770)

George Whitefield was an influential itinerant English preacher who traveled throughout the American colonies where he initially condemned the institution of slavery. The son of a tavern keeper, Whitefield never lost the common touch that would make his preaching uniquely appealing. After graduating from Oxford University in 1736, he embarked on a series of far-flung evangelical tours that confirmed him as a lynchpin of early Methodism in Britain and the spearhead of the Great Awakening in the colonies.

Whitefield's canny self-marketing facilitated his unprecedented success as a preacher—he deployed commercial and entrepreneurial devices very effectively to deliver the message of salvation in Christ. By judiciously distributing printed sermons, journals and other advance publicity, Whitefield ensured himself a reception so enthusiastic that he frequently preached out-of-doors to crowds of thousands. Most of his sermons were structured to make his hearers painfully conscious of their moral failings, to emphasize the grace of God, and to communicate the joy of deliverance through faith. By the mid-1740s, thanks to his perfectly crafted theatrical performances and the appeal of his spiritually egalitarian message, Whitefield was one of the best-known figures in the British Empire—known, if not always respected, by people throughout the colonies.

Whitefield believed depravity and decadence were rife in the populations of the Lower South. In 1740, he focused his attention on South Carolina, which he sought to convert to evangelical Calvinism. Whitefield and his reforming allies felt that the godliness of Southern society was jeopardized by a variety of dangers including an unregenerate clergy, an immoral population fixed on extravagance, and the presence of a cruel slavery.

To the twenty-three-year-old Englishman who would spend his life emphasizing that all souls should be receptive to salvation, the huge number of

George Whitefield. Courtesy of the Library of Congress.

heathen blacks working in appalling physical and spiritual conditions on low-country rice plantations shocked him: "my blood has frequently almost run cold within me to consider how many of your slaves had neither convenient food to eat, nor proper raiment to put on." In June of 1740, Whitefield published an open letter to the planters of the Southern colonies concerning "the treatment of their Negroes." He campaigned for more humane treatment of slaves, warning that unchristian behavior would summon God's disfavor, possibly through slave uprisings, which he suggested *might* be just punishments. But this caveat little moved Carolina planters who perennially feared black insurrection, having only recently suffered the Stono Rebellion of 1739, which killed near twenty whites. While a minority of these planters was persuaded that converting and educating their slaves was a worthy and safe undertaking, most feared that Christianity would offer blacks a dangerous elevated status and the opportunity to justify and coordinate conspiracies. Those planters who did follow Whitefield offered their slaves limited privileges after they converted including church membership, baptism, formalized marriages, and Christian burial. A small minority of reforming planters, warily observed by their counterparts, sought to limit excessive corporal punishments, and some would later permit blacks to minister to their bondspeople.

George Whitefield's advocacy of an improvement in black treatment and education, however, never extended as far as challenging slavery itself. Indeed, within ten years of his arrival, Whitefield was ardently championing the extension of the institution from South Carolina into the fledgling colony of Georgia, where slavery was initially prohibited. For him, a condition of human bondage was justified in Holy Scripture, and therefore lawful, though he deplored the excesses of the slave trade and the brutal abuses that accompanied plantation slavery. When slavery was finally legalized in Georgia, where Whitefield had established an orphanage, he rejoiced that he would have the opportunity to convert to Christ those enslaved on his own estate—the ends justified the means. For a man renowned for his booming voice, Whitefield's silence on slavery after initially condemning the barbarous treatment of slaves represented more of a shift in strategy than a reversal: his will to reform slavery diminished as other projects such as extending evangelism to Southern slaveholders and supporting his orphanage swelled. Yet George Whitefield later became the Countess of Huntingdon's chaplain, and his achievements were commemorated in the first poem written by the freed slave, Phillis Wheatly, after his death in 1770, in which Whitefield not only spoke to "Americans" but also to "Africans," reminding them that God is an "Impartial Saviour." *See also* Antislavery Evangelical Protestantism; First Great Awakening and Antislavery.

Further Readings: Cashin, Edward J. *Beloved Bethesda: A History of George Whitefield's Home for Boys, 1740–2000*. Macon, GA: Mercer University Press, 2001; Gallay, Alan. "The Great Sellout: George Whitefield on Slavery." In W.B. Moore, Jr. and J.F. Tripp, eds., *Looking South: Chapters in the Story of an American Region*. New York: Greenwood Press, 1989; Mason, Julian D., ed. *The Poems of Phillis Wheatley*. Chapel Hill: University of North Carolina Press, 1989; Whitefield, George. *The Works of the Reverend George Whitefield*. 6 vols. London, 1772.

Ben Marsh

Wilberforce, William (1759–1833)

William Wilberforce was a Member of Parliament (MP), an author and Britain's best-known abolitionist. He belonged to one of Kingston-upon-Hull's most affluent merchant families. Wilberforce was gifted intellectually, although his health and eyesight were poor throughout his life. He entered St. John's College, Cambridge in October 1766 and proved an able and popular student. In 1780, Wilberforce became the Member of Parliament for his hometown at twenty-one—the minimum age at which one could run—and was later elected in 1784 as MP for the large, prestigious county seat of Yorkshire. From his earliest days, Wilberforce was regarded as an eloquent speaker.

He had a dramatic religious experience in 1785 when he converted to evangelical Christianity. It transformed his life and his politics. In 1787, he founded the Proclamation Society for the reformation of individual and societal morals. At about the same time, Wilberforce met **Thomas Clarkson** whose research on the Atlantic slave trade shocked him. His friend, Prime Minister **William Pitt the Younger**, also an abolitionist, encouraged Wilberforce to spearhead the issue in the House of Commons. Wilberforce and Clarkson prepared evidence for the Privy Council in 1788. Ill health forced Wilberforce to withdraw temporarily from his political duties, and Pitt presented their findings to Parliament. This resulted in an act that restricted the number of slaves a vessel might carry based on the ship's tonnage. Although popular sentiment continued to mount against the slave trade, George III's mental illness and the resulting Regency Bill Crisis trumped other issues during the winter of 1788–89. The king's recovery in the spring allowed abolition to return to the agenda.

In 1789, Wilberforce, with Pitt's cooperation, brought a bill forward once again to abolish Great Britain's involvement in the Atlantic slave trade. His speech was praised as being one of the most powerful ever heard in the House. In January 1790, abolition was proving a very time-consuming issue and the matter was given to a Select Committee. By the fall, Wilberforce had 1,400 pages of evidence to present to the House. Many abolitionists argued their case on humanitarian and Christian grounds, but Wilberforce also attempted to destroy the notion that Africans were inferior. He became an ardent supporter of the often troubled **Sierra Leone** project to

William Wilberforce. Courtesy of the Library of Congress.

repatriate freed blacks to West Africa. He hoped its success would demonstrate that free Africans could establish a well-ordered society.

Wilberforce addressed the Commons on April 18, 1791, but the bill was defeated yet again. He and his fellow abolitionists pressed on, urging more petitions, meetings, pamphlets, sermons, and public education. Their campaign had always been hampered by powerful economic interests that wanted to defeat, or at least delay, abolition. By the early 1790s, the abolitionists lost ground as public and political opinion recoiled from the excesses of the French Revolution and the St. Domingue slave uprising. The issue was revisited in 1792 in the House; Wilberforce received support for gradual abolition but the House of Lords postponed the issue. Once again the "West Indian interest" of powerful planters employed successful delaying tactics.

Despite the downturn in public and political support for abolition, Wilberforce reintroduced the Abolition Bill almost every year in the 1790s. Much to Wilberforce's dismay, even Pitt's enthusiasm cooled during this period. It was not until 1804 that the tide began to turn. Napoleon's hostility to emancipation became known and the cause was helped by the inclusion of new Irish MPs who favored abolition. However, Wilberforce reintroduced the bill in 1804 and 1805 without success. Finally, Parliament voted overwhelmingly in its favor and the Abolition Act received Royal Assent on March 25, 1807. It became illegal to trade in slaves, although stamping out slavery in British colonies would prove far more difficult to effect.

Troubled by multiple health complaints, Wilberforce resigned his seat of Yorkshire in 1812 for the pocket borough of Bramber, Sussex, which he hoped would be a less demanding constituency. He began work on the Slave Registration Bill, which would help monitor slave traffic and ensure compliance with the Abolition Act. Once again, he encountered significant resistance. Despite his failing health, he continued to speak and publish tracts attacking slavery, which led to the founding of the **Anti-Slavery Society** in 1823 and the campaign to emancipate the slaves in all British colonies. The Society believed in educating and mobilizing popular pressure to overcome remaining opposition. By 1830, it had published half a million tracts.

In 1821, Wilberforce selected his replacement: leadership of the parliamentary campaign passed to **Thomas Fowell Buxton**. In 1825, Wilberforce resigned from the House of Commons. Despite his lengthy career in politics, he never once enjoyed office. Wilberforce's retirement was spent at Mill Hill, north of London, with his family, although he did suffer significant financial setbacks during this time. His last public appearance was in

1830 at a meeting of the Anti-Slavery Society. Wilberforce lived to see the Emancipation bill gain support and was on his deathbed when it received its final Commons reading on July 26, 1833. He died three days later and is buried in Westminster Abbey.

Wilberforce was involved in many humanitarian causes before Parliament, such as Catholic Emancipation, as well as several causes outside of the House. Although Wilberforce is the best known of the abolitionists, he did not act alone. There were many inside and outside of Parliament who fought for this cause. He found great support from his friends and fellow Christians centered in the village of Clapham, south of London. They were nicknamed the "Saints" by their detractors and later tagged the "Clapham Sect." Nevertheless, Wilberforce was the prime mover of the group and was instrumental in the fight to liberate slaves in Britain and internationally. *See also* Atlantic Slave Trade and British Abolition; British Slavery, Abolition of; French Colonies, Emancipation of; St. Domingue, French Defeat in.

Further Readings: Wilberforce, Robert Isaac and Samuel Wilberforce. *Life of William Wilberforce*, 5 vols. London: John Murray, 1838; Furneaux, Robin. *William Wilberforce*. London: Hamish Hamilton, 1974; Lean, Garth. *God's Politician: William Wilberforce's Struggle*. London: Darton, Longman and Todd, 1980; Pollock, John. *William Wilberforce*. London: Constable, 1977.

Cheryl Fury

Williams, Eric Eustace (1911–1981)

Eric Williams is one of a handful of professional historians who made lasting contributions to historical scholarship as well as to national and international politics. For most people, Williams will be remembered as the first prime minister of Trinidad and Tobago, who governed that Caribbean nation for twenty-five years, from its political independence in 1956 to his death in 1981. But historians and related scholars will remember him as a brilliant historian, whose work has had a continuing and unmatched impact on historical scholarship. This entry focuses on his contribution to historical scholarship—specifically, his contribution to the study of slavery and abolition—and not on his contributions in politics and related fields, information on which can be found in the voluminous writings on the man and his time.

Williams's contributions to the study of slavery and abolition began with a 1938 Oxford University doctoral dissertation entitled, "The Economic Aspects of the Abolition of the West Indian Slave Trade and Slavery." Subsequently, Williams moved to the United States where he took a position as assistant professor of social and political science at Howard University in Washington, D.C. For a brief period, he set aside the doctoral work to undertake research leading to the publication of his first book, *The Negro in the Caribbean* (1942). He returned thereafter to the subject of his dissertation, which he expanded to include the contribution of the **Atlantic slave trade** and Caribbean slavery to the development of capitalism in England. The expanded work was published in 1944 under the title *Capitalism* *and Slavery.* In all, Williams wrote seven scholarly books and several journal articles. But his contribution to the study of slavery centers on *Capitalism and Slavery.* The historical scholarship provoked by this seminal work is the focus of this entry.

There are two specific ways the contribution of a scholarly work to the advancement of a disciplinary theme can be measured. One is the lasting relevance of the questions raised and the amount of further research on the theme provoked by the arguments developed. It does not matter whether the new research praises or criticizes the work. The sheer volume of scholarly production responding to the arguments advanced and exploring further the issues articulated is an important measure of scholarly contribution. The other is the extent to which the validity of the conclusions reached stands the test of time after being subjected to sustained scrutiny, with accumulated new evidence and the application of advances in conceptual sophistication. Again, it does not matter whether some or all of the arguments are found to be wrong or inadequate. If the accumulation of new evidence and the application of advances in an analytical framework uphold the conclusions reached in the work under sustained critique, that is a significant measure of scholarly contribution, particularly if the conclusions are radically different from preceding dominant ones. These two measures provide the context for the discussion in this article.

In *Capitalism and Slavery,* Eric Williams explored three main hypotheses that historians have debated for more than six decades: First, that economics, not racism, gave rise to the transatlantic slave trade and the enslavement of Africans in the Americas; ultimately, anti-African racism evolved from African enslavement. Second, that the slave trade and slavery in the British Caribbean contributed greatly to the development of industrial capitalism in England. And, third, that the socio-economic and political conditions created by expanding industrialism in England, not humanitarianism, were the principal factors in the abolition of the slave trade and the emancipation of the enslaved Africans. Each of these three propositions has remained important in the literature on slavery. But, for Williams, and for his protagonists also, the main focus was on the economics and politics of the abolition of the British slave trade and the emancipation of the enslaved Africans in the British Caribbean by the British Government. On this subject, Williams framed his argument in the context of two contending propositions:

- that abolition and emancipation were the product of humanitarian pressures arising from the spread in England of moral condemnation of the slave trade and slavery;
- that abolition and emancipation were primarily the product of power shifts among interest groups with bargaining power in England, brought about by structural changes in the English economy and general changes in the evolving global economy.

The historiography of slavery and abolition had been dominated in Britain for decades by the first argument. It was promoted vigorously by the school of imperial history established at Oxford University by Reginald Coupland. The argument was presented in a manner suggestive of national pride in the triumph of morality over material greed in England. As Williams wrote in his *British Historians and the West Indies* (1964: 233), "The British historians wrote almost as if Britain had introduced Negro slavery solely for the satisfaction of abolishing it." Williams advanced the second argument as a counter. He praised the abolitionists, especially **Thomas Clarkson**, for their selfless crusade against the evils and injustice of slavery and for their service to Africa. But he contended that the importance of the abolitionists, whom he accepted as "saints," has been erroneously argued and grossly exaggerated. The moral sentiments they expressed, he argued, were not sufficiently widespread and deeply felt by the majority of people in eighteenth- and early nineteenth-century England to form the main basis of state policy in an emerging democracy. It was changes in the relative strengths and weaknesses of interest groups with bargaining power, brought about by changes in some groups' perception of their self-interests and the emergence of new groups with bargaining power (e.g., industrial capitalists) following the growth of industrial capitalism that altered the power equation against proslavery interests (e.g., the West India interests and their allies, especially the agrarian aristocracy) and in favor of abolition. Without these fundamental structural changes, Williams contended, the abolitionists would not have been able to secure enough support in Parliament to pass legislation outlawing the slave trade and slavery no matter how much and how well they fought.

Although the three issues articulated by Williams may have been raised by other historians before him, no historian before Williams brought these issues together and developed lines of argument with anything close to the same degree of originality, detail, and clarity. No modern historian before Williams provoked a noteworthy debate on any of these issues. Williams framed the issues and developed his arguments in a manner that made them relevant to the concerns of people in the Commonwealth and beyond during the post-war decades of the 1950s and 1960s. The economic conditions of the British Caribbean in particular, and the entire West Indies in general, had been deteriorating since the nineteenth century. In the post-war decades, the most important exports from the Caribbean had become its people, instead of products, as lack of employment opportunities provoked large-scale migration. People in the Caribbean wanted to know how they got to that situation. Eric Williams's argument served well this yearning for historical explanation. His argument concerning the relative decline over time of the bargaining power of the West India interests in British politics is both original and logically consistent with the broader argument that, while slavery enriched the planters privately and contributed socially to industrial development in England, the economics of slavery created a one-way movement of resources—from the plantations (the Caribbean) to the mercantile centers (England, in this case)—thus preventing in the Caribbean the creation of conditions for self-sustained growth in the long run. The contemporary relevance of the issues, and the clarity and logical consistency of the argument explain the great appeal of the work to the educated public and scholars in the Caribbean.

In fact, the contemporary relevance of the issues and the appeal of the arguments were not limited to the Caribbean. They extended to all countries in the Americas where enslaved Africans were an important part of the historical process between the seventeenth and nineteenth centuries, particularly the United States and Brazil. What is more, even though the circumstances were different, the mercantile argument concerning the contradiction between one-way resource flow and long-run self-sustained development resonated with anticolonial crusaders across the globe, especially in Asia and Africa in the 1950s and 1960s. Like the people of the Caribbean, the educated public in colonized countries in Africa and Asia yearned for an historical explanation of their contemporary relative economic backwardness. Scholars concerned with these countries found that the Williams analytical framework, with appropriate modifications, could be applied logically to the study of the consequences of colonialism for long-run socio-economic development in those countries. In fact, it may be fair to argue that dependency theory evolved out of a continuous refinement of the Williams framework; or, at least, that the two approaches share some common conceptual elements.

While *Capitalism and Slavery* received a warm embrace in the Caribbean and the rest of the Third World—and in the socialist bloc too—it came under relentless attack in the Western world, especially in Britain and North America. Not only did Williams's attack on the Coupland school bring into question the humanitarian basis of abolition and emancipation, but the argument that slavery contributed immensely to the development of capitalism also appears, to some Western historians, to bring into disrepute the moral foundation of Western civilization. The history of this feeling is difficult to trace and explain. Early eighteenth-century writers in England did not see anything immoral in linking economic development in England to the employment of enslaved Africans in the Americas. The ideological battle between capitalism and socialism for moral superiority during the Cold War, and the charge of colonial exploitation by the anticolonial crusaders in Africa and Asia in the 1950s and 1960s, may be partly the explanation. Whatever the origin, the attacks on Williams's work stimulated considerable interest in the subject and gave rise to more questions and research. Few modern historians have stimulated as much research as Williams.

Given the extensive and sustained scrutiny, have Williams's arguments and conclusions stood the test of time? As already suggested, much of the scrutiny came from the Western world, and most of it focused on showing that all Williams's arguments and conclusions are wrong. For decades, no serious efforts were made to determine whether or not the validity of all or some of the conclusions could be demonstrated through the employment of modes of analysis different from those employed by Williams. In other words, most critics and their critiques did not differentiate between arguments and conclusions; they showed little awareness that conclusions may be historically valid even if the arguments leading to them can be shown to be wrong or inadequate. The general tendency was to demonstrate that Williams's arguments are wrong and proceed to say that his conclusions are, therefore, also wrong. However, even this negative approach has not been effective in undermining Williams's arguments in all cases. This is particularly so in respect of the origins of the transatlantic slave trade and the conditions which facilitated the adoption and implementation of abolition policy by the British government.

On the issue of abolition and emancipation, where the debate has been most heated and the amount of research and publication probably most extensive, Williams's arguments have been subjected to detailed evaluation, and some have not faired well. In several instances, Williams' use of evidence has been faulted. Statistical evidence has been amassed and deployed to disprove Williams's argument concerning economic decline in the British Caribbean following the American Revolution. It is argued that the British slave trade and the British Caribbean slave plantations continued to be profitable in the late-eighteenth century. Hence, it is concluded, the British government committed economic suicide—"econocide"—when it signed legislation abolishing the slave trade. Without doubt, this creative research has brought much needed balance to the analysis and raised more questions for further research.

While the narrowly framed debate on the decline issue appears to remain open, as prodecline publications are still appearing in the opening years of the twenty-first century, it must be said that the critique appears to have overlooked the central point in Williams's analysis—relative decline both in reality and in perception. The critique contains no detailed macroeconomic analysis of the changing weight of the British Caribbean economies relative to the English economy that will enable us to assess what was happening to the relative bargaining power of the West India interest in British politics. Even if the argument is correct that the British slave trade and the British Caribbean slave plantations remained profitable in the late-eighteenth century, the evidence is clear enough that the growth of the British Caribbean economies from the 1780s to the early nineteenth century lagged considerably behind the rapidly industrializing economy of England during the period. The sectoral changes in the industrializing economy of England meant that commerce and industry grew disproportionately relative to agriculture, raising the resource weight of the industrial interest groups at the expense of the old agrarian aristocracy. Thus, at the same time that the slave plantation economies of the British Caribbean lagged and became a diminishing proportion of the British imperial economy over time, the agricultural sector lost ground over time in the English economy. In reality, therefore, the weight of the West India interest in English society diminished over time, along with that of their agrarian allies, during the period. Worse still for the West India interest, the interaction of the ongoing structural changes in England with those in the evolving global economy precipitated changes in several interest groups' perception of what was in their self-interest, changes in perception that were detrimental to the political fortunes of the West India interest.

The foregoing observations are in accord with the evidence gathered in the painstaking efforts made by the British government to ascertain before hand the likely consequences of abolishing the slave trade for the English economy in the long run. While the slave traders and the allied plantation interests assembled evidence to show the long-run adverse consequences of abolition for the English economy, what may be taken as the "official mind" of abolition was offered by the inspector general of exports and imports of Great Britain, Thomas Irving, in 1791. Generally acclaimed as the most meticulous of the eighteenth-century inspector generals, his views on the subject were considered sufficiently weighty to warrant the movement of the Parliamentary Select Committee appointed to conduct the investigation to his house where he was recovering from a serious illness. In the long interview, covering several printed pages (with statistical tables), Irving took pains to demonstrate that abolition was likely to produce more positive than adverse consequences for the English economy in the long run.

The perception concerning the declining importance of the British West Indies, right or wrong in reality, appears not to have been uncommon among the informed public in England in the late-eighteenth and early nineteenth centuries. And there is evidence that the British government began to seriously consider changes in commercial policy following the political independence of the United States. Thus, a plan to reorient British trade, drawn up in 1783 by a Henry Trafford and submitted to Lord Grantham, notes that the loss of the North American colonies had compelled "His Majesty's Ministers and the Parliament to take into their most serious consideration what alterations and improvements" needed to be made "in our commercial system." Trafford's plan, submitted to the ministers to assist them in their task, made a strong case for transforming Africa from its subordination to the Americas into the center of British commerce. A somewhat similar view was expressed in 1812 by the managing committee of the English Company of Merchants Trading to Africa, a regulating company of individual British traders.

That these perceptions and structural changes in England significantly influenced British government policy is made even clearer by evidence from the most recent discussion of the issues. The evidence is the more significant, because it comes from Seymour Drescher, one of the most meticulous and energetic critics of the Williams abolition thesis. In *The Mighty Experiment* (2002), Drescher shows the role of social science arguments in the contest leading to the enactment of laws abolishing the British slave trade and slavery in the British Caribbean. Drescher's narrative suggests that **Adam Smith**'s pronouncement that slave labor was more costly than free wage labor, leading to the prediction of the inevitable triumph of free labor, and Thomas Malthus's demographic theory, which implied that emancipation would enable labor to reproduce itself naturally in the British Caribbean, were applied to good effect by the abolitionists to make the British public and the government have overly optimistic expectations about the economic effects of abolition and emancipation. Both the British public and the government were made to believe that free labor would be more profitable than slave labor.

It was only after the abolition and emancipation laws had been enacted that the editor of the 1835 edition of Adam Smith's *Wealth of Nations*, Edward Gibbon Wakefield, exposed the contradiction between Smith's argument that gang organization permitted a greater division of labor (thus greater productivity) and his general statement of the superiority of free over slave labor. Wakefield demonstrated that wherever cheap access to land existed gang organization of free labor for staple production was not possible; only coerced labor would allow gang organization under such conditions. Because these conditions prevailed in the plantation zone of the Americas, Wakefield contended, Smith's generalization, though valid for densely populated regions like Western Europe, was not valid for the plantation Americas. Ultimately, the empirical evidence after abolition and emancipation—from **Sierra Leone** in Africa to the plantation zone of the Americas—turned out to be contrary to the expectations of the abolitionists and the British government; it rather supported Wakefield's analysis. In consequence, as Drescher narrates, the observed economic consequences of British abolition worked against its global extension. In the end, that extension had to be forcefully imposed by state power. What is more, as the unexpected economic consequences of abolition and emancipation unfolded, the British public turned against the abolitionists, leading to their humiliating defeat in Parliament in the 1840s.

Drescher's evidence also confirms the declining bargaining power of the West India interest in British politics. The constitutional reforms of 1832 that extended the franchise (largely a function of the growing economic and political power of the rising industrial capitalists and their entrepreneurial and labor connections) effectively destroyed the so-called rotten boroughs of agrarian England. In consequence, there was "a much reduced West Indian presence in the reformed Parliament."

On the issue of abolition and emancipation, therefore, it can be said that the main arguments and conclusions of Eric Williams have stood the test of time rather well. Several of the individual arguments have been shown to be wrong or inadequately supported by evidence. But, taken together, the central issues raised and the main arguments developed have not been disproved by the sustained research of six decades inspired by Williams. The evidence produced by recent research shows that from the 1780s to the 1830s the bargaining power of the West India interest in British politics declined under the impact of growing industrial capitalism and changes in the emerging global economy, as Williams argued. What is more, perception even far exceeded reality; the public and the government were made to believe that abolition and emancipation would increase prosperity. The recent research thus shows, among other things, that the "official mind of abolition" can only be discovered by focusing on what the government actually knew and believed at the time the laws were enacted. What the deployment of statistics can tell us today may be different; but that is not important if what we want to know is the origin of state policy.

On the issue of whether economics or anti-African racism caused the exclusive focus of New World demand for slave labor on sub-Saharan Africa—a somewhat peripheral issue in *Capitalism and Slavery*—the same conclusion can be reached that Williams's argument and conclusion have stood admirably well the test of time. Initially, this issue did not receive much attention. But in the last two decades or so it has been attracting growing attention. To disprove Williams's argument that the enslavement of Africans in the Americas gave rise to anti-African racism, some participants in the debate sought to show that anti-African racism in the Western world predated the transatlantic slave trade. This stimulated some fascinating research and exchanges in the leading journals in history in the 1980s and 1990s. Biblical evidence featured prominently, especially the history of Noah and his offspring. While that debate continues, it is fair to say that the more persuasive arguments center on the invention of ideological rationalizations long after the event—the mythical curse of Noah on his son, Ham (that his children will be enslaved because of his alleged transgression), was invoked long after the actual fact of the enslavement of a people. Thus, the Slavs of central Europe became identified as the children of Ham after centuries of enslavement. As enslavement shifted from central Europe to sub-Saharan Africa, Africans became the children of Ham. A careful scholarly scrutiny of the history of the Bible has offered no support for this reconstruction of ethnicity and racial identity.

A stronger cultural argument, based on insider-outsider theory, has also failed to disprove the Williams argument. The imaginatively constructed cultural argument was put forward in the 1990s. It attempts to show that it would have been cheaper for New World employers of slave labor to enslave Europeans, but this did not happen because of the ideological constraint that prevented the enslavement of Europeans by other Europeans. This cultural explanation has been effectively critiqued for having overlooked the political situation in Europe at the time. The export of European slaves to the Middle East ended when the rise of relatively strong centralized states, more or less equally matched militarily, ended political fragmentation in Europe and raised for the leaders of European nations the political cost of exporting captives. Widespread political fragmentation in Africa, similar to the earlier situation in Europe, on the other hand, permitted a sustained response to expanding demand for captives to be enslaved in the Americas. No pan-European identity existed in Europe when the Atlantic slave trade began in the sixteenth and seventeenth centuries, just as no pan-African identity existed at the time. It is important to note, in the context of the ideological charges sometimes made, that the issues raised and the arguments developed in this section of *Capitalism and Slavery* place Western civilization in a better moral light, racially speaking, than the counter arguments do. In the final analysis, however, it is safe to say that Williams's arguments and conclusions on these issues remain important and are yet to be disproved.

Second in importance to the issue of abolition and emancipation, at least from Williams's point of view, is the issue of the role of the slave trade and British Caribbean slavery in the development of industrial capitalism in England. On this subject, while the issues raised and the arguments developed by Williams are wide-ranging, ultimately the argument centers on the contribution of profits from the slave trade and Caribbean slavery to the stream of capital that financed the Industrial Revolution in England. For this reason, the voluminous literature inspired by *Capitalism and Slavery* on the role of slavery in the Industrial Revolution focused almost exclusively on the issue of profits. The debate followed two tracks. One measured the rate and the absolute magnitude of profits, quite often from the slave trade alone, and the other computed the percentage of total national industrial capital investment contributed by profits from slavery in the late-eighteenth century. The consistent verdict is that Williams grossly exaggerated the magnitude of the profits. In any case, the critics argue, even if Williams's magnitude of profits is accepted, when related to the total national capital invested in industry during the period the percentage contributed by profits from slavery was inconsequential. From this the conclusion is reached that the Williams arguments and conclusions are wrong. For decades no serious thought was given to the possibility that a reformulation of the issues and the application of new developments in theorizing could produce new sets of data and a new mode of analysis that would support the main conclusion that the slave trade and enslaved Africans in the Americas were critical to the Industrial Revolution.

The research and publications of the last decades of the twentieth century proceeded in that direction. The importance of profits was recognized and the profitability of the slave trade and slavery was demonstrated. But it is stated unequivocally that the emphasis on profits was misplaced. Instead, emphasis shifted to the role of slavery in the growth of Atlantic commerce, and the Industrial Revolution is presented as a function of expanding Atlantic commerce. The geographical dimension, within which the analysis is conducted, is also radically altered, from the British Caribbean alone to the entire Atlantic economy. The new direction of investigation and analysis is completed with the application of new advances in growth theory, combined with neglected insights from classical development theory. The result is strong support for the conclusion that the Atlantic slave trade and enslaved Africans in the Americas were critical to the successful completion of the industrialization process in England from the mid-seventeenth to the mid-nineteenth century.

In the main, therefore, Williams's conclusion that slavery contributed immensely to the development of industrial capitalism in England remains valid. We can agree that Williams's analysis centered on profits did not provide a solid proof for the conclusion. On this, the critics made some valid points. But the critics committed a fatal error in dismissing the conclusion entirely on that basis. They should have been more positive and probed deeper to see if an alternative mode of investigation and analysis could lead to the same conclusion as has now been shown.

Based on the two criteria for measuring the contribution of a scholar's work to historical scholarship specified in the opening paragraphs of the article—the lasting relevance of the issues articulated and the amount of further research inspired, and the degree to which the conclusions stand the test of time—we can infer from the foregoing discussion that *Capitalism and Slavery* has made, and continues to make, an immeasurable contribution to the study of slavery and abolition. Thanks to the way Eric Williams framed the issues, the question of African slavery in the Americas remains very much alive today not only among scholars, but also among the reading public across the globe. The series of mega conferences organized over the years to honor the man and his scholarly work, probably the most important of which was the Golden Jubilee celebration of *Capitalism and*

Slavery in Trinidad in 1996, and the translation of the book into seven languages, including Russian, Chinese, and Japanese, testify to that. The growing popularity of Atlantic World history, a byproduct of the scholarship he inspired, and the ongoing debate on reparation for the lingering adverse economic consequences of slavery for diasporic Africans in the Americas and for continental Africans will ensure the continued relevance of the issues raised by Williams and the research he inspired. What is more, the establishment of the Eric Williams Memorial Collection in Trinidad (named to UNESCO's *Memory of the World Register* in 1999), the product of the indefatigable efforts of his daughter, Erica Williams Connell, adds to the resources available to sustain research on the subject. *See also* British Slavery, Abolition of; Bible and Slavery; West Indies Emancipation Day.

Further Readings: Braude, Benjamin. "The Sons of Noah and the Construction of Ethnic and Geographic Identities in the Medieval and Early Modern Periods." *William and Mary Quarterly* 54 (January 1997): 103–142; Cateau, Heather, and S.H.H. Carrington, eds. *Capitalism and Slavery Fifty Years Later: Eric Eustace Williams—A Reassessment of the Man and His Work*. New York: Peter Lang, 2000; Drescher, Seymour. *The Mighty Experiment: Free Labor versus Slavery in British Emancipation*. Oxford: Oxford University Press, 2002; Eltis, David. "Europeans and the Rise and Fall of African Slavery in the Americas: An Interpretation." *American Historical Review* 98, 5 (1993): 1399–1423; Evans, William McKee. "From the Land of Canaan to the Land of Guinea: The Strange Odyssey of the Sons of Ham." *American Historical Review* 85 (February 1980): 15–43; Inikori, Joseph E. *Africans and the Industrial Revolution in England: A Study in International Trade and Economic Development*. Cambridge: Cambridge University Press, 2002; Inikori, Joseph E. "The Struggle Against the Trans-Atlantic Slave Trade: The Role of the Stat." In Sylviane A. Diouf, ed. *Fighting the Slave Trade: West African Strategies*. Athens: Ohio University Press, 2003, pp. 170–198; Inikori, Joseph E. *The Chaining of a Continent: Export Demand for Captives and the History of Africa South of the Sahara, 1450–1870*. Kingston, Jamaica: Institute of Social and Economic Research, University of the West Indies, 1992; Solow, Barbara L., and Stanley L. Engerman, eds. *British Capitalism and Caribbean Slavery: The Legacy of Eric Williams*. Cambridge: Cambridge University Press, 1987; Williams, Eric. *Capitalism and Slavery*. Chapel Hill: University of North Carolina Press, 1944; Williams, Eric. *British Historians and the West Indies*. London: Deutsch, 1964.

Joseph E. Inikori

Women. *See* Abolitionist Women; Women and Antislavery; Women's Antislavery Societies; Women's Rights and Antislavery

Women's Antislavery Societies

Ladies' antislavery societies that surfaced in the 1830s played a seminal role in raising women's consciousness about their own lack of political, economic, and other civil rights. They posed the first organized, gender-specific challenge to slavery and racism. Their aggressiveness in the male-controlled public sphere made the societies flashpoints for debates on women's place. Members' experiences fermented a feminist culture that set the stage for the first women's rights convention at Seneca Falls in 1848.

The first female-only, antislavery society comprised a group of black women in Salem, Massachusetts, who organized on February 22, 1832, in response to an invitation in **William Lloyd Garrison**'s *The Liberator*. Later that year, a dozen women organized the racially integrated Boston Female Anti-Slavery Society, followed by the Philadelphia Female Anti-Slavery Society in 1833. Integration between the sexes remained more elusive, and the first of three annual all-female antislavery conventions in 1837 drew eighty-one participants from twelve states. By 1838, at least thirty-three female antislavery societies existed throughout the Northeast.

Members shook off the ridicule and violence that greeted women's entrance into politics. The praise they won for resisting a mob in 1835 emboldened the Boston women to move farther into the public sphere, appearing at political meetings to support antislavery measures. The women sued Southerners who brought slaves to their city and organized fundraisers for male abolitionists. In 1836, they coordinated an antislavery petition drive across New England that firmly planted women in politics. Female exercise of the constitutional right to petition was a crucial early bridge between the separate spheres that broadened both sexes' conception of women's role as citizens.

The Boston group's boldness appalled many Americans, however, illuminating cultural beliefs about separate spheres so deeply inscribed that even some antislavery women spurned equal rights with men. The clergy also pounced upon the ladies' antislavery societies because their techniques trespassed traditional male prerogatives, most notoriously by the radical act of women speaking in public. The Boston society sponsored the groundbreaking speaking tour of **Angelina** and Sarah **Grimké**, for instance, which ignited the famous exchanges between the South Carolina sisters and the Massachusetts clergy on women's place.

The "woman question" split the abolition movement in 1840, when Garrison supporters won control of the **American Anti-Slavery Society**. Foes of women's expanding role walked out to form their own organization, followed by the Ladies' New York City Anti-Slavery Society. Ironically, although it decried women speaking in public and linking abolition to women's rights, the New York women had hosted the Grimkés' first speaking engagements as abolition agents in "parlor talks" to women only. The ladies' society withdrew to fund-raising and domestic activities such as antislavery needlework.

The female breach into politics nonetheless widened. **Lucretia Mott**, **Lydia Maria Child,** and Maria Weston Chapman filled the male defectors' seats on the American Anti-Slavery Society's executive committee. In June 1840, Mott was among female delegates refused recognition because of their sex at the **World's Anti-Slavery Convention** in London. Her indignation set Mott and sister abolitionist **Elizabeth Cady Stanton** on the road to Seneca Falls. *See also* Garrisonians; Gender and Slave Emancipation; Gender Relations within Abolitionism; Seneca Falls Convention.

Further Readings: Flexner, Eleanor. *Century of Struggle: The Woman's Rights Movement in the United States*. New York: Atheneum, 1971 (originally published by The Belknap Press of Harvard University Press, 1958); Yellin, Jean Fagan, and

John C. Van Horne, eds. *The Abolitionist Sisterhood: Women's Political Culture in Antebellum America*. Ithaca, NY: Cornell University Press. 1994.

Linda J. Lumsden

World's Anti-Slavery Convention (1840)

The first World's Anti-Slavery Convention was organized by the **British and Foreign Anti-Slavery Society** (BFASS) and held from June 12 to June 23, 1840, in London. The Convention offers historians a snapshot of British antislavery activities in the immediate aftermath of West Indian emancipation, but it was also a snapshot of divisions within the Anglo-American antislavery movement, particularly regarding the participation of women in abolitionist organizations.

Calling the Convention was the first major action of the BFASS. Formed in 1839, the Society's purpose was to turn its attention from British abolition, which had been achieved the year before in the West Indies, to "universal" abolition, to stamping out vestiges of the international slave trade, and to undermining American slavery. Although the idea for an international conference to discuss such issues was broached by Joshua Leavitt, an American, in March 1839, the BFASS embraced the notion as consonant with its global aims. In the summer of 1839, they printed a circular inviting abolitionists from all nations to a "General Anti-Slavery Convention." Despite its global aspirations, British and American delegates predominated at the Convention. Over 200 official members were British, with a majority from England, and about 50 were American. By contrast, only half a dozen French abolitionists attended, along with a handful from continental Europe and the Caribbean.

American abolitionists initially united in welcoming the invitation. One of them, John Greenleaf Whittier, praised the "World's Convention" in a poem by that title. But discord within the American movement was soon amplified in discussions about the conference. **Garrisonians**, who favored the full participation of women in antislavery organizations, disagreed with other abolitionists, generally identified with **Lewis Tappan**, not only on the question of women's rights, but on the legitimacy of political action. When supporters of Tappan's wing notified the BFASS that Garrisonians planned to send women to the Convention, the Society issued a second circular, in February 1840, that explicitly invited "Gentlemen." In May, Tappan's followers seceded from the Garrisonian **American Anti-Slavery Society** (AASS) to form the **American and Foreign Anti-Slavery Society**, which bore more than a nominal resemblance to the BFASS. One month later, at the World's Convention, wounds from the schism were still fresh.

The controversy over women came to a head when seven women delegates, including **Lucretia Mott**, presented credentials in London from Garrisonian societies in the United States. A few weeks earlier, the BFASS had made a final pronouncement excluding women from the meeting, but on the opening day, **Wendell Phillips** moved to rescind this decision. Almost the entire day was taken up with debate on the motion, while Mott and other women looked on from the visitors' gallery. Very few British delegates supported Phillips's motion; **Daniel O'Connell** was one of them, but the Garrisonians' longtime ally, **George Thompson**, called for compromise. Finally the motion was defeated. In protest, **William Lloyd Garrison**, along with Nathaniel P. Rogers and black abolitionist Charles L. Remond, sat in the gallery with the excluded women, after arriving six days late to the Convention, straight from the contentious meeting that had split the American society in May.

While representing new possibilities for transatlantic antislavery, the Convention also represented its limits, delineated by fractious issues like women's rights. But the presence of American women at the Convention did have a formative influence on women's movements. In meetings held outside the Convention, women like Mott met with European antislavery feminists and articulated the need for a movement of their own. **Elizabeth Cady Stanton**, who visited the Convention while honeymooning with her husband, a Tappan supporter, later recalled the event as the genesis of her own commitment to women's suffrage.

The Convention also reflected various strands in British abolitionism following West Indian emancipation. **Thomas Clarkson's** honorary selection as the president of the Convention symbolically represented the passing of the torch from veteran reformers to a new generation of British abolitionists. It also represented the conviction of both generations, but especially the younger, that England's antislavery mission was worldwide. "Mohammedan" slavery in Africa, Spanish slavery in Cuba, and Portuguese slavery in Brazil were prominent subjects of discussion at the Convention. Antislavery addresses to foreign heads of governments were issued. The persistence of slavery in the British Empire, specifically in India, and the continuation of illegal slave trading, despite attempts to suppress it, were also on the agenda.

If the Convention summarized the problems that British abolitionists saw remaining to be solved, it also revealed the diversity of potential solutions. Debates over strategy centered on the effects of emancipation on population growth, production, and profitability. Ardent defenders of free labor believed its superiority had been proven by West Indian emancipation; some favored competition between free-grown produce in the British Empire with slave-grown produce elsewhere. More conservative delegates argued for the maintenance of Britain's protectionist duties on sugar until its price dropped and stabilized. Such debates about free labor and free trade occupied abolitionists throughout the next two decades, including at a second international convention called by the BFASS in 1843, which was boycotted by Garrisonians. Other roads ultimately not taken by most British abolitionists, such as the **free produce movement**, the African Civilization Society, and plans to foster competition between free-grown East Indian cotton and American cotton, were still very much on the map at the 1840 meeting.

Further Readings: Kennon, Donald R. "'An Apple of Discord': The Woman Question at the World's Anti-Slavery Convention of 1840." *Slavery and Abolition* 5 (1984): 244–266; Sklar, Kathryn Kish. "'Women Who Speak for an Entire Nation': American and British Women at the World Anti-Slavery Convention, London, 1840."

In Jean Fagan Yellin & John C. Van Horne, eds., *The Abolitionist Sisterhood: Women's Political Culture in Antebellum America*. Ithaca, NY: Cornell University Press, 1994, pp. 301–333; Temperley, Howard. *British Anti-Slavery, 1833–1870*. London: Longman, 1972.

W. Caleb McDaniel

Wright, Henry Clarke (1797–1870)

Henry Clarke Wright was a prolific American abolitionist and a radical advocate on a variety of reforms, including pacifism, women's rights, children's rights, marriage, and health care.

Wright's studies began at the Andover Theological Seminary in 1819. After his ordination in 1823, Wright started his professional life as a minister in West Newbury, Massachusetts. A decade later, Wright felt he was not doing enough for the improvement of society and quit his flock, leaving him free to write and lecture on multiple agendas, which he did with a fervent passion.

Wright was always sympathetic to the unjust treatment of slaves and free blacks, but it was not until 1835 that he made the conversion to an extreme abolitionist. He was greatly influenced by **William Lloyd Garrison**, the **American Anti-Slavery Society**, and their notion of "immediatism," which challenged colonizationism, a popular idea that freed slaves should be deported to Africa and that their former owners should be compensated. Wright's abolitionist efforts led him to join the Massachusetts Anti-Slavery Society and the American Union for the Moral and Intellectual Improvement of the Colored Race.

Infatuated with the concept of religious pilgrimage, Wright longed to travel to exotic locales, especially Africa. Various obligations guided his travels through the eastern United States, but Wright never got past Chicago. However, he seized the opportunity to go to Great Britain in 1842 for a world's antislavery convention. The convention never happened, but Wright stayed in Europe for five years. Wright worked to revive Great Britain's non-resistance movement, while traveling extensively with two American abolitionists, James Buffum and **Frederick Douglass**.

Perhaps Wright's most important campaign while in Great Britain was the "Send Back the Money" operation. Various churches in Scotland had cut ties with the Calvinists and had formed the Free Kirk. To finance their movement, members of the Free Kirk visited the United States and brought back $3,000 from American Presbyterians. When word got out that a great deal of the money came from Southern slave owners, the result of exploitation and suffering, abolitionists were livid. Wright and other abolitionists traveled throughout Scotland, lamenting that the only acceptable thing to do would be to "send back the money." The campaign deepened Wright's conviction that, by condoning slavery, churches and clergy betrayed their Christianity.

Once Wright was no longer affiliated with the ministry, he was able to voice his radical views more forcefully. Along with his extreme abolitionism, Wright was a controversial pacifist. He worked for the American Peace

Society and the New England Non-Resistance Society. Yet, Wright's pacifist beliefs did not interfere with his support for the Union in the Civil War or antislavery crusader John Brown's violent tactics. Wright continued his hectic schedule of traveling and lectures until his death in 1870, leaving behind a vast collection of writing that covered multiple progressive social movements. *See also* Immediate Emancipation.

Further Reading: Perry, Lewis. *Childhood, Marriage, and Reform.* Chicago: University of Chicago Press, 1980.

Ashley Whitmore

SELECTED BIBLIOGRAPHY

The following bibliography represents only a selection of some of the most important works on antislavery, abolition, and emancipation. Readers should also consult the numerous additional titles that appear at the end of each entry under the heading "Further Readings."

Anstey, Roger. *The Atlantic Slave Trade and British Abolition 1766–1810*. Atlantic Highlands, NJ: Humanities Press, 1975.

Aptheker, Herbert. *American Negro Slave Revolts*. 5th ed. New York: Columbia University Press, 1987.

Bales, Kevin. *Disposable People: New Slavery in the Global Economy*. Berkeley: University of California Press, 1999.

Beckles, Hilary, and Verene Shepherd, eds. *Caribbean Freedom: Economy and Society from Emancipation to the Present*. Princeton, NJ: Markus Weiner, 1996.

Berlin, Ira, et al. *Slaves No More: Three Essays on Emancipation and the Civil War*. Cambridge: Cambridge University Press, 1992.

Blackburn, Robin. *The Overthrow of Colonial Slavery, 1776–1848*. London: Verso Press, 1988.

Blanchard, Peter. *Slavery and Abolition in Early Republican Peru*. Lanham, MD: SR Books, 1992.

Bolt, Christine, and Seymour Drescher, eds. *Anti-Slavery, Religion, and Reform: Essays in Memory of Roger Anstey*. Hamden, CT: Archon Press, 1980.

Bradley, Keith R. *Slavery and Rebellion in the Roman World, 140BC–70BC*. London: B. T. Batsford, 1989.

Carretta, Vincent, ed. *Unchained Voices: An Anthology of Black Authors in the English-Speaking World of the Eighteenth Century*. Lexington: University of Kentucky Press, 1996.

Clarence-Smith, William, ed. *The Economics of the Indian Ocean Slave Trade in the Nineteenth Century*. London: Frank Cass Publishers, 1989.

Conforti, Joseph A. *Samuel Hopkins and the New Divinity Movement: Calvinism, the Congregational Ministry, and Reform in New England between the Great Awakenings*. Grand Rapids, MI: Wm. B. Eerdmans Publishing Company, 1981.

Conrad, Robert. *The Destruction of Brazilian Slavery, 1850–1888*. Berkeley: University of California Press, 1972.

Cooper, Frederick. *From Slaves to Squatters. Plantation Labor and Agriculture in Zanzibar and Coastal Kenya, 1890–1925*. New Haven, CT: Yale University Press, 1980.

Corwin, Arthur F. *Spain and the Abolition of Slavery in Cuba, 1817–1886*. Austin: University of Texas, 1967.

Costa, Emilia Viotti da. *Crowns of Glory, Tears of Blood: The Demerara Slave Rebellion of 1823*. Oxford: Oxford University Press, 1994.

Cover, Robert M. *Justice Accused: Antislavery and the Judicial Process*. New Haven, CT: Yale University Press, 1975.

Craton, Michael. *Testing the Chains: Resistance to Slavery in the British West Indies*. Ithaca, NY: Cornell University Press, 1982.

Davis, David Brion. "The Emergence of Immediatism in British and American Antislavery Thought." *Mississippi Valley Historical Review* 49 (September 1962): 209–230.

——. *The Problem of Slavery in the Age of Revolution, 1770–1823*. 2nd ed. Oxford: Oxford University Press, 1999.

——. *The Problem of Slavery in Western Culture*. New York: Oxford University Press, 1966.

Dillon, Merton L. *Abolitionists: The Growth of a Dissenting Minority*. DeKalb: Northern Illinois University Press, 1974.

Drescher, Seymour. *Capitalism and Antislavery: British Mobilisation in Comparative Perspective*. Oxford: Oxford University Press, 1986.

——. *Econocide: British Slavery and the Slave Trade in the Era of Abolition*. Pittsburgh: University of Pittsburgh Press, 1977.

——. *The Mighty Experiment: Free Labor versus Slavery in British Emancipation*. Oxford: Oxford University Press, 2002.

duBois, Laurent. *A Colony of Citizens: Revolution & Slave Emancipation in the French Caribbean, 1787–1804*. Chapel Hill: University of North Carolina Press, 2004.

Egerton, Douglas R. *Gabriel's Rebellion: The Virginia Slave Conspiracies of 1800 and 1802*. Chapel Hill: University of North Carolina Press, 1993.

——. *He Shall Go Out Free: The Lives of Denmark Vesey*. Madison: Madison House, 1999.

Emmer, Pieter. *The Dutch in the Atlantic Economy, 1580–1880. Trade, Slavery and Emancipation*. Aldershot, England: Ashgate, 1998.

Erdem, Y. Hakan. *Slavery in the Ottoman Empire and its Demise, 1800–1909*. London: Macmillan, 1996.

Fehrenbacher, Don E. *The Slaveholding Republic: An Account of the United States Government's Relations to Slavery*. Completed and edited by Ward M. McAfee. New York: Oxford University Press, 2001.

Field, Daniel. *The End of Serfdom, Nobility and Bureaucracy in Russia, 1855–1861*. Cambridge, MA: Harvard University Press, 1976.

Finkelman, Paul. *An Imperfect Union*. Chapel Hill: University of North Carolina Press, 1981.

——. *Slavery and the Founders: Race and Liberty in the Age of Jefferson*. 2nd ed. Armonk, NY: M.E. Sharpe, 2001.

Finley, Moses I. *Ancient Slavery and Modern Ideology*. Expanded edition edited by Brent D. Shaw. Princeton, N.J., Markus Wiener Publishers, 1998.

Fladeland, Betty. *Men and Brothers: Anglo-American Anti-Slavery Cooperation*. Urbana: University of Illinois Press, 1972.

Foner, Eric. *Free Soil, Free Labor, Free Men*. New York: Oxford University Press, 1970.

——. *Reconstruction: America's Unfinished Revolution, 1863–1877*. New York: Harper & Row, Publishers, 1988.

Gara, Larry. *The Liberty Line: The Legend of the Underground Railroad*. Lexington: University Press of Kentucky, 1961.

Garnsey, Peter. *Ideas of Slavery from Aristotle to Augustine*. Cambridge: Cambridge University Press, 1996.

Genovese, Eugene. *From Rebellion to Revolution: Afro-American Slave Revolts in the Making of the Modern World*. Baton Rouge: Louisiana State University Press, 1979.

Getz, Trevor. *Slavery and Reform in West Africa: Toward Emancipation in Nineteenth-Century Senegal and the Gold Coast*. Athens: Ohio University Press, 2004.

Grover, Kathryn. *The Fugitive's Gibraltar: Escaping Slaves and Abolitionism in New Bedford, Massachusetts*. Amherst: University of Massachusetts Press, 2001.

Hall, Neville. *Slave Society in the Danish West Indies*. B.W. Higman, ed. Jamaica: University of the West Indies Press. 1992.

Heuman, Gad, ed. *Out of the House of Bondage. Runaways, Resistance and Marronage in Africa and the New World*. London: Frank Cass, 1986.

Hutson, Alaine. "Enslavement and Manumission in Saudi Arabia, 1926–38." *Critique: Critical Middle Eastern Studies* 11, 1 (Spring 2002): 49–70.

Jacobs, Donald M., ed. *Courage and Conscience: Black and White Abolitionists in Boston*. Bloomington: Indiana University Press, 1993.

James, C.L.R. *The Black Jacobins: Toussaint L'Ouverture and the San Domingo Revolution*. 2nd ed. New York: Vintage, 1963. Originally published 1938.

Jennings, Lawrence C. *French Anti-Slavery. The Movement for the Abolition of Slavery in France, 1802–1848*. Cambridge: Cambridge University Press, 2000.

Jones, Howard. *Mutiny on the* Amistad. New York: Oxford University Press, 1987.

Kachun, Mitch. *Festivals of Freedom: Memory and Meaning in African American Emancipation Celebrations, 1808–1915*. Amherst: University of Massachusetts, 2003.

Klein, Martin. *Slavery and Colonial Rule in French West Africa*. Cambridge: Cambridge University Press, 1998.

Klingberg, Frank J. *The Anti-Slavery Movement in England*. New Haven, CT: Yale University Press, 1926.

Kraut, Alan M., ed. *Crusaders and Compromisers: Essays on the Relationship of the Antislavery Struggle to the Antebellum Party System*. Westport, CT: Greenwood Press, 1983.

Lal, K.S. *Muslim Slave System in Medieval India*. New Delhi: Aditya Prakashan, 1994.

Locke, Mary Staughton. *Anti-slavery in America from the Introduction of African Slaves to the Prohibition of the Slave-Trade*. Boston: Ginn and Company, 1901; reprint, Johnson Reprint Corporation, 1968.

Lombardi, John. *The Decline and Abolition of Negro Slavery in Venezuela*. Westport, CT: Greenwood, 1971.

Lovejoy, Paul, and Jan Hogendorn. *Slow Death for Slavery: The Course of Abolition in Northern Nigeria, 1897–1936*. Cambridge: Cambridge University Press, 1993.

Loveland, Anne C. "Evangelicalism and 'Immediate Emancipation' in American Antislavery Thought." *Journal of Southern History* 32 (1966): 172–188.

McCalman, Iain. "Anti-Slavery and Ultra Radicalism in Early Nineteenth Century England." *Slavery and Abolition* 7 (September 1986): 99–117.

McInerney, Daniel J. *The Fortunate Heirs of Freedom: Abolition and Republican Thought*. Lincoln: University of Nebraska Press, 1994.

McKivigan, John R. *The War against Proslavery Religion: Abolitionism and the Northern Churches*. Ithaca, NY: Cornell University Press, 1984.

McPherson, James. *The Negro's Civil War: How American Negroes Felt and Acted During the War for the Union*. Champagne-Urbana: University of Illinois Press, 1982.

——. *The Struggle for Equality, Abolitionists and the Negro in the Civil War and Reconstruction*. Princeton, NJ: Princeton University Press, 1964.

Mason, John. *Social Death and Resurrection: Slavery and Emancipation in South Africa*. Charlottesville: University of Virginia Press, 1999.

Mayer, Henry. *All on Fire: William Lloyd Garrison and the Abolition of Slavery*. New York: St. Martin's Griffin, 1998.

Midgley, Clare. *Women Against Slavery: The British Campaigns, 1780–1870*. New York: Routledge, 1992.

Miers, Suzanne. *Slavery in the Twentieth Century: The Evolution of a Global Problem*. Walnut Creek: AltaMira Press, 2003.

Miers, Suzanne, and Richard Roberts, eds. *The End of Slavery in Africa*. Madison: University of Wisconsin Press, 1988.

Miller, William Lee. *Arguing about Slavery: The Great Battle in the United States Congress*. New York: Alfred A. Knopf, 1995.

Minkema, Kenneth. "Jonathan Edwards's Defense of Slavery." *Massachusetts Historical Review* 4 (2002): 23–59.

Moon, David. *The Abolition of Serfdom in Russia 1762–1907*. Longman: Harlow and London, 2001.

Morton, Fred. *Children of Ham: Freed Slaves and Fugitive Slaves on the Kenya Coast, 1873 to 1907*. Boulder, CO: Westview, 1990.

Nash, Gary B. *Race and Revolution*. Madison, WI: Madison House, 1990.

Nash, Gary, and Jean Soderlund. *Freedom by Degrees: Emancipation and Its Aftermath in Pennsylvania*. New York: Oxford University Press, 1991.

Newman, Richard S. *The Transformation of American Abolitionism: Fighting Slavery in the Early Republic*. Chapel Hill: University of North Carolina Press, 2002.

Northrup, David. *Indentured Labor in the Age of Imperialism, 1834–1922*. New York: Cambridge University Press, 1996.

Nuremberger, Ruth Ketring. *The Free Produce Movement: A Quaker Protest Against Slavery*. Durham, NC: Duke University Press, 1942.

O'Phelan, Scarlett. *Rebellions and Revolts in Eighteenth Century Peru and Upper Peru*. Koln, Böhlau Verlag, 1985.

Oubre, Claude F. *Forty Acres and a Mule: The Freedmen's Bureau and Black Land Ownership*. Baton Rouge: Louisiana State University Press, 1978.

Painter, Nell Irvin. *Exodusters: Black Migration to Kansas after Reconstruction*. New York: W.W. Norton & Co., 1992.

——. *Sojourner Truth: A Life, A Symbol*. New York: W.W. Norton & Co., 1996.

Patterson, Orlando. *Slavery and Social Death: A Comparative Study*. Cambridge, MA: Harvard University Press, 1982.

Pease, Jane, and William Pease. *Bound With Them in Chains: A Biographical History of the Antislavery Movement*. Westport, CT: Greenwood Press, 1972.

Peebles, Patrick. *Plantation Tamils of Ceylon*. London: Leicester University Press, 2001.

Perry, Lewis. *Radical Abolitionism: Anarchy and the Government of God in Antislavery Thought*. Ithaca, N: Cornell University Press, 1973.

Perry, Lewis, and Michael Fellman, eds., *Antislavery Reconsidered*. Baton Rouge: Louisiana State University Press, 1979.

Quarles, Benjamin. *Black Abolitionists*. New York: Oxford University Press, 1969.

Rabinowitz, Howard N. *Race Relations in the Urban South, 1865–1890*. Athens: University of Georgia Press, 1996.

Reid, Anthony, ed. *Slavery, Bondage and Dependency in Southeast Asia*. St. Lucia: University of Queensland Press, 1983.

Rice, C. Duncan. *The Scots Abolitionists, 1833–1861*. Baton Rouge: Louisiana State University Press, 1981.

Richards, Leonard L. *Gentlemen of Property and Standing: Anti-Abolition Mobs in Jacksonian America*. New York: Oxford University Press, 1970.

Ripley, C. Peter, ed. *The Black Abolitionist Papers*. 5 vols. Chapel Hill: University of North Carolina Press, 1985.

Roediger, David. *The Wages of Whiteness: Race and the Making of the American Working Class*. New York: Verso, 1999.

Rose, Willie Lee. *Rehearsal for Reconstruction: The Port Royal Experiment*. New York: Oxford University Press, 1964.

Saillant, John. *Black Puritan, Black Republican: The Life and Thought of Lemuel Haynes, 1753–1833*. New York: Oxford University Press, 2003.

Schmidt-Nowara, Christopher. *Empire and Anti-Slavery: Spain, Cuba and Puerto Rico, 1833–1874*. Pittsburgh: Pittsburgh University Press, 1999.

Scott, Rebecca. *Slave Emancipation in Cuba* Princeton, NJ: Princeton University Press, 1985.

Scully, Pamela. *Liberating the Family? Gender and British Slave Emancipation in the Rural Western Cape, 1823–1853*. Portsmouth, NH: Heinemann, 1997.

Scully, Pamela, and Diana Paton, eds. *Gender and Slave Emancipation in the Atlantic World*. Durham, NC: Duke University Press, 2005.

Seeber, Edward. *Anti-Slavery Opinion in France during the Second Half of the Eighteenth Century*. Baltimore: The Johns Hopkins Press, 1937.

Sewell, Richard H. *Ballots for Freedom: Antislavery Politics in the United States, 1837–1860*. New York: Oxford University Press, 1976.

Sikainga, Ahmad. *Slaves into Workers: Emancipation and Labor in Colonial Sudan*. Austin: University of Texas Press, 1996.

Soderlund, Jean. *Quakers and Slavery: A Divided Spirit*. Princeton, NJ: Princeton University Press, 1985.

Solow, Barbara L., and Stanley L. Engerman, eds. *British Capitalism and Caribbean Slavery: The Legacy of Eric Williams*. Cambridge: Cambridge University Press, 1987.

Staudenraus, Philip J. *The African Colonization Movement, 1816–1865*. New York: Columbia University Press, 1961.

Stauffer, John. *The Black Hearts of Men: Radical Abolitionists and the Transformation of Race*. Cambridge, MA: Harvard University Press, 2002.

Stewart, James Brewer. *Holy Warriors: The Abolitionists and American Slavery*. New York: Hill and Wang, 1996.

Stouffer, Allen P. *The Light of Nature and the Law of God: Antislavery in Ontario, 1833–1877*. Montreal and Kingston: McGill-Queen's University Press, 1992.

Swift, David E. *Black Prophets of Justice: Activist Clergy before the Civil War*. Baton Rouge: Louisiana State University Press, 1989.

Temperley, Howard. *British Antislavery, 1833–1870*. London: Longman, 1972.

Toledano, Ehud. *Slavery and Abolition in the Ottoman Middle East*. Seattle: University of Washington Press, 1998.

——. *The Ottoman Slave Trade and its Suppression, 1840–1890*. Princeton, NJ: Princeton University Press, 1982.

Van Horne, John C., ed. *Religious Philanthropy and Colonial Slavery: The American Correspondence of the Associates of Dr. Bray, 1717–1777*. Chicago: University of Illinois Press, 1985.

Vorenberg, Michael. *Final Freedom: The Civil War, the Abolition of Slavery, and the Thirteenth Amendment*. Cambridge: Cambridge University Press, 2001.

Walker, James W. St. G. *The Black Loyalists: The Search for a Promised Land in Nova Scotia and Sierra Leone, 1783–1870*. 2nd ed. Toronto: University of Toronto Press, 1992.

Walters, Ronald G. *The Antislavery Appeal: American Abolitionism after 1830*. New York: W.W. Norton & Co., 1984; Baltimore: Johns Hopkins University Press, 1978.

Walvin, James. *England, Slaves and Freedom 1776–1838*. Oxford: University Press of Mississippi, 1987.

——, ed. *Slavery and British Society, 1776–1846*. Baton Rouge: Louisiana State University Press, 1982.

Whitman, T. Stephen. *The Price of Freedom: Slavery and Manumission in Baltimore in Early National Maryland*. Lexington: University Press of Kentucky, 1997.

Whyte, Iain. *Scotland and the Abolition of Black Slavery 1756–1838*. Edinburgh: University Press, 2006.

Wiecek, William M. *The Sources of Antislavery Constitutionalism in America, 1760–1848*. Ithaca, NY: Cornell University Press, 1977.

Williams, Eric. *Capitalism and Slavery*. Chapel Hill: University of North Carolina Press, 1944.

Willis, John Ralph, ed. *Islam and the Ideology of Slavery*. Vol. I of *Slaves and Slavery in Muslim Africa*. London: Frank Cass, 1985.

Wyatt-Brown, Bertram. *Lewis Tappan and the Evangelical War Against Slavery*. Cleveland: Case Western Reserve University Press, 1969.

Yellin, Jean Fagan. *Women and Sisters: The Antislavery Feminists in American Culture*. New Haven, CT: Yale University Press, 1989.

Zilversmit, Arthur. *The First Emancipation: The Abolition of Slavery in the North*. Chicago: University of Chicago Press, 1967.

INDEX

ABOUT THE EDITORS
AND CONTRIBUTORS

Patricia Acerbi
The Cesar Chavez Middle School and
    Aztlan Academy
Tucson, Arizona

Wayne Ackerson
Salisbury University
Salisbury, Maryland

Chitra Aiyar
Brennan Center for Justice at NYU
    School of Law
New York, New York

William H. Alexander
Norfolk State University
Norfolk, Virginia

Henrice Altink
University of York
York, England, United Kingdom

Jayne R. Beilke
Ball State University
Muncie, Indiana

James D. Bilotta
Brock University
St. Catherines, Ontario, Canada

Emily V. Blanck
Glassboro, New Jersey

Ellesia A. Blaque
CUNY Queensborough Community College
Bayside, New York

Jamie Bronstein
New Mexico State University
Las Cruces, New Mexico

William H. Brown
Clayton, North Carolina

Stephen P. Budney
Pikeville College
Pikeville, Kentucky

Eric Burin
University of North Dakota
Grand Forks, North Dakota

Noah Butler
Northwestern University
Evanston, Illinois

Barry Cahill
Public Archives of Nova
    Scotia
Halifax, Nova Scotia, Canada

Antoine Capet
University of Rouen
Mont-Saint-Aignan, France

Dianne Wheaton Cappiello
Binghamton University
Binghamton, New York

Johnathan L. Carter
Flint, Michigan

Robert F. Castro .
California State University, Fullerton
Fullerton, California

Abdin Chande
Adelphi University
Garden City, New York

William L. Chew III
Vesalius College, Vrije Universiteit Brussel
Brussels, Belgium

Kenneth G. Cleaver
Homewood, Illinois

A. Glenn Crothers
University of Louisville
Louisville, Kentucky

Edward Daniels
Stanford University
Stanford, California

Mary Darcy
The University of Virginia's College at Wise
Wise, Virginia

Hugh Davis
Southern Connecticut State University
New Haven, Connecticut

Chris Dixon
University of Newcastle
Callaghan, New South Wales, Australia

Vicki L. Eaklor
Alfred University
Alfred, New York

Marcela Echeverri
New York University
New York, New York

Douglas R. Egerton
LeMoyne College
Syracuse, New York

Richard J. Ellis
University of Birmingham
Birmingham, England, United Kingdom

Pieter C. Emmer
University of Leiden
Leiden, The Netherlands

Patrick M. Erben
College of William and Mary
Williamsburg, Virginia

Carol Faulkner
SUNY Geneseo
Geneseo, New York

Andrew Lee Feight
Shawnee State University
Portsmouth, Ohio

Frank Felsenstein
Ball State University
Muncie, Indiana

Paul Finkelman
University of Tulsa
Tulsa, Oklahoma

Susan Fletcher
Indiana University-Purdue University
    Indianapolis
Indianapolis, Indiana

James C. Foley
University of Mississippi
Oxford, Mississippi

Andrew K. Frank
Florida Atlantic University
Boca Raton, Florida

Christopher Frank
University of Manitoba
Winnipeg, Manitoba, Canada

Bernard K. Freamon
Seton Hall University School of Law
Newark, New Jersey

John French
University of Wyoming
Laramie, Wyoming

A. James Fuller
University of Indianapolis
Indianapolis, Indiana

Cheryl Fury
St. Stephen's University
St. Stephen, New Brunswick,
    Canada

Gene C. Gerard
Garland, Texas

Gloria-Yvonne
University of Illinois at Chicago
Chicago, Illinois

Luis Gomez
Stony Brook University
Stony Brook, New York

David M. Greenspoon
North Vancouver, British Columbia,
   Canada

Nicole Hallett
Yale University
New Haven, Connecticut

Jennifer Harrison
Indianapolis, Indiana

Stanley Harrold
South Carolina State University
Orangeburg, South Carolina

Mohammed Hassanali
Shaker Heights, Ohio

Robert W. Haynes
Texas A&M International University
Laredo, Texas

Donald E. Heidenreich, Jr.
Lindenwood University
St. Charles, Missouri

Alexia Helsley
Past President, South Carolina Archival
   Association
Columbia, South Carolina

Peter P. Hinks
Wethersfield, Connecticut

Graham Russell Gao Hodges
Colgate University
Hamilton, New York

Nadine Hunt
York University
Toronto, Ontario, Canada

Iris Hunter
Alexandria, Virginia

Joseph E. Inikori
University of Rochester
Rochester, New York

Matthew Isham
Pennsylvania State University
State College, Pennsylvania

Susan B. Iwanisziw
Philadelphia, Pennsylvania

Maurice Jackson
Georgetown University
Washington, D.C.

Michael Jerryson
University of California, Santa Barbara
Goleta, California

Fábio Duarte Joly
University of Sao Paulo
Sao Paulo, Brazil

Ralph Keen
University of Iowa
Iowa City, Iowa

Martin A. Klein
University of Toronto
Toronto, Ontario, Canada

Helen J. Knowles
Boston University
Boston, Massachusetts

Daniel P. Kotzin
Kutztown University
Kutztown, Pennsylvania

Raymond James Krohn
Purdue University
West Lafayette, Indiana

Lori Lee
Syracuse University
Syracuse, New York

Jean-Pierre Le Glaunec
University of Paris VII-Denis Diderot
Paris, France

William J. Leonhirth
Middle Tennessee State University
Murfreesboro, Tennessee

Jennifer Lofkrantz
York University
Toronto, Ontario, Canada

Sonja Lovelace
Irvine Valley College
Irvine, California

Linda J. Lumsden
Western Kentucky University
Bowling Green, Kentucky

Richard MacMaster
University of Florida
Gainesville, Florida

Ben Marsh
Sterling University
Sterling, Scotland, United
    Kingdom

Matthew Mason
Brigham Young University
Provo, Utah

Kate Masur
Northwestern University
Evanston, Illinois

Erik Mathisen
University of Pennsylvania
Philadelphia, Pennsylvania

Tim Matthewson
Alexandria, Virginia

Gerald L. Mattingly
Johnson Bible College
Knoxville, Tennessee

Leslie A. Mattingly
Johnson Bible College
Knoxville, Tennessee

W. Caleb McDaniel
Johns Hopkins University
Baltimore, Maryland

John R. McKivigan
Indiana University-Purdue University
    Indianapolis
Indianapolis, Indiana

Heather K. Michon
Palmyra, Virginia

Suzanne Miers
Professor Emerita
Ohio University
Athens, Ohio

Neil Brody Miller
Southeast Missouri State University
Cape Girardeau, Missouri

C.S. Monaco
Micanopy, Florida

Wesley Moody
Jonesboro, Georgia

David Moon
Durham University
Durham, England

Shawn Mosher
Baylor University
Waco, Texas

William H. Mulligan, Jr.
Murray State University
Murray, Kentucky

Jeffrey Mullins
St. Cloud State University
St. Cloud, Minnesota

Brian Murphy
Clifton, New Jersey

David Murray
University of Guelph
Guelph, Ontario, Canada

Steve Napier
West Chester, Ohio

Robert K. Nelson
College of William and Mary
Williamsburg, Virginia

Richard Newman
Rochester Institute of Technology
Rochester, New York

Michelle Orihel
Syracuse University
Syracuse, New York

Shelinda Pattison
University of Arkansas at Little Rock
Little Rock, Arkansas

Jared Peatman
Virginia Polytechnic Institute and
    State University
Blacksburg, Virginia

Patrick Peebles
University of Missouri at Kansas City
Kansas City, Missouri

Claire Phelan
Texas Christian University
Fort Worth, Texas

Jennifer J. Pierce
Graham, North Carolina

Michael D. Pierson
University of Massachusetts Lowell
Lowell, Massachusetts

Parbattie S. Ramsarran
York University
Toronto, Ontario, Canada

Jeremy Rich
Cabrini College
Radnor, Pennsylvania

R. Volney Riser
University of Alabama
Tuscaloosa, Alabama

Cathy Rodabaugh
Canfield, Ohio

James R. Rohrer
University of Nebraska at Kearney
Kearney, Nebraska

Sarah N. Roth
Widener University
Chester, Pennsylvania

Michael A. Rutz
University of Wisconsin—Oshkosh
Oshkosh, Wisconsin

Jennifer Rycenga
San Jose State University
San Jose, California

John Saillant
Western Michigan University
Kalamazoo, Michigan

Christopher Saunders
University of Cape Town
Cape Town, South Africa

Andrew M. Schocket
Bowling Green State University
Bowling Green, Ohio

Marc L. Schwarz
University of New Hampshire
Durham, New Hampshire

Pamela Scully
Emory University
Atlanta, Georgia

Lumumba H. Shabaka
Providence, Rhode Island

Jeff Shantz
York University
Toronto, Ontario, Canada

Verene Shepherd
University of the West Indies
Mona, Kingston, Jamaica

Juliet Shields
Ohio State University
Columbus, Ohio

John David Smith
University of North Carolina at
    Charlotte
Charlotte, North Carolina

Robert W. Smith
Marshfield, Massachusetts

John Stauffer
Harvard University
Cambridge, Massachusetts

Paul Stewart
Underground Railroad History Project
Albany, New York

Jerome Teelucksingh
University of the West Indies
St. Augustine, Trinidad and Tobago

Gordon C. Thomasson
SUNY Broome Community College
Binghamton, New York

Michael Vorenberg
Brown University
Providence, Rhode Island

Marilyn Walker
University of Illinois at Urbana-
    Champaign
Urbana-Champaign, Illinois

James Walvin
University of York
York, England, United Kingdom

Kimberly Welch
University of Redlands
Redlands, California

Judith Wellman
Professor Emerita
SUNY Oswego
Oswego, New York

Susannah C. West
John Rankin House
Ripley, Ohio

Fred Whitehead
Kansas City, Kansas

Ashley Whitmore
Wayne State University
Detroit, Michigan

Iain Whyte
Fife, Scotland, United Kingdom

R. Owen Williams
Yale University
New Haven, Connecticut

John J. Zaborney
University of Maine at Presque Isle
Presque Isle, Maine

Kathy Zeisel
New York University School
    of Law
New York, New York